Frommer's®
San Francisco

My San Francisco

by Matthew R. Poole

ESSENTIALLY I'M A PROFESSIONAL TOURIST. MY FULL-TIME JOB IS TO

eat at restaurants, stay at hotels, stroll through museums, and take sightseeing tours. I never intended to be a travel writer—I just sort of fell into it. When your best talents are eating, sleeping, and criticizing, your career options are pretty limited.

The point is, because my job is to travel, I can live anywhere. But I *choose* to live in San Francisco, because no other city I've been to combines such a wonderfully cosmopolitan atmosphere with such spectacular scenery. Every time I drive across the majestic Golden Gate Bridge as the sparkling city unfolds in the background I'm reminded of how lucky I am to live here, to be able to travel around the world—visiting dim sum parlors, trattorias, tapas bars, Irish pubs, and Japanese spas—without having to leave the city limits. It's an incredible opportunity.

But don't take my word for it. All you need to do is browse through these photos and skim the "Best of San Francisco" chapter to see why San Francisco is continually voted America's favorite city.

Epicenter of the 1960s peace movement in America, **HAIGHT-ASHBURY (left)** is where the flower got its power, love was free, and the culture was countered by local music legends such as Janis Joplin, Jimi Hendrix, and Jerry Garcia. Okay, so the vibe these days is more about commercialism than spiritual enlightenment, but vestiges of the hippie '60s still remain, and those tie-dyed T-shirts sold along Haight Street sure make great souvenirs.

Despite the ever-encroaching plight of gentrification, the gritty **MISSION DISTRICT (above)** is still a predominately Latin community where taco shops and roving mariachi bands rub shoulders with trendy tapas bars and angst-ridden wannabe novelists. For good insight into the Mission District culture, take one of the Precita Eyes Mural Arts Center's self-guided tours to see nearly 60 power-to-the-people murals in an 8-block walk.

SAN FRANCISCO (above) is so condensed that it's easy to explore multiple districts in a single day, but even after 15 years of living here I'm still constantly surprised by all the architectural and cultural gems that are hidden throughout this amazing city.

At the foot of Market Street is the Ferry Building Marketplace, an architectural jewel filled with artisan food shops, wine bars, ethnic delis, and gourmet coffee shops offering gorgeous views of the bay. But what really lures folks here is the weekend **FARMERS MARKET (right)**, an organic ode to small-scale family farmers. On Saturday mornings, this is where you want to be.

I've crossed the **GOLDEN GATE BRIDGE** at least a thousand times and I still marvel at its majesty. Whether you walk it, bike it, drive it, or view it from a distance, San Francisco's most famous landmark commands attention. The bridge is a visual wonder in itself, but its back-drop of the woodsy Presidio to the south, rugged Mann Headlands to the north, and glistening waters of the Golden Gate below makes it utterly magical to behold.

© Cliff House

I'm the first to admit the historic **CLIFF HOUSE (left)** restaurant is a tourist trap, but the ocean view is so extraordinary—particularly at sunset—that it's worth the inflated prices.

San Franciscans love to ridicule any new civic building project, but I've yet to meet anyone who doesn't take pride in our beautiful ballpark by the bay: **AT&T PARK (below)**. You don't need to know a single thing about baseball to enjoy a sunny afternoon munching on garlic fries and kettle corn while the Giants play down on the field.

Chinatown is not only a world unto itself, it's a city within a city. In fact, this Land of Little Pink Bags is the largest Chinese city outside of Asia. It's not some shiny Disney version of Asian life but the real deal, complete with authentic **TEA HOUSES (above right)**, delectable **DIM SUM (below right)**, the clatter of Mahjong tiles, exotic food markets—yes, that's a box of dead armadillos for sale—and, as of late, a more tasteful selection of trinkets along Grant Avenue.

© Lee Foster/Lonely Planet Images

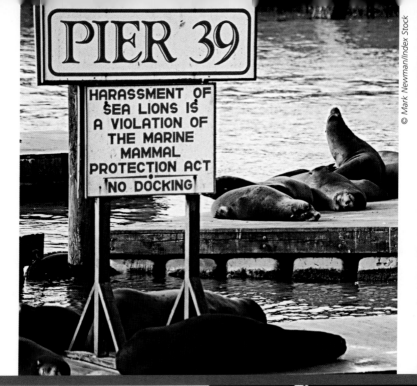

Locals love to loathe PIER 39. But despite the abundance of tchotchke shops, mediocre restaurants, and kitschy attractions, there are some must-see sights at Fisherman's Wharf, particularly the shamelessly lethargic **SEA LIONS (above)** that sunbath on the docks all day, barking at God-knows-what. Even jaded San Franciscans can't deny their charm.

Of all the city's edible delights, Dungeness crab is my favorite seasonal indulgence. Availability varies from year to year, but the season usually begins in November and ends in April. If you're in town during crab season, you absolutely must head to the odiferous sidewalk crab stands at **FISHER-MAN'S WHARF (right)** for a paper plate piled with fresh crab meat topped with tangy cocktail sauce and a side of sourdough bread. Heaven, people, heaven.

San Francisco's architecture is as diverse as its population, but the city is best known for its Victorian houses. The strip of **HOUSES ALONG ALAMO SQUARE (right)** that is often ogled for its picture-perfect side-by-side positioning and pristine upkeep.

The long lines to board **SAN FRANCISCO'S CABLE CARS (below)** ensure that most locals don't take them regularly. But on the rare occasion that I hop on one, I am instantly reminded of why they are so popular. As these antiquated behemoths lunge noisily up and down the city's steep hills, you can't help but revel in the romance, nostalgia, and thrill of it all.

California's bucolic **WINE COUNTRY** (below) is one of the most decadent places on earth. The entire region is dedicated solely to Bacchanalian pleasures: world-class wines, outstanding cuisine, and leisure pursuits such as spas, golf, **BIKE TOURS** (left), and—my favorite—getting comfortably buzzed on a chauffeured wine tasting tour with your friends. Both Napa Valley and Sonoma Valley are only an hour's drive from San Francisco and the perfect complement to the bustling city scene, so be sure to schedule a visit during your vacation.

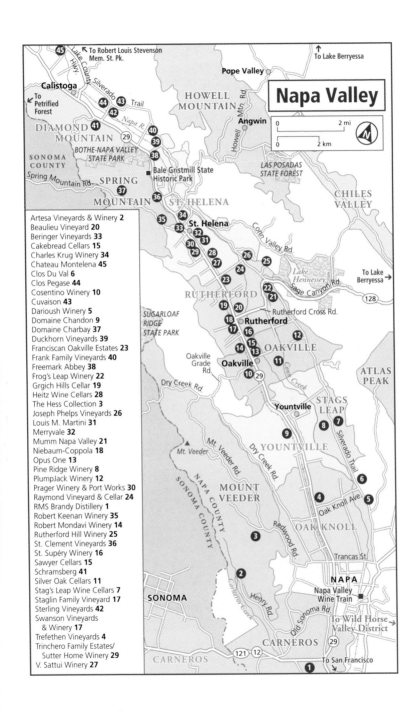

Napa Valley

To Robert Louis Stevenson Mem. St. Pk.
To Lake Berryessa
Pope Valley
Calistoga
To Petrified Forest
HOWELL MOUNTAIN
Angwin
DIAMOND MOUNTAIN
SONOMA COUNTY
BOTHE-NAPA VALLEY STATE PARK
Spring Mountain Rd
SPRING MOUNTAIN
Bale Gristmill State Historic Park
ST. HELENA
St. Helena
LAS POSADAS STATE FOREST
CHILES VALLEY
RUTHERFORD
Lake Hennessey
Sage Canyon Rd.
To Lake Berryessa
128
Rutherford Cross Rd.
SUGARLOAF RIDGE STATE PARK
Rutherford
OAKVILLE
Oakville Grade Rd.
Oakville
Dry Creek Rd.
ATLAS PEAK
STAGS LEAP
Yountville
Mt. Veeder Rd.
Mt. Veeder
MOUNT VEEDER
SONOMA COUNTY
YOUNTVILLE
Silverado Trail
Dry Creek Rd.
OAK KNOLL
Oak Knoll Ave.
Trancas St.
Redwood Rd.
NAPA
Napa Valley Wine Train
SONOMA
CARNEROS
Carneros Creek
Henry Rd.
Old Sonoma Rd.
121
12
CARNEROS
To Wild Horse Valley District
To San Francisco
29

0   2 mi
0   2 km

Artesa Vineyards & Winery **2**
Beaulieu Vineyard **20**
Beringer Vineyards **33**
Cakebread Cellars **15**
Charles Krug Winery **34**
Chateau Montelena **45**
Clos Du Val **6**
Clos Pegase **44**
Cosentino Winery **10**
Cuvaison **43**
Darioush Winery **5**
Domaine Chandon **9**
Domaine Charbay **37**
Duckhorn Vineyards **39**
Franciscan Oakville Estates **23**
Frank Family Vineyards **40**
Freemark Abbey **38**
Frog's Leap Winery **22**
Grgich Hills Cellar **19**
Heitz Wine Cellars **28**
The Hess Collection **3**
Joseph Phelps Vineyards **26**
Louis M. Martini **31**
Merryvale **32**
Mumm Napa Valley **21**
Niebaum-Coppola **18**
Opus One **13**
Pine Ridge Winery **8**
PlumpJack Winery **12**
Prager Winery & Port Works **30**
Raymond Vineyard & Cellar **24**
RMS Brandy Distillery **1**
Robert Keenan Winery **35**
Robert Mondavi Winery **14**
Rutherford Hill Winery **25**
St. Clement Vineyards **36**
St. Supéry Winery **16**
Sawyer Cellars **15**
Schramsberg **41**
Silver Oak Cellars **11**
Stag's Leap Wine Cellars **7**
Staglin Family Vineyard **17**
Sterling Vineyards **42**
Swanson Vineyards & Winery **17**
Trefethen Vineyards **4**
Trinchero Family Estates/ Sutter Home Winery **29**
V. Sattui Winery **27**

San Francisco Bay

Exploratorium/
Palace of Fine Arts

101

GOLDEN GATE
NAT'L REC. AREA—
FORT MASON

Beach St.

Bay St.

**MARINA
DISTRICT**

Moscone
Playground

Francisco St.
Chestnut St.

San Francisco
Neighborhoods

Lombard St.

101

Greenwich St.

**COW
HOLLOW**

Lyon St.

Baker St.

Broderick St.

Divisadero St.

Scott St.

Pierce St.

Steiner St.

Fillmore St.

Webster St.

Buchanan St.

Laguna St.

Octavia St.

Gough St.

Franklin St.

GOLDEN GATE
NAT'L REC. AREA–
THE PRESIDIO

**PACIFIC
HEIGHTS**

Pacific Ave.

Pacific Ave.

Jackson St.

Arguello Blvd.

**PRESIDIO
HEIGHTS**

Walnut St.

Presidio Ave.

Washington St.

Clay St.

Alta Plaza
Park

Pacific
Medical
Center

Lafayette
Park

Sacramento St.

California St.

Pine St.

Bush St.

Euclid Ave.

**LAUREL
HEIGHTS**

Sutter St.

Post St.

JAPANTOWN

Japan Center

Geary Blvd.

Geary Blvd.

O'Farrell St.

Anza St.

Parker Ave.

Masonic Ave.

**ANZA
VISTA**

Ellis St.

Eddy St.

Pierce St.

Steiner St.

Fillmore St.

Webster St.

Buchanan St.

Laguna St.

Jefferson
Square

Turk Blvd.

Golden Gate Ave.

McAllister St.

Central Ave.

**WESTERN
ADDITION**

Fulton St.

Cole St.

Clayton St.

Grove St.

Hayes St.

Lyon St.

Baker St.

Broderick St.

Fulton St.

Alamo
Square

Grove St.

**HAYES
VALLEY**

Hayes St.

Gough St.

Franklin St.

THE PANHANDLE

Fell St.

Oak St.

Octavia Blvd.

GOLDEN GATE PARK

Stanyan St.

Shrader St.

Ashbury St.

Masonic Ave.

HAIGHT-ASHBURY

Page St.

Haight St.

Divisadero St.

Scott St.

Pierce St.

Page St.

Haight St.

Waller St.

Frederick St.

Buena Vista
Park

Duboce
Park

Hermann St.

Duboce Ave.

Market St.

**To
The Castro**
↓

**To the
Mission
District**
↓

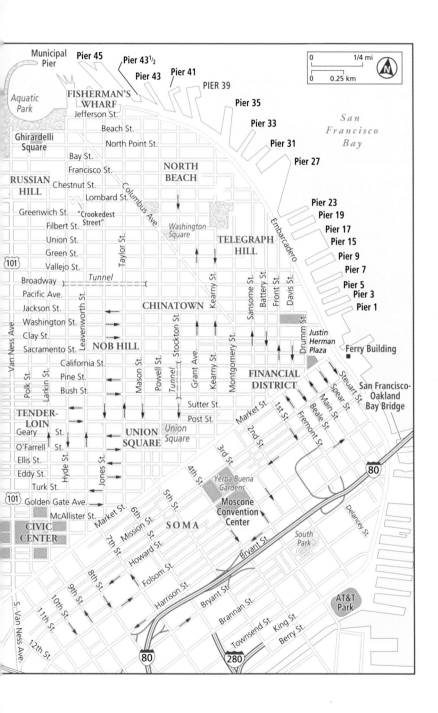

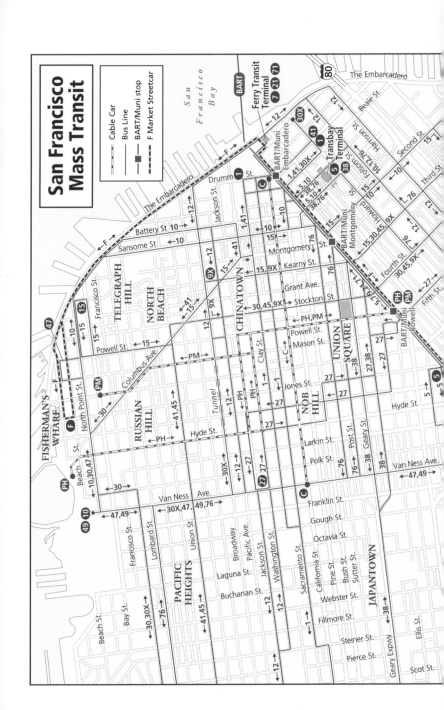

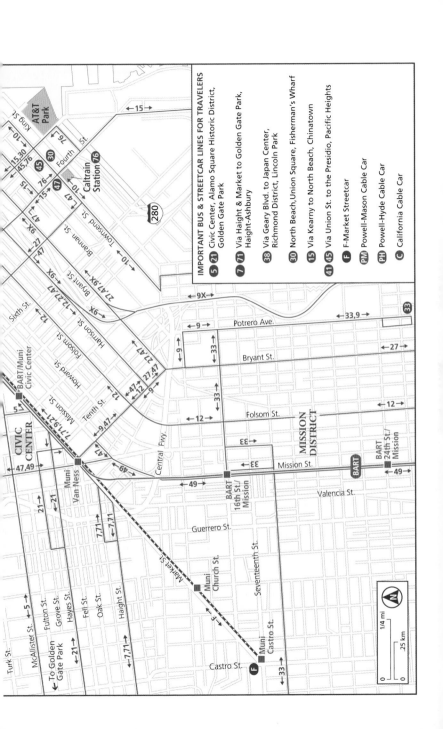

IMPORTANT BUS & STREETCAR LINES FOR TRAVELERS

5 21 Civic Center, Alamo Square Historic District, Golden Gate Park

7 71 Via Haight & Market to Golden Gate Park, Haight-Ashbury

38 Via Geary Blvd. to Japan Center, Richmond District, Lincoln Park

30 North Beach, Union Square, Fisherman's Wharf

15 Via Kearny to North Beach, Chinatown

41 45 Via Union St. to the Presidio, Pacific Heights

F F-Market Streetcar

PM Powell-Mason Cable Car

PH Powell-Hyde Cable Car

C California Cable Car

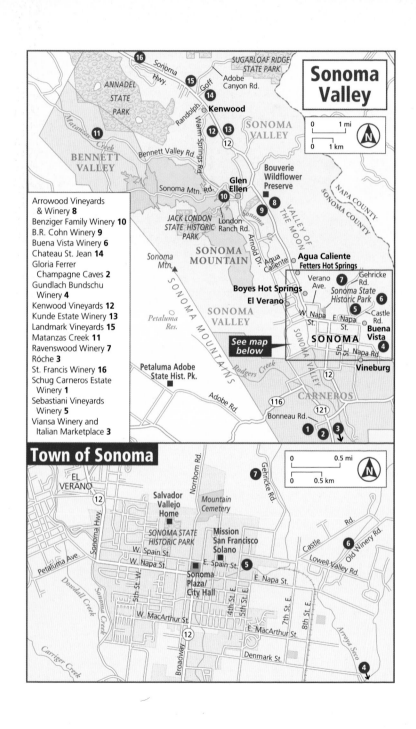

Sonoma Valley

| 0 | 1 mi |
| 0 | 1 km |

Arrowood Vineyards
  & Winery **8**
Benziger Family Winery **10**
B.R. Cohn Winery **9**
Buena Vista Winery **6**
Chateau St. Jean **14**
Gloria Ferrer
  Champagne Caves **2**
Gundlach Bundschu
  Winery **4**
Kenwood Vineyards **12**
Kunde Estate Winery **13**
Landmark Vineyards **15**
Matanzas Creek **11**
Ravenswood Winery **7**
Róche **3**
St. Francis Winery **16**
Schug Carneros Estate
  Winery **1**
Sebastiani Vineyards
  Winery **5**
Viansa Winery and
  Italian Marketplace **3**

SUGARLOAF RIDGE
STATE PARK

Sonoma Hwy.
Adobe Canyon Rd.
Goff
Kenwood

ANNADEL
STATE
PARK

Randolph
Warm Springs Rd.
Matanzas Creek

SONOMA
VALLEY

BENNETT
VALLEY
Bennett Valley Rd.

Bouverie
Wildflower
Preserve

Sonoma Mtn. Rd.
**Glen
Ellen**

NAPA COUNTY
SONOMA COUNTY

VALLEY
OF
THE
MOON

JACK LONDON
STATE HISTORIC
PARK
London
Ranch Rd.

SONOMA
MOUNTAIN

Sonoma
Mtn.

SONOMA
MOUNTAINS

Petaluma
Res.

Arnold Dr.
Agua
Caliente

Agua Caliente
Fetters Hot Springs

Gehricke Rd.
Verano
Ave.
7
Sonoma State
Historic Park
6
5
Castle
Rd.
**Buena
Vista**
4

Boyes Hot Springs
El Verano

W. Napa
St.
E. Napa
St.

SONOMA

5th St.
Napa Rd.

Vineburg

SONOMA
VALLEY

**See map
below**

Petaluma Adobe
State Hist. Pk.

Rodgers Creek
Adobe Rd.

116
121
Bonneau Rd.

CARNEROS

12

1 **2** **3**

Town of Sonoma

| 0 | 0.5 mi |
| 0 | 0.5 km |

EL
VERANO
12

Norrbom Rd.

Gehricke Rd.
7

Salvador
Vallejo
Home

Mountain
Cemetery

Sonoma Hwy.

SONOMA STATE
HISTORIC PARK

Mission
San Francisco
Solano

W. Spain St.
W. Napa St.

Petaluma Ave.

5th St. W.

E. Spain St.
5
**Sonoma
Plaza/
City Hall**
E. Napa St.

4th St. E.
5th St. E.
7th St. E.
8th St. E.

Rd.
Castle
Lowell Valley Rd.
Old Winery Rd.
6

Dowdall Creek

W. MacArthur St.
E. MacArthur St.

Broadway
12

Denmark St.

Carriger Creek

Arroyo Seco

4

Frommer's®

San Francisco

2009

by Matthew Richard Poole & Erika Lenkert

Here's what the critics say about Frommer's:

"Amazingly easy to use. Very portable, very complete."

—*Booklist*

"Detailed, accurate, and easy-to-read information for all price ranges."
—*Glamour Magazine*

"Hotel information is close to encyclopedic."

—*Des Moines Sunday Register*

"Frommer's Guides have a way of giving you a real feel for a place."
—*Knight Ridder Newspapers*

WILEY
Wiley Publishing, Inc.

Published by:

Wiley Publishing, Inc.

111 River St.
Hoboken, NJ 07030-5774

ISBN 978-0-470-28773-6
Editor: Marc Nadeau
Production Editor: Jonathan Scott
Cartographer: Liz Puhl
Photo Editor: Richard Fox
Production by Wiley Indianapolis Composition Services

Front cover photo: Golden Gate Bridge at dusk
Back cover photo: Columbus Street: Man reading book outside Vesuvio Café

For information on our other products and services or to obtain technical support, please contact our Customer Care Department within the U.S. at 800/762-2974, outside the U.S. at 317/572-3993 or fax 317/572-4002.

Wiley also publishes its books in a variety of electronic formats. Some content that appears in print may not be available in electronic formats.

Manufactured in the United States of America

5   4   3   2   1

Contents

List of Maps

An Invitation to the Reader

In researching this book, we discovered many wonderful places—hotels, restaurants, shops, and more. We're sure you'll find others. Please tell us about them, so we can share the information with your fellow travelers in upcoming editions. If you were disappointed with a recommendation, we'd love to know that, too. Please write to:

Frommer's San Francisco 2009
Wiley Publishing, Inc. • 111 River St. • Hoboken, NJ 07030-5774

An Additional Note

Please be advised that travel information is subject to change at any time—and this is especially true of prices. We therefore suggest that you write or call ahead for confirmation when making your travel plans. The authors, editors, and publisher cannot be held responsible for the experiences of readers while traveling. Your safety is important to us, however, so we encourage you to stay alert and be aware of your surroundings. Keep a close eye on cameras, purses, and wallets, all favorite targets of thieves and pickpockets.

About the Author

Matthew Richard Poole, a native Californian, has authored more than two dozen travel guides to California, Hawaii, and abroad, and is a regular contributor to radio and television travel programs, including numerous guest appearances on the award-winning *Bay Area Backroads* television show. Before becoming a full-time travel writer and photographer, he worked as an English tutor in Prague, a ski instructor in the Swiss Alps, and a scuba instructor in Maui and Thailand. He currently lives in San Francisco but spends most of his time on the road searching for new adventures. His other Frommer's titles include *California,* the *Irreverent Guide to San Francisco,* and *Portable Disneyland.*

A native San Franciscan, **Erika Lenkert** divides her time between San Francisco and Napa Valley, where she is forever seeking the next best restaurant, hotel room, and fun way to savor the region. She frequently writes *InStyle* magazine's party guides and offers up tasty tips on the region for *Food & Wine* magazine. In her spare time she pays visits to local and national television news programs, where she gives entertaining and cooking tips based on her book *The Last-Minute Party Girl: Fashionable, Fearless, and Foolishly Simple Entertaining.*

Other Great Guides for Your Trip:

Frommer's California
Frommer's Portable California Wine Country
Frommer's California's Best-Loved Driving Tours
Suzy Gershman's Born to Shop San Francisco
California For Dummies

Frommer's Star Ratings, Icons & Abbreviations

Every hotel, restaurant, and attraction listing in this guide has been ranked for quality, value, service, amenities, and special features using a **star-rating system.** In country, state, and regional guides, we also rate towns and regions to help you narrow down your choices and budget your time accordingly. Hotels and restaurants are rated on a scale of zero (recommended) to three stars (exceptional). Attractions, shopping, nightlife, towns, and regions are rated according to the following scale: zero stars (recommended), one star (highly recommended), two stars (very highly recommended), and three stars (must-see).

In addition to the star-rating system, we also use **seven feature icons** that point you to the great deals, in-the-know advice, and unique experiences that separate travelers from tourists. Throughout the book, look for:

Finds	Special finds—those places only insiders know about
Fun Fact	Fun facts—details that make travelers more informed and their trips more fun
Kids	Best bets for kids and advice for the whole family
Moments	Special moments—those experiences that memories are made of
Overrated	Places or experiences not worth your time or money
Tips	Insider tips—great ways to save time and money
Value	Great values—where to get the best deals

The following **abbreviations** are used for credit cards:

AE	American Express	DISC	Discover	V	Visa
DC	Diners Club	MC	MasterCard		

Frommers.com

Now that you have this guidebook to help you plan a great trip, visit our website at **www.frommers.com** for additional travel information on more than 4,000 destinations. We update features regularly to give you instant access to the most current trip-planning information available. At Frommers.com, you'll find scoops on the best airfares, lodging rates, and car rental bargains. You can even book your travel online through our reliable travel booking partners. Other popular features include:

- Online updates of our most popular guidebooks
- Vacation sweepstakes and contest giveaways
- Newsletters highlighting the hottest travel trends
- Podcasts, interactive maps, and up-to-the-minute events listings
- Opinionated blog entries by Arthur Frommer himself
- Online travel message boards with featured travel discussions

What's New in San Francisco

One of the greatest challenges of producing a quality travel guide is staying on top of the never-ending changes that take place in San Francisco, a city that is always in a state of flux. This section highlights the latest trends, attractions, and openings. There's some great stuff here, so be sure to add it to your to-do list while exploring the city.

HOTELS   What's been the norm in L.A. and New York for the past half decade has finally permeated the San Francisco hospitality industry: hip boutique hotels created by cutting-edge design companies with destination bar/lounges and restaurants run by celebrity chefs. In this edition I've added five formerly frumpy Union Square hotels that have been transmogrified from just a place to stay to the place to *be*.

Take the new **Hotel Vertigo** (940 Sutter St.; ✆ 800/553-1900) for instance. It has a playful, eclectic decor by Thomas Schoos Design, Inc., and food by celebrity chef Tyler Florence. The **Hotel Frank** (386 Geary St.; ✆ 800/553-1900) followed suit with a major renovation in the fall of 2008 that incorporated a blend of popular design trends through the decades, from turn-of-the-century Beaux Art classicism to '40s Art Deco and retro '60s chic.

Other examples include the newly renovated **Villa Florence** (225 Powell St.; (✆ 866/823-4669) with its slick new Bar Norcini wine bar; the **Hotel Metropolis** (25 Mason St. (✆ 800/553-1900) and its yin/yang combo of cheeky decor and Zen ambience; and my new favorite, the **Hotel**

Union Square (114 Powell St.; ✆ 800/553-1900), built in 1913 for the 1915 Pan Pacific Exposition yet now one of the sexiest hotels in the city. If lace curtains and teddy bears just won't do, any of these five new hotels will satisfy the snob in you.

RESTAURANTS   For the first time in decades someone has finally opened a true destination restaurant on the Embarcadero. Heck, they built two. The duo of **EPIC Roasthouse** (369 Embarcadero; ✆ 415/369-9955) and the adjacent **Waterbar** (399 Embarcadero; ✆ 415/284-9922) has managed to get even us restaurant-jaded locals excited. Design genius Pat Kuleto worked his magic yet again to create two of the sexiest restaurants in the city. Even if the prices are beyond your budget, you really need to stop by both restaurants and admire what money, style, and setting can produce.

Two other restaurant newcomers that are getting national press are **Ducca** (50 Third St.; ✆ 415/977-0271) and **Spruce** (3640 Sacramento St.; ✆ 415/931-5100). The former is my new favorite Italian restaurant in the city—the things Executive Chef Richard J. Corbo can do with buffalo mozzarella is humbling—while the latter is the new darling of the Pacific Heights ladies-who-lunch crowd and worth the drive across town just for the burger and fries.

SIGHTSEEING   It took, like, forever, but the city finally got around to opening the new **California Academy of Sciences** (55 Concourse Dr.; ✆ 415/379-8000).

Four years and $500 million dollars later, but the results will wow you. It's the only institution in the world to combine an aquarium, planetarium, natural history museum, and scientific research program under one roof, and what a roof it is—a 2½-acre undulating garden canopy carpeted with over a million plants and flowers. There's much to see and do at the Academy that you could easily spend an entire day roaming amongst the high-tech exhibits. Along with the brilliant de Young Museum and beautiful Conservatory of Flowers, it's yet another reason why everyone who's vacationing in San Francisco should spend at least one full day in Golden Gate Park.

NIGHTLIFE The more things change.... Your grandparents might remember when San Francisco's Fillmore Corridor was the swingingest jazz venue in the 1940s and '50s. Though not quite back to its halcyon days, this revitalized stretch of Fillmore Street just south of Geary Boulevard is once again the top West Coast destination for jazz music now that the new **Yoshi's Jazz Club** (1330 Fillmore St.; ℂ **415/655-5600**), has opened. The two-story, 28,000-square-foot jazz venue is attracting some of the finest jazz artists in the world: Stanton Moore, Branford Marsalis, Diana Krall, et al. Even if you're not a jazz fan, it's still worth the trip to revel in the coolness of it all.

On an entirely different note, I've also added some info about the best drag shows in the city. If you're out on a Friday night and looking for something to do that's decidedly off the straight-laced path, head to the **Cinch** (1723 Polk St.; ℂ **415/776-4162**), for its weekly **Charlie Horse** drag show, or bring grandma to a brunch she'll never forget at **Harry Denton's Starlight Room** (450 Powell St.; ℂ **415/395-8595**). Their weekly **Sunday's a Drag** brunch performance is fit for a queen.

The Best of San Francisco

In a city where parade themes include "Weapons of Ass Destruction" and starting your holiday with an Irish coffee at the Buena Vista Café is de rigueur, it's pretty much guaranteed that you'll have a fun time vacationing in San Francisco. Where else in the world will you find a restaurant whose servers are all gorgeous transvestites? Where it's considered good, clean fun to get airborne in your car? Or where locals don't even pause for earthquakes under 5.0 on the Richter scale?

And it's always been this way: San Francisco's reputation as a rollicking city where almost anything goes dates back to the boom-or-bust days of the California Gold Rush. The result is a wee bit o' heaven for everyone: In a city that is so beautiful, exciting, and cosmopolitan there's always something enjoyable to see and do no matter how long you're staying. I've lived here for 14 years and I'm still discovering new things about this city almost every day.

There are, however, three things you should know before coming to San Francisco that will help you blend in with the locals. First, don't call it 'Frisco. (You wouldn't call New York just "York," would you?) Second, please don't call our beloved cable cars "trolleys." A trolley is a British shopping cart. Third, always dress warmly. Bob Hope once remarked that San Francisco is the city of four seasons—every day. Temperatures can drop darn quick when the fog rolls in, so be prepared.

But the best advice I can give you about San Francisco is to just *go*. Enjoy the cool blast of salty air as you stroll across the Golden Gate. Stuff yourself with dim sum in Chinatown. Browse the secondhand shops along Haight Street. Recite poetry in a North Beach coffeehouse. Walk along the beach, skate through Golden Gate Park, ride the cable cars, tour a Victorian mansion, explore Alcatraz Island, go to a Giants ballgame: Like an eternal world's fair, it's all happening in San Francisco, and everyone's invited. All you have to do is arrive with an open mind, this guidebook, and a sense of adventure—the rest is waiting for you.

Right then. Let's get this vacation started.

1 The Best Only-in-San Francisco Experiences

- **A Powell-Hyde Cable-Car Ride:** Skip the less-scenic California line and take the Powell-Hyde cable car down to Fisherman's Wharf—the ride is worth the wait. When you reach the top of Nob Hill, grab the rail with one hand and hold your camera with the other, because you're about to see a view of the bay that'll make you all weepy. See p. 158.

- **An Adventure at Alcatraz:** Even if you loathe tourist attractions, you'll dig Alcatraz. Just looking at The Rock from across the bay is enough to give you the heebie-jeebies—and the park rangers have put together an excellent audio tour. Heck, even the boat ride across the bay is worth the price. See p. 153.

- **A Walk across the Golden Gate Bridge:** Don your windbreaker and walking shoes and prepare for a wind-blasted, exhilarating journey across San Francisco's most famous landmark. It's simply one of those things you have to do at least once in your life. See p. 163.

- **A Stroll through Chinatown:** Chinatown is a trip. I've been through it at least 100 times, and it has never failed to entertain me. Skip the ersatz camera and luggage stores and head straight for the food markets, where a cornucopia of critters that you'll never see at Safeway sit in boxes waiting for the wok. (Is that an armadillo?) Better yet, take one of Shirley Fong-Torres's Wok Wiz Tours of Chinatown (p. 175).

- **Watching the San Francisco Giants play at AT&T Park:** If it's baseball season, then you *must* spend an afternoon or evening watching the National League's Giants lose at one of the finest ballparks in America. For only $10 you can buy a bleacher-seat ticket on the day of a game. Even if the season's over, you can still take a guided tour of the stadium. See p. 197.

2 The Best Splurge Hotels

- **The Ritz-Carlton,** 600 Stockton St., Nob Hill (© **800/241-3333** or 415/296-7465; www.ritzcarlton.com), is the sine qua non of luxury hotels, offering near-perfect service and every possible amenity. Even if you can't afford a guest room, come for the mind-blowing Sunday brunch. See p. 80.

- **Four Seasons Hotel San Francisco,** 757 Market St., SoMa (© **800/819-5053** or 415/633-3000; www.fourseasons.com), is the perfect combination of opulence, hipness, and class. I can't afford it either, but I sure love to hang out at the bar and pretend. See p. 82.

- **The Mandarin Oriental,** 222 Sansome St., Financial District (© **800/622-0404** or 415/276-9888; www.mandarinoriental.com/sanfrancisco), is perched so high above the city that the fog rolls in *below* you. It's surreal. Maybe I really did die and go to heaven? See p. 90.

- **The St. Regis Hotel,** 125 Third St., SoMa (© **877/787-3447** or 415/284-4000; www.stregis.com/sanfrancisco), has these touch-screen remote controls that let you operate everything in your room—without leaving your bed. Add a destination restaurant and a fabulous two-floor spa, and why would you ever want to leave? See p. 86.

3 The Best Moderately Priced Hotels

- **Laurel Inn,** 444 Presidio Ave., Pacific Heights (© **800/552-8735** or 415/567-8467; www.thelaurelinn.com), may be off the beaten track, but it's one of the best affordable, fashionable hotels in the city. Just outside of the southern entrance to the Presidio in the midst of residential Presidio Heights, it's a chic motel with soothing, contemporary decor and equally calming prices. See p. 95.

- **Hotel Bohème,** 444 Columbus Ave. (© **415/433-9111;** www.hotelboheme.com), is the perfect mixture of art, style, class, romance, and location—just steps from the sidewalk cafes of North Beach. If Bette Davis were alive today, this is where she'd stay. See p. 93.

- **Hotel Union Square,** 114 Powell St. (© **415/397-3000;** www.hotelunion square.com), has the perfect combination of history, style, and location. A $5 million dollar renovation in the spring of 2008 has melded contemporary elements with classic San Francisco features dating back from 1915. See p. 74.

- **Hotel Adagio,** 550 Geary St., Union Square (© **800/228-8830** or 415/775-5000; www.thehoteladagio.com), is far more chic and hip than its category counterparts. The 1929 Spanish Revival building has sexy streamlined rooms swathed in rich shades of brown, and a very chic restaurant and bar on the ground level. See p. 68.

- **The Golden Gate Hotel,** 775 Bush St. (© **800/835-1118** or 415/392-3702; www.goldengatehotel.com), receives nothing but kudos from satisfied guests. Just 2 blocks from Union Square, this 1913 Edwardian hotel is a real charmer and a fantastic value. See p. 76.

4 The Best Dining Experiences

- **The Best of the City's Fine Dining:** Restaurant **Michael Mina,** 335 Powell St., Union Square (© **415/397-9222**), is the place to go for Union Square fine dining. Dozens of fancifully presented small portions add up to a delightfully long, lavish meal. And then there's **Restaurant Gary Danko,** 800 North Point St., Fisherman's Wharf (© **415/749-2060**), always a sure bet for a perfect contemporary French meal complete with polished service and flambéed finales. See p. 106 and p. 132, respectively.

- **Best Classic San Francisco Dining Experience:** The lovable loudmouths working behind the narrow counter of the **Swan Oyster Depot,** 1517 Polk St. (© **415/673-1101**), have been satisfying patrons with fresh crab, shrimp, oysters, and clam chowder since 1912. My dad doesn't care much for visiting San Francisco ("Too crowded!") but he loves having lunch at this beloved seafood institution. See p. 122.

- **Best Dining on Dungeness Crab:** Eating fresh Dungeness crabmeat straight from Fisherman's Wharf seafood vendors' boiling pots at the corner of Jefferson and Taylor streets is the quintessential San Francisco experience.

- **Best Dim Sum Feast:** If you like Chinese food and the current small-plates craze, you'll love to "do dim sum." At the city's best dim sum house, **Ton Kiang,** 5821 Geary Blvd., the Richmond (© **415/387-8273**), p. 152, you'll be wowed by the variety of dumplings and mysterious dishes. For downtown dim sum, the venerable **Yank Sing,** 101 Spear St. (© **415/957-9300**), p. 114, offers an exotic edible surprise on every cart that's wheeled to your table.

- **Best Breakfast:** We have a tie: **Dottie's True Blue Café,** 522 Jones St. (© **415/885-2767**), p. 109, has taken the classic American breakfast to a new level—maybe the best I've ever had. Crummy neighborhood, superb food. **Ella's,** 500 Presidio Ave. (© **415/441-5669**), is far more yuppie, equally divine, and in a much better neighborhood, but it's so popular that the wait on weekend mornings is brutal. See p. 137.

- **Best Funky Atmosphere:** That's an easy one: **Tommy's Joynt,** 1101 Geary Blvd. (© **415/775-4216**). The interior looks like a Buffalo Bill museum that imploded, the exterior paint job looks like a circus tent on acid, and the huge trays of *hofbrau* classics will make your arteries harden just by looking at them. See p. 144.

- **Best Family-Style Restaurant:** Giant platters of classic Italian food and carafes filled with table wine are placed on long wooden tables by motherly waitresses while Sinatra classics play to the festive crowd of contented diners. Welcome to North Beach–style family dining at **Capp's Corner,** 1600 Powell St. (© **415/ 989-2589**). See p. 128.

- **Best Surreal Dining Experience:** This has to be sitting cross-legged on a pillow, shoes off, smoking apricot tobacco out of a hookah, eating baba ghanouj, and drinking spiced wine in an exotic Middle Eastern setting while beautiful, sensuous belly dancers glide across the dining room.

Unwind your mind at **Kan Zaman,** 1793 Haight St. (© **415/751-9656**). See p. 149.

- **Best Wine Country Dining:** If you're a foodie, you already know that one of the top restaurants in the world, **French Laundry,** 6640 Washington St. (© **707/944-2380**), p. 305, is about 1½ hours north of the city in Wine Country's tiny town of Yountville. Only die-hard diners need apply: You'll need to fight for a reservation 2 months in advance. A more relaxed alternative is **Terra,** 1345 Railroad Ave., St. Helena (© **707/963-8931**), where award-winning chef Hiro Sone shows his culinary creativity and mastery of French, Italian, and Japanese cuisine within a historic fieldstone split dining room. See p. 308.

5 The Best Things to Do for Free (or Almost)

- **Meander along the Marina's Golden Gate Promenade and Crissy Field.** There's something about strolling the promenade that just feels right. The combination of beach, bay, boats, Golden Gate views, and clean cool breezes is good for the soul. See p. 185.

- **Wake up with North Beach coffee.** One of the most pleasurable smells of San Francisco is the aroma of roasted coffee beans wafting down Columbus Avenue in the early morning. Start the day with a cup of Viennese on a sidewalk table at **Caffè Grecco** (423 Columbus Ave.; © **415/397-6261**), followed by a walk down Columbus Avenue to the bay.

- **Browse the Haight.** Though the power of the flower has wilted, the Haight is still, more or less, the Haight: a sort of resting home for aging hippies, ex-Deadheads, skate

punks, and an eclectic assortment of young panhandlers. Think of it as a people zoo as you walk down the rows of used-clothing stores, hip boutiques, and leather shops, trying hard not to stare at that girl (at least I *think* it's a girl) with the pierced eyebrows and shaved head. End the mystery tour with a pitcher of sangria and a plate of mussels at **Cha Cha Cha** (p. 148), one of my favorite restaurants that's a bargain to boot.

- **Pretend to be a guest at the Palace or Fairmont hotels.** You may not be staying the night, but you can certainly feel like a million bucks in the public spaces at **The Palace Hotel** (p. 83). The extravagant creation of banker "Bonanza King" Will Ralston in 1875, The Palace Hotel has one of the grandest rooms in the city: the **Garden Court.** Running a close second is the magnificent lobby at

Nob Hill's **Fairmont San Francisco** (p. 78).

- **Sip a cocktail in the clouds.** Some of the greatest ways to view the city are from top-floor lounges in fine hotels such as the Sir Francis Drake, Union Square (p. 71), the Grand Hyatt San Francisco (p. 64), and The Mark Hopkins InterContinental, Nob Hill (p. 79). Drinks aren't cheap, but it beats paying for a dinner. Besides, if you nurse your drink (or order something like tea or coffee), the combo of atmosphere, surroundings, and view is a bargain.

6 The Best Outdoor Activities

- **A Day in Golden Gate Park:** Exploring Golden Gate Park is a crucial part of the San Francisco experience. Its arboreal paths stretch from the Haight all the way to Ocean Beach, offering dozens of fun things to do along the way. Top sights are the Conservatory of Flowers, the Japanese Tea Garden, and the fabulous new de Young Museum (p. 167). The best time to go is Sunday, when portions of the park are closed to traffic (rent a bike for the full effect). Toward the end of the day, head west to the beach and watch the sunset. See p. 180.

- **A Walk along the Coastal Trail:** Stroll the forested Coastal Trail from Cliff House to the Golden Gate Bridge, and you'll see why San Franciscans put up with living on a fault line. Start at the parking lot just above Cliff House and head north. On a clear day, you'll have incredible views of the Marin Headlands, but even on foggy days, it's worth the trek to scamper over old bunkers and relish the cool, salty air (dress warmly). See "The Presidio & Golden Gate National Recreation Area," beginning on p. 182, for more on this area.

- **A Wine Country Excursion:** It'll take you about an hour to get there, but once you arrive you'll want to hopscotch from one winery to the next, perhaps picnic in the vineyards, or have an alfresco lunch at someplace atmospheric like Tra Vigne. And consider this: When the city is fogged in and cold, Napa and Sonoma are almost always sunny and warm. See chapter 13 for more information.

- **A Climb up or down the Filbert Street Steps:** San Francisco is a city of stairs, and the crème de la crème of steps is on Filbert Street between Sansome Street and the east side of Telegraph Hill. The terrain is so steep here that Filbert Street becomes Filbert Steps, a 377-step descent that wends its way through flower gardens and some of the city's oldest and most varied housing. It's a beautiful walk down, and great exercise going up.

- **A Visit to Muir Woods, Stinson Beach, and Point Reyes:** If you have wheels, reserve a day for a trip across the Golden Gate Bridge. Take the Stinson Beach exit off Highway 101, and spend a few hours gawking at the monolithic redwoods at Muir Woods (this place is amazing). Next, head up

The Best Activities for Families

For a list of San Francisco attractions that appeal to kids of all ages, see the "Especially for Kids" box on p. 190 of chapter 8.

the coast to the spectacular Point Reyes National Seashore. Rain or shine, it's a day trip you'll never forget. See "Muir Woods & Mount Tamalpais" and "Point Reyes National Seashore," beginning on p. 270 and p. 271, respectively.

7 The Best Places to Hang with the Locals

- **A Feast at the Ferry Building:** During Farmers' Market days, this bayfront alfresco market is packed with local shoppers vying for the freshest in local produce, breads, and flowers—or just mingling during their lunch breaks. But the building itself has become a mecca for food lovers who browse the outstanding artisan food shops and restaurants daily and then linger over glasses of wine at the festive wine bar. See p. 160.

- **Cafe-Hopping in North Beach:** It's a classic San Francisco experience: lingering at a sidewalk cafe on Columbus Avenue, watching people from all over the world walk by. Start the day with a latte at Café Greco, then wander over to Caffè Trieste, a haven for true San Francisco characters. See "Walking Tour 2: Getting to Know North Beach," beginning on p. 204, for a walking tour of the area.

8 The Best Offbeat Travel Experiences

- **A Soul-Stirring Sunday Morning Service at Glide Memorial Church:** Every city has churches, but only San Francisco has the Glide. An hour or so with Reverend Cecil Williams and his exuberant gospel choir will surely shake your soul and let the glory out, no matter what your religious beliefs may be—everybody leaves this Tenderloin church spiritually uplifted and slightly misty-eyed. See p. 186.

- **A Cruise through the Castro:** The most populated and festive street in the city is not just for gays and lesbians (although the best cruising in town *is* right here). Although there are some great shops and cafes, it's the people-watching here that makes the trip a must. If you have time, catch a flick at the beautiful 1930s Spanish colonial movie palace, the Castro Theatre (p. 178). See "Neighborhoods Worth a Visit," beginning on p. 174, for more on the Castro.

- **Skating through Golden Gate Park on a Weekend:** C'mon! When's the last time you've been skating? And if you've never tried skating before, there's no better place to learn than on the wide, flat main street through Golden Gate Park, which is closed to vehicles on weekends.

- **Catching Big Air in Your Car:** Relive *Bullitt* or *The Streets of San Francisco* as you careen down the center lane of Gough Street between Ellis and Eddy streets, screaming out "Wooooeee!" as you feel the pull of gravity leave you momentarily, followed by the thump of the car suspension bottoming out. Wimpier folk can settle for driving down the steepest street in San Francisco: Filbert Street, between Leavenworth and Hyde streets.

- **AsiaSF:** The gender-bending waitresses—mostly Asian men dressed *very* convincingly as hot-to-trot women—will blow your mind with their lip-synched show tunes, which take place every night. Bring the parents—they'll love it. See p. 120.

2

San Francisco in Depth

Unlike most American cities that have evolved in a more measured fashion, San Francisco has been molded politically, socially, and physically by a variety of (literally) earth-shaking events. In this chapter, we give you a little rundown on the history of the City by the Bay along with some other useful background on local views and customs that give an insight into the city and its inhabitants.

1 San Francisco Today

Shaken but not stirred by the Loma Prieta earthquake in 1989, San Francisco has witnessed a spectacular rebound in recent years. The seaside Embarcadero, once plagued by a horrendously ugly freeway overpass, has been revitalized by a multimillion-dollar facelift, complete with palm trees, a new trolley line, and wide cobblestone walkways. SoMa, the once shady neighborhood south of Market Street, has exploded with new development, including the world-class Museum of Modern Art, the beautiful Yerba Buena Gardens, and a slew of hip new clubs and cafes. South Beach is the new darling of young professionals living the condo-in-the-city life, and the spectacular new California Academy of Sciences and de Young Museum have given even the locals two new reasons to visit Golden Gate Park.

All that glitters is not the Golden Gate, however. At the end of World War II, San Francisco was the largest and wealthiest city on the West Coast. Since then, it has been demoted to the fourth-largest city in California, home to only 750,000 people, less than 5% of the state's total. The industrial heart of the city has been knocked out and shipped off to less costly locations such as Oakland and Los Angeles, and increasingly San Francisco has had to fall back on tourism as a major source of revenue. If the process continues unabated, the city may someday become another Las Vegas, whose only raison d'être will be pleasing its visitors like one vast Fisherman's Wharf—a frightening premonition. Then, of course, there are the typical big-city problems: Crime is up along with drug use, and despite efforts to curb homelessness and panhandling, it's still a thorny issue.

But as a whole, San Francisco is doing just fine these days. Its convention halls are fully booked, the real estate market has hardly been affected by the subprime housing debacle, Mayor Gavin Newsome has brought fresh ideas and renewed energy to the City—even the Giants are batting 500. It's hard to think of a whole city as having its ups and downs, but after nearly a decade of getting thumped by the recession and poor management (among other things), San Francisco is on a definite upswing. Though it may never relive its heady days as the king of the West Coast, San Francisco will undoubtedly retain the title as most everyone's favorite California city.

2 Looking Back at San Francisco

IN THE BEGINNING

Born as an out-of-the-way backwater of colonial Spain and blessed with a harbor that would have been the envy of any of the great cities of Europe, San Francisco boasts a story that is as varied as the millions of people who have passed through its Golden Gate.

THE AGE OF DISCOVERY   After the "discovery" of the New World by Columbus in 1492, legends of the fertile land of California were discussed in the universities and taverns of Europe, even though no one really understood where the mythical land was. (Some evidence of arrivals in California by Chinese merchants hundreds of years before Columbus's landing has been unearthed, although few scholars are willing to draw definite conclusions.) The first documented visit by a European to northern California, however, was by the Portuguese explorer João Cabrilho, who circumnavigated the southern tip of South America as far north as the Russian River in 1542. Nearly 40 years later, in 1579, Sir Francis Drake landed on the northern California coast, stopping for a time to repair his ships and to claim the territory for Queen Elizabeth I of England. He was followed several years later by another Portuguese, Sebastian Cermeño, "discoverer" of Punta de los Reyes (King's Point) in the mid-1590s. Ironically, all three adventurers completely missed the narrow entrance to San Francisco Bay, either because it was enshrouded in fog or, more likely, because they simply weren't looking for it. Believe it or not, the bay's entrance is nearly impossible to see from the open ocean.

It would be another two centuries before a European actually saw the bay that would later extend Spain's influence over much of the American West. Gaspar de Portolá, a soldier sent from Spain to meddle in a rather ugly conflict between the Jesuits and the Franciscans, accidentally stumbled upon the bay in 1769, en route to somewhere else, but then stoically plodded on to his original destination, Monterey Bay, more than 100 miles to the south. Six years later, Juan Ayala, while on a mapping expedition for the Spanish, actually sailed into San Francisco Bay, and immediately realized the enormous strategic importance of his find.

Colonization quickly followed. Juan Bautista de Anza and around 30 Spanish-speaking families marched through the deserts from Sonora, Mexico, arriving after many hardships at the northern tip

Dateline

- **1542** Juan Cabrillo sails up the California coast.
- **1579** Sir Francis Drake lands near San Francisco, missing the entrance to the bay.
- **1769** Members of the Spanish expedition led by Gaspar de Portolá become the first Europeans to see San Francisco Bay.
- **1775** The *San Carlos* is the first European ship to sail into San Francisco Bay.
- **1776** Captain Juan Bautista de Anza establishes a presidio (military fort); San Francisco de Asis Mission opens.
- **1821** Mexico wins independence from Spain and annexes California.
- **1835** The town of Yerba Buena develops around the port; the United States tries unsuccessfully to purchase San Francisco Bay from Mexico.
- **1846** Mexican-American War.
- **1847** Americans annex Yerba Buena and rename it San Francisco.

of modern-day San Francisco in June 1776. They immediately claimed the peninsula for Spain. (Ironically, their claim of allegiance to Spain occurred only about a week before the 13 English-speaking colonies of North America's eastern seaboard, a continent away, declared their independence from Britain.) Their headquarters was an adobe fortress, the Presidio, built on the site of today's park with the same name. The settlers' church, built a mile to the south, was the first of five Spanish missions later developed around the edges of San Francisco Bay. Although the name of the church was officially *Nuestra Señora de Dolores,* it was dedicated to St. Francis of Assisi and nicknamed San Francisco by the Franciscan priests. Later, the name was applied to the entire bay.

In 1821, Mexico broke away from Spain, secularized the Spanish missions, and abandoned all interest in the Indian natives. Freed of Spanish restrictions, California's ports were suddenly opened to trade. The region around San Francisco Bay supplied large numbers of hides and tallow for transport around Cape Horn to the tanneries and factories of New England and New York. The prospects for prosperity persuaded an English-born sailor, William Richardson, to jump ship in 1822 and settle on the site of what is now San Francisco. To impress the commandant of the Presidio, whose daughter he loved, Richardson converted to Catholicism and established the beginnings of what would soon became a thriving trading post and colony. Richard named his trading post *Yerba Buena* (or "good herb") because of a species of wild mint that grew there, near the site of today's Montgomery Street. (The city's original name was recalled with endless mirth 120 years later during San Francisco's hippie era.) He conducted a profitable hide-trading business and eventually became harbormaster and the city's first merchant prince. By 1839, the place was a veritable town, with a mostly English-speaking populace and a saloon of dubious virtue.

Throughout the 19th century, armed hostilities between English-speaking settlers from the eastern seaboard and the Spanish-speaking colonies of Spain and Mexico erupted in places as widely scattered as Texas, Puerto Rico, and along the frequently shifting U.S.-Mexico border. In 1846, a group of U.S. Marines from the warship *Portsmouth* seized the sleepy main plaza of Yerba Buena, ran the U.S. flag up a pole, and declared California an American territory. The Presidio (occupied by about a dozen unmotivated Mexican soldiers) surrendered without a fuss. The first

- **1848** Gold is discovered in Coloma, near Sacramento.
- **1849** In the year of the gold rush, San Francisco's population swells from about 800 to 25,000.
- **1851** Lawlessness becomes acute before attempts are made to curb it.
- **1869** The transcontinental railroad reaches San Francisco.

- **1873** Andrew S. Hallidie invents the cable car.
- **1906** The Great Earthquake strikes, and the resulting fire levels the city.
- **1915** The Panama Pacific International Exposition celebrates San Francisco's restoration and the completion of the Panama Canal.
- **1936** The Bay Bridge is built.
- **1937** The Golden Gate Bridge is completed.

- **1945** The United Nations Charter is drafted and adopted by the representatives of 50 countries meeting in San Francisco.
- **1950** The beat generation moves into the bars and cafes of North Beach.
- **1967** A free concert in Golden Gate Park attracts 20,000 people, ushering in the Summer of Love and the hippie era.

continues

move the new, mostly Yankee citizenry made was to officially adopt the name of the bay as the name of their town.

THE GOLD RUSH The year 1848 was one of the most pivotal years in European history, with unrest sweeping through Europe, horrendous poverty in Ireland, and widespread disillusionment about the hopes for prosperity throughout Europe and the eastern coast of the United States. Stories about the golden port of San Francisco and the agrarian wealth of the American West filtered slowly east, attracting slow-moving groups of settlers. Ex-sailor Richard Henry Dana extolled the virtues of California in his best-selling novel *Two Years Before the Mast,* and helped fire the public's imagination about the territory's bounty, particularly that of the Bay Area.

The first overland party crossed the Sierra and arrived in California in 1841. San Francisco grew steadily, reaching a population of approximately 900 by April 1848, but nothing hinted at the population explosion that was to follow. Historian Barry Parr has referred to the California gold rush as the most extraordinary event to ever befall an American city in peacetime. In time, San Francisco's winning combination of raw materials, healthful climate, and freedom would have attracted thousands of settlers even

without the lure of gold. But the gleam of the soft metal is said to have compressed 50 years of normal growth into less than 6 months. In 1848, the year gold was first discovered, the population of San Francisco jumped from under 1,000 to 26,000 in less than 6 months. As many as 100,000 more passed through San Francisco in the space of less than a year on their way to the rocky hinterlands where the gold was rumored to be.

If not for the discovery of some small particles of gold at a sawmill that he owned, Swiss-born John Augustus Sutter's legacy would have been far less flamboyant. Despite Sutter's wish to keep the discovery quiet, his employee, John Marshall, leaked word of the discovery to friends. It eventually appeared in local papers, and smart investors on the East Coast took immediate heed. The rush did not start, however, until Sam Brannan, a Mormon preacher and famous charlatan, ran through the streets of San Francisco shouting, "Gold! Gold in the American River!" (Brannan, incidentally, bought up all of the harbor-front real estate he could get, and cornered the market on shovels, pickaxes, and canned food, just before making the announcement that was heard around the world.)

A world on the brink of change responded almost frantically. The gold

- **1974** BART's high-speed transit system opens the tunnel linking San Francisco with the East Bay.
- **1978** Harvey Milk, a city supervisor and America's first openly gay politician, is assassinated, along with Mayor George Moscone, by political rival Dan White.
- **1989** An earthquake registering 7.1 on the Richter scale hits San Francisco

during a World Series baseball game, as 100 million watch on TV; the city quickly rebuilds.
- **1991** Fire rages through the Berkeley/Oakland hills, destroying 2,800 homes.
- **1993** Yerba Buena Center for the Arts opens.
- **1995** New San Francisco Museum of Modern Art opens.

- **1996** Former Assembly Speaker Willie Brown elected mayor of San Francisco.
- **2000** Pacific Bell Park (now AT&T Park), the new home to the San Francisco Giants, opens.
- **2002** The San Francisco Giants make it to the World Series but lose to the Anaheim Angels in Game 7.

rush was on. Shop owners hung "Gone to the Diggings" signs in their windows. Flotillas of ships set sail from ports throughout Europe, South America, Australia, and the East Coast, sometimes nearly sinking with the weight of mining equipment. Townspeople from the Midwest headed overland, tent cities sprang up, and the sociology of a nation was transformed almost overnight. Not since the Crusades of the Middle Ages had so many people been mobilized in so short a period of time. Daily business stopped; ships arrived in San Francisco and were almost immediately deserted by their crews. News of the gold strike spread like a plague through every discontented hamlet in the known world. Although other settlements were closer to the gold strike, San Francisco was the famous name, and therefore, where the gold-diggers disembarked. Tent cities sprung up, demand for virtually everything skyrocketed, and although some miners actually found gold, smart merchants quickly discovered that more enduring hopes lay in servicing the needs of the thousands of miners who arrived ill-equipped and ignorant of the lay of the land. Prices soared. Miners, faced with staggeringly inflated prices for goods and services, barely scraped a profit after expenses. Most prospectors failed, many died of hardship, others committed suicide at the alarming rate of 1,000 a year. Yet despite the tragedies, graft, and vice associated with the gold rush, within mere months San Francisco was forever transformed from a tranquil Spanish settlement into a roaring, boisterous boomtown.

BOOMTOWN FEVER By 1855, most of California's surface gold had already been panned out, leaving only the richer but deeper veins of ore, which individual miners couldn't retrieve without massive capital investments. Despite that, San Francisco had evolved into a vast commercial magnet, sucking into its warehouses and banks the staggering riches that overworked newcomers had dragged, ripped, and distilled from the rocks, fields, and forests of western North America.

Investment funds were being lavished on more than mining, however. Speculation on the newly established San Francisco stock exchange could make or destroy an investor in a single day, and several noteworthy writers (including Mark Twain) were among the young men forever influenced by the boomtown spirit. The American Civil War left California firmly in the Union camp, ready, willing, and able to receive hordes of disillusioned soldiers fed up with the internecine war-mongering of the eastern

- **2004** Thirty-six-year-old supervisor Gavin Newsom becomes the city's 42nd mayor and quickly makes headlines by authorizing city hall to issue marriage licenses to same-sex couples. Six months later, the state supreme court invalidates 3,955 gay marriages.
- **2005** The new, seismically correct $202-million de

- Young museum opens in Golden Gate Park.
- **2006** 100 year commemoration of the great earthquake and fire of 1906, the greatest disaster ever to befall an American metropolis.
- **2007** Tiger escapes from its pen at the San Francisco Zoo, killing one man and injuring two others before the police shoot and kill it.

- **2008** The California Supreme Court overturns overturning ban on same-sex marriage, touching off celebrations at San Francisco City Hall.

seaboard. In 1869, the transcontinental railway linked the eastern and western seaboards of the United States, ensuring the fortunes of the barons who controlled it. The railways, however, also shifted economic power bases as cheap manufactured goods from the east undercut the high prices hitherto charged for goods that sailed or steamed their way around the tip of South America. Ownership of the newly formed Central Pacific and Southern Pacific railroads was almost completely controlled by the "Big Four," all iron-willed capitalists—Leland Stanford, Mark Hopkins, Collis P. Huntington, and Charles Crocker—whose ruthlessness was legendary. (Much of the bone-crushing labor for their railway was executed by low-paid Chinese newcomers, most of whom arrived in overcrowded ships at San Francisco ports.) As the 19th century came to a close, civil unrest became more frequent as the monopolistic grip of the railways and robber barons became more obvious. Adding to the discontent were the uncounted thousands of Chinese immigrants, who fled starvation and unrest in Asia at rates rivaling those of the Italians, Poles, Irish, and British.

During the 1870s, the flood of profits from the Comstock Lode in western Nevada diminished to a trickle, a cycle of droughts wiped out part of California's agricultural bounty, and local industry struggled to survive against the flood of manufactured goods imported via railway from the well-established factories of the East Coast and Midwest. Often, discontented workers blamed their woes on the now-unwanted hordes of Chinese workers, who by preference and for mutual protection had congregated into teeming all-Asian communities.

Despite these downward cycles, the city enjoyed other bouts of prosperity around the turn of the century thanks to the Klondike gold rush in Alaska and the Spanish-American War. Long accustomed to making a buck off gold fever, San Francisco managed to position itself as a point of embarkation for supplies bound for Alaska. Also during this time emerged the Bank of America, which eventually evolved into the largest bank in the world. Founded in North Beach in 1904, Bank of America was the brainchild of Italian-born A. P. Giannini, who later funded part of the construction for a bridge that many critics said was preposterous: the Golden Gate.

THE GREAT FIRE   On the morning of April 18, 1906, San Francisco changed for all time. The city has never experienced an earthquake as destructive as the one that hit at 5:13am (scientists estimate its strength at 8.1 on the Richter scale). All but a handful of the city's 400,000 inhabitants lay fast asleep when the ground beneath the city went into a series of convulsions. As one eyewitness put it, "The earth was shaking . . . it was undulating, rolling like an ocean breaker." The quake ruptured every water main in the city, and simultaneously started a chain of fires that rapidly fused into one gigantic conflagration. The fire brigades were helpless, and for three days San Francisco burned.

Militia troops finally stopped the flames from advancing by dynamiting entire city blocks, but not before more than 28,000 buildings lay in ruins. Minor tremors lasted another three days. The final damage stretched across a path of destruction 450 miles long and 50 miles wide. In all, 497 city blocks were razed, or about one-third of the city. As Jack London wrote in a heartrending newspaper dispatch, "The city of San Francisco is no more." The earthquake and subsequent fire so decisively changed the city that post-1906 San Francisco bears little resemblance to the town before the quake. Out of the ashes rose a bigger, healthier, and more beautiful town, though latter-day urbanologists regret that the rebuilding that followed the San Francisco earthquake did not follow a more enlightened plan. So eager was the city to rebuild that the old, somewhat unimaginative gridiron plan was reinstated, despite the opportunities for more daring visions that the aftermath of the quake afforded.

In 1915, in celebration of the opening of the Panama Canal and to prove to the world that San Francisco was restored to it full glory, the city hosted the Panama Pacific International Exhibition, a world's fair that exposed hundreds of thousands of visitors to the city's unique charms. The general frenzy of civic boosterism, however, reached its peak during the years just before World War I, when investments and civic pride might have reached an all-time high. Despite Prohibition, speak-easies did a thriving business in and around the city, and building sprees were as high-blown and lavish as the profits on the San Francisco stock exchange.

WORLD WAR II   The Japanese attack on Pearl Harbor on December 7, 1941, mobilized the United States into a massive war machine, with many shipyards strategically positioned along the Pacific Coast, including San Francisco. Within less than a year, several shipyards were producing up to one new warship per day, employing hundreds of thousands of people working in 24-hour shifts (the largest, Kaiser Shipyards in Richmond, employed more than 100,000 workers alone). In search of work and the excitement of life away from their villages and cornfields, workers flooded into the city from virtually everywhere, forcing an enormous boom in housing. Hundreds found themselves separated from their small towns for the first time in their lives and reveled in their newfound freedom.

After the hostilities ended, many soldiers remembered San Francisco as the site of their finest hours and returned to live there permanently. The economic prosperity of the postwar years enabled massive enlargements of the city, including freeways, housing developments, a booming financial district, and pockets of counterculture enthusiasts such as the beatniks, gays, and hippies.

THE 1950s: THE BEATS   San Francisco's reputation as a rollicking place where anything goes dates from the Barbary Coast days when gang warfare, prostitution, gambling, and drinking were major city pursuits, and citizens took law and order into their own hands. Its more modern role as a catalyst for social change and the avant-garde began in the 1950s when a group of young writers, philosophers, and poets challenged the materialism and conformity of American society by embracing anarchy and Eastern philosophy, expressing their notions in poetry. They adopted a uniform of jeans, sweater, sandals, and beret, called themselves beats, and hung out in North Beach where rents were low and cheap wine was plentiful. *San Francisco Chronicle* columnist Herb Caen, to whom they were totally alien, dubbed them *beatniks* in his column.

Allen Ginsberg, Gregory Corso, and Jack Kerouac had begun writing at Columbia University in New York, but it wasn't until they came west and hooked up with Lawrence Ferlinghetti, Kenneth Rexroth, Gary Snyder, and others that the movement gained national attention. The bible of the beats was Ginsberg's *Howl,* which he first read at the Six Gallery on October 13, 1955. By the time he finished reading Ginsberg was crying, the audience was chanting, and his fellow poets were announcing the arrival of an epic bard. Ferlinghetti published *Howl,* which was deemed obscene, in 1956. A trial followed, but the court found that the book had redeeming social value, thereby reaffirming the right of free expression. The other major work, Jack Kerouac's *On the Road*, was published in 1957, instantly becoming a best seller (he had written it as one long paragraph in 20 days in 1951). The freedom and sense of possibility that this book conveyed became the bellwether for a generation.

While the beats gave poetry readings and generated controversy, two clubs in North Beach were making waves, notably the hungry i and the Purple Onion, where everyone who was anyone or became anyone on the entertainment scene appeared—Mort Sahl, Dick Gregory, Lenny Bruce, Barbra Streisand, and Woody Allen all worked here. Maya Angelou appeared as a singer and dancer at the Purple Onion. The cafes of North Beach were the center of bohemian life in the fifties: the Black Cat, Vesuvio's, Caffè Trieste and Caffè Tosca, and Enrico's Sidewalk Cafe. When the tour buses started rolling in, rents went up, and Broadway was turned into a sex club strip in the early 1960s. Thus ended an era, and the beats moved on. The alternative scene shifted to Berkeley and the Haight.

THE 1960s: THE HAIGHT The torch of freedom had been passed from the beats and North Beach to Haight-Ashbury and the hippies, but it was a radically different torch. The hippies replaced the beats' angst, anarchy, negativism, nihilism, alcohol, and poetry with love, communalism, openness, drugs, rock music, and a back-to-nature philosophy. Although the scent of marijuana wafted everywhere—on the streets, in the cafes, in Golden Gate Park—the real drugs of choice were LSD (a tab of good acid cost $5) and other hallucinogens. Timothy Leary experimented with its effects and exhorted youth to turn on, tune in, and drop out. Instead of hanging out in coffeehouses, the hippies went to

concerts at the Fillmore or the Avalon Ballroom to dance. The first Family Dog Rock 'n' Roll Dance and Concert, "A Tribute to Dr. Strange," was given at the Longshoreman's Hall in fall 1965, featuring the Jefferson Airplane, the Marbles, the Great Society, and the Charlatans. At this event, the first major happening of the 1960s, Ginsberg led a snake dance through the crowd. In January 1966, the three-day Trips Festival, organized by rock promoter Bill Graham, was also held at the Longshoreman's Hall. The climax came with Ken Kesey and the Merry Pranksters Acid Test show, which used five movie screens, psychedelic visions, and the sounds of the Grateful Dead and Big Brother and the Holding Company. The "be-in" followed in the summer of 1966 at the polo grounds in Golden Gate Park, when an estimated 20,000 heard the Jefferson Airplane perform and Ginsberg chant, while the Hell's Angels acted as unofficial police. It was followed by the Summer of Love in 1967 as thousands of young people streamed into the city in search of drugs and sex.

The sixties Haight scene was very different from the fifties beat scene. The hippies were much younger than the beats had been, constituting the first youth movement to take over the nation. Ironically, they also became the first generation of young, independent, and moneyed consumers to be courted by corporations. Ultimately, the Haight and the hippie movement deteriorated from love and flowers into drugs and crime, drawing a fringe of crazies like Charles Manson and leaving only a legacy of sex, drugs, violence, and consumerism. As early as October 1967, the "Diggers," who had opened a free shop and soup kitchen in the Haight, symbolically buried the dream in a clay casket in Buena Vista Park.

The end of the Vietnam War and the resignation of President Nixon took the edge off politics. The last fling of the mentality that had driven the 1960s occurred in 1974 when Patty Hearst was kidnapped from her Berkeley apartment by the Symbionese Liberation Army and taken on a bank-robbing spree before surrendering in San Francisco.

THE 1970s: GAY RIGHTS The homosexual community in San Francisco developed at the end of World War II, when thousands of military personnel were discharged back to the United States via San Francisco. A substantial number of those men were homosexual and decided to stay on in San Francisco. A gay community grew up along Polk Street between Sutter and California. Later, the larger community moved into the Castro, where it remains today.

The gay political protest movement is usually dated from the 1969 Stonewall raid that occurred in Greenwich Village. Although the political movement started in New York, California had already given birth to two major organizations for gay rights: the Mattachine Society, founded in 1951 by Henry Hay in Los Angeles, and the Daughters of Bilitis, a lesbian organization founded in 1955 in San Francisco.

After Stonewall, the Committee for Homosexual Freedom was created in spring 1969 in San Francisco; a Gay Liberation Front chapter was organized at Berkeley. In fall 1969, Robert Patterson, a columnist for the *San Francisco Examiner*, referred to homosexuals as "semi males, drag darlings," and "women who aren't exactly women." On October 31 at noon a group began a peaceful picket of the *Examiner*. Peace reigned until someone threw a bag of printer's ink from an *Examiner* window. Someone wrote "Fuck the Examiner" on the wall, and the police moved in to clear the crowd, clubbing them as they went. The remaining pickets retreated to Glide Methodist Church and then marched on city hall. Unfortunately, the mayor was away. Unable to air their grievances, they started a sit-in that lasted until 5pm, when they were ordered to leave. Most did, but three remained and were arrested.

Later that year, an anti-Thanksgiving rally was staged at which gays protested against several national and local businesses: Western and Delta airlines, the former for firing lesbian flight attendants, the latter for refusing to sell a ticket to a young man wearing a Gay Power button; KFOG, for its antihomosexual broadcasting; and also some local gay bars for exploitation. On May 14, 1970, a group of gay and women's liberationists invaded the convention of the American Psychiatric Association in San Francisco to protest the reading of a paper on aversion therapy for homosexuals, forcing the meeting to adjourn.

The rage against intolerance was appearing on all fronts. At the National Gay Liberation conference held in August 1970 in the city, Charles Thorp, chairman of the San Francisco State Liberation Front, called for militancy and issued a challenge to come out with a rallying cry of "Blatant is beautiful." He also argued for the use of what he felt was the more positive, celebratory term *gay* instead of *homosexual,* and decried the fact that homosexuals were kept in their place at the three B's: the bars, the beaches, and the baths. As the movement grew in size and power, debates on strategy and tactics occurred, most dramatically between those who wanted to withdraw into separate ghettos and those who wanted to enter mainstream society. The most extreme proposal was made in California by Don Jackson, who proposed establishing a gay territory in California's Alpine County, about 10 miles south of Lake Tahoe. It would have had a totally gay administration, civil service, university, museum—everything. The residents of Alpine County were not pleased with the proposal. But before the situation turned really ugly, Jackson's idea was abandoned because of lack of support in the gay community. In the end, the movement would concentrate on integration and civil rights, not separatism. They would elect politicians who were sympathetic to their cause and celebrate their new identity by establishing National Gay Celebration Day and Gay Pride Week, the first of which was celebrated in June 1970 when 1,000 to 2,000 marched in New York, 1,000 in Los Angeles, and a few hundred in San Francisco.

By the mid-1970s, the gay community craved a more central role in San Francisco politics. Harvey Milk, owner of a camera store in the Castro, decided to run as an openly gay man for the board of supervisors. He won, becoming the first gay person to hold a major public office. He and liberal Mayor George Moscone developed a gay rights agenda, but in 1978 both were killed by former Supervisor Dan White, who shot them after Moscone refused his request for reinstatement. White, a Catholic and former police officer, had consistently opposed Milk's and Moscone's more liberal policies. At his trial, White successfully pleaded temporary insanity caused by additives in his fast-food diet. The media dubbed it a "Twinkie defense," but the murder charges against White were reduced to manslaughter. On that day, angry and grieving, the gay community rioted, overturning and burning police cars in a night of rage. To this day a candlelight memorial parade is held on November 27. Milk's martyrdom was both a political and a practical inspiration to gay candidates across the country.

The emphasis in the gay movement shifted abruptly in the 1980s when the AIDS epidemic struck the community.

AIDS has had a dramatic impact on the Castro. While it's still a thriving and lively community, it's no longer the constant party that it once was. The hedonistic lifestyle that had played out in the discos, bars, baths, and streets changed as the seriousness of the epidemic sunk in and the number of deaths increased. Political efforts have shifted away from enfranchisement and toward demanding money for social services and research money to deal with the AIDS crisis. The gay community has developed its own organizations, such as Project Inform and Gay Men's Health Crisis, to publicize information about the disease, treatments available, and safe sex. Though new cases of AIDS within the gay community are on the decline in San Francisco, it still remains a serious problem.

THE 1980s: THE BIG ONE, PART 2

The eighties may have arrived in San Francisco with a whimper (compared to previous generations), but they went out with quite a bang. At 5:04pm on Tuesday, October 17, 1989, as more than 62,000 fans filled Candlestick Park for the third game of the World Series—and the San Francisco Bay Area commute moved into its heaviest flow—an earthquake of magnitude 7.1 struck. Within the next 20 seconds, 63 lives would be lost, $10 billion in damage would occur, and the entire Bay Area community would be reminded of their humble insignificance. Centered about 60 miles south of San Francisco within the Forest of Nisene Marks, the deadly temblor was felt as far away as San Diego and Nevada.

Though scientists had predicted an earthquake would hit on this section of the San Andreas Fault, certain structures that were built to withstand such an earthquake failed miserably. The most catastrophic event was the collapse of the elevated Cypress Street section of Interstate

880 in Oakland, where the upper level of the freeway literally pancaked the lower level, crushing everything with such force that cars were reduced to inches. Other structures heavily damaged included the San Francisco–Oakland Bay Bridge, shut down for months when a section of the roadbed collapsed; San Francisco's Marina district, where several multimillion-dollar homes collapsed on their weak, shifting bases of landfill and sand; and the Pacific Garden Mall in Santa Cruz, which was completely devastated.

President Bush declared a disaster area for the seven hardest-hit counties, where 63 people died, at least 3,700 people were reported injured, and more than 12,000 were displaced. More than 18,000 homes were damaged and 963 others destroyed. Although fire raged within the city and water supply systems were damaged, the major fires sparked within the Marina district were brought under control within three hours, due mostly to the heroic efforts of San Francisco's firefighters.

After the rubble had finally settled, it was unanimously agreed that San Francisco and the Bay Area had pulled through miraculously well—particularly when compared to the more recent earthquake in Kobe, Japan, which killed thousands and displaced an entire city. After the quake, a feeling of esprit de corps swept the city as neighbors helped each other rebuild and donations poured in from all over the world. Though it's been nearly a decade since, San Francisco is still feeling the effects of the quake, most noticeably during rush hour as commuters take a variety of detours to circumvent freeways that were damaged or destroyed and are still under construction. That another "big one" will strike is inevitable: It's the price you pay for living on a fault line. But if there is ever a city that is prepared for a major shakedown, it's San Francisco.

THE 1990s: THE NEW GOLD RUSH

During the 1990s, the nationwide recession influenced the beginning of the decade, while the quiet rumblings of the new frontier in Silicon Valley escaped much notice. By the middle of the decade, San Francisco and the surrounding areas were the site of a new kind of gold rush—the birth of Internet industry.

Not unlike the gold fever of the 1800s, people flocked to the western shores to strike it rich—and they did. In 1999, the local media reported that each day 64 Bay Area residents were gaining millionaire status. Long before the last year of the millennium, real estate prices went into the stratosphere, and the city's gentrification financially squeezed out many of those residents who didn't mean big business (read: many of the alternative types, elderly, and minorities who made the city colorful). New business popped up everywhere—especially in the SoMa area, where startup companies jammed warehouse spaces to the rafters.

As the most popular post-education destination for MBAs and the leader in the media of the future, San Francisco no longer opened its Golden Gate to everyone looking for the legendary alternative lifestyle—unless they could afford a $1,000 studio apartment and $20-per-day fees to park their cars.

The new millennium was christened with bubbly in hand, foie gras and caviar on the linen tablecloth, and seemingly everyone in the money. New restaurants charging $35 per entree were all the rage, hotels were renovated, the new bayfront ballpark was packed, and stock market tips were as plentiful as new million-dollar SoMa condos and high-rises. Though there were whispers of a stock market correction, San Franciscans were too busy raking in the dough and working and playing hard to heed the writing on the wall.

3 San Francisco in Popular Culture: Books, Films & Music

Getting acquainted with San Francisco through the work of authors and filmmakers will provide an extra dimension to your trip and perhaps some added excitement when you happen upon a location you recognize from a favorite cinematic moment or literary passage. San Francisco's own Chronicle Books publishes a great variety of material on the city, for children, cooks, art and architecture students, and readers of memoir and fiction. One of Chronicle's best books to stimulate your interest and curiosity is *San Francisco Stories: Great Writers on the City,* edited by John Miller. This collection of short pieces covers the personal and the political as recalled by acclaimed authors including Mark Twain, Jack Kerouac, Tom Wolfe, and Amy Tan. To find out about a smaller, more intimate city, check out *Good Life in Hard Times: San Francisco in the '20s and '30s,* by former journalist and San Francisco native Jerry Flamm (published by Chronicle Books).

One of the more famous and beloved pieces of modern fiction based in San Francisco is Armistead Maupin's *Tales of the City* (published by Perennial). If you've seen the miniseries, and especially if you haven't, this is a "must read" for a leisurely afternoon—or bring it with you on the plane. Maupin's 1970s soap opera covers the residents of 28 Barbary Lane (Macondry Lane on Russian Hill was the inspiration), melding sex, drugs, and growing self-awareness with enormous warmth and humor.

A work of fiction featuring San Francisco during the Gold Rush is *Daughter of Fortune,* by acclaimed novelist and Marin County resident Isabel Allende (published by HarperTorch). Allende's depiction of life in California during the mid–19th century is vividly described and is one of the novel's strengths.

As one of the loveliest spots on the planet, San Francisco has been a favorite of location scouts since the beginning of the film industry. Hundreds of movies and television shows have been shot or placed in San Francisco, making the hills and bridges among the most recognized of backgrounds. It may be difficult to locate at your local video store, but the 1936 Clark Gable/Jeanette MacDonald romance, *San Francisco,* is lauded for its dramatic reenactment of the 1906 earthquake and for MacDonald's rendition of the song of the same name. *The Maltese Falcon* (1941), Dashiell Hammett's classic detective story, with Humphrey Bogart starring as Sam Spade, includes shots of the Bay Bridge, the Ferry Building, and Burrit Alley (above the Stockton Tunnel). **John's Grill,** mentioned in the novel, continues to flog its association with Hammett's hero from its location at 63 Ellis St. (btw. Stockton and Powell streets).

Alfred Hitchcock's *Vertigo* (1958), starring James Stewart and Kim Novak, is admittedly an obvious choice on the list of great San Francisco films, but it's always worth viewing. Stewart plays a former detective hired to tail the wife of an old college friend, but the woman's identity is less than clear-cut. In the meantime, Stewart becomes obsessed with his prey as they make their way around the **Palace of the Legion of Honor, Fort Point, Mission Dolores,** and the detective's apartment at **900 Lombard St.** The city also fared well in the 1968 thriller *Bullitt,* starring a young Steve McQueen. Along with the hair-raising car chase over many hills, you'll see the Bay Bridge from a recognizable point on the **Embarcadero, Mason Street** heading north next to the **Fairmont Hotel,** the front of the **Mark Hopkins Hotel, Grace Cathedral,** and the fairly unchanged **Enrico's Sidewalk Café.**

For a change of pace and no tragic law-enforcement characters, screen the romantic comedy *What's Up, Doc?* (1972) with Barbra Streisand and Ryan O'Neal. Along with being a very funny film, there's another car chase scene that includes **Lombard Street** and **Chinatown** and ends at **Alta Plaza Park** in **Pacific Heights.** If you have kids to rev up, the 1993 comedy *Mrs. Doubtfire,* starring Sally Field and the city's favorite son, Robin Williams, shows San Francisco under blue skies and cable cars with plenty of room. The house where the character's estranged wife and children live is located at **2640 Steiner St.** (at Broadway), in case you care to gawk.

Finally, *24 Hours on Craigslist* is a documentary that covers a day in the life of this Internet community bulletin-board phenom. The filmmaker posted an ad on Craigslist, followed up with a handful of volunteers—an Ethel Merman impersonator seeking a Led Zeppelin cover band; a couple looking for others to join a support group for diabetic cats; a single, older woman needing a sperm donor—and sent film crews to cover their stories. Unlike other films that show the physical splendors of San Francisco, *24 Hours on Craigslist* will give you a sense of the city's psyche, or at least offer an explanation of why non–San Franciscans think the place is populated with . . . uh . . . unusual types.

SOUNDS OF THE '60S

During its heyday in the 1950s and 1960s, San Francisco was the place to be for anyone who eschewed the conventional American lifestyle. From moody beatniks to political firebrands, the city was a vortex for poets, writers, actors, and a bewildering assortment of free thinkers and activists. Drawn by the city's already liberal views on life, liberty, and the pursuit of happiness, thousands of the country's youth—including some of America's most talented musicians—headed west to join the party. What culminated in the 1960s was San Francisco's hat trick of rock legends: It was able to lay claim to three of the rock era's most influential bands: the Grateful Dead, Big Brother and the Holding Company and Janis Joplin, and the Jefferson Airplane.

THE GRATEFUL DEAD   Easily the most influential band to be spawned from the 1960s' psychedelic movement was San Francisco's music guru, the Grateful Dead. Described as the "house band for the famous acid tests that transformed the City by the Bay into one endless freak-out," the Dead's music was played simultaneously on so many stereo systems (and at such high volumes) that the group almost seemed to have set the tone for one enormous, citywide jam session.

Though the group disbanded in 1995 after the death of its charismatic lead vocalist, Jerry Garcia, the group's devoted fans had already elevated the Grateful Dead to cult empire status. Tie-dyed "Deadheads" (many of whom followed the band on tour for decades) can still be found tripping within the Haight, reminiscing about the good old days when the group never traveled with a sound system weighing less than 23 tons. In fact, more than any other band produced during the 1960s, the Grateful Dead were best appreciated during live concerts, partly because of the love-in mood that frequently percolated through the acidic audiences. Many rock critics remember with nostalgia that the band's most cerebral and psychedelic music was produced in the 1960s in San Francisco, but in the 1980s and 1990s, permutations of their themes were marketed in repetitive, less threatening forms that delighted their aficionados and often baffled or bored virtually everyone else.

For better or for worse, the Grateful Dead was a musical benchmark, expressing in new ways the mood of San Francisco during one of its drug-infused and most creatively fertile periods. But the days of the Dancing Bear and peanut butter sandwiches will never be quite over: Working from a proven formula, thousands of bands around the world continue to propagate the Dead's rhythmical standards.

But reading about the Grateful Dead is like dancing to architecture: If you're looking for an album whose title best expresses the changing artistic premises of San Francisco and the ironies of the pop culture that developed here, look for its award-winning retrospective *What a Long Strange Trip It's Been* at any of the city's record stores.

BIG BROTHER AND THE HOLDING COMPANY AND JANIS JOPLIN

The wide-open moral and musical landscape of San Francisco was almost unnervingly fertile during the 1960s. Despite competition from endless numbers of less talented singers, Texas-born Janis Joplin formulated much of her vocal technique before audiences in San Francisco. Her breakthrough style was first acknowledged at the Monterey Jazz Festival in 1967. Audiences reached out to embrace a singer whose rasping, gravely, shrieking voice expressed the generational angst of thousands of onlookers. *Billboard* magazine characterized her sound as composed of equal portions of honey, Southern Comfort, and gall. She was backed up during her earliest years by Big Brother and the Holding Company, a group she eventually outgrew.

Warned by specialists that her vocal technique would ruin her larynx before she was 30, Janis shrieked, wailed, gasped, and staggered over a blues repertoire judged as the most raw and vivid ever performed. Promoters frantically struggled to market (and protect) Janis and her voice for future artistic endeavors but, alas, her talent was simply too huge for her to handle, the time and place too

destructive for her raw-edged psyche. Her style is best described as "the desperate blues," partly because it never attained the emotional nonchalance of such other blues singers as Bessie Smith or Billie Holiday.

Parts of Janis's life were the subject of such lurid books as *Going Down with Janis,* and stories of her substance abuse, sexual escapades, and general raunchiness litter the emotional landscape of modern-day San Francisco. The star died of a heroin overdose at the age of 27, a tragedy still mourned by her thousands of fans, who continue to refer to her by her nickname, "Pearl." Contemporary photographs taken shortly before her death show a ravaged body and a face partially concealed behind aviator's goggles, long hair, and a tough but brittle facade. Described as omnisexual—and completely comfortable with both male and female partners—she once (unexpectedly) announced to a group of nightclub guests her evaluation of the sexual performance of two of the era's most visible male icons: Joe Namath (not particularly memorable) and Dick Cavett (absolutely fantastic). The audience (like audiences in concert halls around California) drank in the anecdotes that followed as "Gospel According to Janis."

JEFFERSON AIRPLANE

In the San Francisco suburbs of the late 1960s, hundreds of suburban bands dreamed of attaining stardom. Of the few that succeeded, none expressed the love-in ethic of that time in San Francisco better than the soaring vocals and ferocious guitar-playing of Jefferson Airplane. Singers Grace Slick and Marty Balin—as well as bass guitar player Jack Cassady—were considered at the top of their profession by their peers and highly melodic even by orchestral standards. Most importantly, all members of the band, especially Paul Kantner and Jorma Kaukonen, were songwriters. Their fertile mix of musical styles and creative energies led to songs that still reverberate in the minds of anyone who owned an AM radio during the late 1960s. The intense and lonely songs such as "Somebody to Love" and "White Rabbit" became the musical anthems of at least one summer, as American youth emerged into a highly psychedelic kind of consciousness within the creatively catalytic setting of San Francisco.

Although in 1989 the group reassembled its scattered members for a swan song as Jefferson Starship, the output was considered a banal repetition of earlier themes, and the energy of those long-faded summers of San Francisco in the late 1960s was never recovered. But despite its decline in its later years, Jefferson Airplane is still considered a band inextricably linked to the Bay Area's historic and epoch-changing Summer of Love.

3

Planning Your Trip to San Francisco

Although the best vacations are the ones that allow for spontaneity, there's no substitute for a little pre-trip research when it comes to planning a great vacation. Ergo, this entire chapter contains practical information to help you prepare the perfect trip to San Francisco, including megabytes of topical websites, recommended pre-trip arrangements, ideal times to visit, and local resources for those with specialized needs.

For additional help in planning your trip and for more on-the-ground resources in San Francisco, please turn to the "Fast Facts" appendix on p. 329.

1 Visitor Information

The **San Francisco Visitor Information Center,** on the lower level of Hallidie Plaza, 900 Market St., at Powell Street (✆ **415/391-2000;** www.onlyinsanfrancisco.com), is the best source of specialized information about the city. Even if you don't have a specific question, you might want to request the free *Visitors Planning Guide* and the *San Francisco Visitors* kit. The kit includes a 6-month calendar of events; a city history; shopping and dining information; and several good, clear maps; plus lodging information. The bureau highlights only its members' establishments, so if it doesn't have what you're looking for, that doesn't mean it's nonexistent.

You can also get the latest on San Francisco at the following online addresses:

- The *Bay Guardian,* the city's free weekly paper: **www.sfbg.com**
- *SF Gate,* the city's *Chronicle* newspaper: **www.sfgate.com**
- CitySearch: **http://sanfrancisco.city search.com**

2 Entry Requirements

PASSPORTS

New regulations issued by the Department of Homeland Security now require virtually every air traveler entering the U.S. to show a passport. As of January 23, 2007, all persons, including U.S. citizens, traveling by air between the United States and Canada, Mexico, Central and South America, the Caribbean, and Bermuda are required to present a valid passport. As of January 31, 2008, U.S. and Canadian citizens entering the U. S. at land and sea ports of entry from within the western hemisphere will need to present government-issued proof of citizenship, such as a birth certificate, along with a government issued photo ID, such as a driver's license. A passport is not required for U.S. or Canadian citizens entering by land or sea, but it is highly encouraged to carry one.

Value Money-Saving Tourist Passes

If you're the type who loves to cram as many tourist attractions as possible in one trip, then you might want to consider purchasing a **San Francisco City-Pass** or **GO San Francisco Card**. The **CityPass** includes 7 days of unlimited public transportation (including cable cars, Metro streetcars, and the entire bus system), and access some of the city's major attractions: the California Palace of the Legion of Honor and de Young museums, Aquarium of the Bay, the Asian Art Museum, the San Francisco Museum of Modern Art, the Exploratorium, and a Blue & Gold Fleet bay cruise. Discounts and coupons to other tourist-related attractions and activities are included as well. You can buy a CityPass at any of the above attractions or online at www.citypass.net. Current rates are $54 for adults and $44 for kids 5 to 17. For more informa-tion, visit the CityPass website at **www.citypass.net** or send an e-mail to info@citypass.com. For recorded information, call © 888/330-5008.

I think the better deal, however, is the **GO San Francisco Card** (© 800/887-9103; www.gosanfranciscocard.com). It offers free or discounted admis-sion to more than 45 of the most popular attractions, activities, and tours throughout the Bay Area and Wine Country; has far more flexibility (avail-able in 1-, 2-, 3-, 5-, and 7-day increments over a 14-day period); and comes with a nifty little full-color guidebook that fits in your back pocket. In addi-tion, some stores and restaurants offer discounts of up to 20% to Go San Francisco Card holders. The Go Cards are smart-technology enabled, which means they operate by calendar day and are activated the first time they are swiped, so you'll want to start your touring early in the morning to get the most value. The 2-day card costs $75 for adults ($35 for kids 3–12), and doesn't need to be used on consecutive days. You can purchase the GO Cards via their website or at the San Francisco Visitor Information Center (p. 24), Red & White Fleet Ticket Booth (p. 192), or Wax Museum (p. 162).

For information on how to obtain a passport, go to "**Passports**" in the "**Fast Facts**" appendix (p. 329).

VISAS

The U.S. State Department has a **Visa Waiver Program (VWP)** allowing citizens of the following countries to enter the United States without a visa for stays of up to 90 days: Andorra, Australia, Austria, Belgium, Brunei, Denmark, Finland, France, Germany, Iceland, Ireland, Italy, Japan, Liechtenstein, Luxembourg, Monaco, the Netherlands, New Zealand, Norway, Portugal, San Marino, Singapore, Slovenia, Spain, Sweden, Switzerland, and the United Kingdom. (*Note:* This list was accurate at press time; for the most up-to-date list of countries in the VWP, consult www.travel.state.gov/visa.) Canadian citi-zens may enter the United States without visas; they will need to show passports (if traveling by air) and proof of residence, however. *Note:* Any passport issued on or after October 26, 2006, by a VWP coun-try must be an **e-Passport** for VWP trav-elers to be eligible to enter the U.S. without a visa. Citizens of these nations also need to present a round-trip air or cruise ticket upon arrival. E-Passports con-tain computer chips capable of storing bio-metric information, such as the required digital photograph of the holder. (You can identify an e-Passport by the symbol on the bottom center cover of your passport.) If your passport doesn't have this feature, you can still travel without a visa if it is a valid passport issued before October 26, 2005, and includes a machine-readable zone, or between October 26, 2005, and October 25, 2006, and includes a digital photograph. For more information, go to **www.travel.state.gov/visa**.

Citizens of all other countries must have (1) a valid passport that expires at least 6 months later than the scheduled end of their visit to the U.S., and (2) a tourist visa, which may be obtained without charge from any U.S. consulate.

As of January 2004, many international visitors traveling on visas to the United States will be photographed and fingerprinted on arrival at Customs in airports and on cruise ships in a program created by the Department of Homeland Security called **US-VISIT.** Exempt from the extra scrutiny are visitors entering by land or those (mostly in Europe; see p. 25) who don't require a visa for short-term visits. For more information, go to the Homeland Security website at **www.dhs.gov/dhspublic**.

MEDICAL REQUIREMENTS

Unless you're arriving from an area known to be suffering from an epidemic (particularly cholera or yellow fever), inoculations or vaccinations are not required for entry into the United States.

CUSTOMS
WHAT YOU CAN BRING INTO THE U.S.

Every visitor more than 21 years of age may bring in, free of duty, the following: (1) 1 liter of wine or hard liquor; (2) 200 cigarettes, 100 cigars (but not from Cuba), or 3 pounds of smoking tobacco; and (3) $100 worth of gifts. These exemptions are offered to travelers who spend at least 72 hours in the United States and who have not claimed them within the preceding 6 months. It is forbidden to bring into the country almost any meat products (including canned, fresh, and dried meat products such as bullion, soup mixes, and so on). Generally, condiments including vinegars, oils, spices, coffee, tea, and some cheeses and baked goods are permitted. Avoid rice products, as rice can often harbor insects. Bringing fruits and vegetables is not advised, though not prohibited. Customs will allow produce depending on where you got it and where you're going after you arrive in the U.S. Foreign tourists may carry in or out up to $10,000 in U.S. or foreign currency with no formalities; larger sums must be declared to U.S. Customs on entering or leaving, which includes filing form CM 4790. For details regarding U.S. Customs and Border Protection, consult your nearest U.S. embassy or consulate, or **U.S. Customs** (www.customs.ustreas.gov).

WHAT YOU CAN TAKE HOME FROM SAN FRANCISCO:

Canadian Citizens: For a clear summary of Canadian rules, write for the booklet I Declare, issued by the Canada Border Services Agency (© **800/461-9999** in Canada, or 204/983-3500; **www.cbsa-asfc.gc.ca**).

U.K. Citizens: For information, contact **HM Customs & Excise** at © **0845/ 010-9000** (from outside the U.K., 020/8929-0152), or consult their website at **www.hmce.gov.uk**.

Australian Citizens: A helpful brochure available from Australian consulates or Customs offices is *Know Before You Go.* For more information, call the **Australian Customs Service** at © **1300/ 363-263,** or log on to **www.customs. gov.au**.

New Zealand Citizens: Most questions are answered in a free pamphlet available at New Zealand consulates and Customs offices: *New Zealand Customs Guide for Travellers, Notice no. 4.* For more information, contact **New Zealand Customs,** The Customhouse, 17–21 Whitmore St., Box 2218, Wellington (© **04/473-6099** or 0800/428-786; **www.customs.govt.nz**).

3 When to Go

If you're dreaming of convertibles, Frisbee on the beach, and tank-topped evenings, change your reservations and head to Los Angeles. Contrary to California's sunshine-and-bikini image, San Francisco's weather is "mild" (to put it nicely) and can often be downright bone-chilling because of the wet, foggy air and cool winds—it's nothing like that of Southern California. Summer, the most popular time to visit, is often characterized by damp, foggy days; cold, windy nights; and crowded tourist destinations. A good bet is to visit in spring or, better yet, autumn. Every September, right about the time San Franciscans mourn being cheated (or fogged) out of another summer, something wonderful happens: The thermometer rises, the skies clear, and the locals call in sick to work and head for the beach. It's what residents call "Indian summer." The city is also delightful during winter, when the opera and ballet seasons are in full swing; there are fewer tourists, many hotel prices are lower, and downtown bustles with holiday cheer.

CLIMATE

San Francisco's temperate, marine climate usually means relatively mild weather year-round. In summer, chilling fog rolls in most mornings and evenings, and if temperatures top 70°F (21°C), the city is ready to throw a celebration. Even when autumn's heat occasionally stretches into the 80s (upper 20s Celsius) and 90s (lower 30s Celsius), you should still dress in layers, or by early evening you'll learn firsthand why sweatshirt sales are a great business at Fisherman's Wharf. In winter, the mercury seldom falls below freezing and snow is almost unheard of, but that doesn't mean you won't be whimpering if you forget your coat. Still, compared to most of the states' weather conditions, San Francisco's are consistently pleasant.

It's that beautifully fluffy, chilly, wet, heavy, sweeping fog that makes the city's weather so precarious. A rare combination of water, wind, and topography creates Northern California's summer fog bank. It lies off the coast, and rising air currents pull it in when the land heats up. Held back by coastal mountains along a 600-mile front, the low clouds seek out any passage they can find. The easiest access is the slot where the Pacific Ocean penetrates the continental wall—the Golden Gate.

San Francisco's Average Temperatures & Rainfall

	Jan	Feb	Mar	Apr	May	June	July	Aug	Sept	Oct	Nov	Dec
High °F	56	59	61	64	67	70	71	72	73	70	62	56
Low °F	43	46	47	48	51	53	55	56	55	52	48	43
High °C	13	15	16	18	19	21	22	22	23	21	17	13
Low °C	6	8	8	9	11	12	13	13	13	11	9	6
Rain (in.)	4.5	4.0	3.3	1.2	0.4	0.1	0.1	0.1	0.2	1.0	2.5	2.9
Rain (mm)	113.0	101.9	82.8	30.0	9.7	2.8	0.8	1.8	5.1	26.4	63.2	73.4

Tips **Travel Attire**

Even if it's sunny out, don't forget to bring a jacket; the weather can change almost instantly from sunny and warm to windy and cold in San Francisco.

SAN FRANCISCO CALENDAR OF EVENTS

For more information, visit www.onlyinsan francisco.com for an annual calendar of local events.

February

Chinese New Year, Chinatown. In 2009, public celebrations will again spill onto every street in Chinatown. Festivities begin with the "Miss Chinatown USA" pageant parade, and climax a week later with a celebratory parade of marching bands, rolling floats, barrages of fireworks, and a block-long dragon writhing in and out of the crowds. The revelry runs for several weeks and wraps up with a memorable parade through Chinatown that starts at Market and Second streets and ends at Kearny Street. Arrive early for a good viewing spot on Kearny Street. You can purchase bleacher seats online starting in December. Make your hotel reservations early. For dates and information, call ✆ **415/982-3000** or visit www.chineseparade.com.

March

St. Patrick's Day Parade, Union Square and Civic Center. Everyone's an honorary Irish person at this festive affair, which starts at 11:30am at Market and Second streets and continues to City Hall. But the party doesn't stop there. Head down to the Civic Center for the post-party, or venture to The Embarcadero's Harrington's bar (245 Front St.) and celebrate with hundreds of the Irish-for-a-day yuppies as they gallivant around the closed-off streets and numerous pubs. For information,

call ✆ **415/675-9885;** www.sfst patricksdayparade.com. Sunday before March 17.

April

Cherry Blossom Festival, Japantown. Meander through the arts-and-crafts and food booths lining the blocked-off streets around Japan Center and watch traditional drumming, flower arranging, origami making, or a parade celebrating the cherry blossom and Japanese culture. Call ✆ **415/563-2313** for information. Mid- to late April.

San Francisco International Film Festival, around San Francisco with screenings at the AMC Kabuki 8 Cinemas (Fillmore and Post sts.), and at many other locations. Begun in 1957, this is America's oldest film festival. It features close to 200 films and videos from more than 50 countries. Tickets are relatively inexpensive, and screenings are accessible to the public. Entries include new films by beginning and established directors. For a schedule or information, call ✆ **415/561-5000** or visit www.sffs.org. Mid-April to early May.

May

Cinco de Mayo Festival, Mission District. This is when the Latino community celebrates the victory of the Mexicans over the French at Puebla in 1862; mariachi bands, dancers, food, and a parade fill the streets of the Mission. In 2008 the parade started at 9:30am at 24th and Harrison streets and down Mission Street. Check their website for the 2009 route. Contact the Mission Neighborhood Center for more information at (C) **415/206-0577;** www.carnavalsf.com. Fourth Sunday in May.

Bay to Breakers Foot Race, The Embarcadero through Golden Gate Park to Ocean Beach. Even if you don't participate, you can't avoid this run from downtown to Ocean Beach, which stops morning traffic throughout the city. More than 75,000 entrants gather—many dressed in wacky, innovative, and sometimes X-rated costumes—for the approximately 7.5-mile run. If you don't want to run, join the throng of spectators who line the route. Sidewalk parties, bands, and cheerleaders of all ages provide a good dose of true San Francisco fun. For recorded information, call (C) **415/359-2800,** or check their website, www.baytobreakers.com. Third Sunday of May.

Carnaval Festival, Harrison Street between 16th and 23rd streets. The Mission District's largest annual event, held from 9:30am to 6pm, is a day of festivities that includes food, music, dance, arts and crafts, and a parade that's as sultry and energetic as the Latin American and Caribbean people behind it. For one of San Franciscans' favorite events, more than half a million spectators line the parade route, and samba musicians and dancers continue to entertain on 14th Street, near Harrison, at the end of the march where you'll find food and craft booths, music, and more revelry. Call the hot line at (C) **415/920-0125** for information. Celebrations are held Saturday and Sunday of Memorial Day weekend, but the parade is on Sunday morning only. See www.carnavalsf.com for more information.

June

Union Street Art Festival, Pacific Heights, along Union Street from Steiner to Gough streets. This outdoor fair celebrates San Francisco with themes, gourmet food booths, music, entertainment, and a juried art show featuring works by more than 250 artists. It's a great time and a chance to see the city's young well-to-dos partying it up. Call the **Union Street Association** ((C) **415/441-7055**) for more information or see www.unionstreetfestival.com. First weekend of June.

Haight-Ashbury Street Fair, Haight-Ashbury. A far cry from the froufrou Union Street Fair, this grittier fair features alternative crafts, ethnic foods, rock bands, and a healthy number of hippies and street kids whooping it up and slamming beers in front of the blaring rock-'n'-roll stage. The fair usually extends along Haight between Stanyan and Ashbury streets. For details and the exact date, call (C) **415/863-3489** or visit www.haightstreetfair.org.

North Beach Festival, Grant Avenue, North Beach. In 2008, this party celebrated its 54th anniversary; organizers claim it's the oldest urban street fair in the country. Close to 100,000 city folk meander along Grant Avenue, between Vallejo and Union streets, to eat, drink, and browse the arts-and-crafts booths, poetry readings, swing-dancing venue, and *arte di gesso* (sidewalk chalk art). But the most enjoyable parts of the event are listening to music and people-watching. Call (C) **415/989-2220** or visit www.northbeachfestival.com for details. Usually Father's Day weekend, but call to confirm.

Stern Grove Music Festival, Sunset District. Pack a picnic and head out early to join the thousands who come here to lie in the grass and enjoy classical, jazz, and ethnic music and dance in the grove, at 19th Avenue and Sloat Boulevard. The Festival's 70th year was marked in 2007. The free concerts take place every Sunday at 2pm between mid-June and August. Show up with a lawn chair or blanket. There are food booths if you forget snacks, but you'll be dying to leave if you don't bring warm clothes—the Sunset District can be one of the coldest parts of the city. Call ✆ **415/252-6252** for listings; www.sterngrove.org. Sundays, mid-June through August.

San Francisco Lesbian, Gay, Bisexual, Transgender Pride Parade & Celebration, downtown's Market Street. This prideful event draws up to one million participants who celebrate all of the above—and then some. The parade proceeds west on Market Street until it gets to the Civic Center, where hundreds of food, art, and information booths are set up around several soundstages. Call ✆ **415/864-3733** or visit www.sfpride.org for information. Usually the third or last weekend of June.

July

Fillmore Jazz Festival, Pacific Heights. July starts with a bang, when the upscale portion of Fillmore closes to traffic and the blocks between Jackson and Eddy are filled with arts and crafts, gourmet food, and live jazz from 10am to 6pm. Call ✆ **510/970-3217** for more information; www.fillmore jazzfestival.com. First weekend in July.

Fourth of July Celebration & Fireworks, Fisherman's Wharf. This event can be something of a joke—more often than not, fog comes into the city, like everyone else, to join in the festivities. Sometimes it's almost impossible to view the million-dollar pyrotechnics from Pier 39 on the northern waterfront. Still, it's a party, and if the skies are clear, it's a darn good show. Visit www.4thofjulysf.com for more info.

San Francisco Marathon, San Francisco and beyond. This is one of the largest marathons in the world. It starts and ends at the Ferry Building at the base of Market Street, winds 26-plus miles through virtually every neighborhood in the City, and crosses the Golden Gate Bridge. For entry information, visit www.runsfm.com. Usually the last weekend in July.

September

Sausalito Art Festival, Sausalito. A juried exhibit of more than 20,000 original works of art, this festival includes music—provided by jazz, rock, and blues performers from the Bay Area and beyond—and international cuisine, enhanced by wines from some 50 Napa and Sonoma producers. Parking is impossible; take the **Blue & Gold Fleet ferry** (✆ **415/705-5555**) from Fisherman's Wharf to the festival site. For more information, call ✆ **415/332-3555** or log on to www.sausalito artfestival.org. Labor Day weekend.

Opera in the Park, usually in Sharon Meadow, Golden Gate Park. Each year the San Francisco Opera launches its season with a free concert featuring a selection of arias. Call ✆ **415/861-4008** to confirm the location and date. Usually the Sunday after Labor Day.

San Francisco Blues Festival, on the grounds of Fort Mason, the Marina. The largest outdoor blues music event on the West Coast was 35 years old in 2007 and continues to feature local and national musicians performing back-to-back during the 3-day extravaganza. You can charge tickets by phone at ✆ **415/421-8497** or online at www.ticketmaster.com. For information, call ✆ **415/979-5588** or visit www.sfblues.com. Usually in late September.

Folsom Street Fair, along Folsom Street between 7th and 12th streets, SoMa, from 11am to 6pm. This is a local favorite for its kinky, outrageous, leather-and-skin gay-centric blowout celebration. It's hard-core, so only open-minded and adventurous types need head into the leather-clad and partially dressed crowds. For info call ✆ **415/861-3247** or visit www.folsom streetfair.org. Last Sunday of September.

October

Fleet Week, Marina and Fisherman's Wharf. Residents gather along the Marina Green, The Embarcadero, Fisherman's Wharf, and other vantage points to watch incredible (and loud!) aerial performances by the Blue Angels, flown in tribute to our nation's marines. Call ✆ **650/599-5057** or visit www.fleetweek.us/fleetweek for details and dates.

Artspan Open Studios, various San Francisco locations. Find an original piece of art to commemorate your trip, or just see what local artists are up to by grabbing a map to over 800 artists' studios that are open to the public during weekends in October. Call ✆ **415/861-9838** or visit www.artspan.org for more information.

Castro Street Fair, the Castro. Celebrate life in the city's most famous gay neighborhood. Call ✆ **415/841-1824** or visit www.castrostreetfair.org for information. First Sunday in October, from 11am to 6pm.

Italian Heritage Parade, North Beach and Fisherman's Wharf. The city's Italian community leads the festivities around Fisherman's Wharf, celebrating Columbus's landing in America. The year 2008 marks the festival's 140th,

and as usual includes a parade along Columbus Avenue. But for the most part, it's a great excuse to hang out in North Beach and people-watch. For information, call ✆ **415/587-8282** or visit www.sfcolumbusday.org. Observed the Sunday before Columbus Day.

Exotic Erotic Halloween Ball, the Cow Palace, on the southern outskirts of San Francisco. Thousands come here dressed in costume, lingerie, and sometimes even less than that. It's a wild fantasy affair with bands, dancing, and costume contests. *Beware:* It can be somewhat cheesy. Advance tickets range from $60 to $125 per person. For information, call ✆ **415/567-BALL** or visit www.exoticeroticball.com. One or two Friday or Saturday nights before Halloween.

Halloween, the Castro. This is a huge night in San Francisco, especially in the flamboyant gay community of the Castro. Drop by for music, costume contests, and all-around revelry when streets are shut down and filled with a mixed crowd reveling in costumes of extraordinary imagination. For info visit www.halloweeninthecastro.com. October 31.

San Francisco Jazz Festival, various San Francisco locations. This festival presents eclectic programming in an array of fabulous jazz venues throughout the city. With close to 3 weeks of nightly entertainment and dozens of performers, the jazz festival is a hot ticket. Past events have featured Herbie Hancock, Dave Brubeck, the Modern Jazz Quartet, Wayne Shorter, and Bill Frisell. For information, call ✆ **800/850-SFJF** or 415/788-7353; or visit www.sfjazz.org. Also check the website for other events throughout the year. Late October and early November.

December

The Nutcracker, War Memorial Opera House, Civic Center. The **San Francisco Ballet** (📞 **415/865-2000**) performs this Tchaikovsky classic annually. Order tickets to this holiday tradition well in advance. Visit www.sfballet.org for information.

For an exhaustive list of events beyond those listed here, check http://events.frommers.com, where you'll find a searchable, up-to-the-minute roster of what's happening in cities all over the world.

4 Getting There & Getting Around

GETTING TO SAN FRANCISCO BY PLANE

The northern Bay Area has two major airports: San Francisco International and Oakland International.

SAN FRANCISCO INTERNATIONAL AIRPORT Almost four dozen major scheduled carriers serve **San Francisco International Airport** or **SFO** (📞 **650/821-8211;** www.flysfo.com), 14 miles directly south of downtown on U.S. 101. Travel time to downtown during commuter rush hour is about 40 minutes; at other times, it's about 20 to 25 minutes.

You can also call **511** or visit www.511.org for up-to-the-minute information about public transportation and traffic.

OAKLAND INTERNATIONAL AIRPORT About 5 miles south of downtown Oakland, at the Hegenberger Road exit of Calif. 17 (U.S. 880; if coming from south, take 98th Ave.), **Oakland International Airport** (📞 **800/247-6255** or 510/563-3300; www.oaklandairport.com) primarily serves passengers with East Bay destinations. Some San Franciscans prefer this less-crowded, more accessible airport, although it takes about half an hour to get there from downtown San Francisco (traffic permitting). The airport is also accessible by BART via a shuttle bus.

Arriving at the airport IMMIGRATION & CUSTOMS CLEARANCE International visitors arriving by air, no matter what the port of entry, should cultivate patience and resignation before setting foot on U.S. soil. U.S. airports have considerably beefed up security clearances in the years since the terrorist attacks of September 11, and clearing Customs and Immigration can take as long as 2 hours.

GETTING INTO TOWN FROM SAN FRANCISCO INTERNATIONAL AIRPORT

The fastest and cheapest way to get from SFO to the city is to take **BART** (Bay Area Rapid Transit; 📞 **415/989-2278;** www.bart.gov), which offers numerous stops within downtown San Francisco. This route, which takes about 35 minutes, avoids traffic on the way and costs a heck of a lot less than taxis or shuttles (about $6 each way, depending on exactly where you're going). Just jump on the airport's free shuttle bus to the International terminal, enter the BART station there, and you're on your way to San Francisco. Trains leave approximately every 15 minutes.

A **cab** from the airport to downtown costs $35 to $40, plus tip, and takes about 30 minutes, traffic permitting.

SuperShuttle (📞 **800/BLUE-VAN** or 415/558-8500; www.supershuttle.com) is a private shuttle company that offers door-to-door airport service, in which you share a van with a few other passengers. They will take you anywhere in the city, charging $15 per person to a residence or business. On the return trip, add $8 to $15 for each additional person depending on whether you're traveling from a hotel or a residence. The shuttle stops at least every 20 minutes, sometimes sooner, and picks up passengers from the marked areas outside the terminals' upper levels. Reservations are required for the return trip to the airport only and should be made 1 day before departure. These shuttles often demand they pick you up 2 hours before your domestic flight and 3 hours before international flights and during holidays. Keep in mind that you could be the first one on and the last one off, so this trip could take a while; you might want to ask before getting in. For $65, you can either charter the entire van for up to seven people or an Execucar private sedan for up to four people. For more info on the Execucar, call ⓒ **800/410-4444.**

The San Mateo County Transit system, **SamTrans** (ⓒ **800/660-4287** in Northern California, or 650/508-6200; www.samtrans.com), runs two buses between the San Francisco Airport and the Transbay Terminal at First and Mission streets. Bus no. 292 costs $1.50 and makes the trip in about 55 minutes. The KX bus costs $4 and takes just 35 minutes but permits only one carry-on bag. Both buses run daily. The no. 292 starts at 5:25am Monday through Friday and 5:30am on weekends; both run until 1am and run every half-hour until 7:30pm, when they run hourly. The KX starts at 5:53am and ends at 10:37pm Monday through Friday. On weekends, service runs from 7:19am to 9:30pm, runs every half-hour until 6:30pm, and then changes to an hourly schedule.

GETTING INTO TOWN FROM OAKLAND INTERNATIONAL AIRPORT

Taxis from the Oakland Airport to downtown San Francisco are expensive—approximately $50, plus tip.

Bayporter Express (ⓒ **877/467-1800** in the Bay Area, or 415/467-1800 elsewhere; www.bayporter.com) is a shuttle service that charges $26 for the first person and $12 for each additional person for the ride from the Oakland Airport to downtown San Francisco. Children under 12 pay $7. The fare for outer areas of San Francisco is higher. The service accepts advance reservations. To the right of the Oakland Airport exit, there are usually shuttles that take you to San Francisco for around $20 per person. The shuttles in this fleet are independently owned, and prices vary.

The cheapest way to reach downtown San Francisco is to take the shuttle bus from the Oakland Airport to **BART** (Bay Area Rapid Transit; ⓒ **510/464-6000;** www.bart.gov). The AirBART shuttle bus runs about every 15 minutes Monday through Saturday from 5am to 12:05am and Sunday from 8am to 12:05am. It makes pickups in front of terminals 1 and 2 near the ground transportation signs. Tickets must be purchased at the Oakland Airport's vending machines prior to boarding. The cost is $2 for the 10-minute ride to BART's Coliseum station in Oakland. BART fares vary, depending on your destination; the trip to downtown San Francisco costs $3.15 and takes 15 minutes once you're on board. The entire excursion should take around 45 minutes.

LONG-HAUL FLIGHTS: HOW TO STAY COMFORTABLE

- Your choice of airline and airplane will definitely affect your leg room. Find more details about U.S. airlines at **www.seatguru.com**. For international airlines, the research firm Skytrax has posted a list of average seat pitches at **www.airlinequality.com**.
- Emergency exit seats and bulkhead seats typically have the most legroom. Emergency exit seats are usually left unassigned until the day of a flight (to ensure that someone able-bodied fills the seats); it's worth checking in online at home (if the airline offers that option) or getting to the ticket counter early to snag one of these

spots for a long flight. Many passengers find that bulkhead seating offers more legroom, but keep in mind that bulkhead seats have no storage space on the floor in front of you.

- To have two seats for yourself in a three-seat row, try for an aisle seat in a center section toward the back of coach. If you're traveling with a companion, book an aisle and a window seat. Middle seats are usually booked last, so chances are good you'll end up with three seats to yourselves. And in the event that a third passenger is assigned the middle seat, he or she will probably be more than happy to trade for a window or an aisle.

- To sleep, avoid the last row of any section or the row in front of an emergency exit, as these seats are the least likely to recline. Avoid seats near highly trafficked toilet areas. Avoid seats in the back of many jets—these can be narrower than those in the rest of coach. Or reserve a window seat so you can rest your head and avoid being bumped in the aisle.

- Get up, walk around, and stretch every 60 to 90 minutes to keep your blood flowing. This helps avoid **deep vein thrombosis,** or "economy-class syndrome." See the box "Avoiding 'Economy Class Syndrome,'" p. 41.

- Drink water before, during, and after your flight to combat the lack of humidity in airplane cabins. Avoid caffeine and alcohol, which will dehydrate you.

BY CAR

San Francisco is easily accessible by major highways: **Interstate 5,** from the north, and **U.S. 101,** which cuts south–north through the peninsula from San Jose and across the Golden Gate Bridge to points north. If you drive from Los Angeles, you can take the longer coastal route (437 miles and 11 hr.) or the inland route (389 miles and 8 hr.). From Mendocino, it's 156 miles and 4 hours; from Sacramento, 88 miles and 1½ hours; from Yosemite, 210 miles and 4 hours.

If you are driving and aren't already a member, it's worth joining the **American Automobile Association** (AAA; ✆ 800/922-8228; www.csaa.com). It charges $49 to $79 per year (with an additional one-time joining fee), depending on where you join, and provides roadside and other services to motorists. **Amoco Motor Club** (✆ 800/334-3300; www.bpmotorclub.com) is another recommended choice.

For listings of the major car rental agencies in San Francisco, please see p. 37.

BY TRAIN

Traveling by train takes a long time and usually costs as much as, or more than, flying. Still, if you want to take a leisurely ride across America, rail may be a good option.

San Francisco–bound **Amtrak** (✆ 800/872-7245 or 800/USA-RAIL; www.amtrak.com) trains leave from New York and cross the country via Chicago. The journey takes about 3½ days, and seats sell quickly. At this writing, the lowest round-trip fare costs about $300 from New York and $270 from Chicago. Round-trip tickets from Los Angeles range from $120 to as much as $200. Trains arrive in Emeryville, just north of Oakland, and connect with regularly scheduled buses to San Francisco's Ferry Building and the Caltrain station in downtown San Francisco.

Caltrain (✆ 800/660-4287 or 415/546-4461; www.caltrain.com) operates train service between San Francisco and the towns of the peninsula. The city depot is at 700 Fourth St., at Townsend Street.

⟨Value⟩ Muni Discounts

Muni discount passes, called **Passports,** entitle holders to unlimited rides on buses, streetcars, and cable cars. A Passport costs $11 for 1 day, $18 for 3 days, and $24 for 7 consecutive days. Another option is buying a **CityPass,** which entitles you to unlimited Muni rides for 7 days, plus admission to the numerous attractions (see p. 25). Passports are also sold every day from 8am to midnight at the information booths in the baggage claim areas at San Francisco International Airport. You can also buy a Passport or CityPass at the San Francisco Visitor Information Center, Powell/Market cable car booth, Holiday Inn Civic Center, and TIX Bay Area booth at Union Square, among other outlets.

GETTING AROUND

For a map of San Francisco's public transportation options, see the "San Francisco Mass Transit" color map in the insert of this book. You can also call 511 for current transportation and traffic information or check www.511.org.

BY PUBLIC TRANSPORTATION

The **San Francisco Municipal Transportation Agency,** 1 S. Van Ness Ave., better known as "Muni" (© **415/673-6864;** www.sfmuni.com), operates the city's cable cars, buses, and streetcars. Together, these three services crisscross the entire city. Fares for buses and streetcars are $1.50 for adults; 50¢ for seniors over 65, children 5 to 17, and riders with disabilities. Cable cars, which run from 6:30am to 12:50am, cost a whopping $5 for all people over 5 ($1 for seniors and riders with disabilities 9pm–7am). Needless to say, they're packed primarily with tourists. Exact change is required on all vehicles except cable cars. Fares are subject to change. If you're standing waiting for Muni and have wireless Web access (or from any computer), check www.nextmuni.com to get up-to-the-minute information about when the next bus or streetcar is coming. Muni's NextBus uses satellite technology and advanced computer modeling to track vehicles on their routes. Each vehicle is fitted with a satellite tracking system so the information is constantly updated.

For detailed route information, phone Muni or consult the Muni map at the front of the San Francisco Yellow Pages. If you plan to use public transportation extensively, you might want to invest in a comprehensive transit and city map ($2), sold at the San Francisco Visitor Information Center (p. 24), Powell/Market cable car booth, and many downtown retail outlets. Also, see the "Muni Discounts" box for more information.

CABLE CAR   San Francisco's cable cars might not be the most practical means of transport, but the rolling historic landmarks are a fun ride. The three lines are concentrated in the downtown area. The most scenic, and exciting, is the **Powell-Hyde line,** which follows a zigzag route from the corner of Powell and Market streets, over both Nob Hill and Russian Hill, to a turntable at gaslit Victorian Square in front of Aquatic Park. The **Powell-Mason line** starts at the same intersection and climbs Nob Hill before descending to Bay Street, just 3 blocks from Fisherman's Wharf. The least scenic is the **California Street line,** which begins at the foot of Market Street and runs a straight course through Chinatown and over Nob Hill to Van Ness Avenue. All riders must exit at the last stop and wait in line for the return trip. The cable car system operates from approximately 6:30am to 12:50am, and each ride costs $5.

BUS   Buses reach almost every corner of San Francisco and beyond—they even travel over the bridges to Marin County and Oakland. Overhead electric cables power some buses; others use conventional gas engines. All are numbered and display their destinations on the front. Signs, curb markings, and yellow bands on adjacent utility poles designate stops, and most bus shelters exhibit Muni's transportation map and schedule. Many buses travel along Market Street or pass near Union Square and run from about 6am to midnight. After midnight, there is infrequent all-night "Owl" service. For safety, avoid taking buses late at night.

Popular tourist routes include bus nos. 5, 7, and 71, all of which run to Golden Gate Park; 41 and 45, which travel along Union Street; and 30, which runs between Union Square and Ghirardelli Square. A bus ride costs $1.50 for adults and 50¢ for seniors over 65, children 5 to 17, and riders with disabilities.

STREETCAR   Five of Muni's six streetcar lines, designated J, K, L, M, and N, run underground downtown and on the streets in the outer neighborhoods. The sleek rail cars make the same stops as BART (see below) along Market Street, including Embarcadero Station (in the Financial District), Montgomery and Powell streets (both near Union Square), and the Civic Center (near City Hall). Past the Civic Center, the routes branch off: The J line takes you to Mission Dolores; the K, L, and M lines run to Castro Street; and the N line parallels Golden Gate Park and extends all the way to The Embarcadero and AT&T Park. Streetcars run about every 15 minutes, more frequently during rush hours. They operate Monday through Friday from 5am to 12:15am, Saturday from 6am to approximately 12:15am, and Sunday from approximately 8am to 12:20am. The L and N lines operate 24 hours a day, 7 days a week, but late at night, regular buses trace the L and N routes, which are normally underground, from atop the city streets. Because the operation is part of Muni, the fares are the same as for buses, and passes are accepted.

The most recent new line to this system is not a newcomer at all, but is, in fact, an encore performance of San Francisco's beloved rejuvenated 1930s streetcar. The beautiful, retro multicolored F-Market streetcar runs from 17th and Castro streets to Beach and Jones streets; every other streetcar continues to Jones and Beach streets in Fisherman's Wharf. This is a quick and charming way to get up- and downtown without any hassle.

BART   BART, an acronym for **Bay Area Rapid Transit** (© **415/989-2278;** www.bart.gov), is a futuristic-looking, high-speed rail network that connects San Francisco with the East Bay—Oakland, Richmond, Concord, and Fremont. Four stations are on Market Street (see "Streetcar," above). Fares range from $1.45 to $7.35, depending on how far you go. Machines in the stations dispense tickets that are magnetically encoded with a dollar amount. Computerized exits automatically deduct the correct fare. Children 4 and under ride free. Trains run every 15 to 20 minutes, Monday through Friday from 4am to midnight, Saturday from 6am to midnight, and Sunday from 8am to midnight. In keeping with its futuristic look, BART now offers online trip planners that you can download to your PDA, iPod, or phone.

The 33-mile BART extension, which extends all the way to San Francisco International Airport, opened in June 2003. See earlier in this chapter for information on getting into town from the airport.

BY TAXI

This isn't New York, so don't expect a taxi to appear whenever you need one—if at all. If you're downtown during rush hour or leaving a major hotel, it won't be hard to hail a cab; just look for the lighted sign on the roof that indicates the vehicle is free. Otherwise, it's a good idea to call one of the following companies to arrange a ride; even then, there's been more than one time when the cab never came for me. What to do? Call back if your cab is late and insist on attention, but don't expect prompt results on weekends, no matter how nicely you ask. The companies are: **Veteran's Cab** (© 415/552-1300), **Luxor Cabs** (© 415/282-4141), **De Soto Cab** (© 415/970-1300), and **Yellow Cab** (© 415/626-2345). Rates are approximately $2.85 for the first mile and 45¢ each fifth of a mile thereafter.

BY CAR

You don't need a car to explore downtown San Francisco. In fact, with the city becoming more crowded by the minute, a car can be your worst nightmare—you're likely to end up stuck in traffic with lots of aggressive and frustrated drivers, pay upwards of $30 a day to park (plus a whopping new 14% parking lot tax), and spend a good portion of your vacation looking for a parking space. Don't bother. However, if you want to venture outside the city, driving is the best way to go.

Before heading outside the city, especially in winter, call © 800/427-7623 for California **road conditions.** You can also call 511 for current traffic information.

CAR RENTALS   All the major rental companies operate in the city and have desks at the airports. When we last checked, you could get a compact car for a week for anywhere from $165 to $315, including all taxes and other charges, but prices change dramatically on a daily basis and depend on which company you rent from.

Some of the national car-rental companies operating in San Francisco include **Alamo** (© 800/327-9633; www.alamo.com), **Avis** (© 800/331-1212; www.avis.com), **Budget** (© 800/527-0700; www.budget.com), **Dollar** (© 800/800-4000; www.dollar.com), **Enterprise** (© 800/325-8007; www.enterprise.com), **Hertz** (© 800/654-3131; www.hertz.com), **National** (© 800/227-7368; www.nationalcar.com), and **Thrifty** (© 800/367-2277; www.thrifty.com).

Car-rental rates vary even more than airline fares. Prices depend on the size of the car, where and when you pick it up and drop it off, the length of the rental period, where and how far you drive it, whether you buy insurance, and a host of other factors. A few key questions can save you hundreds of dollars, but you have to ask—reservations agents don't often volunteer money-saving information:

- Are weekend rates lower than weekday rates? Ask if the rate is the same for pickup Friday morning, for instance, as it is for Thursday night. Reservations agents won't volunteer this information, so don't be shy about asking.
- Does the agency assess a drop-off charge if you don't return the car to the same location where you picked it up?
- Are special promotional rates available? If you see an advertised price in your local newspaper, be sure to ask for that specific rate; otherwise, you could be charged the standard rate. Terms change constantly.
- Are discounts available for members of AARP, AAA, frequent-flier programs, or trade unions? If you belong to any of these organizations, you may be entitled to discounts of up to 30%.
- How much tax will be added to the rental bill? Will there be local tax and state tax?

Tips Safe Driving

Keep in mind the following handy driving tips:

- California law requires that both drivers and passengers wear seat belts.
- You can turn right at a red light (unless otherwise indicated), after yielding to traffic and pedestrians, and after coming to a complete stop.
- Cable cars always have the right of way, as do pedestrians at intersections and crosswalks.
- Pay attention to signs and arrows on the streets and roadways, or you might suddenly find yourself in a lane that requires exiting or turning when you want to go straight. What's more, San Francisco's many one-way streets can drive you in circles, but most road maps of the city indicate which way traffic flows.

- How much does the rental company charge to refill your gas tank if you return with the tank less than full? Most rental companies claim their prices are "competitive," but fuel is almost always cheaper in town, so you should try to allow enough time to refuel the car before returning it.

Some companies offer "refueling packages," in which you pay for an entire tank of gas upfront. The cost is usually fairly competitive with local prices, but you don't get credit for any gas remaining in the tank. If a stop at a gas station on the way to the airport will make you miss your plane, then by all means take advantage of the fuel purchase option. Otherwise, skip it.

Most agencies enforce a minimum-age requirement—usually 25. Some also have a maximum-age limit. If you're concerned that these limits might affect you, ask about rental requirements at the time of booking to avoid problems later.

Make sure you're insured. Hasty assumptions about your personal auto insurance or a rental agency's additional coverage could end up costing you tens of thousands of dollars, even if you are involved in an accident that is clearly the fault of another driver.

If you already have your own car insurance, you are most likely covered in the United States for loss of or damage to a rental car and liability in case of injury to any other party involved in an accident. Be sure to check your policy before you spend extra money (around $10 or more per day) on the **collision damage waiver (CDW)** offered by all agencies.

Most major credit cards (especially gold and platinum cards) provide some degree of coverage as well—if they were used to pay for the rental. Terms vary widely, however, so be sure to call your credit card company directly before you rent and rely on the card for coverage. If you are uninsured, your credit card may provide primary coverage as long as you decline the rental agency's insurance. If you already have insurance, your credit card may provide secondary coverage, which basically covers your deductible. However, note that *credit cards will not cover liability*, which is the cost of injury to an outside party and/or damage to an outside party's vehicle. If you do not hold an insurance policy, you should seriously consider buying additional liability insurance from your rental company, even if you decline the CDW.

PARKING   If you want to have a relaxing vacation, don't even attempt to find street parking on Nob Hill, in North Beach, in Chinatown, by Fisherman's Wharf, or on Telegraph Hill. Park in a garage or take a cab or a bus. If you do find street parking, pay attention to street signs that explain when you can park and for how long. Be especially careful not to park in zones that are tow areas during rush hours. And be forewarned, San Francisco has instituted a 14% parking tax, so don't be surprised by that garage fee!

Curb colors also indicate parking regulations. *Red* means no stopping or parking; *blue* is reserved for drivers with disabilities who have a disabled plate or placard; *white* means there's a 5-minute limit; *green* indicates a 10-minute limit; and *yellow* and *yellow-and-black* curbs are for stopping to load or unload passengers or luggage only. Also, don't park at a bus stop or in front of a fire hydrant, and watch out for street-cleaning signs. If you violate the law, you might get a hefty ticket or your car might be towed; to get your car back, you'll have to get a release from the nearest district police department and then go to the towing company to pick up the vehicle.

When parking on a hill, apply the hand brake, put the car in gear, and *curb your wheels*—toward the curb when facing downhill, away from the curb when facing uphill. Curbing your wheels not only prevents a possible "runaway" but also keeps you from getting a ticket—an expensive fine that is aggressively enforced.

BY FERRY

TO/FROM SAUSALITO, TIBURON, OR LARKSPUR The **Golden Gate Ferry Service** fleet (© **415/455-2000;** www.goldengateferry.org) shuttles passengers daily between the San Francisco Ferry Building, at the foot of Market Street, and downtown Sausalito and Larkspur. Service is frequent, departing at reasonable intervals every day of the year except January 1, Thanksgiving Day, and December 25. Phone or check the website for an exact schedule. The ride takes half an hour, and one-way fares are $6.45 for adults; $3.35 for seniors, passengers with disabilities, and youth 6 to 18. Children 5 and under travel free when accompanied by a full-fare paying adult (limit two children per adult). Family rates are available on weekends.

Ferries of the **Blue & Gold Fleet** (© **415/773-1188** for recorded info, or 415/705-5555 for tickets; www.blueand goldfleet.com) also provide round-trip service to downtown Sausalito and Tiburon, leaving from Fisherman's Wharf at Pier 41. The one-way cost is $8.50 for adults, $4.50 for kids 5 to 11. Boats run on a seasonal schedule; phone for departure information. Tickets can be purchased at Pier 41.

5 Money & Costs

It's always advisable to bring money in a variety of forms on a vacation: a mix of cash, credit cards, and ATM cards. You should also have enough petty cash upon arrival to cover airport incidentals, tipping, and transportation to your hotel before you leave home. You can always withdraw money upon arrival at an airport ATM, but you'll still need to make smaller change for tipping.

The most common bills are the $1 (a "buck"), $5, $10, and $20 denominations. There are also $2 bills (seldom encountered), $50 bills, and $100 bills (the last two are usually not welcome as payment for small purchases).

Coins come in seven denominations: 1¢ (1 cent, or a penny); 5¢ (5 cents, or a nickel); 10¢ (10 cents, or a dime); 25¢ (25 cents, or a quarter); 50¢ (50 cents, or a half dollar); the gold-colored Sacagawea coin, worth $1; and the rare silver dollar.

ATMs

In San Francisco and nationwide, the easiest and best way to get cash away from home is from an ATM (automated teller machine), sometimes referred to as a "cash machine," or "cashpoint." The **Cirrus** (© **800/424-7787;** www.mastercard. com) and **PLUS** (© **800/843-7587;** www.visa.com) networks span the country; you can find them even in remote regions. Go to your bank card's website to find ATM locations at your destination. Be sure you know your daily withdrawal limit before you depart.

Note: Many banks impose a fee every time you use a card at another bank's ATM, and that fee is often higher for international transactions (up to $5 or more) than for domestic ones (where they're rarely more than $2). In addition, the bank from which you withdraw cash may charge its own fee. To compare banks' ATM fees within the U.S., use **www.bankrate.com**. Visitors from outside the U.S. should also find out whether their bank assesses a 1% to 3% fee on charges incurred abroad.

Tip: One way around these fees is to ask for cash back at grocery, drug, and convenience stores that accept ATM cards and don't charge usage fees (be sure to ask). Of course, you'll have to purchase something first.

CREDIT CARDS & DEBIT CARDS

Credit cards are the most widely used form of payment in the United States: **Visa** (Barclaycard in Britain), **Master-Card** (Eurocard in Europe, Access in Britain, Chargex in Canada), **American Express, Diners Club,** and **Discover.**

They also provide a convenient record of all your expenses, and offer relatively good exchange rates. You can withdraw cash advances from your credit cards at banks or ATMs, but high fees make credit-card cash advances a pricey way to get cash.

It's highly recommended that you travel with at least one major credit card. You must have a credit card to rent a car, and hotels and airlines usually require a credit card imprint as a deposit against expenses.

TRAVELER'S CHECKS

Traveler's checks are something of an anachronism from the days before the ATM made cash accessible at any time. Traveler's checks used to be the only sound alternative to traveling with dangerously large amounts of cash. They were as reliable as currency, but, unlike cash, could be replaced if lost or stolen.

These days, traveler's checks are less necessary because most cities have 24-hour ATMs that allow you to withdraw small amounts of cash as needed. However, keep in mind that you will likely be charged an ATM withdrawal fee if the bank is not your own, so if you're withdrawing money every day, you might be better off with traveler's checks—provided that you don't mind showing identification every time you want to cash one. Visitors should make sure that traveler's checks are denominated in U.S. dollars; foreign-currency checks are often difficult to exchange.

6 Health

STAYING HEALTHY

Yes, the water's okay to drink in San Francisco, but you can spend your vacation in your hotel room if you wear shoes impractical for hiking the city's hills, or catch a cold because you didn't dress for winter weather in mid-July.

The United States **Centers for Disease Control and Prevention** (© **800/311-3435;** www.cdc.gov) provides up-to-date information on health hazards by region or country and offers tips on food safety. The website **www.tripprep.com**, sponsored by a consortium of travel medicine

Avoiding "Economy Class Syndrome"

Deep vein thrombosis, or as it's know in the world of flying, "economy-class syndrome," is a blood clot that develops in a deep vein. It's a potentially deadly condition that can be caused by sitting in cramped conditions—such as an airplane cabin—for too long. During a flight (especially a long-haul flight), get up, walk around, and stretch your legs every 60 to 90 minutes to keep your blood flowing. Other preventative measures include frequent flexing of the legs while sitting, drinking lots of water, and avoiding alcohol and sleeping pills. If you have a history of deep vein thrombosis, heart disease, or another condition that puts you at high risk, some experts recommend wearing compression stockings or taking anticoagulants when you fly; always ask your physician about the best course for you. Symptoms of deep vein thrombosis include leg pain or swelling, or even shortness of breath.

practitioners, **Travel Health Online,** may also offer helpful advice on traveling abroad. You can find listings of reliable clinics overseas at the **International Society of Travel Medicine** (www.istm.org).

WHAT TO DO IF YOU GET SICK AWAY FROM HOME

If you worry about getting sick away from home, you may want to consider **medical travel insurance.** In most cases, however, your existing health plan will provide all the coverage you need, but be sure to carry your identification card with you at all times. We list **additional emergency numbers** in the "Fast Facts" appendix, p. 330.

If you suffer from a chronic illness, consult your doctor before your departure. Pack **prescription medications** in your carry-on luggage, and carry them in their original containers, with pharmacy labels—otherwise they won't make it through airport security. Visitors from outside the U.S. should carry generic names of prescription drugs. For U.S. travelers, most reliable health-care plans provide coverage if you get sick away from home. Foreign visitors may have to pay all medical costs upfront and be reimbursed later. See "Medical Insurance," under "Insurance," in Appendix A.

7 Safety

STAYING SAFE

For a big city, San Francisco is relatively safe, and requires only that you use common sense (for example, don't leave your new video camera on the seat of your parked car). However, in neighborhoods such as Lower Haight, the Mission, the Tenderloin (a few blocks west of Union Sq.), and Fisherman's Wharf (at night especially), it's a good idea to pay attention to yourself and your surroundings.

Avoid carrying valuables with you on the street, and don't display expensive cameras or electronic equipment. Hold on to your pocketbook, and place your billfold in an inside pocket. In theaters, restaurants, and other public places, keep your possessions in sight.

Remember also that hotels are open to the public, and in a large hotel, security may not be able to screen everyone entering. Always lock your room door—don't assume that inside your hotel you are automatically safe.

Driving safety is important, too. Ask your rental agency about personal safety, and ask for a traveler-safety brochure when you pick up your car. Ask for written directions to your destination or a map with the route clearly marked. (Many agencies offer the option of renting a cellphone for the duration of your car rental; check with the rental agent when you pick up the car.) Try to arrive and depart during daylight hours.

Recently, more crime has involved cars and drivers. If you drive off a highway into a doubtful neighborhood, leave the area as quickly as possible. If you have an accident, even on the highway, stay in your car with the doors locked until you assess the situation or until the police arrive. If you're bumped from behind on the street or are involved in a minor accident with no injuries, and the situation appears to be suspicious, motion to the other driver to follow you. Never get out of your car in such situations. Go directly to the nearest police precinct, well-lit service station, or 24-hour store.

Always try to park in well-lit and well-traveled areas. Never leave any packages or valuables in sight. If someone attempts to rob you or steal your car, don't try to resist the thief or carjacker. Report the incident to the police department immediately by calling ℂ **911.** This is a free call, even from pay phones.

8 Specialized Travel Resources

TRAVELERS WITH DISABILITIES

Most disabilities shouldn't stop anyone from traveling. There are more options and resources out there than ever before.

Most of San Francisco's major museums and tourist attractions have wheelchair ramps. Many hotels offer special accommodations and services for wheelchair users and other visitors with disabilities. As well as the ramps, they include extra-large bathrooms and telecommunication devices for hearing-impaired travelers. The San Francisco Visitor Information Center (p. 24) should have the most up-to-date information.

Travelers in wheelchairs can request special ramped taxis by calling **Yellow Cab** (ℂ **415/626-2345**), which charges regular rates for the service. Travelers with disabilities can also get a free copy of the *Muni Access Guide,* published by the San Francisco Municipal Transportation Agency, Accessible Services Program, One South Van Ness, third floor (ℂ **415/ 923-6142**), which is staffed weekdays from 8am to 5pm. Many of the major car-rental companies offer hand-controlled cars for drivers with disabilities. **Alamo** (ℂ **800/651-1223**), **Avis** (ℂ **800/331-1212,** ext. 7305), and **Budget** (ℂ **800/314-3932**) have special hot lines that help provide such a vehicle at any of their U.S. locations with 48 hours' advance notice; **Hertz** (ℂ **800/654-3131**) requires between 24 and 72 hours' advance notice at most locations.

Organizations that offer a vast range of resources and assistance to disabled travelers include **MossRehab** (ℂ **800/ CALL-MOSS;** www.mossresourcenet. org); the **American Foundation for the Blind** (**AFB;** ℂ **800/232-5463;** www. afb.org); and **SATH (Society for Accessible Travel & Hospitality;** ℂ **212/ 447-7284;** www.sath.org). **AirAmbulanceCard.com** is now partnered with SATH and allows you to preselect topnotch hospitals in case of an emergency.

Access-Able Travel Source (ℂ **303/ 232-2979;** www.access-able.com) offers a comprehensive database on travel agents from around the world with experience in accessible travel; destination-specific access information; and links to such resources as service animals, equipment rentals, and access guides.

Many travel agencies offer customized tours and itineraries for travelers with disabilities. Among them are **Flying Wheels Travel** (© 507/451-5005; www.flyingwheelstravel.com); and **Accessible Journeys** (© 800/846-4537 or 610/521-0339; www.disabilitytravel.com).

Flying with Disability (www.flying-with-disability.org) is a comprehensive information source on airplane travel. **Avis Rent a Car** (© 888/879-4273) has an "Avis Access" program that offers services for customers with special travel needs. These include specially outfitted vehicles with swivel seats, spinner knobs, and hand controls; mobility scooter rentals; and accessible bus service. Be sure to reserve well in advance.

Also check out the quarterly magazine *Emerging Horizons* (www.emerging horizons.com), available by subscription ($16.95 year U.S.; $21.95 outside U.S.).

The "Accessible Travel" link at **Mobility-Advisor.com** (www.mobility-advisor.com) offers a variety of travel resources to disabled persons.

British travelers should contact **Holiday Care** (© 0845-124-9971 in U.K. only; www.holidaycare.org.uk) to access a wide range of travel information and resources for disabled and elderly people.

GAY & LESBIAN TRAVELERS

If you head down to the Castro—an area surrounding Castro Street near Market Street—you'll understand why the city is a mecca for gay and lesbian travelers. Since the 1970s, this unique part of town has remained a colorfully festive neighborhood, teeming with "out" city folk who meander the streets shopping, eating, partying, or cruising. If anyone feels like an outsider in this part of town, it's heterosexuals, who, although warmly welcomed in the community, may feel uncomfortable or downright threatened if they harbor any homophobia or aversion to being checked out. For many San Franciscans, it's just a fun area (especially on Halloween) with some wonderful shops.

Gays and lesbians make up a good deal of San Francisco's population, so it's no surprise that clubs and bars all over town cater to them. Although lesbian interests are concentrated primarily in the East Bay (especially Oakland), a significant community resides in the Mission District, around 16th and Valencia streets.

Several local publications concentrate on in-depth coverage of news, information, and listings of goings-on around town for gays and lesbians. The *Bay Area Reporter* (www.ebar.com) has the most comprehensive listings, including a weekly calendar of events. Distributed free on Thursday, it can be found stacked at the corner of 18th and Castro streets and at Ninth and Harrison streets, as well as in bars, bookshops, and stores around town. It may also be available in gay and lesbian bookstores elsewhere in the country.

GUIDES & PUBLICATIONS For a good book selection, contact **Giovanni's Room,** 345 S. 12th St., Philadelphia, PA 19107 (© 215/923-2960; www.giovanis room.com); and **A Different Light Bookstore,** 489 Castro St., San Francisco, CA 94114 (© 415/431-0891; www.adlbooks.com).

The **International Gay and Lesbian Travel Association (IGLTA;** © 800/448-8550 or 954/776-2626; www.iglta.org) is the trade association for the gay and lesbian travel industry, and offers an online directory of gay- and lesbian-friendly travel businesses and tour operators.

Many agencies offer tours and travel itineraries specifically for gay and lesbian travelers. **Above and Beyond Tours** (© 800/397-2681; www.abovebeyond tours.com) are gay Australia tour specialists. San Francisco–based **Now, Voyager** (© 800/255-6951; www.nowvoyager. com) offers worldwide trips and cruises; and **Olivia** (© 800/631-6277; www. olivia.com) offers lesbian cruises and resort vacations.

Gay.com Travel (© **800/929-2268** or 415/644-8044; www.gay.com/travel or www.outandabout.com) is an excellent online successor to the popular *Out & About* print magazine. It provides regularly updated information about gay-owned, gay-oriented, and gay-friendly lodging, dining, sightseeing, nightlife, and shopping establishments in every important destination worldwide. British travelers should click on the "Travel" link at **www.uk.gay.com** for advice and gay-friendly trip ideas.

The Canadian website **GayTraveler** (**www.gaytraveler.ca**) offers ideas and advice for gay travel all over the world.

The following travel guides are available at many bookstores, or you can order them from any online bookseller: *Spartacus International Gay Guide* (Bruno Gmünder Verlag; www.spartacusworld.com/gayguide) and *Odysseus: The International Gay Travel Planner* (www.odyusa.com); and the *Damron* guides (www.damron.com), with separate, annual books for gay men and lesbians.

For more gay and lesbian travel resources visit frommers.com.

SENIOR TRAVEL

Nearly every attraction in San Francisco offers a senior discount; age requirements vary, and specific prices are listed in chapter 8. Public transportation and movie theaters also have reduced rates. Don't be shy about asking for discounts, but always carry some kind of identification, such as a driver's license, that shows your date of birth.

Members of **AARP**, 601 E St. NW, Washington, DC 20049 (© **888/687-2277**; www.aarp.org), get discounts on hotels, airfares, and car rentals. AARP offers members a wide range of benefits, including *AARP The Magazine* and a monthly newsletter. Anyone over 50 can join.

Recommended publications offering travel resources and discounts for seniors include: the quarterly magazine *Travel 50 & Beyond* (www.travel50andbeyond.com) and the bestselling paperback *Unbelievably Good Deals and Great Adventures That You Absolutely Can't Get Unless You're Over 50* (McGraw-Hill), by Joann Rattner Heilman.

Frommers.com offers more information and resources on travel for seniors.

FAMILY TRAVEL

If you have enough trouble getting your kids out of the house in the morning, dragging them thousands of miles away may seem like an insurmountable challenge. But family travel can be immensely rewarding, giving you new ways of seeing the world through smaller pairs of eyes.

San Francisco is full of sightseeing opportunities and special activities geared toward children. See "Especially for Kids," in chapter 8, beginning on p. 190, for information and ideas for families. Also watch for the "Kids" icon throughout this guide.

Recommended family travel websites include **Family Travel Forum** (www.familytravelforum.com), a comprehensive site that offers customized trip planning; **Family Travel Network** (www.familytravelnetwork.com), an online magazine providing travel tips; and **Travel WithYourKids.com,** a comprehensive site written by parents for parents offering sound advice for long-distance and international travel with children.

PUBLICATIONS *Frommer's San Francisco with Kids* (Wiley Publishing, Inc.) is a good source of kid-specific information for your trip. The *Unofficial Guide to California with Kids* is also a useful resource if you plan to travel throughout the state.

For a list of more family-friendly travel resources, turn to the experts at frommers.com.

STUDENT TRAVEL

A valid student ID will often qualify students for discounts on airfare, accommodations, entry to museums, cultural events, movies, and more. Check out the **International Student Travel Confederation (ISTC;** www.istc.org) website for comprehensive travel services information and details on how to get an **International Student Identity Card (ISIC),** which qualifies students for substantial savings on rail passes, plane tickets, entrance fees, and more. It also provides students with basic health and life insurance and a 24-hour helpline. The card is valid for a maximum of 18 months. You can apply for the card online or in person at **STA Travel** (© **800/781-4040** in North America; © 132-782 in Australia; © 0871/2-300-040 in the U.K.; www.statravel.com), the biggest student travel agency in the world; check out the website to locate STA Travel offices worldwide. If you're no longer a student but are still under 26, you can get an **International Youth Travel Card (IYTC)** from the same people, which entitles you to some discounts. **Travel CUTS** (© **800/592-2887;** www.travelcuts.com) offers similar services for both Canadians and U.S. residents. Irish students may prefer to turn to **USIT** (© **01/602-1904;** www.usit.ie), an Ireland-based specialist in student, youth, and independent travel.

TRAVELING WITH PETS

If you're thinking of taking your pet along with you to romp on a California beach, make sure you do a little research. For one thing, dogs are restricted from running free on most public beaches in the San Francisco area (though the law is often ignored). To find out where you can bring man's best friend, check out the online **Pets Welcome** service (www.petswelcome.com), which lists accommodations that allow pets. The site also lists pet-related publications, medical travel tips, and links to other pet-related websites.

A good book to carry along is *The California Dog Lover's Companion: The Insider's Scoop on Where to Take Your Dog* (Avalon Travel Publishing), a 900-page source for complete statewide listings of fenced dog parks, dog-friendly beaches, and other indispensable information.

Also note that San Francisco has strict leash laws (including stiff penalties for failing to pick up waste). In the event that your pet requires medical care while you're visiting, call or visit the **SF/SPCA Animal Hospital,** 2500 16th St. at Harrison Street (© **415/554-3030;** www.sfspca.org). The **San Francisco Veterinary Specialists,** located at 600 Alabama St. at 18th Street (© **415/401-9200;** www.sfvs.net), is open 24 hours, 7 days a week.

For more resources about traveling with pets, go to www.frommers.com.

9 Sustainable Tourism

Sustainable tourism is conscientious travel. It means being careful with the environments you explore, and respecting the communities you visit. Two overlapping components of sustainable travel are **ecotourism** and **ethical tourism.** The **International Ecotourism Society (TIES)** defines ecotourism as responsible travel to natural areas that conserves the environment and improves the well-being of local people. TIES suggests that ecotourists follow these principles:

- Minimize environmental impact.
- Build environmental and cultural awareness and respect.
- Provide positive experiences for both visitors and hosts.
- Provide direct financial benefits for conservation and for local people.

• Raise sensitivity to host countries' political, environmental, and social climates.
• Support international human rights and labor agreements.

You can find some eco-friendly travel tips and statistics, as well as touring companies and associations—listed by destination under "Travel Choice"—at the **TIES** website, www.ecotourism.org. Also check out **Ecotravel.com,** which lets you search for sustainable touring companies in several categories (water-based, land-based, spiritually oriented, and so on).

While much of the focus of ecotourism is about reducing impacts on the natural environment, ethical tourism concentrates on ways to preserve and enhance local economies and communities, regardless of location. You can embrace ethical tourism by staying at a locally owned hotel or shopping at a store that employs local workers and sells locally produced goods.

Responsible Travel (www.responsible travel.com) is a great source of sustainable travel ideas; the site is run by a spokesperson for ethical tourism in the travel industry. **Sustainable Travel International** (www.sustainabletravelinternational.org) promotes ethical tourism practices, and manages an extensive directory of sustainable properties and tour operators around the world.

In the U.K., **Tourism Concern** (www. tourismconcern.org.uk) works to reduce social and environmental problems connected to tourism. The **Association of Independent Tour Operators** (AITO; www.aito.co.uk) is a group of specialist operators leading the field in making holidays sustainable.

10 Staying Connected

TELEPHONES
Generally, hotel surcharges on long-distance and local calls are astronomical, so you're better off using your **cellphone** or a **public pay telephone.** Many convenience groceries and packaging services sell **prepaid calling cards** in denominations up to $50; for international visitors these can be the least expensive way to call home. Many public pay phones at airports now accept American Express, MasterCard, and Visa credit cards. **Local calls** made from pay phones in most locales cost either 25¢ or 35¢ (no pennies, please).

Most long-distance and international calls can be dialed directly from any phone. **For calls within the United States and to Canada,** dial 1 followed by the area code and the seven-digit number.

Tips Hey, Google, did you get my text message?

It's bound to happen: The day you leave this guidebook back at the hotel for an unencumbered stroll through Pacific Heights, you'll forget the address of the lunch spot you had earmarked. If you're traveling with a mobile device, send a text message to ℭ **46645 (GOOGL)** for a lightning-fast response. For instance, type "carnegie deli new york" and within 10 seconds you'll receive a text message with the address and phone number. This nifty trick works in a range of search categories: Look up weather ("weather miami"), movie times ("harry potter 60605"), and more. If your search results are off, be more specific ("the abbey gay bar west hollywood"). For more tips and search options, see www.google.com/intl/en_us/mobile/sms.

For other international calls, dial 011 followed by the country code, city code, and the number you are calling.

Calls to area codes **800, 888, 877,** and **866** are toll-free. However, calls to area codes **700** and **900** (chat lines, bulletin boards, "dating" services, and so on) can be very expensive—usually a charge of 95¢ to $3 or more per minute, and they sometimes have minimum charges that can run as high as $15 or more.

For **reversed-charge or collect calls,** and for person-to-person calls, dial the number 0 then the area code and number; an operator will come on the line, and you should specify whether you are calling collect, person-to-person, or both. If your operator-assisted call is international, ask for the overseas operator.

For **local directory assistance** ("information"), dial 411; for long-distance information, dial 1, then the appropriate area code and 555-1212.

4

Suggested
San Francisco Itineraries

If you've left your brain at the office and want someone else to make all the tough decisions during your vacation, you'll love this chapter. It's where I tell you what *I* think you should see and do during your vacation in San Francisco. It's broken down into 1 Day, 2 Day, and 3 Day sections, depending on how long you're in town. If you've already made your way through "The Best in 1 Day," the 2 Day tour starts where the 1 Day schedule left off, and so on. But if you really want to enjoy even a fraction of what San Francisco has to offer, you should plan on staying at least 3 days, preferably a week. And because renting a car in the city is an expensive hassle (and driving in the city is insane), we're going to do all our transportation via foot, bus, and bike. Right, then: Let's get started.

1 The Best of San Francisco in 1 Day

If you've got only 1 day to explore the city, put on your walking shoes and start early. You've got a lot of ground to cover just to get to the must-sees, but luckily, condensed geography (and hopefully weather) are in your favor. The whirlwind tour starts with a scenic ride on a cable car followed by a tour of Alcatraz Island. Next you'll hoof it up to two of the city's most colorful neighborhoods—Chinatown and North Beach— for lunch, shopping, browsing, cocktails, dinner, and cappuccino. Get an early start, because you're about to have a long yet wonderful day in the city by the bay. *Start: Bus no. 2, 3, 4, 30, 45, or 76 to Union Square.*

❶ Union Square

Union Square—which was named for a series of pro-union mass demonstrations staged here on the eve of the Civil War— isn't an attraction in itself, but it's the epicenter of the city's shopping district. Macy's, Saks, Tiffany's, Victoria's Secret, and company are located here, and are surrounded by blocks crammed with hundreds of other high-end boutiques. There are very few shopping bargains here, but it's fun to play lookey-loo. Just 3 blocks down, at Powell and Market streets, is the cable car turnaround where you'll embark on a ride on the nation's only moving National Historic Landmark. See p. 56.

❷ Cable Cars & Lombard Street ✸✸✸

Don't be intimidated by the line of people at the cable car turnaround at Market and Powell streets—the ride is worth the wait. The $5 thrill ride starts with a steep climb up Nob Hill, then passes through Chinatown and Russian Hill before plummeting down Hyde Street to Fisherman's Wharf. It's an experience you'll

The Best of San Francisco in 1 & 2 Days

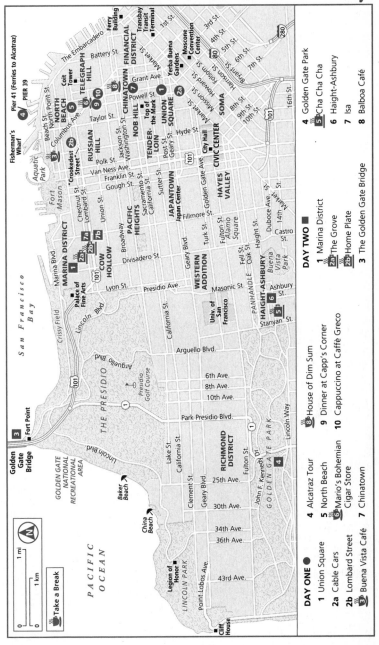

DAY ONE ●

1 Union Square
2a Cable Cars
2b Lombard Street
☕ Buena Vista Café

4 Alcatraz Tour
5 North Beach
6 Mario's Bohemian Cigar Store
7 Chinatown

8 House of Dim Sum
9 Dinner at Capp's Corner
10 Cappuccino at Caffè Greco

DAY TWO ■

1 Marina District
2a The Grove
2b Home Plate
3 The Golden Gate Bridge

4 Golden Gate Park
5 Cha Cha Cha
6 Haight-Ashbury
7 Isa
8 Balboa Café

Take a Break

N

0 ___ 1 mi
0 ___ 1 km

49

never forget. (*Note:* If you want to check out the famous winding stretch of Lombard Street, hop off the cable car at the intersection of Hyde and Lombard streets and, when you've seen enough, either walk the rest of the way down to Fisherman's Wharf or take the next cable car that comes along.) For maximum thrill, stand during the ride and hold onto the brass rail. See p. 158.

BUENA VISTA CAFÉ

After you've completed your first Powell-Hyde cable car ride, it's a San Francisco tradition to celebrate with an Irish coffee at the Buena Vista Café, located at 2765 Hyde St. across from the cable car turnaround (*(*✆*) 415/474-5044*). The first Irish coffees served in America were mixed here in 1952, and they're still the best in the Bay Area. See p. 243.

❹ Alcatraz Tour ✰✰✰

To tour "The Rock," the Bay Area's famous abandoned prison on its own island, you must first get there, and that's half the fun. The brief but beautiful ferry ride offers captivating views of the Golden Gate Bridge, the Marin Headlands, and the city. Once inside, an excellent audio tour guides you through cell blocks and offers a colorful look at the prison's historic past as well as its most infamous inmates. Book well in advance because these tours consistently sell out in the summer. Bring snacks and beverages—the ferry's pickings are slim and expensive, and nothing is available on the island. See p. 153.

❺ North Beach ✰✰✰

One of the best ways to get the San Francisco vibe is to mingle with the locals, and one of my favorite places to do so is in San Francisco's "Little Italy." Dozens of Italian restaurants and coffeehouses continue to flourish in what is still the center of the city's Italian community. A stroll along Columbus Avenue will take you past eclectic little cafes, delis, bookstores, bakeries, and coffee shops that give North Beach its Italian-bohemian character. See p. 204.

Tip: Be sure to see chapter 9, "City Strolls," for highlights of North Beach and Chinatown.

MARIO'S BOHEMIAN CIGAR STORE

Okay, so the menu's limited to coffee drinks and a few sandwiches (the meatball is my favorite), but the convivial atmosphere and large windows that are perfect for people-watching make this tiny, pie-shaped cafe a favorite even with locals. 566 Columbus Ave.; *(*✆*) 415/362-0536*. See p. 129.

❼ Chinatown ✰✰

One block from North Beach is a whole other world: Chinatown. San Francisco has one of the largest communities of Chinese people in the United States, with more than 80,000 people condensed around Grant Avenue and Stockton Street. Although frequented by tourists, the area caters mostly to the Chinese community, who crowd the vegetable and herb markets, restaurants, and shops carrying those ubiquitous pink plastic bags. It's worth a peek if only to see the Stockton Street markets hawking live frogs, armadillos, turtles, and odd sea creatures destined for tonight's dinner table. *Tip:* The dozens of knickknack shops are a great source of cheap souvenirs. See p. 198.

HOUSE OF DIM SUM

You can't visit Chinatown and not sample dim sum. Walk to 735 Jackson St. to the House of Dim Sum (*(*✆*) 415/399-0888*) and order shrimp dumplings, pork dumplings, sweet buns, turnip cake, and the sweet rice with chicken wrapped in a lotus leaf. Find an empty table, pour a side of soy sauce, and dig in.

9 Dinner at Capp's Corner ☆

What I love about North Beach are its old-school restaurants—those dusty, frumpy, loud, and over-sauced bastions of bacchanal. **Capp's Corner** (1600 Powell St; ☎ **415/989-2589**) is one of my favorites, where patrons sit at long tables and dine family-style via huge platters of Italian comfort food served by brusque waitresses while Frank croons his classics on the jukebox. See p. 128.

10 Cappuccino at Caffè Greco ☆

By now you should be stuffed and exhausted. Good. End the night with a cappuccino at **Caffè Greco** (423 Columbus Ave.; ☎ **415/397-6261**). Sit at one of the sidewalk tables and reminisce on what a great day you had in San Francisco.

2 The Best of San Francisco in 2 Days

On your second day, get familiar with other famous landmarks around the city. Start with breakfast, a science lesson, and a pleasant bayside stroll in the Marina District. Next, cross the famed Golden Gate Bridge on foot, then take a bus to Golden Gate Park. After a stroll through the city's beloved park, it's time for lunch and power shopping on Haight Street, followed by dinner and cocktails back in the Marina District. Smashing. *Start: Bus no. 22, 28, 30, 30X, 43, 76, or 82X.*

1 Good Morning Marina District

The area that became famous for its destruction during the 1989 earthquake has long been one of the most picturesque and coveted patches of local real estate. Here, along the northern edge of the city, multimillion-dollar homes back up against the bayfront Marina, where a flotilla of sailboats and the mighty Golden Gate Bridge make for a magnificent backdrop for a morning stroll.

Start the day with good cup of coffee on Chestnut Street (see "Take a Break" below), then walk to the Palace of Fine Arts building, built for the Panama-Pacific Exhibition of 1915 and home of the Exploratorium (p. 168). Spend a few hours being thoroughly entertained at the "best science museum in the world" (kids *love* this place), then walk over to Crissy Field (p. 185), where restored wetlands and a beachfront path lead to historic Fort Point (p. 185) and the footpath that will take you up to the southern end of the Golden Gate Bridge.

> **2 BREAKFAST**
> If you can't jumpstart your brain properly without a good cup of coffee, then begin your day at **The Grove** (2250 Chestnut St.; ☎ **415/474-4843**; p. 139), located in the Marina District—it's as cozy as an old leather couch.

3 The Golden Gate Bridge ☆☆☆

It's one of those things you have to do at least once in you life—walk across the fabled Golden Gate Bridge, the most photographed man-made structure in the world (p. 163). As you would expect, the views along the span are spectacular and the wind a wee bit chilly, so bring a light jacket. It takes at least an hour to walk northward to the vista point and back. When you return to the southern end, board either Muni bus no. 28 or no. 29 (be sure to ask the driver if the bus is headed toward Golden Gate Park).

❹ Golden Gate Park ★★★

Stretching from the middle of the city to the Pacific Ocean and comprising 1,017 acres, Golden Gate Park is one of the city's greatest attributes. Since its development in the late 1880s, it has provided San Franciscans with urban respite via dozens of well-tended gardens, museums, and great grassy expanses prime for picnicking, lounging, or tossing a Frisbee.

Have the bus driver drop you off near John F. Kennedy Drive. Walking eastward on JFK Drive, you'll pass three of the park's most popular attractions: Stow Lake, the newly renovated de Young Museum, and the wonderful Conservatory of Flowers (a must-visit). See p. 180.

> ☕ **CHA CHA CHA** ★★
>
> By now you're probably starving, so walk out of the park and into the Haight to **Cha Cha Cha** (1801 Haight St.; ℂ **415/386-7670;** p. 148), one of my favorite restaurants in the city. Order plenty of dishes from the tapas-style menu and dine family-style. Oh, and don't forget a pitcher of sangria—you've earned it.

❻ Exploring the Haight-Ashbury District ★★★

Ah, the Haight. Birthplace of the Summer of Love and Flower Power, shrine to the Grateful Dead, and the place where America's nonconformists still congregate over beers, bongos, and buds. Spend at least an hour strolling up Haight Street (p. 178), browsing the cornucopia of used clothes stores, leather shops, head shops, and poster stores. There are some great bargains to be found here, especially for vintage clothing. When you get to the intersection of Haight and Masonic streets, catch the Muni no. 43 bus heading north, which will take you through the Presidio and back to the Marina District.

❼ Dinner & Drinks

You've had a full day, my friend, so rest your weary bones at the back patio at **Isa** (3324 Steiner St.; ℂ **415/567-9588;** p. 138), a fantastic and surprisingly affordable French restaurant in the Marina. If there's still gas in your tank after dinner, walk over to the **Balboa Café** (3199 Fillmore St.; ℂ **415/921-3944**) and practice your pick-up lines among the young-and-restless who practically live here.

<hr/>

3 The Best of San Francisco in 3 Days

If we weren't on a tight budget I'd have you rent a car and head to the Wine Country for a day of wine tasting, but that would probably blow your budget (if not, skip to the Wine Country chapter; see p. 276). Instead, we're going to do one of my all-time favorite things to do on my day off—ride a bike from Fisherman's Wharf to Sam's Anchor Cafe in Tiburon (that small peninsula just north of Alcatraz Island). The beautiful and exhilarating ride takes you over the Golden Gate Bridge, through the heart of Sausalito, and along the scenic North Bay bike path, ending with a frosty beer and lunch at the best outdoor cafe in the Bay Area. And here's the best part: You don't have to bike back. After lunch, you can take the passenger ferry across the bay to Fisherman's Wharf—right to your starting point. Brilliant. *Start: Powell-Hyde cable-car line. Bus no. 10, 19, 30, or 47.*

<hr/>

❶ Rent a Bicycle

Walk, take a bus, or ride the Powell-Hyde cable car (which goes right by it) to **Blazing Saddles** bicycle rental shop at 2715 Hyde St, between Beach and North Point streets near Ghirardelli Square (ℂ **415/202-8888;** p. 195). Rent a single or tandem bike for a full day, and be sure to ask for: 1) a free map pointing out the route

1 Bike rental from Blazing Saddles
2 The Warming Hut
3 Bike across the Golden Gate Bridge
4 Sausalito Tour
5 Horizons
6 North Bay Tour
7 Lunch at Sam's Anchor Café
8 Ferry from Tiburon to San Francisco (Pier 39)

Take a Break

to Sam's in Tiburon, 2) ferry tickets, 3) a bicycle lock, and 4) a bottle of water. Bring your own sunscreen, a hat (for the deck at Sam's), and a light jacket—no matter how warm it is right now, the weather can change in minutes. Each bike has a small pouch hooked to the handlebars where you can stuff your stuff.

Fun Tip: While you're here, ask about the GoCar rentals—they're a blast to drive and a great way to explore the city. (See the GoCar sidebar on p. 163 for more info.)

❷ The Warming Hut

Start pedaling along the map route to Golden Gate Bridge. You'll encounter one short, steep hill right from the start at Aquatic Park, but it's okay to walk your

bike (hey, you haven't had your coffee fix yet). Keep riding westward through Fort Point and the Marina Green to Crissy Field. At the west end of Crissy Field, alongside the bike path, is the Warming Hut, a white, barnlike building where you can fuel up with a light snack and coffee drinks. (Don't eat too much.) Several picnic tables nearby offer beautiful views of the bay.

❸ Biking the Golden Gate

After your break, there's one more steep hill up to the bridge. Follow the bike path to the west side of the bridge (pedestrians must stay on the east side), cross the bridge, and take the road to your left heading downhill and crossing underneath Highway 101. Coast all the way to Sausalito.

❹ Exploring Sausalito

You'll love Sausalito. Coasting your bike onto Bridgeway is like being transported to one of those seaside towns on the French Riviera (p. 266). Lock the bikes and mosey around on foot for a while.

☕ **⁵ HORIZONS**

If you're thirsty, ask for a table on the bay-side deck at **Horizons** (558 Bridgeway; ℂ **415/331-3232**) and order a Bloody Mary, but don't eat yet. See p. 269.

---

❻ North Bay Tour

Back on the bike, head north again on the bike path as it winds along the bay. When you reach the Mill Valley Car Wash at the end of the bike path, turn right onto East Blithedale Avenue, which will cross Highway 101 and turn into Tiburon Boulevard. (This is the only sucky part of the ride where you'll encounter traffic.) About a mile past Highway 101 you'll enter a small park called Blackie's Pasture. (Look for the life-size bronze statue erected in 1995 to honor Tiburon's beloved "mascot" Blackie.) Now it's an easy cruise on the bike path all the way to Sam's.

❼ Lunch at Sam's Anchor Cafe

Ride your bike all the way to the south end of Tiburon and lock your bike at the bike rack near the ferry dock. Walk over to the ferry loading dock and check the ferry departure schedule for "Tiburon to Pier 39/Fisherman's Wharf." Then walk over to **Sam's Anchor Cafe** (27 Main St.; ℂ **415/435-4527;** p. 266), request a table on the back patio overlooking the harbor, and relax with a cool drink—you've earned it.

❽ Ferry Ride Back to San Francisco

When it's time to leave, board the ferry with your bike (bike riders board first, so don't stand in line) and enjoy the ride from Tiburon to San Francisco, with a short stop at Angel Island State Park. From Pier 39 it's a short ride back to the rental shop.

After all this adventuring, it's time to reenergize your body and soul with an Irish whiskey at the **Buena Vista Cafe** (2765 Hyde St.; ℂ **415/474-5044,** across from the cable car turnaround), a short walk from the bike rental shop. After libations, take the cable car back to your hotel for some rest and a shower, then spend the rest of the evening enjoying dinner.

If this isn't one of the best days you've had on your vacation, send me this book and I'll eat it.

5

Getting to Know San Francisco

This chapter offers useful information on how to become better acquainted with San Francisco, even though half the fun of becoming familiar with this city is wandering around and haphazardly stumbling upon great shops, restaurants, and vistas that even locals might not know about. You'll find that although the city is metropolitan, San Francisco is still a small town at heart—one where you won't feel like a stranger for long.

If you get disoriented, just remember that downtown is east and the Golden Gate Bridge is north—and even if you do get lost, you probably won't go too far, since water surrounds three sides of the city. The most difficult challenge you'll have, if you're traveling by car (which I suggest you avoid), is mastering the maze of one-way streets.

1 Orientation

VISITOR INFORMATION

The **San Francisco Visitor Information Center,** on the lower level of Hallidie Plaza, 900 Market St., at Powell Street (© **415/391-2000;** www.onlyinsanfrancisco.com), has brochures, discount coupons, and advice on restaurants, sights, and events in the city; their website offers an incredible amount of information as well. The on-site staff can provide answers in German, Japanese, French, Italian, and Spanish. To find the office, descend the escalator at the cable car turnaround. The office is open Monday through Friday from 9am to 5pm, and Saturday and Sunday from 9am to 3pm, May through October. However, it is closed on Sundays during winter and Easter, Thanksgiving Day, and Christmas Day. Phones are answered in person Monday through Friday only. Otherwise, dial © **415/391-2001** any time, day or night, for a recorded message about current cultural events, theater, music, sports, and other special happenings.

Pick up a copy of the *Bay Guardian* (www.sfbg.com) or the *S.F. Weekly* (www.sfweekly.com), the city's free alternative papers, to get listings of all city happenings. You'll find them in kiosks throughout the city and in most cafes.

For specialized information on Chinatown's shops and services, and on the city's Chinese community in general, contact the **Chinese Chamber of Commerce,** 730 Sacramento St. (© **415/982-3000**), open daily from 9am to 5pm.

CITY LAYOUT

San Francisco occupies the tip of a 32-mile peninsula between San Francisco Bay and the Pacific Ocean. Its land area measures about 46 square miles, although the city is often referred to as being 7 square miles. At more than 900 feet high, towering Twin Peaks (which are, in fact, two neighboring peaks), mark the geographic center of the city and make a great place to take in a vista of San Francisco.

Tips **Finding Your Way**

For a full-color map of San Francisco and its public transportation, see the "San Francisco Neighborhoods" and "San Francisco Mass Transit" maps in the color insert at the beginning of this book.

With lots of one-way streets, San Francisco might seem confusing at first, but it will quickly become easy to negotiate. The city's downtown streets are arranged in a simple grid pattern, with the exceptions of Market Street and Columbus Avenue, which cut across the grid at right angles to each other. Hills appear to distort this pattern, however, and can disorient you. As you learn your way around, the hills will become your landmarks and reference points.

MAIN ARTERIES & STREETS   **Market Street** is San Francisco's main thoroughfare. Most of the city's buses travel this route on their way to the Financial District from the outer neighborhoods to the west and south. The tall office buildings clustered downtown are at the northeast end of Market; 1 block beyond lies The Embarcadero and the bay.

The Embarcadero ★—an excellent strolling, skating, and biking route (thanks to recent renovations)—curves along San Francisco Bay from south of the Bay Bridge to the northeast perimeter of the city. It terminates at Fisherman's Wharf, the famous tourist-oriented pier. Aquatic Park, Fort Mason, and Golden Gate National Recreation Area are on the northernmost point of the peninsula.

From the eastern perimeter of Fort Mason, **Van Ness Avenue** runs due south, back to Market Street. The area just described forms a rough triangle, with Market Street as its southeastern boundary, the waterfront as its northern boundary, and Van Ness Avenue as its western boundary. Within this triangle lie most of the city's main tourist sights.

FINDING AN ADDRESS   Because most of the city's streets are laid out in a grid pattern, finding an address is easy when you know the nearest cross street. Numbers start with 1 at the beginning of the street and proceed at the rate of 100 per block. When asking for directions, find out the nearest cross street and your destination's neighborhood, but be careful not to confuse numerical avenues with numerical streets. Numerical avenues (Third Ave. and so on) are in the Richmond and Sunset districts in the western part of the city. Numerical streets (Third St. and so on) are south of Market Street in the east and south parts of town.

NEIGHBORHOODS IN BRIEF

For further discussion of some of the neighborhoods below, see the "Neighborhoods Worth a Visit" section of chapter 8, beginning on p. 174. For a color map of the city, see the "San Francisco Neighborhoods" map in the color insert of this book.

Union Square Union Square is the commercial hub of San Francisco. Most major hotels and department stores are crammed into the area surrounding the actual square, which was named for a series of violent pro-union mass demonstrations staged here on the eve of the Civil War. A plethora of upscale boutiques, restaurants, and galleries occupy the spaces tucked between the larger buildings. A few blocks west is the **Tenderloin** neighborhood, a patch of poverty and blight where you should keep your wits about you. The **Theater District** is 3 blocks west of Union Square.

The Financial District East of Union Square, this area, bordered by the Embarcadero and by Market, Third, Kearny, and Washington streets, is the city's business district and the stamping grounds for many major corporations. The pointy Transamerica Pyramid, at Montgomery and Clay streets, is one of the district's most conspicuous architectural features. To its east sprawls the Embarcadero Center, an 8½-acre complex housing offices, shops, and restaurants. Farther east still is the old Ferry Building, the city's pre-bridge transportation hub. Ferries to Sausalito and Larkspur still leave from this point. However, in 2003, the building became an attraction in itself when it was completely renovated, jampacked with outstanding restaurant and gourmet food- and wine-related shops, and surrounded by a farmers' market a few days a week, making it a favorite place of San Francisco's residents seeking to stock their kitchens.

Nob Hill & Russian Hill Bounded by Bush, Larkin, Pacific, and Stockton streets, Nob Hill is a genteel, well-heeled district still occupied by the city's major power brokers and the neighborhood businesses they frequent. Russian Hill extends from Pacific to Bay and from Polk to Mason. It contains steep streets, lush gardens, and high-rises occupied by both the moneyed and the bohemian.

Chinatown A large red-and-green gate on Grant Avenue at Bush Street marks the official entrance to Chinatown. Beyond lies a 24-block labyrinth, bordered by Broadway, Bush, Kearny, and Stockton streets, filled with restaurants, markets, temples, shops, and, of course, a substantial percentage of San Francisco's Chinese residents. Chinatown is a great place for exploration all along Stockton and Grant streets, Portsmouth Square, and the alleys that lead off them, like Ross and Waverly. This district has a maddening combination of incessant traffic and horrible drivers, so don't even think about driving around here.

North Beach This Italian neighborhood, which stretches from Montgomery and Jackson to Bay Street, is one of the best places in the city to grab a coffee, pull up a cafe chair, and do some serious people-watching. Nightlife is equally happening in North Beach; restaurants, bars, and clubs along Columbus and Grant avenues attract folks from all over the Bay Area, who fight for a parking place and romp through the festive neighborhood. Down Columbus toward the Financial District are the remains of the city's Beat Generation landmarks, including Ferlinghetti's City Lights Bookstore and Vesuvio's Bar. Broadway—a short strip of sex joints—cuts through the heart of the district. **Telegraph Hill** looms over the east side of North Beach, topped by Coit Tower, one of San Francisco's best vantage points.

Fisherman's Wharf North Beach runs into Fisherman's Wharf, which was once the busy heart of the city's great harbor and waterfront industries. Today it's a kitschy and mildly entertaining tourist area with little, if any, authentic waterfront life, except for a small fleet of fishing boats and some lethargic sea lions. What it does have going for it are activities for the whole family, with attractions, restaurants, trinket shops, and beautiful views and walkways everywhere you look.

The Marina District Created on landfill for the Pan Pacific Exposition of 1915, the Marina District boasts some of the best views of the Golden Gate, as well as plenty of grassy fields alongside San Francisco Bay. Elegant Mediterranean-style homes and apartments, inhabited by the city's well-to-do singles and wealthy families, line the streets. Here, too, are the Palace of Fine Arts, the Exploratorium, and Fort Mason Center. The main street is Chestnut, between Franklin and Lyon, which abounds with shops, cafes, and boutiques. Because of its landfill foundation, the Marina was one of the hardest-hit districts in the 1989 quake.

Cow Hollow Located west of Van Ness Avenue, between Russian Hill and the Presidio, this flat, grazable area supported 30 dairy farms in 1861. Today, Cow Hollow is largely residential and largely yuppie. Its two primary commercial thoroughfares are Lombard Street, known for its many relatively inexpensive motels, and Union Street, a flourishing shopping sector filled with restaurants, pubs, cafes, and shops.

Pacific Heights The ultra-elite, such as the Gettys and Danielle Steel—and those lucky enough to buy before the real-estate boom—reside in the mansions and homes in this neighborhood. When the rich meander out of their fortresses, they wander down to Union Street and join the pretty people who frequent the street's long stretch of chic boutiques and lively neighborhood restaurants, cafes, and bars.

Japantown Bounded by Octavia, Fillmore, California, and Geary, Japantown shelters only a small percentage of the city's Japanese population, but exploring these few square blocks and the shops and restaurants within them is still a cultural experience.

Civic Center Although millions of dollars have gone toward brick sidewalks, ornate lampposts, and elaborate street plantings, the southwestern section of Market Street can still feel a little sketchy due to the large number of homeless who wander the area. The Civic Center at the "bottom" of Market Street, however, is a stunning beacon of culture and refinement. This large complex of buildings includes the domed and dapper City Hall, the Opera House, Davies Symphony Hall, and the Asian Art Museum. The landscaped plaza connecting the buildings is the staging area for San Francisco's frequent demonstrations for or against just about everything.

SoMa No part of San Francisco has been more affected by recent development than the area south of Market Street (dubbed "SoMa"), the area within the triangle of the Embarcadero, Highway 101, and Market Street. Until a decade ago it was a district of old warehouses and industrial spaces, with a few scattered underground nightclubs, restaurants, and shoddy residential areas. But when it became the hub of dot-commercialization and half-million-dollar-plus lofts, its fate changed forever. Today, though dot-coms don't occupy much of the commercial space, the area is jumping thanks to fancy loft residences, the baseball stadium, and surrounding businesses, restaurants, and nightclubs in addition to urban entertainment such as the Museum of Modern Art, Yerba Buena Gardens, Metreon, and a slew of big-bucks hotels that make tons of money from businesspeople. Though still gritty in some areas, it's growing more glittery by the year.

Mission District This is another area that was greatly affected by the city's new wealth. The Mexican and Latin

American populations here, with their cuisine, traditions, and art, make the Mission District a vibrant area to visit. Some parts of the neighborhood are still poor and sprinkled with the homeless, gangs, and drug addicts, but young urbanites have also settled in the area, attracted by its "reasonably" (a relative term) priced rentals and endless oh-so-hot restaurants and bars that stretch from 16th and Valencia streets to 25th and Mission streets. Less adventurous tourists may just want to duck into Mission Dolores, cruise by a few of the 200-plus amazing murals, and head back downtown. But anyone who's interested in hanging with the hipsters and experiencing the hottest restaurant and bar nightlife should definitely beeline it here. Don't be afraid to visit this area, but do use caution at night.

The Castro One of the liveliest streets in town, the Castro is practically synonymous with San Francisco's gay community (even though it is technically a street in the Noe Valley District). Located at the very end of Market Street, between 17th and 18th streets, the Castro has dozens of shops, restaurants, and bars catering to the gay community. Open-minded straight people are welcome, too.

Haight-Ashbury Part trendy, part nostalgic, part funky, the Haight, as it's most commonly known, was the soul of the psychedelic, free-loving 1960s and the center of the counterculture movement. Today, the gritty neighborhood straddling upper Haight Street on the eastern border of Golden Gate Park is more gentrified, but the commercial area still harbors all walks of life. Leftover aging hippies mingle with grungy, begging street kids outside Ben & Jerry's Ice Cream Store (where they might still be talking about Jerry Garcia), nondescript marijuana dealers whisper "Buds" as shoppers pass, and many people walking down the street have Day-Glo hair. But you don't need to be a freak or wear tie-dye to enjoy the Haight—the ethnic food, trendy shops, and bars cover all tastes. From Haight Street, walk south on Cole Street for a more peaceful and quaint neighborhood experience.

Richmond & Sunset Districts San Francisco's suburbs of sorts, these are the city's largest and most populous neighborhoods, consisting mainly of small (but expensive) homes, shops, and neighborhood restaurants. Although they border Golden Gate Park and Ocean Beach, few tourists venture into "the Avenues," as these areas are referred to locally, unless they're on their way to the Cliff House, zoo, or Palace of the Legion of Honor.

6

Where to Stay

Whether you want a room with a view or just a room, San Francisco is more than accommodating to its 15.7 million annual guests. Most of the city's 200-plus hotels cluster near Union Square, but some smaller independent gems are scattered around town.

When reading over your options, keep in mind that prices listed are "rack" (published) rates. At big, upscale hotels, almost no one actually pays them, and there are always deals to be had. Therefore, you should always ask for special discounts or, even better, vacation packages. It's often possible to get the room you want for $100 less than what is quoted here, except when the hotels are packed (usually during summer and due to conventions) and bargaining is close to impossible. Use the rates listed here for the big hotels as guidelines for comparison only; prices for inexpensive choices and smaller B&Bs are closer to reality, however.

Hunting for hotels in San Francisco can be a tricky business, particularly if you're not a seasoned traveler. What you don't know—and the reservations agent may not tell you—could very well ruin your vacation, so keep the following

pointers in mind when it comes time to book a room:

- Prices listed below do not include state and city taxes, which total 14%. Other hidden extras include parking fees, which can be up to $45 per day (also subject to 14% tax!), and hefty surcharges—up to $1 per local call—for telephone use.
- San Francisco is Convention City, so if you want a room at a particular hotel during high season (summer, for example), book well in advance.
- Be sure to have a credit card in hand when making a reservation, and know that you may be asked to pay for at least 1 night in advance. (This doesn't happen often, though.)
- Hotels usually hold reservations until 6pm. If you don't tell the staff you're arriving late, you might lose your room.
- Almost every hotel in San Francisco requires a credit card imprint for "incidentals" (and to prevent walk-outs). If you don't have a credit card, be sure to make special arrangements with the management before you hang up the phone, and make a note

Pricing Categories

The accommodations listed below are classified first by area, and then by price, using the following categories: **Very Expensive,** more than $250 per night; **Expensive,** $200 to $250 per night; **Moderate,** $150 to $200 per night; and **Inexpensive,** less than $150 per night. These categories reflect the rack rates for an average double room during the high season, which runs approximately from April to September.

⌒Value Dial Direct

When booking a room in a chain hotel, call the hotel's local line and the toll-free number and see where you get the best deal. A hotel makes nothing on a room that stays empty. The clerk who runs the place is more likely to know about vacancies than someone from the toll-free number and will often grant deep discounts in order to fill up rooms.

of the name of the person with whom you spoke.

• When you check in, if your room isn't up to snuff, politely inform the front desk of your dissatisfaction and ask for another. If the hotel can accommodate you, they almost always will—and sometimes will even upgrade you!

Read the following entries carefully: Many hotels also offer rooms at rates above and below the price category that applies to most of the units. If you like the sound of a place that's a bit over your budget, it never hurts to call and ask a few questions. Also note that we do not list single rates. Some hotels, particularly more affordable choices, do charge lower rates for singles, so inquire about them if you are traveling alone.

San Francisco is a popular destination year-round, so although there are bargains available, rooms here will still seem expensive compared to those in many other U.S. destinations. Still, you should always ask about weekend discounts, corporate rates, and family plans. Most larger hotels, and many smaller ones, offer them, but many reservations agents don't mention them unless you ask about them specifically.

You'll find nonsmoking rooms available in all larger hotels and many smaller hotels; reviews indicate establishments that are entirely nonsmoking. Nowadays, the best advice for smokers is to confirm a smoking-permitted room in advance, and if there's a special cleaning charge per night.

Although you'll find that most accommodations have an abundance of amenities (including phones, unless otherwise noted), don't be alarmed by the lack of air-conditioned guest rooms. San Francisco's weather is so mild, you'll hardly ever need it.

Most larger hotels can accommodate guests who use wheelchairs and those who have other special needs. Ask when you make a reservation to ensure that your hotel can accommodate your needs, especially if you are interested in a bed-and-breakfast.

HELPING HANDS Having reservations about your reservations? Leave it up to the pros:

San Francisco Reservations, 360 22nd St., Suite 300, Oakland, CA 94612 (🕾 **800/677-1500** or 510/628-4450; www.hotelres.com), arranges reservations for more than 150 of San Francisco's hotels and often offers discounted rates. Their nifty website allows Internet users to make reservations online.

Other good online sites with discounted rates include **www.hotels.com** and **www.placestostay.com**.

1 The Best Hotel Bets

• **Best for Families:** Kids like the **Westin St. Francis,** 335 Powell St. (🕾 **866/500-0038** or 415/397-7000), because upon arrival, children under 12 get the travel-themed Westin Kids Club backpack filled with a make-your-own postcard kit, colored pencils, a travelogue, a map of the world, and a safari hat. Parents with babies get a rubber duck, a night light, and an emergency kit. At the nautically themed **Argonaut,** 495 Jefferson St. (© **866/415-0704** or 415/563-0800), kids get to pick a toy out of the "treasure chest," and parents will appreciate the free cribs and strollers. But the place kids will probably love the most is the **Hotel Del Sol,** 3100 Webster St. (© **877/433-5765** or 415/921-5520), with its "Kids are VIPs" program that includes a lending library of books, toys, and videos; evening cookies and milk; and a plethora of toys to use by the heated outdoor pool. Parents will love the bonded babysitting services and the three baby-proofed rooms, among many other perks for families. See p. 65, 92, and 95, respectively.

- **Best for Romance:** Oozing with bohemian romance is the **Hotel Bohème,** 444 Columbus Ave. (© **415/433-9111**). See p. 93.
- **Best Public Space in a Historic Hotel:** The **Palace Hotel,** 2 New Montgomery St. (© **888/625-5144** or 415/512-1111), the extravagant creation of banker "Bonanza King" Will Ralston in 1875, has one of the grandest rooms in the city: the Garden Court. Equally eye-catching is the magnificent lobby at Nob Hill's the **Fairmont San Francisco,** 950 Mason St. (© **866/540-4491** or 415/772-5000). See p. 83 and 78, respectively.
- **Best Trendy Scene:** If you want to shack up with the tragically hip, head to **Clift Hotel,** 495 Geary St. (© **800/697-1791** or 415/775-4700), which promises upscale flirting at its bar, the Redwood Room. See p. 64. Less chichi and funkier in style and location is the **Phoenix Hotel,** 601 Eddy St. (© **800/248-9466** or 415/776-1380), where guests lounge poolside or hang at the too-cool Bambuddha Lounge. See p. 98.
- **Best Service and Amenities:** As usual, the **Ritz-Carlton,** 600 Stockton St. (© **800/241-3333** or 415/296-7465), corners the market in ultimate luxury, from its stunning ground-floor bathrooms to its fabulous restaurant to everything in between. Of course such pampering comes at a cost, but if you can afford it, it's worth the splurge. See p. 80. While it doesn't have quite the number of perks that the Ritz has, the **St. Regis Hotel,** 125 Third St. (© **877/787-3447** or 415/284-4000), is a fabulous place to stay. From its state-of-the-art rooms swathed in browns and creams to its huge spa, gym, hopping bar scene, and destination-restaurant Ame—not to mention its location next to the Museum of Modern Art—it's one of my favorite hotels in the city. See p. 86.

2 Union Square

VERY EXPENSIVE

Campton Place Hotel 𝒜𝒜 This luxury boutique hotel offers some of the best accommodations in town—not to mention the most expensive. Rooms are compact but comfy, with limestone, pear wood, and Italian-modern decor. The two executive suites and one luxury suite push the haute envelope to even more luxurious heights. Discriminating returning guests will still find superlative service, California king-size beds, exquisite bathrooms, bathrobes, top-notch toiletries, slippers, and every other necessity and extra that's made Campton Place a favored temporary address. Alas, Campton Place Restaurant lost its award-winning chef Daniel Humm in 2005, but the restaurant still offers a respectable French/California menu. The jury's still out on whether it's a destination in its own right.

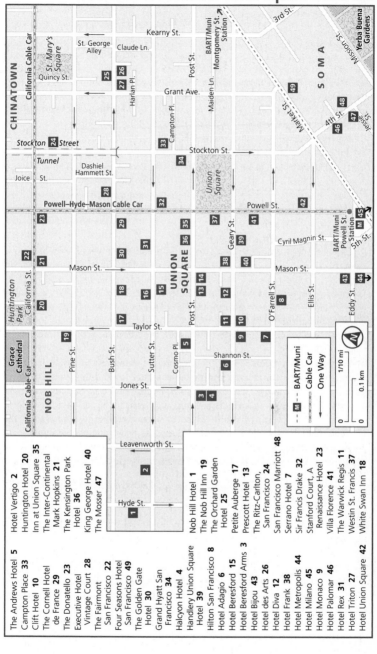

Accommodations near Union Square & Nob Hill

The Andrews Hotel **5**
Campton Place **33**
Clift Hotel **10**
The Cornell Hotel
de France **29**
The Donatello **23**
Executive Hotel
Vintage Court **28**
The Fairmont
San Francisco **22**
Four Seasons Hotel
San Francisco **49**
The Golden Gate
Hotel **30**
Grand Hyatt San
Francisco **34**
Halcyon Hotel **4**
Handlery Union Square
Hotel **39**
Hilton San Francisco **8**
Hotel Adagio **6**
Hotel Beresford **15**
Hotel Beresford Arms **3**
Hotel Bijou **43**
Hotel des Arts **26**
Hotel Diva **12**
Hotel Frank **38**
Hotel Metropolis **44**
Hotel Milano **45**
Hotel Monaco **9**
Hotel Palomar **46**
Hotel Rex **31**
Hotel Triton **27**
Hotel Union Square **42**

Hotel Vertigo **2**
Huntington Hotel **20**
Inn at Union Square **35**
The Inter-Continental
Mark Hopkins **21**
The Kensington Park
Hotel **36**
King George Hotel **40**
The Mosser **47**

Nob Hill Hotel **1**
The Nob Hill Inn **19**
The Orchard Garden
Hotel **25**
Petite Auberge **17**
Prescott Hotel **13**
The Ritz-Carlton,
San Francisco **24**
San Francisco Marriott **48**
Serrano Hotel **7**
Sir Francis Drake **32**
Stanford Court, A
Renaissance Hotel **23**
Villa Florence **41**
The Warwick Regis **11**
Westin St. Francis **37**
White Swan Inn **18**

Legend:
- **M** — BART/Muni
- Cable Car
- One Way

1/10 mi

0.1 km

340 Stockton St. (btw. Post and Sutter sts.), San Francisco, CA 94108. ℂ 866/332-1670 or 415/781-5555. Fax 415/955-5536. www.camptonplace.com. 110 units. $350–$485 double; $585–$2,000 suite. American breakfast $18. AE, DC, MC, V. Valet parking $38. Bus: 2, 3, 4, 30, 38, or 45. Cable car: Powell–Hyde or Powell–Mason lines (1 block west). BART: Market St. **Amenities:** Restaurant; outdoor fitness terrace; concierge; secretarial services; room service; laundry service; same-day dry cleaning. *In room:* A/C, TV w/pay movies, dataport, T1 line, minibar, hair dryer, iron, safe.

Clift Hotel 🖈   Ian Schrager, king of such ultrahip hotels as New York's Royalton and Paramount, L.A.'s Mondrian, and Miami's Delano, renovated this classic old luxury property a few years back. Young trendsetters now flock here for overpriced mono-chrome lavender streamlined rooms with often-minuscule bathrooms, glamorous atmosphere, and a heavy dose of attitude. Its best attribute is the renovated historic Redwood Room, complete with sexy redwood walls (all made from one tree!) and Deco lighting from 1933 and a luxurious and rather uncomfortable interior designed by Philippe Starck. The equally trendy, expensive, and mediocre Asia de Cuba restaurant adjoins the swank lounge. If you ask me, the only reason to pay the high prices here is if you're interested in being surrounded by the young and hip. Otherwise, there are far better rooms around town at a similar or lower price.

> **Fun Fact Inflation at the Clift**
>
> When it first opened in 1915 the Clift Hotel charged a mere $2 per night.

495 Geary St. (at Taylor St.), San Francisco, CA 94102. ℂ 800/697-1791 or 415/775-4700. Fax 415/441-4621. www.clifthotel.com. 363 units. $325–$460 double; from $455 studio suite; from $950 deluxe suite. AE, DC, DISC, MC, V. Valet parking $45. Bus: 2, 3, 4, 30, 38, or 45. Cable car: Powell–Hyde or Powell–Mason lines (2 blocks east). **Amenities:** Restaurant; bar; exercise room; concierge; room service; same-day laundry service/dry cleaning. *In room:* TV/DVD, Wi-Fi ($10/day), minibar, hair dryer.

Grand Hyatt San Francisco 🖈   If the thought of a 10-second walk to Saks Fifth Avenue makes your pulse race, this high-rise luxury hotel is the place for you. The Grand Hyatt sits amid all the downtown shopping while also boasting some of the best views in the area. The lobby is indeed grand, with Chinese artifacts and enormous ceramic vases. Thankfully, the well-kept rooms were recently renovated; they're swankier than they used to be, and now feature the Hyatt's signature Grand Bed with pillow top mattresses, ultra-plush pillows and down (or down alternative) duvets. Each room has a lounge chair as well as a small desk and sitting area. Views from most of the 36 floors are truly spectacular.

Rates for concierge-level Regency Club rooms ($50 extra) include access to the lounge, honor bar, continental breakfast, and evening hors d'oeuvres. Three floors hold business-plan guest rooms, which for $25 extra get you 24-hour access to a printer, a photocopier, and office supplies; free local calls and credit card phone access; and a daily newspaper.

345 Stockton St. (btw. Post and Sutter sts.), San Francisco, CA 94108. ℂ 888/591-1234 or 415/398-1234. Fax 415/391-1780. www.sanfrancisco.grand.hyatt.com. 685 units. $199–$329 double; Regency Club $50 additional. AE, DC, DISC, MC, V. Valet parking $41. Bus: 2, 3, 4, 30, 38, or 45. Cable car: Powell–Hyde or Powell–Mason lines (2 blocks west). **Amenities:** Restaurant; bar; health club; concierge; business center; Wi-Fi in public areas; secretarial services; limited room service; laundry service; same-day dry cleaning. *In room:* A/C, TV w/pay movies, dataport, high-speed Internet access ($9.95/day), minibar, coffeemaker, hair dryer, iron, safe, 2 phone lines with speaker capability.

Hotel Monaco 🖈🖈   This remodeled 1910 Beaux Arts building has plenty of atmos-phere thanks to a whimsically ethereal lobby with a two-story French inglenook fire-place. The guest rooms, which were upgraded in 2006, follow suit, with canopy beds,

Asian-inspired armoires, bamboo writing desks, lively stripes, and vibrant color. Everything is bold but tasteful, and as playful as it is serious, with nifty extras like flatscreen TVs, complimentary Wi-Fi, and two-line cordless phones. The decor, combined with the truly grand neighboring Grand Café restaurant that's ideal for cocktails and mingling (but also serves breakfast and lunch), would put this place on my top-10 list if it weren't for rooms that tend to be too small (especially for the price) and the lack of a sizable gym. That said, it's a fine Union Square option, which happens to include complimentary wine and cheese tasting accompanied by shoulder and neck massages. *Tip:* If you were/are a big fan of Jefferson Airplane, inquire about their Grace Slick Shrine Suite.

501 Geary St. (at Taylor St.), San Francisco, CA 94102. © 866/622-5284 or 415/292-0100. Fax 415/292-0111. www.monaco-sf.com. 201 units. $229–$409 double; $279–$619 suite. Rates include evening wine and cheese tasting. Call for discounted rates. AE, DC, DISC, MC, V. Valet parking $39. Bus: 2, 3, 4, 27, or 38. Pets accepted. **Amenities:** Restaurant; exercise room; spa; Jacuzzi; sauna; steam room; concierge; courtesy car; business center; room service; in-room massage; laundry service; dry cleaning. *In room:* A/C, TV, CD player, dataport, Wi-Fi, minibar, coffeemaker w/Starbucks coffee, hair dryer, iron, safe.

Prescott Hotel 🎔🎔 It may be small and lack common areas, but the boutique Prescott Hotel has some big things going for it. The staff treats you like royalty, rooms are attractively unfrilly and masculine, the location (just a block from Union Square) is perfect, and limited room service is provided by Wolfgang Puck's restaurant Postrio. Ralph Lauren fabrics in dark tones of green, plum, and burgundy and crisp white Italian linens blend well with the cherrywood furnishings in each of the soundproof rooms; the view, alas, isn't so pleasant. The very small bathrooms contain terry robes and Aveda products, and the suites have Jacuzzi bathtubs. Concierge-level guests are pampered with a free continental breakfast and evening cocktails and hors d'oeuvres.

545 Post St. (btw. Mason and Taylor sts.), San Francisco, CA 94102. © 866/271-3632 or 415/563-0303. Fax 415/563-6831. www.prescotthotel.com. 164 units. $245–$350 double; $280 concierge-level double (including breakfast and evening cocktail reception); from $365 suite. AE, DC, DISC, MC, V. Valet parking $40. Bus: 2, 3, 4, 30, 38, or 45. Cable car: Powell–Hyde or Powell–Mason lines (1 block east). **Amenities:** Restaurant; bar; small exercise room; concierge; limited courtesy car; limited room service. *In room:* TV w/pay movies, dataport, Wi-Fi, minibar, hair dryer, iron, safe, video games.

Westin St. Francis 🎔🎔 *Kids* At the turn of the 20th century, Charles T. Crocker and a few of his wealthy buddies decided that San Francisco needed a world-class hotel, and up went the St. Francis. Since then, hordes of VIPs have hung their hats and hosiery here, including Emperor Hirohito of Japan, Queen Elizabeth II of England, Mother Teresa, King Juan Carlos of Spain, the shah of Iran, and all the U.S. presidents from Taft through Clinton. In 1972, the hotel gained the 32-story Tower, doubling its capacity and adding banquet and conference centers. The older rooms of the main building vary in size and have more old-world charm than the newer rooms, but the Tower is remarkable for its great views of the city (including from the glass elevators) from above the 18th floor.

Although the St. Francis is too massive to offer the personal service you get at the smaller deluxe hotels on Nob Hill, few other hotels in San Francisco can match its majestic aura. Stroll through the vast, ornate lobby, and you can feel 100 years of history oozing from its hand-carved redwood paneling. The hotel has done massive renovations costing $185 million over the past decade, replacing the carpeting, furniture, and bedding in every main-building guest room; gussying up the lobby; restoring the facade; and adding one of the hottest downtown dining spots, the very expensive and fancy Michael Mina (p. 106).

The Westin makes kids feel right at home, too, with a goody bag upon check-in. The tower's Grandview Rooms evoke a contemporary design along the lines of the W Hotel. The historic main building accentuates its history with traditional, more elegant ambience, high ceilings, and crown molding. Alas, the venerable Compass Rose tearoom is no longer.

335 Powell St. (btw. Geary and Post sts.), San Francisco, CA 94102. © **866/500-0038** or 415/397-7000. Fax 415/774-0124. www.westinstfrancis.com. 1,195 units. Main building: $229–$529 double; Tower (Grand View): $219–$559 double; from $650 suite (in either building). Extra person $30. Continental breakfast $15–$18. AE, DC, DISC, MC, V. Valet parking $42. Bus: 2, 3, 4, 30, 38, 45, or 76. Cable car: Powell–Hyde or Powell–Mason lines (direct stop). Pets under 40 lb. accepted (dog beds available on request). **Amenities:** 2 restaurants; elaborate health club and spa; concierge; car-rental desk; business center; room service. *In room:* A/C, TV, dataport, high-speed Internet access ($15), Wi-Fi ($9.95/day), minibar, fridge available upon request, hair dryer, iron, cordless phones.

EXPENSIVE

The Donatello ☆ *Value* If you're not looking for trendy lodgings or an anonymous business hotel but want old-world elegance, book a room here. The Donatello is, in a word, dignified. The lobby is classy, with Italian marble and a serious staff. The airy, contemporary Art Nouveau rooms, which are some of the largest in the city (an average of 400 sq. ft.), were overhauled in 2006 with new bedding, carpet, and furniture and feature original art, king-size mattresses, and textiles. Unfortunately, most of the extra-large windows lack great views, but if it's fresh air you're after, the fifth floor has seven terrace rooms.

501 Post St. (at Mason St.), San Francisco, CA 94102. © **800/227-3184** or 415/441-7100. Fax 415/885-8842. www.thedonatellosf.com. 94 units. $139–$295 double. Children under 12 stay free in parent's room. AE, DC, DISC, MC, V. Valet parking $28. Bus: 2, 3, 4, 30, 38, or 45. Cable car: Powell–Hyde or Powell–Mason lines (1 block west). **Amenities:** Restaurant; bar; exercise room; concierge; limited room service; same-day laundry service/dry cleaning; 2 meeting spaces. *In room:* A/C, TV w/pay movies, dataport, free Wi-Fi, fridge, microwave, toaster, coffeemaker, hair dryer, iron, CD player.

Executive Hotel Vintage Court ☆ *Value* Consistent personal service and great value attract a loyal clientele at this European-style hotel 2 blocks north of Union Square. The chocolate-brown lobby, accented with comfy couches, is welcoming enough to actually spend a little time in, especially when California wines are being poured each evening from 5 to 6pm free of charge (each week a local vintner is on hand to do the pouring).

But the varietals don't stop at ground level. Each tidy, quiet, and comfortable room is named after a winery and boasts a modern country look (think Pottery Barn meets Napa Valley), where greens and earth tones reign supreme, with cream duvets and lovely mahogany-slat blinds. Niebaum-Coppola Penthouse Suite (named after the winery owned by the movie maverick), the deluxe two-room penthouse suite, has an original 1912 stained-glass skylight, wood-burning fireplace, whirlpool tub, complete entertainment center, and panoramic views of the city. Smokers, book a room elsewhere because puffing is prohibited in all rooms here. On the bright side, pets are welcome.

Masa's, one of the city's more upscale restaurants, serves very expensive contemporary French dinners here.

650 Bush St. (btw. Powell and Stockton sts.), San Francisco, CA 94108. © **888/388-3932** or 415/392-4666. Fax 415/433-4065. www.executivehotels.net/vintagecourt. 107 units. $159–$229 double; $325–$395 penthouse suite. Rates include continental breakfast and evening wine reception. AE, DC, DISC, MC, V. Valet parking $37; self-parking $27. Bus: 2, 3, 4, 30, 45, or 76. Cable car: Powell–Hyde or Powell–Mason lines (direct stop). **Amenities:** Restaurant; access to off-premises health club ($14/day); concierge; in-room massage; same-day laundry service/dry cleaning. *In room:* A/C, TV, dataport, Wi-Fi, minibar, coffeemaker, hair dryer, iron, video games.

Handlery Union Square Hotel ☆ *Kids*   A mere half-block from Union Square, the Handlery was already a good deal frequented by European travelers before the 1908 building underwent a complete overhaul a few years ago. Now you'll find every amenity you could possibly need, plus lots of extras, in the extremely tasteful and modern (although sedate and a little dark) rooms. Rooms range from coral and gray in the historic building to taupe and tan in the newer club-level building. In between is a heated outdoor pool. Literally everything was replaced in the rooms: mattresses, alarm radios, refrigerators, light fixtures, paint, carpets, and furnishings. Perks include adjoining L.A.-based chain restaurant the Daily Grill (which is unfortunately not as good as its sister restaurants down south) and club-level options (all in the newer building) that include larger rooms, a complimentary morning newspaper, a bathroom scale, robes, two two-line phones, and adjoining doors that make the units great choices for families. Downsides? Not a lot of direct light, no grand feeling in the lobby, and lots of trekking if you want to go to and from the adjoining buildings that make up the hotel. All in all, it's a good value for downtown, but, personally, this would be a choice second to the less expensive Warwick Regis.

351 Geary St. (btw. Mason and Powell sts.), San Francisco, CA 94102. ℭ **800/843-4343** or 415/781-7800. Fax 415/781-0269. www.handlery.com. 377 units. $249–$269 double; Club section $249–$289 double; Owner's Suite $600. Extra person $10. AE, DC, DISC, MC, V. Parking $32. Bus: 2, 3, 4, 30, 38, or 45. Cable car: Powell–Hyde or Powell–Mason lines (direct stop). **Amenities:** Restaurant; heated outdoor swimming pool; access to nearby health club ($10/day); sauna; barbershop; room service; babysitting; same-day laundry service. *In room:* Central air, TV w/Nintendo and pay movies, dataport, Wi-Fi, fridge, free coffee/tea-making facilities, hair dryer, iron, safe, voice mail.

Hilton San Francisco   Complete with bustling conventioneers and a line to register that resembles airport check-in, the Hilton's lobby is so enormous and busy that it feels more like a convention hall than a hotel. The three connecting buildings (the original 19-story main structure, a 46-story tower topped by a panoramic restaurant, and a 23-story landmark with 386 luxurious rooms and suites) bring swarms of visitors. Even during quieter times, the sheer enormity of the place makes the Hilton somewhat overwhelming.

After you get past the sweeping grand lobby, jump on an elevator, and wind through endless corridors to your room, you're likely to find the mystique ends with clean but run-of-the-mill standard-size corporate accommodations. That said, some of the views from the floor-to-ceiling windows in the main tower's rooms are memorable. All rooms have flatscreen TVs, bathrooms with walk-in showers (no tubs), Serta Suite Dreams beds, and a pillow menu that ensures you get a pillow that suits your firmness preference.

Still, the overall feel and decor of the hotel are impersonal and plain—perfect for conventioneers, but not for a romantic weekend. One bonus is the 13,000-square-foot health club and day spa. The Hilton has four restaurants: Cityscape, on the 46th floor, offers classic California cuisine and a breathtaking 360-degree view; Intermezzo serves Mediterranean-style food; the Café offers a buffet; and Kiku of Tokyo offers—you guessed it—Japanese food. The Lobby Bar also offers bar snacks.

333 O'Farrell St. (btw. Mason and Taylor sts.), San Francisco, CA 94102. ℭ **800/445-8667** or 415/771-1400. Fax 415/771-6807. www.sanfrancisco.hilton.com. 1,908 units. $195–$409 double; $315–$3,700 junior suite. Children stay free in parent's room. AE, DC, DISC, MC, V. Parking $47 (some oversize vehicles cannot be accommodated, depending on height). Bus: 2, 3, 4, 7, 9, 21, 27, 30, 38, 45, or 71. Cable car: Powell–Hyde or Powell–Mason lines (1 block east). **Amenities:** 4 restaurants; bar; outdoor pool; outdoor whirlpool; health club; spa; sauna; concierge; tour desk; car-rental desk; business center; Wi-Fi in public spaces; secretarial services; room service; laundry service; dry cleaning. *In room:* A/C, 27-in. flatscreen TV, dataport, high-speed Internet access, minibar, coffeemaker, hair dryer, iron.

Hotel Adagio 🐈🐈 *Value* Our local hip-hotel company, Joie de Vivre, revamped every one of this 1929 Spanish Revival hotel's 171 large, bright guest rooms in gorgeous modern style. They're real lookers, each with a walnut brown and mocha color palette and dark wood furnishings. Other plusses include firm mattresses, double-paned windows that open, quiet surroundings, voice mail, and plenty of elbowroom. Executive floors (7–16) also come with robes, upscale amenities, makeup mirrors, and stereos with iPod ports. Bathrooms are old but spotless, and have resurfaced tubs. Feel like splurging? Go for one of the two penthouse-level suites; one has lovely terraces with a New York vibe. Another good reason to stay here is the restaurant/bar **Cortez,** which draws a lively crowd of locals who meet here after work to nosh on small plates in the groovy lounge. *Tip:* Rooms above the eighth floor have good, but not great, views of the city.

550 Geary St., San Francisco, CA 94102. ✆ **800/228-8830** or 415/775-5000. Fax 415/775-9388. www.thehoteladagio. com. 171 units. $189–$279 double. AE, DISC, MC, V. Valet parking $35. **Amenities:** Restaurant; bar; fitness center; concierge; business center w/free Wi-Fi; room service; laundry service; dry cleaning; luggage storage room. *In room:* TV w/Nintendo and pay movies, CD player, dataport, free high-speed Internet access, minibar, fridge, hair dryer, iron, safe.

Hotel Diva 🐈 *Kids* A showbiz darling when it opened in 1985, the Diva is so sleek and ultramodern it won "Best Hotel Design" from *Interiors* magazine not long after it opened and is still as svelte as ever. A profusion of curvaceous glass, marble, and steel marks the lobby, and the minimalist rooms are spotless and neat, with cobalt blue carpets and Euro-chic furnishings of monochromatic colors, silver accents, and rolled steel. Each room is equipped with 36-inch flatscreen TVs, iPod alarm clocks, and blond-wood desks. The downside is that the rooms have views that make you want to keep the chic curtains closed. Services abound, ranging from fitness and business centers to four themed Diva Lounges for business (including 24-hour free use of a computer) and pleasure. Families should inquire about their two-room Little Divas Suite designed for kids that can accommodate a family of four. A nice touch for music-lovers, iPods are available at the front desk for $10 to $15 per day, complete with special Diva music mixes.

440 Geary St. (btw. Mason and Taylor sts.), San Francisco, CA 94102. ✆ **800/553-1900** or 415/885-0200. Fax 415/346-6613. www.hoteldiva.com. 116 units. $159–$359 double; $199–$799 suite. AE, DC, DISC, MC, V. Valet parking $30. Bus: 38 or 38L. Cable car: Powell–Mason line. **Amenities:** Coffee/tea service 6:30–10am; exercise room; concierge; free Wi-Fi; laundry service; dry cleaning. *In room:* A/C, TV/DVD/CD, dataport, hair dryer, iron, safe.

Hotel Rex 🐈 Joie de Vivre, the most creative hotel group in the city, is the brains behind this cleverly restored historic building, a restoration that was inspired by the San Francisco art and literary salons of the 1920s and '30s. JDV kept some of the imported furnishings and the European boutique hotel ambience, but gave the lobby and rooms a major face-lift, adding the decorative flair that makes its hotels among the most popular in town. The clublike lobby lounge is modeled after a 1920s literary salon and is, like all the group's properties, cleverly stylish. (They even host jazz artists Fri 6–8pm.) The guest rooms are above average in size, decorated with custom wall coverings, hand-painted lampshades, and works by local artists. If you have one of the rooms in the back, you'll look out over a shady, peaceful courtyard. It's also in a great location, situated near several fine galleries, theaters, and restaurants.

562 Sutter St. (btw. Powell and Mason sts.), San Francisco, CA 94102. ✆ **800/433-4434** or 415/433-4434. Fax 415/433-3695. www.thehotelrex.com. 94 units. $159–$269 double; $400 suite. AE, DC, DISC, MC, V. Valet parking $34. Bus: 2, 3, 4, 30, 38, or 45. Cable car: Powell–Hyde or Powell–Mason lines (1 block east). **Amenities:** Access to

nearby health club; concierge; business center; room service (7am–11pm); same-day laundry service/dry cleaning. *In room:* TV w/pay movies, CD player, dataport, free high-speed Internet access and Wi-Fi throughout, minibar, hair dryer, iron.

Hotel Triton ✮   Described as vogue, chic, retrofuturistic, and even neo-baroque, this Kimpton Group property is whimsy at its boutique-hotel best. The completely renovated lobby features a 360-degree mural by emerging artist Kari Pei (yes, from *that* Pei family–she's I. M. Pei's daughter-in-law) that relates the history of San Francisco and Triton. The funky-fun (if not a wee bit too small) designer suites named after musicians and artists like Jerry Garcia, Wyland (the ocean artist), and Santana, along with all the other rooms, are eco-friendly, featuring filtered water and air, all-natural linens, recycle trash cans, and water conservation fixtures. Even the cleaning products used in the hotel are environmentally sensitive to please the tree-hugger in all of us. All the rooms include modern touches like armoires hiding Sony flatscreen TVs and iPod iH5 docking stations that double as clock radios. Not to be outdone, the fitness center touts DirecTV in the cardio machines.

The hotel serves coffee and tea each morning, and freshly baked cookies at 3 and 8pm. Wine, tarot readings, and chair massages are available each evening (included in the room rate) in the lobby. The bustling and casual Café de la Presse has a cool French cafe vibe but overpriced food.

342 Grant Ave. (at Bush St.), San Francisco, CA 94108. ✆ **800/800-1299** or 415/394-0500. Fax 415/394-0555. www.hoteltriton.com. 140 units. $179–$239 double; $279–$379 suite. AE, DC, DISC, MC, V. Parking $37, oversize vehicles an additional $2. Cable car: Powell–Hyde or Powell–Mason lines (2 blocks west). Pets stay free with conditional agreement. **Amenities:** Cafe; fitness center; business center (fee); room service; same-day laundry service/dry cleaning. *In room:* A/C, flatscreen TV, web TV, dataport, free Wi-Fi, minibar, coffeemaker on request, hair dryer, iron.

The Inn at Union Square ✮✮   As narrow as an Amsterdam canal house, the Inn at Union Square is the antithesis of the big, impersonal hotels that surround Union Square. If you need plenty of elbowroom, skip this one. But if you're looking for an inn whose staff knows each guest's name, read on. One-half block west of the square, this six-story inn makes up for its small stature by spoiling guests with a pile of perks. Mornings start with a continental breakfast served in lounges stocked with daily newspapers, and evening emerges with appetizers of wine, cheese, fruit, and chocolates served in sweet little fireplace lounges at the end of each hall. There's also unlimited use of a nearby full-service health club with heated lap pool. The handsome rooms are individually decorated with Georgian reproductions, goose-down pillows, and floral fabrics, and they are smaller than average but infinitely more appreciated than the cookie-cutter rooms of most larger hotels. Smoking is not allowed anywhere in the hotel.

440 Post St. (btw. Mason and Powell sts.), San Francisco, CA 94102. ✆ **800/288-4346** or 415/397-3510. Fax 415/989-0529. www.unionsquare.com. 30 units. $169–$219 double; from $370 suite. Rates include continental breakfast; all-day tea and cider, afternoon wine and hors d'oeuvres; and evening cookies. AE, DC, DISC, MC, V. Valet parking $36. Bus: 2, 3, 4, 30, 38, or 45; all Market St. buses. Cable car: Powell–Hyde or Powell–Mason lines. **Amenities:** Access to nearby health club (for a nominal fee); concierge; secretarial services; laundry service; dry cleaning. *In room:* TV, dataport, free Wi-Fi, hair dryer, iron.

Kensington Park Hotel ✮   Housed in a stately 1925 Moorish/Gothic-style building that also houses the Post Street Theatre and popular Farallon seafood restaurant (p. 104), the Kensington underwent a $1.5 million dollar renovation in the spring of '08 and is now one of the best mid-priced lodging deals near Union Square. Exuding old-school San Francisco charm, the lobby features hand-painted ceilings, mosaic tile, and classic Queen Anne antiques accented by crystal chandeliers and palm trees. Large guest rooms on the 5th through 12th floors have a mix of classic and contemporary furnishings such as 36-inch flatscreen TVs and iPod alarm clocks, and the bathrooms, though small, are sweetly appointed in brass and marble. If you want the royal treatment, book The Royal Suite, which features a canopy bed, formal dining room, living room, whirlpool bath, two fireplaces, and wonderful views of Union Square. The hotel lacks a fitness center, but guests have complimentary use of the adjacent Hotel Diva fitness center. *Tip:* For the best city views request an upper corner room.

450 Post St. (btw. Powell and Mason sts.), San Francisco, CA 94102. © 800/553-1900 or 415/788-6400. Fax 415/399-9484. www.kensingtonparkhotel.com. 92 units. $159–$349 double; $199–$389 Royal Court Rooms; from $399 suite. Rates include morning coffee and tea and afternoon tea and sherry. AE, DC, DISC, MC, V. Valet parking $35; extra charge for oversize cars. Cable car: Powell–Hyde or Powell–Mason lines (½ block east). **Amenities:** Restaurant; coffee/tea service 7–10am; concierge; business center; same-day dry cleaning. *In room:* TV w/pay movies, dataport, free Wi-Fi, newspaper, hair dryer, iron.

The Orchard Garden Hotel 𝒦𝒦   If Al Gore was a hotelier, this would be his hotel. The new $25-million-dollar Orchard Garden Hotel is California's first generation of truly "green" hotels and the only hotel in the state that was built to the nationally accepted standards for green buildings developed by the U.S. Green Building Council (USGBC). From the eco-friendly construction materials to an in-room recycling system and the use of organic, citrus-based cleaning products, just about every aspect of this vanguard property is geared toward creating a healthy environment for guests and staff. It's also the first hotel in the city to use the European-style keycard system that turns power off to the entire room each time you leave, thereby saving about 20% in energy consumption. But going green doesn't mean you have to cut back on comfort—yes, that's Egyptian cotton linen on the king-size bed, real feather down in the pillows, and plush spa-style robes in the closet. The 86 guest rooms are super-insulated (and very quiet), and decorated in natural wood tones with soothing light colors. Spacious bathrooms come with Aveda bath products (organic, of course). High-tech toys include HD LCD TVs, DVD/CD players, iPod docking stations, and dual-line cordless telephones on large work desks. The hotel also has a pleasant rooftop garden, a small fitness center (and $15 passes to Club One), and the lobby-level **Roots Restaurant,** which serves contemporary American cuisine made from locally sourced organic products for breakfast, lunch, and dinner. The hotel's location at Bush and Grant streets is ideal, with Chinatown, Union Square, and the Financial District all just a short walk away. *Note:* If the hotel is fully booked, inquire about their sister property—the Orchard Hotel—up the street.

466 Bush St. (at Grant St.), San Francisco, CA 94108. © 888/717-2881 or 415/399-9807. Fax 415/393-9917. www.theorchardgardenhotel.com. 82 units. $169–$499 double. AE, DC, DISC, MC, V. Valet parking $24. Cable car: Powell–Hyde or Powell–Mason lines. **Amenities:** Restaurant; fitness center; concierge; morning car service to Financial District; bicycle storage; business center; evening turndown; free DVD library. *In room:* A/C, flatscreen HD TV, DVD/CD player dataport, Wi-Fi, minibar, coffeemaker, hair dryer, iron, safe, robes, iPod docking station, cordless phone.

Petite Auberge 𝒦𝒦   Nobody does French provincial like the Petite Auberge: handcrafted armoires, delicate sheer curtains, cozy little fireplaces in most rooms, and an adorable array of antiques and knickknacks. Honeymooners should splurge on the petite suite, which has a private entrance, deck, and spa tub. The breakfast room, with its mural of a country market scene, terra-cotta tile floors, and gold-yellow tablecloths, opens onto a small garden. California wines, tea, and hors d'oeuvres (included in

the room rates) are served each afternoon, and guests have free rein of the fridge stocked with soft drinks. Bathers take note: Eight rooms have showers only, while others have tubs.

863 Bush St. (btw. Taylor and Mason sts.), San Francisco, CA 94102. ② **800/365-3004** or 415/928-6000. Fax 415/673-7214. www.petiteaubergesf.com. 26 units. $199–$239 double; $269 petite suite. Rates include full breakfast and afternoon reception. AE, DC, DISC, MC, V. Parking $32. Bus: 2, 3, 4, 30, 38, or 45. Cable car: Powell–Hyde or Powell–Mason lines. **Amenities:** Access to small exercise room next door; concierge; babysitting; same-day laundry service/dry cleaning. *In room:* TV, dataport, Wi-Fi ($7.95/day), high-speed Internet available at sister hotel next door, the **White Swan Inn** (p. 72), hair dryer, robes.

Serrano Hotel ♠   Los Angeles designer Cheryl Rowley (who also designed the Hotel Monaco; p. 64) swathed this 17-story 1920s hotel in her trademark vibrant color and added a playful dash of Moroccan flair while preserving the building's Spanish Revival integrity. Original architectural elements dot the colorful lobby, with its whimsically painted beams, high ceilings, large ornate fireplace, and dramatic colonnade. Equally vibrant guest rooms (sometimes small) have oversize windows and high ceilings, cherrywood headboards, terry robes, and theater-themed artwork. The hotel is in the heart of the Theater District, right off Union Square, and is pet-friendly.

405 Taylor St. (at O'Farrell St.), San Francisco, CA 94102. ② **866/289-6561** or 415/885-2500. Fax 415/474-4879. www.serranohotel.com. 236 units. From $199 double; from $329 suite. Rates include morning coffee and tea service and afternoon beverages. AE, DC, DISC, MC, V. Valet parking $39. Bus: 2, 3, 4, 27, or 38. Cable car: Powell or Market. Pets accepted. **Amenities:** Restaurant/bar; exercise room; sauna; concierge; courtesy car; business center w/fax; Wi-Fi in meeting rooms and public spaces; limited room service; babysitting by referral; same-day laundry service/dry cleaning. *In room:* A/C, TV w/pay movies, dataport, free Wi-Fi, minibar, hair dryer, iron, safe.

Sir Francis Drake ♠♠   This landmark hotel is one of San Francisco's grand dames, operating continuously since 1928 in the heart of Union Square. The Kimpton Hotel company has done a wonderful job renovating the hotel (which has been sorely needed since I was a kid), giving this elegant lady a much-needed makeover. I've always been a fan of the Hotel Monaco's modern, slightly offbeat interiors with bold patterns and custom furnishings, and they've incorporated a similar style at this property, though with a cream and sage green color scheme. It's always a pleasure to have Tom Sweeny, the ebullient (and legendary) Beefeater doorman, handle your bags as you enter the elegant, captivating lobby with its gilded high ceilings, glittering crystal chandeliers, and massive curved marble staircase that leads to a mezzanine overlooking bustling Powell Street. It's a grand entrance experience you won't soon forget.

Scala's Bistro (p. 109), one of the most festive restaurants downtown, serves good Italian cuisine in a stylish setting on the first floor; the Italian-style Caffe Espresso does an equally commendable job serving coffees, pastries, and sandwiches daily in its spot adjacent to the hotel. Harry Denton's Starlight Room (p. 241), on the 21st floor, offers cocktails, entertainment, and dancing nightly with a panoramic view of the city.

Fun Fact **A Living Legend**

Tom Sweeny, the head doorman at the Sir Francis Drake hotel, is a living San Francisco historical monument. Dressed in traditional Beefeater's attire (you can't miss those $1,400 duds), he's been the subject of countless snapshots—an average 200 per day for the past 25 years—and has shaken hands with every president since Jerry Ford.

450 Powell St. (at Sutter St.), San Francisco, CA 94102. © **800/795-7129** or 415/392-7755. Fax 415/391-8719. www.sirfrancisdrake.com. 417 units. $239–$289 double; from $5,200 suite. AE, DC, DISC, MC, V. Valet parking $38. Bus: 2, 3, 4, 45, or 76. Cable car: Powell–Hyde or Powell–Mason lines (direct stop). Pets welcome. **Amenities:** 2 restaurants; bar; exercise room; concierge; Wi-Fi; limited room service; same-day laundry service/dry cleaning. *In room:* A/C, TV w/movies on demand, dataport, free Wi-Fi, minibar, hair dryer, iron.

Villa Florence 🏨🏨 Located ½ block south of Union Square, fronting the Powell Street cable car line, this seven-story hotel is in one of the liveliest sections of the city (no need to drive, 'cause you're already here). The Villa Florence provides guests a taste of contemporary Italian decor with cherrywood furniture, plantation shutters, windows that actually open, and perks such as flatscreen TVs with DVD players and CD players. You'll like the large, comfortable beds draped in down comforters with Frette duvets, as well as such luxury touches as Aveda bath products and Frette bathrobes. The hotel's ground-floor restaurant, Kuleto's (p. 108), is one of downtown's most bustling and stylish Italian restaurants. That and Bar Norcini wine bar help make the hotel a worthy contender among Union Square's boutique inns—as if the location alone weren't reason enough to book a room. *Note:* A complete interior/exterior remodel should be completed by October 2008.

225 Powell St. (btw. Geary and O'Farrell sts.), San Francisco, CA 94102. © **866/823-4669** or 415/397-7700. Fax 415/397-1006. www.villaflorence.com. 183 units. $199–$249 double; $249–$299 studio suites. Rates include evening wine. AE, DC, DISC, MC, V. Valet parking $35, plus an extra $10–$15 per day for oversize vehicles and SUVs. Bus: 2, 3, 4, 30, 38, or 45. Cable car: Powell–Hyde or Powell–Mason lines (direct stop). **Amenities:** Access to nearby health club ($15/day); concierge; courtesy car; business center; secretarial services; babysitting on request; same-day laundry service/dry cleaning; in-room spa services. *In room:* A/C, ceiling fan, flatscreen TV w/pay movies, CD player, dataport, free Wi-Fi, minibar, fridge, coffeemaker, hair dryer, iron.

The Warwick Regis 🏨🏨 *Value* Louis XVI might have been a rotten monarch, but he certainly had taste. Fashioned in the style of pre-Revolutionary France, the Warwick is awash with pristine French and English antiques, Italian marble, chandeliers, four-poster beds, hand-carved headboards, and the like. The result is an expensive-looking hotel that, for all its pleasantries and perks, is surprisingly affordable when compared to its Union Square contemporaries. Rooms can be on the small side; nonetheless, they're some of the city's most charming. Honeymooners should splurge on the fireplace rooms with four-poster beds—ooh la la! Adjoining the lobby is La Scene Restaurant and Bar, a beautiful place to start your day with a latte and end it with a nightcap.

490 Geary St. (btw. Mason and Taylor sts.), San Francisco, CA 94102. © **800/203-3232** or 415/928-7900. Fax 415/441-8788. www.warwicksf.com. 74 units. $199–$299 double; $299–$399 suite. AE, DC, DISC, MC, V. Parking $29. Bus: 2, 3, 4, 27, or 38. Cable car: Powell–Hyde or Powell–Mason lines. **Amenities:** Restaurant; access to nearby health club ($15/day); concierge; business center; secretarial services; 24-hr. room service; babysitting; laundry service; dry cleaning. *In room:* TV, dataport, Wi-Fi, minibar, hair dryer, iron, safe.

White Swan Inn 🏨🏨 From the moment you're buzzed into this well-secured inn, you'll know you're not in a generic bed-and-breakfast. The romantically homey rooms are warm and cozy—the perfect place to snuggle up with a good book. They're also quite big, with hardwood entryways, rich dark-wood furniture, working fireplaces, and an assortment of books tucked in nooks. The decor is English elegance at its best, if not to excess (floral prints and ceramic bric-a-brac abound). The luxury king suites are not much better than regular rooms, just a wee bit bigger, and feature perks like evening turndown, bathrobes, and a wet bar stocked with complimentary beverages. Each morning, a breakfast buffet is served in a common room just off a tiny garden. Afternoon reception, consisting of hors d'oeuvres, sherry, wine, and home-baked pastries, can be enjoyed in front of the fireplace while you browse through the books in the library or in the parlor.

The inn's location—2½ blocks from Union Square—makes this nonsmoking 1900s building a charming and serene choice, with service and style that will please travelers of all ages.

845 Bush St. (btw. Taylor and Mason sts.), San Francisco, CA 94108. ℂ 800/999-9570 or 415/775-1755. Fax 415/775-5717. www.whiteswaninnsf.com. 26 units. $229–$319 double; $269 luxury king suite; $319 2-room suite. Extra person $20. Rates include breakfast and afternoon wine and hors d'oeuvres. AE, DC, DISC, MC, V. Valet parking $32. Bus: 1, 2, 3, 4, 27, or 45. Cable car: Powell St. line (1 block north). **Amenities:** Small exercise room; concierge; same-day laundry service; Internet station in conference room (20¢/min.). *In room:* Dataport, Wi-Fi ($7.95/day), fridge w/free beverages, coffeemaker, hair dryer, iron.

MODERATE

Hotel Beresford Arms *Value*   The bargain prices are the main reason I recommend this dependable, if unfashionable, hotel. On the plus side, suites have bidets, whirlpool bathtubs, and a wet bar or fully equipped kitchenette—an advantage for families—and a continental breakfast is included in the price of all rooms. All accommodations include plenty of in-room perks, including an afternoon "Social Hour" with wine, tea, and snacks. The location, between the Theater District and Union Square, in a quieter section of San Francisco, is ideal for visitors without cars, and the price for what you get is hard to beat. The on-site **White Horse Tavern,** a quaint replica of an old English pub, serves dinner Tuesday through Saturday. *Tip:* Rooms that face Post Street might be a bit noisier than others, but they're also larger and sunnier, and some have window seats.

701 Post St. (at Jones St.), San Francisco, CA 94109. ℂ 800/533-6533 or 415/673-2600. Fax 415/929-1535. www.beresford.com. 95 units. $99–$279 double. Extra person $10. Children under 12 stay free in parent's room. Rates include pastry, coffee, afternoon wine and tea. Senior and AAA discounts available. AE, DC, DISC, MC, V. Valet parking $20. Bus: 2, 3, 4, 27, or 38. Cable car: Powell–Hyde line (3 blocks east). **Amenities:** Access to nearby health club ($10/day); free Internet access in lobby; laundry service. *In room:* TV, dataport, minibar, hair dryer upon request, iron.

Hotel Frank *✦✦*   Its location—only a block from Union Square—and chic-boutique makeover are the two main reasons this former Maxwell Hotel is the new darling amongst hip business travelers and serious shoppers. A major renovation in the fall of 2008 brought the hotel to a far more upscale, boutique-hotel standard. A clever interior makeover by one of the country's most cutting-edge designers, Thomas Schoos Design, Inc., incorporates a blend of popular design trends through the decades, from turn-of-the-century Beaux Art classicism to '40s Art Deco and retro '60s chic (yes, I know, it sounds odd, but it works). The guestrooms—each with 32-inch flat-screen TVs and iPod docking stations—exude a custom designed look: houndstooth-patterned carpeting, elongated emerald green headboards in crocodile-patterned leather, sleek white leather couches, vintage 1930s artwork. Even the bathrooms are outfitted in floor-to-ceiling Carrera marble. The hotel's 28 roomy junior suites offer excellent value despite the slightly audible elevator noise, but best of all are the pair of one-bedroom penthouses on the 13th floor, both of which offer separate living rooms and exceptional views of the city.

386 Geary St. (at Mason St.), San Francisco, CA 94102. ℂ 800/553-1900 or 415/986-2000. www.personalityhotels.com. 153 units. $169–$399 double; $209–$469 Jr. suite; $499–$1,200 penthouse suits. AE, DC, DISC, MC, V. Valet parking $30. Bus: 2, 3, 4, 30, 38, or 45. Cable car: Powell–Hyde or Powell–Mason lines (1 block east). **Amenities:** Concierge; 24-hour business center; meeting facilities; room service; same-day dry cleaning; express check-out. *In room:* A/C, TV w/pay movies, free Wi-Fi, hair dryer, iron, safe, bathrobes, honor bar, turndown service.

Hotel Metropolis ☆ *Kids* *Finds*   Located just off of Market Street, a few blocks from Union Square, the Hotel Metropolis is ideal for people who dread staying at boring, corporate-frumpy McHotels. The lobby alone tells the story: Adorning the walls are more than 80 works of colorful (and curiously abstract) art created by the children, yet a Zen-like feel permeates throughout the hotel, starting with the lobby's cascading slate-wall waterfall. The result is a yin/yang combo of playfulness and serenity. As with most downtown hotels, the rooms are on the small side, but all are vibrant and cheery, with vivid colors, custom African Limba-wood furnishings, and comfy beds with wave-shaped headboards with portholes. The six Executive Rooms on the 10th floor are upgraded with feather beds and pillows, iPod alarm clocks, and robes, while the three-room Urban Explorers Kids Suite, which sleeps up to six adults and three children, is filled with pint-sized furniture, bunk beds, a computer, a chalkboard wall, toys and rubber ducky decor in the bathroom. After a busy day in the city, you can relax with a bit of yoga or meditation in the hotel's "well-being room" complete with a miniature rock and sand garden, or enjoy a cup of tea and a good read in the book-filled loft/library. Additional perks include complimentary room service via the adjacent Farmer Brown's restaurant ("farm-fresh soul food"), a 24-hour business center with complimentary computers and laser printers, free Wi-Fi, and a 24-hour exercise room. All this and rates starting at $99 makes the Hotel Metropolis is a real find.

25 Mason St. (at Turk and Market sts.), San Francisco, CA 94102. ℂ **800/553-1900** or 415/775-4600. www.hotel metropolis.com. 105 units. $99–$289 double; $159–$369 suite. AE, DC, DISC, MC, V. Valet parking $30. Bus: All Market St. buses. Streetcar: Powell St. station. **Amenities:** Exercise room; business center; room service; same-day laundry service/dry cleaning. *In room:* TV w/PPV, free Wi-Fi, hair dryer, iron.

Hotel Milano ☆   Neoclassical Italian design patterned after Giorgio Armani's villa in Milan, elegantly streamlined rooms (with double-paned soundproof windows), moderate prices, and a central location next to the San Francisco Centre make Hotel Milano a popular choice for tourists and businesspeople alike. The hotel also has a film-production facility and private screening room to entice media types. Corporate travelers come for the spacious guest rooms, which feature everything an executive could want, from Wi-Fi to video game systems and work desks. Suites have spa tubs and bidets.

55 Fifth St. (btw. Market and Mission sts.), San Francisco, CA 94103. ℂ **800/398-7555** or 415/543-8555. Fax 415/543-5885. www.hotelmilanosf.com. 108 units. $109–$199 double. Extra person $20. AE, DC, DISC, MC, V. Valet parking $33. Bus: All Market St. buses. **Amenities:** Fitness room; spa; steam room and sauna; concierge; laundry service; valet. *In room:* A/C, TV w/video games, fax, dataport, Wi-Fi ($9.95/day), fridge, hair dryer, iron, safe.

Hotel Union Square ☆☆   After a $5 million dollar renovation in the spring of 2008, the Hotel Union Square has achieved that rare hotel hat-trick of history, style, and location. History: It's San Francisco's first boutique hotel, built in 1913 for the 1915 Pan Pacific Exposition. Style: The renovation has juxtaposed contemporary and classic San Francisco, with original 1915 Egyptian-motif mosaic murals, signature staircases, and opulent moldings contrasted by sleek furnishings, completely remodeled bathrooms, and state-of-the-art technology. Location: It's only a half-block from Union Square, in the heart of the city with the cable cars passing by your window. The guestrooms feel more like urban apartments, each outfitted with platform beds with custom-made leather headboards, 600-thread count linens, sleek dark-wood desks, velvety chaise lounges, flatscreen televisions, and custom lighting. Many have an open loft-like layout with exposed brick walls and floating white paneled ceiling installations, while the two rooftop penthouses are the ultimate in San Francisco chic with large living rooms, wet bars, and expansive redwood decks with city views. There's also a custom Kids Suite, a Dashiell Hammett-themed suite (the third man will cost you an extra $10), and "Sleep & Soak" rooms on each floor that feature spa-like bathrooms outfitted with corner soaking tubs and chaise lounges. The hotel lacks a fitness center, but guests have complimentary use of the adjacent Hotel Diva fitness center, and there's even complimentary room delivery from the adjacent Tad's Steakhouse.

114 Powell St. (btw. O'Farrell and Ellis sts.), San Francisco, CA 94102. © **800/553-1900** or 415/397-3000. www.hotel unionsquare.com. 131 units. $149–$349 double; $199–$499 suite; $229–$799 penthouse suites. Rates include morning coffee and tea and weekday wine reception. AE, DC, DISC, MC, V. Valet parking $30. Bus: 2, 3, 4, 30, 38, 45, or 76. Cable car: Powell–Hyde or Powell–Mason lines. Streetcar: Powell St. station. **Amenities:** 24-hour business center; room service; same-day laundry service/dry cleaning; on-site currency exchange. *In room:* TV w/PPV, free Wi-Fi, hair dryer, iron.

Hotel Vertigo 🕭🕭   I don't normally write reviews of hotels that haven't opened yet, but I have insider info that the York Hotel, currently under renovation and scheduled to reopen in the fall of '08 as Hotel Vertigo, will be *the* hot new place to stay and play in San Francisco. Combining big-name designers with celebrity chefs is the new trend in high-end hospitality, so locally-based Personality Hotels paired cutting-edge design company Thomas Schoos Design, Inc., with celebrity chef Tyler Florence (who will open his first-ever restaurant, Bar Florence, within the hotel) to create a hotel with instant celebrity status. It's a clever concept: The restaurant's salon-style seating and Florence's shared-plates menu will bring in the locals, while Schoos' stylistic design elements will attract tourists and business travelers looking for an alternative to the W Hotel. There's even some colorful history involved as well—the hotel occupies the former site of the Empire Hotel made famous in Alfred Hitchcock's Vertigo, hence the name. Guest rooms will feature playful, eclectic design features such as white tufted-leather headboards, custom wingback chairs in vibrant orange, and crocodile-patterned tiles in the bathrooms. iPod docking stations and 36-inch flatscreen TVs will be standard as well. With room rates starting at $169 (half that of the W), it's a safe bet that the Vertigo will be one of the hottest new hotels in town.

940 Sutter St. (btw. Leavenworth and Hyde sts.), San Francisco, CA 94109. © **800/553-1900** or 415/885-6800. www.personalityhotels.com. 97 units. $169–$399 double; $350–$495 suites. Rates include morning beverages in lobby and express breakfast. AE, DISC, MC, V. Valet parking $30. Bus: 2, 3, or 4. **Amenities:** Fitness room; concierge; business center; room service; same-day dry cleaning; turn-down service; overnight shoe shine; daily newspaper. *In room:* TV w/pay movies, free Wi-Fi, hair dryer, iron, safe, robes.

King George Hotel 🕭 *(Value*   Built in 1914 for the Panama–Pacific Exhibition (when rooms went for $1 per night), the boutique King George has fared well over the years with its mostly European clientele. The location—surrounded by cable car lines, the Theater District, Union Square, and dozens of restaurants—is superb, and the rooms are surprisingly quiet for such a busy spot (sadly, the interior noise is definitely audible through thin, old walls). The guest rooms can be very small (in the smallest rooms it can be difficult for two people to maneuver at the same time), but they still manage to find room for writing desks, private bathrooms, and king or queen pillow-top beds with down comforters. A big hit since it started a few years back is the hotel's English afternoon tea, served in the Windsor Tea Room Saturday, Sunday, and holidays from 1 to 4pm. Recent additions include a pub, a 24-hour business center, and an upgraded "executive" level.

334 Mason St. (btw. Geary and O'Farrell sts.), San Francisco, CA 94102. ℭ **800/288-6005** or 415/781-5050. Fax 415/835-5991. www.kinggeorge.com. 153 units. $175 double; $195 suite. Breakfast $9.95–$13. Special-value packages available seasonally. AE, DC, DISC, MC, V. Valet parking $26; self-parking $23. Bus: 1, 2, 3, 4, 5, 7, 30, 38, 45, 70, or 71. Cable car: Powell–Hyde or Powell–Mason lines (1 block west). **Amenities:** Tearoom; evening lounge/bar; $12 access to health club ½ block away; concierge; 24-hr. business center; Wi-Fi in lobby; secretarial services; room service; same-day laundry service/dry cleaning. *In room:* TV w/video games and pay movies, dataport, free Wi-Fi, hair dryer, iron, safe.

INEXPENSIVE

The Andrews Hotel   For the location, price, and service, the Andrews is a safe bet for an enjoyable stay in San Francisco. Two blocks west of Union Square, the Andrews was a Turkish bath before its conversion in 1981. As is typical in Euro-style hotels, the rooms are small but well maintained and comfortable, with nice touches like white lace curtains and fresh flowers. Continued upgrades help keep things fresh, but large bathroom lovers beware—the facilities here are tiny. A bonus is the adjoining Fino Bar and Ristorante, which offers respectable Italian fare and free wine to hotel guests in the evening.

624 Post St. (btw. Jones and Taylor sts.), San Francisco, CA 94109. ℭ **800/926-3739** or 415/563-6877. Fax 415/928-6919. www.andrewshotel.com. 48 units, some with shower only. $92–$142 double; $139–$179 superior rooms. Rates include continental breakfast, coffee in lobby, and evening wine. AE, DC, MC, V. Valet parking $25. Bus: 2, 3, 4, 30, 38, or 45. Cable car: Powell–Hyde or Powell–Mason lines (3 blocks east). **Amenities:** Restaurant; access to nearby health club; concierge; room service (5:30–10pm); babysitting; nearby self-service laundromat; laundry service; dry cleaning. *In room:* TV/VCR w/video library, CD player in suites only, dataport, free Wi-Fi, fridge, hair dryer on request, iron.

The Cornell Hotel de France   Its quirks make this small French-style hotel more charming than many others in its price range. Pass the office, where a few faces will glance in your direction and smile, and embark on a ride in the old-fashioned elevator (we're talking seriously old-school here) to get to your basic room. Each floor is dedicated to a French painter and decorated with reproductions. Rooms are all plain and comfortable, with desks and chairs, and are individually and simply decorated. Smoking is not allowed. The full American breakfast included in the rate is served in the cool cavernlike provincial basement restaurant, Jeanne d'Arc. Union Square is just a few blocks away.

715 Bush St. (btw. Powell and Mason sts.), San Francisco, CA 94108. ℭ **800/232-9698** or 415/421-3154. Fax 415/399-1442. www.cornellhotel.com. 55 units. $85–$155 double. Rates include full American breakfast. AE, DC, DISC, MC, V. Parking across the street $17. Bus: 2, 3, 4, 30, or 45. Cable car: Powell–Hyde or Powell–Mason lines. **Amenities:** Restaurant; computer w/Internet in lobby. *In room:* TV, dataport, Wi-Fi (for a fee), hair dryer.

The Golden Gate Hotel ✦ *Value*   San Francisco's stock of small hotels in historic turn-of-the-20th-century buildings includes some real gems, and the Golden Gate Hotel is one of them. It's 2 blocks north of Union Square and 2 blocks down (literally) from the crest of Nob Hill, with cable car stops at the corner for easy access to Fisherman's Wharf and Chinatown. The city's theaters and best restaurants are also within walking distance. But the best thing about the 1913 Edwardian hotel—which definitely has a B&B feel—is that it's family run: John and Renate Kenaston and daughter Gabriele are hospitable innkeepers who take obvious pleasure in making their guests comfortable. Each individually decorated room has recently been repainted and carpeted and has handsome antique furnishings (plenty of wicker) from the early 1900s, quilted bedspreads, and fresh flowers. Request a room with a clawfoot tub if you enjoy a good, hot soak. Afternoon tea is served daily from 4 to 7pm, and guests are welcome to use the house fax and computer with Wi-Fi free of charge.

775 Bush St. (btw. Powell and Mason sts.), San Francisco, CA 94108. ℂ **800/835-1118** or 415/392-3702. Fax 415/392-6202. www.goldengatehotel.com. 25 units, 14 with bathroom. $85–$105 double without bathroom; $150 double with bathroom. Rates include continental breakfast and afternoon tea. AE, DC, MC, V. Self-parking $20. Bus: 2, 4, 30, 38, or 45. Cable car: Powell–Hyde or Powell–Mason lines (1 block east). BART: Powell and Market. **Amenities:** Access to health club 1 block away; activities desk; laundry service/dry cleaning next door. *In room:* TV, dataport, free Wi-Fi, hair dryer and iron upon request.

Halcyon Hotel *(Value)*   Inside this small, four-story brick building is a penny-pincher's dream come true, the kind of place where you'll find everything you need yet won't have to pay through the nose to get. The small but clean studio guest rooms are equipped with microwave ovens, refrigerators, flatware and utensils, toasters, alarm clocks, coffeemakers and coffee, phones with free local calls, mail delivery, and voice mail—all the comforts of home in the heart of Union Square (you can even bring your pet!). A coin-operated washer and dryer are located in the basement, along with free laundry soap and irons. The managers are usually on hand to offer friendly, personal service, making this option all in all an unbeatable deal. Be sure to ask about special rates for weekly stays.

649 Jones St. (btw. Geary and Post sts.), San Francisco, CA 94102. ℂ **800/627-2396** or 415/929-8033. Fax 415/441-8033. www.halcyonsf.com. 25 units. $79–$99 double year-round; $450–$600 weekly. AE, DC, DISC, MC, V. Parking garage nearby $14–$16 per day. Bus: 2, 3, 4, 9, 27, or 38. Pets accepted. **Amenities:** Access to nearby health club; concierge; tour desk; laundry facilities; free fax available in lobby. *In room:* TV, dataport, kitchen, fridge, coffeemaker, hair dryer, iron, voice mail.

Hotel Beresford   The small, less expensive sister property of the Hotel Beresford Arms (see above), the seven-floor Hotel Beresford is another good, moderately priced choice near Union Square. Perks are the same: satellite TV, phone, radio, private bathrooms with either a tub or shower, and stocked fridges. The guest rooms are decorated in Victorian style and very well kept, with plenty of personal touches you don't often find in a budget hotel. Rates even include continental breakfast. The on-site **White Horse Tavern,** a quaint replica of an old English pub, serves dinner Tuesday through Saturday and is a favorite for folks who like less trendy hullabaloo with their meal.

635 Sutter St. (near Mason St.), San Francisco, CA 94102. ℂ **800/533-6533** or 415/673-9900. Fax 415/474-0449. www.beresford.com. 114 units. $89–$165 double. Extra person $10. Rates include continental breakfast. Children under 12 stay free in parent's room. AE, DC, DISC, MC, V. Valet parking $20. Bus: 2, 3, 4, 30, 38, or 45. Cable car: Powell–Hyde line (1 block east). **Amenities:** Restaurant/pub; access to nearby health club ($10/day); free high-speed Internet access in kiosk in lobby; laundry service. *In room:* TV, dataport, minibar, hair dryer upon request, iron.

Hotel Bijou *(★)* *(Value)*   Three words sum up this hotel: clean, colorful, and cheap. Although it's on the periphery of the gritty Tenderloin (just 3 blocks off Union Sq.), once inside this gussied-up 1911 hotel, all's cheery, bright, and perfect for budget travelers who want a little style with their savings. Joie de Vivre hotel group disguised the hotel's age with lively decor, a Deco theater theme, and a heck of a lot of vibrant paint. To the left of the small lobby is a "theater" where guests can watch San Francisco–based double features nightly (it has cute old-fashioned theater seating, though it's just a basic TV showing videos). Upstairs, rooms named after locally made films are small, clean, and colorful (think buttercup, burgundy, and purple), and have all the basics from clock radios, dressers, and small desks to tiny bathrooms (one of which is so small you have to close the door to access the toilet). Alas, a few mattresses could be firmer, and there's only one small and slow elevator. But considering the price, and perks like the continental breakfast and friendly service, you can't go wrong here.

111 Mason St., San Francisco, CA 94102. ☎ **800/771-1022** or 415/771-1200. Fax 415/346-3196. www.hotel bijou.com. 65 units. $99–$159 double. Rates include continental breakfast. AE, DC, DISC, MC, V. Valet parking $27. Bus: All Market St. buses. Streetcar: Powell St. station. **Amenities:** Concierge; DSL access in lobby ($4/20 min); limited room service; same-day laundry service/dry cleaning. *In room:* TV, dataport, high-speed Internet, Wi-Fi ($7.95/day), hair dryer, iron.

Hotel Carlton ★ *Value* If you're looking for wonderfully cheap, attractive, and clean accommodations and don't mind being in the gritty center of the city, book a room here. The Joie de Vivre hotel group is behind this 163-room hotel that was built in 1927 and revamped in May 2004 in "global vintage" decor. The interior design is globally eclectic, with travel photographs from the American Himalayan Foundation, tribal figurines, Oriental rugs, a vibrant sari-like color scheme, imported hand-painted Moroccan tables, and cool Lucite-beaded table lamps in the guest rooms. Outside, the neighborhood is drab, but it's only a 7-block walk to Union Square, and with doubles starting at a mere $93, you can splurge for a taxi with the money saved. Or stick nearby and try **Saha,** their Arabian-fusion restaurant (think hummus, pizza, Yemenese meatballs, and seared scallops), which serves breakfast and dinner. Heck, they even throw in a complimentary evening wine hour in the lobby.

1075 Sutter St. (btw. Larkin and Hyde sts.), San Francisco, CA 94109. ☎ **800/922-7586** or 415/673-0242. Fax 415/673-4904. www.jdvhospitality.com. 163 units. $93–$199 double. Rates include evening wine reception. AE, MC, V. Valet parking $30; self parking $25. Bus: 2, 3, 4, 19, or 76. **Amenities:** Restaurant; concierge; laundry service; dry cleaning. *In room:* TV, free Wi-Fi, coffeemaker, hair dryer, iron, safe.

Hotel des Arts ★★ *Value* While this bargain find has the same floor plan as San Francisco's numerous other Euro-style hotels—small lobby, narrow hallways, cramped rooms—the owners of the des Arts have made an obvious effort to distance themselves from the competition by including a visually stimulating dose of artistic license throughout the hotel. The lobby, for example, hosts a rotating art gallery featuring contemporary works by emerging local artists and is outfitted with groovy furnishings, while the guest rooms are soothingly situated with quality furnishings and tasteful accouterments. There's one suite that can sleep up to four persons at no additional charge. You'll love the lively location as well: right across the street from the entrance to Chinatown and 2 blocks from Union Square. There's even a French brasserie right downstairs. Considering the price (rooms with a very clean shared bathroom start at $59), quality, and location, it's quite possibly the best budget hotel in the city. *Tip:* Log onto the hotel's website to check out the "Painted Rooms" designed by local artists, then call the hotel directly to book your favorite.

447 Bush St. (at Grant St.), San Francisco, CA 94108. ☎ **800/956-4322** or 415/956-3232. Fax 415/956-0399. www. sfhoteldesarts.com. 51 units, 26 with private bathroom. $79–$159 with bathroom; $59–$79 double without bathroom. Rates include continental breakfast. AE, DC, MC, V. Nearby parking $18. Cable car: Powell–Hyde and Powell–Mason lines. **Amenities:** 24-hr. concierge, fax, and copy services; laundry and valet service. *In room:* TV, 2-line direct-dial telephone w/dataport and voice mail, minifridge and microwave in many rooms, hair dryer, iron and board.

3 Nob Hill

VERY EXPENSIVE

The Fairmont San Francisco ★★★ *Kids* The granddaddy of Nob Hill's elite cadre of ritzy hotels—and the only spot in San Francisco where each of the city's cable car lines meet—the century-old Fairmont is a must-visit if only to marvel at the incredibly glamorous lobby with its vaulted ceilings, Corinthian columns, a spectacular spiral staircase, and rococo furniture (it's easy to feel underdressed in such opulent surroundings). And yes, such decadence carries to the guest rooms where luxuries abound: oversized marble bathrooms, thick down blankets, goose-down king pillows, extra-long mattresses, and large walk-in closets. Because it's perched at the top of Nob Hill, there are spectacular city views from every guest room, but nuances such as a health club and spa, a 24-hour concierge, twice-daily maid service, babysitting services, and a business center enhance every guest's stay. Within the lobby is the ornate **Laurel Court** restaurant and lounge, which serves as the hotel's centerpiece. (It's fun to indulge in afternoon tea here, served daily 2:30–4:30pm.) A local institution that's been around since I was a kid is the hotel's **Tonga Room,** a fantastically kitsch Disneyland-like tropical bar and restaurant where happy hour hops and "rain" falls every 30 minutes.

950 Mason St. (at California St.), San Francisco, CA 94108. (C) **866/540-4491** or 415/772-5000. Fax 415/772-5086. www.fairmont.com. 591 units. Main building $229–$349 double; from $500 suite. Tower $289–$469 double; from $750 suite. Penthouse $12,500. Extra person $30. AE, DC, DISC, MC, V. Parking $43. Cable car: California St. line (direct stop). **Amenities:** 2 restaurants/bars; health club (free for Fairmont President's Club members; $15/day or $20/2 days, non-members); concierge; tour desk; car-rental desk; business center; Wi-Fi in lobby; shopping arcade; salon; room service; massage; babysitting; same-day laundry service/dry cleaning. *In room:* A/C, TV w/pay movies and video games available, dataport, high-speed Internet access, kitchenette in some units, minibar, hair dryer, iron, safe.

The Huntington Hotel ★★

One of the kings of Nob Hill, the stately Huntington Hotel has long been a favorite retreat for Hollywood stars and political VIPs who desire privacy and security. Family-owned since 1924—an extreme rarity among large hotels—the Huntington eschews pomp and circumstance; absolute privacy and unobtrusive service are its mainstays. Although the lobby, decorated in grand 19th-century style, is rather petite compared to its Nob Hill neighbors, the guest rooms are like spacious apartments; they feature Brunschwig & Fils fabrics and bed coverings, antique French furnishings, and dreamy views of the city. Be warned, however, that they are also quirky and sprinkled with downscale items; one room where I recently stayed had motel-quality doorknobs and a tiny, plain bathroom. Where they make up for the room deficiencies is a genuinely gracious staff and the celestial **Nob Hill Spa** (the best in the city). The lavish suites, so opulent that they've been featured in *Architectural Digest,* are individually decorated with custom-made furnishings. Prices are steep, as you would expect, but special offers such as the Romance Package, which includes champagne, specialty teas, limousine service, and two 50-minute massages from their spa, make the Huntington worth considering for a special occasion. **The Big Four** restaurant offers expensive contemporary American cuisine, including the best $16 chicken pot pie I've ever had. Live piano music is played nightly in the lounge.

1075 California St. (btw. Mason and Taylor sts.), San Francisco, CA 94108. (C) **800/227-4683** or 415/474-5400. Fax 415/474-6227. www.huntingtonhotel.com. 135 units. $350–$500 single or double; $600–$1,350 suite. Continental breakfast $14. Special packages available. AE, DC, DISC, MC, V. Valet parking $29. Bus: 1. Cable car: California St. line (direct stop). **Amenities:** Restaurant; lounge; indoor heated pool (ages 16 and up); health club; spa; Jacuzzi; steam room; sauna; yoga and Pilates room; concierge; massage; babysitting; same-day laundry service/dry cleaning. *In room:* A/C, TV w/pay movies, dataport, Wi-Fi ($9.95/day). kitchenettes in some units, minibar, fridges in some units, hair dryer, iron, safe.

InterContinental Mark Hopkins ★★★

Built in 1926 on the spot where railroad millionaire Mark Hopkins's turreted mansion once stood, the 19-story Mark Hopkins gained global fame during World War II when it was de rigueur for Pacific-bound servicemen to toast their goodbye to the States in the Top of the Mark cocktail lounge. Nowadays, this grand hotel caters mostly to convention-bound corporate executives, since its prices often require corporate charge accounts. Each neoclassical room is exceedingly comfortable and comes with all the fancy amenities you'd expect from a world-class hotel, including custom furniture, plush fabrics, sumptuous bathrooms, Frette bathrobes, and extraordinary views of the city. The luxury suites are twice the size of most San Francisco apartments and cost close to a month's rent per night. A minor caveat: The hotel has only three guest elevators, making a quick trip to your room difficult during busy periods.

The **Top of the Mark** (p. 246), a fantastic bar/lounge (open daily), offers dancing to live jazz or swing, Sunday brunch, and cocktails in swank, old-fashioned style. (Romantics, this place is for you, but keep in mind that there's a $10 cover fee Fri–Sat after 8:30pm for the live nightly entertainment.) The Nob Hill Restaurant offers California cuisine nightly and breakfast on Sunday.

1 Nob Hill (at California and Mason sts.), San Francisco, CA 94108. (C) **800/972-3124** or 415/392-3434. Fax 415/421-3302. www.markhopkins.net. 380 units. $399–$599 double; from $650 suite; from $3,000 luxury suite. Breakfast $17 for juice, coffee, and pastry to $23 for full buffet. AE, DC, DISC, MC, V. Valet parking $44, some oversize vehicles prohibited. Bus: 1. Cable car: California St. or Powell lines (direct stop). **Amenities:** 2 restaurants; bar; exercise room; concierge; business center; secretarial services; room service; babysitting; laundry service; dry cleaning; concierge-level floors. *In room:* A/C, TV w/pay movies, VCR/DVD in suites only, dataport, Wi-Fi in all rooms for nominal fee, minibar, coffeemaker, hair dryer, iron, safe.

The Ritz-Carlton, San Francisco ✦✦✦   Ranked among the top hotels in the world, The Ritz-Carlton San Francisco has been the benchmark for the city's luxury hotels since it opened in 1991. A Nob Hill landmark, the former Metropolitan Insurance headquarters stood vacant for years until The Ritz-Carlton company acquired it and embarked on a $100-million, 4-year renovation. The interior was completely gutted and restored with fine furnishings, fabrics, and artwork, including a pair of Louis XVI blue marble urns with gilt mountings, and 19th-century Waterford candelabras. And just to make sure they stay on top, the rooms were completely upgraded last year to the tune of $12.5 million, and now include 32-inch LCD TVs, DVD/CD players, Wi-Fi, and two cordless phones. The Italian marble bathrooms offer every possible amenity: double sinks, telephone, name-brand toiletries, and plush terry robes. The more expensive rooms take advantage of the hotel's location—the south slope of Nob Hill—and have good views of the city. Clubrooms, on the top floors, have a dedicated concierge, separate elevator-key access, and complimentary small plates throughout the day. No restaurant in town has more formal service than this hotel's **Dining Room,** which serves modern French cuisine with a Japanese influence. The less formal **Terrace Restaurant** offers contemporary Mediterranean cuisine and the city's best Sunday brunch. The Lobby lounge serves classic afternoon tea and cocktails with low-key live entertainment daily, and sushi Wednesday through Saturday.

600 Stockton St. (btw. Pine and California sts.), San Francisco, CA 94108. (C) **800/241-3333** or 415/296-7465. Fax 415/986-1268. www.ritzcarlton.com. 336 units. $445–$480 double; $600–$850 club-level double; from $750–$850 executive suite. Buffet breakfast $32; Sun champagne brunch $65. Weekend discounts and packages available. AE, DC, DISC, MC, V. Parking $55. Cable car: California St. cable car line (direct stop). **Amenities:** 2 restaurants; 3 bars; indoor pool; outstanding fitness center; Jacuzzi; steam room; concierge; courtesy car; business center; secretarial services; room service; in-room massage and manicure; same-day laundry service/dry cleaning. *In room:* A/C, TV w/pay movies, dataport, high-speed Internet access and Wi-Fi ($13/day), minibar, hair dryer, iron, safe.

Stanford Court, A Renaissance Hotel ✦✦   The Stanford Court has maintained a long and discreet reputation as one of San Francisco's most exclusive hotels. Keeping company with the Ritz, Fairmont, Mark Hopkins, and Huntington hotels atop Nob Hill, it's frequented mostly by corporate execs. The foundation was originally the mansion of Leland Stanford, whose legacy lives on in the many portraits and biographies that adorn the rooms. At first, the guest rooms come across as austere and antiquated compared to those at most other top-dollar business hotels, but the quality and comfort of the furnishings are so superior that you're forced to admit there's little room for improvement. The Stanford Court also prides itself on its impeccable service. The lobby, furnished in 19th-century style with Baccarat chandeliers, French antiques, and a gorgeous stained-glass dome, makes for a grand entrance.

Many of the guest rooms have partially canopied beds; all have writing desks and feature the new signature Renaissance bedding with new linens and down duvets and oak armoires that conceal the television sets. Bathrooms contain robes, telephones, and heated towel racks. Deluxe rooms have Frette linens. A thoughtful perk: There is no charge for toll-free or credit card calls made from your room, and complimentary coffee and tea are available with a wake-up call request.

905 California St. (at Powell St.), San Francisco, CA 94108. (℄ **800/HOTELS** or 415/989-3500. Fax 415/391-0513. www.stanfordcourt.com. 393 units. $299 double; from $550 suite. Continental breakfast $17–$22; American breakfast $21–$26. AE, DC, DISC, MC, V. Valet parking $41. Bus: 1. Cable car: Powell–Hyde, Powell–Mason, or California–Van Ness lines (direct stop). **Amenities:** Restaurant; lounge; 24-hr. fitness center; concierge; free car to downtown destinations; business center; room service; same-day laundry service/dry cleaning. *In room:* A/C, TV w/pay movies and Web TV, dataport, $9.95 high-speed Internet access, hair dryer, iron, local call package.

MODERATE

Nob Hill Hotel *(Value)*   The Nob Hill Hotel is an amazing deal for such an over-the-top Victorian inn, with rates around $130 peak season (and often less). Located in a quiet area between the Tenderloin and Nob Hill (aka Tendernob), it was built in 1906 and fully restored in 1998, and whoever renovated the lobby did a smashing job restoring it to its original "Old San Francisco Victorian" splendor, complete with original marble flooring, high ceilings with decorative moldings, and stained-glass panels and alabaster dating from about 1892. Though the rooms are small, they are all handsomely decorated with old-fashioned furnishings such as Victorian antique armoires, rich carpeting, marble bathrooms, brass beds with comforters, and carved-wood nightstands. A pleasant oxymoron: All the rooms are equipped with a plethora of high-tech amenities such as Internet access and personal voice mail. Complimentary pastries and coffee are served each morning, and there's even free evening wine tasting. The adjacent **Il Bacio** restaurant is a good place to refuel on regional Italian cuisine before venturing down the street to Union Square. *Tip:* The hotel's website offers a Priceline-style "Name Your Own Rate" option that might save you big bucks on your room.

835 Hyde St. (btw. Bush and Sutter sts.), San Francisco, CA 94109. (℄ **877/662-4455** or 415/885-2987. Fax 415/921-1648. www.nobhillhotel.com. 53 units. $130–$150 double. Rates include continental breakfast. DC, DISC, MC, V. Parking $24. Bus: 2, 3, or 4. **Amenities:** Adjoining restaurant (Italian); 24-hr. fitness passes available; copy, fax, and e-mail services; laundry service. *In room:* TV w/pay movies, dataport, microwave, hair dryer, iron, CD/radio alarm clocks; suites have Jacuzzi tubs, fax.

The Nob Hill Inn *(✿)*   Built in 1907 as a private home, this four-story inn has been masterfully refurbished with Victorian-style antiques, expensive fabrics, reproduction artwork, and a magnificent etched-glass European-style lift. Even the low-priced Gramercy rooms receive equal attention: with good-size bathrooms (with claw-foot tubs), antique furnishings, faux-antique phones, discreetly placed televisions, and comfortable full-size beds. Granted, the cheaper rooms are quite small, but they're so charming that it's tough to complain, especially when you consider that rates include continental breakfast, afternoon tea and sherry, and the distinction of staying in one

> ## *Value* Accommodations with Free Parking
>
> Despite my exhortations to leave the driving to locals and use the public transportation system to get around, I know that some of you will still want to drive the crazy streets of San Francisco, or at least arrive by car. But with parking fees averaging $30 to $40 a night at most hotels, the extra charges can add up for visitors with wheels. So if you're going to rent a car or bring your own, you might want to consider staying at one of these hotels that offers free parking:
>
> - Beck's Motor Lodge, the Castro, p. 99
> - Cow Hollow Motor Inn & Suites, Marina District/Cow Hollow, p. 96
> - Hostelling International San Francisco—Fisherman's Wharf, p. 97
> - Hotel Del Sol, Marina District/Cow Hollow, p. 95
> - Laurel Inn, Marina District/Cow Hollow, p. 95
> - Marina Motel, Marina District/Cow Hollow, p. 97
> - Phoenix Hotel, Civic Center, p. 98
> - San Francisco Airport North Travelodge, Near the Airport, p. 101
> - Seal Rock Inn, Richmond District, p. 91
> - The Wharf Inn, North Beach/Fisherman's Wharf, p. 94

of the city's most prestigious neighborhoods. *Tip:* Ideal for families of four are the inn's one-bedroom apartment-style suites, which include a stocked kitchenette, a private master bedroom, and a parlor with a sofa sleeper.

1000 Pine St. (at Taylor St.), San Francisco, CA 94109. © **415/673-6080.** Fax 415/673-6098. www.nobhillinn.com. 21 units. $125–$195 double; $245–$275 suite. Rates include continental breakfast, afternoon tea, and sherry. AE, DC, DISC, MC, V. Parking $25–$35 per day in nearby garages. Bus: 1. Cable car: California St. line. **Amenities:** Concierge. *In room:* TV, kitchenette in some, hair dryer, iron.

4 SoMa

VERY EXPENSIVE

Four Seasons Hotel San Francisco 🦋🦋🦋   What makes this überluxury hotel that opened in late 2001 one of my favorites in the city is its perfect combination of elegance, trendiness, and modern luxury. The entrance, either off Market or through a narrow alley off Third Street, is deceptively underwhelming, although it does tip you off to the hotel's overall discreetness. Take the elevators up to the lobby and you're instantly surrounded by calm, cool, and collected hotel perfection. After all, what's not to love about dark mood lighting, comfy leather chairs, bottomless bowls of olives and spicy wasabi-covered peanuts, a tempting cocktail list, and a pianist playing jazz standards intermingled with No Doubt and Cold Play? Many of the oversize rooms (starting at 460 sq. ft. and including 46 suites) overlook Yerba Buena Gardens. Not too trendy, not too traditional, they're just right, with custom-made mattresses and pillows that guarantee the all-time best night's sleep, beautiful works of art, and huge luxury marble bathrooms with deep tubs and L'Occitane toiletries. Hues of taupe, beige, and green are almost as soothing as the impeccable service. Adding to the perks are free access to the building's huge Sports Club L.A. (the best hotel gym in the city), round-the-clock business services, a 2-block walk to Union Square and the Moscone Convention Center, and a vibe that combines sophistication with a hipness far more refined than the W or the Clift. Its only contender in that department is the St. Regis.

757 Market St. (btw. Third and Fourth sts.), San Francisco, CA 94103. © **800/819-5053** or 415/633-3000. Fax 415/633-3001. www.fourseasons.com/sanfrancisco. 277 units. $450–$855 double; $825 executive suite. AE, DC, DISC, MC, V. Parking $39. Bus: All Market St. buses. Streetcar: F, and all underground streetcars. BART: All trains. **Amenities:** Restaurant; bar; huge fitness center; spa; concierge; high-tech business center; Wi-Fi in lobby; secretarial services; salon; room service; in-room massage; overnight laundry service/dry cleaning. *In room:* A/C, TV w/pay movies, fax, dataport, high-speed Internet access ($13/day), minibar, hair dryer, safe.

Hotel Palomar 🏨🏨   The Kimpton Boutique Hotels' most luxurious downtown property occupies the top five floors of a refurbished 1907 landmark office building. As the group's most refined boutique property, the Art Deco–inspired interior designed by Cheryl Rowley features rooms with an updated twist on 1930s modern design—artful, understated textural elements such as emerald-tone velvets, fine woods, and raffia. Tailored lines and rich textures throughout lend a sophisticated, fresh aspect to the overall air of elegance. Rooms, however, can range from very cozy (read: small) to soothingly spacious (try for a corner room overlooking Market St.); they're also bound to be in mint condition thanks to soft-goods upgrades in 2007. There's not much in the way of public spaces, but the hotel makes up for it with its rooms' fab-factor, homey luxuries like DVD/CD players and flatscreen TVs, and its dining room, the **Fifth Floor Restaurant,** which is one of the most expensive and upscale restaurants in town. That said, if you want the full-blown luxury hotel experience—with every hotel amenity under the sun—you're better off with one of the Nob Hill or Union Square big boys.

12 Fourth St. (at Market St.), San Francisco, CA 94103. © **866/373-4941** or 415/348-1111. Fax 415/348-0302. www.hotelpalomar.com. 198 units. From $369 double; from $569 suite. Continental breakfast $22. AE, DC, DISC, MC, V. Parking $44. Streetcar: F, and all underground streetcars. BART: All trains. Pets welcome. **Amenities:** Restaurant; fitness center; concierge; courtesy car; business center; secretarial services; room service; in-room massage; babysitting; same-day laundry service/dry cleaning. *In room:* A/C, TV, CD player, dataport, free high-speed Internet and Wi-Fi, minibar, fridge, hair dryer, iron, safe.

The Palace Hotel 🏨   The original 1875 Palace was one of the world's largest and most luxurious hotels, and every time you walk through the doors here, you'll be reminded how incredibly majestic old luxury really is. Rebuilt after the 1906 quake, its most spectacular attributes remain the regal lobby and the Garden Court, a San Francisco landmark restaurant that was restored to its original 1909 grandeur. A double row of massive Italian-marble Ionic columns flank the court, and 10 huge chandeliers dangle above. The real heart-stopper, however, is the 80,000-pane stained-glass ceiling (good special effects made Michael Douglas look like he fell through it in the movie *The Game*). Regrettably, the rooms aren't *quite* as grand. But they're vastly improved and emulate yesteryear's refinement with mahogany beds, warm gold paint and upholstery, and tasteful artwork.

The **Garden Court** is famous for its elaborate brunch on special holidays and a scaled-down version on regular weekends. Maxfield's Restaurant, a traditional San Francisco grill, serves lunch and dinner. Kyo-ya, an authentic Japanese restaurant, is highly regarded; and the Pied Piper Bar is named after the $2.5-million Maxfield Parrish mural that dominates the room.

Accommodations Around Town

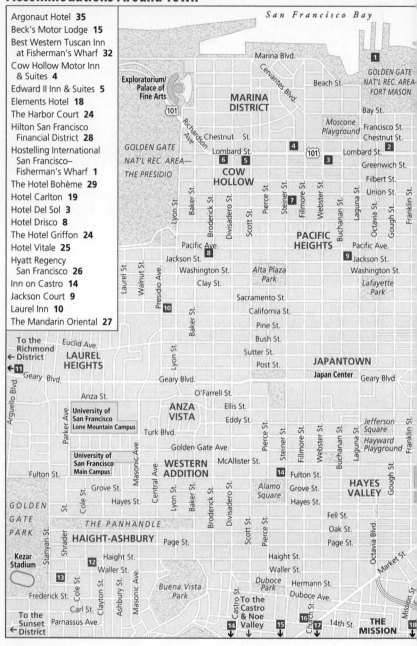

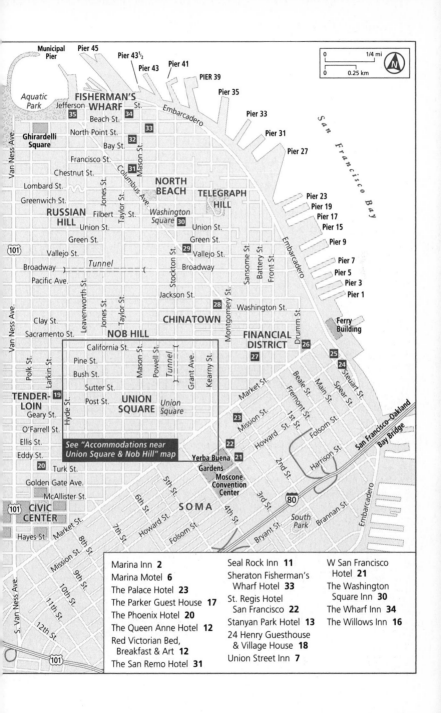

Marina Inn **2**
Marina Motel **6**
The Palace Hotel **23**
The Parker Guest House **17**
The Phoenix Hotel **20**
The Queen Anne Hotel **12**
Red Victorian Bed,
  Breakfast & Art **12**
The San Remo Hotel **31**

Seal Rock Inn **11**
Sheraton Fisherman's
  Wharf Hotel **33**
St. Regis Hotel
  San Francisco **22**
Stanyan Park Hotel **13**
24 Henry Guesthouse
  & Village House **18**
Union Street Inn **7**

W San Francisco
  Hotel **21**
The Washington
  Square Inn **30**
The Wharf Inn **34**
The Willows Inn **16**

2 New Montgomery St. (at Market St.), San Francisco, CA 94105. © **888/625-5144** or 415/512-1111. Fax 415/543-0671. www.sfpalace.com. 552 units. $550–$650 double; from $775 suite. Extra person $40. Children under 18 sharing existing bedding stay free in parent's room. Weekend rates and packages available. AE, DC, DISC, MC, V. Parking $40. Bus: All Market St. buses. Streetcar: All Market St. streetcars. **Amenities:** 4 restaurants; bar; health club w/skylight-covered, heated lap pool; spa; Jacuzzi; sauna; concierge; 24-hr. business center; Wi-Fi in lobby; conference rooms w/Wi-Fi; room service; laundry service; dry cleaning. *In room:* A/C, TV w/pay movies, dataport, high-speed Internet access ($16/day), minibar, hair dryer, iron, safe.

St. Regis Hotel 🐸🐸🐸 The latest in full-blown high-tech luxury is yours at this überchic 40-story SoMa tower, which debuted in late 2005. Strategically located near the Museum of Modern Art and Yerba Buena Gardens, this shrine to urban luxury welcomes guests (and residents willing to pay upwards of $2 million for an apartment) with a 16-foot-long gas fireplace and streamlined lobby bar that's frequented by city socialites. A "personal butler" will take you to your room and show you how to use its coolest feature: a touch-screen control panel that works everything, from the phone to the drapes to the temperature to the lights. Decor is minimalist, with dark woods, cream, taupes, and sexy touches like Barcelona benches, 42-inch plasma TVs, and leather paneling (at least in the suites). Bathrooms beckon with deep soaking tubs, 13-inch LCD TVs, rainforest showerheads, and fancy toiletries. You may want to lounge on a chaise and can peek into the happenings of downtown bustle or the green patch of grass that marks Yerba Buena Gardens, but definitely leave your room for an afternoon at the posh two-floor **Remède Spa,** the huge pool and fitness center, and restaurant **Ame,** where chef Hiro Sone, who also owns Terra in Napa Valley, presides over an Asian-influenced menu that includes delicacies such as hamachi sashimi and decadences like foie gras and unagi (eel) over mushroom risotto.

125 Third St. (at Mission St.), San Francisco, CA 94103. © **877/787-3447** or 415/284-4000. Fax 415/284-4100. www.stregis.com/sanfrancisco. 260 units. Double from $529–$679; suites from $1,050–$8,500. AE, DC, DISC, MC, V. Parking $45 per day. Bus: 15, 30, or 45. Streetcar: J, K, L, or M to Montgomery. **Amenities:** 2 restaurants; bar; health club w/heated lap pool; giant spa; steam room; sauna; whirlpool; 24-hr. concierge; 24-hr. business center; Wi-Fi ($15/day); conference rooms; room service; laundry service; dry cleaning. *In room:* A/C, 2 TVs w/pay movies, fax, dataport, high-speed Internet access ($15/day), printer, scanner, copier, minibar, hair dryer, iron upon request, safe.

W San Francisco Hotel 🐸🐸 Starwood Hotels & Resorts' 31-story property is as modern and hip as its fashionable clientele. Sophisticated, slick, and stylish, it suits its neighbors, which include the Museum of Modern Art, the Moscone Center, and the Metreon entertainment center. The striking gray granite facade, piped with polished black stone, complements the octagonal three-story glass entrance and lobby. The hip, urban style extends to the guest rooms, which have a residential feel. Each contains a feather bed with a goose-down comforter and pillows, Waterworks linens, an oversize dark-wood desk, an upholstered chaise longue, and louvered blinds that open to (usually) great city views. Each room also contains a compact media wall complete with a Sony CD/DVD player, an extensive CD library, and a 27-inch color TV with optional high-speed Internet service (and an infrared keyboard) at $15 per day. Bathrooms are super-sleek and stocked with Bliss products. Furthering the cool vibe is a bi-level **XYZ** bar and restaurant, which serves wonderful Californian cuisine within a beautiful modern interior. In 2005, the W welcomed a 5,000-square-foot outpost of NYC's **Bliss Spa** to the premises. All in all, this is one of the top places to stay in San Francisco, particularly if you enjoy the nightlife scene.

181 Third St. (btw. Mission and Howard sts.), San Francisco, CA 94103. © **877/WHOTELS** or 415/777-5300. Fax 415/817-7823. www.whotels.com/sanfrancisco. 410 units. From $359 double; $1,800–$2,500 suite. AE, DC, DISC, MC, V. Valet parking $40. Bus: 15, 30, or 45. Streetcar: J, K, L, or M to Montgomery. **Amenities:** Restaurant; 2 bars; heated

Finds **Elements: A Hip Mission District Hotel**

Bad credit? No problem. There's finally a place for the perpetually young and broke to stay and play in the heart of the Mission District. The **Elements Hotel** is sort of a cross between a boutique hotel and a hostel, offering both private rooms and shared dorms, all with private bathrooms. Add to that Wi-Fi Internet access throughout the hotel, a free Internet lounge, rooftop parties, free movie nights, lockers, free continental breakfast, luggage storage and laundry facilities, free linens, TVs (in private rooms), a lively restaurant and lounge called Medjool, and a plethora of inexpensive ethnic cafes in the neighborhood, and baby, you've got it made. The hotel is at 2524 Mission St., between 21st and 22nd streets (© **866/327-8407** or 415/647-4100; www.elementssf.com). Rates per person are between $25 and $30; expect higher rates and minimum stays during holidays.

atrium pool and Jacuzzi; fitness center; spa; concierge; business center; Wi-Fi in public spaces; secretarial services; 24-hr. room service; same-day laundry service/dry cleaning. *In room:* A/C, TV w/pay movies, CD/DVD player, fax (in some rooms), dataport, high-speed Internet access, minibar, coffeemaker, hair dryer, iron, safe.

EXPENSIVE

The Harbor Court ✯✯   When the Embarcadero Freeway was torn down after the Big One in 1989, one of the major benefactors was the "wellness-themed" Harbor Court hotel: The 1926 landmark building's backyard view went from a wall of cement to a dazzling vista of the Bay Bridge (be sure to request a bay-view room, for an extra fee). Located just off the Embarcadero at the edge of the Financial District, this former YMCA books a lot of corporate travelers, but anyone who seeks stylish, high-quality accommodations—half-canopy beds, large armoires, writing desks, soundproof windows, and 27-inch LCD TVs—with a superb view and lively scene will be perfectly content here. A major bonus is the free use of the adjoining fitness club, a top-quality YMCA facility with a giant indoor swimming pool. Two more reasons to stay here are the daily hosted evening wine reception and the adjacent **Ozumo Sushi Bar and Robata Grill,** which has a hugely popular happy hour, a cool vibe, and wonderful cuisine.

165 Steuart St. (btw. Mission and Howard sts.), San Francisco, CA 94105. © **866/792-6283** or 415/882-1300. Fax 415/882-1313. www.harborcourthotel.com. 131 units. $195–$425 double. Continental breakfast $10. AE, DC, DISC, MC, V. Parking $35. Bus: 14 or 80X. Streetcar: Embarcadero. Pets accepted. **Amenities:** Access to adjoining health club and large, heated indoor pool; courtesy car weekday mornings; room service (breakfast only); same-day laundry service/dry cleaning; safe. *In room:* A/C, TV, dataport, free Wi-Fi, minibar, hair dryer, iron.

The Hotel Griffon ✯✯   Among San Francisco's small boutique hotels, this is a top contender. Ideally situated on the historic waterfront and steps from the heart of the Financial District and Ferry Building Marketplace (p. 160), the Griffon is impeccably outfitted with a soothing design sensibility. Completely renovated in 2007, it boasts contemporary features such as 32-inch flatscreen TVs, lofty ceilings, marble vanities, Aveda bath products, cozy window seats, and plush bedding (really, this place is smooth). Be sure to request a bay-view room overlooking the Bay Bridge—the added perks and view make it well worth the extra cost. Smokers, book a room elsewhere—there's no puffing allowed here.

155 Steuart St. (btw. Mission and Howard sts.), San Francisco, CA 94105. (✆) **800/321-2201** or 415/495-2100. Fax 415/495-3522. www.hotelgriffon.com. 62 units. $189–$295 double; $385–$445 suite. Rates include extended continental breakfast and newspaper and free Mon–Fri morning town car service within the Financial District. AE, DC, DISC, MC, V. Parking $28. All Market St. buses and streetcars, BART, and ferries. **Amenities:** Restaurant; access to large health club and pool next door (for a fee); concierge; morning car service to downtown; free Wi-Fi in lobby and restaurant; secretarial services; limited room service; in-room massage; laundry service; dry cleaning. *In room:* TV, dataport, free high-speed Internet access, minibar, coffeemaker, hair dryer, iron, safe.

Hotel Vitale ★★ Perched at the foot of the Embarcadero with outstanding waterfront and Bay Bridge views from east-facing rooms, this 199-unit hotel opened in early 2005 to instant popularity. In addition to its prime location across from the Ferry Building Marketplace (p. 160), Hotel Vitale looks pretty darned chic, from the clean-lined lobby, lounge, and decent but not destination-worthy **Americano** restaurant (with a hopping after-work bar scene), to the modern and masculine rooms awash in earth tones and armed with contemporary perks like flatscreen TVs, CD players with groovy compilations, gourmet minibars and for-sale bath products, huge bathrooms with walk-in showers, and nature-themed pop art. Despite excellent service from the well-trained staff, there are a few subtleties that separate Vitale from true luxury hotel status: For example, my fancy flatscreen TV didn't face the bed or the couch and wasn't on hinges that allowed it to be adjusted—very annoying—and the fitness room is flat-out lame with three cardio machines and a few weights. However, they're now offering complimentary access to the nearby YMCA health club, which has all the workout essentials. So, if you can live with a few quirks, it's a very attractive place to stay—my NYC friend loves this hotel—especially if you book one of the suites with 270-degree San Francisco views.

8 Mission St. (at Embarcadero), San Francisco, CA 94105. (✆) **888/890-8868** or 415/278-3700. Fax 415/278-3750. www.hotelvitale.com. 199 units. $269–$399 double; from $699 suite. Rates include morning paper, free morning yoga, and free courtesy car to downtown locations on weekdays. AE, DC, DISC, MC, V. Valet parking $42. Bus: 2, 7, 14, 21, 71, or 71L. **Amenities:** Restaurant; exercise room; spa; concierge; business center; free Internet salon; free Wi-Fi; room service; laundry service; dry cleaning. *In room:* A/C, TV w/pay movies, CD player, dataport, high-speed Internet access, Wi-Fi, minibar, hair dryer, iron, safe.

San Francisco Marriott ★★ Some call it a masterpiece; others liken it to the world's biggest parking meter. In either case, the Marriott is one of the largest buildings in the city, making it a popular stop for convention-goers and those looking for a room with a view. Fortunately, the controversy does not extend to the rooms, which are pleasant, vibrant, and contemporary with large bathrooms and exceptional city vistas. *Tip:* Upon arrival, enter from Fourth Street, between Market and Mission, to avoid a long trek to the registration area.

55 Fourth St. (btw. Market and Mission sts.), San Francisco, CA 94103. (✆) **800/228-9290** or 415/896-1600. Fax 415/486-8101. www.marriott.com/sfodt. 1,598 units. $199–$349 double; $499–$3,250 suite. AE, DC, DISC, MC, V. Parking $46. Bus: All Market St. buses. Streetcar: All Market St. streetcars. Cable car: Powell–Hyde or Powell–Mason lines (3 blocks west). **Amenities:** 2 restaurants; 2 bars; indoor pool; health club; tour desk; car rental; business center; Wi-Fi in select areas; dry cleaning. *In room:* A/C, TV w/pay movies, dataport, high-speed Internet ($13/day), hair dryer, iron.

MODERATE

The Mosser ★ *Value* "Hip on the Cheap" might best sum up the Mosser, a highly atypical budget hotel that incorporates Victorian architecture with modern interior design. It originally opened in 1913 as a luxury hotel only to be dwarfed by the far more modern sky-rise hotels that surround it. But a major multimillion-dollar renovation a few years back transformed this aging charmer into a sophisticated, stylish,

The Best Family-Friendly Hotels

Argonaut Hotel (p. 92)   Not only is it near all the funky kid fun of Fisherman's Wharf and the National Maritime Museum, but this bayside hotel, a winner for the whole family, also has kid-friendly perks like the opportunity for each child to grab a gift from the hotel's "treasure chest."

Cow Hollow Motor Inn & Suites (p. 96)   Two-bedroom suites allow kids to shack up in style instead of camping on the pull-out couch.

Hotel Diva (p. 68)   The Diva is so sleek and ultramodern that it won "Best Hotel Design" from *Interiors* magazine not long after it opened and is still as svelte as ever. Families should inquire about their two-room Little Divas Suite, designed for kids, that can accommodate a family of four.

The Fairmont San Francisco (p. 78)   While the glamorous lobby and spectacular city views will please parents, kids will be thrilled by the hotel's **Tonga Room,** a fantastically kitsch Disneyland-like tropical bar and restaurant where "rain" falls every 30 minutes.

Handlery Union Square Hotel (p. 67)   Never mind that it's been completely renovated. The real kid-friendly kickers here are the adjoining rooms in the "newer" addition; a heated, clean, outdoor pool; and the adjoining restaurant, the Daily Grill, which offers the gamut of American favorites.

Hotel Del Sol (p. 95)   It's colorful enough to represent a Crayola selection, but tots are more likely to be impressed by the "Kids are VIPs" program that includes a lending library, toys and videos, evening cookies and milk, and accouterments for the heated pool (think sunglasses, visors, beach balls). Parental perks include access to a bonded babysitting service and three baby-proofed rooms and family suite (three adjoining rooms).

Hotel Metropolis (p. 74)   The lobby walls at this playful yet serene hotel are covered with more than 80 works of colorful (and curiously abstract) art created by children. The three-room Urban Explorers Kids Suite, which sleeps up to six adults and three children, is filled with pint-sized furniture, bunk beds, a computer, a chalkboard wall, toys, and rubber ducky decor in the bathroom.

San Francisco Airport North Travelodge (p. 101)   It's nothing fancy, but if you've got an early flight out, want to stay near the airport, and don't want to rent an extra room to accommodate the little ones, this place (with pull-out couches in 20 out of the 199 rooms) is a good bet.

Stanyan Park Hotel (p. 100)   Plenty of elbowroom and a half-block walk to Golden Gate Park's Children's Playground make this a prime spot for crashing family style. But the biggest bonuses are the suites, which come with one or two bedrooms, a full kitchen, and a dining area.

Westin St. Francis (p. 65)   A classic San Francisco hotel down to its hospitality, the Westin welcomes the little ones with fun gifts and free drink refills at its restaurants.

and surprisingly affordable SoMa lodging. Guest rooms are replete with original Victorian flourishes—bay windows and hand-carved moldings—that juxtapose well with the contemporary custom-designed furnishings, granite showers, stainless steel fixtures, ceiling fans, Frette linens, double-paned windows, and modern electronics. The least expensive rooms are quite small and share a bathroom, but are an incredible deal for such a central location. The hotel's restaurant, Annabelle's Bar & Bistro, serves lunch and dinner, and the Mosser even houses Studio Paradiso, a state-of-the-art recording studio. The location is excellent as well—3 blocks from Union Square, 2 blocks from the MOMA and Moscone Convention Center, and half a block from the cable car turnaround. It also borders on a "sketchy" street, but then again, so do most hotels a few blocks west of Union Square.

54 Fourth St. (at Market St.), San Francisco, CA 94103. ✆ 800/227-3804 or 415/986-4400. Fax 415/495-7653. www.themosser.com. 166 units, 112 with bathroom. $169–$259 double with bathroom; $79–$99 double without bathroom. Rates include safe-deposit boxes at front desk. AE, DC, DISC, MC, V. Parking $30, plus $10 for oversize vehicles. Streetcar: F, and all underground Muni. BART: All trains. **Amenities:** Restaurant; bar; 24-hr. concierge; same-day laundry service/dry cleaning. *In room:* Ceiling fan, TV, AM/FM stereo w/CD player, dataport, Wi-Fi ($9.95/day), hair dryer, iron/ironing board, voice mail.

5 The Financial District

VERY EXPENSIVE

The Mandarin Oriental 🏨🏨🏨   No hotel combines better ultra-luxury digs with incredible views than this gem. The only reason to pause in the lobby or mezzanine is for the traditional tea service or cocktails. Otherwise, heaven begins after a rocketing ride on the elevators to the rooms, all of which are located between the 38th and 48th floors of a high-rise. The opulent rooms also feature contemporary Asian-influenced decor, but the best details by far are the huge windows with superb city views, particularly when the fog rolls in below you. Not all rooms have tub-side views (incredible and standard with the signature rooms), but every one does have a luxurious marble bathroom stocked with terry and cotton cloth robes, a makeup mirror, and silk slippers. An added bonus: The restaurant, **Silks,** has a kitchen crew working wonders with the Asian-influenced menu. If the dining room weren't so awkwardly empty, it'd be a recommended destination. That said, even without the whole package, it's an excellent place to dine.

222 Sansome St. (btw. Pine and California sts.), San Francisco, CA 94104. ✆ 800/622-0404 or 415/276-9888. Fax 415/433-0289. www.mandarinoriental.com. 158 units. $375–$725 double; $645–$695 signature rooms; from $1,450 suite. Continental breakfast $21; American breakfast $32. AE, DC, DISC, MC, V. Valet parking $36. Bus: All Market St. buses. Streetcar: J, K, L, or M to Montgomery. **Amenities:** Restaurant; bar; fitness center; concierge; car rental; business center; Wi-Fi; room service; in-room massage; laundry service; same-day dry cleaning. *In room:* A/C, TV w/pay movies, CD player, fax on request, dataport, Wi-Fi ($13/day), minibar, hair dryer, iron, safe.

EXPENSIVE

Hilton San Francisco Financial District 🏨   Finally there's a good reason to stay in Chinatown. Reopened in 2006 after a $40-million renovation, this upscale hotel geared toward the needs of the business traveler is a good choice for anyone seeking a convenient downtown location perfect for forays into Chinatown, North Beach, and beyond. All of the comfortably modern rooms feature either city or bay views, so you really can't go wrong. The panoramic bay views of Coit Tower, Telegraph Hill, and Alcatraz are wholly unobstructed as you look straight down the Columbus Avenue thoroughfare to Ghirardelli Square. The in-room contemporary decor includes dark muted earth-tone carpets; warm honey-colored wood; and lush, pristine palette beds

(Finds) Sleeping Seaside

You would think that a city surrounded on three sides by water would have a slew of seaside hotels. Oddly enough, it has very few, one of which is the **Seal Rock Inn**. It's about as far from Union Square and Fisherman's Wharf as you can place a hotel in San Francisco, but that just makes it all the more unique. The motel fronts Sutro Heights Park, which faces Ocean Beach. Most rooms in the four-story structure have at least partial views of the ocean; at night, the sounds of the surf and distant foghorns lull guests to sleep. The rooms, although large and spotless, are old and basic, with rose and teal floral accents. Only some rooms have kitchenettes, but phones, TVs, fridges, covered parking, and use of the enclosed patio and pool area are standard. On the ground floor of the inn is a small old-fashioned restaurant serving breakfast and lunch. Golden Gate Park and the Presidio are both nearby, and the Geary bus—which snails its way to Union Square and Market Street—stops right out front and takes at least a half-hour to get downtown.

The Seal Rock Inn (© **888/732-5762** or 415/752-8000; fax 415/752-6034; www.sealrockinn.com) is at 545 Point Lobos Ave. (at 48th Ave.), San Francisco, CA 94121. Double rooms range from $105 to $143.

with crisp white linens and featherbeds swathed in masculine dusty blue, tan, and slate-gray pillows and accents. All units boast modern goodies such as MP3-compatible alarm clocks and flatscreen TVs. All signature-floor accommodations have balconies. The seven suites have bamboo floors, fireplaces, balconies, and large luxurious bathrooms, some with nice touches like sleek yours-and-mine sinks. For concierge-floor guests, a complimentary breakfast is served in a private lounge. A coffee bar in the lobby is perfect for getting your morning fix on the fly, and the renowned day spa, trū, offers world-class treatments, a variety of them in their one-of-a-kind rainforest room with walk-through waterfall. The restaurant, Seven Fifty, blends Mediterranean and Californian cuisine, while the high-backed *Star Trek*–esque chairs in the lounge make you feel like you are commander of the fleet.

750 Kearny St., at Washington St., San Francisco, CA 94108. © **800/HILTONS** or 415/433-6660. Fax 415/765-7891. www.sanfranciscofinancialdistrict.hilton.com. 549 units. $199–$429 double; $989–$1,200 suite. AE, DC, DISC, MC, V. Valet parking $42. Bus: 1, 9AX, 9BX, or 15. Cable car: California. **Amenities:** Restaurant; bar; coffee bar; fitness room; spa; concierge; free car service to downtown; 24-hr. business center; secretarial services; room service; laundry service; same-day dry cleaning; foreign currency exchange; notary public. *In room:* A/C, TV w/pay movies, dataport, Wi-Fi ($9.95), minibar, hair dryer, iron, safe.

Hyatt Regency San Francisco ⨉   The Hyatt Regency, a convention favorite, rises from the edge of The Embarcadero Center at the foot of Market Street. The gray concrete structure, with a 1970s, bunkerlike facade, is shaped like a vertical triangle, serrated with long rows of jutting balconies. The 17-story atrium lobby, illuminated by museum-quality theater lighting, has a waterway flowing through it.

Rooms are furnished in "contemporary decor" à la corporate hotel fashion. Bonuses include ergonomic workstation chairs; textiles in shades of gold, charcoal gray, and celadon; and coffeemakers. Definitely not a standout choice for shacking up.

The Eclipse Café serves breakfast and lunch daily; during evenings it becomes A Cut Above steakhouse. The 13-Views Lounge serves cocktails and bar food for dinner. **The Equinox,** a revolving rooftop restaurant and bar that's open for cocktails and dinner, has 360-degree city views.

5 Embarcadero Center, San Francisco, CA 94111. © **888/591-1234** or 415/788-1234. Fax 415/398-2567. www.san franciscoregency.hyatt.com. 802 units. $189–$349 double; extra $50 for executive suite. Continental breakfast $18. AE, DC, DISC, MC, V. Valet parking $41. Bus: All Market St. buses. Streetcar: All Market St. streetcars. **Amenities:** Restaurant; cafe; bar; fitness center; concierge; car rental; business center; dry cleaning. *In room:* A/C, TV w/pay movies, dataport, Wi-Fi ($9.95/day), minibar, hair dryer, safe.

6 North Beach/Fisherman's Wharf

EXPENSIVE

Argonaut Hotel ★★ *Kids*   The Kimpton Hotel Group is behind Fisherman's Wharf's best hotel, a true boutique gem that's ideally located at San Francisco Maritime National Historical Park (p. 170) near Fisherman's Wharf and half a block from the bay. The four-story timber and brick landmark building was originally built in 1908 as a warehouse for the California Fruit Canners Association, and later used by William Randolph Hearst to store items that eventually ended up inside his Hearst Castle in San Simeon. Its 239 rooms and 13 suites are whimsically decorated to emulate a luxury cruise ship in cheerful nautical colors of blue, white, red, and yellow (though evidence of its modest past appears in original brick walls, large timbers, and steel warehouse doors). Along with all the standard hotel amenities are special touches such as flatscreen TVs, DVD/CD players, Aveda toiletries, and—get this—leopard-spotted bathrobes. All guests are welcome at weekday evening wine receptions and can use the lobby's two popular (and free) Internet terminals. Suites have wonderful views and come fully loaded with telescopes and spa tubs. If possible, try to book a "view" room, which overlooks the wharf or bay (some rooms offer fabulous views of Alcatraz and the Golden Gate Bridge). If you're bringing the kids, know that the Argonaut's friendly staff goes out of their way to make little ones feel at home and allows each pint-size guest to pick a new plaything from the hotel's "treasure chest." With so many offerings it's no surprise the hotel was awarded a Four Diamond rating from AAA. *Tip:* The concierge seems to be able to work wonders when you need tickets to Alcatraz—even when the trips are officially sold out.

495 Jefferson St (at Hyde St.), San Francisco, CA 94109. © **866/415-0704** or 415/563-0800. Fax 415/563-2800. www.argonauthotel.com. 252 units. $189–$389 double; $489–$1,089 suite. Rates include evening wine in the lobby, daily newspaper, and kid-friendly perks like cribs and strollers. AE, DC, DISC, MC, V. Parking $39. Bus: 10, 30, or 47. Streetcar: F. Cable car: Powell–Hyde line. **Amenities:** Restaurant; bar; fitness center; concierge; Wi-Fi in public areas; laundry service; dry cleaning; yoga video and mats. *In room:* A/C, flatscreen TV w/Nintendo and pay movies, Web TV, DVD and CD players, free high-speed Internet access, minibar, coffeemaker, hair dryer, iron, safe.

Sheraton Fisherman's Wharf Hotel   Built in the mid-1970s, this contemporary, four-story hotel offers the reliable comforts of a Sheraton in San Francisco's most popular tourist area. In other words, the clean, modern rooms are comfortable and well equipped but nothing unique to the city. On the bright side, they have a heated outdoor pool (a rarity in San Francisco). A corporate floor caters exclusively to business travelers.

2500 Mason St. (btw. Beach and North Point sts.), San Francisco, CA 94133. © **800/325-3535** or 415/362-5500. Fax 415/956-5275. www.sheratonatthewharf.com. 529 units. $199–$299 double; $550–$1,000 suite. Extra person $20. Continental breakfast $13. AE, DC, DISC, MC, V. Valet parking $36. Bus: 10 or 49. Streetcar: F. Cable car:

Powell–Mason line (1 block east, 2 blocks south). **Amenities:** Restaurant; bar; outdoor heated pool; exercise room; concierge; car-rental desk; business center; limited room service; laundry service; dry cleaning. *In room:* A/C, TV, fax (in suites only), dataport, high-speed Internet ($9.95/day), coffeemaker, hair dryer.

MODERATE

Best Western Tuscan Inn at Fisherman's Wharf 🟊🟊

Like an island of respectability in a sea of touristy schlock, this boutique Best Western is one of the best midrange hotels at Fisherman's Wharf. It continues to exude a level of style and comfort far beyond that of its neighboring competitors. For example, every evening in the plush lobby warmed by a grand fireplace, a wine reception is hosted by the manager, and the adjoining **Café Pescatore** serves wonderful pizzas and grilled meats from their wood-burning oven. The rooms are a definite cut above competing Fisherman's Wharf hotels: All are handsomely decorated and have writing desks and armchairs. The only caveat is the lack of scenic views—a small price to pay for a good hotel in a great location.

425 North Point St. (at Mason St.), San Francisco, CA 94133. ℂ **800/648-4626** or 415/561-1100. Fax 415/561-1199. www.tuscaninn.com. 221 units. $129–$369. Rates include coffee, tea, and evening wine reception. AE, DC, DISC, MC, V. Parking $36. Bus: 10, 15, or 47. Cable car: Powell–Mason line. Pets welcome for $50 fee. **Amenities:** Access to nearby gym; concierge; courtesy car; secretarial services; limited room service; same-day laundry service/dry cleaning. *In room:* A/C, TV w/video games and pay movies, dataport, free Wi-Fi, minibar, coffeemaker, hair dryer, iron.

The Hotel Bohème 🟊🟊 *Finds*

Romance awaits at the intimate Hotel Bohème. Although it's located on the busiest avenue in the neighborhood, once you climb the staircase to this narrow second-floor boutique hotel, you'll discover a style and demeanor reminiscent of a home in upscale Nob Hill. Alas, there are no common areas other than a little booth for check-in and concierge, but rooms, though small, are truly sweet, with gauze-draped canopies, stylish decor such as ornate parasols shading ceiling lights, and walls dramatically colored with lavender, sage green, black, and pumpkin. The staff is ultra-hospitable, and bonuses include sherry in the lobby each afternoon. Some fabulous cafes, restaurants, bars, and shops along Columbus Avenue are just a few steps away, and Chinatown and Union Square are within easy walking distance. *Note:* Although the bathrooms are spiffy, they're also tiny and have showers only. Also, request a room off the street side, which is quieter.

444 Columbus Ave. (btw. Vallejo and Green sts.), San Francisco, CA 94133. ℂ **415/433-9111.** Fax 415/362-6292. www. hotelboheme.com. 15 units. $164–$184 double. Rates include afternoon sherry. AE, DC, DISC, MC, V. Parking $12–$31 at nearby public garages. Bus: 12, 15, 30, 41, 45, or 83. Cable car: Powell–Mason line. **Amenities:** Concierge. *In room:* TV, dataport, free Wi-Fi, hair dryer, iron.

The Washington Square Inn 🟊

This small, comely, European-style bed-and-breakfast is ideal for older couples who prefer a quieter, more subdued environment than the commotion of downtown San Francisco. It's across from Washington Square in North Beach—a coffee-craver's haven—and within walking distance of Fisherman's Wharf and Chinatown. All rooms feature European antiques, ceiling fans, flatscreen TVs, and private bathrooms, while some have fireplaces or sitting areas in bay windows. A light breakfast is served in your room or the lobby, and in the evening hors d'oeuvres are served with wine.

1660 Stockton St. (btw. Filbert and Union sts.), San Francisco, CA 94133. ℂ **800/388-0220** or 415/981-4220. Fax 415/397-7242. www.wsisf.com. 15 units. $149–$289 double. Rates include continental breakfast and afternoon tea, wine, and hors d'oeuvres. AE, DISC, MC, V. Valet parking $35; self parking $15. Bus: 15, 30, 41, or 45. **Amenities:** Limited room service. *In room:* Flatscreen TV, CD player, dataport, free Wi-Fi, hair dryer, iron on request.

INEXPENSIVE

The San Remo Hotel *Value*   This small, European-style *pensione* is one of the best budget hotels in San Francisco. In a quiet North Beach neighborhood, within walking distance of Fisherman's Wharf, the Italianate Victorian structure originally served as a boardinghouse for dockworkers displaced by the great fire of 1906. As a result, the rooms are small and bathrooms are shared, but all is forgiven when it comes time to pay the bill. Rooms are decorated in cozy country style, with brass and iron beds; oak, maple, or pine armoires; and wicker furnishings. The immaculate shared bathrooms feature tubs and brass pull-chain toilets with oak tanks and brass fixtures. If the penthouse—which has its own bathroom, TV, fridge, and patio—is available, book it: You won't find a more romantic place to stay in San Francisco for so little money.

2237 Mason St. (at Chestnut St.), San Francisco, CA 94133. © 800/352-7366 or 415/776-8688. Fax 415/776-2811. www.sanremohotel.com. 62 units, 61 with shared bathroom. $65–$90 double; $175–$185 penthouse suite. AE, DC, MC, V. Self-parking $13–$14. Bus: 10, 15, 30, or 47. Streetcar: F. Cable car: Powell–Mason line. **Amenities:** Access to nearby health club; 2 massage chairs; Internet kiosk in lobby; self-service laundry; TV room. *In room:* Ceiling fan.

The Wharf Inn *Value*   My top choice for good-value/great-location lodging at Fisherman's Wharf, the Wharf Inn offers above-average accommodations at one of the most popular tourist attractions in the world. The well-stocked rooms are done in handsome tones of earth, muted greens, and burnt orange, but more importantly, they are situated smack-dab in the middle of the wharf, a mere two blocks from Pier 39 and the cable car turnaround, and within walking distance of the Embarcadero and North Beach. The inn is ideal for car-bound families because parking is free (that saves at least $25 a day right off the bat).

2601 Mason St. (at Beach St.), San Francisco, CA 94133. © 877/275-7889 or 415/673-7411. Fax 415/776-2181. www.wharfinn.com. 51 units. $99–$209 double; $299–$439 penthouse. AE, DC, DISC, MC, V. Free parking. Bus: 10, 15, 39, or 47. Streetcar: F. Cable car: Powell–Mason or Powell–Hyde lines. **Amenities:** Access to nearby health club ($10/day); concierge; tour desk; free coffee/tea and newspapers. *In room:* TV, dataport, free Wi-Fi, hair dryer on request, iron on request.

7 The Marina/Pacific Heights/Cow Hollow

EXPENSIVE

Hotel Drisco *Finds*   Located on one of the most sought-after blocks of residential property in all of San Francisco, the Drisco, built in 1903, is one of the city's best small hotels. Refinements by interior designer Glenn Texeira (who also did the Ritz-Carlton in Manila) are evident from the very small lobby and sitting areas to the calming atmosphere of the cream, yellow, and green guest rooms. As in the neighboring mansions, traditional antique furnishings and thick, luxurious fabrics abound here. The hotel's comfy beds will make you want to loll late into the morning before primping in the large marble bathrooms, complete with robes and slippers. Each suite has a couch that unfolds into a bed (although you would never guess from the looks of it), an additional phone and TV, and superior views. A 24-hour coffee and tea service is available on the ground floor, in the same comfy rooms where breakfast is served. If you're arriving by car, however, you may not want to stay here as there is no hotel parking.

2901 Pacific Ave. (at Broderick St.), San Francisco, CA 94115. © 800/634-7277 or 415/346-2880. Fax 415/567-5537. www.hoteldrisco.com. 48 units. $249 double; $369–$399 suite. Rates include buffet breakfast and evening wine hour. AE, DC, DISC, MC, V. No parking available. Bus: 3 or 24. **Amenities:** Exercise room and free pass to YMCA; concierge; business center; limited room service; same-day laundry service/dry cleaning. *In room:* TV/VCR, CD player, dataport, free high-speed Internet access, minibar, fridge, hair dryer, iron, safe.

MODERATE

Hotel Del Sol ★★ *Kids* *Value*   The cheeriest motel in town is located just 2 blocks off the Marina District's bustling section of Lombard. Three-level Hotel del Sol is all about festive flair and luxury touches. The sunshine theme extends from the Miami Beach–style use of vibrant color, as in the yellow, red, orange, and blue exterior, to the heated courtyard pool, which beckons the youngish clientele as they head for their cars parked (for free!) in cabana-like spaces. This is also one of the most family-friendly places to stay, with a "Kids are VIPs" program, including a family suite (three adjoining rooms with bunks and toys); a lending library of kids' books, toys, and videos; childproofing kits; three rooms that have been professionally baby-proofed; bonded babysitting services; evening cookies and milk; and pool toys; and sunglasses and visors for the young ones. Fair-weather fun doesn't stop at the front door of the hotel, which boasts 57 spacious rooms (updated with all new bedding, paint, carpets, drapes, and sofas in 2006) with equally perky interior decor (read: loud and colorful) as well as unexpected extras like CD players, Aveda products, and tips on the town's happenings and shopping meccas. Suites also include minifridges and DVD players.

3100 Webster St. (at Greenwich St.), San Francisco, CA 94123. ℂ 877/433-5765 or 415/921-5520. Fax 415/931-4137. www.thehoteldelsol.com. 57 units. $139–$199 double; $179–$239 suite. Rates include continental breakfast and free newspapers in the lobby. AE, DC, DISC, MC, V. Free parking. Bus: 22, 28, 41, 43, 45, or 76. **Amenities:** Heated outdoor pool; same-day dry cleaning. *In room:* TV/VCR, CD player, dataport, Wi-Fi ($7.95/day), kitchenettes in 3 units, fridge and DVD in suites only, iron.

Jackson Court ★★   The Jackson Court, a stately three-story brownstone Victorian mansion, is in one of San Francisco's most exclusive neighborhoods, Pacific Heights. Its only fault—that it's far from the action—is also its blessing: If you crave a blissfully quiet vacation in elegant surroundings, this is the place. The rooms are individually furnished with superior-quality antique furnishings; two have wood-burning fireplaces (whose use is de rigueur in the winter) and two have gas fireplaces. The Blue Room features an inviting window seat; the Garden Court Suite has handcrafted wood paneling, a king bed, and a large picture window looking onto the private garden patio. After a continental breakfast of muffins, scones, croissants, oatmeal, juice, and fruit, spend the day browsing the shops along nearby Union and Fillmore streets and return in time for afternoon tea.

2198 Jackson St. (at Buchanan St.), San Francisco, CA 94115. ℂ 415/929-7670. Fax 415/929-1405. www.jacksoncourt.com. 10 units. $160–$225 double. Rates include continental breakfast and afternoon tea. AE, MC, V. Parking on street only. Bus: 1, 3, 12, or 22. **Amenities:** Concierge; guests allowed to use high-speed Internet in office; dry cleaning. *In room:* TV, dataport, hair dryer, iron available on request.

Laurel Inn ★★ *Value*   If you don't mind being out of the downtown area, this hip hotel is one of the most tranquil and affordably high-style places to rest your head. Tucked just beyond the southernmost tip of the Presidio and Pacific Heights, the outside is nothing impressive—just another motor inn. And that's what it was until the Joie de Vivre hotel company breathed new life into the place. Now decor is *très* chic and modern, with Zen-like influences (think W Hotel at half the price). The rooms, some of which have excellent city views, are smartly designed and decorated in the style of a contemporary studio apartment. The continental breakfast is fine, but why bother when you're across the street from **Ella's** (p. 137), which serves San Francisco's best breakfast? Other thoughtful touches: 24-hour coffee and tea service, pet-friendly rooms, a CD and video lending library, and indoor parking. There's also great shopping a block away at

Sacramento Street; and the new and hip **G Bar,** which serves libations and a surprisingly active slice of glamorous young Pacific Heights–style revelry.

444 Presidio Ave. (at California Ave.), San Francisco, CA 94115. ☎ 800/552-8735 or 415/567-8467. Fax 415/928-1866. www.thelaurelinn.com. 49 units. $169–$209 double. Rates include continental breakfast and afternoon lemonade and cookies. AE, DC, DISC, MC, V. Free parking. Bus: 1, 3, 4, or 43. Pets accepted. **Amenities:** Adjoining bar; access to the mind-blowing JCC gym across the street at $10 per day; concierge; same-day laundry/dry cleaning. *In room:* TV/VCR, CD player, dataport, Internet access and Wi-Fi ($8/day), kitchenette in some units, hair dryer, iron.

Union Street Inn 🏵🏵 Who would have guessed that one of the most delightful B&Bs in California would be in San Francisco? This two-story 1903 Edwardian fronts perpetually busy (and trendy shopping and bar-hopping stop) Union Street, but is as quiet as a church on the inside. The individually decorated rooms are furnished with down comforters, fresh flowers, fruit baskets, and bay windows (beg for one with a view of the garden). A few even have Jacuzzi tubs for two. An extended full breakfast is served in the parlor, in your room, or on an outdoor terrace overlooking a lovely English garden. The ultimate honeymoon retreat is the private carriage house behind the inn, but any room at this warm, friendly inn is guaranteed to please.

2229 Union St. (btw. Fillmore and Steiner sts.), San Francisco, CA 94123. ☎ 415/346-0424. Fax 415/922-8046. www.unionstreetinn.com. 5 units, 1 cottage. $179–$289 double. Rates include breakfast, hors d'oeuvres, and evening beverages. AE, DISC, MC, V. Nearby parking $15. Bus: 22, 28, 41, or 45. *In room:* TV, CD/DVD player, free Wi-Fi.

INEXPENSIVE

Cow Hollow Motor Inn & Suites 🄺🄸🄳🄴 If you're less interested in being downtown than in playing in and around the beautiful bayfront Marina, check out this modest brick hotel on busy Lombard Street. There's no fancy theme, but each room has cable TV, free local phone calls, free covered parking, and a coffeemaker. Families will appreciate the one- and two-bedroom suites, which have full kitchens and dining areas as well as antique furnishings and surprisingly tasteful decor.

2190 Lombard St. (btw. Steiner and Fillmore sts.), San Francisco, CA 94123. ☎ 415/921-5800. Fax 415/922-8515. www.cowhollowmotorinn.com. 129 units. $72–$125 double. Extra person $10. AE, DC, MC, V. Free parking. Bus: 28, 30, 43, or 76. **Amenities:** Laundry and dry cleaning within a block. *In room:* A/C, TV, dataport, free high-speed DSL and Wi-Fi, full kitchens in suites only, coffeemaker, hair dryer.

Edward II Inn & Suites 🏵 This three-story "English country" inn has a room for almost anyone's budget, ranging from *pensione* units with shared bathrooms to luxuriously appointed suites and cottages with whirlpool bathtubs and fireplaces. Originally built to house guests who attended the 1915 Pan-Pacific Exposition, it's still a good place to stay in spotless and comfortably appointed rooms with cozy antique furnishings. They've recently added a small fitness center and the Café Maritime, a seafood restaurant open for dinner. Room prices even include a full continental breakfast. Nearby Chestnut and Union streets offer some of the best shopping and dining in the city. The adjoining pub serves drinks nightly. The only caveat is that the hotel's Lombard Street location is usually congested with traffic.

3155 Scott St. (at Lombard St.), San Francisco, CA 94123. ☎ 800/473-2846 or 415/922-3000. Fax 415/931-5784. www.edwardii.com. 29 units, 21 with bathroom. $69–$99 double with shared bathroom; $115–$139 double with private bathroom; $179–$199 junior suite. Extra person $25. Rates include continental breakfast and evening sherry. AE, DISC, MC, V. Self-parking $12 1 block away. Bus: 28, 30, 43, or 76. **Amenities:** Pub; fitness center ($10/day); computer station (for nominal fee). *In room:* TV, free high-speed Internet access and Wi-Fi, hair dryer and iron available on request.

Hostelling International San Francisco—Fisherman's Wharf *(Finds*   Unbeliev-able but true—you can get front-row bay views for a mere $23 a night. This hostel, on national park property, provides dorm-style accommodations and offers easy access to the Marina's shops and restaurants. Rooms sleep 2 to 12 people and there are 10 private rooms available; communal space includes a fireplace, kitchen, dining room, coffee bar, pool table, and foosball. The breakfast alone practically makes it worth the price. Make reservations well in advance.

Fort Mason, Building 240, San Francisco, CA 94123. © **415/771-7277.** Fax 415/771-1468. www.sfhostels.com. 150 beds. $23–$29 per person per night; kids $15–$17 per night. Rates include breakfast. MC, V. Free limited parking. Bus: 28, 30, 47, or 49. **Amenities:** Self-service laundry and kitchen; meeting room; free Wi-Fi; computer kiosks for small fee; baggage storage; secure lockers.

Marina Inn *(Value*   Marina Inn is one of the best low-priced hotels in San Fran-cisco. How it offers so much for so little is mystifying. Each guest room in the 1924 four-story Victorian looks like something from a country furnishings catalog, com-plete with rustic pinewood furniture, a four-poster bed with silky-soft comforter, pretty wallpaper, and soothing tones of rose, hunter green, and pale yellow. You also get remote-control televisions discreetly hidden in pine cabinetry—all for as little as $75 a night. Combine that with continental breakfast, friendly service, a business cen-ter in the lobby with an Internet kiosk, free Wi-Fi, and an armada of shops and restau-rants within easy walking distance, and there you have it: one of my top choices for best overall value. *Note:* Traffic can be a bit noisy here, so the hotel added double panes on windows facing the street. Still, if you're a light sleeper you might want to stay at the Union Street Inn (see above).

3110 Octavia St. (at Lombard St.), San Francisco, CA 94123. © **800/274-1420** or 415/928-1000. Fax 415/928-5909. www.marinainn.com. 40 units. Nov–Feb $75–$115 double; Mar–May $85–$135 double; June–Oct $95–$145 double. Rates include continental breakfast. AE, DC, DISC, MC, V. Bus: 28, 30, 43, or 76. *In room:* TV, free Wi-Fi, hair dryer and iron on request.

Marina Motel   Established in 1939, the Marina Motel is one of San Francisco's first motels, built for the opening of the Golden Gate Bridge. The same family has owned this peach-colored, Spanish-style stucco building for three generations, and they've taken exquisite care of it. All rooms look out onto an inner courtyard, which is awash with beautiful flowering plants and wall paintings by local artists. Though the rooms show minor signs of wear and tear, they're all quite clean, bright, quiet, and pleasantly decorated with framed lithographs of old San Francisco—a thoughtful touch that adds to the motel's old-fashioned character and which makes these budget accommo-dations stand out from all the rest along busy Lombard Street. Two-bedroom suites with fully equipped kitchens are also available. Location-wise, the Presidio and Marina Green are mere blocks away, and you can easily catch a bus downtown. The only downside is the street noise, which is likely to burden light sleepers. **Bonus:** All rooms include a breakfast coupon valid for two entrees for the price of one at **Judy's Restau-rant,** a short walk from the motel.

2576 Lombard St. (btw. Divisadero and Broderick sts.), San Francisco, CA 94123. © **800/346-6118** or 415/921-9406. Fax 415/921-0364. www.marinamotel.com. 38 units. $89–$159 double; $199 suite. Lower rates in winter. Rates include 2-for-1 breakfast coupon at nearby cafe. AE, DISC, MC, V. Free covered parking. Bus: 28, 29, 30, 43, or 45. Dogs accepted with $10 nightly fee. *In room:* Dataport, fridge, coffeemaker, hair dryer, iron.

8 Japantown & Environs

The Queen Anne Hotel ☆☆ ⒱alue   This majestic 1890 Victorian charmer was once a grooming school for upper-class young women. Restored in 1980 and renovated in early 2006, the four-story building recalls San Francisco's golden days. Walk under rich red draperies to the lavish "grand salon" lobby replete with English oak wainscoting and period antiques and it's not hard to imagine that you've been transported to a different era. Guest rooms also contain a profusion of antiques—armoires, marble-top dressers, and other Victorian-era pieces. Some have corner turret bay windows that look out on tree-lined streets, as well as separate parlor areas and wet bars; others have cozy reading nooks and fireplaces. All rooms have phones and nice bath amenities in their marble-tiled bathrooms. Guests can relax in the parlor, with two fireplaces, or in the hotel library. If you don't mind staying outside the downtown area, this hotel is highly recommended and very classic San Francisco.

1590 Sutter St. (btw. Gough and Octavia sts.), San Francisco, CA 94109. ☎ **800/227-3970** or 415/441-2828. Fax 415/775-5212. www.queenanne.com. 48 units. $110–$199 double; $169–$350 suite. Extra person $10. Rates include continental breakfast on weekday mornings, local free limousine service (weekday mornings), afternoon tea and sherry, and morning newspaper. AE, DC, DISC, MC, V. Parking $14. Bus: 2, 3, or 4. **Amenities:** Access to nearby health club for $10; 24-hr. concierge; business center; same-day dry cleaning; front desk safe. *In room:* TV, dataport, free Internet access in some rooms and Wi-Fi throughout, hair dryer, iron.

9 Civic Center

MODERATE

The Phoenix Hotel ☆☆   If you'd like to tell your friends back home that you stayed in the same hotel as Linda Ronstadt, David Bowie, Keanu Reeves, Moby, Franz Ferdinand, and Interpol, this is the place to go. On the fringes of San Francisco's less-than-pleasant Tenderloin District, which is rife with the homeless and crack addicts, this well-sheltered retro 1950s-style hotel is a gathering place for visiting rock musicians, writers, and filmmakers who crave a dose of Southern California—hence the palm trees and pastel colors. The focal point of the Palm Springs–style hotel is a small, heated outdoor pool adorned with a mural by artist Francis Forlenza and ensconced in a modern-sculpture garden.

The rooms are more pop than plush, with bright island-inspired furnishings and original local art; every room faces the pool. In addition to the usual amenities, the hotel offers movies on request and a party vibe that's not part of the package at most city hotels. Some big bonuses: free parking and the hotel's restaurant and club, the groovy and very hip **Bambuddha Lounge** (☎ **415/885-5088**), which serves Southeast Asian cuisine with cocktail-lounge flair. If you want luxury and quiet, stay elsewhere, but if you're looking for a great scene and fun vibe, head to the Phoenix.

601 Eddy St. (at Larkin St.), San Francisco, CA 94109. ☎ **800/248-9466** or 415/776-1380. Fax 415/885-3109. www.thephoenixhotel.com. 44 units. $149–$169 double; $219–$399 suite. Rates include continental breakfast. AE, DC, MC, V. Free parking. Bus: 19, 31, 38, or 47. **Amenities:** Bar; heated outdoor pool; concierge; tour desk; in-room massage; same-day laundry service/dry cleaning. *In room:* TV, VCR on request, dataport, high-speed Internet and Wi-Fi ($7.95/day), fridge and microwave in some rooms, hair dryer, iron.

10 The Castro

Though most accommodations (usually converted homes) in the Castro cater to a gay and lesbian clientele, everyone is welcome. Unfortunately, there are few choices, and their amenities don't really compare to those at most of the better (and much larger) hotels throughout San Francisco.

MODERATE

The Parker Guest House ⚄⚄   This is the best B&B option in the Castro, and one of the best in the entire city. In fact, even some of the better hotels could learn a thing or two from this fashionable, gay-friendly, 5,000-square-foot, 1909 beautifully restored Edwardian home and adjacent annex a few blocks from the heart of the Castro's action. Within the bright, cheery urban compound, period antiques abound. But thankfully, the spacious guest rooms are wonderfully updated with smart patterned furnishings, voice mail, robes, and spotless private bathrooms (plus amenities) en suite or, in two cases, across the hall. A fire burns nightly in the cozy living room, and guests are also welcome to make themselves at home in the wood-paneled common library (with fireplace and piano), sunny breakfast room overlooking the garden, and spacious garden with fountains and a steam room. Animal lovers will appreciate the companionship of the house pugs Porter and Pasty.

520 Church St. (btw. 17th and 18th sts.), San Francisco, CA 94114. © **888/520-7275** or 415/621-3222. Fax 415/621-4139. www.parkerguesthouse.com. 21 units. $129–$199 double; $219 junior suite. Rates include extended continental breakfast and evening wine and cheese. AE, DISC, MC, V. Self-parking $17. Bus: 22 or 33. Streetcar: J Church. **Amenities:** Access to nearby health club; steam room; concierge. *In room:* TV, dataport, free Wi-Fi, hair dryer, iron.

INEXPENSIVE

Beck's Motor Lodge   In a town where DINK (double income, no kids) tourists happily spend fistfuls of money, you'd think someone would create a gay luxury hotel—or even a moderate hotel, for that matter. But absurdly, the most commercial and modern accommodations in the touristy Castro is this run-of-the-mill motel. Standard but contemporary, the ultra-tidy rooms include low-Levitz furnishings, a sun deck overlooking upper Market Street's action, and free parking. Unless you're into homey B&Bs, this is really your only choice in the area—fortunately, it's very well maintained. But be warned that this is a party spot; party people stay here, and the staff can be brusque.

2222 Market St. (at 15th St.), San Francisco, CA 94114. © **800/227-4360** in the U.S., except CA, 800/955-2325 within CA or 415/621-8212. Fax 415/241-0435. www.becksmotorlodgesf.com. 58 units. $93–$151 double. AE, DC, DISC, MC, V. Free parking. Bus: 8 or 37. Streetcar: F. **Amenities:** Coin-operated washing machines. *In room:* TV, dataport, free Wi-Fi, fridge, coffeemaker.

Inn on Castro ⚄   One of the better choices in the Castro, half a block from all the action, is this Edwardian-style inn decorated with contemporary furnishings, original modern art, and fresh flowers throughout. It definitely feels more like a home than an inn, so if you like less commercial abodes, this place is for you. Most rooms share a small back patio, and the suite has a private entrance and outdoor sitting area. The inn also offers access to six individual nearby apartments ($125–$190) with complete kitchens. Note that rates include a full breakfast, and that the least expensive rooms share a bathroom.

321 Castro St. (at Market St.), San Francisco, CA 94114. © **415/861-0321.** Fax 415/861-0321. www.inn oncastro.com. 8 units, 2 with bathroom across the hall; 6 apts. $105–$165 double. Rates include full breakfast and evening brandy. AE, DC, MC, V. Streetcar: F, K, L, or M. **Amenities:** Hall fridges stocked w/free sodas and water. *In room:* Flatscreen TV, DVD/CD, dataport, free Wi-Fi, hair dryer.

The Willows Inn ✿   Right in the heart of the Castro, the all-nonsmoking Willows Inn employs a staff eager to greet and attend to visitors. The country and antique willow furnishings don't strictly suit a 1903 Edwardian home, but everything's quite comfortable—especially considering the extras, which include an expanded continental breakfast (fresh fruit, yogurt, baked goods, gourmet coffee, eggs, assorted teas, and orange juice), the morning paper, nightly cocktails, a sitting room (with a DVD player), and a pantry with limited kitchen facilities. The homey rooms vary in size from large (queen-size bed) to smaller (double bed) and are priced accordingly. Each room has a vanity sink, and all the rooms share eight water closets and shower rooms.

710 14th St. (near Church and Market sts.), San Francisco, CA 94114. ✆ 800/431-0277 or 415/431-4770. Fax 415/431-5295. www.willowssf.com. 12 units, none with bathroom. $105–$135 double; $145 suite. Rates include continental breakfast. AE, DC, DISC, MC, V. Bus: 22 or 37. Streetcar: Church St. station (across the street) or F. *In room:* TV/VCR, free Wi-Fi, fridge.

11 Haight-Ashbury

MODERATE

Red Victorian Bed, Breakfast & Art ✿ *(Finds)*   Still having flashbacks from the 1960s? Or want to? No problem. A room at the Red Vic, in the heart of the Haight, will throw you right back into the Summer of Love (minus, of course, the free-flowing LSD). Owner Sami Sunchild has re-created this historic hotel and "Peace Center" as a living museum honoring the bygone era. The rooms are inspired by San Francisco's sights and history, and are decorated accordingly. The Flower Child Room has a sun on the ceiling and a rainbow on the wall, while the bed sports a hand-crocheted shawl headboard. The Peacock Suite, though pricey, is one funky room, with red beads, a canopy bed, and multicolored patterns throughout. The clincher is its bedroom bathtub, which has a circular pass-through looking into the sitting area. Four guest rooms have private bathrooms; the rest share four bathrooms down the hall. In general, the rooms and bathrooms are clean and the furnishings lighthearted. Rates for longer stays are a great deal. A family-style continental breakfast is a gathering place for a worldly array of guests, and there's a gift shop called the Meditation Room and Peace Center. Be sure to check out Sami's website to get a sneak peek at the weird and wonderful guest rooms.

1665 Haight St. (btw. Cole and Belvedere sts.), San Francisco, CA 94117. ✆ 415/864-1978. Fax 415/863-3293. www.redvic.com. 18 units, 4 with private bathroom. $89–$110 double with shared bathroom; $129–$149 double with private bathroom; $229 suite. Rates include continental breakfast and afternoon tea. Lower rates for stays of 3 days or more. AE, DISC, MC, V. Guarded parking lot nearby. Metro: N line. Bus: 7, 66, 71, or 73.

Stanyan Park Hotel ✿✿ *(Kids) (Value)*   The only real hotel on the east end of Golden Gate Park and the west end of funky-chic Haight Street, this small inn offers classic San Francisco–style living at a very affordable price. The Victorian structure, which has operated as a hotel under a variety of names since the turn of the 20th century and is on the National Register of Historic Places, offers good-size rooms all done in period decor. Its three stories are decorated with antique furnishings; Victorian wallpaper; and pastel quilts, curtains, and carpets. Families will appreciate the six one- and two-bedroom suites, each of which has a full kitchen and formal dining and living rooms and can sleep up to six comfortably. Tea is served each afternoon from 4 to 6pm. Continental breakfast is served in the dining room off the lobby from 6 to 10am. All rooms are nonsmoking.

750 Stanyan St. (at Waller St.), San Francisco, CA 94117. ℂ **415/751-1000.** Fax 415/668-5454. www.stanyanpark. com. 36 units. $135–$209 double; $265–$335 suite. Rates include continental breakfast and afternoon and evening tea service. Rollaway $20; cribs free. AE, DISC, MC, V. Off-site parking $14. Bus: 7, 33, 43, 66, or 71. Streetcar: N. *In room:* TV, dataport, free Wi-Fi, kitchen (in suites only), hair dryer, iron in suites or on request.

12 Near San Francisco International Airport

MODERATE

Embassy Suites ✿ If you've stayed at an Embassy Suites before, you know the drill. But this hotel is one of the best airport options, if only for the fact that every room is a suite. But there is more: The property has an indoor pool, whirlpool, courtyard with fountain, palm trees, and bar/restaurant. Each tastefully decorated two-room suite has comfy linens and mattresses and nice additions such as two TVs. Additionally, a complimentary breakfast of your choice is available before you're whisked to the airport on the free shuttle—all that and the price is still right.

250 Gateway Blvd., South San Francisco, CA 94080. ℂ **800/362-2779** or 650/589-3400. Fax 650/589-1183. www. embassysuites.com. 312 units. $139–$199 double. Rates include breakfast and free evening beverages. AE, DC, MC, V. **Amenities:** Restaurant; bar; indoor pool; Jacuzzi; airport shuttle. *In room:* A/C, TV, Wi-Fi ($9.95/day), fridge, microwave, coffeemaker, hair dryer, iron.

INEXPENSIVE

San Francisco Airport North Travelodge *Kids*   The Travelodge is a good choice for families, mainly because of the hotel's large heated pool. The rooms are as ordinary as you'd expect from a Travelodge. Still, they're comfortable and come with plenty of perks like Showtime and free toll-free and credit card calls. Each junior suite has a microwave and refrigerator. The clincher is the 24-hour complimentary shuttle, which makes the 2-mile trip to the airport in 5 minutes.

326 S. Airport Blvd. (off Hwy. 101), South San Francisco, CA 94080. ℂ **800/578-7878** or 650/583-9600. Fax 650/ 873-9392. www.sfotravelodge.com. 199 units. $89–$139 double. AE, DC, DISC, MC, V. Free parking. **Amenities:** Restaurant; heated outdoor pool; courtesy shuttle to airport; fax and copier services; high-speed Internet access at computer station (for fee); dry cleaning. *In room:* A/C, TV w/pay movies, microwave available, coffeemaker, hair dryer, iron, safe.

7

Where to Dine

For more than a decade the readers of *Bon Appétit* magazine have named San Francisco their top city for dining out. And for good reason—with more than 3,500 restaurants offering cuisines from around the globe, San Francisco has more restaurants per capita than any other city in the United States.

San Francisco also attracts some of the world's most talented chefs, drawn not only to the creative freedom that has always defined San Francisco's culinary scene, but also to the year-round access to Northern California's unparalleled abundance of organic produce, seafood, free-range meats, and wine.

Afghan, Cajun, Burmese, Moroccan, Persian, Cambodian, Basque, vegan—whatever you're in the mood for, this town has it covered, which is why more San Franciscans eat out than any other city's residents in the U.S. And all you need to join America's largest dinner party is an adventurous palate, because half the fun of visiting San Francisco is the opportunity to sample the flavors of the world in one fell swoop.

Although dining in San Francisco is almost always a hassle-free experience, you should keep a few things in mind:

- If you want a table at the restaurants with the best reputations, you

probably need to book 6 to 8 weeks in advance for weekends, and a couple of weeks ahead for weekdays.
- If there's a long wait for a table, ask if you can order at the bar, which is often faster and more fun.
- Don't leave *anything* valuable in your car while dining, particularly in or near high-crime areas such as the Mission, downtown, or—believe it or not—Fisherman's Wharf. (Thieves know tourists with nice cameras and a trunkful of mementos are headed there.) Also, it's best to give the parking valet only the key to your car, *not* your hotel room or house key.
- ***Remember:*** It is against the law to smoke in any restaurant in San Francisco, even if it has a separate bar or lounge area. You're welcome to smoke outside, however.
- This ain't New York: Plan on dining early. Most restaurants close their kitchens around 10pm.
- If you're driving to a restaurant, add extra time to your itinerary for parking, which can be an especially infuriating exercise in areas like the Mission, Downtown, the Marina, and, well, pretty much everywhere. And expect to pay at least $10 to $13 for valet service, *if* the restaurant offers it.

⸢Tips⸥ E-Reservations

Want to book your reservations online? Go to **www.opentable.com**, where you can save seats in San Francisco and the rest of the Bay Area in real time.

Pricing Categories
The restaurants listed below are classified first by area, then by price, using the following categories: **Very Expensive,** dinner from $75 per person; **Expensive,** dinner from $50 per person; **Moderate,** dinner from $35 per person; and **Inexpensive,** dinner less than $35 per person. These categories reflect prices for an appetizer, main course, dessert, and glass of wine.

1 The Best Dining Bets

- **Best Hotel Restaurant: Ame,** 689 Mission St. (© **415/284-4040**), located in the swank St. Regis Hotel, means "rain" in Japanese. But the only drops you'll see coming down here are tears of joy from local foodies who no longer have to drive to St. Helena to enjoy a meal by Hiro Sone, James Beard Award winner and master of Japanese, French, and Italian cuisine. See p. 115.
- **Best for Impressing Clients:** Show your business associates you've got class—and deep pockets—by reserving a table at the Financial District's **Aqua,** 252 California St. (© **415/956-9662**). See p. 111.
- **Best Romantic Spot:** Anyone who loves classic French cooking will be seduced at **Fleur de Lys,** 777 Sutter St. (© **415/673-7779**), under the rich burgundy-tented canopy that swathes the elegant room in romance. There's lots of question-popping here, too. See p. 104.
- **Best for a Celebration:** Great food, a full bar, and a lively atmosphere are the key ingredients that make **Boulevard,** 1 Mission St. (© **415/543-6084**), the place to celebrate. See p. 118. Or celebrate Latino-style with pitchers of sangria at the Haight's **Cha Cha Cha,** 1801 Haight St. (© **415/386-7670**). See p. 148.
- **Best Decor:** Celeb restaurant designer Pat Kuleto spent a week sketching sea life at the Monterey Bay Aquarium before applying his genius to whimsical **Farallon,** 450 Post St. (© **415/956-6969**). See p. 104. Two more Kuleto design feats are within **Waterbar,** 399 Embarcadero (© **415/284-9922**) and the **Grand Café,** 501 Geary St. (© **415/292-0101**), where the old-world European ballroom meets Art Nouveau glamour. See p. 119 and 106.
- **Best Wine List:** Renowned sommelier Rajat Parr, at **Michael Mina,** 335 Powell St. (© **415/397-9222**), will pour liquid heaven provided you can swallow the steep prices. See p. 106. Another sip-worthy spot is **bacar,** 448 Brannan St. (© **415/904-4100**), which offers 60 wines by the glass.
- **Best Pizza: Pauline's,** 260 Valencia St. (© **415/552-2050**), p. 145, does two things—pizzas and salads—but does them both better than any other restaurant in the city.
- **Best Dim Sum:** Downtown and Chinatown dim sum restaurants may be more centrally located, but that's all they've got on **Ton Kiang,** 5821 Geary Blvd. (© **415/387-8273**), where carts bring the best Chinese dumplings and other dim sum delicacies to your table. See p. 152.
- **Best Vegetarian Food:** For excellent farm-fresh food and an equally stunning view of the Golden Gate, go to **Greens Restaurant,** Building A, Fort Mason Center (© **415/771-6222**). See p. 137. Also check out **Millennium,** 580 Geary St. (© **415/345-3900**).

> **Tips** **Multicourse Dining**
>
> Ordering a "fixed-price," "prix-fixe," or "tasting" menu can be a good bargain as well as a great way to sample lots of dishes at one sitting. Many dining rooms in town offer these multicourse menus, which tend to cost around $75 for four courses, including dessert.

- **Best Cafe:** If you want to know what life was like before Starbucks, spend some time at North Beach's beloved **Mario's Bohemian Cigar Store,** 566 Columbus Ave. (© **415/362-0536**); and **Caffè Trieste,** 601 Vallejo St. (© **415/392-6739**). See p. 129.
- **Best Dive:** Anyone who's a connoisseur of funky little ethnic eateries will love **Sam Wo,** 813 Washington St. (© **415/982-0596**), my favorite Chinatown dive. See p. 125.

2 Union Square

VERY EXPENSIVE

Farallon ⊕ SEAFOOD   Although this seafood restaurant is hands-down the most whimsical with its stunning oceanic decor, the high price tag, and fine, but not mind-blowing, food make it a better cocktail-and-appetizer stop than dinner choice. The multimillion-dollar attraction's outrageous decor follows the "coastal" cuisine theme; hand-blown jellyfish lamps, kelp bed–like backlit columns, glass clamshells, sea-urchin light fixtures, a sea-life mosaic floor, and a tentacle-encircled bar set the scene. (Thankfully, designer Pat Kuleto's impressive renovation of the 1924 building left the original Gothic arches intact.)

Executive chef Mark Franz, who opened the once-famous restaurant Stars with Jeremiah Tower, orchestrates the cuisine. He offers starters ranging from the expected (a variety of very expensive oysters) to the more ambitious (seared breast of squab with roasted foie gras, leg confit raviolo, and rhubarb chutney)—with a few meat and game items stuck in for good measure. The whimsy-meets-sophistication extends only as far as the food—the service and wine lists (more than 400 by the bottle; 30 by the glass) are seriously professional. Personally, I prefer stopping in for appetizers at the bar. The scene may be swank, but for seafood, Aqua (p. 111) is worlds better.

450 Post St. (btw. Mason and Powell sts., adjoining the Kensington Park Hotel). © **415/956-6969.** www.farallon restaurant.com. Reservations recommended. Pre-theater 3-course prix-fixe dinner menu $45; main courses $30–$39 dinner. AE, DC, DISC, MC, V. Mon 5:30–10pm; Tues–Wed 5:30–10:30pm; Fri–Sat 5:30–11pm; Sun 5–10pm. Valet parking $12. Bus: 2, 3, 4, or 38.

Fleur de Lys ⊕⊕ FRENCH   Fleur de Lys is the city's most traditional and formal classic French affair. Draped in 900 yards of rich patterned fabric mood-lit with dim French candelabras and accented with an extraordinary sculptural floral centerpiece, this restaurant is a romantic spot, so long as your way of wooing includes donning a dinner jacket, which is "appreciated" but not required. Equally formal is the cuisine of chef Hubert Keller (former President Clinton's first guest chef at the White House), who is usually in the kitchen preparing the menus and watching a closed-circuit TV of the dining room to ensure all goes smoothly. Diners in favor of grazing should start

Dining in Union Square & the Financial District

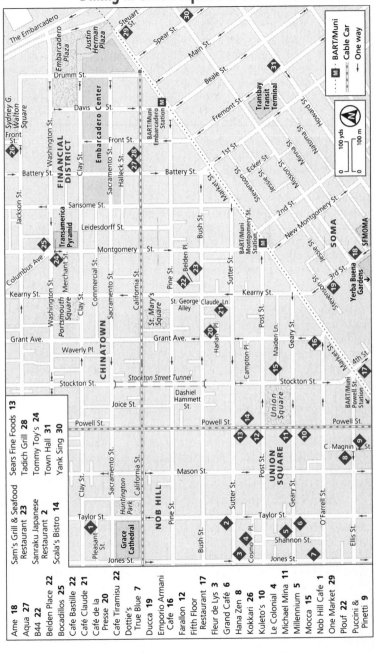

Legend:
- **M** BART/Muni
- Cable Car
- → One way

Ame **18**
Aqua **27**
B44 **22**
Belden Place **22**
Bocadillos **25**
Cafe Bastille **22**
Café Claude **21**
Café de la
Presse **20**
Cafe Tiramisu **22**
Dottie's
True Blue **7**
Ducca **19**
Emporio Armani
Cafe **16**
Farallon **12**
Fifth Floor
Restaurant **17**
Fleur de Lys **3**
Grand Café **6**
Hana Zen **8**
Kokkari **26**
Kuleto's **10**
Le Colonial **4**
Michael Mina **11**
Millennium **5**
Mocca **15**
Nob Hill Cafe **1**
One Market **29**
Plouf **22**
Puccini &
Pinetti **9**

Sam's Grill & Seafood
Restaurant **23**
Sanraku Japanese
Restaurant **2**
Scala's Bistro **14**
Sears Fine Foods **13**
Tadich Grill **28**
Tommy Toy's **24**
Town Hall **31**
Yank Sing **30**

105

with the "Symphony" appetizer, a culinary medley with bite-size samplings of roasted beet and anchovies, pistachio-crusted foie gras, Maine lobster tartare, and butternut squash vichyssoise. Other sure things include radicchio-wrapped salmon with cannellini beans and Banyuls vinegar and olive oil; and lamb loin with roasted potato stew, whole-grain mustard, and honey and red-wine reduction. The selection of around 700 French, California, and Northwestern wines is also impressive.

777 Sutter St. (at Jones St.). ✆ 415/673-7779. www.fleurdelyssf.com. Reservations required. 3-course menu $70; 4-course $77; 5-course $88; vegetarian tasting menu $68. Vegan option available with advance notice. AE, DC, MC, V. Mon–Thurs 6–9:30pm; Fri 5:30–10:30pm; Sat 5–10:30pm. Valet parking $13. Bus: 2, 3, 4, 27, or 38.

Michael Mina ✿✿✿ AMERICAN   Chef Michael Mina, who became a celebrity chef while overseeing Aqua (p. 111) and was *Bon Appétit* Chef of the Year for 2005–2006, takes the small-plate dining concept to extremes at this sexy, swank spot. Previously the Compass Rose tearoom in the Westin St. Francis hotel, the cream-on-cream room, with deep leather lounge chairs and tables that are too wide for romance, sets the scene for this formal prix-fixe affair. But rather than three dishes, courses arrive as a trio of different renditions of the same theme (plus three sides to match) on custom Mina-designed modular china. That's six different preparations per dish or a total of 18 different flavors over the course of an evening. It's a bit fussy for anyone who prefers to order a few things that sound good and eat lots of bites of them, but if the idea of sampling lots of styles and flavors appeals to you, this edible food-combination case study is likely to be a culinary wonder. Take diver scallops for example. One preparation is accented with lemon Osetra caviar while the other two pair them with yellow corn and summer truffles and smoked tomato and Maine lobster—not to mention three different "chilled salads" in tiny glasses. You might also find crispy pork loin done with risotto, as pulled pork with apple ravioli, and as barbecue with a corn fritter. Some dishes hit, some miss, but in all cases this is a swank affair with an incredible wine list by Rajat Parr.

335 Powell St. (at Geary St.). ✆ 415/397-9222. www.michaelmina.net. Reservations recommended. 3-course tasting menu $98; seasonal classic tasting menu $135. AE, DC, DISC, MC, V. Dinner Mon–Sat 5:30–10pm; Sun 5:30–9:30pm. Valet parking $17. Bus: 2, 3, 4, 30, 38, 45, or 76.

EXPENSIVE

Grand Café ✿ FRENCH   If you aren't interested in exploring restaurants beyond those in Union Square and want a huge dose of atmosphere with your seared salmon, Grand Café is your best bet. Its claims to fame? The grandest dining room in San Francisco, an enormous 156-seat, turn-of-the-20th-century grand-ballroom-like dining oasis that's a magnificent combination of old Europe and Art Nouveau. To match the surroundings, chef Ron Boyd, a San Francisco native and Domaine Chandon alum, serves dressed-up French-inspired California dishes such as sautéed salmon with French lentils and house-cured bacon or salade niçoise. You can also drop by for a lighter meal in the more casual front room, the Petit Café, which offers a raw bar and similar dishes for about half the price. In fact, I prefer to hang out in the cafe and nosh on pizzas from the wood-burning oven or a big bowl full of mussels swimming in broth with a side of sourdough bread—it's twice the atmosphere at half the price. There's also a wonderful selection of small-batch American whiskeys and single-malt Scotches.

501 Geary St. (at Taylor St., adjacent to the Hotel Monaco). ✆ 415/292-0101. www.grandcafe-sf.com. Reservations recommended. Main courses $18–$28. AE, DC, DISC, MC, V. Mon–Fri 7–10:30am; Sat 8am–2:30pm; Sun 9am–2:30pm; Mon–Fri 11:30am–2:30pm; Sun–Thurs 5:30–10pm; Fri–Sat 5:30–11pm. Valet parking free at brunch, $15 for 3 hr. at dinner, $3 each additional half-hour. Bus: 2, 3, 4, 27, or 38.

Le Colonial ★ *Finds* VIETNAMESE   Viet-chic environs—picture slowly spinning ceiling fans, tropical plants, rattan furniture, and French Colonial decor—and quality French Vietnamese food make this an excellent choice for folks who want to nosh at one of the sexiest restaurants in town. The upstairs lounge (which opens at 4:30pm) is where romance reigns, with cozy couches, seductive surroundings, and a well-dressed cocktail crowd of post-work professionals who nosh on coconut-crusted crab cakes and Vietnamese spring rolls. In the tiled downstairs dining room and along the stunning heated front patio, guests savor the vibrant flavors of coconut curry with black tiger prawns, mangos, eggplant, and Asian basil and tender wok-seared beef tenderloin with watercress onion salad.

20 Cosmo Place (off Taylor St., btw. Post and Sutter sts.). © 415/931-3600. www.lecolonialsf.com. Reservations recommended. Main courses $20–$38. AE, DC, MC, V. Sun–Wed 5:30–10pm; Thurs–Sat 5:30–11pm. Public valet parking $6 1st hr., $2 each additional half-hour. Bus: 2, 3, 4, or 27.

MODERATE

Bocadillos ★★ *Finds* SPANISH/BASQUE TAPAS   The sister to Piperade (p. 126) is flat-out fabulous if you're in the mood for tapas or Spanish-influenced small plates. Executive chef Gerald Hirigoyen celebrates his Basque roots with outstanding calamari with creamy tomato-and-garlic romesco sauce, scallops "mole cortado" with sherry and orange, sautéed hot peppers, tuna carpaccio, decadent foie gras sushi rolls, and astoundingly tasty warm chocolate cake with sautéed bananas. Just watch your budget—at up to $12 per plate the tab can creep up on you. You might also want to check out their breakfast, which includes baked eggs with chorizo and manchego cheese. But don't come anticipating a formal dining environment or a cocktail: This small Financial District space is cafe-casual and serves beer-and-wine only.

710 Montgomery St. (at Washington St.). © 415/982-2622. www.bocasf.com. Breakfast items $2–$6; lunch and dinner small items $3–$12. AE, DC, DISC, MC, V. Mon–Fri 7am–11pm; Sat 5–11pm. Closed Sun. Bus: 15, 30X, or 41.

Café Claude ★ FRENCH   Euro transplants love Café Claude, a crowded and lively restaurant tucked into a narrow (and very European feeling) side street near Union Square. Seemingly everything—every table, spoon, saltshaker, and waiter—is imported from France. With prices topping out at about $22 on the menu featuring classics like steak tartare; steamed mussels; duck confit; escargot; steak with spinach gratin and crisp potatoes; and quail stuffed with pine nuts, sausage, and wild rice, Café Claude offers an affordable slice of Paris without leaving the city. But beware: On my last visit the service was rather . . . er . . . French as well. There's live jazz on Thursdays, Fridays, and Saturdays from 7:30 to 10:30pm, and atmospheric sidewalk seating is available when the weather permits.

7 Claude Lane (off Sutter St.). © 415/392-3515. www.cafeclaude.com. Reservations recommended. Main courses $8–$12 lunch, $14–$22 dinner. AE, DC, DISC, MC, V. Mon–Sat 11:30am–10:30pm; Sun 5:30–10:30pm. Bus: 30. Cable car: Powell–Mason.

Hana Zen ★ *Finds* JAPANESE   Even most locals don't know about this Japanese restaurant, mistaking it for just another touristy sushi bar. Sure, they serve good sushi, but what makes this place special is the yakitori bar, which cranks out savory skewered and grilled meats and veggies that we can never seem to get enough of. It's all prepared Benihana style, with acrobatic chefs whirling knives around and making lots of *"Hai!"* "ahhh," and "ooohh" sounds. My favorite dishes are the asparagus spears wrapped in thinly sliced pork, and the grilled marinated shiitake mushrooms. A few tables are perched beside windows overlooking downtown San Francisco, but the best seats are at the long, arched yakitori bar, where the deft chefs spear together nearly 30 versions of the meal-on-a-stick. You can order either one pair at a time if you like the show, or all at once for a feast; about a half dozen make a meal. The terminally indecisive can opt for the Yakitori Dinner Set for $20, which makes an interesting light meal for two.

115 Cyril Magnin St. (at Ellis St.). ✆ 415/421-2101. Sushi/yakitori items $4–$6. AE, DC, MC, V. Lunch daily 11:30am–5pm; dinner Sun–Thurs 5pm–midnight, Fri–Sat 5pm–1am. Bus: 27 or 38.

Kuleto's ✿ ITALIAN   Kuleto's is one of downtown's Italian darlings. Muscle your way into a seat at the antipasto bar or at the chef's counter overlooking the kitchen and fill up on Italian specialties and selections from the wine list featuring 30 by-the-glass options. Or partake in the likes of penne pasta drenched in tangy lamb-sausage marinara sauce, clam linguine (generously overloaded with fresh clams), or any of the grilled fresh-fish specials in the casually refined dining room. If you don't arrive by 6pm, expect to wait—this place fills up fast. Not to worry though, you can always cross the hotel lobby to the wine bar, which also serves the full menu and is open from 6 to 10pm daily. Don't have time to sit down? Try Cafe Kuleto's, which is located just outside and serves panini, pastries, salads, and espresso to go, open daily from 7am to 8pm.

In the Villa Florence Hotel, 221 Powell St. (btw. Geary and O'Farrell sts.). ✆ 415/397-7720. www.kuletos.com. Reservations recommended. Breakfast $5–$15; main courses $12–$25. AE, DC, DISC, MC, V. Mon–Fri 7–10:30am; Sat–Sun 8–10:30am; daily 11:30am–11pm. Bus: 2, 3, 4, or 38. Streetcar: All streetcars. Cable car: Powell–Mason or Powell–Hyde lines.

Millennium ✿✿ VEGAN   Banking on the trend toward lighter, healthier cooking, chef Eric Tucker and his band of merry waiters set out to prove that a meatless menu doesn't mean you have to sacrifice taste. In a narrow, handsome, Parisian-style dining room with checkered tile flooring, French windows, and sponge-painted walls, Millennium has had nothing but favorable reviews for its egg-, butter-, and dairy-free creations since the day it opened. Favorites include Balinese-style salt and pepper-crusted oyster mushrooms with blood orange chile jam, and main courses such as truffled potato Wellington stuffed with shiitake mushroom duxelles served with spring onion and lentil sugo, seared asparagus, blood orange, and capers; or *masala dosa,* a lentil rice crepe with South Indian chickpea and red chard curry, sweet and spicy papaya chutney, and mint raita. No need to divert from PC dining with your wine choice—all the selections here are organic.

In the Savoy Hotel, 580 Geary St. (at Jones St.). ✆ 415/345-3900. www.millenniumrestaurant.com. Reservations recommended. Main courses $18–$22. AE, DC, DISC, MC, V. Sun–Thurs 5:30–9:30pm; Fri–Sat 5:30–10pm. Bus: 38. Streetcar: All Muni lines. BART: Powell St.

Puccini & Pinetti ✿ *Kids* ITALIAN   It takes some *buco bravado* to open yet another Italian restaurant in San Francisco, but partners Bob Puccini and Steve Pinetti obviously did their homework—this trendy little trattoria has been packed since the day it opened. The formula isn't exactly unique: large portions of good food at fair prices. What really makes it work, though, is the upbeat yet casual ambience, colorful decor, busy exhibition kitchen, and convenient corner location near Union Square. The menu doesn't take any chances either: Italian standbys—pastas, salads, thin-crust wood-fired–oven pizzas, grilled meats—dominate the menu. The fresh-baked focaccia sandwiches do well during lunch, as do the grilled portobello mushrooms with fresh mozzarella, roasted peppers, and mixed baby greens. The creamy tiramisu and devil's food cake both make for a proper finish. *Tip:* This is one of the few places in the Union Square area that actually welcomes kids—in fact, they get to make their own pizza.

129 Ellis St. (at Cyril Magnin St.). © 415/392-5500. www.pucciniandpinetti.com. Reservations recommended. Main courses $8–$20. AE, DC, DISC, MC, V. Mon–Thurs 11:30am–10pm; Fri–Sat 11:30am–11pm; Sun 5–10pm. Cable car: Powell-Mason line. Bus: 27 or 38.

Scala's Bistro ✴✴ FRENCH/ITALIAN   Firmly entrenched at the base of the refurbished Sir Francis Drake hotel, this downtown favorite blends Italian-bistro and old-world atmosphere with jovial and bustling results. With just the right balance of elegance and informality, this is a perfect place to have some fun (and apparently most people do). Of the tempting array of Italian and French dishes, it's de rigueur to start with the "Earth and Surf" calamari appetizer with grilled portobello mushrooms. Golden beet salad and garlic cream mussels are also good bets. Generous portions of moist, rich duck-leg confit will satisfy hungry appetites, but if you can order only one thing, make it Scala's signature dish: seared salmon. Resting on a bed of creamy buttermilk mashed potatoes and accented with a tomato, chive, and white-wine sauce, it's downright delicious. Finish with Bostini cream pie, a dreamy combo of vanilla custard and orange chiffon cake with a warm chocolate glaze.

In the Sir Francis Drake hotel, 432 Powell St. (at Sutter St.). © 415/395-8555. www.scalasbistro.com. Reservations recommended. Breakfast $7–$10; main courses $12–$24 lunch and dinner. AE, DC, DISC, MC, V. Daily 8–10:30am and 11:30am–midnight. Bus: 2, 3, 4, 30, 45, or 76. Cable car: Powell-Hyde line.

Straits Restaurant ✴ SINGAPOREAN   Straits is the place to go if you're in the mood for some adventurous Asian-inspired dining. I'm a huge fan of Chef Chris Yeo's spicy Malaysian-Indian-Chinese offerings, such as *murtabak* (stuffed Indian bread), chile crab, basil chicken, *nonya daging rendang* (beef simmered in lime leaves), *ikan pangang* (banana leaf–wrapped barbecued salmon with chile paste), and, hottest of all, his green curry (prawns, scallops, and mussels simmered in a jalapeño-based curry). The stylish restaurant—practically glowing with its profusion of polished woods, stainless steel accents, and gleaming open kitchen—is located on the fourth floor of the fancy new San Francisco Centre (right above Bloomingdale's in fact), so you can squeeze in an afternoon of power shopping before your culinary adventure begins.

San Francisco Centre, 845 Market St., Suite 597. © 415/668-1783. www.straitsrestaurants.com. Reservations recommended. Main courses $10–$27. AE, DC, MC, V. Daily 11am–2am. Bus: 2, 3, 4, or 38.

INEXPENSIVE

Café de la Presse FRENCH/AMERICAN   Parisians will find this 1930s-style French bistro and international newsstand familiarly comforting. But you needn't hail from across the pond to enjoy freshly baked pastries, coffee drinks, sidewalk seating, and French-speaking staff. Its location, directly across from the Chinatown gates, makes it one of the best places in the Union Square area to sit and enjoy the busy downtown vibe. The menu offers light fare for breakfast—at somewhat inflated prices—and meatier bistro-style entrees such as duck leg confit and braised beef stew for lunch and dinner. But the main reason to come here isn't to indulge your appetite, it's to browse the foreign magazine and newspaper racks for a bit, then rest your weary feet, nurse a cappuccino, nibble on a pastry, and soak up the street-side scene.

352 Grant Ave. (at Bush St.). © 415/398-2680. Breakfast $6.25–$10; lunch and dinner main courses (other than fish and meat) $9–$13; fish and meat main courses $15–$20. AE, DC, DISC, MC, V. Breakfast Mon–Fri 7:30–10am, Sat–Sun 8–11:30am; lunch Mon–Fri 11:30am–2:30pm; dinner Mon–Thurs 5:30–9:30pm, Fri–Sun 5:30–10pm; brunch Sat–Sun 11:30am–4pm. Bus: 9X, 15, 30, or 45.

Dottie's True Blue Café ✴ *Kids* AMERICAN/BREAKFAST   This family-owned breakfast restaurant is one of my favorite downtown diners. This is the kind of place you'd expect to see off Route 66, where most customers are on a first-name basis with the staff and everyone is welcomed with a hearty hello and steaming mug of coffee. Dottie's serves far-above-average American morning fare (big portions of French toast, pancakes, bacon and eggs, omelets, and the like), delivered to tables laminated with old movie star photos on rugged, diner-quality plates. Whatever you order arrives with delicious homemade bread, muffins, or scones, as well as house-made jelly. There are also daily specials and vegetarian dishes.

In the Pacific Bay Inn, 522 Jones St. (at O'Farrell St.). © 415/885-2767. Reservations not accepted. Breakfast $5–$11. DISC, MC, V. Wed–Mon 7:30am–3pm (lunch 11:30am–3pm). Bus: 2, 3, 4, 27, or 38. Cable car: Powell–Mason line.

Emporio Armani Cafe ⭑ ITALIAN   All the hobnobbing of an elite luncheon comes at a moderate price at the Armani Cafe. This upscale-casual cafe consists of a circular counter in the middle of Armani's ever-fashionable (and expensive) clothing store, a few tables on a mezzanine, and some crowded sidewalk seats when the weather's agreeable. Yes, it's a bit unusual to be eating amongst the racks of clothes, but that's what makes this cafe such a great place to take a break from Union Square shopping. Local favorites include the antipasto *misto,* panini, salads, and daily pizza specials. And just in case you need a stiff drink after seeing the prices of their designer suits, the bar stays open until 7pm.

1 Grant Ave. (at O'Farrell St., off Market St.). © 415/677-9010. Reservations accepted. Main courses $9–$17. AE, DC, DISC, MC, V. Mon–Sat 11am–4pm, Sun noon–4pm. Bus: All Union Sq. buses.

Mocca ⭑ ITALIAN   If you're like me and can't be bothered with a long lunch when there's serious shopping to be done, head to this classic Italian deli on foot-traffic-only Maiden Lane. Here it's counter service and cash only for sandwiches, caprese (Italian tomato and mozzarella salad), and big leafy salads. You can enjoy them at the few indoor tables or the umbrella-shaded tables on the pedestrian-only street-front which look onto Union Square.

175 Maiden Lane (at Stockton St.). © 415/956-1188. Reservations not accepted. Main courses $7–$13. No credit cards. Pastry and coffee daily 10:30am–5:30pm; lunch daily 11am–5:30pm. Bus: All Union Sq. buses.

Sanraku Japanese Restaurant ⭑ *Value* JAPANESE/SUSHI   A perfect combination of great cooked dishes and sushi at bargain prices makes this straightforward, bright, and busy restaurant the best choice in the area for Japanese food. The friendly, hardworking staff does its best to keep up with diners' demands, but the restaurant gets quite busy during lunch, when a special box lunch of the likes of California roll, soup, salad, deep-fried salmon roll, and beef with noodles with steamed rice comes at a very digestible $9.50. The main menu, which is always available, features great sesame chicken with teriyaki sauce and rice; tempura; a vast selection of *nigiri* (raw fish sushi) and rolls; and delicious combination plates of sushi, sashimi, and teriyaki. Dinner sees brisk business, too, but there always seems to be an available table.

704 Sutter St. (at Taylor St.). © 415/771-0803. www.sanraku.com. Main courses $7–$13 lunch, $10–$26 dinner; 7-course fixed-price dinner $55. AE, DC, DISC, MC, V. Mon–Sat lunch 11am–4pm, dinner 4–10pm; Sun dinner 4–10pm. Bus: 2, 3, 4, 27, or 38. Cable car: Powell–Mason line.

Sears Fine Foods ⭑ *Kids* AMERICAN   Sears is not just another downtown diner—it's an old-fashioned institution, famous for its crispy, dark-brown waffles, light sourdough French toast served with house-made strawberry preserves, and silver dollar–size Swedish pancakes (18 per serving!). As the story goes, Ben Sears, a retired clown, founded the diner in 1938. His Swedish wife, Hilbur, was responsible for the legendary pancakes, which, although the restaurant is under new ownership, are still whipped up according to her family's secret recipe. Sears also offers classic lunch and dinner fare—try the Reuben for lunch and cod fish and chips for dinner, followed by a big slice of pie for dessert. Breakfast is served until 3pm every day, and plan on a brief wait to be seated on weekends.

439 Powell St. (btw. Post and Sutter sts.). (C) 415/986-0700. www.searsfinefood.com. Reservations accepted for parties of 6 or more. Breakfast $3–$8; salads and soups $3–$8; main courses $6–$10. AE, DC, MC, V. Daily 6:30am–10pm (breakfast until 3pm). Cable car: Powell-Mason and Powell-Hyde lines. Bus: 2, 3, 4, or 38.

3 Financial District

VERY EXPENSIVE

Aqua ☆☆ SEAFOOD   At San Francisco's finest seafood restaurant, heralded chef Laurent Manrique dazzles customers with a bewildering juxtaposition of earth and sea. Under his care, the artfully composed dishes are delicately decadent: the ahi tartare with fresh herbs, Moroccan spices, and lemon confit is divine and one of the best I've ever had. Other favorites are the celery root soup with black truffle flan, frogs' legs, and rock shrimp; the Alaskan black cod wrapped in smoked bacon and accompanied by tomato and date chutney and glazed carrots; and the braised veal cheeks with smoked foie gras and beef consommé—all perfectly paired with wines chosen by the sommelier. The large dining room with high ceilings, elaborate floral displays, and oversized mirrors is pleasing to the eye if not to the ear. (It can get quite loud on busy nights.) Steep prices prevent most people from making a regular appearance, but for special occasions or billable lunches, Aqua is highly recommended.

252 California St. (near Battery). (C) 415/956-9662. www.aqua-sf.com. Reservations recommended. Main courses $29–$39; 3-course menu $68; 6-course tasting menu $95; vegetarian tasting menu $65. AE, DC, DISC, MC, V. Mon–Fri 11:30am–2pm; Mon–Sat 5:30–10:30pm; Sun 5:30–9:30pm. Valet parking (dinner only) $10. Bus: All Market St. buses.

EXPENSIVE

Kokkari ☆☆ GREEK/MEDITERRANEAN   The funny thing is, I've been to Athens, and the food there wasn't nearly as good as what they're serving at Kokkari (Ko-*kar*-ee), one of my favorite restaurants in the city. My love affair starts with the setting: a beautifully rustic dining area with a commanding fireplace and oversize furnishings. Past the tiny bar, the other main room is pure rustic revelry with exposed wood beams, pretty standing lamps, and a view of the glass-enclosed private dining room. Then there are the wonderful, traditional Aegean dishes. A must-order appetizer is the *Marithes Tiganites,* a beautiful platter of whole crispy smelts enhanced with garlic-potato *skordalia* (a traditional Greek dip) and lemon. Other favorites are the *pikilia* (a sampling of traditional Greek spreads served with dolmades and house-made pitas) and the fabulous mesquite-grilled octopus salad. Try not to overindulge before the main courses, which include grilled whole petrale sole with lemon, olive oil, and braised greens; to-die-for moussaka (eggplant, lamb, potato, and béchamel); and lamb chops with oven-roasted lemon-oregano potatoes. Also consider the rotisserie specialties such as a rotisserie-roasted pork loin.

200 Jackson St. (at Front St.). (C) 415/981-0983. www.kokkari.com. Reservations recommended. Main courses $14–$23 lunch, $19–$35 dinner. AE, DC, DISC, MC, V. Lunch Mon–Fri 11:30am–2:30pm; bar menu 2:30–5:30pm; dinner Mon–Thurs 5:30–10pm, Fri 5:30–11pm, Sat 5–11pm. Valet parking (dinner only) $8. Bus: 12, 15, 41, or 83.

One Market ☆☆ CALIFORNIA   Some of the city's best food has been served at this popular Embarcadero restaurant since 1993. Amid the airy main dining room

Finds **The Sun on Your Face at Belden Place**

San Francisco has always been woefully lacking in the alfresco dining department. One exception is **Belden Place,** an adorable little brick alley in the heart of the Financial District that is open only to foot traffic. When the weather is agreeable, the restaurants that line the alley break out the big umbrellas, tables, and chairs, and *voilà*—a bit of Paris just off Pine Street.

A handful of cafes line Belden Place and offer a variety of cuisines all at moderate prices. There's **Cafe Bastille,** 22 Belden Place (© **415/986-5673**), a classic French bistro and fun speak-easy basement serving excellent crepes, mussels, and French onion soup; it schedules live jazz on Fridays. **Cafe Tiramisu,** 28 Belden Place (© **415/421-7044**), is a stylish Italian hot spot serving addictive risottos and gnocchi. **Plouf,** 40 Belden Place (© **415/986-6491**), specializes in big bowls of mussels slathered in your choice of seven sauces, as well as fresh seafood. **B44,** 44 Belden Place (© **415/986-6287**), serves up a side order of Spain alongside its revered paella and other seriously zesty Spanish dishes.

Conversely, come at night for a Euro-speak-easy vibe with your dinner.

with its open exhibition kitchen, cozy banquettes, mahogany trim, and slate flooring is a sea of diners feasting from a farm-fresh menu put together by Chef Mark Dommen, who has a passion for using only the freshest local ingredients—they helped establish the Ferry Plaza Farmers' Market across the street and now support it by shopping there—to create highly original dishes. During my last visit, my table was wowed by the truly divine beet carpaccio, shellfish, and seafood sampler (*not* your everyday platter), and a superb crispy skin pork saddle with fava beans and chorizo broth. Whatever you choose, you're bound to find a perfectly accompanying wine from the "cellar," which has over 500 selections of American vintages. Arrive early to mingle with the spirited corporate crowd that convenes from 4:30 to 7pm for happy hour at the bar—it's a fun scene.

1 Market St. (at Stuart St., across from Justin Herman Plaza). © **415/777-5577.** www.onemarket.com. Reservations recommended. Lunch $16–$23; dinner $20–$33. AE, DC, DISC, MC, V. Mon–Fri 11:30am–2pm and 5:30–9pm; Sat 5:30–10pm. Valet parking $10. Bus: All Market St. buses. Bart: All BART trains.

The Slanted Door ★★ VIETNAMESE   What started in 1995 as an obscure little family-run restaurant in the Mission District has become one of the most popular and written-about restaurants in the city. Due to its meteoric rise—helped along by celebrity fans such as Mick Jagger, Keith Richards, and Quentin Tarantino—it's been relocated within a beautiful bay-inspired, custom-designed space at the Ferry Building Marketplace. What hasn't changed is a menu filled with incredibly fresh and flavorful Vietnamese dishes such as catfish clay-pot flavored with cilantro, ginger, and Thai chilies; an amazing green papaya salad with roasted peanuts; and fragrant peppercorn duck served with apples and watercress. If the cellophane noodles with fresh Dungeness crab meat are on the menu, *definitely* order them. Be sure to start the feast with a pot of tea from their eclectic collection.

1 Ferry Plaza (at the Embarcadero and Market). ℂ **415/861-8032.** www.slanteddoor.com. Reservations recommended. Lunch main courses $8.50–$17; most dinner dishes $15–$27; 7-item fixed-price dinner $45 (parties of 7 or more only). AE, MC, V. Daily 11am–2:30pm; Sun–Thurs 5:30–10pm; Fri–Sat 5:30–10:30pm. Bus: All Market Street buses. Streetcar: F, N-Judah line.

Tommy Toy's ⓕ CHINESE   If you want romantic, extravagant Chinese, come to Tommy's. Fashioned after the 19th-century quarters of the Empress Dowager's sitting room and replete with mood-lit candelabras and antique paintings, it's perhaps the only Chinese restaurant in the city where dressing up is apropos. Most evenings, the dining room is filled mostly with tourists and traveling business types, while locals are more likely to come for the fixed-price lunches (the multi-course "Executive Luncheon" is a bargain at $23). Not much changes on the expensive, French-influenced Chinese menu, but that's fine with the loyalists who return year after year for such beautifully presented dishes as minced squab in leaves of lettuce; sautéed lobster with mushrooms, chives, and angel-hair crystal noodles; and puff-pastry–topped creamy lobster bisque. During my visits, the food has varied from fine to very good, but the portions are always substantial and the decor is definitely memorable.

655 Montgomery St. (at Clay and Washington sts.). ℂ **415/397-4888.** www.tommytoys.com. Reservations recommended. Main courses $17–$23; fixed-price lunch $23; fixed-price dinner $58–$65. AE, DC, DISC, MC, V. Mon–Fri 11:30am–2:30pm; daily 5:30–9:30pm. Valet parking (dinner only) $8. Bus: 9AX, 9BX, 12, 15, or 41.

Waterfront Restaurant CALIFORNIA   Bay Bridge views, a sunny patio, a sleek industrial-chic dining room, and great food made the Waterfront an instant hit after its renovation and reopening in late 1997. Unfortunately, the parade of chefs in and out of the kitchen has made what was a sure thing now more of an interesting gamble. Still, the atmosphere alone can induce idyllic San Francisco memories—especially when you're seated outdoors on a sunny day. Fortunately, the menu's now trying to stick with safe classics such as Dungeness crab cakes; sautéed chicken breast with herbed polenta, spinach, and truffle rosemary pan sauce; and salads, pizzas, and wood-fired grill items. The wine list includes many selections starting at just $27.

Pier 7 (on the Embarcadero near Broadway). ℂ **415/391-2696.** www.waterfrontsf.com. Reservations recommended. Main courses $18–$30. AE, DC, DISC, MC, V. Daily 11:30am–10:30pm. Valet parking $7. Streetcar: F.

MODERATE

Sam's Grill & Seafood Restaurant ⓕ (Finds) SEAFOOD   Power-lunching at Sam's is a San Francisco tradition, and Sam's has done a brisk business with Financial District suits since—get this—1867. Even if you're not carrying a briefcase, this is the place to come for time-capsule dining at its most classically San Francisco. Pass the crowded entrance and small bar to get to the main dining room—packed with virtually all men—kick back, and watch yesteryear happen today. (Or conversely, slide into a curtained booth and see nothing but your dining companion.) Tuxedo-clad waiters race around, doling out big crusty cuts of sourdough bread and distributing salads overflowing with fresh crab and Roquefort vinaigrette, towering plates of seafood pasta with marinara, charbroiled fish, roasted chicken, and old-school standbys like calves' liver with bacon and onions or Salisbury steak. Don't worry—they didn't forget classic creamed spinach. The restaurant's mildly salty service and good old-fashioned character make everything on the menu taste that much better.

374 Bush St. (btw. Montgomery and Kearny sts.). ℂ **415/421-0594.** Reservations recommended for dinner and for 6 or more at lunch. Main courses $12–$24. AE, DC, DISC, MC, V. Mon–Fri 11am–9pm. Bus: 15, 45, or 76.

Tips Fast Food from Around the World

Catering to the dense population of downtown white-collar workers, the **Rincon Center's Food Court** at the corner of Spear and Mission streets has about a dozen to-go places serving cheap, respectable fare running the gastronomic gamut: Korean, American, Mexican, pizza, coffee and cookies, Indian, Thai, sandwiches, Middle Eastern, and Chinese. Seat-yourself tables are dispersed throughout the indoor courtyard. Most of the restaurants are open Monday through Friday from 11am to 3pm, but some remain open until early evening.

Similar inexpensive eats can be found at the **Ferry Building Marketplace** (p. 160) and **Justin Herman Plaza,** both at the foot of Market Street at the Embarcadero.

Tadich Grill ⊛ SEAFOOD   Not that the veteran restaurant needed more reason to be beloved, but the city's ongoing loss of local institutions makes 158-year-old Tadich the last of a long-revered dying breed. This business began as a coffee stand during the 1849 gold rush and claims to be the very first to broil seafood over mesquite charcoal back in the early 1920s. An old-fashioned power-dining restaurant to its core, Tadich boasts its original mahogany bar, which extends the length of the restaurant, and seven booths for private powwows. Big plates of sourdough bread top the tables.

You won't find fancy California cuisine here. The novella-like menu features a slew of classic salads such as sliced tomato with Dungeness crab or prawn Louis, meats and fish from the charcoal broiler, and even casseroles. The seafood cioppino is a specialty, as is the baked casserole of stuffed turbot with crab and shrimp à la Newburg, and the petrale sole with butter sauce. Everything comes with a heaping side of fries, but if you crave something green, order the creamed spinach.

240 California St. (btw. Battery and Front sts.). ✆ **415/391-1849.** Reservations not accepted. Main courses $14–$20. MC, V. Mon–Fri 11am–9:30pm; Sat 11:30am–9:30pm. Bus: All Market St. buses. Streetcar: All Market St. streetcars. BART: Embarcadero.

Tsar Nicoulai Caviar Cafe ⊛ CAVIAR   Tsar Nicoulai is a wonderful little U-shaped 15-seat counter within the Ferry Building Marketplace where all sorts of caviar, champagne by the glass, and roe-related snacks are served to fans of fish roe. Drop by without reservations for the best American and imported caviars (served by the taste or the ounce), blinis hot off the griddle, caviar and champagne samplers, and specials like seafood salads and truffled scrambled eggs. If you haven't yet done so elsewhere, try the fun, colorful varieties of whitefish roe, which come in flavors of beet and saffron, ginger, wasabi, and truffle.

Ferry Building Marketplace, 1 Ferry Building no. 12 (at the Embarcadero and Market St.). ✆ **415/288-8630.** www.tsarnicoulai.com. Reservations not accepted. Caviar $10–$76 for samplers or 1–gram portions. Salads and such $10–$18. AE, MC, V. Mon–Fri 11am–7pm; Sat 9am–6pm; Sun 11am–5pm. Bus: All Market St. buses. Streetcar: F or N-Judah line.

Yank Sing ⊛⊛ CHINESE/DIM SUM   Loosely translated as "a delight of the heart," Yank Sing is widely regarded as the best dim sum restaurant in the downtown area. The servers are good at guessing your gastric threshold as they wheel stainless steel carts carrying small plates of exotic dishes around the vast dining room; if they whiz right by your table there's probably a good reason. If you're new to dim sum (which, translated, means "to touch the heart"), stick with the safe, recognizable classics such as spareribs, stuffed crab claws, scallion pancakes, shrimp balls, pork buns, and steamed dumplings filled with delicious concoctions of pork, beef, fish, or vegetables. A second location, open Monday through Friday from 11am to 3pm, is at 49 Stevenson St., off First Street (© **415/541-4949**) in SoMa, and has outdoor seating for fair-weather dining.

101 Spear St. (at Mission St. at Rincon Center). © **415/957-9300.** www.yanksing.com. Dim sum $3.65–$9.30 for 2–6 pieces. AE, DC, MC, V. Mon–Fri 11am–3pm; Sat–Sun and holidays 10am–4pm. Validated parking in Rincon Center Garage. Bus: 1, 12, 14, or 41. Streetcar: F. Cable car: California St. line. BART: Embarcadero.

4 SoMa

For a map of restaurants in this section, see the "Dining Around Town" map on p. 116.

VERY EXPENSIVE

Ame ✦✦✦ NEW AMERICAN   Restaurateurs Hiro Sone and Lissa Doumani, the owners of the sensational Napa Valley restaurant Terra, have blessed us foodies with an equally fantastic restaurant in the city. Located on the ground level of the new and *très* chic St. Regis Hotel, the L-shaped dining room with its mesquite flooring, red accents, and long striped curtains fits right in with the hotel's minimalist theme. Sone, a master of Japanese, French, and Italian cuisines, offers an array of exotic selections that are utterly tempting: ragout of sweetbreads with salsify and forest mushrooms; Japanese egg custard with lobster and urchin; mushroom risotto topped with foie gras; grilled Wagyu beef with fried Miyagi oysters and rémoulade sauce. If you can't figure out where to start on a menu where everything looks wonderful, opt for Sone's A Taste of Ame, an $81 five-course tasting menu that, for an additional $60, is paired with a bevy of wines by the glass. After dinner, be sure to enjoy an aperitif at the hotel's swank bar where the city's elite congregate nightly

689 Mission St. (at Third St.). © **415/284-4040.** www.amerestaurant.com. Reservations recommended. Main courses $19–$25 lunch, $22–$35 dinner. AE, DC, DISC, MC, V. Daily 5:30–10pm. Valet parking $12 for the 1st 3 hr. Bus: 15, 30, or 45. Streetcar: J, K, L, or M to Montgomery.

bacar ✦✦ AMERICAN BRASSERIE   No other dining room makes wine as integral to the meal as popular bacar. Up to 250 eclectic, fashionable diners pack into this warehouse-restaurant's three distinct areas—the casual (loud) downstairs salon; the bustling lounge, bar, and main dining room; or the more quiet upstairs mezzanine, which looks down on the lounge and bar's action—for the creamy salt-cod and crab *brandade* (purée) and zesty roasted mussels with a chile-and-garlic sauce that begs to be soaked up by the accompanying grilled bread. Ditto the grilled mesquite pork chop with mashed yams and pineapple-mango chutney. Just as much fun is the wine selection, which gives you more than 1,400 choices. Around 65 wines are served by the glass, 2-ounce pour, or 250- or 500-milliliter decanter. If you want a festive night out, this is the place to come—especially when jazz is playing Monday through Saturday evenings. *Note:* bacar is open only 1 day per week (Fri) for lunch.

448 Brannan St. (at Third St.). © **415/904-4100.** www.bacarsf.com. Reservations recommended. Lunch 3-course fixed-price menu $22; main courses dinner $22–$38. AE, DC, DISC, MC, V. Sun 5:30–10pm; Mon–Thurs 5:30–11pm; Fri 11:30am–2:30pm and 6:30pm–midnight; Sat 5:30pm–midnight. Valet parking (Mon–Sat from 5:30pm) $10. Bus: 15, 30, 45, 76, or 81.

Dining Around Town

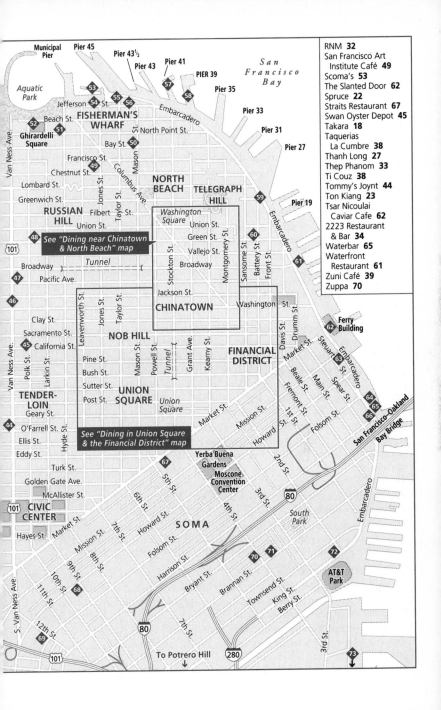

RNM **32**
San Francisco Art
  Institute Café **49**
Scoma's **53**
The Slanted Door **62**
Spruce **22**
Straits Restaurant **67**
Swan Oyster Depot **45**
Takara **18**
Taquerias
  La Cumbre **38**
Thanh Long **27**
Thep Phanom **33**
Ti Couz **38**
Tommy's Joynt **44**
Ton Kiang **23**
Tsar Nicoulai
  Caviar Cafe **62**
2223 Restaurant
  & Bar **34**
Waterbar **65**
Waterfront
  Restaurant **61**
Zuni Café **39**
Zuppa **70**

Municipal Pier
Pier 45
Pier 43½
Pier 43
Pier 41
PIER 39
Pier 35
Pier 33
Pier 31
Pier 27

San Francisco Bay

Aquatic Park

Jefferson St.
FISHERMAN'S WHARF
Beach St.
Ghirardelli Square
Bay St.
Francisco St.
Chestnut St.
Lombard St.
Greenwich St.
RUSSIAN HILL
Filbert St.
Union St.
See "Dining near Chinatown & North Beach" map
Broadway
Tunnel
Pacific Ave.
Clay St.
Sacramento St.
California St.
Pine St.
NOB HILL
Bush St.
Sutter St.
UNION SQUARE
Post St.
TENDER-LOIN
Geary St.
O'Farrell St.
Ellis St.
Eddy St.
Turk St.
Golden Gate Ave.
McAllister St.
CIVIC CENTER
Hayes St.
Market St.

Van Ness Ave.
Polk St.
Larkin St.
Hyde St.
Leavenworth St.
Jones St.
Taylor St.
Mason St.
Powell St.
Grant Ave.
Kearny St.

North Point St.
Embarcadero
NORTH BEACH
TELEGRAPH HILL
Washington Square
Union St.
Green St.
Vallejo St.
Broadway
Jackson St.
CHINATOWN
Washington St.
FINANCIAL DISTRICT
Tunnel
Union Square
Market St.
Mission St.
Howard St.

Stockton St.
Columbus Ave.
Montgomery St.
Sansome St.
Battery St.
Front St.
Davis St.
Drumm St.
Embarcadero

See "Dining in Union Square & the Financial District" map

Yerba Buena Gardens
Moscone Convention Center

Ferry Building

Market St.
Steuart St.
Beale St.
Main St.
Spear St.
Fremont St.
1st St.
Folsom St.

San Francisco–Oakland Bay Bridge

SOMA
5th St.
6th St.
7th St.
8th St.
9th St.
10th St.
11th St.
12th St.
S. Van Ness Ave.
Mission St.
Howard St.
Folsom St.
Harrison St.
Bryant St.
Brannan St.
Townsend St.
King St.
Berry St.
2nd St.
3rd St.
4th St.

South Park

AT&T Park

Embarcadero

To Potrero Hill

San Francisco Bay

117

Boulevard 🍷🍷 AMERICAN   Master restaurant designer Pat Kuleto and chef Nancy Oakes are behind one of San Francisco's most beloved restaurants. Inside, the dramatically artistic Belle Epoque interior, with vaulted brick ceilings, floral banquettes, a mosaic floor, and tulip-shaped lamps, is the setting for Oakes's equally impressive sculptural and mouthwatering dishes. Starters alone could make a perfect meal, especially if you indulge in pan-seared day boat sea scallops with sautéed fresh hearts of palm, pomelo, basil, toasted shallots, and macadamia nuts, or the pan-seared foie gras with rhubarb syrup on whole grain toast. The nine or so main courses are equally creative and might include grilled Pacific sea bass with fresh gulf prawns, grilled artichoke, spring asparagus, and green garlic purée; or fire-roasted Angus filet with crispy Yukon gold potatoes, béarnaise sauce, sautéed spinach and crimini mushrooms, and red wine *jus*. Finish with warm chocolate cake with a chocolate caramel center, caramel corn, and butterscotch ice cream. Three levels of formality—bar, open kitchen, and main dining room—keep things from getting too snobby. Although steep prices prevent most from making Boulevard a regular gig, you'd be hard-pressed to find a better place for a special, fun-filled occasion.

1 Mission St. (btw. the Embarcadero and Steuart sts.). ✆ 415/543-6084. www.boulevardrestaurant.com. Reservations recommended. Main courses $14–$22 lunch, $28–$39 dinner. AE, DC, DISC, MC, V. Mon–Fri 11:30am–2pm; Sun–Thurs 5:30–10pm; Fri–Sat 5:30–10:30pm. Valet parking $12 lunch, $10 dinner. Bus: 12, 15, 30, 32, or 41. BART: Embarcadero.

Ducca 🍷🍷🍷 ITALIAN   If you've never experienced what a talented chef can do with *mozzarella di bufala*, you owe it to yourself to visit Ducca. Executive Chef Richard J. Corbo learned his trade at the Apicus culinary institute in Florence, then refined it at Restaurant Gary Danko (see p. 132), before being asked to run his own kitchen at Ducca. Since then he's earned nothing but kudos for his simple, seasonal Italian dishes seasoned with a hint of California influences, such as his veal chop Milanese with a fennel pollen-breadcrumb crust and preserved lemon vinaigrette, ricotta gnocchi with fava beans and fungi, and a superb yellowtail crudo with pine nuts, currants, and mint. Corbo also offers a modest selection of *cichetti*, Italian-style bar snacks such as white anchovies, salt cod crostini, risotto fritters, et al. You'll enjoy the ambience as well, as it's smartly arranged into three inviting areas: a stylish bar and lounge, an alfresco terrace, and an airy dining room with embossed columns, cream-colored banquettes, and a bustling open kitchen. Be sure to arrive a bit early to enjoy a Campari and soda in the circular lounge or outdoors by the fireplace.

50 Third St. (btw. Market and Mission sts., adjacent to the Westin San Francisco Market Street hotel). ✆ 415/977-0271. www.duccasf.com. Main courses $23–$51. AE, DISC, MC, V. Daily breakfast 6:30–10:30am; lunch 11:30am–2pm; dinner 5:30–10:30pm. Valet parking $12. Bus: 15, 30, or 45. Streetcar: J, K, L, or M.

EPIC Roasthouse 🍷🍷 STEAKHOUSE   Why it took so long is a mystery, but for the first time in decades someone has finally built and opened a true destination restaurant on the Embarcadero. Two, actually. Location is everything, and the EPIC Roasthouse and its adjoining sister restaurant Waterbar (see below) were both built from the ground up on perhaps the most prime piece of real estate in the city—right on the Embarcadero with spectacular views of the Bay Bridge, Treasure Island, and city skyline. They both opened on the eve of January 29, 2008 to such fanfare that the opening party was a debacle (everyone invited showed up). At EPIC it's all about steak. Renowned chef and co-owner Jan Birnbaum, a New Orleans man who knows his meat, runs the show within his huge exhibition kitchen, perspiring at the wood-fired hearth to make sure your $76 rib eye-for-two is cooked to your specs. The restaurant's Pat

Kuleto-designed interior makes for a grand entrance: Only when you're done marveling at the bold industrial elements of leather, stone, mahogany, and massive cast iron gears do you notice the phenomenal view of the Bay Bridge from the two-story-tall wall of windows. Perhaps the only thing prettier than the scenery is Birnbaum's sizzling 26 oz. bone-in porterhouse on your plate ("Every steak comes with a handle," claims Jan). If you don't have a reservation, the upstairs Quiver Bar serves both bar and full menus, but the upstairs crowd usually consists of obnoxious businessmen and Gucci-toting gold-diggers from across the bridge. Better to call ahead and dine below. *Tip:* On sunny days beg the hostess for a table on the bay-view patio.

369 Embarcadero (at Harrison St.). ℂ 415/369-9955. www.epicroasthousesf.com. Reservations recommended. Main courses $27–$54. AE, MC, V. Lunch Mon–Fri 11:30am–2pm; dinner Sun–Thurs 5–10:30pm, Fri–Sat 5pm–midnight; brunch Sat–Sun 10:30am–3pm. Valet parking $15 lunch, $10 dinner. Bus: 1, 12, 14, or 41. Streetcar: F. BART: Embarcadero.

Waterbar ✿✿ SEAFOOD   Built in tandem with the EPIC Roasthouse (see above), Waterbar is the surf to EPIC's turf. As with EPIC, Waterbar was built from the ground up on perhaps the most prime piece of real estate in the city along the Embarcadero. Whereas renowned restaurant designer Pat Kuleto went with a moderately conservative industrial look at the EPIC steakhouse, at Waterbar he unleashed his imagination and created the most visually playful decor since he opened Farallon in 1997 (p. 104). The focal point of the restaurant is a pair of radiant 19-foot floor-to-ceiling circular aquariums filled with fish and marine critters from the Pacific Ocean. The aquatic theme ebbs along on with a beautiful glass "caviar" chandelier and a horseshoe-shaped raw bar that has too few of the most coveted seats in town. Even the open kitchen is visually—and aromatically—pleasing. The menu offers a wide selection of market-driven, sustainable seafood such as Dover sole served whole (a whopping $80) and local halibut poached in milk with grilled asparagus, but more fun can be had at the raw bar noshing on oysters and small plates. Either way, be sure to start off with the superb sea scallop ceviche infused with sweet potato, smoked salt, and paprika. If the weather is agreeable, ask the hostess for a table on the patio

399 Embarcadero (at Harrison St.). ℂ 415/284-9922. www.waterbarsf.com. Reservations recommended. Main courses $28–$36. AE, DISC, MC, V. Daily 11:30am–2pm and 5:30–10:00pm. Valet parking $15 lunch, $10 dinner. Bus: 1, 12, 14, or 41. Streetcar: F. BART: Embarcadero.

EXPENSIVE

MoMo's AMERICAN   With an abundance of patio seating, a huge swank-yet-casual dining room, and proximity to AT&T Park baseball stadium, festive MoMo's hits a home run if you're headed to a Giants game, but is not a destination in itself. Crowds of upscale sports fans make this a fun place to hang out on the patio and chow down on greasy-good thin-sliced onion rings, refreshing seared ahi salad, thin-crust pizza, and awesome burgers. Come sundown, there are dozens of other restaurants where I'd prefer to spend my money, but singles appreciate the bar scene. Happy hour is hopping Monday through Friday in the baseball off season—especially during sunny weather. If you're headed here on a game day, make a reservation or arrive early, because party people form a line around the block to get in, and it's no fun trying to eat standing at the bar or wrestling for one of the coveted patio tables.

760 Second St. (at King St.). ℂ 415/227-8660. www.sfmomos.com. Reservations recommended. Main courses $12–$39. AE, DC, DISC, MC, V. Sun–Wed 11:30am–9pm; Thurs–Sat 11:30am–10pm. Valet parking $8 lunch, $11 dinner, $20 game hours. Bus: 15, 30, 45, or 80x. Streetcar: F or N.

Town Hall ✿ AMERICAN   Mitchell and Steven Rosenthal (Postrio) and front man Doug Washington (Vertigo, Jardinière, and Postrio) are behind this SoMa warehouse hot spot featuring an attractive and rustically glitzy interior and huge portions of hearty American regional cuisine. The homey food is good and might include the likes of ale-batter fish and chips, duck confit enchiladas, and slow-braised lamb shank with creamy polenta and natural *jus*.

342 Howard St. (at Fremont St.). ✆ **415/908-3900.** www.townhallsf.com. Reservations recommended. Main courses $10–$17 lunch, $18–$26 dinner. AE, MC, V. Lunch Mon–Fri 11:30am–2:30pm; dinner Sun–Thurs 5:30–10pm, Fri–Sat 5:30–11pm. Bus: 10, 14, or 76.

MODERATE

Gordon Biersch Brewery Restaurant ✿ CALIFORNIA   Popular with the young Republican crowd (loose ties and tight skirts predominate), this modern, two-tiered brewery and restaurant eschews traditional brewpub fare—no cheesy nachos on this menu—in an attempt to attract a more upscale clientele. And it works. Goat cheese ravioli is a bestseller, followed by the pecan-crusted half-chicken with garlic mashed potatoes. Start with the delicate and crunchy fried calamari appetizer or, if you're a garlic hound, the tangy Caesar salad. Most dishes can be paired with one of the brewery's lagers or ales. Couples bent on a quiet, romantic dinner can skip this place; when the lower-level bar fills up, you practically have to shout to be heard. Beer-lovers who want to pair their suds with decent grub, however, will be quite content.

2 Harrison St. (on the Embarcadero). ✆ **415/243-8246.** www.gordonbiersch.com. Reservations recommended. Main courses $10–$23. AE, DC, DISC, MC, V. Sun–Thurs 11:30am–midnight; Fri–Sat 11:30am–2am. Bus: 32.

Zuppa ✿✿ ITALIAN   If you're looking for a casual-chic dinner spot with good affordable food, lively ambience, and a somewhat hip crowd, Zuppa is it. Located among the warehouses of SoMa, this warm industrial room is awash with dark wood tables and features a back-wall bar orchestrated by on-site owners Joseph and Mary (yes, really). Joe, whose career launched from Spago Hollywood more than 2 decades ago, oversees the menu while Mary works the front of the house. With a menu of items that don't top $20, this is the way San Francisco dining used to be—if you can't decide between the antipasti of lemon-cured tuna with veggies, pizza with clams and garlic, or bone-in rib-eye, you can order all of them and not break the bank. A selection of cured meats, pizzas, and antipasti make it easy to snack through a meal, but don't. The pastas—particularly the pork ragu—are fantastic and shouldn't be missed, and the entrees are great as well—especially when paired with an Italian wine. *Take note:* Parking in local lots around here costs more on game days (the Giants ballpark is nearby)—expect to pay around $15. Otherwise, it's very affordable.

564 Fourth St. (btw. Brannan and Bryant sts.). ✆ **415/777-5900.** www.zuppa-sf.com. Reservations recommended. Main courses $16–$19. AE, DC, DISC, MC, V. Lunch Mon–Fri 11:30am–2:30pm; dinner Mon–Thurs 5:30–10pm, Fri–Sat 5:30–11pm, Sun 5–9pm. Street parking or pay at nearby lots. Bus: 9X, 12, 30, 45, or 76.

INEXPENSIVE

AsiaSF ✿ ASIAN/CALIFORNIA   Part restaurant, part gender-illusionist musical revue, AsiaSF manages to be both entertaining and satisfying. As you're entertained by mostly Asian men dressed as women (who lip-sync show tunes when they're not waiting on tables), you can nibble on superb grilled shrimp and herb salad; baby back pork ribs with honey tamarind glaze, pickled carrots, and sweet-potato crisps; or filet mignon with Korean dipping sauce, miso eggplant, and fried potato stars. The full bar, *Wine Spectator* award–winning wine list, and sake list add to the festivities. Fortunately, the food and the atmosphere are as colorful as the staff, which means a night here is more than a meal—it's a very happening event.

201 Ninth St. (at Howard St.). ✆ 415/255-2742. www.asiasf.com. Reservations recommended. Main courses $9–$20. AE, DISC, MC, V (Mon–Wed $25 minimum). Sun–Thurs 6–10pm; Fri 6:45–10pm; Sat 5–10pm; cocktails and dancing until 2am on weekends. Bus: 9, 12, or 47. Streetcar: Civic Center on underground streetcar. BART: Civic Center.

Manora's ✿ THAI   Manora's cranks out some of the best Thai food in town and is well worth a jaunt to SoMa. But this is no relaxed affair: It's perpetually packed (unless you come early), and you'll be seated sardinelike at one of the cramped but well-appointed tables. During the dinner rush, the noise level can make conversation among larger parties almost impossible, but the food is so darned good, you'll probably prefer to turn toward your plate and stuff your face anyway. Start with a Thai iced tea or coffee and tangy soup or chicken satay, which comes with decadent peanut sauce. Follow these with any of the wonderful dinner dishes—which should be shared—and a side of rice. There are endless options, including a vast array of vegetarian plates. Every remarkably flavorful dish arrives seemingly seconds after you order it, which is great if you're hungry, a bummer if you were planning a long, leisurely dinner. *Tip:* Come before 7pm or after 9pm if you don't want a loud, rushed meal.

1600 Folsom St. (at 12th St.). ✆ 415/861-6224. www.manorathai.com. Reservations recommended for 4 or more. Main courses $7–$12. MC, V. Mon–Fri 11:30am–2:30pm; Mon–Sat 5:30–10:30pm; Sun 5–10pm. Bus: 9, 12, or 47.

5 Nob Hill/Russian Hill

For a map of restaurants in this section, see the "Dining Around Town" map on p. 116.

VERY EXPENSIVE

La Folie ✿✿✿ *Finds* FRENCH   I call this unintimidating, cozy, intimate French restaurant "the house of foie gras." Why? Because on my first visit, virtually every dish overflowed with the ultrarich delicacy. Subsequent visits proved that foie gras still reigns here, but more than that, it reconfirmed La Folie's long-standing reputation as one of the city's very best fine dining experiences—and without any stuffiness to boot. Chef/owner Roland Passot, who unlike many celebrity chefs is actually in the kitchen each night, offers melt-in-your-mouth starters such as seared foie gras with caramelized pineapple and star anise vanilla muscat broth. Generous main courses include rôti of quail and squab stuffed with wild mushrooms and wrapped in crispy potato strings; butter-poached lobster with glazed blood oranges and shiso, scallion, carrot, and toasted almond salad; and roast venison with vegetables, quince, and huckleberry sauce. The staff is extremely approachable and knowledgeable, and the new surroundings (think deep wood paneling, mirrors, long, rust-colored curtains, and gold-hued Venetian plaster) are now as elegant as the food. Best of all, the environment is relaxed, comfortable, and intimate. Finish with any of the delectable desserts. If you're not into the three-, four-, or five-course tasting menu, don't be deterred; the restaurant tells me they'll happily price out individual items.

2316 Polk St. (btw. Green and Union sts.). ✆ 415/776-5577. www.lafolie.com. Reservations recommended. 3-course tasting menu $65; 4-course tasting menu $75; 5-course chef's tasting menu $85; vegetarian tasting menu $65. AE, DC, DISC, MC, V. Mon–Sat 5:30–10:30pm. Valet parking $15. Bus: 19, 41, 45, 47, 49, or 76.

EXPENSIVE

House of Prime Rib ✿✿ STEAKHOUSE   Anyone who loves a huge slab of meat and old-school–style dining will feel right at home at this shrine to prime (rib). It's a fun and ever-packed affair within the men's clublike dining rooms (fireplaces included), where drinks are stiff, waiters are loose, and all the beef is roasted in rock salt, sliced tableside, and served with salad dramatically tossed tableside. This is followed by creamed spinach and either mashed potatoes or a baked potato and Yorkshire pudding, which accompany the entree. To placate the occasional non-meat eater, they offer a fish-of-the-day special.

1906 Van Ness Ave. (near Washington St.). (©) 415/885-4605. Reservations recommended. Complete dinners $28–$33. AE, MC, V. Mon–Thurs 5:30–10pm; Fri 5–10pm; Sat 4:30–10pm; Sun 4–10pm. Valet parking $7. Bus: 47 or 49.

MODERATE

Nob Hill Cafe *Finds* ITALIAN/PIZZA Considering the steep cost and formality of most Nob Hill restaurants, it's no wonder that residents don't mind waiting around for a table to open up at this cozy neighborhood bistro. This is the kind of place where you can come wearing jeans and sneakers, tuck into a large plate of linguine with clams and a glass of pinot, and leave fulfilled without blowing a wad of dough (pastas are in the humble $9–$12 range). The dining room is split into two small, simple rooms, with windows looking onto Taylor Street and bright local art on the walls. Service is friendly, and one of the owners is almost always on hand to make sure everyone's content. When the kitchen is "on," expect hearty Northern Italian comfort fare worth at least twice its price; even on off days, it's still a bargain. Start with a salad or the decadent polenta with pesto and parmigiano, and then fill up on the veal piccata, any of the pastas or pizzas, or petrale sole. *Tip:* Parking can be difficult in Nob Hill; fortunately, they offer valet parking a block away at the corner of Washington and Taylor streets.

1152 Taylor St. (btw. Sacramento and Clay sts.). (©) 415/776-6500. www.nobhillcafe.com. Reservations not accepted. Main courses $7–$16. DC, MC, V. Daily 11:30am–3pm and 5–10pm. Bus: 1.

Swan Oyster Depot *Finds* SEAFOOD Turning 96 years old in 2008, Swan Oyster Depot is a classic San Francisco dining experience you shouldn't miss. Opened in 1912, this tiny hole in the wall, run by the city's friendliest servers, is little more than a narrow fish market that decided to slap down some bar stools. There are only 20 or so stools here, jammed cheek-by-jowl along a long marble bar. Most patrons come for a quick cup of chowder or a plate of oysters on the half shell that arrive on crushed ice. The menu is limited to fresh crab, shrimp, oyster, clam cocktails, a few types of smoked fish, Maine lobster, and Boston-style clam chowder, all of which are exceedingly fresh. *Note:* Don't let the lunchtime line dissuade you—it moves fast.

1517 Polk St. (btw. California and Sacramento sts.). (©) 415/673-1101. Reservations not accepted. Seafood cocktails $7–$15; clams and oysters on the half-shell $7.95 per half-dozen. No credit cards. Mon–Sat 8am–5:30pm. Bus: 1, 19, 47, or 49.

6 Chinatown

For a map of restaurants in this section, see the "Dining near Chinatown & North Beach" map on p. 123.

INEXPENSIVE

Brandy Ho's Hunan Food CHINESE Fancy black-and-white granite tabletops and a large, open kitchen give you the first clue that the food at this casual restaurant is a cut above the usual Hunan fare. Take my advice and start immediately with fried dumplings (in sweet-and-sour sauce) or cold chicken salad and then move on to fish-ball soup with spinach, bamboo shoots, noodles, and other goodies. The best main

Dining near Chinatown & North Beach

Bix **20**	House of Nanking **17**	Pasta Pomodoro **1**
Bocadillos **21**	Hunan Home's **18**	R&G Lounge **22**
Brandy Ho's	Il Pollaio **3**	Sam Wo **23**
Hunan Food **16**	L'Osteria del Forno **5**	Sodini's Green Valley
Caffè Macaroni **19**	Mario's Bohemian	Restaurant **8**
Caffè Sport **6**	Cigar Store **2**	Steps of Rome Caffe **12**
Capp's Corner **4**	Maykadeh **10**	Stinking Rose The **13**
Gold Mountain **14**	Mo's Gourmet Burgers **11**	Tommaso's **15**
Golden Boy Pizza **7**	North Beach Pizza **9**	
Great Eastern **24**	Oriental Pearl **25**	

course is Three Delicacies, a combination of scallops, shrimp, and chicken with onion, bell pepper, and bamboo shoots, seasoned with ginger, garlic, and wine, and served with black-bean sauce. Most dishes are quite hot and spicy, but the kitchen will adjust the level to meet your specifications. A full bar includes Asian-food–friendly libations like plum wine and sake from 11:30am to 11pm. *Note:* There's a second location in the Castro at 4068 18th St. (at Castro St.; © **415/252-8000**).

217 Columbus Ave. (at Pacific Ave.). © **415/788-7527.** www.brandyhos.com. Reservations recommended. Main courses $8–$13. AE, DISC, MC, V. Sun–Thurs 11:30am–11pm; Fri–Sat 11:30am–midnight. Paid parking available at 170 Columbus Ave. Bus: 15 or 41.

Gold Mountain ⊛ *Finds* *Kids* CHINESE/DIM SUM   This gymnasium-size restaurant is a must-visit for anyone who's never experienced what it's like to dine with hundreds of Chinese-speaking patrons conversing loudly at enormous round tables among glittering chandeliers and gilded dragons while dozens of white-shirted waitstaff push around stainless steel carts filled with small plates of exotic-looking edible adventures (Was that sentence long enough for you?). Chicken feet, pork buns, shrimp dumplings, honey-walnut prawns (yum), the ubiquitous chicken-in-foil, and a myriad of other quasi-recognizable concoctions that range from appealing to revolting (never ate beef tripe, never will) whiz about at eye-level. I remember coming here as a little kid on late Saturday mornings and being infatuated with the entire cacophonous event. And even if you eat until you're ill, you'll never put down more than $20 worth of food, making Gold Mountain a real bargain as well, especially for large groups. Don't even bother with the regular menu: it's the dim sum service from 8am to 3pm on weekends and 10:30am to 3pm on weekdays that you want.

664 Broadway (btw. Grant Ave. and Stockton St.). © **415/296-7733.** Main courses $3–$9. AE, MC, V. Mon–Fri 10:30am–3pm and 5–9:30pm; Sat–Sun 8am–3pm and 5–9:30pm. Bus: 12, 15, 30, or 83.

Great Eastern ⊛ *Finds* CHINESE   If you like seafood and Chinese food and have an adventurous palate, you're going to love Great Eastern, which is well known among serious foodies for serving hard-to-find seafood pulled straight from the myriad of tanks that line the walls. Rock cod, steelhead, sea conch, sea bass, shrimp, frogs, softshell turtle, abalone—if it's even remotely aquatic and edible, it's on the menu at this popular Hong Kong–style dinner house that's mostly frequented by Chinese locals (so you know its good). The day's catch, sold by the pound, is listed on a board. Both upper- and lower-level dining rooms are stylish in a Chinatown sort of way, with shiny black and emerald furnishings. The dim sum is excellent here as well—some say it's even better than the venerable Yank Sing (p. 114)—so give it a try as well. *Tip:* Unless you can translate an authentic Hong Kong menu, order a set dinner (the crab version is fantastic) or point to another table and say, "I want that."

649 Jackson St. (btw. Kearny St. and Grant Ave.). © **415/986-2500.** Most main courses $8–$13. AE, MC, V. Daily 10am–1am. Bus: 15, 30, 41, or 45.

House of Nanking ⊛ CHINESE   This place would be strictly a tourist joint if it weren't for the die-hard fans who happily wait—sometimes up to an hour—for a coveted seat at this inconspicuous little restaurant serving Shanghai-style cuisine. Order the requisite pot stickers, green-onion-and-shrimp pancakes with peanut sauce, or any number of pork, rice, beef, seafood, chicken, or vegetable dishes from the menu, but I suggest you trust the waiter when he recommends a special. Even with an expansion that doubled the available space, seating is tight, so prepare to be bumped around a bit and don't expect perky or attentive service—it's all part of the Nanking experience.

919 Kearny St. (at Columbus Ave.). ℂ **415/421-1429**. Reservations accepted for groups of 8 or more. Main courses $6–$12. MC, V. Mon–Fri 11am–10pm; Sat–Sun noon–10pm. Bus: 9, 12, 15, or 30.

Hunan Home's ✯✯ CHINESE   One of Chinatown's best restaurants, Hunan Home's is a feast for the eyes—ubiquitous pink-and-white walls lined with big wall-to-wall mirrors that reflect armies of fish tanks and tacky chandeliers—as well as the palate. The rule of thumb here is not to put anything in your mouth until you're armed with a glass of water, because most every dish is *ooooweeeee* hot! Start with Home's excellent hot-and-sour soup (the acid test of every Chinese restaurant) or wonton soup (chock-full of shrimp, chicken, barbecued pork, squid, and vegetables), followed by the succulent bread appetizer, a platter of prawns with honeyed walnuts, and the scallops à la Hunan (sautéed along with snow peas, baby corn, celery, and mushrooms). Photographs of the more popular dishes are posted out front, though it's hard to tell which ones will singe your nose hairs.

622 Jackson St. (btw. Kearny St. and Grant Ave.). ℂ **415/982-2844**. Main courses $7.95–$12. AE, DC, DISC, MC, V. Daily 11:30am–2:30pm and 5–9:30pm. Bus: 15, 30, 41, or 45.

Oriental Pearl ✯ CHINESE/DIM SUM   Wherever the Chiu Chow region in southern China is, one thing's for sure: They're eating well there! Oriental Pearl specializes in regional Chiu Chow cuisine, a variation of Cantonese that's unlike anything you've ever seen or tasted, such as the house special chicken meatball—a delicate mix of shrimp, chicken, water chestnuts, and ham wrapped in a thin veneer of egg whites. Other recommended choices are the *pei pa* tofu with shrimp, seafood chow mein, and spicy braised prawns, all served by spiffy waiters wearing white shirts and black bow ties. The roomy, spotless restaurant is so obscurely located on the second floor of a business complex that it must rely almost exclusively on repeat and word-of-mouth clientele; but the word must be spreading, because it's usually packed. Unlike most other restaurants in Chinatown, dim sum is ordered via a menu, which isn't as fun but guarantees freshness (the steaming baskets of shrimp and scallop dumplings are excellent). Prices are slightly higher than average, but most definitely worth the extra money.

760 Clay St. (btw. Kearny St. and Grant Ave.). ℂ **415/433-1817**. Main courses $8.25–$9.50. AE, DC, DISC, MC, V. Daily 11am–3pm and 5–9:30pm. Bus: 15, 30, 41, or 45.

R&G Lounge ✯ CHINESE   It's tempting to take your chances and duck into any of the exotic restaurants in Chinatown, but if you want a sure thing, go directly to the three-story R&G Lounge. During lunch, all three floors are packed with hungry neighborhood workers who go straight for the $5.50 rice-plate specials. Even then, you can order from the dinner menu, which features legendary deep-fried salt-and-pepper crab (a little greasy for my taste); and wonderful chicken with black-bean sauce. A personal favorite is melt-in-your-mouth R&G Special Beef, which explodes with the tangy flavor of the accompanying sauce. I was less excited by the tired chicken salad, house specialty noodles, and bland spring rolls. But that was just fine since I saved room for generous and savory seafood in a clay pot and classic roast duck.

631 Kearny St. (at Clay St.). ℂ **415/982-7877**. www.rnglounge.com. Reservations recommended. Main courses $9.50–$30. AE, DC, DISC, MC, V. Daily 11am–9:30pm. Parking validated across the street at Portsmouth Sq. garage 24 hr. or Holiday Inn after 5pm. Bus: 1, 9AX, 9BX, or 15. Cable Car: California.

Sam Wo CHINESE   Very handy for late-nighters, Sam's is a total dive that's usually packed at one in the morning with party people trying to sober up (I've been pulling all-nighters here since I was a teen). The century-old restaurant's two pocket-size dining rooms are located on top of each other, on the second and third floors—take the stairs past the grimy first-floor kitchen. You'll probably have to share a table, but this place is for mingling almost as much as for eating (the bossy waitresses are pure comedy). The house specialty is *jook,* known as *congee* in its native Hong Kong—a thick rice gruel flavored with fish, shrimp, chicken, beef, or pork; the best is Sampan, made with rice and seafood. Try sweet-and-sour pork rice, wonton soup with duck, or a roast-pork/rice-noodle roll. More traditional fried noodles and rice plates are available, too, but I always end up ordering the same thing: tomato beef with noodles and house special chow mein.

813 Washington St. (by Grant Ave.). (℗ 415/982-0596. Reservations not accepted. Main courses $3.50–$6. No credit cards. Mon–Sat 11am–3am; Sun 11am–9:30pm in summer and on holidays. Bus: 9x, 15, 30, or 45.

7 North Beach/Telegraph Hill

For a map of restaurants in this section, see the "Dining near Chinatown & North Beach" map on p. 123.

EXPENSIVE

Bix 🏰🏰 *Moments* AMERICAN/CALIFORNIA   The martini lifestyle may now be *en vogue,* but it was never out of style in this glamorous retro '30s-era supper club. Bix is utterly stylish, with curving mahogany paneling, giant silver pillars, and dramatic lighting, all of which sets the stage for live music and plenty of hobnobbing. Though the sleek setting has overshadowed the food in the past, the legions of diners entranced by the Bix experience don't seem to care—and it seems as of late Bix is "on" again. Chicken hash has been a menu favorite for the past 19 years, but newer luxury comfort-food dishes—such as caviar service, marrowbones with toast and shallot confit, steak tartare, and pan-roasted seasonal fish dishes—are developing their own fan clubs. ***Bargain tip:*** At lunch a three-course prix-fixe menu goes for $25.

56 Gold St. (btw. Sansome and Montgomery sts.). (℗ 415/433-6300. www.bixrestaurant.com. Reservations recommended. Main courses $12–$15 lunch, $16–$32 dinner. AE, DC, DISC, MC, V. Mon–Thurs 4:30–11pm; Fri 11:30am–2pm and 5:30pm–midnight; Sat 5:30pm–midnight; Sun 6–10pm. Valet parking $10. Bus: 15, 30, 41, or 45.

MODERATE

Maykadeh PERSIAN/MIDDLE EASTERN   If you're looking to add a little exotic adventure to your North Beach dinner plans, this is the place to go. Surrounded by a sea of Italian bistros, Maykadeh is one of San Francisco's best and most elegant Persian restaurants. The Middle East may no longer be the culinary capital of the world, but at Maykadeh you can still sample the exotic flavors that characterize Persian cuisine. Of the dozen or so appetizers, some of the best are eggplant with mint garlic sauce; stuffed grape leaves; and lamb tongue with lime juice, sour cream, and saffron (c'mon, live a little). About eight mesquite-grilled items are on the menu, including filet of lamb marinated in lime, homemade yogurt, saffron, and onions. House specialties include half a dozen vegetarian dishes, among them eggplant braised with saffron, fresh tomato, and dried lime.

470 Green St. (btw. Kearny St. and Grant Ave.). (℗ 415/362-8286. www.maykadehrestaurant.com. Reservations recommended. Main courses $13–$27. MC, V. Mon–Thurs 11:45am–10:30pm; Fri–Sat 11:45am–11pm; Sun 11:45am–10pm. Valet parking $7 lunch, $8 dinner. Bus: 15, 30, or 41.

Piperade 🏰🏰 BASQUE   Chef Gerald Hirigoyen takes diners on a Basque adventure in this charming, small restaurant. Surrounded by a low wood-beam–lined ceiling, oak floors, and soft sconce lighting, it's a casual affair where diners indulge in small and large plates of Hirigoyen's superbly flavorful West Coast Basque cuisine. Your edible odyssey starts with small plates—or plates to be shared—like my personal favorites: piquillo peppers stuffed with goat cheese; and a bright and simple salad of garbanzo beans with calamari, chorizo, and piquillo peppers. Share entrees, too. Indulge in New York steak with braised shallots and french fries or sop up every drop of the sweet and savory red-pepper sauce with the braised seafood and shellfish stew. Save room for orange blossom beignets: Light and airy with a delicate and moist web of dough within and a kiss of orange essence, the beignet is dessert at its finest. There's a communal table for drop-in diners and front patio seating during warmer weather.

1015 Battery St. (at Green St.). © **415/391-2555**. www.piperade.com. Reservations recommended. Main courses $17–$24. AE, DC, DISC, MC, V. Mon–Fri 11:30am–3pm and 5:30–10:30pm; Sat 5:30–10:30pm; closed Sun. Bus: 10, 12, 30, or 82x.

The Stinking Rose ITALIAN   Garlic is the "flower" from which this restaurant gets its name. From soup to ice cream, the supposedly healthful herb is a star ingredient in almost every dish. ("We season our garlic with food," exclaims the menu.) From a gourmet point of view, the Stinking Rose is unremarkable. Pizzas, pastas, and meats smothered in simple, overpowering sauces are tasty, but they're memorable only for their singular garlicky intensity. That said, this is a fun place; the restaurant's lively atmosphere and odoriferous aroma combine for good entertainment. The best dishes include iron-skillet–roasted mussels, shrimp, and crab with garlic sauce; smoked mozzarella, garlic, and tomato pizza; salt-roasted tiger prawns with garlic parsley glaze; and 40-clove garlic chicken (served with garlic mashed potatoes, of course). *Note:* For those who are not garlic-inclined, they offer garlic-free "Vampire Fare."

325 Columbus Ave. (btw. Vallejo and Broadway). © **415/781-7673**. www.thestinkingrose.com. Reservations recommended. Main courses $13–$30. AE, DC, DISC, MC, V. Daily 11am–11pm. Bus: 15, 30, 41, or 45.

INEXPENSIVE

Caffè Macaroni ✦ *Finds* ITALIAN   You wouldn't know it from the looks (or name) of it, but this tiny, funky restaurant on busy Columbus Avenue is one of the best southern Italian restaurants in the city. It looks as though it can hold only two customers at a time, and if you don't duck your head when entering the upstairs dining room, you might as well ask for one lump or two. Fortunately, the kitchen also packs a wallop, dishing out a large variety of antipasti and excellent pastas. The spinach-and-cheese ravioli with wild-mushroom sauce and the gnocchi are outstanding. The owners and staff are always vivacious and friendly, and young ladies in particular will enjoy the attentions of the charming Italian men manning the counter. If you're still pondering whether you should eat here, consider that most entrees are under $15.

124 Columbus Ave. (at Jackson St.). © **415/956-9737**. www.caffemacaroni.com. Reservations accepted. Main courses $9–$15. AE, MC, V. Mon–Sat 11am–2:30pm and 5:30–11pm; Sun noon–10pm. Bus: 15 or 41.

Caffè Sport ✦ ITALIAN   People either love or hate this stodgy, garlic-smelling Sicilian eatery. Every square inch is cluttered with hanging hams, fishnets, decorative plates, dolls, mirrors, and over 2 decades' worth of dust, Caffè Sport was once a culinary landmark. Now it's better known for its surly staff and eclectic ambience than for its good—though cream- and butter-heavy—food. Still, the fare is served up with hearty portions of tongue-in-cheek attitude along with huge garlic-laden pasta dishes. Lunch is tame in comparison to dinner, when the Sport is mobbed and lively, and strangers might be packed together family style. Disregard the menu and just accept the waiter's "suggestions." Whatever arrives—whether calamari, mussels, or shrimp in tomato-garlic sauce, or pasta in pesto sauce—it's bound to be *bene*. Bring a huge appetite and plenty of cash (they don't take credit cards), but above all, don't be late if you have a reservation.

574 Green St. (btw. Grant and Columbus aves.). © **415/981-1251.** Reservations recommended. Main courses $15–$30. No credit cards. Tues–Sat noon–2pm and 5–10:30pm. Bus: 15, 30, 41, or 45.

Capp's Corner ★ ⍰*Value* ITALIAN

Capp's is a place of givens: It's a given that high-spirited regulars are hunched over the bar and that you'll be served huge portions of straightforward Italian fare at low prices in a raucous atmosphere that prevails until closing. The waitresses are usually brusque and bossy, but always with a wink. Long tables are set up for family-style dining: bread, soup, salad, and choice of around 20 classic main dishes (herb-roasted leg of lamb, spaghetti with meatballs, *osso buco* with polenta, fettuccine with prawns and white-wine sauce)—all for $15 or $17 or so per person, around $10 for kids. You might have to wait awhile for a table, but if you want fun and authentic old-school dining without pomp or huge prices, you'll find the wait worthwhile.

1600 Powell St. (at Green St.). © **415/989-2589.** www.cappscorner.com. Reservations accepted. Complete dinners $15–$17. AE, DC, MC, V. Daily 11:30am–2:30pm; Mon–Fri 4:30–10:30pm; Sat–Sun 4–11pm. Bus: 15, 30, or 41.

Golden Boy Pizza ★ ⍰*Value* ITALIAN/PIZZA

Pass by Golden Boy when the bars are hopping in North Beach and you'll find a crowd of inebriated sots savoring steamy slices of wondrously gooey pizza. But you don't have to be on a red wine buzz to enjoy the big, doughy squares of Italian-style pizzas, each enticingly placed in the front windows (the aroma alone is deadly). Locals have flocked here for years to fill up on one of the cheapest and cheesiest meals in town. Expect to take your feast to go on busy nights, as there are only a few bar seats inside.

542 Green St. (btw. Stockton St. and Grant Ave.). © **415/982-9738.** Pizza slice $2.50–$3.50. No credit cards. Sun–Thurs 11:30am–11pm; Fri–Sat 11:30am–2am. Bus: 15, 30, 45, 39, or 41.

Il Pollaio ★ ⍰*Value* ITALIAN/ARGENTINE

Simple, affordable, and consistently good is the winning combination at Il Pollaio. When I used to live in the neighborhood I ate here at least once a week and I still can't make chicken this good. Seat yourself in the tiny, unfussy room, order, and wait expectantly for the fresh-from-the-grill lemon-infused chicken, which is so moist it practically falls off the bone. Each meal comes with a choice of salad or fries. If you're not in the mood for chicken, you can opt for rabbit, lamb, pork chop, or Italian sausage. On a sunny day, get your goods to-go and picnic across the street at Washington Square.

555 Columbus Ave. (btw. Green and Union sts.). © **415/362-7727.** Reservations not accepted. Main courses $8–$15. DISC, MC, V. Mon–Sat 11:30am–9pm. Bus: 15, 30, 39, 41, or 45. Cable car: Powell–Mason line.

L'Osteria del Forno ★★ ITALIAN

L'Osteria del Forno might be only slightly larger than a walk-in closet, but it's one of the top three authentic Italian restaurants in North Beach. Peer in the window facing Columbus Avenue, and you'll probably see two Italian women with their hair up, sweating from the heat of the oven, which cranks out the best focaccia (and focaccia sandwiches) in the city. There's no pomp or circumstance here: Locals come strictly to eat. The menu features a variety of superb pizzas, salads, soups, and fresh pastas, plus a good selection of daily specials (pray for the roast pork braised in milk), which includes a roast of the day, pasta, and ravioli.

Small baskets of warm focaccia keep you going until the arrival of the entrees, which should always be accompanied by a glass of Italian red. Good news for folks on the go: You can get pizza by the slice. Note that it's cash-only here.

519 Columbus Ave. (btw. Green and Union sts.). © 415/982-1124. www.losteriadelforno.com. Reservations not accepted. Sandwiches $6–$7; pizzas $10–$18; main courses $6–$14. No credit cards. Sun–Mon and Wed–Thurs 11:30am–10pm; Fri–Sat 11:30am–10:30pm. Bus: 15, 30, 41, or 45.

Mario's Bohemian Cigar Store 🎯 *Finds* ITALIAN   Across the street from Washington Square is one of North Beach's most venerable neighborhood hangouts. The century-old corner cafe—small, well worn, and perpetually busy—is one of the oldest and best original cappuccino cafes in United States. I stop by at least once a month for a meatball or eggplant focaccia sandwich and a slice of Mario's house-made ricotta cheesecake, and then recharge with a cappuccino as I watch the world stroll by the picture windows. And no, they don't sell cigars.

566 Columbus Ave. (at Union St.). © 415/362-0536. Sandwiches $7.75–$8.50. MC, V. Mon–Sat 10am–midnight; Sun 10am–11pm. Bus: 15, 30, 41, or 45.

Mo's Gourmet Burgers 🎯🎯 *Kids* AMERICAN   This simple diner offers a straightforward but winning combination: big, thick, grilled patties of fresh-ground, best-quality, center-cut chuck; fresh french fries; and choice of cabbage slaw, sautéed garlic mushrooms, or chili. *Voilà!* You've got the city's burger of choice (Zuni Café's is a contender, but at almost twice the price—p. 144). The other food—spicy chicken sandwiches; steak with veggies, garlic bread, and potatoes; and token veggie dishes—is also up to snuff, but that messy, memorable burger is what keeps the carnivores captivated (the sinisterly sweet shakes are fantastic, too). Bargain-diners will appreciate prices, with burgers ranging from $5.95 for a classic to $7.95 for an "Alpine" burger with Gruyère cheese and sautéed mushrooms. Entrees start at $9 for meatloaf with mashed potatoes, garlic bread, and a vegetable, and top out at $17 for New York steak. The classic breakfast menu is also a bargain. A second location at SoMa's Yerba Buena Gardens, 772 Folsom St., between Third and Fourth streets (© 415/957-3779), is open Monday from 10am to 5pm, Tuesday through Friday from 10am to 8pm, Saturday from 9am to 8pm, and Sunday from 9am to 5pm. It features breakfast and burgers.

1322 Grant Ave. (btw. Vallejo and Green sts.). © 415/788-3779. Main courses $5.95–$17. MC, V. Mon–Thurs 11:30am–10:30pm; Fri 11:30am–11:30pm; Sat 9am–11:30pm; Sun 9am–10:30pm. Bus: 9X, 15, 30, 39, 41, or 45.

North Beach Pizza 🎯 *Kids* ITALIAN/PIZZA   Whenever I order a North Beach pizza, I'm always disappointed by the measly amount of toppings that they give you. Then I eat the entire damn thing in one sitting. There's something about that uniquely gooey whole-milk mozzarella and hand-spun dough with thick, chewy edges that's so addictive it's been the most awarded and widely beloved pizza in the city for more than 2 decades. You *can* get a better pizza in the city—Pauline's and Little Star has them beat—but not in North Beach, not via free delivery throughout the city, and not at 2:30am on Saturday when you're drunk, stoned, and starving. Either create your own pizza from their list of 20 fresh ingredients (the sausage with black olives is the *bomb*), or choose from the house's 10 specialties such as the San Francisco Special—clams, garlic, cheese, and one brutal case of halitosis. There are numerous satellite NBPs throughout the city offering fast, free delivery until the wee hours.

1499 Grant St. (at Union St.). © 415/433-2444. www.northbeachpizza.com. Main courses $9–$21. AE, DC, DISC, MC, V. Sun–Thurs 9am–1am; Fri–Sat 9am–3am. Cable car: Powell-Mason line. Bus: 15, 30, 41, or 45.

Pasta Pomodoro ★★ *Kids* *Value* ITALIAN   If you're looking for a good, cheap meal in North Beach—or anywhere else in town, for that matter—this San Francisco chain can't be beat. There can be a short wait for a table, but after you're seated, you'll be surprised at how promptly you're served. Every dish is fresh and sizable and, best of all, costs a third of what you'd pay elsewhere. Winners include spaghetti *frutti di mare* made with calamari, mussels, scallops, tomato, garlic, and wine; and smoked rigatoni, with roast chicken, sun-dried tomatoes, cream, mushrooms, and Parmesan—both under $13. When I don't feel like cooking, I often stop here for angel-hair pasta with tomato and basil and a decadent spinach salad with peppered walnuts and bleu cheese. The tiramisu is huge, delicious, and cheap, too.

655 Union St. (at Columbus Ave.). ✆ **415/399-0300**. www.pastapomodoro.com. Reservations not accepted. Main courses $6–$12. AE, MC, V. Sun–Thurs 11am–10:30pm; Fri–Sat 11am–11pm. Bus: 15, 30, 41, or 45. Cable car: Powell–Mason line. There are 7 other locations, including 2304 Market St., at 16th St. (✆ **415/558-8123**); 3611 California St., btw. Spruce St. and Parker Ave. (✆ **415/831-0900**); and 816 Irving St., btw. Ninth and 10th sts. (✆ **415/566-0900**).

San Francisco Art Institute Café *Finds* AMERICAN   Never in a million years would you stumble upon the Art Institute Café by accident. One of the best-kept secrets in San Francisco, this cafe offers fresh, affordable cafe standards for in-the-know residents and visitors as well as Art Institute students: a wide array of hearty breakfast dishes, fresh salads, sandwiches on homemade bread, daily ethnically inspired specials, and anything with caffeine in it—all priced at or under $7. The view, which extends from Alcatraz Island to Coit Tower and beyond, is so phenomenal that the exterior served as the outside of Sigourney Weaver's chic apartment in the movie *Copycat.* The cafe has an open kitchen, sleek aluminum tables, and weekly rotating student art shows. A large courtyard with cement tables (and the same Hollywood view) is the perfect spot for an alfresco lunch high above the tourist fray.

800 Chestnut St. (btw. Jones and Leavenworth sts.). ✆ **415/749-4567**. Main courses $4–$6. No credit cards. Fall–spring Mon–Thurs 8am–5pm, Fri 8am–4pm; summer Mon–Fri 9am–2pm. Closed Sat–Sun. Hours dependent on school schedule; please call to confirm. Bus: 30 or 49. Cable car: Powell–Hyde or Powell–Mason line.

Sodini's Green Valley Restaurant ★ ITALIAN   Sodini's is everything you would expect from a classic Italian restaurant in North Beach—a family-owned and -operated business run by a friendly, vivacious staff that serves hearty Italian classics on tables topped with wax-encrusted chianti bottle candles while the Chairman of the Board croons love songs in the background. There's usually a wait for a table; fortunately, the bar is a great place to hang out, shoot the breeze with the friendly bartender (most likely one of the owners), and get a little North Beach history lesson. The clientele is a mix of locals and tourists, all getting hungrier by the minute as the aroma of garlic and fresh basil wafts from the kitchen. The large wood-fired pizzas are very good and worth moving that belt one more notch, but their best dish is the light and tender gnocchi. Regardless of what you order, you won't leave hungry or unhappy.

510 Green St. (at Grant St.). ✆ **415/291-0499**. Reservations not accepted. Main courses $10–$23. MC, V. Daily 5–10pm. Cable car: Powell-Mason line. Bus: 15, 30, 41, or 45.

Steps of Rome Caffe ★ ITALIAN   All the vibrancy and flavor of Italy can be found at this affordable and casual North Beach eatery. It's known as much as a meeting point for the young and social as it is for its heaping plates of fresh pasta, so if you head here, expect a lively time. Start with tasty bruschetta, carpaccio, or Caesar or caprese salad, but save room for panini (sandwiches of pressed toasted bread with killer fillings like salmon, tomatoes, and citrus sauce or prosciutto and mozzarella), classic pastas—from Alfredo to pomodoro to crab ravioli—pizzas, or entrees ranging from grilled chicken breast over salad to filet mignon. Should you want the taste without the bustle, the more mild and formal Trattoria is next door. Also, keep this spot in mind for late-night hunger pangs; they serve until 2am weekdays, 3am weekends.

348 Columbus Ave. (btw. Broadway and Vallejo St.). ✆ 415/397-0435. www.stepsofrome.com. Reservations recommended. Main courses $6.95–$20. No credit cards. Sun–Thurs 10am–2am; Fri–Sat 10am–3am. Bus: 15 or 41.

Tommaso's ✦ *Kids* ITALIAN   From the street, Tommaso's looks wholly unappealing—a drab, windowless brown facade sandwiched between sex shops. Then why are people always waiting in line to get in? Because everyone knows that Tommaso's, which opened in 1935, bakes one of San Francisco's best traditional-style pizzas. The center of attention in the downstairs dining room is the chef, who continuously tosses huge hunks of garlic and mozzarella onto pizzas before sliding them into the oak-burning brick oven. Nineteen different toppings make pizza the dish of choice, even though Italian classics such as veal Marsala, chicken cacciatore, superb lasagna, and wonderful calzones are also available. Tommaso's also offers half-bottles of house wines, homemade manicotti, and good Italian coffee. If you can overlook the seedy surroundings, this fun, boisterous restaurant is a great place to take the family.

1042 Kearny St. (at Broadway). ✆ 415/398-9696. www.tommasosnorthbeach.com. Reservations not accepted. Pasta and pizza $14–$24; main courses $11–$18. AE, DC, DISC, MC, V. Tues–Sat 5–10:30pm; Sun 4–9:30pm. Closed Dec 15–Jan 15. Bus: 15 or 41.

8 Fisherman's Wharf

For a map of restaurants in this section, see the "Dining Around Town" map on p. 116.

VERY EXPENSIVE

Forbes Island ✦ *Moments* FRENCH   Been there and done that in every San Francisco dining room? Then it's time for Forbes Island, a wonderfully ridiculous floating restaurant disguised as an island (complete with lighthouse and real 40-ft. palm trees) and unknown to even most locals. The idea's kitschy, but the execution's actually quite wonderful. Here's how it works: Arrive at the dock next to Pier 39, call the restaurant via the courtesy phone, climb aboard its pontoon boat that takes you on a 4-minute journey to the "island" located 75 feet from the city's famed sea lions, and descend into the island's bowels to find a surprisingly classy, Tudor-like wood-paneled dining room. Warmed by a fireplace and amused by fish swimming past the portholes (yes, the dining room is a wee bit underwater), guests dine on surprisingly well-prepared classic French food such as decadent ragout of wild mushrooms, toasted brioche, and soft goat cheese or roasted half-rack of lamb with herbed flageolet beans, minted edamame, and natural lamb reduction *jus*. The added "Sea Lion" room boasts the closest view you'll ever get of the creatures. ***But be warned:*** The menu is very limited, the wine list features basic big-name producers without listing the vintage, and the "island" does gently rock. (Landlubbers need not apply or should take Dramamine a couple of hours beforehand.) ***One annoyance:*** the mandatory $3 shuttle fee since the only other way to get there is to swim.

Water shuttle is just left of Pier 39. ✆ 415/951-4900. www.forbesisland.com. Reservations recommended. Main courses $24–$34. AE, DC, MC, V. Wed–Sun arrive 5–10pm. Validated parking at Pier 39 garage, $8 for up to 6 hr.

Restaurant Gary Danko ✿✿✿ FRENCH   James Beard Award–winning chef Gary Danko presides over my top pick for fine dining. Eschewing the white-glove formality of yesteryear's fine dining, Danko offers impeccable cuisine and perfectly orchestrated service in an unstuffy environment of wooden paneling and shutters and well-spaced tables (not to mention spa-style bathrooms). The three- to five-course fixed-price seasonal menu is freestyle, so whether you want a sampling of appetizers or a flight of meat courses, you need only ask. I am a devoted fan of his trademark buttery-smooth glazed oysters with lettuce cream, salsify, and Osetra caviar; seared foie gras, which may be accompanied by peaches, caramelized onions, and *verjus* (a classic French sauce); horseradish-crusted salmon medallions with dilled cucumbers; and adventurous Moroccan spiced squab with *chermoula* (a Moroccan sauce made with cilantro) and orange-cumin carrots. Truthfully, I've never had a dish here that wasn't wonderful. And wine? The list is stellar, albeit expensive. If after dinner you have the will to pass on the glorious cheese cart or flambéed dessert of the day, a plate of petit fours reminds you that Gary Danko is one sweet and memorable meal. **Tip:** If you can't get a reservation and are set on dining here, slip in and grab a seat at the 10-stool first-come, first-served bar where you can also order a la carte.

800 North Point St. (at Hyde St.). ✆ 415/749-2060. www.garydanko.com. Reservations required except at walk-in bar. 3- to 5-course fixed-price menu $61–$89. AE, DC, DISC, MC, V. Daily 5:30–10pm; bar open 5pm. Valet parking $10. Bus: 10. Streetcar: F. Cable car: Hyde.

Scoma's ✿ SEAFOOD   A throwback to the dining of yesteryear, Scoma's eschews trendier trout preparations and fancy digs for good old-fashioned seafood served in huge portions amid a very casual windowed waterfront setting. Gourmands should skip this one. But if your idea of heaven is straightforward seafood classics—fried calamari, raw oysters, pesto pasta with rock shrimp, crab cioppino, lobster thermidor—served with a generous portion of old-time hospitality, then Scoma's is as good as it gets. Unfortunately, a taste of tradition will cost you big time. Prices are as steep as those at some of the finest restaurants in town. Personally, I'd rather splurge at Gary Danko, but many of my out-of-town guests insist we meet at Scoma's, which is fine by me since it's a change of pace from today's chic spots, and the parking's free.

Pier 47 and Al Scoma Way (btw. Jefferson and Jones sts.). ✆ 800/644-5852 or 415/771-4383. www.scomas.com. Reservations not accepted. Most main courses $18–$35. AE, DC, DISC, MC, V. Sun–Thurs 11:30am–10pm; Fri–Sat 11:30am–10:30pm; bar opens 30 min. prior to lunch daily. Free valet parking. Bus: 10 or 47. Streetcar: F.

EXPENSIVE

Alioto's SEAFOOD   One of San Francisco's oldest restaurants, run by one of the city's most prominent families, the Aliotos, this Fisherman's Wharf landmark has a long-standing reputation for great cioppino. The curbside crab stand, Café 8, and the outdoor crab market are great for quick, inexpensive doses of San Francisco's finest. For more formal surroundings, continue up the stairs to the multilevel, harbor-view dining room. Don't mess around with the menu: If you're here, you're after Dungeness crab. Cracked, caked, stuffed, or stewed, it's impossible to get your fill, so bring plenty of money—particularly if you intend to order from Alioto's prodigious (and pricey) wine list. If you don't care for cracked crab, try the griddle-fried sand dabs or the rex sole served with tartar sauce.

Fisherman's Wharf (at Taylor St.). ✆ 415/673-0183. www.aliotos.com. Reservations recommended. Main courses $15–$30 lunch; most main courses $20–$35 dinner. AE, DC, DISC, MC, V. Daily 11am–11pm. Bus: 10, 15, 39, or 47. Streetcar: F. Cable car: Powell–Hyde line.

Ana Mandara ⓖ VIETNAMESE   Yes, Don Johnson is part owner. But more important, this Fisherman's Wharf favorite serves fine Vietnamese food in an outstandingly beautiful setting. Amid a shuttered room with mood lighting, palm trees, and Vietnamese-inspired decor, diners (mostly tourists) splurge on crispy rolls, lobster ravioli with mango and coconut sauce, and wok-charred tournedos of beef tenderloin with sweet onions and peppercress. There is no more expensive Vietnamese dining room in town, but, along with the enjoyable fare, diners pay for the atmosphere, which, if they're in the neighborhood and want something more exotic than the standby seafood dinner, is worth the price.

891 Beach St. (at Polk St.). ⓒ 415/771-6800. www.anamandara.com. Reservations recommended. Main courses $19–$32. AE, DC, DISC, MC, V. Mon–Fri 11:30am–2pm; Sun–Thurs 5:30–9:30pm; Fri–Sat 5:30–10:30pm; bar until 1am. Valet parking Tues–Sun $9. Bus: 19, 30, or 45.

MODERATE

Cafe Pescatore ⓖ ITALIAN   This cozy trattoria is one of the better bets in Fisherman's Wharf. Two walls of sliding glass doors offer pseudo-sidewalk seating when the weather's warm, although heavy vehicular traffic can detract from the alfresco experience. All the classics are well represented here: crisp Caesar salad; fried calamari; bruschetta; cioppino; pastas; chicken Marsala; and veal saltimbocca (sautéed veal scaloppini) with whipped baby potatoes, spinach, prosciutto and lemon-caper butter sauce. The consensus is to order anything that's cooked in the open kitchen's wood-fired oven, such as pizza (Margherita), roasts (sea bass with pine-nut crust, or Atlantic salmon), or panini (lunch only; grilled chicken or grilled veggies). They serve a darn good breakfast, too.

2455 Mason St. (at North Point St., adjoining the Tuscan Inn). ⓒ 415/561-1111. www.cafepescatore.com. Reservations recommended. Main courses $6.50–$12 breakfast, $9–$22 lunch and dinner. AE, DC, DISC, MC, V. Daily 7am–10pm. Bus: 15, 39, or 42. Streetcar: F. Cable car: Powell–Mason line.

Fog City Diner ⓖ AMERICAN   The Fog City Diner gets a lot of mixed reviews among locals for service and food, but I've always had a satisfying experience dining here. The restaurant looks like a genuine American metallic diner—but only from the outside. Inside, dark polished woods, inspired lighting, and a well-stocked raw bar tell you this is no hash-slinger. Here dressed-up diner dishes include juicy gourmet burgers with house-made pickles, huge salads, "warm breads," soups, sandwiches, cioppino, macaroni and Gouda cheese, and pork chops. Fancier fish and meat meals include grilled catches of the day and thick-cut steaks. Light eaters can make a meal out of the long list of "small plates," which include crab cakes and quesadillas with asparagus and leek. They've recently opened for weekend brunch as well. The food is fine, but if your heart is set on coming here, do so at lunch or early evening cocktails and appetizers—you'll be better off elsewhere if you want a special dinner.

1300 Battery St. (at the Embarcadero.). ⓒ 415/982-2000. www.fogcitydiner.com. Reservations recommended. Main courses $11–$22. DC, DISC, MC, V. Mon–Thurs 11am–10pm; Fri 11am–11pm; Sat 10:30am–11pm; Sun 10:30am–10pm. Bus: 42.

Lou's Pier 47 STEAK/SEAFOOD/CAJUN   This popular restaurant and blues club is one of the few establishments on Fisherman's Wharf that locals will admit they've been to at least once. The bottom floor consists of a bar and bistro-style dining room, while the upstairs hosts blues bands every night of the week, with the occasional Motown, country, and R&B act thrown in for variety. Lunch and dinner items range from a variety of Cajun classics such as gumbo ya ya, jambalaya, and shrimp Creole to baby back ribs, steamed Dungeness crab, blackened swordfish, and New York steak. There's a lengthy starters menu if you just want to nosh on a Jamaica jerk salad, Louisiana crawfish bowl, or "peel 'em and eat" shrimp. *Budget tip:* The Saturday blues show from noon to 3pm is free; otherwise, the upstairs club cover is $3 to $10.

300 Jefferson St. (near Pier 47). 🄲 **415/771-5687.** www.louspier47.com. Main courses $11–$18. AE, DC, MC, V. Daily 11am–11pm (club remains open until 2am). Cable car: Powell-Hyde line. Bus: 32.

INEXPENSIVE

Boudin at the Wharf DELI/AMERICAN This industrial-chic Fisherman's Wharf shrine to the city's famous tangy French-style bread is impossible to miss. Even if you're not hungry, drop in to see bakers at work making 3,000 loaves daily or take the tour and learn about the city sourdough bread's history (Boudin is the city's oldest continually operating business). Good, strong coffee is served at **Peet's Coffee** (another Bay Area great), and at **Bakers Hall** you'll find picnic possibilities such as handcrafted cheeses, fruit spreads, and chocolates, as well as a wall map highlighting the town's best places to spread a blanket and feast. There's also a casual **self-serve cafe** serving sandwiches, clam chowder bowls, salads, and pastries, and the more formal **Bistro Boudin** restaurant, which offers Alcatraz views with its Dungeness crab Louis, pizza, crab cakes, and burgers on sourdough buns.

160 Jefferson St., near Pier 43½. 🄲 **415/928-1849.** www.boudinbakery.com. Reservations recommended at bistro. Main courses cafe $6–$10, bistro $11–$33. AE, DC, DISC, MC, V. Cafe daily 8am–10pm; bistro Mon–Fri noon–10pm; Sat 11:30am–10pm; Sun 11:30am–9pm. Bus: 10, 15, or 47. Streetcar: F.

Hard Rock Cafe *Kids* AMERICAN I hate to plug chains, and this loud, rock-nostalgia-laden place would be no exception if it didn't serve a fine burger and overall decent heaping plates of food at such moderate prices. For many, the real draw—more than 20 years past the time when it was hip to wear the restaurant's logo—is the merchandise shop, but a shopper's gotta eat. The menu offers burgers, fajitas, baby back ribs, grilled fish, chicken, salads, and sandwiches, the munching of which tend to be muffled by blaring music. Although nothing unique to San Francisco, the Hard Rock is a fine place to bring the kids and grab a bite.

Pier 39. 🄲 **415/956-2013.** www.hardrock.com. Reservations accepted for groups of 25 or more. Main courses $8–$23. AE, DC, DISC, MC, V. Sun–Thurs 11am–11pm; Fri–Sat 11am–midnight. Validated parking for 1 hr. during lunch and 2 hr. after 6pm at Pier 39 lot. Bus: 10, 15, or 47. Streetcar: F.

9 The Marina/Pacific Heights/Cow Hollow

For a map of restaurants in this section, see the "Dining Around Town" map on p. 116.

VERY EXPENSIVE

Harris' *Finds* STEAKHOUSE Every big city has a great steak restaurant, and in San Francisco it's Harris'—a comfortably elegant establishment where the seriously handsome and atmospheric wood-paneled dining room has high-backed booths, banquettes, high ceilings, hunting murals, stately waiters, a convivial bar scene with live jazz Thursday through Saturday, and even a meat counter for the carnivore on the go. Here, the point, of course, is steak, which can be seen hanging in a glass-windowed aging room off Pacific Avenue. The cuts are thick—New York–style or T-bone—and are served with a baked potato and seasonal vegetables. You'll also find classic French onion soup, spinach and Caesar salads, and sides of delicious creamed spinach, sautéed shiitake mushrooms, or caramelized onions. Harris' also offers lamb chops, fresh fish, lobster, and occasionally venison, buffalo, and other seasonal game. Desserts, such as a sculptural beehive-like baked Alaska, are surprisingly good. If you're debating between this place and House of Prime Rib, consider that aside from specializing in aged meats, this place is more "upscale," while HOPR features prime rib and a classic old-school vibe.

2100 Van Ness Ave. (at Pacific Ave.). © 415/673-1888. www.harrisrestaurant.com. Reservations recommended. Most main courses $24–$42. AE, DC, DISC, MC, V. Mon–Thurs 5:30–9:30pm; Fri 5:30–10pm; Sat 5–10pm; Sun 5–9:30pm. Valet parking $10. Bus: 12, 47, or 49.

Spruce ✿ CONTEMPORARY AMERICAN   If you haven't heard of San Francisco's Pacific Heights neighborhood, it's where most of the city's old money lives, and now the ladies-who-lunch have a new place to hang their cloches: Spruce. Housed in a beautifully restored 1930s-era auto barn, Spruce consists of a restaurant, cafe, bar, and lounge under a single roof, making it both a destination restaurant and neighborhood hangout. As you enter there's a library nook on one side filled with newspapers, cookbooks, and so on, and a cafe on the other side offering gourmet takeaway items. Further inside is an elegant bar to the right and 70-seat restaurant to left, both topped with a vast cathedral ceiling highlighted by a glass-and-steel skylight. With mohair couches, faux-ostrich chairs, and a black-and-chocolate decor it's all quite visually appealing, but, alas, the cuisine isn't quite as impressive. The organic, locally sourced produce is wonderfully fresh, but many of the dishes we tried—spearmint and nettle ravioli, leek and fennel soup with salt cod dumplings, honey lacquered duck breast— were lacking in flavor, and the service suffered from mysteriously long spells of absence. Spruce is still one of the exciting new restaurants in San Francisco, but it's best enjoyed from a seat at the bar while tucking into their fantastic all-natural burger and fries while pondering which wine to choose from their 70 by-the-glass selections.

3640 Sacramento Street (at Spruce St.). © 415/931-5100. www.sprucesf.com. Reservations recommended. Main courses $25–$40. AE, DC, DISC, MC, V. Mon–Fri 11:30am–11pm, Sat–Sun 5–11pm. Valet parking $12 dinner only. Bus: 1, 2, or 4.

EXPENSIVE

Quince ✿✿ CALIFORNIA/ITALIAN   Its discreet location in a quiet residential neighborhood hasn't stopped this tiny and predominantly white-hued restaurant from becoming one of the city's hardest reservations to get. With only 15 tables, diners are clamoring for a seat to savor the nightly changing Italian-inspired menu by Michael Tusk, who mastered the art of pasta while working at the East Bay's famed Chez Panisse and Oliveto restaurants. Regardless, it's worth the effort—especially if you love simple food that honors a few high-quality, organic ingredients. Dining divinity might start with a pillowy spring garlic soufflé or white asparagus with a lightly fried egg and brown butter, but it really hits heavenly notes with the pasta course, be it garganelli with English peas and prosciutto, tagliatelle with veal ragout and fava beans, or artichoke ravioli. Meat and fish selections don't fall short either, with delicately prepared mixed grill plates, tender Alaskan halibut with fava beans, and juicy lamb with fennel and olives. Desserts aren't quite as celestial, but the trio of citrus sorbets make for a light, pleasant finish to a wonderful meal.

1701 Octavia St. (at Bush St.). © 415/775-8500. www.quincerestaurant.com. Reservations required. Main courses $16–$29. AE, MC, V. Mon–Thurs 5:30–10pm; Fri–Sat 5–10pm. Valet parking $8. Bus: 1, 31, or 38.

MODERATE

Ace Wasabi's Rock 'n' Roll Sushi ✪ JAPANESE/SUSHI   What differentiates this Marina hot spot from the usual sushi spots around town are the unique combinations, the varied menu, and the young, hip atmosphere. The innovative rolls are a nice change for those bored with traditional styles, but don't worry if someone in your party isn't a raw fish fan: There are also plenty of non-seafood and cooked items on the menu. Don't miss the rainbow "Three Amigos" roll, or the "Flying Kamikaze" with spicy albacore tuna wrapped around asparagus and topped with ponzu and scallions. The service, like the surroundings, is jovial.

3339 Steiner St. (at Chestnut St.). ✆ 415/567-4903. Reservations not accepted. Sushi $4–$14. AE, MC, V. Mon–Thurs 5:30–10:30pm; Fri–Sat 5:30–11pm; Sun 5–10pm. Bus: 30.

A16 ✪✪ ITALIAN   This sleek, casual, and wonderfully lively spot is one of San Francisco's best and busiest restaurants, featuring Neapolitan-style pizza and cuisine from the region of Campania. Named after the motorway that traverses the region, the divided space boasts a wine and beer bar up front, a larger dining area and open kitchen in the back, and a wall of wines in between. But its secret weapon is the creative menu of outstanding appetizers, pizza, and entrees, which are orchestrated by chef Nate Appleman with the same perfection as they were by opening chef Christophe Hille. Even if you must hoard the insanely good braised pork shoulder to yourself, start by sharing roasted asparagus with walnut cream and pecorino tartuffo or artichoke and tuna conserva with grilled bread and chiles. Co-owner and wine director Shelley Lindgren guides diners through one of the city's most exciting wine lists, featuring 40 wines by the half-glass, glass, and carafe. Oddly enough, their desserts are consistently mediocre, but perhaps that will change by the time you visit.

2355 Chestnut St. (btw. Divisadero and Scott sts.). ✆ 415/771-2216. www.a16sf.com. Reservations recommended. Main courses $8–$13 lunch, $14–$20 dinner. AE, DC, MC, V. Wed–Fri 11:30am–2:30pm; Sun–Thurs 5–10pm; Fri–Sat 5–11pm. Bus: 22, 30, or 30X.

Betelnut ✪ SOUTHEAST ASIAN   Although San Francisco is teeming with Asian restaurants, few offer the posh, fashionable dining environment of this restaurant on upscale Union Street. As the menu explains, the restaurant is themed after Pejui Wu, a traditional Asian beer house offering local brews and savory dishes. But with the bamboo paneling, red Formica countertops, and low-hanging lamps, the place feels less like an authentic harbor restaurant and more like a set out of *Shanghai Surprise*. Still, the atmosphere is en vogue, with dimly lit booths, ringside seating overlooking the bustling stir-fry chefs, sidewalk tables (weather permitting), and body-to-body flirting at the cramped but festive bar. Starters include sashimi and tasty salt-and-pepper whole gulf prawns; main courses offer wok-seared Mongolian beef and Singapore chile crab (seasonal). Whatever you do, order their heavenly signature dessert: a mouthwatering tapioca pudding with sweet red adzuki beans.

2030 Union St. (at Buchanan St.). ✆ 415/929-8855. www.betelnutrestaurant.com. Reservations recommended. Main courses $9–$16. DC, DISC, MC, V. Sun–Thurs 11:30am–11pm; Fri–Sat 11:30am–midnight. Bus: 22, 41, or 45.

Chez Nous ✪✪ FRENCH   Diners get crammed into the 40-seat dining area of this bright, cheery, small, and bustling dining room, but the eclectic tapas are so delicious and affordable, no one seems to care. Indeed, this friendly and fast-paced neighborhood haunt has become a blueprint for other restaurants that understand the allure of small plates. But Chez Nous stands out as more than a petite-portion trendsetter. The clincher is that most of its Mediterranean dishes taste so clean and fresh you can't wait to come back and dine here again. Start with the soup, whatever it is; don't skip tasty french fries with *harissa* (Tunisian hot sauce) aioli; savor the lamb chops with lavender sea salt; and save room for their famed dessert, the minicustard-cakelike *canneles de Bordeaux*.

1911 Fillmore St. (btw. Pine and Bush sts.). © 415/441-8044. Reservations accepted, but walk-ins welcome. Small dishes $5–$13. AE, MC, V. Daily 11:30am–3pm and 5:30–10pm (Fri–Sat until 11pm). Bus: 22, 41, or 45.

E'Angelo Restaurant ☞ ITALIAN

Back when I was barely making enough to cover my rent, I would often treat myself to a night out at E'Angelo. All the house specialties, pastas, and pizzas cost less than $19; the atmosphere is casual and fun; tables are cozy-cramped; and the Italian staff is friendly. For me, the combination made not only for a hearty meal, but for an opportunity to mingle with San Francisco: to live a little, eavesdrop on neighbors' conversations, and perhaps even run into local celebrities such as Robin Williams with his family. While years have passed, not much has changed at this traditional Italian hot spot: The place still won't take reservations or credit cards. It still serves decent portions of pastas, veal, lamb, chicken, and fish; a carafe of red or white wine for about 18 bucks (thrifty by-the-bottle prices, too); and one heck of a rich eggplant parmigiana. And unlike those at most of the neighboring restaurants, desserts are dirt-cheap.

2234 Chestnut St. (btw. Pierce and Scott sts.). © 415/567-6164. Reservations not accepted. Main courses $13–$19. No credit cards. Tues–Sun 5–10pm. Bus: 22, 30, or 30X.

Ella's ☞☞ AMERICAN/BREAKFAST

Well known throughout town as the undisputed queen of breakfasts, this restaurant's acclaim means you're likely to wait in line up to an hour on weekends. But midweek and in the wee hours of morning, it's possible to slide onto a counter or table seat in the colorful split dining room and lose yourself in outstanding and generous servings of chicken hash, crisped to perfection and served with eggs any way you like them, with a side of fluffy buttermilk biscuits. Pancakes, omelets, and the short list of other breakfast essentials are equally revered. Alas, service can be woefully slow, but at least the busboys and -gals are quick to fill coffee cups. Come lunchtime, solid entrees like salads, chicken potpie, and grilled salmon with mashed potatoes remind you what's great about American cooking.

500 Presidio Ave. (at California St.). © 415/441-5669. www.ellassanfrancisco.com. Reservations accepted for lunch. Main courses $5.50–$10 breakfast, $6–$12 lunch. AE, DISC, MC, V. Mon–Fri 7am–3pm; Sat–Sun 8:30am–2pm. Bus: 1, 3, or 43.

Greens Restaurant ☞☞ VEGETARIAN

In an old waterfront warehouse, with enormous windows overlooking the bridge, boats, and the bay, Greens is one of the most renowned vegetarian restaurants in the country. Executive chef Annie Somerville (author of *Fields of Greens*) cooks with the seasons, using produce from local organic farms. Within the quiet dining room, a weeknight dinner might feature such appetizers as mushroom soup with Asiago cheese and tarragon; or grilled portobello and endive salad. Entrees run the gamut from pizza with wilted escarole, red onions, lemon, Asiago, and Parmesan, to Vietnamese yellow curry or risotto with black trumpet mushrooms, leeks, savory spinach, white-truffle oil, Parmesan Reggiano, and thyme. Those interested in the whole shebang should make reservations for the $48 four-course dinner served on Saturday only. Lunch and brunch are equally fresh and tasty. The adjacent Greens To Go sells sandwiches, soups, salads, and pastries.

Building A, Fort Mason Center (enter Fort Mason opposite the Safeway at Buchanan and Marina sts.). © 415/771-6222. www.greensrestaurant.com. Reservations recommended. Main courses $9.50–$14 lunch, $15–$20 dinner, fixed-price dinner $48; Sun brunch $8–$14. AE, DISC, MC, V. Tues–Sat noon–2:30pm; Sun 10:30am–9pm; Mon–Sat 5:30–9pm. Greens To Go Mon–Thurs 8am–8pm; Fri–Sat 8am–5pm; Sun 10:30am–4pm. Parking in hourly lot $4 for up to 2½ hours. Bus: 28 or 30.

Isa 𝄞𝄞 FRENCH   Luke Sung, who trained with some of the best French chefs in the city, has captured many locals' hearts by creating the kind of menu we foodies dream of: a smattering of small dishes, served a la carte family-style, that allow you to try numerous items in one sitting. It's a good thing the menu, considered "French tapas," offers small portions at reasonable prices. After all, it's asking a lot to make a diner choose between mushroom ragout with veal sweetbreads, seared foie gras with caramelized apples, potato-wrapped sea bass in brown butter, and rack of lamb. Here, a party of two can choose all of these plus one or two more and not be rolled out the door afterward. Adding to the allure is the warm boutique dining environment—70 seats scattered amid a small dining room in the front, and a large tented and heated patio out back that sets the mood with a warm yellow glow. Take a peek at the "kitchen," a shoebox of a cooking space, to appreciate Sung's accomplishments that much more. Cocktailers, take note: You'll only find beer, wine, and shoju cocktails (shoju is a smooth alcohol made from sweet potato that is used like vodka).

3324 Steiner St. (btw. Lombard and Chestnut sts.). ℂ 415/567-9588. www.isarestaurant.com. Reservations recommended. Main courses $9–$16. MC, V. Mon–Thurs 5:30–10pm; Fri–Sat 5:30–10:30pm. Bus: 22, 28, 30, 30X, 43, or 76.

Pane e Vino 𝄞 ITALIAN   While the rest of the city tries to modernize their manicotti, this ultracasual Italian spot focuses on huge helpings of classics that are fine for the traditional diner, but not fabulous for the gourmand. That said, prices are reasonable, and the mostly Italian-accented staff is always smooth and efficient under pressure (you'll see). The menu offers a wide selection of appetizers, including a fine carpaccio, *vitello tonnato* (sliced roasted veal and capers in lemony tuna sauce), and the hugely popular chilled artichoke stuffed with bread and tomatoes and served with vinaigrette. The broad selection of pastas includes flavorful *penne putanesca* with tomatoes, capers, anchovies, garlic, and olives. Other specialties are grilled fish and meat dishes, including chicken breast marinated in lime juice and herbs. Top dessert picks are any of the Italian ice creams, panna cotta, and (but of course) creamy tiramisu.

1715 Union St. (btw. Gough and Octavia sts.). ℂ 415/346-2111. www.paneevinotrattoria.com. Reservations highly recommended. Main courses $10–$24. AE, MC, V. Mon–Thurs 5–10pm; Fri–Sat 11:30am–10pm; Sun 5–9pm. No parking. Bus: 41 or 45.

PlumpJack Café 𝄞 CALIFORNIA/FRENCH/MEDITERRANEAN   Wildly popular among San Francisco's style-setters, this small, 55-seat Cow Hollow restaurant, with a hint of whimsical Shakespearean decor, is one of the neighborhood's most "in" places to dine—partly because the place was founded and is frequented by Mayor Gavin Newsom. A typical dinner may start with Sonoma foie gras sweetened with Khalas dates and sweet vermouth, local Delta asparagus with smoked ham hock rillette, poached and roasted guinea fowl with a side of caramelized endive and parsnips, and for dessert a bananas Foster with vanilla bean ice cream. The extraordinarily extensive California wine list—gleaned from the PlumpJack wine shop down the street—is sold at next to retail prices, with many wines available by the glass.

3127 Fillmore St. (btw. Filbert and Greenwich sts.). ℂ 415/563-4755. www.plumpjack.com. Reservations recommended. Main courses $13–$16 lunch, $20–$34 dinner. AE, DC, DISC, MC, V. Mon–Fri 11:30am–2pm; daily 5:30–10pm. Valet parking $14 for 3 hr. after 6pm. Bus: 22, 41, or 45.

INEXPENSIVE

Andalé Taqueria ✿ *Kids* *Value* MEXICAN   Andalé (Spanish for "hurry up") offers *muy bueno* high-end fast food for the health-conscious and the just plain hungry. As the long menu explains, this small California chain prides itself on its fresh ingredients and low-cal options. Lard, preservatives, and canned items are eschewed; Andalé favors salad dressings made with double virgin olive oil, whole vegetarian beans (not refried), skinless chicken, salsas and *aguas frescas* made from fresh fruits and veggies, and mesquite-grilled meats. Add the location (on a sunny shopping stretch), sophisticated decor, full bar, and check-me-out patio seating (complete with corner fireplace), and it's no wonder that good-looking, fitness-fanatic Marina District residents consider this place home. Cafeteria-style service keeps prices low.

2150 Chestnut St. (btw. Steiner and Pierce sts.). ✆ **415/749-0506.** Reservations not accepted. Most dishes $4.25–$11. MC, V. Daily 10am–10pm. Bus: 22, 28, 30, 30X, 43, 76, or 82X.

Barney's Gourmet Hamburgers ✿ *Kids* HAMBURGERS   If you're on a perpetual quest for the best burger in America, a mandatory stop is Barney's Gourmet Hamburgers. Once you get past all the framed awards for the Bay Area's best burger, you're bombarded by a mind-boggling menu of beef, chicken, turkey, and vegetarian burgers to choose from, as well as sandwiches and salads. The ultimate combo is a humungous basket of fries (enough for a party of three), one-third-pound burger, and thick shake. Popular versions are the California Burger with jack cheese, bacon, Ortega chiles, and sour cream, or the Popeye Burger made with chicken, sautéed spinach, and feta cheese. Be sure to dine alfresco in the hidden courtyard in back.

3344 Steiner St. (btw. Chestnut and Lombard sts.). ✆ **415/563-0307.** www.barneyshamburgers.com. Main courses $5–$8. No credit cards. Mon–Thurs 11am–9:30pm; Fri–Sat 11am–10pm; Sun 11am–9pm. Bus: 22, 28, 30, 30X, 43, 76, or 82X.

Eliza's ✿ *Value* CHINESE   Despite the curiously colorful design of modern architecture, whimsy, and glass art, this perennially packed neighborhood haunt serves some of the freshest California-influenced Chinese food in town. Unlike comparable options, here the atmosphere (albeit unintentionally funky) and presentation parallel the food. The fantastically fresh soups, salads, seafood, pork, chicken, duck, and such specials as spicy eggplant are outstanding and are served on beautiful English and Japanese plates. (Get the sea bass with black-bean sauce and go straight to heaven!) I often come at midday and order the wonderful kung pao chicken lunch special (available weekdays only): a mixture of tender chicken, peanuts, chile peppers, subtly hot sauce, and perfectly crunchy vegetables. It's one of 32 main-course choices that come with rice and soup for around $6. The place is also jumping at night, so prepare to stand in line. A second location, in Potrero Hill at 1457 18th St. (✆ **415/648-9999**), is open Monday through Friday 11am to 3pm and daily 5 to 9pm.

2877 California St. (at Broderick St.). ✆ **415/621-4819.** Reservations accepted for parties of 4 or more. Main courses $5.30–$6.15 lunch, $7.15–$15 dinner. MC, V. Mon–Thurs 11am–3pm and 5–9:30pm; Fri 11am–3pm and 5–10pm; Sat 4:30–10pm; Sun 4:30–9pm. Bus: 1 or 24.

The Grove ✿ CAFE   The Grove is the kind of place you go just to hang out and enjoy the fact that you're in San Francisco. That the heaping salads, lasagna, pasta, sandwiches, and daily specials are predictably good is an added bonus. I like coming here on weekday mornings for the easy-going vibe, strong coffee, and friendly, fast service. Inside you can sit at one of the dark wood tables on the scuffed hardwood floor and people-watch through the large open windows, but on sunny days the most coveted seats are along the sidewalk. It's the perfect place to read the newspaper, sip an enormous mug of coffee, and be glad you're not at work right now. A second Pacific Heights location is at 2016 Fillmore St. between California and Pine streets (© **415/ 474-1419**).

2250 Chestnut St. (btw. Scott and Pierce sts.). © **415/474-4843**. Most main courses $6–$7. MC, V. Mon–Fri 7am–11pm; Sat–Sun 8am–11pm. Bus: 22, 28, 30, 30X, 43, 76, or 82X.

Home Plate ⭐ *Finds* BREAKFAST   Dollar for dollar, Home Plate just may be the best breakfast place in San Francisco. Many Marina residents kick off their hectic weekends by carbo-loading here on big piles of buttermilk pancakes and waffles smothered with fresh fruit, or hefty omelets stuffed with everything from apple wood–smoked ham to spinach. You'll always start off with a coveted plate of freshly baked scones, best eaten with a bit of butter and a dab of jam. Be sure to look over the daily specials scrawled on the little green chalkboard before you order. And as every fan of this tiny cafe knows, it's best to call ahead and ask to have your name put on the waiting list before you slide into Home Plate.

2274 Lombard St. (at Pierce St.). © **415/922-HOME**. Main courses $3.95–$7. DC, DISC, MC, V. Daily 7am–4pm. Bus: 28, 30, 43, or 76.

La Méditerranée ⭐ *Value* MEDITERRANEAN   With an upscale-cafe ambience and quality food, La Méditerranée has long warranted its reputation as one of the most appealing inexpensive restaurants on upper Fillmore. Here you'll find freshly prepared traditional Mediterranean food that's worlds apart from the Euro-eclectic fare many restaurants now call "Mediterranean." Baba ghanouj, tabbouleh, dolmas, and hummus start out the menu. My favorite dish here is the chicken Cilicia, a phyllo-dough dish that's hand-rolled and baked with cinnamony spices, almonds, chickpeas, and raisins. Also recommended are the zesty chicken pomegranate drumsticks on a bed of rice. Both come with green salad, potato salad, or soup for around $9.50. Ground lamb dishes, quiches, and Middle Eastern combo plates round out the affordable menu, and wine comes by the glass and in half- or full liters. A second location is at 288 Noe St., at Market Street (© **415/431-7210**).

2210 Fillmore St. (at Sacramento St.). © **415/921-2956**. www.cafelamed.com. Main courses $7–$10 lunch, $8–$12 dinner. AE, MC, V. Sun–Thurs 11am–10pm; Fri–Sat 11am–11pm. Bus: 1, 3, or 22.

Mel's Drive-In ⭐ *Kids* AMERICAN   Sure, it's contrived, touristy, and nowhere near healthy, but when you get that urge for a chocolate shake and banana cream pie at the stroke of midnight—or when you want to entertain the kids—no other place in the city comes through like Mel's Drive-In. Modeled after a classic 1950s diner, right down to the jukebox at each table, Mel's harkens back to the halcyon days when cholesterol and fried foods didn't jab your guilty conscience with every greasy, wonderful bite. Too bad the prices don't reflect the '50s; a burger with fries and a Coke costs about $12.

Another Mel's at 3355 Geary St., at Stanyan Street (© **415/387-2244**), is open from 6am to 1am Sunday through Thursday and 6am to 3am Friday and Saturday. Additional locations are: 1050 Van Ness (© **415/292-6357**), open Sunday through Thursday 6am to 3am and Friday through Sunday 6am to 4am; and 801 Mission St. (© **415/227-4477**), open Sunday through Wednesday 6am to 1am, Thursday 6am to 2am, and Friday and Saturday 24 hours.

2165 Lombard St. (at Fillmore St.). © **415/921-3039**. www.melsdrive-in.com. Main courses $6.50–$12 breakfast, $7–$10 lunch, $8–$15 dinner. MC, V. Sun–Wed 6am–1am; Thurs 6am–2am; Fri–Sat 24 hr. Bus: 22, 30, or 43.

Pluto's ⭐ *Value* CALIFORNIA   Catering to the Marina District's DINK (double income, no kids) crowd, Pluto's combines assembly-line efficiency with high quality. The result is cheap, fresh fare: huge salads with a dozen choices of toppings; oven-roasted poultry and grilled meats (the tri-tip is great); sandwiches; and a wide array of sides like crispy garlic potato rings, seasonal veggies, and barbecued chicken wings. Pluto's serves teas, sodas, bottled brews, and Napa wines as well as homemade desserts. The ordering system is bewildering to newcomers: Grab a checklist, and then hand it to the servers who check off your order and relay it to the cashier. Seating is limited during the rush, but the turnover is fairly fast. A second Inner Sunset location is at 627 Irving St., at Eighth Avenue (📞 **415/753-8867**).

3258 Scott St. (at Chestnut St.). 📞 **415/7-PLUTOS**. www.plutosfreshfood.com. Reservations not accepted. Main courses $3.50–$5.75. MC, V. Mon–Fri 11am–10pm; Sat–Sun 10:30am–10pm. Bus: 28, 30, or 76.

10 Japantown

MODERATE

Takara ⭐ JAPANESE/SUSHI   When I'm in the mood for sushi, I often head to this unassuming restaurant tucked at the eastern end of Japantown. Not only is it large enough that you don't have to wait in a long line (unlike other local sushi spots), but the fish is extremely fresh and affordable and the other offerings are fantastic. Along with standard nigiri, I always go for the seaweed with fabulously tangy vinegar and a floating quail egg. But on the occasions that I can curb my sushi craving, I get more than my fill with their *yosenabe*. A meal for two that's under $20, it's a giant pot of soup brought to the table on a burner accompanied by a plate of fresh raw meat or seafood and vegetables. After you push the food into the liquid and briefly let it cook, you ladle it out and devour it. Even after serving two hungry people, there are always leftovers. Other favorites are anything with shrimp—pulled live from the tank—and sukiyaki, another tableside cooking experience. Bargain hunters should come for a lunch plate.

22 Peace Plaza no. 202 (in Japan Center Miyako Mall). 📞 **415/921-2000**. Reservations recommended. Main courses: $15–$23. MC, V. Daily lunch 11:30am–2:30pm; dinner 5:30–10pm.

11 Civic Center

For a map of restaurants in this section, see the "Dining Around Town" map on p. 116.

VERY EXPENSIVE

Jardinière ⭐⭐ CALIFORNIA/FRENCH   Jardinière is a pre- and post-symphony favorite, and it also happens to be the perfect setting for enjoying a cocktail with your significant other. A culinary dream team created the elegant dining room and sophisticated menu: owner-designer Pat Kuleto, who created the beautiful champagne-inspired decor, and owner-chef Traci Des Jardins, one of the city's most popular chefs. On most evenings the bi-level brick structure is abuzz with an older crowd (including ex-mayor Brown, a regular) who sip cocktails at the centerpiece mahogany bar or watch the scene discreetly from the circular balcony. The restaurant's champagne theme extends to twinkling lights and clever ice buckets built into the balcony railing, making the atmosphere conducive to splurging in the best of style—especially when live jazz is playing (at 7:30pm nightly). The daily changing menu might include seared scallops with truffled potatoes and truffle reduction; sautéed petrale sole with Alsatian cabbage and Riesling sauce; or venison with celery root, red wine, braised cabbage,

Finds   **Hidden Treasures**

They're on the way to nowhere, but because they're among the city's most unique, it would be a crime to leave out these destination restaurants. If you're not familiar with the streets of San Francisco, be sure to call first to get directions; otherwise, you'll spend more time driving than dining.

Thanh Long ☆, 4101 Judah St. (at 46th Ave.; ℰ **415/665-1146**; www. anfamily.com; streetcar: N), is an out-of-the-way Sunset District Vietnamese standout that, long after my mom started taking me here as a tot for excellent roasted crab and addictive garlic noodles, has remained a San Francisco secret. Since the owners, the An family, have become rather famous for their aforementioned signature dishes now that they're served in sister restaurants Crustacean Beverly Hills and S.F., suffice it to say the crab's out of the bag. But this location is still far enough on the outskirts of the city to keep it from becoming overcrowded. The restaurant is more visually pleasing than most Southeast Asian outposts (white tablecloths, tastefully exotic decor), but the extra glitz is reflected in the prices of luxury dishes (main courses run from $14–$34) such as charbroiled tiger prawns with those famed garlic noodles and steamed sea bass with scallions and ginger sauce. On the plus side, unlike the cheaper options around town, there's a full bar here, too, serving fun cocktails such as the Pineapple and Litchi vodka infusion. Reservations are recommended. Thanh Long is open Sunday and Tuesday through Thursday from 4:30 to 10pm, Friday and Saturday from 4:30 to 11pm, and is closed on Mondays.

The Ramp, 855 China Basin (at the end of Mariposa St.; ℰ **415/621-2378**; www.ramprestaurant.com; bus: 22 or 48), is an out-of-the-way mecca for seaside snacks, dancing, and drinking that's at its best when the sun is shining.

and juniper sauce. There's also an outstanding cheese selection and superb wine list—many by the glass, and over 500 bottles.

300 Grove St. (at Franklin St.). ℰ **415/861-5555**. www.jardiniere.com. Reservations recommended. Main courses $26–$38; 6-course tasting menu $79. AE, DC, DISC, MC, V. Sun–Wed 5–10:30pm; Thurs–Sat 5–11:30pm. Valet parking $10. Bus: 19 or 21.

MODERATE

Absinthe ☆ FRENCH   This Hayes Valley hot spot is sexy, fun, reasonably priced, and frequented by everyone from the theatergoing crowd to the young and chic. Decor is all brasserie, with French rattan cafe chairs, copper-topped tables, a pressed-tin ceiling, soft lighting, period art, and a rich use of color and fabric, including leather and mohair banquettes. It's always a pleasure to unwind at the bar with a Ginger Rogers—gin, mint, lemon juice, ginger ale, and a squeeze of lime. The lengthy lunch menu offers everything from oysters and caviar to Caesar salad and a respectable burger, but I always end up getting the same thing: their outstanding open-faced smoked-trout sandwich on grilled Italian bread. In the divided dining room, main courses are equally satisfying, from coq au vin and steak frites to roasted whole Dungeness crab with poached leeks in mustard vinaigrette, salt roasted potatoes, and aioli.

If you're lucky enough to be in San Francisco on one of those rare hot days, head to this bayside hangout. The fare is of the basic pub grub variety— burgers, sandwiches, salads, and soups from $8 to $13—but the rustic boat-yard environment and patio seating make this a relaxing place to dine in the sun. In summer, the place really rocks when live bands perform (4:30–8:30pm Fri–Sun Apr–Oct) and tanned, cocktailing singles prowl the area. It's open for lunch Monday through Friday from 11am to 3:30pm, and for brunch Satur-day and Sunday from 8:30am to 4pm. The bar is open until 9pm on weekdays and later on weekends. From April to October, an outdoor barbecue is offered Saturday and Sunday from 4 to 7:30pm.

   Little Star Pizza 𝒢𝒢, 846 Divisadero St. (at McAllister St.; ℂ **415/441-1118;** www.littlestarpizza.com; bus: 5 or 24), may be on a dreary strip of busy Divisadero Street and feel like a bohemian speak-easy with its dark col-ored walls, low ceilings, and jukebox, but this joint is cranking out the best pizza in town. You're likely to have to wait for a seat at one of the well-spaced tables and you may have to strain to chat over the music and dining din, but there's little I wouldn't endure for one of Little Star's deep dish cornmeal-crust pizzas ($11–$22). Rather than inches of dough, these pies are thin and crisp with high sides that coddle fillings such as chicken, tomatoes, artichoke hearts, red bell peppers, sausage, and feta. These babies take about 25 minutes to bake, which is a great excuse to order chicken wings and a glass of wine for the wait. The place serves dinner Sunday and Tues-day through Thursday from 5 to 10pm, Friday and Saturday from 5 to 11pm, and is closed on Mondays. *Note:* There's a second location in the Mission Dis-trict at 400 Valencia St. at 15th St. (ℂ **415/551-7827**).

The best item on the weekend brunch menu is the creamy polenta with mascarpone, maple syrup, bananas, and toasted walnuts.

398 Hayes St. (at Gough St.). ℂ 415/551-1590. www.absinthe.com. Reservations recommended. Brunch $8–$14; most main courses $12–$22 lunch, $18–$28 dinner. AE, DC, DISC, MC, V. Tues–Fri 11:30am–midnight (bar until 2am Fri); Sat 11am–midnight (bar until 2am); Sun 11am–10pm (bar until midnight). Valet parking (Tues–Sat after 5pm) $10. Bus: 21.

Hayes Street Grill 𝒢 SEAFOOD   For well over a decade, this small, no-nonsense seafood restaurant (owned and operated by revered food writer and chef Patricia Unterman) has maintained a solid reputation among San Francisco's picky epicureans for its impeccably fresh and straightforwardly prepared fish. The concise menu offers a dozen appetizers—most of which are fresh and lively salads—a half-dozen grilled fish selections cooked to perfection and matched with your sauce of choice (Szechuan peanut, tomatillo salsa, herb-shallot butter), and a side of signature fries. Fancier seafood specials, which change with the seasons and range from mahimahi (with Viet-namese dipping sauce, baby spinach, roasted peanuts, and basmati rice) to classic paella, are balanced by a few meat-driven dishes, which may include Niman Ranch (organic and wonderful) flatiron steak with mustard butter and balsamic onions. Fin-ish your meal with the outstanding crème brûlée.

320 Hayes St. (near Franklin St.). © 415/863-5545. www.hayesstreetgrill.com. Reservations recommended. Main courses $14–$20 lunch, $16–$23 dinner. AE, DISC, MC, V. Mon–Fri 11:30am–2pm; Mon–Thurs 5–9:30pm; Fri 5–10:30pm; Sat 5:30–10:30pm; Sun 5–8:30pm. Bus: 19, 21, 31, or 38.

Zuni Café ★★ *Finds* MEDITERRANEAN   Zuni Café embodies the best of San Francisco dining: Its clientele spans young hipsters to hunky gays, the cuisine is consistently terrific, and the atmosphere is electric. Its expanse of windows overlooking Market Street gives the place a sense of space despite the fact that it's always packed. For the full effect, stand at the bustling, copper-topped bar and order a glass of wine and a few oysters from the oyster menu (a dozen or so varieties are on hand at all times). Then, because *of course* you made advance reservations, take your seat in the stylish exposed-brick two-level maze of little dining rooms or on the patio. Then do what we all do: Splurge on chef Judy Rodgers' Mediterranean-influenced menu. Although the ever-changing menu always includes meat (such as hanger steak), fish (grilled or braised on the kitchen's wood grill), and pasta (tagliatelle with nettles, applewood-smoked bacon, butter, and Parmesan), it's almost sinful not to order her brick-oven roasted chicken for two with Tuscan-style bread salad. I rarely pass up the polenta with mascarpone and a proper Caesar salad. But then again, if you're there for lunch or after 10pm, the hamburger on grilled rosemary focaccia bread is a strong contender for the city's best. Whatever you decide, be sure to order a stack of shoestring potatoes.

1658 Market St. (at Franklin St.). © 415/552-2522. www.zunicafe.com. Reservations recommended. Main courses $10–$19 lunch, $15–$29 dinner. AE, MC, V. Tues–Sat 11:30am–midnight; Sun 11am–11pm. Valet parking $10. Bus: 6, 7, or 71. Streetcar: All Market St. streetcars.

INEXPENSIVE

Frjtz Fries ★ BELGIAN   Although they serve great sandwiches and salads, Frjtz is best known for its addictively crisp french fries, piled high in a paper cone (how Euro) and served with a barrage of exotic dipping sauces such as chipotle rémoulade and balsamic mayo. I'm also a fan of their crepes—try the grilled rosemary chicken and Swiss cheese—their big, leafy salad, or the chunky focaccia sandwich packed with roasted peppers, red onions, pesto mayo, grilled eggplant, and melted Gorgonzola. Wash it down with creamy Chimay Belgian ale. *Note:* There's also a second Frjtz Fries at 590 Valencia St. (at 17th St.; © 415/863-8272) in the Mission.

581 Hayes St. (at Laguna St.). © 415/864-7654. www.frjtzfries.com. Reservations not accepted. Fries $3–$4.50; crepes $5–$8; sandwiches $7–$8.25. AE, DC, DISC, MC, V. Mon–Thurs 11am–10pm; Fri–Sat 11am–midnight; Sun 11am–9pm. Bus: 21.

Tommy's Joynt *Value* *Kids* AMERICAN   With its colorful mural exterior, it's hard to miss Tommy's Joynt, a 58-year-old haven for cholesterol-be-damned hold-outs from America's halcyon days and a late-night favorite for those in search of a cheap and hearty meal. The restaurant's exterior is tame in comparison to the interior, which looks like a Buffalo Bill museum that imploded: a wild collage of stuffed birds, a mounted buffalo head, an ancient piano, rusty firearms, fading prints, a beer-guzzling lion, and Santa Claus masks. The hofbrau-style buffet offers a cornucopia of rib-clinging a la carte dishes such as their signature buffalo stew (via a buffalo ranch in Wyoming), which resides under heat lamps among the stainless steel trays of turkeys, hams, sloppy Joes, oxtails, corned beef, meatballs, mashed potatoes, and other classics. There's also a slew of seating on two levels, almost 100 varieties of beer, and a most interesting clientele of almost exclusively 50-something pre-cardiac-arrest males (some of whom have been coming to the "Joynt" for more than 40 years). It's all good stuff in a 'merican kind of way, the kind of place you take Grandpappy when he's in town just to show him that San Francisco's not entirely sissy.

1101 Geary Blvd. (at Van Ness Ave.). ℂ 415/775-4216. www.tommysjoynt.com. Reservations not accepted. Main courses $4–$7. No credit cards. Daily 10am–2am. Bus: 2, 3, 4, or 38.

12 Mission District

For a map of restaurants in this section, see the "Dining Around Town" map on p. 116.

MODERATE

Delfina 𝒢𝒢 ITALIAN   Unpretentious warehouse-chic atmosphere, reasonable prices, and chef/co-owner Craig Stoll's superb seasonal Italian cuisine have made this family-owned restaurant one of the city's most cherished. Stoll, who was one of *Food & Wine*'s Best New Chefs in 2001 and a 2005 James Beard Award nominee, changes the menu daily, while his wife Annie works the front of the house (when she's not being a mom). Standards include Niman Ranch flatiron steak with french fries, and roasted chicken with Yukon Gold mashed potatoes and royal trumpet mushrooms. The winter menu might include slow-roasted pork shoulder or gnocchi with squash and chestnuts, while spring indulgences can include sand dabs with frisée, fingerling potatoes, and lemon-caper butter; or lamb with polenta and sweet peas. Trust me—order the buttermilk *panna cotta* (custard) if it's available. *A plus:* A few tables and counter seating are reserved for walk-in diners. Delfina also has a heated and covered patio that's used mid-March through November.

3621 18th St. (btw. Dolores and Guerrero sts.). ℂ 415/552-4055. www.delfinasf.com. Reservations recommended. Main courses $13–$22. MC, V. Mon–Thurs 5:30–10pm; Fri–Sat 5:30–11pm; Sun 5:30–10pm. Parking lot at 18th and Valencia sts, $8. Bus: 26 or 33. Streetcar: J.

Foreign Cinema 𝒢𝒢 MEDITERRANEAN   This place is so chic and well-hidden that it eludes me every time I drive past it on Mission Street (*hint:* look for the valet stand). The "cinema" here is a bit of a gimmick: It's an outdoor dining area (partially covered and heated, but still chilly) where mostly foreign films are projected onto the side of an adjoining building without any audio. What's definitely not a gimmick, however, is the superb Mediterranean-inspired menu created by husband-and-wife team John Clark and Gayle Pirie. Snackers like me find solace at the oyster bar with a half-dozen locally harvested Miyagi oysters and a devilishly good *brandade* (fish purée) gratin. Heartier eaters can opt for grilled halibut with chanterelles and roasted figs in a fig vinaigrette; fried Madras curry-spiced chicken with gypsy peppers; or grilled natural rib-eye with Tuscan-style beans and rosemary-fried peppercorn sauce— all made from seasonal, sustainably farmed, organic ingredients when possible. Truth be told, even if the food weren't so good, I'd still come here—it's just that cool. If you have to wait for your table, consider stepping into their adjoining bar, Laszlo.

2534 Mission St. (btw. 21st and 22nd sts.). ℂ 415/648-7600. www.foreigncinema.com. Reservations recommended. Main courses $17–$26. AE, MC, V. Mon–Thurs 6–10pm; Fri–Sat 6–11pm; Sun 5–10pm; brunch Sat–Sun 11am–3pm. Valet parking $10. Bus: 14, 14L, or 49.

Pauline's 𝒢 PIZZA   Housed in a cheery yellow double-decker building that stands out like a beacon in a somewhat seedy neighborhood, Pauline's does only three things—pizzas, salads, and desserts—but it does them better than most restaurants in the city. Running the gauntlet of panhandlers for a slice of Louisiana Andouille pizza topped with Andouille sausage, bell peppers, and fontina cheese is completely worth it. Other gourmet toppings include house-made chicken sausage, French goat cheese, roasted eggplant, Danish fontina cheese, and *tasso* (spiced pork shoulder). The salads are equally amazing: certified organic, handpicked by California growers, and topped with fresh and dried herbs (including edible flowers) from Pauline's own gardens in Berkeley. Don't forget to leave room for the house-made ice cream and sorbets or chocolate mousse and butterscotch pudding. The wine list offers a smart selection of low-priced wines, where Star Canyon Vineyards, yet another of the owners' pursuits, is showcased. Yes, prices are a bit steep (small pizzas start at $14), but what a paltry price to pay for perfection.

260 Valencia St. (btw. 14th St. and Duboce Ave.). ✆ 415/552-2050. www.paulinespizza.com. Reservations accepted for parties of 8 or more. Pizzas $12–$25. MC, V. Tues–Sat 5–10pm. Bus: 14, 26, or 49.

INEXPENSIVE

Taquerias La Cumbre MEXICAN   If San Francisco commissioned a flag honoring its favorite food, we'd probably all be waving a banner of the Golden Gate Bridge bolstering a giant burrito—that's how much we love the mammoth tortilla-wrapped meals. Taquerias La Cumbre has been around forever and still retains its "Best Burrito" title, each deftly constructed using fresh pork, steak, chicken, or vegetables, plus cheese, beans, rice, salsa, and maybe a dash of guacamole or sour cream. The fact that it's served in a cafeteria-like brick-lined room with overly shellacked tables featuring a woman with overflowing cleavage makes it taste even better.

515 Valencia St. (btw. 16th and 17th sts.). ✆ 415/863-8205. Reservations not accepted. Tacos and burritos $3.50–$6.50; dinner plates $5–$7. No credit cards. Mon–Sat 11am–9pm; Sun noon–9pm. Bus: 14, 22, 33, 49, or 53. BART: Mission.

Ti Couz 🐸 CREPES   At Ti Couz (pronounced "Tee Cooz"), one of the most architecturally stylish and popular restaurants in the Mission, the headliner is simple: the delicate, paper-thin crepe. More than 30 choices of fillings make for infinite expertly executed combinations. The menu advises you how to enjoy these wraps: Order a light crepe as an appetizer, a heftier one as a main course, and a drippingly sweet one for dessert. Recommended combinations are listed, but you can build your own from the 15 main-course selections (such as smoked salmon, mushrooms, sausage, ham, scallops, and onions) and over 15 dessert options (caramel, fruit, chocolate, Nutella, and more). Soups and salads are equally stellar; the seafood salad, for example, is a delicious and generous compilation of shrimp, scallops, and ahi tuna with veggies and five kinds of lettuce.

3108 16th St. (at Valencia St.). ✆ 415/252-7373. Reservations not accepted. Crepes $2–$12. MC, V. Mon and Fri 11am–11pm; Tues–Thurs 5–10pm; Sat–Sun 10am–11pm. Bus: 14, 22, 26, 33, 49, or 53. BART: 16th or Mission.

13 The Castro

For a map of restaurants in this section, see the "Dining Around Town" map on p. 116.

EXPENSIVE

Mecca 🐸 NEW AMERICAN   In 1996, Mecca entered the San Francisco dining scene in a decadent swirl of chocolate-brown velvet, stainless steel, cement, and brown leather. It's an industrial-chic supper club that makes you want to order a martini just so you'll match the ambience. The eclectic city clientele (with a heavy dash of same-sex couples) mingles at the oval centerpiece bar. A night here promises a live DJ spinning hot grooves, and a globally inspired New American meal prepared by chef Randy Lewis and served at tables tucked into several nooks. Lewis's menu items are as varied and interesting as his clientele: Moroccan-spiced lamb meatballs; "Last-Night's-Red-Wine-by-the-Glass Braised Short Ribs"; pan-seared Scottish salmon served with gnocchi, mustard seed vinaigrette, and pecan-apple relish; and a wickedly good Angus cheeseburger with tomato marmalade and garlic aioli on a brioche bun. When the place is jumping on a weekend night it's a great opportunity for tourists to experience an only-in-San Francisco vibe.

2029 Market St. (by 14th and Church sts.). ✆ 415/621-7000. www.sfmecca.com. Reservations recommended. Main courses $22–$34. AE, DC, MC, V. Tues–Thurs 5–10pm; Fri–Sat 5pm–midnight; Sun 4–10pm. Valet parking $10. Bus: 8, 22, 24, or 37. Streetcar: F, K, L, or M.

MODERATE

2223 Restaurant & Bar 𝒢 CALIFORNIA

Surrounded by hardwood floors, candles, streamlined modern light fixtures, and loud music, a festive mixed crowd comes here for heavy-handed specialty drinks, grilled pork chops, the ever-popular roasted chicken with roasted potatoes, and sour cherry bread pudding. Along with Mecca (see above), this is one of the hottest dining and schmoozing spots in the area—and definitely one of the better Sunday brunch spots.

2223 Market St. (btw. Sanchez and Noe sts.). ✆ 415/431-0692. www.2223restaurant.com. Reservations recommended. Main courses $4.75–$11 brunch, $9–$20 dinner. AE, DC, MC, V. Sun–Thurs 5:30–9:30pm; Fri–Sat 5:30–11pm; Sun brunch 10:30am–2:30pm. Bus: 8, 22, 24, or 37. Streetcar: F, K, L, or M.

INEXPENSIVE

Café Flore Ⓥalue CALIFORNIA

Because of its large and lively patio overlooking a busy section of Market Street intersection, Café Flore is the top sunny-day meet-me-for-coffee spot within the Castro community. And boy is the people-watching good here—leather-wrapped bears, drag queens, trannies (Dad, is that you?), gym bunnies, and other anti-establishment types saunter down Market Street in full glory. As for dining at the cafe, here's how it works: You order drinks and desserts inside at the bar, then find a seat indoors or outside on the patio or sidewalk and claim a spot. Next, go to the kitchen counter (there are no waiters), place your meal order and get a number, and the food will be delivered to your table. Many of the menu items are composed of mostly organic ingredients and include a succulent version of roasted chicken over rice, Niman Ranch hamburgers, soups, salads, and pastas. Breeders are always welcome as long as they behave, and breakfast is served until 3pm.

2298 Market St. (at Noe St.). ✆ 415/621-8579. Reservations not accepted. American breakfast $5.95; main courses $4.50–$10. MC, V. Sun–Thurs 7am–11:30pm; Fri–Sat 7am–midnight. Metro: F.

Chow 𝒢 Ⓥalue AMERICAN

Chow claims to serve American cuisine, but the management must be thinking of today's America, because the menu is not exactly meatloaf and apple pie. And that's just fine for eclectic and cost-conscious diners. After all, what's not to like about starting with a Cobb salad before moving on to Thai-style noodles with steak, chicken, peanuts, and spicy lime-chile garlic broth, or cioppino? Better yet, everything except the fish of the day costs under $15, especially the budget-wise daily sandwich specials, which range from meatball with mozzarella (Sun) to grilled tuna with Asian-style slaw, pickled ginger, and a wasabi mayonnaise (Mon); both come with salad, soup, or fries. Although the food and prices alone would be a good argument for coming here, beer on tap, a great inexpensive wine selection, and the fun, tavernlike environment clinch the deal. A second location, **Park Chow,** is at

1240 Ninth Ave. (© **415/665-9912**). You can't make reservations unless you have a party of eight or more, but if you're headed their way, you can call ahead to place your name on the wait list (recommended).

215 Church St. (near Market St.). © **415/552-2469**. Reservations not accepted except for parties of 8 or more. Main courses $7–$15. DISC, MC, V. Mon–Thurs 11am–11pm; Fri 11am–midnight; Sat 10am–midnight; Sun 10am–11pm; brunch served Sat–Sun 10–2:30pm. Bus: 8, 22, or 37. Streetcar: F, J, K, L, or M.

Firewood Café ⟨★⟩ ⟨*Value*⟩ AMERICAN/ITALIAN   One of the sharpest rooms in the neighborhood, the colorful Firewood put its money in the essentials and eliminated extra overhead. There are no waiters or waitresses; everyone orders at the counter and then relaxes at the single family-style table, at one of the small tables facing the huge street-side windows, or in the cheery back dining room. Management didn't skimp on the cozy-chic atmosphere and inspired but limited menu: The fresh salads come with a choice of three "fixin's," ranging from caramelized onions to spiced walnuts, and three gourmet dressing options. Then there are the pastas—three tortellini selections, such as roasted chicken and mortadella—and gourmet pizzas. Or how about herb-roasted half or whole chicken ($8.25 or $15, respectively) with roasted new potatoes? Wines cost $4.95 to $5.95 by the glass and a reasonable $15 to $22 per bottle. Draft and bottled beers are also available, and desserts top off at $4.

4248 18th St. (at Diamond St.). © **415/252-0999**. www.firewoodcafe.com. Main courses $7–$15. MC, V. Sun–Thurs 11am–10pm; Fri–Sat 11am–11pm. Bus: 8, 33, 35, or 37. Streetcar: F, K, L, or M.

14 Haight-Ashbury

For a map of restaurants in this section, see the "Dining Around Town" map on p. 116.

MODERATE

RNM ⟨★⟩ AMERICAN   Lower Haight is hardly known for glamour, and that's just what makes this hip little restaurant such a pleasant surprise. Beyond the full-length silver mesh curtain is a glitzy dual-level dining room that looks like it belongs in New York City rather than this funky 'hood. Warmly lit with dark-wood floors and tables, a cool full bar, and lounge mezzanine, it's a pleasant setting for an Italian- and French-inspired American meal by chef Justine Miner, who sharpened her culinary skills and knives at San Francisco's Postrio, Café Kati, and Globe. Start with appetizers such as ahi tuna tartare with waffle chips, quail egg, and microgreens; the charcuterie plate; and caramelized onion and wild-mushroom pizza with fontina cheese and truffle oil. Entrees range from porcini-crusted day boat scallops on a purée of artichokes, to pan roasted rib-eye steak with pancetta-wrapped red Irish potatoes and shaved black Himalayan truffles. It's not a destination restaurant, but if you're in the area or want to go off the beaten dining path, this is a good choice. *Tip:* A $28 prix fixe menu is offered daily from 5:30 to 7pm.

598 Haight St. (at Steiner St.). © **415/551-7900**. www.rnmrestaurant.com. Reservations recommended. Small plates and pizza $7–$14; main courses $12–$22. AE, MC, V. Tues–Thurs 5:30–10pm; Fri–Sat 5:30–11pm. Valet Thurs–Sat. Closed Sun–Mon. Bus: 7 or 22.

INEXPENSIVE

Cha Cha Cha ⟨★★⟩ ⟨*Value*⟩ CARIBBEAN   This is one of my all-time favorite places to get festive, but it's not for everybody. Dining at Cha Cha Cha is not about a meal, it's about an experience. Put your name on the waiting list, crowd into the minuscule bar, and sip sangria while you wait. When you do get seated (it can take up to two pitchers of sangria, but by then you really don't care), you'll dine in a loud—and I mean *loud*—dining room with Santería altars, banana trees, and plastic tropical-themed tablecloths. The best thing to do is order from the tapas menu and share the dishes family-style. Fried calamari, fried new potatoes, Cajun shrimp, and mussels in saffron broth are all bursting with flavor and accompanied by luscious sauces—whatever you choose, you can't go wrong. This is the kind of place where you take friends in a partying mood and make an evening of it. If you want the flavor without the festivities, come during lunch. Their second, larger location, in the Mission District, at 2327 Mission St., between 19th and 20th streets (℃ **415/648-0504**), is open for dinner only and has a full bar specializing in mojitos.

1801 Haight St. (at Shrader St.). ℃ **415/386-7670**. www.cha3.com. Reservations not accepted. Tapas $5–$9; main courses $12–$15. MC, V. Daily 11:30am–4pm; Sun–Thurs 5–11pm; Fri–Sat 5–11:30pm. Bus: 6, 7, or 71. Streetcar: N.

Citrus Club ⚡ NOODLES   When you're a starving writer you quickly discover that the cheapest, healthiest, and most satisfying things to eat in San Francisco are burritos and noodles. Citrus Club does noodles. Large, heaping bowls of thick Asian noodles, served hot in bone-warming broth or cool, minty, and refreshing. In typical Upper Haight fashion, the Club has sort of a cheap-Polynesian-chic feel—love those Vietnamese straw hat lamps—a young, hip staff and clientele, and the omnipresent world beat rhythms. Most items on the menu are unlike anything you've seen before, so take my advice and walk around the two dining rooms to see what looks good before ordering. A refreshing starter is the citrus salad made with mixed greens, mint, fried noodles, and a tangy citrus vinaigrette. Popular cold noodle selections are the spicy lime and coconut, and the orange-mint. For hot noodles, try the marmalade shrimp or sweet chile-glazed tofu and greens. If you're in a party mood, order a sake margarita; otherwise, a big pot of ginger tea goes well with any of the noodle dishes.

1790 Haight St. (at Shrader St.). ℃ **415/387-6366**. Main courses $6–$10. MC, V. Mon–Thurs and Sun 11:30am–10pm; Fri–Sat 11:30am–11pm. Muni Metro: N. Bus: 6, 7, 66, 71, or 73.

Kan Zaman ⚡ *Finds* MIDDLE EASTERN   An evening dining at Kan Zaman is one of those quintessential Haight-Ashbury experiences that you can't wait to tell your friends about back in Ohio. As you pass through glass-beaded curtains, you're led by the hostess to knee-high tables under a billowed canopy tent. Shoes removed, you sit cross-legged with your friends in cushioned comfort. The most adventurous of your group requests an *argeeleh*, a large hookah pipe filled with fruity honey or apricot tobacco. Reluctantly at first, everyone simultaneously sips the sweet smoke from the cobra-like tendrils emanating from the hookah, then dinner arrives—inexpensive platters offering a variety of classic Middle Eastern cuisine: smoky baba ghanouj, kibbe (cracked wheat with spiced lamb) meat pies, Casablanca beef couscous, spicy hummus with pita bread, succulent lamb and chicken kabobs. The spiced wine starts to take effect, just in time for the beautiful, sensuous belly dancers who glide across the dining room, mesmerizing the rapt audience with their seemingly impossible gyrations. The evening ends, the bill arrives: $17 each. Perfect. *Note:* Belly dancing starts at 9pm Thursday though Saturday only.

1793 Haight St. (at Shrader St.). ℃ **415/751-9656**. Main courses $4–$14. MC, V. Mon–Thurs 5pm–midnight; Fri 5pm–2am; Sat noon–2am; Sun noon–midnight. Metro: N. Bus: 6, 7, 66, 71, or 73.

Thep Phanom ⚡ THAI   It's the combination of fresh ingredients, attractive decor, and friendly service, and that heavenly balance of salty, sweet, hot, and sour flavors, that have made Thep Phanom one of the city's most beloved Thai restaurants. Those who like to play it safe will be more than happy with standards such as pad Thai, coconut-lemon-grass soup, and prawns in red curry sauce, but consider diverting from the usual suspects for such house specialties as Thaitanic Beef (stir-fried beef and string beans in a spicy sauce), prawns with eggplant and crisped basil, and *ped sawan*—duck with a delicate honey sauce served over spinach. There's good people-watching here as well—the restaurant's reputation attracts a truly diverse San Francisco crowd. Be sure to make reservations or prepare for a long wait on weekend nights, and don't leave anything even remotely valuable in your car.

400 Waller St. (at Fillmore St.). © **415/431-2526.** www.thepphanom.com. Reservations recommended. Main courses $9–$13. AE, DC, DISC, MC, V. Daily 5:30–10:30pm. Bus: 6, 7, 22, 66, or 71.

15 Richmond/Sunset Districts

Yes, it's a long haul from Downtown to "the Avenues," but these restaurants wouldn't be in the guidebook if they weren't worth the trip. For a map of restaurants in this section, see the "Dining Around Town" map on p. 116.

MODERATE

Aziza ★★ MOROCCAN   If you're looking for something really different—or a festive spot for a large party—head deep into the Avenues for an exotic taste of Morocco. Chef-owner Mourad Lahlou creates an excellent dining experience through colorful and distinctly Moroccan surroundings combined with a modern yet authentic take on the cuisine of his homeland. In any of the three opulently adorned dining rooms (the front room features private booths, the middle room is more formal, and the back has lower seating and a Moroccan lounge feel), you can indulge in the seasonal five-course tasting menu ($49) or individual treats such as kumquat-enriched lamb shank; saffron guinea hen with preserved lemon and olives; or Paine Farm squab with wild mushrooms, bitter greens, and a *ras el hanout* reduction (a traditional Moroccan blend of 40 or so spices). Consider finishing off with my favorite dessert (if it's in season): rhubarb galette with rose- and geranium-scented crème fraîche, vanilla aspic, and rhubarb consommé.

5800 Geary Blvd. (at 22nd Ave.). © **415/752-2222.** www.aziza-sf.com. Reservations recommended. Main courses $10–$22; 5-course menu $39. MC, V. Wed–Mon 5:30–10:30pm. Valet parking $8 weekdays, $10 weekends. Bus: 29 or 38.

Beach Chalet Brewery & Restaurant ★ AMERICAN   While Cliff House (see below) has more historical character and better ocean views, the Beach Chalet down the road has far better food, drinks, and atmosphere (ergo, it's where the locals go). The Chalet occupies the upper floor of a historic public lounge adorned with WPA frescos that originally opened in 1900 and has been fully restored. Dinner is pricey, and the ocean view disappears with the sun, so come for lunch or an early dinner when you can eat your hamburger, buttermilk fried calamari, or grilled Atlantic salmon with one of the best vistas around. It the evening it's a more local crowd, especially on Tuesday through Sunday evenings when live bands accompany the cocktails and house-brewed ales. Breakfast is served here as well. *Note:* Be careful getting into the parking lot (accessible only from the northbound side of the highway)—it's a quick, sandy turn.

In early 2004, owners Lara and Greg Truppelli added the adjoining **Park Chalet** restaurant to the Beach Chalet. The 3,000-square-foot glass-enclosed extension behind the original landmark building offers more casual fare—with entrees ranging from $11 to $23—including rib-eye steak, fish and chips, roasted chicken, and pizza. Other reasons to come? Retractable glass walls reveal Golden Gate Park's landmark Dutch windmill, a fireplace warms the room on chillier evenings, and live music is performed Tuesday and Thursday through Sunday evenings. Weather permitting, you can eat out back on the lawn; there's even a weekend barbecue from 11am to dusk in the summer. The restaurant opens at 11am daily in the summer (noon in winter) and, like the Beach Chalet, has varying closing times, so call ahead.

1000 Great Hwy. (at west end of Golden Gate Park, near Fulton St.). ℂ 415/386-8439. www.beachchalet.com. Main courses $8–$17 breakfast, $11–$27 lunch/dinner. AE, MC, V. Beach Chalet: Breakfast Mon–Fri 9–11am; lunch daily 11am–5pm; dinner Sun–Thurs 5–10pm, Fri–Sat 5–11pm; brunch Sat–Sun 9am–2pm. Park Chalet: Lunch Mon–Fri noon–9pm; dinner Sun–Thurs 5–9pm, Fri–Sat 5–11pm; brunch Sat–Sun 11am–2pm. Bus: 18, 31, or 38. Streetcar: N.

Cliff House ⓖ CALIFORNIA/SEAFOOD   In the old days (we're talking way back), Cliff House was *the* place to go for a romantic night on the town. Nowadays, the revamped San Francisco landmark caters mostly to tourists who arrive to gander at the Sutro Baths remains next door or dine at the two remodeled restaurants. The more formal (and pricey) **Sutro's** has contemporary decor, spectacular panoramic views, and a fancy seafood-influenced American menu that showcases local ingredients. The food, while nothing revolutionary, is well prepared and features the likes of roasted organic beet salad; lobster and crab cakes with shaved fennel, romesco sauce, and caramelized Meyer lemon; and a mighty fine grilled lamb sirloin sandwich (at lunch). The same spectacular views in less dramatic but still beautiful surroundings can be found at the **Bistro,** which offers big salads, sandwiches, burgers, and other soul-satisfiers. For the most superb ocean views, come for sunset, so long as it looks like the fog will let up. Alternatively, overindulge to the tune of live harp music at the Sunday champagne buffet in the **Terrace Room.** (Reserve well in advance; it's a popular event.)

1090 Point Lobos (at Merrie Way). ℂ 415/386-3330. www.cliffhouse.com. Reservations accepted for Sutro's only. Bistro main courses $9–$26 breakfast/lunch, $13–$26 dinner; Sutro main courses $18–$25 lunch, $18–$30 dinner; 3-course prix-fixe $25 lunch and $35 dinner (Mon–Fri only). AE, DC, DISC, MC, V. Bistro: Mon–Sat 9am–9:30pm; Sat–Sun 9am–10pm. Sutro: daily 11:30am–3:30pm and 5–9:30pm; brunch Sun 10am–2pm. Bus: 18 or 38.

Khan Toke Thai House ⓖⓖ *Value* THAI   Khan Toke Thai is so traditional you're asked to remove your shoes before being seated. Popular for special occasions, this Richmond District fixture is easily the prettiest Thai restaurant in the city; lavishly carved teak interiors evoke the ambience of a Thai temple. To start, I suggest ordering the *tom yam gong* soup of lemon grass, shrimp, mushroom, tomato, and cilantro. Follow with such well-flavored dishes as ground pork with fresh ginger, green onion, peanuts, and lemon juice; prawns with hot chiles, mint leaves, lime juice, lemon grass, and onions; or chicken with cashews, crispy chiles, and onions. For a real treat, have the deep-fried pompano topped with sautéed ginger, onions, peppers, pickled garlic, and yellow-bean sauce; or deep-fried red snapper with "three-flavors" sauce and basil leaves. A complete dinner, including appetizer, soup, salad, two main courses, dessert, and coffee, is a great value.

5937 Geary Blvd. (btw. 23rd and 24th aves.). ℂ 415/668-6654. Reservations recommended Fri–Sat for parties of 3 or more. Main courses $6–$13; fixed-price dinner $20. AE, MC, V. Daily 5–10pm. Bus: 38.

INEXPENSIVE

Burma Superstar ⓖⓖ *Value* BURMESE   Despite its gratuitous name, this basic dining room garners two-star status by offering exceptional Burmese food at rock-bottom prices. Unfortunately, the allure of the tealeaf salad, Burmese-style curry with potato, and sweet-tangy sesame beef is one of the city's worst-kept secrets. Add to that a no-reservations policy and you can count on waiting in line for up to an hour. (FYI, parties of two are seated more quickly than larger groups, and it's less crowded at lunch.) On the bright side, you can pencil your cellphone number onto the waiting list and browse the Clement Street shops until you receive a call.

309 Clement St. (at Fourth Ave.). © 415/387-2147. www.burmasuperstar.com. Reservations not accepted. Main courses $8–$16. MC, V. Mon–Thurs 11am–3:30pm and 5:30–9:30pm; Fri–Sat 11am–3:30pm and 5:30–10pm; Sun 11am–3:30pm and 5:30–9:30pm. Bus: 2, 4, 38, or 44.

Ton Kiang ★★ CHINESE/DIM SUM   Ton Kiang is the number one place in the city to have dim sum (served daily), only partially due to the fact that they make all their sauces, pickles, and other delicacies in-house. The experience goes like this: Wait in line (which is out the door 11am–1:30pm on weekends), get a table on the first or second floor, and get ready to say yes to dozens of delicacies, which are brought to the table for your approval. From stuffed crab claws, roast Beijing duck, and a gazillion dumpling selections (including scallop and vegetable, shrimp, and beef) to the delicious and hard-to-find *doa miu* (snow pea sprouts flash-sautéed with garlic and peanut oil) and a mesmerizing mango pudding, every tray of morsels coming from the kitchen is an absolute delight. Though it's hard to get past the dim sum, which is served all day every day, the full menu of Hakka cuisine is worth investigation as well—fresh and flavorful soups; an array of seafood, beef, and chicken; and clay-pot specialties.

5821 Geary Blvd. (btw. 22nd and 23rd aves.). © 415/387-8273. www.tonkiang.net. Reservations accepted for parties of 8 or more. Dim sum $2–$5.50; main courses $9–$25. AE, DC, DISC, MC, V. Mon–Thurs 10am–10pm; Fri 10am–10:30pm; Sat 9:30am–10:30pm; Sun 9am–10pm. Bus: 38.

8

Exploring San Francisco

San Francisco's parks, museums, tours, and landmarks are favorites for travelers the world over and offer an array of activities to suit every visitor. But no particular activity or place makes the city one of the most popular destinations in the world. It's San Francisco itself—its charm, its atmosphere, its perfect blend of big metropolis with small-town hospitality. No matter what you do while you're here—whether you spend all your time in central areas like Union Square or North Beach, or explore the outer neighborhoods—you're bound to discover the reason millions of visitors keep leaving their hearts in San Francisco.

1 Famous San Francisco Sights

Alcatraz Island ★★★ (Kids)   Visible from Fisherman's Wharf, Alcatraz Island (also known as the Rock) has seen a checkered history. Juan Manuel Ayala was the first European to discover it in 1775 and named it after the many pelicans that nested on the island. From the 1850s to 1933, when the army vacated the island, it served as a military post, protecting the bay's shoreline. In 1934, the government converted the buildings of the military outpost into a maximum-security prison. Given the sheer cliffs, treacherous tides and currents, and frigid water temperatures, it was believed to be a totally escape-proof prison. Among the famous gangsters who occupied cell blocks A through D were Al Capone, Robert Stroud, the so-called Birdman of Alcatraz (because he was an expert in ornithological diseases), Machine Gun Kelly, and Alvin Karpis. It cost a fortune to keep them imprisoned here because all supplies, including water, had to be shipped in. In 1963, after an apparent escape in which no bodies were recovered, the government closed the prison. In 1969, a group of Native Americans chartered a boat to the island to symbolically reclaim the island for the Indian people. They occupied the island until 1971, the longest occupation of a federal facility by Native Americans to this day, when they were forcibly removed by the U.S. government (see www.nps.gov/archive/alcatraz/indian.html for more information on the Native American occupation of Alcatraz). The next year the island became part of the Golden Gate National Recreation Area. The wildlife that was driven away during the military and prison years has begun to return—the black-crested night heron and other seabirds are nesting here again—and a trail passes through the island's nature areas. Tours, including an audio tour of the prison block and a slide show, are given by the park's rangers, who entertain guests with interesting anecdotes.

Allow about 2½ hours for the round-trip boat ride and the tour. Wear comfortable shoes (the National Park Service notes that there are a lot of hills to climb on the tour) and take a heavy sweater or windbreaker, because even when the sun's out, it's cold there. You should also bring snacks and drinks with you if you think you'll want them. Although there is a beverage-and-snack bar on the ferry, the options are limited and

Major San Francisco Attractions

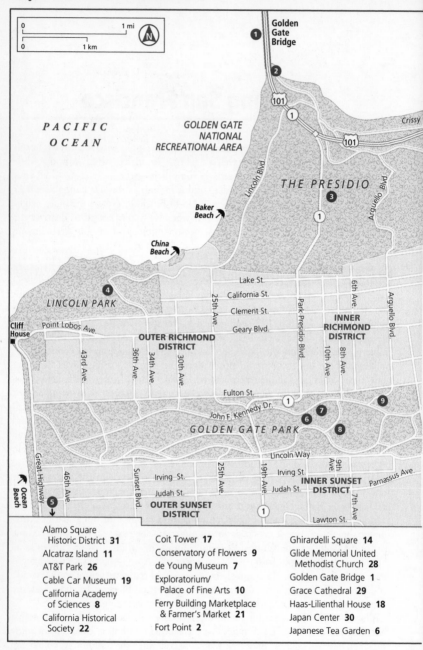

Alamo Square
 Historic District **31**

Alcatraz Island **11**

AT&T Park **26**

Cable Car Museum **19**

California Academy
 of Sciences **8**

California Historical
 Society **22**

Coit Tower **17**

Conservatory of Flowers **9**

de Young Museum **7**

Exploratorium/
 Palace of Fine Arts **10**

Ferry Building Marketplace
 & Farmer's Market **21**

Fort Point **2**

Ghirardelli Square **14**

Glide Memorial United
 Methodist Church **28**

Golden Gate Bridge **1**

Grace Cathedral **29**

Haas-Lilienthal House **18**

Japan Center **30**

Japanese Tea Garden **6**

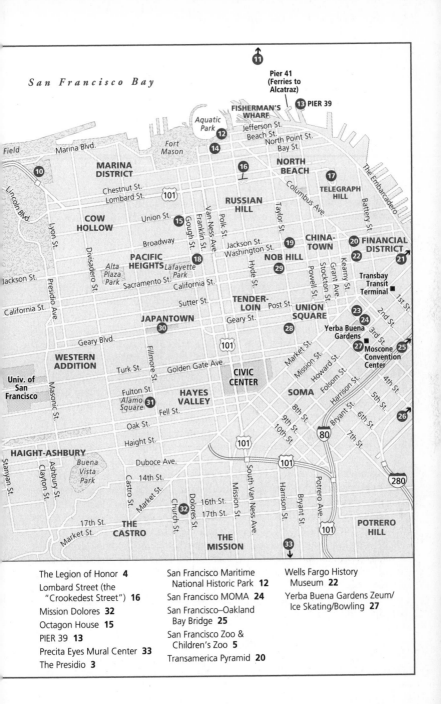

San Francisco Bay

Pier 41 (Ferries to Alcatraz)
13 PIER 39

FISHERMAN'S WHARF
Jefferson St.
Aquatic Park **12**
Beach St.
North Point St.
Bay St.

Field
Marina Blvd.
Fort Mason

10
Lincoln Blvd

MARINA DISTRICT

16

NORTH BEACH

17 TELEGRAPH HILL

Chestnut St.
Lombard St. **101**
Union St. **15**

COW HOLLOW

Columbus Ave.

Battery St.

The Embarcadero

Lyon St.
Divisadero St.
Gough St.
Franklin St.
Van Ness Ave.
Polk St.

Broadway

PACIFIC HEIGHTS
Alta Plaza Park
Lafayette Park

RUSSIAN HILL

Taylor St.

Jackson St.
Washington St.
Hyde St.

NOB HILL
19
29

CHINA-TOWN

Grant Ave.
Stockton St.
Kearny St.
Powell St.

20 **FINANCIAL DISTRICT**
22 **21**

Transbay Transit Terminal

Jackson St.
Presidio Ave.
Masonic Ave.

California St.

Sacramento St.
California St.

Sutter St.

JAPANTOWN
30

TENDER-LOIN
Post St.

Geary St.

UNION SQUARE
28

2nd St.
1st St.

23
24

Yerba Buena Gardens
27 Moscone Convention Center
25

Geary Blvd.

WESTERN ADDITION

Fillmore St.

101

CIVIC CENTER

Mission St.
Howard St.
Folsom St.

3rd St.
4th St.

26

Univ. of San Francisco

Turk St.
Golden Gate Ave.

Fulton St.
Alamo Square **31**
Oak St.

HAYES VALLEY

Fell St.

SOMA

8th St.
9th St.
10th St.

Harrison St.
Bryant St.

5th St.
6th St.
7th St.

80

Haight St.

HAIGHT-ASHBURY
Buena Vista Park

Duboce Ave.
14th St.

101
101

South Van Ness Ave.
Harrison St.
Bryant St.
Potrero Ave.

280

Stanyan St.
Ashbury St.
Clayton St.
Castro St.
Market St.

16th St.
17th St.

Church St.
Dolores St.
Mission St.

32

17th St.
Market St.

THE CASTRO

THE MISSION

33

POTRERO HILL

101

Tips Finding Your Way

When asking for directions in San Francisco, be careful not to confuse numerical avenues with numerical streets. Numerical avenues (Third *Avenue* and so on) are in the Richmond and Sunset districts in the western part of the city. Numerical streets (Third *Street* and so on) are south of Market St. in the eastern and southern parts of the city. Get this wrong and you'll be an hour late for dinner.

expensive, and only water is available on the island. The excursion to Alcatraz is very popular and space is limited, so purchase tickets as far in advance as possible (up to 90 days) via the **Alcatraz Cruises** website at www.alcatrazcruises.com. You can also purchase tickets in person by visiting the Hornblower Alcatraz Landing ticket office at Pier 33. The first departure, called the "Early Bird," leaves at 9am, and ferries depart about every half-hour afterward until 2pm. Night tours (highly recommended) are also available Thursday through Monday and are a more intimate and wonderfully spooky experience.

For those who want to get a closer look at Alcatraz without going ashore, two boat-tour operators offer short circumnavigations of the island (see "Self-Guided & Organized Tours" on p. 191 for complete information).

Pier 41, near Fisherman's Wharf. © 415/981-7625. www.alcatrazcruises.com or www.nps.gov/alcatraz. Admission (includes ferry trip and audio tour) $25 adults; $23 seniors 62 and older; $15 children 5–11. Night tours cost $32 adults; $29 seniors 62 and older; $19 children 5–11. Arrive at least 20 min. before departure time.

AT&T Park ★★ *Moments* If you're a baseball fan, you'll definitely want to schedule a visit to the magnificent AT&T Park, home of the San Francisco Giants and hailed by the media as one of the finest ballparks in America. From April through October, a sell-out crowd of 40,800 fans pack the $319-million ballpark for nearly every game—which has a smaller, more intimate feel than Monster Park (where the 49ers play) and prime views of San Francisco Bay—and root for their National League Giants.

During the Major League season, tickets to the game are usually hard to come by (and expensive when you find them), but you can try to join the Bleacher Bums by purchasing one of the 500 bleacher-seat tickets sold every day before the game. They make you work for it, however: You have to show up at the ballpark 4 hours early to get a lottery number, and then come back 2 hours before the game to get your tickets (maximum four per person). The upside is that the tickets are only $8.50 to $10.

If you can't even get bleacher seats, you can always join the "knothole gang" at the Portwalk (located behind right field) to catch a free glimpse of the game through cut-out portholes into the ballpark. In the spirit of sharing, Portwalk peekers are encouraged to take in only an inning or two before giving way to fellow fans.

One guaranteed way to get into the ballpark is to take a **guided tour of AT&T Park** and go behind the scenes where you'll see the press box, the dugout, the visitor's clubhouse, a luxury suite, and more. All tours run daily at 10:30am and 12:30pm. Ticket prices are $10 for adults, $8 for seniors over 55, and $6 for kids 12 and under. There are no tours on game days, and limited tours on the day of night games. To buy tickets online log onto www.sfgiants.com, and then click on "AT&T Park" and "Ballpark Tours" from the drop-down list. You can also buy tour tickets at any Giants Dugout Store or Tickets.com outlet. For more tour information call © 415/972-2400.

Fisherman's Wharf & Vicinity

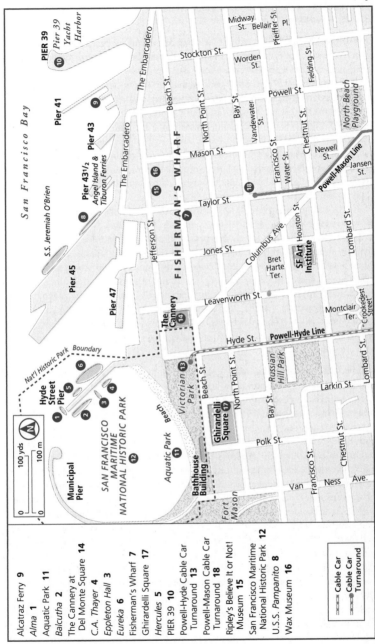

Alcatraz Ferry **9**
Alma **1**
Aquatic Park **11**
Balcutha **2**
The Cannery at
  Del Monte Square **14**
C.A. Thayer **4**
Eppleton Hall **3**
Eureka **6**
Fisherman's Wharf **7**
Ghirardelli Square **17**
Hercules **5**
PIER 39 **10**
Powell-Hyde Cable Car
  Turnaround **13**
Powell-Mason Cable Car
  Turnaround **18**
Ripley's Believe It or Not!
  Museum **15**
San Francisco Maritime
  National Historic Park **12**
U.S.S. Pampanito **8**
Wax Museum **16**

Cable Car
Cable Car
Turnaround

At the southeast corner of SoMa at the south end of the Embarcadero (bounded by King, 2nd, and 3rd sts.). ⓒ **415/ 972-2000.** www.sfgiants.com. Metro: N line; Bus: 10, 15, 30, 45, and 47.

Boudin at the Wharf 𝒢   After more than 30 years of being an inconspicuous bread shop in the heart of Fisherman's Wharf, the Boudin Bakery has been super-sized. The new, ultra-modern, 26,000-square-foot flagship baking emporium is nearly half a block long, housing not only their signature demonstration bakery but also a museum, gourmet marketplace, cafe, espresso bar, and restaurant. The Boudin (pro-nounced bo-DEEN) family has been baking sourdough French bread in San Francisco since the Gold Rush, using the same simple recipe and "mother dough" for more than 150 years. About 3,000 loaves a day are baked within the glass-walled bakery; visitors can watch the entire process from a 30-foot observation window along Jefferson Street or from a catwalk suspended directly over the bakery (it's quite entertaining, actually). You'll smell it before you see it, as the heavenly aroma emanating from the bread ovens is purposely blasted down onto the sidewalk.

The best time to arrive is in the morning when the demo bakery is in full swing. Watch (and smell) the action along Jefferson Street; then, when your appetite is stoked, head to the cafe for an inexpensive breakfast of sourdough French toast or their Bread Bowl Scrambler filled with eggs, bacon, cheddar, onions, and bell peppers. After breakfast, spend some time browsing the museum and marketplace. On the upper level is **Bistro Boudin,** a full-service restaurant serving lunch, dinner, and week-end brunch. Tours of the bakery are available as well. *Tip:* If the line at the cafe is too long, walk across the parking lot to the octagon-shaped building, which serves the same items—Boudin chowder bowls, salads, pizzas—in a serve-yourself setting.

160 Jefferson St. (btw. Taylor and Mason sts.). ⓒ **415/928-1849.** www.boudinbakery.com. Bakery/cafe/marketplace daily 10am–7pm.

Cable Cars 𝒢𝒢𝒢 *Moments* *Kids*   Although they may not be San Francisco's most practical means of transportation, cable cars are certainly the best loved and are a must-experience when visiting the city. Designated official historic landmarks by the National Park Service in 1964, they clank up and down the city's steep hills like mobile museum pieces, tirelessly hauling thousands of tourists each day to nowhere in particular.

London-born engineer Andrew Hallidie invented San Francisco's cable cars in 1869. He got the idea by serendipity. As the story goes, Hallidie was watching a team of overworked horses haul a heavily laden carriage up a steep San Francisco slope. As he watched, one horse slipped and the car rolled back, dragging the other tired beasts with it. At that moment, Hallidie resolved that he would invent a mechanical contrap-tion to replace such horses, and just 4 years later, in 1873, the first cable car made its maiden run from the top of Clay Street. Promptly ridiculed as "Hallidie's Folly," the cars were slow to gain acceptance. One early onlooker voiced the general opinion by exclaiming, "I don't believe it—the damned thing works!"

Even today, many visitors have difficulty believing that these vehicles, which have no engines, actually work. The cars, each weighing about 6 tons, run along a steel cable, enclosed under the street in a center rail. You can't see the cable unless you peer straight down into the crack, but you'll hear its characteristic clickity-clanking sound whenever you're nearby. The cars move when the gripper (not the driver) pulls back a lever that closes a pincerlike "grip" on the cable. The speed of the car, therefore, is determined by the speed of the cable, which is a constant 9½ mph—never more, never less.

Tips **The Secret to Catching Cable Cars**

Here's the secret to catching a ride on a cable car: Don't wait in line with all the tourists at the turnaround stops at the beginning and end of the lines. Walk a few blocks up the line (follow the tracks) and do as the locals do: Hop on when the car stops, hang on to a pole, and have your $5 ready to hand to the brakeman (hoping, of course, that he'll never ask). On a really busy weekend, however, the cable cars often don't stop to pick up passengers en route because they're full, so you might have to stand in line at the turnarounds.

The two types of cable cars in use hold a maximum of 90 and 100 passengers, and the limits are rigidly enforced. The best views are from the outer running boards, where you have to hold on tightly when taking curves.

Hallidie's cable cars have been imitated and used throughout the world, but all have been replaced by more efficient means of transportation. San Francisco planned to do so, too, but the proposal met with so much opposition that the cable cars' perpetuation was actually written into the city charter in 1955. The mandate cannot be revoked without the approval of a majority of the city's voters—a distant and doubtful prospect.

San Francisco's three existing cable car lines form the world's only surviving system of cable cars, which you can experience for yourself should you choose to wait in the often long boarding lines (up to a 2-hr. wait in summer). For more information on riding them, see "Getting There & Getting Around," in chapter 3, p. 32.

Powell–Hyde and Powell–Mason lines begin at the base of Powell and Market sts.; California St. line begins at the foot of Market St. $5 per ride.

The Cannery   The Cannery was built by Del Monte in 1907 as the world's largest fruit-canning plant. It was converted into a mall in the 1960s and now contains 30-plus shops and several restaurants, including **Jack's Cannery Bar** (*C* **415/931-6400**). Vendors' stalls and sidewalk cafes occupy the courtyard amid a grove of century-old olive trees, and weather permitting, street performers are usually out in force, entertaining tourists (but very few locals). Shops are open daily at 10am and Sunday at 11am, while the restaurants generally open at 11:30am.

2801 Leavenworth St. (btw. Beach and Jefferson sts.). *C* www.thecannery.com. Bus: 30 or 47. Streetcar: F to Hyde St.

Coit Tower *★★*   In a city known for its great views and vantage points, Coit Tower is one of the best. Located atop Telegraph Hill, just east of North Beach, the round stone tower offers panoramic views of the city and the bay.

Completed in 1933, the tower is the legacy of Lillie Hitchcock Coit, a wealthy eccentric who left San Francisco a $125,000 bequest "for the purpose of adding beauty to the city I have always loved" and as a memorial to its volunteer firemen. She had been saved from a fire as a child and held the city's firefighters in particularly high esteem.

Inside the base of the tower are impressive murals titled *Life in California* and *1934,* which were completed under the WPA during the New Deal. They are the work of more than 25 artists, many of whom had studied under Mexican muralist Diego Rivera.

The only bummer: The narrow street leading to the tower is often clogged with tourist traffic. If you can, find a parking spot in North Beach and hoof it. It's actually a beautiful walk—especially if you take the Filbert Street Steps (p. 195).

> *Tips*   **Earthquake Advice**
>
> Earthquakes are fairly common in California, though most are so minor you won't even notice them. However, in case of a significant shaker, there are a few basic precautionary measures to follow: If you are inside a building, do not run outside into falling debris. Seek cover—stand under a doorway or against a wall, and stay away from windows. If you exit a building after a substantial quake, use stairwells, not elevators. If you're in a car, pull over to the side of the road and stop—but not until you are away from bridges, overpasses, telephone poles, and power lines. Stay in your car. If you're out walking, stay outside and away from trees, power lines, and the sides of buildings. If you're in an area with tall buildings, find a doorway in which to stand. And if you're having cocktails find a straw.

Telegraph Hill. ✆ 415/362-0808. Admission is free to enter; elevator ride to the top is $4.50 adults, $3.50 seniors, $2 children 6–12. Daily 10am–6pm. Bus: 39 (Coit).

Farmers' Market ✶✶✶   If you're heading to the Ferry Building Marketplace or just happen to be in the area at the right time (especially a sunny Sat), make a point of visiting the Farmers' Market, which is held in the outdoor areas in front of and behind the marketplace. This is where San Francisco foodies and many of the best local chefs—including the famed Alice Waters of Chez Panisse—gather, hang out, and peruse stalls hawking the finest Northern California fruits, vegetables, breads, dairy, flowers, readymade snacks, and complete meals by local restaurants. You'll be amazed at the variety and quality, and the crowded scene itself is something to behold. You can also pick up locally made vinegars, preserves, olives, and oils here—they make wonderful gifts. Drop by on Saturday from 9am to noon for a serious social fest, including interviews with local farmers and culinary demos by city chefs.

The Embarcadero, at Market St. ✆ 415/291-3276. www.cuesa.org. Year-round Tues 10am–2pm, Sat 8am–2pm; May–Oct Tues 10am–2pm, Thurs 4–8pm, Sat 8am–2pm, Sun 10am–2pm. Bus: 2, 7, 12, 14, 21, 66, or 71. Streetcar: F. BART: Embarcadero.

Ferry Building Marketplace ✶✶✶ *Finds*   There's no better way to enjoy a San Francisco morning than strolling this gourmet marketplace in the Ferry Building and snacking your way through breakfast or lunch. San Franciscans—myself included—can't get enough of this place; we're still amazed at what a fantastic job they did renovating the interior. The Marketplace is open daily and includes much of Northern California's best gourmet bounty: Cowgirl Creamery's Artisan Cheese Shop, Recchiuti Confections (amazing), Scharffen Berger Chocolate, Acme Breads, Wine Country's gourmet diner Taylor's Refresher, famed Vietnamese restaurant the Slanted Door, and myriad other restaurants, delis, gourmet coffee shops, specialty foods, and wine bars. Check out the Imperial Tea Court where you'll be taught the traditional Chinese way to steep and sip your tea; nosh on premium sturgeon roe at Tsar Nicoulai Caviar, a small Parisian-style "caviar cafe"; buy cooking items at the Sur La Table shop; grab a bite and savor the bayfront views from in- and outdoor tables; or browse the Farmers' Market when it's up and running (see above). Trust me, you'll love this place.

The Embarcadero, at Market St. ✆ 415/693-0996. www.ferrybuildingmarketplace.com. Most stores daily 10am–6pm; restaurant hours vary. Bus: 2, 7, 12, 14, 21, 66, or 71. Streetcar: F. BART: Embarcadero.

Fisherman's Wharf *Kids*   Few cities in America are as adept at wholesaling their historical sites as San Francisco, which has converted Fisherman's Wharf into one of the most popular tourist attractions in the world. Unless you come early in the morning to watch the few remaining fishing boats depart, you won't find many traces of the traditional waterfront life that once existed here—the only trolling going on at Fisherman's Wharf these days is for tourists' dollars. Nonetheless, everyone always seems to be enjoying themselves as they stroll down Pier 39 on a sunny day, especially the kids.

Originally called Meigg's Wharf, this bustling strip of waterfront got its present moniker from generations of fishermen who used to dock their boats here. A small fleet of fewer than 30 fishing boats still set out from here, but basically Fisherman's Wharf has been converted into one long shopping and entertainment mall that stretches from Ghirardelli Square at the west end to Pier 39 at the east.

Accommodating a total of 300 boats, two marinas flank Pier 39 and house the sightseeing ferry fleets, including departures to Alcatraz. In recent years, some 900 California sea lions have taken up residence on the adjacent floating docks. Until they abandon their new playground, which seems more and more unlikely, these playful, noisy (some nights you can hear them all the way from Washington Sq.) *Zalophus californianus* are one of the best free attractions on the wharf. Weather permitting, the **Marine Mammal Center** (✆ **415/289-SEAL**) offers an educational talk at Pier 39 on weekends from 11am to 5pm that teaches visitors about the range, habitat, and adaptability of the California sea lion.

Some people love Fisherman's Wharf; others can't get far enough away from it. Most agree that, for better or for worse, it has to be seen at least once in your lifetime. There are still some traces of old-school San Francisco character here that I will always enjoy, particularly the convivial seafood street vendors who dish out piles of fresh Dungeness, clam chowder, and sourdough bread from their steaming stainless steel carts. Fisherman's Wharf is also one of the few places in the city where kids can be unleashed to roam through the aquarium, crawl through a real World War II submarine, play at the arcade, ride the carousel, and eat junk food galore. In short, there's something for everyone here, even us snobby locals.

At Taylor St. and the Embarcadero. ✆ 415/674-7503. www.fishermanswharf.org. Bus: 15, 30, 32, 39, 42, or 82X. Streetcar: F. Cable car: Powell–Mason to the last stop and walk to the wharf. If you're arriving by car, park on adjacent streets or on the wharf btw. Taylor and Jones sts. for $16 per day, $8 with validation from participating restaurants.

San Francisco Segway Tours

Segways are those weird-looking upright scooters you've probably seen on TV. The two-wheeled "human transporter" is an ingenious electric-powered transportation device that uses gyroscopes to emulate human balance. After the free 40-minute lesson, riding a Segway becomes intuitive: lean forward, go forward; lean back, go back; stand upright, stop. Simple. The **San Francisco Electric Tour Company** offers Segway-powered narrated 2-hour tours of the San Francisco waterfront daily, starting from Fisherman's Wharf and heading out all the way to the Marina Green. For $70 it's not a bad deal, and it's the closest you'll come to being a celebrity (*everyone* checks you out). *Note:* You have be at least 12 years old to join the tour. For more information log onto www.sfelectrictour.com or call ✆ **415/474-3130**.

Kids **Funky Favorites at Fisherman's Wharf**

The following attractions clustered on or near Fisherman's Wharf are great fun for kids, adults, and kitsch-lovers of all ages. My favorite is the ominous-looking World War II submarine **USS *Pampanito,*** Pier 45, Fisherman's Wharf (© 415/775-1943; www.maritime.org), which saw plenty of action in the Pacific. It has been completely restored, and visitors are free to crawl around inside and play Das Boot. Admission, which includes an audio tour, is $9 for those 13 to 61, $5 for seniors 62 and older, $3 for children 6 to 12, and free for children 5 and under; the family pass (two adults, up to four kids) costs $20. The *Pampanito* is open daily at 9am. Also on Pier 45, the free **Musée Mécanique** (p. 171) is worth a look.

Ripley's Believe It or Not! Museum, 175 Jefferson St. (© 415/771-6188; www.ripleysf.com), has drawn curious spectators through its doors for over 30 years. Inside, you'll experience a world of improbabilities: a 1/3-scale matchstick cable car, a shrunken human torso once owned by Ernest Hemingway, a dinosaur made from car bumpers, a walk through a kaleidoscope tunnel, and video displays and illusions. Robert LeRoy Ripley's infamous arsenal may lead you to ponder whether truth is, in fact, stranger than fiction. What it won't do is blow your mind or feel truly worth the money. That said, with the right attitude, it's easy to enjoy an hour here playing amid the goofy and interactive displays with lots of laughs included in the admission price, which is $15 for adults, $9 for children 5 to 12, and free for children 4 and under. The museum is open Sunday through Thursday from 9am to 11pm, and 9am until midnight on Friday and Saturday (open 10am in winter months).

Conceived and executed in the Madame Tussaud mold, San Francisco's **Wax Museum,** 145 Jefferson St. (© 800/439-4305 or 415/202-0402; www.waxmuseum.com), has long been a kitschy tourist trap. The museum has 270 lifelike figures, including Oprah Winfrey, Britney Spears, Marilyn Monroe, John Wayne, former President George Bush and current president George W. Bush, Giants baseball star Barry Bonds, rap artist Eminem, and "Feared Leaders" such as Fidel Castro. The Chamber of Horrors features Dracula, Frankenstein, and a werewolf, along with bloody victims hanging from meat hooks. New additions include pop icons such as Brad Pitt, Angelina Jolie, and Nicole Kidman. Admission is $13 for adults, $9.95 for juniors 12 to 17 and seniors 55 and older, $6.95 for children 6 to 11, and free for children 5 and under. The complex is open Monday through Friday from 10am to 9pm, Saturday and Sunday from 9am to 11pm.

Ghirardelli Square This National Historic Landmark property dates from 1864, when it served as a factory making Civil War uniforms, but it's best known as the former chocolate and spice factory of Domingo Ghirardelli (pronounced "*Gear*-ar-delly"), who purchased it in 1893. The factory has since been converted into an unimpressive three-level mall containing 30-plus stores and five dining establishments. Street performers entertain regularly in the West Plaza and fountain area. Incidentally, the Ghirardelli Chocolate Company still makes chocolate, but its factory is in a lower-rent district in the East Bay. Still, if you have a sweet tooth, you won't be disappointed at the mall's fantastic (and expensive) old-fashioned soda fountain, which is open until midnight. Their "world famous" hot fudge sundae is good, too. (Then again, have you ever had a bad hot fudge sundae?)

900 North Point St. (btw. Polk and Larkin sts.). © **415/775-5500**. www.ghirardellisq.com. Stores generally open daily 10am–9pm in summer; Sun–Fri 10am–6pm, Sat 10am–9pm rest of year. Parking $2 per 20 min. (1–1½ hr. free with purchase and validation, max. $30).

Golden Gate Bridge ★★★ *Kids*   The year 2007 marked the 70th birthday of possibly the most beautiful, and certainly the most photographed, bridge in the world. Often half-veiled by the city's trademark rolling fog, San Francisco's Golden Gate Bridge, named for the strait leading from the Pacific Ocean to the San Francisco Bay, spans tidal currents, ocean waves, and battering winds to connect The City by the Bay with the Redwood Empire to the north.

With its gracefully suspended single span, spidery bracing cables, and zooming twin towers, the bridge looks more like a work of abstract art than one of the 20th century's greatest practical engineering feats. Construction was completed in May 1937 at the then-colossal cost of $35 million (plus another $39 million in interest being financed entirely by bridge tolls).

The 1¾-mile bridge (including the approach), which reaches a height of 746 feet above the water, is awesome to cross. Although kept to a maximum of 45 miles an hour, traffic usually moves quickly, so crossing by car won't give you too much time to see the sights. If you drive from the city, take the last San Francisco exit, right before the toll plaza, park in the southeast parking lot, and make the crossing by foot. Back

---

GoCar Tours of San Francisco

If the thought of walking up and down San Francisco's brutally steep streets has you sweating already, consider renting a talking GoCar instead. The tiny yellow three-wheeled convertible cars are easy and fun to drive—every time I see one of these things the people riding in them are grinning from ear to ear—and they're cleverly guided by a talking GPS (Global Positioning System), which means that the car always knows where you are, even if you don't. The most popular computer-guided tour is a 2-hour loop around the Fisherman's Wharf area, out to the Marina District, through Golden Gate Park, and down Lombard Street, the "crookedest street in the world." As you drive, the talking car tells you where to turn and what landmarks you're passing. Even if you stop to check something out, as soon as you turn your GoCar back on, the tour picks up where it left off. Or you can just cruise around wherever you want (but not across the Golden Gate Bridge). There's a lockable trunk for your things, and the small size makes parking a breeze. You can rent a GoCar from 1 hour (about $44) to a full day. You'll have to wear a helmet, and you must be a licensed driver of at least 18-years of age. The GoCar rental shop is at 2715 Hyde St., between Beach and North Point streets at Fisherman's Wharf. For more information call © **800/91-GoCar** or © **415/441-5695**, or log onto their website at www.gocarsf.com.

in your car, continue to Marin's Vista Point, at the bridge's northern end. Look back, and you'll be rewarded with one of the finest views of San Francisco.

Millions of people visit the bridge each year, gazing up at the tall orange towers, out at the vistas of San Francisco and Marin County, and down into the stacks of ocean-going liners. You can walk out onto the span from either end, but be prepared—it's usually windy and cold, and the traffic is noisy. Still, walking even a short distance is one of the best ways to experience the immense scale of the structure.

Hwy. 101 N. www.goldengatebridge.org. $5 cash toll collected when driving south. Bridge-bound Golden Gate Transit buses ((C) 511) depart hourly during the day for Marin County, starting from Mission and First sts. (across the street from the Transbay Terminal and stopping at Market and Seventh sts., at the Civic Center, along Van Ness Ave., at Lombard and Fillmore sts., and at Francisco and Richardson sts.).

(Fun Fact **Golden Gate Bridge by the Numbers**

Span: 6,450 feet
Total length: 8,981 feet
Completion date: May 28, 1937
Cost: $35 million
Date paid in full: July, 1971
Engineer: Joseph B. Strauss
Road height: 260 feet
Tower height: 746 feet
Swing span: 27 feet
Deepest foundation: 110 feet under water
Cable thickness: 36 1/2 inches
Cable length: 7,650 feet
Steel used: 83,000 pounds
Concrete used: 389,000 cubic yards
Miles of wire cable: 80,000
Gallons of paint annually: 10,000
Color: international orange
Rise, in cold weather: 5 feet
Drop, in hot weather: 10 feet
Traffic: 3 million vehicles per month
Toll: $5 (southbound only)

Lombard Street ⟨ Known (erroneously) as the "crookedest street in the world," this whimsically winding block of Lombard Street draws thousands of visitors each year (much to the chagrin of neighborhood residents, most of whom would prefer to block off the street to tourists). The angle of the street is so steep that the road has to snake back and forth to make a descent possible. The brick-lined street zigzags around the residences' bright flower gardens, which explode with color during warmer months. This short stretch of Lombard Street is one-way, downhill, and fun to drive. Take the curves slowly and in low gear, and expect a wait during the weekend. Save your film for the bottom where, if you're lucky, you can find a parking space and take a few snapshots of the silly spectacle. You can also take staircases (without curves) up or down on either side of the street. In truth, most locals don't understand what the fuss is all about. I'm guessing the draw is the combination of seeing such a famous landmark, the challenge of negotiating so many steep curves, and a classic photo op. *FYI:* Vermont Street, between 20th and 22nd streets in Potrero Hill, is even more crooked, but not nearly as picturesque.

Btw. Hyde and Leavenworth sts.

Pier 39 *(Overrated)* Pier 39 is a multilevel waterfront complex a few blocks east of Fisherman's Wharf. Constructed on an abandoned cargo pier, it is, ostensibly, a re-creation of a turn-of-the-20th-century street scene, but don't expect a slice of old-time maritime life here: Today, Pier 39 is a busy mall welcoming millions of visitors per year. It has more than 110 stores, 13 bay-view restaurants, a two-tiered Venetian carousel, a

Hard Rock Cafe, the Riptide Arcade, and the Aquarium of the Bay (below) for the kids. And everything here is slanted toward helping you part with your travel dollars. This is *the* place that locals love to hate, but kids adore it here. That said, it does have a few perks: absolutely beautiful natural surroundings and bay views, fresh sea air, and hundreds of sunbathing sea lions (about 900 in peak season) lounging along its neighboring docks.

On the waterfront at the Embarcadero and Beach St. ⓒ 415/705-5500. www.pier39.com. Shops daily 10am–8:30pm, with extended weekend hours during summer.

2 Museums

For information on museums in Golden Gate Park, see the "Golden Gate Park" section, beginning on p. 180.

Aquarium of the Bay   This $38-million, 1-million-gallon marine attraction at Pier 39 is filled with sharks, stingrays, and other sea creatures that visitors can watch through clear acrylic tunnels (being here during an earthquake would be *real* interesting). Although the tunnel is an engineering marvel, the overall experience pales in comparison to the Monterey Bay Aquarium, but the kids sure seem to get a kick out of all the fish swimming above and around them.

The Embarcadero at Beach St. ⓒ 888/SEA-DIVE or 415/623-5333. www.aquariumofthebay.com. Aquarium admission $15 adults, $8 seniors and children 3–11, free for children 2 and under. Family (two adults, two children) package $38. Behind-the-scenes tour $21 per person, $14 seniors and children 5–11, including admission to the aquarium. Mon–Thurs 10am–6pm; Fri–Sun 10am–7pm; summer hours 9am–8pm daily. Closed Dec 25.

Asian Art Museum ⚑   Previously in Golden Gate Park and reopened in what was once the Civic Center's Beaux Arts–style central library, San Francisco's Asian Art Museum is one of the Western world's largest museums devoted to Asian art. Its collection boasts more than 15,000 art objects, such as world-class sculptures, paintings, bronzes, ceramics, and jade items, spanning 6,000 years of history and regions of south Asia, west Asia, Southeast Asia, the Himalayas, China, Korea, and Japan. Inside you'll find 40,000 square feet of gallery space showcasing 2,500 objects at any given time. Add temporary exhibitions, live demonstrations, learning activities, Cafe Asia, and a store, and you've got one very good reason to head to the Civic Center.

200 Larkin St. (btw. Fulton and McAllister sts.). ⓒ 415/581-3500. www.asianart.org. Admission $12 adults, $8 seniors 65 and over, $7 youths 13–17 and college students with ID, free for children 12 and under, $5 flat rate for all (except children under 12 who are free) after 5pm Thurs. Free 1st Sun of the month. Tues–Wed and Fri–Sun 10am–5pm; Thurs 10am–9pm. Bus: All Market St. buses. Streetcar: Civic Center.

Cable Car Museum ⚑ *Value* *Kids*   If you've ever wondered how cable cars work, this nifty museum explains (and demonstrates) it all. Yes, this is a museum, but the Cable Car Museum is no stuffed shirt. It's the living powerhouse, repair shop, and storage place of the cable car system and is in full operation. Built for the Ferries and Cliff House Railway in 1887, the building underwent an $18-million reconstruction to restore its original gaslight-era look, install an amazing spectators' gallery, and add a museum of San Francisco transit history.

The exposed machinery, which pulls the cables under San Francisco's streets, looks like a Rube Goldberg invention. Stand in the mezzanine gallery and become mesmerized by the massive groaning and vibrating winches as they thread the cable that hauls the cars through a huge figure-eight and back into the system using slack-absorbing tension wheels. For a better view, move to the lower-level viewing room, where you can see the massive pulleys and gears operating underground.

Also on display here is one of the first grip cars developed by Andrew S. Hallidie, operated for the first time on Clay Street on August 2, 1873. Other displays include an antique grip car and trailer that operated on Pacific Avenue until 1929, and dozens of exact-scale models of cars used on the various city lines. There's also a shop where you can buy a variety of cable car gifts. You can see the whole museum in about 45 minutes.

1201 Mason St. (at Washington St.). ✆ 415/474-1887. www.cablecarmuseum.org. Free admission. Apr–Sept daily 10am–6pm; Oct–Mar daily 10am–5pm. Closed Thanksgiving, Christmas, and New Year's Day. Cable car: Both Powell St. lines.

California Academy of Sciences ★★★ *Kids*   San Francisco's California Academy of Sciences has been entertaining locals and tourists for more than 150 years, and with the grand opening of the all-new Academy on September 27, 2008, it's now going stronger than ever. Four years and $500 million in the making, it's the only institution in the world to combine an aquarium, planetarium, natural history museum, and scientific research program under one roof, and so vastly entertaining that the entire family could easily spend a whole day here. In fact, the spectacular new complex has literally reinvented the role of science museums in the 21st century, where visitors interact with animals, educators, and biologists at hands-on exhibits such as a four-story living rainforest dome and the world's deepest living coral reef display. Even the Academy's 2½-acre undulating garden roof is an exhibit, planted with 1.7 million native California plants, including thousands of flowers (all that's missing are the Teletubbies).

More than 38,000 live animals fill the new Academy's aquarium and natural history exhibits, making it one of the most diverse collections of live animals at any museum or aquarium in the world. Highlights include the **Morrison Planetarium,** the world's largest all-digital planetarium that takes you on a guided tour of the solar system and beyond using current data from NASA to produce the most accurate and interactive digital universe ever created; the **Philippine Coral Reef,** the world's deepest living coral reef tank where 4,000 sharks, rays, sea turtles, giant clams, and other aquatic creatures live in a Technicolor forest of coral; and the **Rainforests of the World,** a living rainforest filled with mahogany and palm trees, croaking frogs, chirping birds, leaf cutter ants, bat caves, chameleons, and hundreds of tropical butterflies. You can climb into the tree-tops of Costa Rica, descend in a glass elevator into the Amazonian flooded forest, and walk along an acrylic tunnel beneath the Amazonian river fish that swim overhead. Pretty cool, eh?

Even the dining options here are first-rate, as both the **Academy Café** and **Moss Room** restaurant are run by two of the city's top chefs, Charles Phan and Loretta Keller, and feature local, organic, sustainable foods. The only thing you won't enjoy here is the entrance fee—a whopping $25 per adult—but it includes access to all the Academy exhibits *and* the Planetarium shows, and if you arrive by public transportation they'll knock $3 off the fee (how very green). Combined with a visit to the spectacular de Young museum across the Concourse, it makes for a very entertaining and educational day in Golden Gate Park.

55 Concourse Dr., Golden Gate Park. ✆ 415/379-8000. www.calacademy.org. Admission $25 adults, $20 seniors 65 and over, $20 youths 12–17, $15 children 7–11, free for children 6 and under. Free to all 3rd Wed of each month. Mon–Sat 9:30am–5pm; Sun 11am–5pm. Closed Thanksgiving and Christmas. Bus: 5, 16AX, 16BX, 21, 44, or 71.

Yerba Buena Gardens & Environs

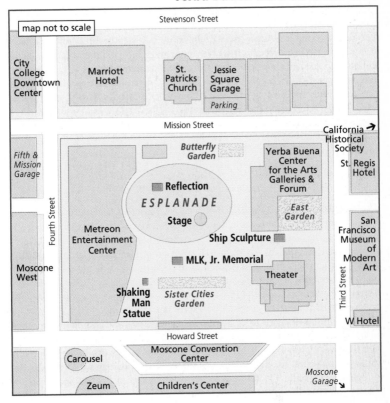

map not to scale

Stevenson Street

City College Downtown Center

Marriott Hotel

St. Patricks Church

Jessie Square Garage

Parking

Mission Street

California →
Historical Society

Fifth & Mission Garage

Butterfly Garden

Yerba Buena Center for the Arts Galleries & Forum

St. Regis Hotel

Fourth Street

Reflection

ESPLANADE

Stage

East Garden

San Francisco Museum of Modern Art

Metreon Entertainment Center

Ship Sculpture

MLK, Jr. Memorial

Moscone West

Theater

Shaking Man Statue

Sister Cities Garden

Third Street

W Hotel

Howard Street

Carousel

Moscone Convention Center

Moscone Garage ↘

Zeum

Children's Center

California Historical Society   As part of the plan to develop the Yerba Buena Gardens area as the city's cultural hub, the **California Historical Society** opened to house a research library, an ever-changing roster of exhibits that pertain to California's rich history, 2-hour walking tours of the Bay Area given by local eccentric Gary L. Holloway, and a museum store. Call or check the website for current exhibit and walking tour information.

678 Mission St. (btw. Third and New Montgomery sts.). ℂ **415/357-1848.** www.californiahistoricalsociety.org. North Baker Research Library Wed–Fri noon–4:30pm; Galleries Wed–Sat noon–4:30pm. Bus: 5, 9, 14, 15, 30, or 45. Streetcar: Powell or Montgomery.

de Young Museum ★★★   After closing for several years, San Francisco's oldest museum (founded in 1895) reopened in late 2005 in its state-of-the-art Golden Gate Park facility. Its vast holdings include one of the finest collections of American paintings in the United States from Colonial times through the 20th century, as well as decorative arts and crafts; western and non-western textiles; and arts from Africa, Oceania, and the Americas. Along with superb revolving exhibitions, the de Young has long been beloved for its educational arts programs for both children and adults, and now it's equally enjoyed for its stunning architecture and sculpture-graced surroundings. The striking facade consists of 950,000 pounds of textured and perforated copper that's intended to patinate with age, while the northeast corner of the building features a 144-foot tower that slowly spirals from the ground floor and culminates with an observation floor offering panoramic views of the entire Bay Area (from a distance it has the surreal look of a rusty aircraft carrier cruising through the park). Surrounding sculpture gardens and lush, grassy expanses are perfect for picnicking. Adding to the allure is surprisingly good and healthy organic fare at the grab-and-go or order-and-wait cafe/restaurant. You'll enjoy browsing through the museum's interesting gift shop as well. *Note:* Underground parking is accessed at 10th Avenue and Fulton Street. Also, admission tickets to the de Young may be used on the same day for free entrance to the Legion of Honor (see below).

50 Hagiwara Tea Garden Dr. (inside Golden Gate Park, 2 blocks from the park entrance at Eighth Ave. and Fulton). ℂ 415/863-3330. www.thinker.org. Adults $10, seniors $7, youths 13–17 and college students with ID $6, children 12 and under free. Free 1st Tues of the month. $2 discount for Muni riders with Fast Pass or transfer receipt. AE, MC, V. Tues–Sun 9:30am–5:15pm. Closed Jan 1, Thanksgiving Day, and Dec 25. Bus: 5, 16AX, 16BX, 21, 44, or 71.

The Exploratorium ★★★ *Kids*   *Scientific American* magazine rated the Exploratorium "the best science museum in the world"—and I couldn't agree more. Inside you'll find hundreds of exhibits that explore everything from giant-bubble blowing to Einstein's theory of relativity. It's like a mad scientist's penny arcade, an educational fun house, and an experimental laboratory all rolled into one. Touch a tornado, shape a glowing electrical current, or take a sensory journey in total darkness in the **Tactile Dome** ($3 extra, and call ℂ **415/561-0362** to make advance reservations)—even if you spent all day here you couldn't experience everything. Every exhibit at the Exploratorium is designed to be interactive, educational, safe and, most importantly, fun. And don't think it's just for kids; parents inevitably end up being the most reluctant to leave. I went here recently and spent 3 hours in just one small section of the museum, marveling like a little kid at all the mind-blowing hands-on exhibits related to light and eyesight. On the way out, be sure to stop in the wonderful gift store, which is chock-full of affordable brain candy.

The museum is in the Marina District at the beautiful **Palace of Fine Arts** ★★, the only building left standing from the Panama-Pacific Exposition of 1915. The adjoining park with lagoon—the perfect place for an afternoon picnic—is home to ducks, swans, seagulls, and grouchy geese, so bring bread.

3601 Lyon St., in the Palace of Fine Arts (at Marina Blvd.). ℂ **415/EXP-LORE,** or 415/561-0360 (recorded information). www.exploratorium.edu. Admission $14 adults; $11 seniors, youth 13–17, visitors with disabilities, and college students with ID; $9 children 4–12; free for children 3 and under. AE, MC, V. Tues–Sun 10am–5pm. Closed Mon except MLK, Jr., Day, Presidents' Day, Memorial Day, and Labor Day. Free parking. Bus: 28, 30, or Golden Gate Transit.

Haas–Lilienthal House   Of the city's many gingerbread Victorians, this handsome Queen Anne house is one of the most flamboyant. The 1886 structure features all the architectural frills of the period, including dormer windows, flying cupolas, ornate trim, and winsome turret. The elaborately styled house is now the only Victorian house museum in the city that has its rooms fully furnished with period pieces. The San Francisco Architectural Heritage maintains the house and offers docent-led 1-hour tours (the only way to see the house), which start every 20 to 30 minutes on Wednesdays, Saturdays, and Sundays.

2007 Franklin St. (at Washington St.). ℂ **415/441-3004.** www.sfheritage.org. 1-hr. guided tour $8 adults, $5 seniors and children 12 and under. Wed and Sat noon–3pm; Sun 11am–4pm. **(Note:** Some Saturdays the house is closed for private functions, so call to confirm.) Bus: 1, 12, 19, 27, 47, or 49. Cable car: California St. line.

Moments Italian-Style Saturday Sing-Along

If you haven't completely fallen in love with San Francisco yet, then show up at **Caffè Trieste** in the North Beach on most Saturdays between 1 and 5pm. That's when the stringed instruments are tuned up, the chairs are scooted against the walls, and the locals entertain the crowd with their lively version of classic Italian operas and heartwarming folk songs. Everybody's so high on caffeine that it quickly becomes one big happy party and the highlight of everyone's vacation. (Even lifelong locals still get a kick out of it.) This family-owned corner institution is one of San Francisco's most beloved cafes—a Beat Generation hangout that's been around since 1956 serving locally roasted Italian coffee. You'll find it at 601 Vallejo St. at Grant Ave. (© **415/392-6739;** www.caffetrieste.com), next to the row of motorcycles. Call to confirm that the show's on.

The Legion of Honor 🔶🔶 Designed as a memorial to California's World War I casualties, this neoclassical structure is an exact replica of the Legion of Honor Palace in Paris, right down to the inscription HONNEUR ET PATRIE above the portal. The exterior's grassy expanses, cliff-side paths, and incredible view of the Golden Gate and downtown make this an absolute must-visit attraction before you even get in the door. The inside is equally impressive: the museum's permanent collection covers 4,000 years of art and includes paintings, sculpture, and decorative arts from Europe, as well as international tapestries, prints, and drawings. The chronological display of 4,000 years of ancient and European art includes one of the world's finest collections of Rodin sculptures. The sunlit Legion Cafe offers indoor and outdoor seating at moderate prices. Plan to spend 2 or 3 hours here.

In Lincoln Park (34th Ave. and Clement St.). © **415/750-3600,** or 415/863-3330 (recorded information). www.thinker.org. Admission $10 adults, $7 seniors 65 and over, $6 youths 13–17 and college students with ID, free for children 12 and under. Fees may be higher for special exhibitions. Free 1st Tues of each month. Free admission with same-day tickets from the de Young Museum. Tues–Sun 9:30am–5:15pm. Bus: 18.

Metreon Entertainment Center *(Kids)* This 350,000-square-foot hi-tech complex houses great movie theaters, an IMAX theater, the only Sony store in the country devoted to PlayStation, the one-of-a-kind Walk of Game (à la Hollywood's stars in the sidewalk, these steel stars honor the icons of the video game industry), a luxurious arcade (think big screens and a pub), a "Taste of San Francisco" food court with decent "international" fare, and lots more shops, many of which are gaming related. The whole place is wired for Wi-Fi, so if you're a true techie and want to hang out with other techies, grab some lunch, find a comfy spot, and log on.

101 Fourth St. (at the corner of Mission St.) © **415/369-6000.** www.metreon.com. Building 10am–10pm daily; individual businesses may have different hours. Bus: 5, 9, 14, 15, 30, or 45. Streetcar: Powell or Montgomery.

Octagon House This unusual, eight-sided, cupola-topped house dates from 1861 and is maintained by the National Society of Colonial Dames of America. Its design was based on a past theory that people living in a space of this shape would live longer, healthier lives. Inside is a small museum where you'll find Early American furniture, portraits, silver, pewter, looking glasses, and English and Chinese ceramics. There are also some historic documents, including signatures of 54 of the 56 signers of the Declaration of Independence. Even if you're not able to visit the inside, this atypical structure is worth a look from the outside.

2645 Gough St. (at Union St.). ℭ 415/441-7512. Free admission; donation suggested. Feb–Dec 2 Sun, and 2nd and 4th Thurs of each month noon–3pm. Tours by appointment are the only way to see the house. Closed holidays. Bus: 41 or 45.

San Francisco Maritime National Historical Park ✿ *Kids*   This park includes several marine-themed sites within a few blocks of each other. Although the park's signature Maritime Museum—on Beach Street at Polk Street, shaped like an Art Deco ship, and filled with sea-faring memorabilia—is undergoing its planned 2006 to 2009 renovations, it's worth walking by just to admire the building. Head 2 blocks east to the corner of Hyde and Jefferson and you'll find SFMNHP's state-of-the-art Visitor's Center, which offers a fun, interactive look at the City's maritime heritage. Housed in the historic Haslett Warehouse building, the Center tells the stories of voyage, discovery, and cultural diversity. Across the street, at the park's Hyde Street Pier, are several historic ships, which are moored and open to the public.

The *Balclutha,* one of the last surviving square-riggers and the handsomest vessel in San Francisco Bay, was built in Glasgow, Scotland, in 1886 and carried grain from California at a near-record speed of 300 miles a day. The ship is now completely restored.

The 1890 *Eureka* still carries a cargo of nostalgia for San Franciscans. It was the last of 50 paddle-wheel ferries that regularly plied the bay; it made its final trip in 1957. Restored to its original splendor at the height of the ferryboat era, the side-wheeler is loaded with deck cargo, including antique cars and trucks.

The black-hulled, three-masted *C. A. Thayer,* built in 1895 and recently restored, was crafted for the lumber trade and carried logs felled in the Pacific Northwest to the carpentry shops of California.

Other historic ships docked here include the tiny two-masted *Alma,* one of the last scow schooners to bring hay to the horses of San Francisco; the *Hercules,* a huge 1907 oceangoing steam tug; and the *Eppleton Hall,* a side-wheel tugboat built in England in 1914 to operate on London's River Thames.

At the pier's small-boat shop, visitors can follow the restoration progress of historic boats from the museum's collection. It's behind the maritime bookstore on your right as you approach the ships.

Visitor's Center: Hyde and Jefferson sts. (near Fisherman's Wharf). ℭ 415/447-5000. www.nps.gov/safr. No fee for Visitor's Center. Tickets to board ships $5, free for children 15 and under. Visitor's Center: Memorial Day to Sept 30 daily 9:30am–5:30pm; Oct 1 to Memorial Day 9:30am–5pm. Ships on Hyde St. Pier: Memorial Day to Sept 30 daily 9:30am–5:30pm; Oct 1 to Memorial Day daily 9am–5pm. Bus: 19, 30, or 47. Cable car: Powell–Hyde St. line to the last stop.

San Francisco Museum of Modern Art (SFMOMA) ✿   Swiss architect Mario Botta, in association with Hellmuth, Obata, and Kassabaum, designed this $65-million museum, which has made SoMa one of the more popular areas to visit for tourists and residents alike. The museum's permanent collection houses the West Coast's most comprehensive collection of 20th-century art, including painting, sculpture, photography, architecture, design, and media arts. The collection features master works by Ansel Adams, Bruce Conner, Joseph Cornell, Salvador Dalí, Richard Diebenkorn, Eva Hesse, Frida Kahlo, Ellsworth Kelly, Yves Klein, Sherrie Levine, Gordon Matta-Clark, Henri Matisse, Piet Mondrian, Pablo Picasso, Robert Rauschenberg, Diego Rivera, Cindy Sherman, Alfred Stieglitz, Clyfford Still, and Edward Weston, among many others, as well as an ever-changing program of special exhibits. Unfortunately, few works are on display at one time, and for the money the experience can be disappointing—especially

> **Finds** **San Francisco's Old-Fashioned Arcade Museum**
>
> "Fun for all ages" isn't a trite expression when describing San Francisco's **Musée Mécanique,** a truly unique penny arcade museum containing one of the largest privately owned collections of antique coin-operated mechanical musical instruments in the world—160 machines dating back from the 1880s through the present (and they still work!). You can pay Grand-Ma Fortune Teller a quarter to see what she has to say about your future, or watch little kids cower in fear as Laughing "Fat Lady" Sal gives her infamous cackle of a greeting. Other yesteryear seaside resort games include antique movie machines, 19th-century music boxes, old-school strength testers, and mechanical cranes. The museum is located at Pier 45 at the end of Taylor Street at Fisherman's Wharf. It's open Monday through Friday from 10am to 7pm and Saturday and Sunday from 10am to 8pm. Admission is free (© **415/ 346-2000;** www.museemechanique.org).

compared to the finer museums of New York. However, this is about as good as it gets in our boutique city, so take it or leave it. Docent-led tours take place daily. Times are posted at the admission desk. Phone or check SFMOMA's website for current details of upcoming special events and exhibitions.

The **Caffè Museo,** to the right of the museum entrance, offers very good-quality fresh soups, sandwiches, and salads. Be sure to visit the **MuseumStore,** which carries a wonderful array of modern and contemporary art books, innovative design objects and furniture, jewelry and apparel, educational children's books and toys, posters, and stationery: It's one of the best shops in town and always carries their famed "Fog-Dome"—a snowglobe with a mini MOMA that gets foggy rather than snowy when you shake it.

151 Third St. (2 blocks south of Market St., across from Yerba Buena Gardens). © 415/357-4000. www.sfmoma.org. Admission $13 adults, $8 seniors, $7 students over 12 with ID, free for children 12 and under. Half-price for all Thurs 6–9pm; free to all 1st Tues of each month. Thurs 11am–8:45pm; Fri–Tues 11am–5:45pm. Closed Wed and major holidays. Bus: 15, 30, or 45. Streetcar: J, K, L, or M to Montgomery.

San Francisco Zoo (& Children's Zoo) *Kids*   Located between the Pacific Ocean and Lake Merced in the southwest corner of the city, the San Francisco Zoo, which once had a reputation for being a bit shoddy and out-of-date, has come a long way in recent years (that is, until the tiger vs. teen incident). Though grown-ups who are into wildlife will enjoy the visit, it's an especially fun trip with kids because they'll really get a kick out of the hands-on Children's Zoo, along with the many other animal attractions (the flock of shockingly pink flamingos near the entrance is especially appealing.)

Founded at its present site near the ocean in 1929, the zoo is spread over 100 acres and houses more than 930 animals, including some 245 species of mammals, birds, reptiles, amphibians, and invertebrates. Exhibit highlights include the Lipman Family Lemur Forest, a forest setting for five endangered species of lemurs from Madagascar that features interactive components for the visitor; Jones Family Gorilla World, a tranquil setting for a family group of western lowland gorillas; Koala Crossing, which connects to the Australian Walkabout exhibit with its kangaroos, wallaroos, and emu;

Penguin Island, home to a large breeding colony of Magellanic Penguins (join them for lunch at 2:30pm daily); and the Primate Discovery Center, home to rare and endangered monkeys. In the South American Tropical Forest building, a large green anaconda can be found as well as other South American reptile and bird species. Puente al Sur (Bridge to the South) has a pair of giant anteaters and some capybaras. The Lion House is home to rare Sumatran and Siberian tigers and African lions. You can see the big cats fed every day at 2pm (except Mon when you are less likely to see them since when they're not eating they like to hang out in secluded areas). African Savanna is a 3-acre mixed-species habitat with giraffes, zebras, antelope, and birds.

The 6-acre Children's Zoo offers kids and their families opportunities for close-up encounters with domestic rare breeds of goats, sheep, ponies, and horses in the Family Farm. Touch and feel small mammals, reptiles, and amphibians along the Nature Trail and gaze at eagles and hawks stationed on Hawk Hill. Visitors can see the inner workings of the Koret Animal Resource Center, a thriving facility that houses the animals used in the educational outreach programs, and visit the incredible Insect Zoo. One of the Children's Zoo's most popular exhibits is the Meerkat and Prairie Dog exhibit, where kids can crawl through tunnels and play in sand, just like these two amazing burrowing species.

Don't miss the Little Puffer miniature steam train, which takes passengers around a ⅓-mile track, and the historic Dentzel Carousel (both $2 per ride). There's a coffee cart by the entrance as well as two decent cafes inside, definitely good enough for a bite with the kids (though the lines can be long and slightly confusing if you're handling food and kid duty at the same time).

Great Highway btw. Sloat Blvd. and Skyline Blvd. ℭ **415/753-7080.** www.sfzoo.org. Admission $11 adults, $8 for seniors 65 and over and youth 12–17, $5 for children 3–11, free for children 2 and under. Free to all 1st Wed of each month, except $2 fee for Children's Zoo. Carousel $2. Daily 10am–5pm, 365 days a year. Bus: 23 or 18. Streetcar: L from downtown Market St. to the end of the line.

Wells Fargo History Museum

Wells Fargo, one of California's largest banks, got its start in the Wild West. Its history museum, at the bank's head office, houses hundreds of genuine relics from the company's whip-and-six-shooter days, including pistols, photographs, early banking articles, posters, a stagecoach, and mining equipment.

420 Montgomery St. (at California St.). ℭ **415/396-2619.** www.wellsfargohistory.com. Free admission. Mon–Fri 9am–5pm. Closed bank holidays. Bus: Any to Market St. Cable car: California St. line. BART: Montgomery St.

Yerba Buena Center for the Arts ℛ *Finds* *Kids*

The **YBCA,** which opened in 1993, is part of the large outdoor complex that takes up a few city blocks across the street from SFMOMA, and sits atop the underground Moscone Convention Center. It's the city's cultural facility, similar to New York's Lincoln Center but far more fun on the outside. The Center's two buildings offer music, theater, dance, and visual arts programs and shows. James Stewart Polshek designed the 755-seat theater, and Fumihiko Maki designed the Galleries and Arts Forum, which features three galleries and a space designed especially for dance. Cutting-edge computer art, multimedia shows, contemporary exhibitions, and performances occupy the center's high-tech galleries.

701 Mission St. ℭ **415/978-ARTS** (box office). www.ybca.org. Admission for gallery $6 adults; $3 seniors, teachers, and students. Free to all 1st Tues of each month. Free for seniors and students with ID every Thurs. Tues–Wed and Sun noon–5pm; Thurs–Sat noon–8pm. Contact YBCA for times and admission to theater. Bus: 5, 9, 14, 15, 30, or 45. Streetcar: Powell or Montgomery.

To beef up attendance and give indigent folk like us travel writers a break, almost all of San Francisco's art galleries and museums are open free to the public 1 day of the week or month (or both), and several never charge admission. Use the following list to plan your week around the museums' free-day schedules; refer to the individual attraction listings in this chapter for more information on each museum.

First Tuesday
- California Palace of the Legion of Honor (p. 169)
- Center for the Arts at Yerba Buena Gardens (p. 172)
- de Young Museum (p. 167)
- San Francisco Museum of Modern Art (p. 170)

First Wednesday
- Exploratorium (p. 168)
- San Francisco Zoo (p. 171)

First Sunday
- Asian Art Museum (p. 165)

Third Wednesday
- California Academy of Sciences (p. 166)

Always Free
- Cable Car Museum (p. 165)
- San Francisco Maritime National Historical Park and Museum (there's a fee to board ships) (p. 170)
- Musée Mécanique (p. 171)
- Wells Fargo History Museum (p. 172)
- Glide Memorial United Methodist Church (p. 186)

Yerba Buena Gardens 🌟   Unless you're at Yerba Buena to catch a performance, you're more likely to visit the 5-acre gardens, a great place to relax in the grass on a sunny day and check out several artworks. The most dramatic outdoor piece is an emotional mixed-media memorial to Martin Luther King, Jr. Created by sculptor Houston Conwill, poet Estella Majozo, and architect Joseph de Pace, it features 12 panels, each inscribed with quotations from King, sheltered behind a 50-foot-high waterfall. There are also several actual garden areas here, including a Butterfly Garden, the Sister Cities Garden (highlighting flowers from the city's 13 sister cities), and the East Garden, blending Eastern and Western styles. May through October, Yerba Buena Arts & Events puts on a series of free outdoor festivals featuring dance, music, poetry, and more by the San Francisco Ballet, Opera, Symphony, and others.

Located on 2 square city blocks bounded by Mission, Folsom, Third, and Fourth sts. www.yerbabuenagardens.com. Daily 6am–10pm. No admission fee. Contact Yerba Buena Arts & Events: ☎ 415/543-1718 or www.ybgf.org for details about the free outdoor festivals. Bus: 5, 9, 14, 15, 30, or 45. Streetcar: Powell or Montgomery.

Zeum/The Yerba Buena Ice Skating and Bowling Center 🌟 Kids   Also in Yerba Buena Gardens you'll find **Zeum,** an innovative, hands-on multimedia, arts and technology museum for kids of all ages. Zeum also features the fabulous 1906 carousel that once graced the city's bygone Oceanside amusement park, Playland-at-the-Beach; the Children's Garden; a cafe; and a fun store. Right behind Zeum, you'll find **The Yerba Buena Ice Skating and Bowling Center,** a great stopover if you're looking for fun indoor activities, including a 12-lane bowling alley and an ice-skating rink with public sessions daily.

Zeum: 221 Fourth St. (at Howard St.) *©* **415/820-3320.** www.zeum.com. Admission $8 adults, $7 seniors and students, $6 youth 3–18, free for children 2 and under. Summer Tues–Sun 11am–5pm; hours during the school year Wed–Sun 11am–5pm. Carousel $3 per person, each ticket good for 2 rides. Daily 11am–6pm. **The Yerba Buena Ice Skating and Bowling Center:** 750 Folsom St. *©* **415/820-3521.** www.skatebowl.com. Bowling alley: $20–$30 per lane/per hour; Sun–Thurs 10am–10pm, Fri–Sat 10am–midnight. Skating rink: call for hours and admission. Bus: 5, 9, 14, 15, 30, or 45. Streetcar: Powell or Montgomery.

3 Neighborhoods Worth a Visit

To really get to know San Francisco, break out of the downtown and Fisherman's Wharf areas to explore the ethnically and culturally diverse neighborhoods. Walk the streets, browse the shops, grab a bite at a local restaurant; you'll find that San Francisco's beauty and charm are around every corner, not just at the popular tourist destinations.

Note: For information on Fisherman's Wharf, see its entry under "Famous San Francisco Sights," on p. 161. For information on San Francisco neighborhoods and districts that aren't discussed here, see "Neighborhoods in Brief," in chapter 5, beginning on p. 56.

NOB HILL

When the cable car started operating in 1873, this hill became the city's exclusive residential area. Newly wealthy residents who had struck it rich in the gold rush (and were known by names such as the "Big Four" and the "Comstock Bonanza kings") built their mansions here, but they were almost all destroyed by the 1906 earthquake and fire. The only two surviving buildings are the Flood Mansion, which serves today as the **Pacific Union Club,** and the **Fairmont Hotel,** which was under construction when the earthquake struck and was damaged but not destroyed. Today, the burned-out sites of former mansions hold the city's luxury hotels—the InterContinental **Mark Hopkins,** the **Stanford Court,** the **Huntington Hotel,** and spectacular **Grace Cathedral,** which stands on the Crocker mansion site. Nob Hill is worth a visit if only to stroll around **Huntington Park,** attend a Sunday service at the cathedral, or ooh and aah your way around The Fairmont's spectacular lobby.

SOUTH OF MARKET (SoMa)

From Market Street to Townsend Street and the Embarcadero to Division Street, SoMa has become the city's newest cultural and multimedia center. The process

---

Fun Fact

San Francisco received the highest score of any city in the United States in Condé Nast Traveler's annual Readers' Choice Awards. This is the 17th time San Francisco has topped the poll's "Top Cities—United States" category since it debuted in 1990. It is the 16th consecutive year that San Francisco has scored the highest (Santa Fe won in 1992).

Finds This City's for the Birds!

If you're walking around San Francisco—especially Telegraph Hill or Russian Hill—and you suddenly hear lots of loud squawking and screeching overhead, look up. You're most likely witnessing a fly-by of the city's famous green flock of wild parrots. These are the scions of a colony that started out as a few wayward house pets—mostly cherry-headed conures, which are indigenous to South America—who found each other, and bred. Years later they've become hundreds strong, traveling in chatty packs through the city (with a few parakeets along for the ride), and stopping to rest on tree branches and delight residents who have come to consider them part of the family. To learn just how special these birds are to the city, check out the book *The Wild Parrots of Telegraph Hill,* or see the heart-warming movie of the same name.

started when alternative clubs began opening in the old warehouses in the area nearly a decade ago. A wave of entrepreneurs followed, seeking to start new businesses in what was once an extremely low-rent area compared to the neighboring Financial District. Today, gentrification and high rents hold sway, spurred by a building boom that started with the **Moscone Convention Center** and continued with the **Yerba Buena Center for the Arts and Yerba Buena Gardens,** the **San Francisco Museum of Modern Art, Four Seasons Hotel, W Hotel, St. Regis Hotel,** and the **Metreon Entertainment Center.** Other institutions, businesses, and museums move into the area on an ongoing basis. A substantial portion of the city's nightlife takes place in warehouse spaces throughout the district.

NORTH BEACH ✦✦✦

In the late 1800s, an enormous influx of Italian immigrants to North Beach firmly established this aromatic area as San Francisco's "Little Italy." Dozens of Italian restaurants and coffeehouses continue to flourish in what is still the center of the city's Italian community. Walk down **Columbus Avenue** on any given morning and you're bound to be bombarded by the wonderful aromas of roasting coffee and savory pasta sauces. Although there are some interesting shops and bookstores in the area, it's the dozens of eclectic little cafes, delis, bakeries, and coffee shops that give North Beach its Italian-bohemian character.

For more perspective on this neighborhood, follow the detailed walking tour in chapter 9 (beginning on p. 204) or sign up for a guided Javawalk with coffee nut Elaine Sosa (see "Walking Tours," on p. 192 in this chapter).

CHINATOWN ✦✦

The first of the Chinese immigrants came to San Francisco in the early 1800s to work as servants. By 1851, 25,000 Chinese people were working in California, and most had settled in San Francisco's Chinatown. Fleeing famine and the Opium Wars, they had come seeking the good fortune promised by the "Gold Mountain" of California, and hoped to return with wealth to their families in China. For the majority, the reality of life in California did not live up to the promise. First employed as workers in the gold mines during the gold rush, they later built the railroads, working as little more than slaves and facing constant prejudice. Yet the community, segregated in the Chinatown ghetto, thrived. Growing prejudice led to the Chinese Exclusion Act of 1882, which halted all Chinese immigration for 10 years and severely limited it thereafter (the Chinese Exclusion Act was not repealed until 1943). Chinese people were also denied the opportunity to buy homes outside the Chinatown ghetto until the 1950s.

Today, San Francisco has one of the largest communities of Chinese people in the United States. More than 80,000 people live in Chinatown, but the majority of Chinese people have moved out into newer areas like the Richmond and Sunset districts. Although frequented by tourists, the area continues to cater to Chinese shoppers, who crowd the vegetable and herb markets, restaurants, and shops. Tradition runs deep here, and if you're lucky, through an open window you might hear women mixing mah-jongg tiles as they play the centuries-old game. (*Be warned:* You're likely to hear lots of spitting around here, too—it's part of local tradition.)

The gateway at Grant Avenue and Bush Street marks the entry to Chinatown. The heart of the neighborhood is Portsmouth Square, where you'll find locals playing board games or just sitting quietly.

On the newly beautified and renovated Waverly Place, a street where the Chinese celebratory colors of red, yellow, and green are much in evidence, you'll find three **Chinese temples:** Jeng Sen (Buddhist and Taoist) at no. 146, Tien Hou (Buddhist) at no. 125, and Norras (Buddhist) at no. 109. If you enter, do so quietly so that you do not disturb those in prayer.

A block west of Grant Avenue, **Stockton Street,** from 1000 to 1200, is the community's main shopping street, lined with grocers, fishmongers, tea sellers, herbalists, noodle parlors, and restaurants. Here, too, is the Buddhist Kong Chow Temple, at no. 855, above the Chinatown post office. Explore at your leisure. A Chinatown walking tour is outlined in chapter 9, beginning on p. 198. Visit www.sanfranciscochinatown.com for more info.

JAPANTOWN

More than 12,000 citizens of Japanese descent (1.4% of the city's population) live in San Francisco, or Soko, as the Japanese who first emigrated here often called it. Initially, they settled in Chinatown and south of Market along Stevenson and Jessie streets from Fourth to Seventh streets. After the earthquake in 1906, SoMa became a light industrial and warehouse area, and the largest Japanese concentration took root

---

Fortune Cookie Factory

At 56 Ross Alley is the **Golden Gate Fortune Cookie Factory,** a tiny Chinatown storefront where, since 1962, three women sit at a conveyer belt, folding messages into thousands of fortune cookies as the manager invariably calls out to tourists, beckoning them to stroll in, watch the cookies being made, and buy a bag of 40 for about $3. Sure, there are other fortune cookie bakeries in the city, but this is the only one left where the cookies are still made by hand the old-fashioned way. You can purchase regular fortunes, unfolded flat cookies without fortunes, or, if you bring your own fortunes, they can create custom cookies (great for dinner parties) at around $6 for 50 cookies—a very cheap way to impress your friends. The factory is open daily 9am to 8:30pm. Admission is free; ℂ **415/781-3956.**

Finds Urban Renewal

- **Kabuki Springs & Spa,** 1750 Geary Blvd. (© **415/922-6000;** www.kabuki springs.com), the Japan Center's most famous tenant, was once an authentic, traditional Japanese bathhouse. The Joie de Vivre hotel group bought and renovated it, however, and it's now more of a pan-Asian spa with a focus on wellness. The deep ceramic communal tubs—at a very affordable $20 to $25 per person—private baths, and shiatsu massages remain. The spa is open from 10am to 10pm daily; joining the baths is an array of massages and ayurvedic treatments, body scrubs, wraps, and facials, which cost from $60 to $150.

- **Spa Radiance,** 3011 Fillmore St. (© **415/346-6281;** www.sparadiance.com), is an utterly San Francisco spa experience due to its unassuming Victorian surroundings and its wonderfully luxurious treatments such as facials, body treatments, massages, manicures, pedicures, Brazilian waxing, spray-tanning, and makeup application by in-house artists.

- A more posh and modern experience is yours at **International Orange,** 2044 Fillmore St., second floor (© **888/894-8811;** www.internationalorange.com). The self-described spa yoga lounge offers just what it says in a chic white-on-white space on the boutique-shopping stretch of Fillmore Street. They've also got a great selection of clothing and face and body products, including one of my personal favorites, locally made In Fiore body balms.

- In the St. Regis Hotel, **Remède Spa,** 125 Third St. (© **415/284-4060;** www. remede.com), has two whole floors dedicated to melting away all your cares, worries, kinks, and knots—not to mention primping. Expect wonderful massage, facials, manis and pedis, waxes, and more. A few doors down in the W Hotel is the city's outpost of New York's **Bliss Spa,** 181 Third St., fourth floor (© **415/281-0990;** www.blissworld.com). The hip version to St. Regis's chic, it offers a similar spa menu, including wedding specialties.

in the Western Addition between Van Ness Avenue and Fillmore Street, the site of today's Japantown, now 100 years old. By 1940, it covered 30 blocks.

In 1913, the Alien Land Law was passed, depriving Japanese Americans of the right to buy land. From 1924 to 1952, the United States banned Japanese immigration. During World War II, the U.S. government froze Japanese bank accounts, interned community leaders, and removed 112,000 Japanese Americans—two-thirds of them citizens—to camps in California, Utah, and Idaho. Japantown was emptied of Japanese people, and war workers took their place. Upon their release in 1945, the Japanese found their old neighborhood occupied. Most of them resettled in the Richmond and Sunset districts; some returned to Japantown, but it had shrunk to a mere 6 or so blocks. Today, the community's notable sights include the **Buddhist Church of San Francisco,** 1881 Pine St. (at Octavia St.), www.bcsfweb.org; the **Konko Church of San Francisco,** 1909 Bush St. (at Laguna St.); the **Sokoji–Soto Zen Buddhist Temple,** 1691 Laguna St. (at Sutter St.); **Nihonmachi Mall,** 1700 block of Buchanan Street between Sutter and Post streets, which contains two steel fountains by Ruth Asawa; and the **Japan Center,** an Asian-oriented shopping mall occupying 3 square blocks bounded by Post, Geary, Laguna, and Fillmore streets. At its center stands the five-tiered **Peace Pagoda,** designed by world-famous Japanese architect Yoshiro

Taniguchi "to convey the friendship and goodwill of the Japanese to the people of the United States." Surrounding the pagoda, through a network of arcades, squares, and bridges, you can explore dozens of shops and showrooms featuring everything from TVs and tansu chests to pearls, bonsai, and kimonos. **Kabuki Springs & Spa** (see the "Urban Renewal" box on p. 177) is the center's most famous tenant. But locals also head to its numerous restaurants, teahouses, shops, and multiplex movie theater.

There is often live entertainment in this neighborhood on summer weekends, including Japanese music and dance performances, tea ceremonies, flower-arranging demonstrations, martial-arts presentations, and other cultural events. **The Japan Center** (© 415/922-6776) is open daily from 10am to midnight, although most shops close much earlier. To get there, take bus nos. 2, 3, or 4 (exit at Buchanan and Sutter sts.) or nos. 22 or 38 (exit at the northeast corner of Geary Blvd. and Fillmore St.).

HAIGHT-ASHBURY

Few of San Francisco's neighborhoods are as varied—or as famous—as Haight-Ashbury. Walk along Haight Street, and you'll encounter everything from drug-dazed drifters begging for change to an armada of the city's funky-trendy shops, clubs, and cafes. Turn anywhere off Haight, and instantly you're among the clean-cut, young urban professionals who can afford the steep rents in this hip 'hood. The result is an interesting mix of well-to-do and well-screw-you aging flower children, former Dead-heads, homeless people, and throngs of tourists who try not to stare as they wander through this most human of zoos. Some find it depressing, others find it fascinating, but everyone agrees that it ain't what it was in the free-lovin' psychedelic Summer of Love. Is it still worth a visit? Not if you are here for a day or two, but it's certainly worth an excursion on longer trips, if only to enjoy a cone of Cherry Garcia at the now-famous Ben & Jerry's Ice Cream Store on the corner of Haight and Ashbury streets, and then to wander and gawk at the area's intentional freaks.

THE CASTRO

Castro Street, between Market and 18th streets, is the center of the city's gay community as well as a lovely neighborhood teeming with shops, restaurants, bars, and other institutions that cater to the area's colorful residents. Among the landmarks are **Harvey Milk Plaza** and the **Castro Theatre** (www.castrotheatre.com), a 1930s movie palace with a Wurlitzer. The gay community began to move here in the late 1960s and early 1970s from a neighborhood called Polk Gulch, which still has a number of gay-oriented bars and stores. Castro is one of the liveliest streets in the city and the perfect place to shop for gifts and revel in free-spiritedness. Check www.castroonline.com for more info.

THE MISSION DISTRICT

Once inhabited almost entirely by Irish immigrants, the Mission District is now the center of the city's Latino community as well as a mecca for young, hip residents. It's an oblong area stretching roughly from 14th to 30th streets between Potrero Avenue on the east and Dolores on the west. In the outer areas, many of the city's finest Victorians still stand, although they seem strangely out of place in the mostly lower-income neighborhoods. The heart of the community lies along 24th Street between Van Ness and Potrero, where dozens of excellent ethnic restaurants, bakeries, bars, and specialty stores attract people from all over the city. The area surrounding 16th Street and Valencia is a hotbed for impressive—and often impressively cheap—restaurants

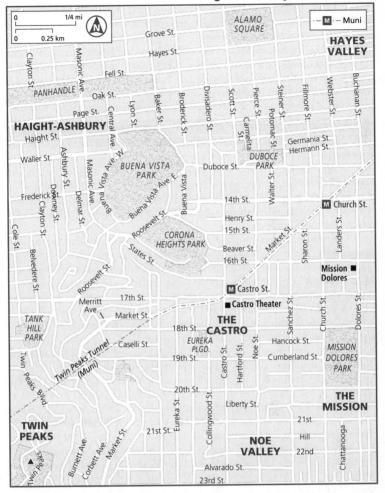

and bars catering to the city's hip crowd. The Mission District at night doesn't feel like the safest place (although in terms of creepiness, the Tenderloin, a few blocks off Union Sq., beats the Mission by far), and walking around the area should be done with caution, but it's usually quite safe during the day and is highly recommended.

For an even better insight into the community, go to the **Precita Eyes Mural Arts Center,** 2981 24th St., between Harrison and Alabama streets (© **415/285-2287;** www.precitaeyes.org), and take one of the 11/2- to 2-hour tours conducted on Saturdays and Sundays at 11am and 1:30pm, where you'll see 60 murals in an 8-block walk. Group tours are available during the week by appointment. The 11am tour costs $10 for adults, $8 for students with ID, $5 for seniors, and $2 for children 17 and under; the 1:30pm tour, which is half an hour longer and includes a slide show, costs $12 for adults, $8 for students with ID, and $5 for seniors and children 17 and under. All but the Saturday-morning tour (which leaves from 3325 24th St. at the Café Venice) leave from the center's 24th Street location.

Other signs of cultural life in the neighborhood are progressive theaters such as Theatre Rhinoceros (www.therhino.org) and Theater Artaud (www.artaud.org). At 16th Street and Dolores is the Mission San Francisco de Asís, better known as **Mission Dolores** (p. 187). It's the city's oldest surviving building and the district's namesake.

4 Golden Gate Park ★★★

Everybody loves **Golden Gate Park**—people, dogs, birds, frogs, turtles, bison, trees, bushes, and flowers. Literally, everything feels unified here in San Francisco's enormous arboreal front yard. Conceived in the 1860s and 1870s, this great 1,017-acre landmark, which stretches inland from the Pacific coast, took shape in the 1880s and 1890s thanks to the skill and effort of John McLaren, a Scot who arrived in 1887 and began landscaping the park.

When he embarked on the project, sand dunes and wind presented enormous challenges. But McLaren had developed a new strain of grass called "sea bent," which he planted to hold the sandy soil along the Firth of Forth back home, and he used it to anchor the soil here, too. Every year the ocean eroded the western fringe of the park, and ultimately he solved this problem, too, though it took him 40 years to build a natural wall, putting out bundles of sticks that the tides covered with sand. He also built the two windmills that stand on the western edge of the park to pump water for irrigation. Under his brilliant eye, the park took shape.

Today the park consists of hundreds of gardens and attractions connected by wooded paths and paved roads. While many worthy sites are clearly visible, there are infinite hidden treasures, so pick up information at **McLaren Lodge and Park Headquarters** (at Stanyan and Fell sts.; ℂ **415/831-2700**) if you want to find the more hidden spots. It's open daily and offers park maps for $3. Of the dozens of special gardens in the park, most recognized are **McLaren Memorial Rhododendron Dell, the Rose Garden, Strybing Arboretum,** and, at the western edge of the park, a springtime array of thousands of tulips and daffodils around the **Dutch windmill.**

In addition to the highlights described in this section, the park contains lots of recreational facilities: tennis courts; baseball, soccer, and polo fields; a golf course; riding stables; and fly-casting pools. The Strawberry Hill boathouse handles boat rentals. The park is also the home of the **M. H. de Young Memorial Museum,** which recently relocated to its spectacular new home at 50 Tea Garden Dr. (ℂ **415/750-3600** or 415/863-3330). For more information see p. 167.

For further information, call the San Francisco Visitor Information Center at ℂ **415/283-0177.** Enter the park at Kezar Drive, an extension of Fell Street; bus riders can take no. 5, 6, 7, 16AX, 16BX, 66, or 71.

PARK HIGHLIGHTS

CONSERVATORY OF FLOWERS ★★ Opened to the public in 1879, this glorious Victorian glass structure is the oldest existing public conservatory in the Western Hemisphere. After a bad storm in 1995 and delayed renovations, the conservatory was closed and visitors were only able to imagine what wondrous displays existed within the striking glass assemblage. Thankfully, a $25-million renovation, including a $4-million exhibit upgrade, was completed a few years ago, and now the Conservatory is a cutting-edge horticultural destination with over 1,700 species of plants. Here you can check out the rare tropical flora of the Congo, Philippines, and beyond within the stunning structure. As one of only four public institutions in the U.S. to house a highland tropics exhibit, its five galleries also include the lowland tropics, aquatic plants, the largest Dracula orchid collection in the world, and special exhibits. It doesn't take long to visit, but make a point of staying a while; outside there are good sunny spots for people-watching as well as paths leading to impressive gardens begging to be explored. If you're around during summer and fall, don't miss the Dahlia Garden to the right of the entrance in the center of what was once a carriage roundabout—it's an explosion of colorful Dr. Seuss–like blooms. The conservatory is open Tuesday through Sunday from 9am to 5pm, closed Mondays. Admission is $5 for adults; $3 for youth 12 to 17 years of age, seniors, and students with ID; $1.50 for children 5 to 11; and free for children 4 and under and for all visitors the first Tuesday of the month. For more information, visit www.conservatoryofflowers.org or call ⓒ **415/ 666-7001.**

JAPANESE TEA GARDEN   John McLaren, the man who began landscaping Golden Gate Park, hired Makoto Hagiwara, a wealthy Japanese landscape designer, to further develop this garden originally created for the 1894 Midwinter Exposition. It's a quiet place with cherry trees, shrubs, and bonsai crisscrossed by winding paths and high-arched bridges over pools of water. Focal points and places for contemplation include the massive bronze Buddha (cast in Japan in 1790 and donated by the Gump family), the Buddhist wooden pagoda, and the Drum Bridge, which, reflected in the water, looks as though it completes a circle. The garden is open daily November through February from 8:30am to 5pm (teahouse 10am–4:30pm), March through October from 8:30am to 6pm (teahouse 10am–5:30pm). For information on admission, call ⓒ **415/752-4227.** For the **teahouse,** call ⓒ **415/752-1171.**

STRAWBERRY HILL/STOW LAKE   Rent a paddle boat or rowboat and cruise around the circular Stow Lake as painters create still lifes, joggers pass along the grassy shoreline, ducks waddle around waiting to be fed, and turtles sunbathe on rocks and logs. Strawberry Hill, the 430-foot-high artificial island and highest point in the park that lies at the center of Stow Lake, is a perfect picnic spot; it boasts a bird's-eye view of San Francisco and the bay. It also has a waterfall and peace pagoda. For the **boathouse,** call ⓒ **415/752-0347.** Boat rentals are available daily from 10am to 4pm, weather permitting; four-passenger rowboats go for $13 per hour, and four-person paddle boats run $17 per hour; fees are cash-only.

STRYBING ARBORETUM & BOTANICAL GARDENS   More than 7,000 plant species grow here, among them some ancient plants in a special "primitive garden," rare species, and a grove of California redwoods. Docent tours begin at 1:30pm daily, with an additional 10:20am tour on weekends. Strybing is open Monday through Friday from 8am to 4:30pm, and Saturday, Sunday, and holidays from 10am to 5pm. Admission is free. For more information, call ⓒ **415/661-1316** or visit www. strybing.org.

Golden Gate Park

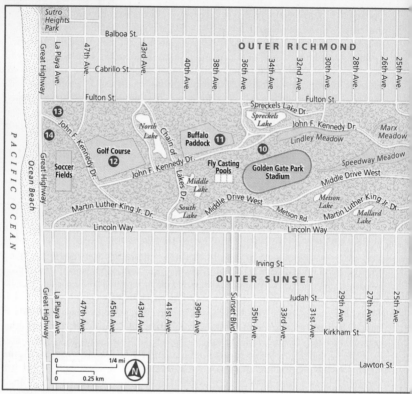

5 The Presidio & Golden Gate National Recreation Area

THE PRESIDIO

In October 1994, the Presidio passed from the U.S. Army to the National Park Service and became one of a handful of urban national parks that combines historical, architectural, and natural elements in one giant arboreal expanse. (It also contains a previously private golf course and a home for George Lucas's production company.) The 1,491-acre area incorporates a variety of terrain—coastal scrub, dunes, and prairie grasslands—that shelter many rare plants and more than 200 species of birds, some of which nest here.

This military outpost has a 220-year history, from its founding in September 1776 by the Spanish under José Joaquin Moraga to its closure in 1994. From 1822 to 1846, the property was in Mexican hands.

During the war with Mexico, U.S. forces occupied the fort, and in 1848, when California became part of the Union, it was formally transferred to the United States. When San Francisco suddenly became an important urban area during the gold rush, the U.S. government installed battalions of soldiers and built Fort Point to protect the entry to the harbor. It expanded the post during the Civil War and during the Indian Wars of the 1870s and 1880s. By the 1890s, the Presidio was no longer a frontier post

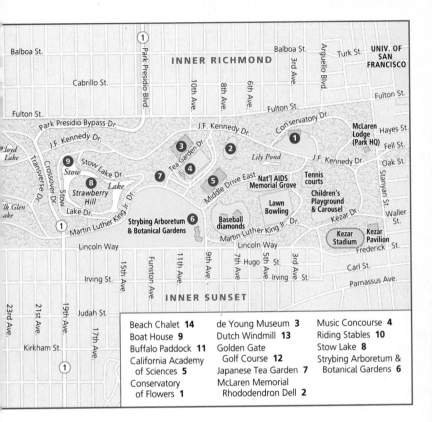

INNER RICHMOND

UNIV. OF SAN FRANCISCO

Balboa St.   Balboa St.

Cabrillo St.

Fulton St.   Fulton St.

Park Presidio Blvd.   Park Presidio Bypass Dr.   J.F. Kennedy Dr.

Lloyd Lake   Transverse Dr.   Crossover Dr.

Stow Lake Dr.   Stow

Strawberry Hill   Stow Lake

Lk Glen ake

Martin Luther King Jr. Dr.

Strybing Arboretum & Botanical Gardens 6

Lincoln Way   Lincoln Way

Irving St.

INNER SUNSET

Judah St.

Kirkham St.

Turk St.

Arguello Blvd.

Hayes St.

Fell St.

Oak St.

McLaren Lodge (Park HQ)

Conservatory Dr.

J.F. Kennedy Dr.

Lily Pond

Tea Garden Dr.

Middle Drive East

Nat'l AIDS Memorial Grove

Tennis courts

Children's Playground & Carousel

Lawn Bowling

Baseball diamonds

Kezar Stadium   Kezar Pavilion

Stanyan St.

Waller St.

Kezar Dr.

Frederick St.

Carl St.

Parnassus Ave.

Hugo St.

Beach Chalet **14**	de Young Museum **3**	Music Concourse **4**
Boat House **9**	Dutch Windmill **13**	Riding Stables **10**
Buffalo Paddock **11**	Golden Gate	Stow Lake **8**
California Academy	Golf Course **12**	Strybing Arboretum &
of Sciences **5**	Japanese Tea Garden **7**	Botanical Gardens **6**
Conservatory	McLaren Memorial	
of Flowers **1**	Rhododendron Dell **2**	

but a major base for U.S. expansion into the Pacific. During the war with Spain in 1898, thousands of troops camped here in tent cities awaiting shipment to the Philippines, and the Army General Hospital treated the sick and wounded. By 1905, 12 coastal defense batteries were built along the headlands. In 1914, troops under the command of Gen. John Pershing left here to pursue Pancho Villa and his men. The Presidio expanded during the 1920s, when Crissy Army Airfield (the first airfield on the West Coast) was established, but the major action was seen during World War II, after the attack on Pearl Harbor. Soldiers dug foxholes along nearby beaches, and the Presidio became the headquarters for the Western Defense Command. Some 1.75 million men were shipped out from nearby Fort Mason to fight in the Pacific; many returned to the Presidio's hospital, whose capacity peaked one year at 72,000 patients. In the 1950s, the Presidio served as the headquarters for the Sixth U.S. Army and a missile defense post, but its role slowly shrank. In 1972, it was included in new legislation establishing the Golden Gate National Recreation Area; in 1989, the Pentagon decided to close the post and transfer it to the National Park Service.

Today, the area encompasses more than 470 historic buildings, a scenic golf course, a national cemetery, 22 hiking trails (to be doubled over the next decade), and a variety of terrain and natural habitats. The National Park Service offers walking and biking tours

Golden Gate National Recreation Area

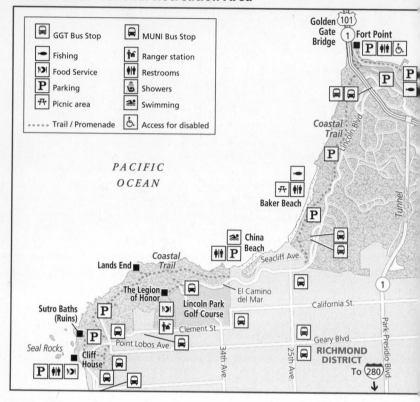

around the Presidio (reservations are suggested) as well as a free shuttle "PresidioGo." For more information, call the **Presidio Visitors Center** at © 415/561-4323. Take bus nos. 28, 45, 76, or 82X to get there.

GOLDEN GATE NATIONAL RECREATION AREA

The largest urban park in the world, GGNRA makes New York's Central Park look like a putting green, covering three counties along 28 miles of stunning, condo-free shoreline. Run by the National Park Service, the Recreation Area wraps around the northern and western edges of the city, and just about all of it is open to the public with no access fees. The Muni bus system provides transportation to the more popular sites, including Aquatic Park, Cliff House, Fort Mason, and Ocean Beach. For more information, contact the **National Park Service** (© 415/561-4700; www.nps.gov/goga). For more detailed information on particular sites, see the "Getting Outside" section, later in this chapter.

Here is a brief rundown of the salient features of the park's peninsula section, starting at the northern section and moving westward around the coastline:

Aquatic Park, adjacent to the Hyde Street Pier, has a small swimming beach, although it's not that appealing (and darned cold). Far more entertaining is a visit to the San Francisco Maritime National Historical Park's Visitor Center a few blocks away (see p. 170 for more information).

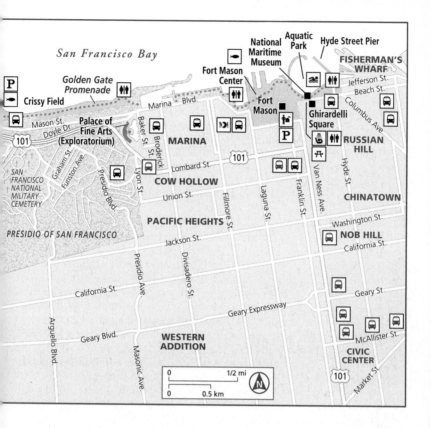

Fort Mason Center, from Bay Street to the shoreline, consists of several buildings and piers used during World War II. Today they hold a variety of museums, theaters, shops, and organizations, and Greens vegetarian restaurant (p. 137), which affords views of the Golden Gate Bridge. For information about Fort Mason events, call ☏ **415/441-3400** or visit www.fortmason.org. The park headquarters is also at Fort Mason.

Farther west along the bay at the northern end of Laguna Street is **Marina Green,** a favorite local spot for kite-flying, jogging, and walking along the Promenade. The St. Francis Yacht Club is also here.

Next comes the 3½-mile paved **Golden Gate Promenade** ⚐, San Francisco's best and most scenic biking, jogging, and walking path. It runs along the shore past **Crissy Field** (www.crissyfield.org) and ends at Fort Point under the Golden Gate Bridge (be sure to stop and watch the gonzo windsurfers and kite surfers, who catch major wind here, and admire the newly restored marshlands). The Crissy Field Café and Bookstore is open from 9am to 5pm Wednesday through Sunday and offers yummy, organic soups, salads, sandwiches, coffee drinks, and a decent selection of outdoor-themed books and cards.

Fort Point ⚐ (☏ **415/556-1693;** www.nps.gov/fopo) was built in 1853 to 1861 to protect the narrow entrance to the harbor. It was designed to house 500 soldiers manning 126 muzzle-loading cannons. By 1900, the fort's soldiers and obsolete guns had been removed, but the formidable brick edifice remains. Fort Point is open Friday through Sunday only from 10am to 5pm, and guided tours and cannon demonstrations are given at the site once or twice a day on open days, depending on the time of year.

Lincoln Boulevard sweeps around the western edge of the bay to **Baker Beach,** where the waves roll ashore—a fine spot for sunbathing, walking, or fishing. Hikers can follow the **Coastal Trail** (www.californiacoastaltrail.org) from Fort Point along this part of the coastline all the way to Lands End.

A short distance from Baker Beach, **China Beach** is a small cove where swimming is permitted. Changing rooms, showers, a sun deck, and restrooms are available.

A little farther around the coast is **Lands End** ★, looking out to Pyramid Rock. A lower and an upper trail offer hiking amid windswept cypresses and pines on the cliffs above the Pacific.

Still farther along the coast lie **Point Lobos,** the **Sutro Baths** (www.sutrobaths.com), and **Cliff House** ★. Cliff House (www.cliffhouse.com), which recently underwent major renovations, has been serving refreshments to visitors since 1863. It's famed for its views of Seal Rocks (a colony of sea lions and many marine birds) and the Pacific Ocean. Immediately northeast of Cliff House you'll find traces of the once-grand Sutro Baths, a swimming facility that was a major summer attraction accommodating up to 24,000 people until it burned down in 1966. (Alas, my favorite Cliff House attraction, the **Musée Mécanique** ★★, an arcade featuring antique games, moved to digs at Pier 45; for more information, call ✆ **415/346-2000** or visit www.museemecanique.org.)

A little farther inland at the western end of California Street is **Lincoln Park,** which contains a golf course and the spectacular Legion of Honor museum (p. 169).

At the southern end of Ocean Beach, 4 miles down the coast, is another area of the park around Fort Funston (✆ **415/561-4700**), where there's an easy loop trail across the cliffs. Here you can watch hang gliders take advantage of the high cliffs and strong winds.

Farther south along Route 280, **Sweeney Ridge** affords sweeping views of the coastline from the many trails that crisscross its 1,000 acres. From here the expedition led by Don Gaspar de Portolá first saw San Francisco Bay in 1769. It's in Pacifica; take Sneath Lane off Route 35 (Skyline Blvd.) in San Bruno.

The GGNRA extends into Marin County, where it encompasses the Marin Headlands, Muir Woods National Monument, and Olema Valley behind the Point Reyes National Seashore. See chapter 12 for information on those areas' highlights.

6 Religious Buildings Worth Checking Out

Glide Memorial United Methodist Church ★★ *Moments*   The best way to spend a Sunday morning in San Francisco is to visit this Tenderloin-area church to witness the exhilarating and lively sermons accompanied by an amazing gospel choir. Reverend Cecil Williams's enthusiastic and uplifting preaching and singing with the homeless and poor of the neighborhood has attracted nationwide fame over the past 40-plus years. In 1994, during the pastor's 30th-anniversary celebration, singers Angela Bofill and Bobby McFerrin joined comedian Robin Williams, author Maya Angelou, and talk-show queen Oprah Winfrey to honor him publicly. Even former President Clinton has joined the crowd. Cecil Williams now shares pastor duties with Douglas Fitch and alternates presiding over the roof-raising Sunday services in front of a diverse audience that crosses all socioeconomic boundaries. Go for an uplifting experience and some hand-clapping, shoulder-swaying gospel choir music—it's an experience you'll never forget. *Tip:* Arrive about 20 minutes early to make sure you get a seat; otherwise it's SRO.

330 Ellis St. (west of Union Sq.). (C) **415/674-6000.** www.glide.org. Services Sun at 9 and 11am. Bus: 27. Streetcar: Powell. BART: Powell.

Grace Cathedral   Although this Nob Hill cathedral, designed by architect Lewis P. Hobart, appears to be made of stone, it is in fact constructed of reinforced concrete beaten to achieve a stonelike effect. Construction began on the site of the Crocker mansion in 1928 but was not completed until 1964. Among the more interesting features of the building are its stained-glass windows, particularly those by the French Loire studios and Charles Counick, depicting such modern figures as Thurgood Marshall, Robert Frost, and Albert Einstein; the replicas of Ghiberti's bronze *Doors of Paradise* at the east end; the series of religious murals completed in the 1940s by Polish artist John de Rosen; and the 44-bell carillon. Along with its magical ambience, Grace lifts spirits with services, musical performances (including organ recitals on many Sundays), and its weekly Forum (Sun 9:30–10:30am except during summer and major holidays), where guests lead discussions about spirituality in modern times and have community dialogues on social issues.

1100 California St. (btw. Taylor and Jones sts.). (C) **415/749-6300.** www.gracecathedral.org.

Mission Dolores   San Francisco's oldest standing structure, the Mission San Francisco de Asís (also known as Mission Dolores), has withstood the test of time, as well as two major earthquakes, relatively intact. In 1776, at the behest of Franciscan missionary Junípero Serra, Father Francisco Palou came to the Bay Area to found the sixth in a series of missions that dotted the California coastline. From these humble beginnings grew what was to become the city of San Francisco. The mission's small, simple chapel, built solidly by Native Americans who were converted to Christianity, is a curious mixture of native construction methods and Spanish-colonial style. A statue of Father Serra stands in the mission garden, although the portrait looks somewhat more contemplative, and less energetic, than he must have been in real life. A 45-minute self-guided tour costs $5; otherwise, admission is $3 for adults and $2 for children.

16th St. (at Dolores St.). (C) **415/621-8203.** www.missiondolores.org. Admission $3 adults, $2 children. Daily 9am–5pm summer; 9am–4pm winter; 9am–4:30pm spring; 9am–noon Good Friday. Closed Thanksgiving, Easter, and Dec 25. Bus: 14, 26, or 33 to Church and 16th sts. Streetcar: J.

7 Architectural Highlights

MUST-SEES FOR ARCHITECTURE BUFFS

ALAMO SQUARE HISTORIC DISTRICT   San Francisco's collection of Victorian houses, known as **Painted Ladies,** is one of the city's most famous assets. Most of the 14,000 extant structures date from the second half of the 19th century and are private residences. Spread throughout the city, many have been beautifully restored and ornately painted. The small area bordered by Divisadero Street on the west, Golden Gate Avenue on the north, Webster Street on the east, and Fell Street on the south—about 10 blocks west of the Civic Center—has one of the city's greatest concentrations of Painted Ladies. One of the most famous views of San Francisco—seen on postcards and posters all around the city—depicts sharp-edged Financial District skyscrapers behind a row of Victorians. This fantastic juxtaposition can be seen from Alamo Square, in the center of the historic district, at Fulton and Steiner streets.

CITY HALL & CIVIC CENTER   Built between 1913 and 1915, City Hall, located in the Civic Center District, is part of this "City Beautiful" complex done in the Beaux Arts style. The dome rises to a height of 306 feet on the exterior and is ornamented with oculi and topped by a lantern. The interior rotunda soars 112 feet and is finished in oak, marble, and limestone, with a monumental marble staircase leading to the second floor. With a major renovation completed in the late 1990s, the building was returned to its former splendor. No doubt you saw it on TV during early 2004, when much of the hoopla surrounding the short-lived and controversial gay marriage proceedings was depicted on the front steps. (Remember Rosie O'Donnell emerging from this very building after getting married to her girlfriend?) Public tours are given Monday through Friday at 10am, noon, and 2pm. Call © **415/554-4933** for details.

OTHER ARCHITECTURAL HIGHLIGHTS

San Francisco is a center of many architecturally striking sights. This section concentrates on a few highlights.

The Union Square and Financial District areas have a number of buildings worth checking out. One is the former **Circle Gallery,** 140 Maiden Lane. Now a gallery housing Folk Art International, Xanadu Tribal Arts, and Boretti Amber & Design, it's the only building in the city designed by Frank Lloyd Wright (in 1948). The gallery was the prototype for the Guggenheim's seashell-shaped circular gallery space, even though it was meant to serve as a retail space for V. C. Morris, a purveyor of glass and crystal. Note the arresting exterior, a solid wall with a circular entryway to the left. Maiden Lane is just off Union Square between Geary and Post streets.

The **Hallidie Building,** 130–150 Sutter St., designed by Willis Polk in 1917, is an ideal example of a glass-curtain building. The vast glass facade is miraculously suspended between the two cast-iron cornices. The fire escapes that course down each side of the building complete the proscenium-like theatrical effect.

Two prominent pieces of San Francisco's skyline are in the Financial District. The **Transamerica Pyramid,** 600 Montgomery St., between Clay and Washington streets, is one of the tallest structures in San Francisco. This corporate headquarters was completed in 1972, stands 48 stories tall, and is capped by a 212-foot spire. The former **Bank of America World Headquarters,** 555 California St., was designed by Wurster, Bernardi, and Emmons with Skidmore, Owings, and Merrill. This carnelian-marble-covered building dates from 1969. Its 52 stories are topped by a panoramic restaurant and bar, the Carnelian Room. The focal point of the building's formal plaza is an abstract black granite sculpture, known locally as the "Banker's Heart," designed by Japanese architect Masayuki Nagare.

The **Medical Dental Building,** 450 Sutter St., is a steel-frame structure beautifully clad in terra cotta. It was designed by Miller and Pflueger in 1929. The entrance and the window frames are elaborately ornamented with Mayan relief work; the lobby ceiling is similarly decorated with gilding. Note the ornate elevators.

At the foot of Market Street you will find the **Ferry Building.** Built between 1895 and 1903, it served as the city's major transportation hub before the Golden Gate and Bay bridges were built; some 170 ferries docked here daily unloading Bay Area commuters until the 1930s. The tower that soars above the building was inspired by the Campanile of Venice and the Cathedral Tower in Seville. In 2003, a 4-year renovation was completed and the building is now a spectacular mixed-use landmark building

featuring a 660-foot-long, skylit nave, which had been partially filled in and destroyed in the 1950s. If you stop by the Ferry Building, you might also want to go to **Rincon Center,** 99 Mission St., to see the WPA murals painted by the Russian artist Refregier in the post office.

Several important buildings are on or near Nob Hill. The **Flood Mansion,** 1000 California St., at Mason Street, was built between 1885 and 1886 for James Clair Flood. Thanks to the Comstock Lode, Flood rose from being a bartender to one of the city's wealthiest men. He established the Nevada bank that later merged with Wells Fargo. The house cost $1.5 million to build at the time; the fence alone cost $30,000. It was designed by Augustus Laver and modified by Willis Polk after the 1906 earthquake to accommodate the Pacific Union Club. Unfortunately, you can't go inside: The building is now a private school.

Built by George Applegarth in 1913 for sugar magnate Adolph Spreckels, the **Spreckels Mansion,** 2080 Washington St., is currently home to romance novelist Danielle Steel (don't even try to get in to see her!). The extraordinary building has rounded-arch French doors on the first and second floors and curved balconies on the second floor. Inside, the original house featured an indoor pool in the basement, Adamesque fireplaces, and a circular Pompeian room with a fountain.

Kids   Especially for Kids

The following San Francisco attractions appeal to kids of all ages:

- Alcatraz Island (p. 153)
- Cable Car Museum (p. 165)
- Cable cars (p. 158)
- California Academy of Sciences (p. 166)
- The Exploratorium (p. 168)
- Golden Gate Bridge (p. 163)
- Golden Gate Park, including the Children's Playground, Bison Paddock, and Japanese Tea Garden (p. 180)
- Maritime Museum (San Francisco Maritime National Historical Park) and the historic ships anchored at Hyde Pier (p. 170)
- The Metreon Entertainment Center (p. 169)
- The San Francisco Zoo (p. 171)

In addition to the sights listed above, a number of playgrounds are of particular interest to kids. One of the most enormous, fun playgrounds for kids is in **Golden Gate Park,** where you'll find a fantastic kids' playground just west of the Stanyan Street entrance. But other playful perks include Stow Lake's boats and peeks at the bison in the bison paddock. Apartment buildings surround the **Cow Hollow Playground,** Baker Street between Greenwich and Filbert streets, on three of four sides. The landscaped playground features a bi-level play area fitted with well-conceived, colorful play structures, including a tunnel, slides, swings, and a miniature cable car. **Huntington Park,** Taylor Street between Sacramento and California streets, sits atop Nob Hill. This tiny play area contains several small structures particularly well suited to children under 5. **Julius Kahn Playground,** West Pacific Avenue at Spruce Street, is a popular playground inside San Francisco's great Presidio Park. Larger play structures and forested surroundings make this area attractive to children and adults alike. Go to www.parks.sfgov.org and click on "Programs" for more info.

Finally, one of San Francisco's most ingenious architectural accomplishments is the **San Francisco–Oakland Bay Bridge.** Although it's visually less appealing than the nearby Golden Gate Bridge (except at night when it's lit up), the Bay Bridge is in many ways more spectacular. The silvery giant that links San Francisco with Oakland is one of the world's longest steel bridges (8¼ miles). It opened in 1936, 6 months before the Golden Gate. Each of its two decks contains five automobile lanes. The Bay Bridge is not a single bridge at all, but a superbly dovetailed series of spans joined mid-bay, at Yerba Buena Island, by one of the world's largest (in diameter) tunnels. To the west of Yerba Buena, the bridge is actually two separate suspension bridges, joined at a central anchorage. East of the island is a 1,400-foot cantilever span, followed by a succession of truss bridges. This east span of the bridge is finally being replaced after being damaged in the 1989 Loma Prieta earthquake and a years-long fight between city residents, planners, and designers. And it looks even more complex than it sounds. You can drive across the bridge (the toll is $3, paid westbound), or you can catch a bus at the Transbay Terminal (Mission at First St.) and ride to downtown Oakland.

8 Self-Guided & Organized Tours

THE 49-MILE SCENIC DRIVE ☺☺

The self-guided, 49-mile drive is an easy way to orient yourself and to grasp the beauty of San Francisco and its extraordinary location. It's also a flat-out stunning and very worthy excursion. Beginning in the city, it follows a rough circle around the bay and passes virtually all the best-known sights, from Chinatown to the Golden Gate Bridge, Ocean Beach, Seal Rocks, Golden Gate Park, and Twin Peaks. Originally designed for the benefit of visitors to San Francisco's 1939 and 1940 Golden Gate International Exposition, the route is marked by blue-and-white seagull signs. Although it makes an excellent half-day tour, this mini-excursion can easily take longer if you decide, for example, to stop to walk across the Golden Gate Bridge or to have tea in Golden Gate Park's Japanese Tea Garden.

The San Francisco **Visitor Information Center,** at Powell and Market streets (p. 55), distributes free route maps, which are handy since a few of the Scenic Drive marker signs are missing. Try to avoid the downtown area during the weekday rush hours from 7 to 9am and 4 to 6pm.

A BART TOUR

One of the world's best commuter systems, **Bay Area Rapid Transit (BART)** runs along 104 miles of rail, linking 43 stations between San Francisco, Millbrae, and the East Bay. Under the bay, BART runs through one of the longest underwater transit tubes in the world. This link opened in September 1972, 2 years behind schedule and 6 months after the general manager resigned under fire. The train cars are 70 feet long and were designed to represent the latest word in public transport luxury. More than 3 decades later, they no longer seem futuristic, but they're still attractively modern, with carpeted floors, tinted picture windows, air-conditioning, and recessed lighting. The trains can hit a top speed of 80 mph; a computerized control system monitors and adjusts their speed.

The people who run BART think so highly of their trains and stations that they sell a $4.65 **"Excursion Ticket,"** which allows you, in effect, to "sightsee" the BART system, or basically ride it. "Tour" the entire system as much as you like for up to 3 hours; you must exit at the station where you entered (if you get out anywhere else along the line, the gate instantly computes the normal fare). For more information, call ℭ **415/ 989-BART** or visit www.bart.gov, where you can also download trip plans directly to your iPod, PDA, or wireless.

BOAT TOURS

One of the best ways to look at San Francisco is from a boat bobbing on the bay. There are several cruises to choose from, and many of them start from Fisherman's Wharf.

Blue & Gold Fleet, Pier 39, Fisherman's Wharf (ℭ **415/773-1188;** www.blueand goldfleet.com), tours the bay year-round in a sleek, 350-passenger sightseeing boat, complete with food and beverage facilities. The fully narrated, 1-hour cruise passes beneath the Golden Gate Bridge and comes within yards of Alcatraz Island. Don a jacket, bring the camera, and make sure it's a clear day for the best bay cruise. Frequent daily departures from Pier 39's West Marina begin at 10:45am daily during winter and 10am daily during summer. Tickets cost $21 for adults, $17 for seniors over 62 and juniors 12 to 18, and $13 for children 5 to 11; children 4 and under are admitted free. There's a $2.25 charge for ordering tickets by phone; discounts are available on their website.

The **Red & White Fleet,** Pier 43½ (© **415/901-5254;** www.redandwhite.com), offers daily "Bay Cruises" tours that leave from Pier 43½. The tour boats cruise along the city waterfront, beneath the Golden Gate Bridge, past Angel Island, and around Alcatraz and are narrated in eight languages. Prices are $21 for adults, $18 for seniors and teens 12 to 17, and $14 for children 5 to 11. Discounts are available through online purchase.

BUS TOURS

Gray Line (© **888/428-6937** or 415/434-8687; www.sanfranciscosightseeing.com) is San Francisco's largest bus-tour operator. It offers numerous itineraries daily (far too many to list here). Free pickup and return are available between centrally located hotels and departure locations. Advance reservations are required for all tours except motorized cable car and trolley tours. Day and evening tours depart from Pier 43½ at Fisherman's Wharf; motorized cable car tours depart from Pier 39 and Pier 41.

SEAPLANE & HELICOPTER TOURS

For those of you seeking a little thrill and adventure during your vacation, consider booking a flight with **San Francisco Seaplane Tours,** the Bay Area's only seaplane tour company. For more than 60 years, this locally owned outfit has provided its customers a bird's-eye view of the city, flying directly over San Francisco at an altitude of about 1,500 feet. Sights you'll see during the narrated excursions include the Golden Gate and Bay Bridges, Alcatraz, Tiburon, and Sausalito. Half the fun, however, is taking off and landing on the water (which is surprisingly smooth). Trips depart from Sausalito, and they offer complimentary shuttle pick-up at Pier 39. Prices range from $139 per person for the 20-minute Golden Gate Tour to $189 for the 30-minute Champagne Sunset Flight, which includes a bottle of bubbly and a cozy backseat for two. Children's rates are also available, and cameras are welcome. (On calm days, the pilot will even roll the window down.) For more information or reservations, log onto www.seaplane.com or call © **415/332-4843.**

Equally thrilling (and perhaps more so if you've never been in a helicopter) is a tour of San Francisco and the bay via **San Francisco Helicopters.** The $140 Vista package includes free shuttle pick-up from your hotel or Pier 39, and a 20-minute tour that takes you under—yes, under—the Golden Gate Bridge, over the city, and past the Bay Bridge and Alcatraz Island. After takeoff, the pilot gives a narrated tour and answers questions while the background music adds a bit of Disney-ride quality to the experience. (*Tip:* The view from the front seat is the best.) Picnic lunch and sunset dinner packages are available as well. For more information or reservations, log onto www.sfhelicopters.com or call © **800/400-2404** or 650/635-4500.

WALKING TOURS

Javawalk is a 2-hour walking tour by self-described "coffeehouse lizard" Elaine Sosa. As the name suggests, it's loosely a coffee walking tour through North Beach, but there's a lot more going on than drinking cups of brew. Javawalk also serves up a good share of historical and architectural trivia, offering something for everyone. The best part of the tour may be the camaraderie that develops among the participants. Sosa keeps the excursion interactive and fun, and it's obvious she knows a profusion of tales and trivia about the history of coffee and its North Beach roots. It's a guaranteed good time, particularly if you're addicted to caffeine. Javawalk is offered Saturday at 10am. The price is $20 per person, $10 for kids 11 and under. For information and reservations, call ✆ **415/673-9255;** or visit www.javawalk.com.

Cruisin' the Castro (✆ **415/255-1821;** www.cruisinthecastro.com) is an informative historical tour of San Francisco's most famous gay quarter, which will give you new insight into the contribution of the gay community to the city's political maturity, growth, and beauty. This fun and easy walking tour is for all ages, highlighting gay and lesbian history from 1849 to present. Stops include America's only Pink Triangle Park and Memorial, the original site of the AIDS Quilt Name Project, Harvey Milk's residence and photo shop, the Castro Theatre, and the Human Rights Campaign and Action Center. Tours run Tuesday through Saturday from 10am to noon and meet at the Rainbow Flag at the Harvey Milk Plaza on the corner of Castro and Market streets above the Castro Muni station. Reservations are required. The tour costs $35 per adult, $25 for children 3 to 12.

On the **Haight-Ashbury Flower Power Walking Tour** (✆ **415/863-1621**), you explore hippie haunts with Pam and Bruce Brennan (the "Hippy Gourmet"). You'll revisit the Grateful Dead's crash pad, Janis Joplin's house, and other reminders of the Summer of Love in 2½ short hours. Tours begin at 9:30am on Tuesdays and Saturdays, and Fridays at 11am. The cost is $20 per person (cash only). Reservations are required. You can purchase tickets online at www.hippygourmet.com (click on the "Walking Tours" link at the bottom left of the webpage) or by calling ✆ 800/979-3370.

San Francisco's Chinatown is always fascinating, but for many visitors with limited time it's hard to know where to search out the "nontouristy" shops, restaurants, and historical spots in this microcosm of Chinese culture. **Wok Wiz Chinatown Walking Tours & Cooking Center,** 250 King St., Suite 268 (✆ **650/355-9657;** www.wok wiz.com), founded over 2 decades ago by author and cooking instructor Shirley Fong-Torres, is the answer. The Wok Wiz tours take you into Chinatown's nooks and crannies. Guides are Chinatown natives, speak fluent Cantonese, and are intimately acquainted with the neighborhood's alleys and small enterprises, as well as Chinatown's history, folklore, culture, and food. Tours are conducted daily from 10am to 1pm and include a 7-course dim sum lunch (a Chinese meal made up of many small plates of food). There's also a less expensive tour that does not include lunch. The walk is easy, as well as fun and fascinating. Groups are generally held to a maximum of 15, and reservations are essential. Prices (including lunch) are $40 for adults and $35 for children 10 and under; without lunch, prices are $28 and $23, respectively. Tickets can be purchased online at Shirley's website, www.wokwiz.com, or by calling ✆ 212/209-3370. Shirley also operates an **I Can't Believe I Ate My Way Through Chinatown** tour. It starts with breakfast, moves to a wok shop, and stops for nibbles at a vegetarian restaurant, dim sum place, and a marketplace, before taking a break for a sumptuous authentic Cantonese luncheon. It's offered on most Saturdays and costs $80 per person, food included. Tickets to either tour can be purchased online at Shirley's website or by calling ✆ 212/209-3370.

Jay Gifford, founder of the **Victorian Homes Historical Walking Tour** (✆ **415/252-9485;** www.victorianwalk.com) and a San Francisco resident for more than 2 decades, communicates his enthusiasm and love of San Francisco throughout this highly entertaining walking tour. The 2½-hour tour, set at a leisurely pace, starts at the corner of Powell and Post streets at Union Square and incorporates a wealth of knowledge about San Francisco's Victorian architecture and the city's history—particularly the periods just before and after the great earthquake and fire of 1906. You'll stroll through Japantown, Pacific Heights, and Cow Hollow. In the process, you'll see more than 200 meticulously restored Victorians, including the sites where *Mrs. Doubtfire* and *Party of Five* were filmed. Jay's guests often find that they are the only ones on the quiet neighborhood streets, where tour buses are forbidden. The tour ends in Cow Hollow, where you can have lunch on your own, or return via bus to Union Square, passing through North Beach and Chinatown. Tours run daily and start at 11am rain or shine; cost is $20 per person (cash only).

9 Getting Outside

Half the fun in San Francisco takes place outdoors. If you're not in the mood to trek it, there are other things to do that allow you to enjoy the surroundings.

BALLOONING   Although you must drive an hour to get to the tour site, hot-air ballooning over the Wine Country is an ethereal experience. **Adventures Aloft,** P.O. Box 2500, Vintage 1870, Yountville, CA 94599 (© **800/944-4408** or 707/944-4408; www.nvaloft.com), is Napa Valley's oldest hot-air balloon company, staffed with full-time professional pilots. Groups are small, and each flight lasts about an hour. The cost of $210 per person includes a post-adventure champagne brunch and a framed "first-flight" certificate. Flights launch daily at sunrise (weather permitting).

BEACHES   Most days it's too chilly to hang out at the beach, but when the fog evaporates and the wind dies down, one of the best ways to spend the day is oceanside in the city. On any truly hot day, thousands flock to the beach to worship the sun, build sandcastles, and throw a ball around. Without a wet suit, swimming is a fiercely cold endeavor and is not recommended. In any case, dip at your own risk—there are no lifeguards on duty and San Francisco's waters are cold and have strong undertows. On the South Bay, **Baker Beach** is ideal for picnicking, sunning, walking, or fishing against the backdrop of the Golden Gate (though pollution makes your catch not necessarily worthy of eating).

   Ocean Beach, at the end of Golden Gate Park, on the westernmost side of the city, is San Francisco's largest beach—4 miles long. Just offshore, at the northern end of the beach, in front of Cliff House, are the jagged Seal Rocks, inhabited by various shorebirds and a large colony of barking sea lions (bring binoculars for a close-up view). To the left, Kelly's Cove is one of the more challenging surf spots in town. Ocean Beach is ideal for strolling or sunning, but don't swim here—tides are tricky, and each year bathers drown in the rough surf.

   Stop by Ocean Beach bus terminal at the corner of Cabrillo and La Playa to learn about San Francisco's history in local artist Ray Beldner's whimsically historical sculpture garden. Then hike up the hill to explore **Cliff House** and the ruins of the **Sutro Baths.** These baths, once able to accommodate 24,000 bathers, were lost to fire in 1966.

BIKING   The San Francisco Parks and Recreation Department maintains two city-designated bike routes. One winds 7½ miles through Golden Gate Park to Lake Merced; the other traverses the city, starting in the south, and continues over the Golden Gate Bridge. These routes are not dedicated to bicyclists, who must exercise caution to avoid crashing into pedestrians. Helmets are recommended for adults and required by law for kids under 18. A bike map is available from the San Francisco Visitor Information Center, at Powell and Mason streets, for $3 (see "Visitor Information" in chapter 5), and from bicycle shops all around town.

   Ocean Beach has a public walk- and bikeway that stretches along 5 waterfront blocks of the Great Highway between Noriega and Santiago streets. It's an easy ride from Cliff House or Golden Gate Park.

Avenue Cyclery, 756 Stanyan St., at Waller Street, in the Haight (© **415/387-3155**), rents bikes for $7 per hour or $28 per day. It's open daily, April through September from 10am to 7pm and October through March from 10am to 6pm. For cruising Fisherman's Wharf and the Golden Gate Bridge, your best bet is **Blazing Saddles** (© **415/202-8888;** www.blazingsaddles.com), which has five locations around Fisherman's Wharf. Bikes rent for $28 per day, including maps, locks, and helmets; tandem bikes are available as well.

BOATING   At the **Golden Gate Park Boat House** (© **415/752-0347**) on Stow Lake, the park's largest body of water, you can rent a rowboat or pedal boat by the hour and steer over to Strawberry Hill, a large, round island in the middle of the lake, for lunch. There's usually a line on weekends. The boathouse is open daily from 10am to 4pm, weather permitting.

Cass' Marina, 1702 Bridgeway, Sausalito; P.O. Box 643; Sausalito, CA 94966 (© **800/472-4595** or 415/332-6789; www.cassmarina.com), is a certified sailing school that rents sailboats measuring 22 to 38 feet. Sail to the Golden Gate Bridge on your own or with a licensed skipper. In addition, large sailing yachts leave from Sausalito on a regularly scheduled basis. Call or check the website for schedules, prices, and availability of sailboats. The marina is open Wednesday through Monday from 9am to sunset.

CITY STAIR CLIMBING ★★   Many health clubs have stair-climbing machines and step classes, but in San Francisco, you need only go outside. The following city stair climbs will give you not only a good workout, but seriously stunning neighborhood, city, and bay views as well. Check www.sisterbetty.org/stairways for more ideas.

Filbert Street Steps, between Sansome Street and Telegraph Hill, are a particular challenge. Scaling the sheer eastern face of Telegraph Hill, this 377-step climb winds through verdant flower gardens and charming 19th-century cottages. Napier Lane, a narrow, wooden plank walkway, leads to Montgomery Street. Turn right and follow the path to the end of the cul-de-sac, where another stairway continues to Telegraph's panoramic summit.

The **Lyon Street Steps,** between Green Street and Broadway, were built in 1916. This historic stairway street contains four steep sets of stairs totaling 288 steps. Begin at Green Street and climb all the way up, past manicured hedges and flower gardens, to an iron gate that opens into the Presidio. A block east, on Baker Street, another set of 369 steps descends to Green Street.

FISHING   **Berkeley Marina Sports Center,** 225 University Ave., Berkeley (© **510/237-3474;** www.berkeleysportfishing.com), makes daily trips for ling cod, rock fish, and many other types of game fish year-round, and it makes trips for salmon runs April through October. Fishing equipment is available; the cost, including boat ride and bait, is about $95 per person. Reservations are required, as are licenses for adults. One-day licenses can be purchased for $11 before departure. Find out the latest on the season by contacting their hot line at © **510/486-8300** (press 3). Excursions run daily from 6am to 4pm. Fish are cleaned, filleted, and bagged on the return trip for a small fee (free for salmon fishing).

GOLF   San Francisco has a few beautiful golf courses. One of the most lavish is the **Presidio Golf Course** (© **415/561-4661;** www.presidiogolf.com). Greens fees are $60 until 12:30pm for residents Monday through Thursday and $96 for nonresidents; rates drop to $50 until 2pm, and then to $35 for the rest of the day for residents and nonresidents. Friday though Sunday, rates are $96 for residents and $108 for nonresidents from 8 to 11am; from 11am to 12:30pm, the cost is $60 for residents. After that it's $50 for everyone until 2pm and $35 for the rest of the day. Carts are included. There are also two decent municipal courses in town.

The 9-hole **Golden Gate Park Course,** 47th Avenue and Fulton Street (© **415/ 751-8987;** www.goldengateparkgolf.com), charges greens fees of $14 per person Monday through Thursday, $18 Friday through Sunday. The 1,357-yard course is par 27. All holes are par 3, and this course is appropriate for all levels. The course is a little weathered in spots, but it's casual, fun, and inexpensive. It's open daily from sunup to sundown.

The 18-hole **Lincoln Park Golf Course,** 34th Avenue and Clement Street (© **415/221-9911;** www.parks.sfgov.org), charges greens fees of $31 per person Monday through Thursday, $36 Friday through Sunday, with rates decreasing after 4pm in summer, 2pm in winter. It's San Francisco's prettiest municipal course, with terrific views and fairways lined with Monterey cypress and pine trees. The 5,181-yard layout plays to par 68, and the 17th hole has a glistening ocean view. This is the oldest course in the city and one of the oldest in the West. It's open daily at daybreak.

HANDBALL   The city's best handball courts are in Golden Gate Park, opposite Seventh Avenue, south of Middle Drive East. Courts are available free, on a first-come, first-served basis.

PARKS   In addition to **Golden Gate Park** and the **Golden Gate National Recreation Area** (p. 180 and p. 184, respectively), San Francisco boasts more than 2,000 acres of parkland, most of which is perfect for picnicking or throwing around a Frisbee.

Smaller city parks include **Buena Vista Park** (Haight St. between Baker and Central sts.), which affords fine views of the Golden Gate Bridge and the area around it and is also a favored lounging ground for gay lovers; **Ina Coolbrith Park** (Taylor St. between Vallejo and Green sts.), offering views of the Bay Bridge and Alcatraz; and **Sigmund Stern Grove** (19th Ave. and Sloat Blvd.) in the Sunset District, which is the site of a famous free summer music festival.

One of my personal favorites is **Lincoln Park,** a 270-acre green on the northwestern side of the city at Clement Street and 34th Avenue. The Legion of Honor is here (p. 169), as is a scenic 18-hole municipal golf course (see "Golf," above). But the best things about this park are the 200-foot cliffs that overlook the Golden Gate Bridge and San Francisco Bay. To get to the park, take bus no. 38 from Union Square to 33rd and Geary streets, and then walk a few blocks.

RUNNING   The **ING Bay to Breakers Foot Race** ✷ (© **415/359-2800;** www.ing baytobreakers.com) is an annual 7½-mile run from downtown to Ocean Beach. About 80,000 entrants take part in it, one of San Francisco's trademark events. Costumed participants and hordes of spectators add to the fun. The event is held on the third Sunday of May.

The San Francisco **Marathon** takes place annually in the middle of July. For more information, visit www.runsfm.com (no phone contact).

Great **jogging paths** include the entire expanse of Golden Gate Park, the shoreline along the Marina, and the Embarcadero.

TENNIS   The **San Francisco Parks and Recreation Department** (© **415/753-7001**) maintains more than 132 free courts throughout the city. Almost all are available free, on a first-come, first-served basis. An additional 21 courts are available in **Golden Gate Park,** which cost $5 for 90 minutes during weekdays and $10 on weekends. Check the website for details on rules for reserving courts (www.parks.sfgov.org).

WALKING & HIKING   The **Golden Gate National Recreation Area** offers plenty of opportunities. One incredible walk (or bike ride) is along the Golden Gate Promenade, from Aquatic Park to the Golden Gate Bridge. The 3.5-mile paved trail heads along the northern edge of the Presidio out to Fort Point, passing the marina, Crissy Field's new restored wetlands, a small beach, and plenty of athletic locals. You can also hike the Coastal Trail all the way from the Fort Point area to Cliff House. The park service maintains several other trails in the city. For more information or to pick up a map of the Golden Gate National Recreation Area, stop by the park service headquarters at Fort Mason; enter on Franklin Street (© **415/561-4700**).

Although most people drive to this spectacular vantage point, a more rejuvenating way to experience **Twin Peaks** is to walk up from the back roads of U.C. Medical Center (off Parnassus) or from either of the two roads that lead to the top (off Woodside or Clarendon aves.). The best time to trek is early morning, when the city is quiet, the air is crisp, and sightseers haven't crowded the parking lot. Keep an eye out for cars, however, because there's no real hiking trail, and be sure to walk beyond the lot and up to the highest vantage point.

10 Spectator Sports

The Bay Area's sports scene includes several major professional franchises. Check the local newspapers' sports sections for daily listings of local events.

MAJOR LEAGUE BASEBALL

The **San Francisco Giants** ★ play at **AT&T Park,** Third and King streets (© **415/ 972-2000;** www.sfgiants.com), in the China Basin section of SoMa. From April to October, 41,503 fans fill the seats here to root for the National League Giants. Tickets are hard to come by, but you can try to obtain some through **Tickets.com** (© **800/225-2277;** www.tickets.com).

The American League's **Oakland Athletics** play across the bay at McAfee Coliseum, at the Hegenberger Road exit from I-880, Oakland (© **510/430-8020;** www.athletics.mlb.com). The stadium holds over 50,000 spectators and is accessible through BART's Coliseum station. Tickets are available from the Coliseum Box Office or by phone through **Tickets.com** (© **800/225-2277;** www.tickets.com).

PRO BASKETBALL

The **Golden State Warriors** of the NBA play at the ORACLE Arena, a 19,200-seat facility at 7000 Coliseum Way in Oakland (© **510/986-2200;** www.nba.com/warriors). The season runs November through April, and most games start at 7:30pm. Tickets are available at the arena, online, and by phone through **Tickets.com** (© **800/225-2277;** www.tickets.com).

PRO FOOTBALL

The **San Francisco 49ers** (www.sf49ers.com) play at Monster Park, Giants Drive and Gilman Avenue, on Sundays August through December; kickoff is usually at 1pm. Tickets sell out early in the season but are available at higher prices through ticket agents beforehand and from "scalpers" (illegal ticket-sellers who are usually at the gates). Ask your hotel concierge for the best way to track down tickets.

The 49ers' archenemies, the **Oakland Raiders** (www.raiders.com), play at McAfee Coliseum, off the I-880 freeway (Nimitz). Call © **800/RAIDERS** for ticket information.

9

City Strolls

Hills schmills. Don't let a few steep slopes deter you from one of San Francisco's greatest pleasures—walking around the neighborhoods and exploring the city for yourself. Here are a couple of introductory walks that hit the highlights of my favorite neighborhoods for touring on foot. For more extensive city walking tours, check out *Frommer's Memorable Walks in San Francisco* (Wiley Publishing, Inc.).

WALKING TOUR 1	CHINATOWN: HISTORY, CULTURE, DIM SUM & THEN SOME

Start:	Corner of Grant Avenue and Bush Street.
Public Transportation:	Bus nos. 2, 3, 4, 9X, 15, 30, 38, 45, or 76.
Finish:	Commercial Street between Montgomery and Kearny streets.
Time:	2 hours, not including museum or shopping stops.
Best Times:	Daylight hours, when the streets are most active.
Worst Times:	Early or late in the day, because shops are closed and no one is milling around.
Hills That Could Kill:	None.

This tiny section of San Francisco, bounded loosely by Broadway and by Stockton, Kearny, and Bush streets, is said to harbor one of the largest Chinese populations outside Asia. Daily proof is the crowds of Chinese residents who flock to the herbal stores, vegetable markets, restaurants, and businesses. Chinatown also marks the spot where the city began its development in the mid-1800s. On this walk, you'll learn why Chinatown remains intriguing to all who wind through its narrow, crowded streets, and how its origins are responsible for the city as we know it.

To begin the tour, make your way to the corner of Bush Street and Grant Avenue, 4 blocks from Union Square and all the downtown buses, where you can't miss the Chinatown Gateway Arch.

❶ Chinatown Gateway Arch

Traditional Chinese villages have ceremonial gates like this one. A lot less formal than those in China, this gate was built more for the benefit of the tourist industry than anything else.

Once you cross the threshold, you'll be at the beginning of Chinatown's portion of Grant Avenue.

❷ Grant Avenue

This is a mecca for tourists who wander in and out of gift shops that offer a variety of unnecessary junk interspersed with quality imports. You'll also find decent restaurants and grocery stores frequented by Chinese residents, ranging from children to the oldest living people you've ever seen.

1 Chinatown Gateway Arch
2 Grant Avenue
3 St. Mary's Square
4 Old St. Mary's Cathedral
5 Canton Bazaar
6 Bank of America
7 Chinatown Kite Shop
8 The Wok Shop
9 The original street of "American" California
10 United Commercial Bank
 Washington Bakery & Restaurant

11 Ten Ren Tea Co., Ltd.
12 Ross Alley
13 Golden Gate Fortune Cookie Company
14 Great China Herb Co.
15 Stockton Street
16 Chinese Historical Society of America Museum
17 Waverly Place and Tin How Temple
18 Portsmouth Square
19 Chinese Cultural Center
20 Joshua A. Norton's home
 R&G Lounge

Tear yourself away from the shops and turn right at the corner of Pine Street. Cross to the other side of Pine, and on your left you'll come to St. Mary's Square.

❸ St. Mary's Square

Here you'll find a huge metal-and-granite statue of Dr. Sun Yat-sen, the founder of the Republic of China. A native of Guangdong (Canton) Province, Sun Yat-sen led the rebellion that ended the reign of the Qing Dynasty.

Note also the second monument in the square, which honors Chinese-American victims of both World Wars.

Walk to the other end of the square, toward California Street, turn left, cross California Street at Grant Street, and you'll be standing in front of Old St. Mary's Cathedral.

❹ Old St. Mary's Cathedral

The first Catholic cathedral in San Francisco and the site of the Chinese community's first English-language school, St. Mary's was built primarily by Chinese laborers and dedicated on Christmas Day 1854.

Step inside to find a written history of the church and turn-of-the-20th-century photos of San Francisco.

Upon leaving the church, take a right and walk to the corner of Grant Avenue and California Street, and then go right on Grant. Here you'll find a shop called Canton Bazaar.

❺ Canton Bazaar

Of the knickknack and import shops lining Grant Avenue, this is one of the most popular; it's located at 616 Grant Ave.

Continue in the same direction on Grant Avenue, and cross Sacramento Street to the northwest corner of Sacramento and Grant. You'll be at the doorstep of the Bank of America.

❻ Bank of America

This bank is an example of traditional Chinese architectural style. Notice the dragons subtly portrayed on many parts of the building.

Head in the same direction (north) on Grant, and a few doors down is the Chinatown Kite Shop.

❼ Chinatown Kite Shop

This store, located at 717 Grant Ave., has an assortment of flying objects, including attractive fish kites, nylon or cotton windsock kites, hand-painted Chinese paper kites, wood-and-paper biplanes, and pentagonal kites.

Cross Grant, and you'll arrive at The Wok Shop.

❽ The Wok Shop

Here's where you can purchase just about any cleaver, wok, cookbook, or vessel you might need for Chinese-style cooking in your own kitchen. It's located at 718 Grant Ave.

When you come out of the Wok Shop, go right. Walk past Commercial Street, and you'll arrive at the corner of Grant Avenue and Clay Street; cross Clay, and you'll be standing on the original street of "American" California.

❾ Original Street of "American" California

Here an English seaman named William Richardson set up the first tent in 1835, making it the first place that an Anglo set up base in California.

Continue north on Grant to Washington Street. Turn right, and at 743 Washington St. you will be standing in front of the former Bank of Canton, now known as the United Commercial Bank.

❿ United Commercial Bank

This building boasts the oldest (from 1909) Asian-style edifice in Chinatown. The three-tiered temple-style building once housed the China Telephone Exchange, known as "China-5" until 1945.

You're probably thirsty by now, so follow Washington Street a few doors down (east); on your right-hand side you will come upon Washington Bakery & Restaurant.

TAKE A BREAK
Washington Bakery & Restaurant is at 733 Washington St. No need to have a full meal here—the service can be abrupt. Do stop in, however, for a little potable adventure: snow red beans with ice cream. The sugary-sweet drink mixed with whole beans and ice cream is not something you're likely to have tried elsewhere, and it happens to be quite tasty. Whatever you do, don't fill up—a few blocks away, some wonderfully fresh dim sum awaits you.

Head back to Grant Avenue, cross Washington Street, cross Grant, and follow the west side of Grant 1 block to Ten Ren Tea Co., Ltd.

⑪ Ten Ren Tea Co., Ltd.

In this amazing shop at 949 Grant Ave., you can sample a freshly brewed tea variety and check out the dozens of drawers and canisters labeled with more than 40 kinds of tea. Like Washington Bakery, Ten Ren offers unusual drinks worth trying: delightful hot or iced milk teas containing giant blobs of jelly or tapioca. Try black tea or green tea and enjoy the outstanding flavors and the giant balls of tapioca slipping around in your mouth.

Leave Ten Ren, make a left, and when you reach Jackson Street, make another left. Follow Jackson Street until you reach Ross Alley, and turn left into the alley.

⑫ Ross Alley

As you walk along this narrow street, just one of the many alleyways that crisscrossed Chinatown to accommodate the many immigrants who jammed into the neighborhood, it's not difficult to believe that this block once was rife with gambling dens.

As you follow the alley south, on the left side of the street you'll encounter the Golden Gate Fortune Cookie Company.

⑬ Golden Gate Fortune Cookie Company

Located at 56 Ross Alley, this store is little more than a tiny place where three women sit at a conveyer belt, folding messages into warm cookies as the manager invariably calls out to tourists, beckoning them to buy a big bag of the fortune-telling treats.

You can purchase regular fortunes, unfolded flat cookies without fortunes, or, if you bring your own fortunes, make custom cookies (I often do this when I'm having dinner parties) at around $6 for 50 cookies—a very cheap way to impress your friends! Or, of course, you can just take a peek and move on.

As you exit the alley, cross Washington Street, take a right heading west on Washington, and you're in front of the Great China Herb Co.

⑭ Great China Herb Co.

For centuries, the Chinese have come to shops like this one, at 857 Washington St., which are full of exotic herbs, roots, and other natural substances. They buy what they believe will cure all types of ailments and ensure good health and long life. Thankfully, unlike owners in many similar area shops, Mr. and Mrs. Ho speak English, so you will not be met with a blank stare when you inquire what exactly is in each box, bag, or jar arranged along dozens of shelves. It is important to note that you should not use Chinese herbs without the guidance of a knowledgeable source such as an herb doctor. They may be natural, but they also can be quite powerful and are potentially harmful if misused.

Take a left upon leaving the store and walk to Stockton Street.

⑮ Stockton Street

The section of Stockton Street between Broadway and Sacramento Street is where most of the residents of Chinatown do their daily shopping.

One noteworthy part of this area's history is **Cameron House** (actually up the hill at 920 Sacramento St., near Stockton St.), which was named after Donaldina Cameron (1869–1968). Called Lo Mo, or "the Mother," by the Chinese, she spent her life trying to free Chinese women who came to America in hopes of marrying well but who found themselves forced into prostitution and slavery. Today, the house still helps women free themselves from domestic violence.

A good stop if you're in the market for some jewelry is **Jade Galore** (1000 Stockton St., at Washington St.). Though the employees aren't exactly warm and fuzzy, they've got the goods. In addition to purveying jade jewelry, the store does a fair trade in diamonds.

After browsing at Jade Galore, you might want to wander up Stockton Street to absorb the atmosphere and street life of this less-tourist-oriented Chinese community before doubling back to Washington Street. At 1068 Stockton St. you'll find **AA Bakery & Café,** an extremely colorful bakery with Golden Gate Bridge–shaped cakes, bright green and pink snacks, moon cakes, and a flow of Chinese diners catching up over pastries. Another fun place at which to peek is **Gourmet Delight B.B.Q.,** at 1045 Stockton St., where barbecued duck and pork are supplemented by steamed pigs' feet and chicken feet. Everything's to go here, so if you grab a snack, don't forget napkins. Head farther north along the street and you'll see live fish and fowl awaiting their fate as the day's dinner.

Meander south on Stockton Street to Clay Street and turn west (right) onto Clay. Continue to 965 Clay St. (Make sure you come Tues–Fri noon–5pm or Sat or Sun noon–4pm.) You've arrived at the museum at 965 Clay St.

⑯ Chinese Historical Society of America Museum

Founded in 1963, this museum (© **415/ 391-1188**) has a small but fascinating collection that illuminates the role of Chinese immigrants in American history, particularly in San Francisco and the rest of California.

The interesting artifacts on display include a shrimp-cleaning machine; 19th-century clothing and slippers of the Chinese pioneers; Chinese herbs and scales; historic hand-carved and painted shop signs; and a series of photographs that document the development of Chinese culture in America.

The goal of this organization is not only to "study, record, acquire, and preserve all suitable artifacts and such cultural items as manuscripts, books, and works of art . . . which have a bearing on the history of the Chinese living in the United States of America," but also to "promote the contributions that Chinese Americans living in this country have made to the United States of America." It's an admirable and much-needed effort, considering what little recognition and appreciation the Chinese have received throughout American history.

The museum is open Tuesday through Friday from noon to 5pm and Saturday and Sunday from noon to 4pm. Admission is $3 for adults, $2 for college students with ID and seniors, and $1 for kids 6 to 17.

Retrace your steps, heading east on Clay Street back toward Grant Avenue. Turn left onto Waverly Place.

⑰ Waverly Place

Also known as "the Street of Painted Balconies," Waverly Place is probably Chinatown's most popular side street or alleyway because of its painted balconies and colorful architectural details—a sort of Chinese-style New Orleans street. And though you can admire the architecture only from the ground, because most of the buildings are private family associations or temples, with a recent beautification and renovation by the City, it's definitely worth checking out.

One temple you can visit (but make sure it's open before you climb the long, narrow stairway) is the **Tin How Temple,** at 125 Waverly Place. Accessible via the stairway three floors up, this incense-laden sanctuary, decorated in traditional black, red, and gold lacquered wood, is a house of worship for Chinese Buddhists, who come here to pray, meditate, and send offerings to their ancestors and to Tin How, the Queen of the Heavens and Goddess of the Seven Seas. There are no scheduled services, but you are welcome to visit. Just remember to quietly respect those who are here to pray, and try to be as unobtrusive as possible. It is customary to give a donation or buy a bundle of incense during your visit.

Once you've finished exploring Waverly Place, walk east on Clay Street, past Grant Avenue, and continue until you come upon the block-wide urban playground that is also the most important site in San Francisco's history.

⑱ Portsmouth Square

This very spot was the center of the region's first township, which was called Yerba Buena before it was renamed San Francisco in 1847. Around 1846, before any semblance of a city had taken shape, this plaza lay at the foot of the bay's eastern shoreline. There were fewer than 50 non–Native American residents in the settlement, there were no substantial buildings to speak of, and the few boats that pulled into the cove did so less than a block from where you're sitting.

In 1846, when California was claimed as a U.S. territory, the marines who landed here named the square after their ship, the USS *Portsmouth*. (Today, a bronze plaque marks the spot where they raised the U.S. flag.)

Yerba Buena remained a modest township until the gold rush of 1849 when, over the next 2 years, the population grew from under 1,000 to over 19,000, as gold seekers from around the world made their way here.

When the square became too crowded, long wharves were constructed to support new buildings above the bay. Eventually, the entire area became landfill. That was almost 150 years ago, but today the square still serves as an important meeting place for neighborhood Chinese—a sort of communal outdoor living room.

Throughout the day, the square is heavily trafficked by children and—in large part—by elderly men, who gamble over Chinese cards. If you arrive early in the morning, you might come across people practicing tai chi.

It is said that Robert Louis Stevenson used to love to sit on a bench here and watch life go by. (At the northeast corner of the square, you'll find a monument to his memory, consisting of a model of the *Hispaniola*, the ship in Stevenson's novel *Treasure Island*, and an excerpt from his "Christmas Sermon.")

Once you've had your fill of the square, exit to the east at Kearny Street. Directly across the street, at 750 Kearny, is the Holiday Inn. Cross the street, enter the hotel, and take the elevator to the third floor, where you'll find the Chinese Culture Center.

⑲ Chinese Culture Center

This center is oriented toward both the community and tourists, offering interesting display cases of Chinese art and a gallery with rotating exhibits of Asian art and writings. The center is open Tuesday through Saturday from 10am to 4pm.

When you leave the Holiday Inn, take a left on Kearny and go 3 short blocks to Commercial Street. Take a left onto Commercial and note that you are standing on the street once known as the site of Joshua A. Norton's Home.

⑳ Joshua A. Norton's Home

Norton, the self-proclaimed "Emperor of the United States and Protector of Mexico," used to walk around the streets in an old brass-buttoned military uniform, sporting a hat with a "dusty plume." He lived in a fantasy world, and San Franciscans humored him at every turn.

Norton was born around 1815 in the British Isles and sailed as a young man to South Africa, where he served as a colonial rifleman. He came to San Francisco in 1849 with $40,000 and proceeded to double and triple his fortune in real estate. Unfortunately for him, he next chose to go into the rice business. While Norton was busy cornering the market and forcing prices up, several ships loaded with rice arrived unexpectedly in San Francisco's harbor. The rice market was suddenly flooded, and Norton was forced into bankruptcy. He left San Francisco for about 3 years and must have experienced a breakdown (or revelation) of some sort, for upon his return, Norton thought he was an emperor.

Instead of ostracizing him, however, San Franciscans embraced him as their own homegrown lunatic and gave him free meals.

When Emperor Norton died in 1880 (while sleeping at the corner of California St. and Grant Ave.), approximately 10,000 people passed by his coffin, which was bought with money raised at the Pacific Union Club, and more than 30,000 people participated in the funeral procession. Today you won't see a trace of his character, but it's fun to imagine him cruising the street.

From here, if you've still got an appetite, you should go directly to 631 Kearny (at Clay St.), home of the R&G Lounge.

 TAKE A BREAK
The **R&G Lounge** is a sure thing for tasty $5 rice-plate specials, chicken with black-bean sauce, and gorgeously tender and tangy R&G Special Beef.

Otherwise, you might want to backtrack on Commercial Street to Grant Avenue, take a left, and follow Grant back to Bush Street, the entrance to Chinatown. You'll be at the beginning of the Union Square area, where you can catch any number of buses (especially on Market St.) or cable cars or do a little shopping. Or you might backtrack to Grant, take a right (north), and follow Grant to the end. You'll be at Broadway and Columbus, the beginning of North Beach, where you can venture onward for our North Beach tour (see below).

WALKING TOUR 2	GETTING TO KNOW NORTH BEACH

Start:	Intersection of Montgomery Street, Columbus Avenue, and Washington Street.
Public Transportation:	Bus no. 10, 12, 15, 30X, or 41.
Finish:	Washington Square.
Time:	3 hours, including a stop for lunch.
Best Times:	Monday through Saturday between 11am and 4pm.
Worst Times:	Sunday, when shops are closed.
Hills That Could Kill:	The Montgomery Street hill from Broadway to Vallejo Street; otherwise, this is an easy walk.

Along with Chinatown, North Beach is one of the city's oldest neighborhoods. Originally the Latin Quarter, it became the city's Italian district when Italian immigrants moved "uphill" in the early 1870s, crossing Broadway from the Jackson Square area and settling in. They quickly established restaurants, cafes, bakeries, and other businesses familiar to them from their homeland. The "Beat Generation" helped put North Beach on the map, with the likes of Jack Kerouac and Allen Ginsberg holding court in the area's cafes during the 1950s. Although most of the original Beat poets are

Walking Tour 2: North Beach

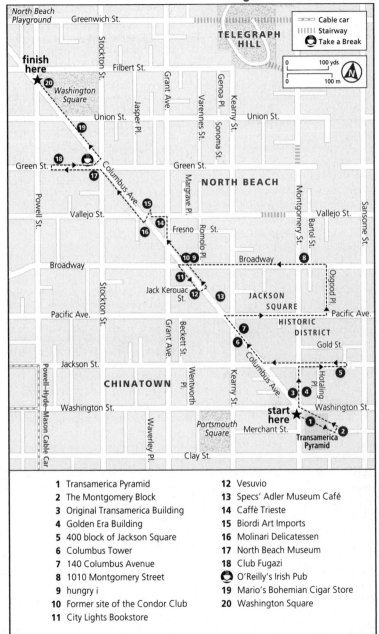

Legend:
- ▭▭▭ Cable car
- ||||| Stairway
- 🔵 Take a Break

North Beach Playground

Greenwich St.

TELEGRAPH HILL

0 — 100 yds
0 — 100 m

finish here ★ 20

Washington Square

Filbert St.

Union St.

Green St. 18

17 🔵

Green St.

NORTH BEACH

Vallejo St. 15

14

16 Fresno St.

Broadway 10 9

Broadway 8

11

Jack Kerouac St. 12 13

JACKSON SQUARE

Pacific Ave.

Pacific Ave.

HISTORIC DISTRICT

7

6

Gold St.

Jackson St.

5

CHINATOWN

Washington St.

start here ★ 3 4

1

Washington St.

Portsmouth Square

Merchant St.

2

Transamerica Pyramid

Clay St.

Stockton St. · Grant Ave. · Genoa Pl. · Kearny St. · Jasper Pl. · Varennes St. · Sonoma St. · Union St. · Columbus Ave. · Margrave Pl. · Montgomery St. · Bartol St. · Sansome St. · Vallejo St. · Powell St. · Romolo Pl. · Osgood Pl. · Stockton St. · Grant Ave. · Beckett St. · Wentworth Pl. · Kearny St. · Columbus Ave. · Hotaling Pl. · Powell-Hyde-Mason Cable Car · Waverley Pl.

1 Transamerica Pyramid	**12** Vesuvio
2 The Montgomery Block	**13** Specs' Adler Museum Café
3 Original Transamerica Building	**14** Caffè Trieste
4 Golden Era Building	**15** Biordi Art Imports
5 400 block of Jackson Square	**16** Molinari Delicatessen
6 Columbus Tower	**17** North Beach Museum
7 140 Columbus Avenue	**18** Club Fugazi
8 1010 Montgomery Street	🔵 O'Reilly's Irish Pub
9 hungry i	**19** Mario's Bohemian Cigar Store
10 Former site of the Condor Club	**20** Washington Square
11 City Lights Bookstore	

gone, their spirit lives on in North Beach, which is still a haven for bohemian artists and writers. The neighborhood, thankfully, retains its Italian village feel; it's a place where residents from all walks of life enjoy taking time for conversation over pastries and frothy cappuccinos.

If there's one landmark you can't miss, it's the familiar building on the corner of Montgomery Street and Columbus Avenue, the Transamerica Pyramid (take bus nos. 15, 30X, or 41 to get there).

❶ Transamerica Pyramid

Noted for its spire (which rises 212 ft. above the top floor) and its "wings" (which begin at the 29th floor and stop at the spire), this pyramid is San Francisco's tallest building and a hallmark of the skyline. You might want to take a peek at one of the rotating art exhibits in the lobby or go around to the right and into ½-acre Redwood Park, which is part of the Transamerica Center.

The Transamerica Pyramid occupies part of the 600 block of Montgomery Street, which once held a historic building called the Montgomery Block.

❷ The Montgomery Block

Originally four stories high, the Montgomery Block was the tallest building in the West when it was built in 1853. San Franciscans called it "Halleck's Folly" because it was built on a raft of redwood logs that had been bolted together and floated at the edge of the ocean (which was right at Montgomery St. at that time). The building was demolished in 1959 but is fondly remembered for its historical importance as the power center of the city. Its tenants included artists and writers of all kinds, among them Jack London, George Sterling, Ambrose Bierce, Bret Harte, and Mark Twain. This is a picturesque area, but there's no particular spot to direct you to. It's worth looking around, however, if only for the block's historical importance.

From the southeast corner of Montgomery and Washington streets, look across Washington to the corner of Columbus Avenue, and you'll see the original Transamerica Building, located at 4 Columbus Ave.

❸ Original Transamerica Building

The original Transamerica Building is a Beaux Arts flatiron-shaped building covered in terra cotta; it was also the home of Sanwa Bank and Fugazi Bank. Built for the Banco Populare Italiano Operaia Fugazi in 1909, it was originally a two-story building and gained a third floor in 1916. In 1928, Fugazi merged his bank with the Bank of America, which was started by A. P. Giannini, who also created the Transamerica Corporation. The building now houses a Church of Scientology.

Cross Washington Street and continue north on Montgomery Street to no. 730, the Golden Era Building.

❹ Golden Era Building

Erected around 1852, this San Francisco historic landmark building is named after the literary magazine, *The Golden Era,* which was published here. Some of the young writers who worked on the magazine were known as "the Bohemians"; they included Samuel Clemens (also known as Mark Twain) and Bret Harte (who began as a typesetter here). Backtrack a few dozen feet and stop for a minute to admire the exterior of the annex, at no. 722, which, after years of neglect and lawsuits, has finally been stabilized and is going to be developed. The Belli Annex, as it is currently known, is registered as a historic landmark.

Continue north on Washington Street, and take the first right onto Jackson Street. Continue until you hit the 400 block of Jackson Square.

⑤ 400 Block of Jackson Square

Here's where you'll find some of the only commercial buildings to survive the 1906 earthquake and fire. The building at no. 415 Jackson (ca. 1853) served as headquarters for the Ghirardelli Chocolate Company from 1855 to 1894. The Hotaling Building (no. 451) was built in 1866 and features pediments and quoins of cast iron applied over the brick walls. At no. 441 is another of the buildings that survived the disaster of 1906. Constructed between 1850 and 1852 with ship masts for interior supporting columns, it served as the French Consulate from 1865 to 1876.

Cross the street, and backtrack on Jackson Street. Continue toward the intersection of Columbus Avenue and Jackson Street. Turn right on Columbus and look across the street for the small triangular building at the junction of Kearny Street and Columbus Avenue, Columbus Tower (also known as the Sentinel Building).

⑥ Columbus Tower

If you walk a little farther, and then turn around and look back down Columbus, you'll be able to get a better look at Columbus Tower. The flatiron beauty, a building shaped to a triangular site, went up between 1905 and 1907. Movie director and producer Francis Ford Coppola bought and restored it in the mid-1970s; it is now home to his film production company, American Zoetrope Studios. The building's cafe showcases all things Rubicon (Coppola's winery)—including olive oil, Parmesan cheese, and wine. It's a great place to stop for a glass of wine, an espresso, or a thin-crusted pizza snack.

Across the street from Columbus Tower on Columbus Avenue is 140 Columbus Ave.

⑦ 140 Columbus Ave.

Although it was closed for a few years, the **Purple Onion** (© **415/956-1653**), famous for its many renowned headliners who often played here before they became famous, is again host to an eclectic mix of music and comedy. Let's hope the next Phyllis Diller, who's now so big that she's

famous for something as simple as her laugh—and who was still struggling when she played a 2-week engagement here in the late 1950s—will catch her big break here, too.

Continue north on Columbus, and then turn right on Pacific Avenue. After you cross Montgomery Street, you'll find brick-lined Osgood Place on the left. A registered historic landmark, it is one of the few quiet—and car-free—little alleyways left in the city. Stroll up Osgood and go left on Broadway to 1010 Montgomery St. (at Broadway).

⑧ 1010 Montgomery St.

This is where Allen Ginsberg lived when he wrote his legendary poem, "Howl," first performed on October 13, 1955, in a converted auto-repair shop at the corner of Fillmore and Union streets. By the time Ginsberg finished reading, he was crying and the audience was going wild. Jack Kerouac proclaimed, "Ginsberg, this poem will make you famous in San Francisco."

Continue along Broadway toward Columbus Avenue. This stretch of Broadway is San Francisco's answer to New York's Times Square, complete with strip clubs and peep shows that are being pushed aside by restaurants, clubs, and an endless crowd of visitors. It's among the most sought-after locations in the city as more and more profitable restaurants and clubs spring up. Keep walking west on Broadway, and on the right side of the street, you'll come to Black Oak Books, 540 Broadway. It sells new and used discount books and is worth a quick trip inside for a good, cheap read. A few dozen yards farther up Broadway is the current location of the hungry i.

⑨ hungry i

Now a seedy strip club (at 546 Broadway), the original hungry i (at 599 Jackson St., which is under construction for senior housing) was owned and operated by the vociferous "Big Daddy" Nordstrom. If you had been here while Enrico Banducci was in charge, you would have found only a plain room with an exposed brick wall and director's chairs around small tables. A who's who of nightclub entertainers fortified their careers at the original hungry i, including Lenny Bruce, Billie Holiday (who sang "Strange Fruit" there), Bill Cosby, Richard Pryor, Woody Allen, and Barbra Streisand.

At the corner of Broadway and Columbus Avenue, you will see the former site of the Condor Club.

❿ Former Site of the Condor Club

The Condor Club was located at 300 Columbus Ave.; this is where Carol Doda scandalously bared her breasts and danced topless for the first time in 1964. Note the bronze plaque claiming the Condor Club as BIRTHPLACE OF THE WORLD'S FIRST TOPLESS & BOTTOMLESS ENTERTAINMENT. Go inside what is now the Condor Sports Bar and have a look at the framed newspaper clippings that hang around the dining room. From the elevated back room, you can see Doda's old dressing room and, on the floor below, an outline of the piano that would descend from the second floor with her atop it.

When you leave the Condor Sports Bar, cross to the south side of Broadway. Note the mural of jazz musicians painted on the entire side of the building directly across Columbus Avenue. Diagonally across the intersection from the Condor Sports Bar is the City Lights bookstore.

⓫ City Lights Booksellers & Publishers

Founded in 1953 and owned by one of the first Beat poets to arrive in San Francisco, Lawrence Ferlinghetti, City Lights is now a city landmark and literary mecca. Located at 261 Columbus Ave., it's one of the last of the Beat-era hangouts in operation. An active participant in the Beat movement, Ferlinghetti established his shop as a meeting place where writers and bibliophiles could (and still do) attend poetry readings and other events. A vibrant part of the literary scene, the well-stocked bookshop prides itself on its collection of art, poetry, and political paperbacks.

Upon exiting City Lights bookstore, turn right, cross aptly named Jack Kerouac Street, and stop by Vesuvio, the bar on your right.

⓬ Vesuvio

Because of its proximity to City Lights bookstore, Vesuvio became a favorite hangout of the Beats. Dylan Thomas used to drink here, as did Jack Kerouac, Ferlinghetti, and Ginsberg. Even today, Vesuvio, which opened in 1949, maintains its original bohemian atmosphere. The bar is located at 255 Columbus Ave. (at Jack Kerouac St.) and dates from 1913. It is an excellent example of pressed-tin architecture.

Facing Vesuvio across Columbus Avenue is another favorite spot of the Beat Generation:

⓭ Spec's Adler Museum Cafe

Located at 12 Saroyan Place, this is one of the city's funkiest bars, a small, dimly lit watering hole with ceiling-hung maritime flags and exposed brick walls crammed with memorabilia. Within the bar is a mini-museum that consists of a few glass cases filled with mementos brought by seamen who frequented the pub from the '40s and onward.

From here, walk back up Columbus across Broadway to Grant Avenue. Turn right on Grant, and continue until you come to Vallejo Street. At 601 Vallejo St. (at Grant Ave.) is Caffè Trieste.

⓮ Caffè Trieste

Yet another favorite spot of the Beats and founded by Gianni Giotta in 1956, Caffè Trieste is still run by family members. The quintessential San Francisco coffeehouse, Trieste features opera on the jukebox, and the real thing, performed by the Giottas, on Saturday afternoons. Any day of the week is a good one to stop in for a cappuccino or espresso—the beans are roasted right next door.

Go left out of Caffè Trieste onto Vallejo Street, turn right on Columbus Avenue, and bump into the loveliest shop in all of North Beach, Biordi Art Imports, located at 412 Columbus Ave.

⓯ Biordi Art Imports

This store has carried imported hand-painted majolica pottery from the hill towns of central Italy for more than 50 years. Some of the colorful patterns date from the 14th century. Biordi handpicks its artisans, and its catalog includes biographies of those who are currently represented.

Across Columbus Avenue, at the corner of Vallejo Street, is the Molinari Delicatessen.

⓰ Molinari Delicatessen

This deli, located at 373 Columbus Ave., has been selling its pungent, air-dried salamis since 1896. Ravioli and tortellini are made in the back of the shop, but it's the mouthwatering selection of cold salads, cheeses, and marinades up front that captures the attention of most folks. Each Italian sub is big enough for two hearty appetites.

Walk north to the lively intersection of Columbus, Green, and Stockton streets, and look for the U.S. Bank at 1435 Stockton St. On the second floor of the bank, you'll find the North Beach Museum.

⓱ North Beach Museum

The North Beach Museum displays historical artifacts that tell the story of North Beach, Chinatown, and Fisherman's Wharf. Just before you enter the museum, you'll find a framed, handwritten poem by Lawrence Ferlinghetti that captures his impressions of this primarily Italian neighborhood. After passing through the glass doors, visitors see many photographs of some of the first Chinese and Italian immigrants, as well as pictures of San Francisco after the 1906 earthquake. You can visit the museum any time the bank is open (unfortunately, it's closed on weekends), and admission is free.

Now backtrack toward Columbus Avenue and go left on Green Street to Club Fugazi, at 678 Green St.

⓲ Club Fugazi

It doesn't look like much from the outside, but Fugazi Hall was donated to the city (and more important, the North Beach area) by John Fugazi, the founder of the Italian bank that was taken over by A. P. Giannini and turned into the original Transamerica Corporation. For many years, Fugazi Hall has been staging the zany and whimsical musical revue *Beach Blanket Babylon*. The show evolved from Steve Silver's Rent-a-Freak service, which consisted of a group of partygoers who would attend parties dressed as any number of characters in outrageous costumes. The fun caught on and soon became *Beach Blanket Babylon*.

If you love comedy, you'll love this show. We don't want to spoil it for you by telling you what it's about, but if you get tickets and they're in an unreserved-seat section, you should arrive fairly early because you'll be seated around small cocktail tables on a first-come, first-served basis. (Two sections have reserved seating, four don't, and all of them frequently sell out weeks in advance; however, sometimes it is possible to get tickets at the last minute on weekdays.) You'll want to be as close to the stage as possible. This supercharged show (see p. 236 for more information) is definitely worth the price of admission.

TAKE A BREAK
Head back the way you came on Green Street. Before you get to Columbus Avenue, you'll see **O'Reilly's Irish Pub** (622 Green St.), a homey watering hole that dishes out good, hearty Irish food and a fine selection of beers (including Guinness, of course) that are best enjoyed at one of the sidewalk tables. Always a conversation piece is the mural of Irish authors peering from the back wall. How many can you name?

As you come out of O'Reilly's, turn left, cross Columbus Avenue, and then take a left onto Columbus. Proceed 1 block northwest to Mario's Bohemian Cigar Store.

⓳ Mario's Bohemian Cigar Store

Located at 566 Columbus Ave., across the street from Washington Square, this is one of North Beach's most popular neighborhood hangouts. No, it does not sell cigars, but the cramped and casual space overlooking Washington Square does sell killer focaccia sandwiches, coffee drinks, beer, and wine.

Our next stop, directly across Union Street, is Washington Square.

⑳ Washington Square

This is one of the oldest parks in the city. The land was designated a public park in 1847 and has undergone many changes since then. Its current landscaping dates from 1955. You'll notice **Saints Peter and Paul Church** (the religious center for the neighborhood's Italian community) on the northwest end. Take a few moments to go inside and check out the traditional Italian interior. Note that this is the church in which baseball great Joe DiMaggio married his first wife, Dorothy Arnold. He wasn't allowed to marry Marilyn Monroe here because he had been divorced. He married Monroe at City Hall and came here for publicity photos.

Today the park is a pleasant place in which to soak up the sun, read a book, or chat with a retired Italian octogenarian who has seen the city grow and change.

From here, you can see the famous Coit Tower at the top of Telegraph Hill to the northwest. If you'd like to get back to your starting point at Columbus and Montgomery streets, walk south (away from the water) on Columbus.

Shopping

Like its population, San Francisco's shopping scene is incredibly diverse. Every style, era, fetish, and financial status is represented here—not in huge, sprawling shopping malls, but in hundreds of boutiques and secondhand stores scattered throughout the city. Whether it's a pair of Jimmy Choo shoes, a Chanel knockoff, or Chinese herbal medicine you're looking for, San Francisco's got it. Just pick a shopping neighborhood, wear some sensible shoes, and you're sure to end up with at least a few take-home treasures.

1 The Shopping Scene

MAJOR SHOPPING AREAS

San Francisco has many shopping areas, but the following places are where you'll find most of the action.

UNION SQUARE & ENVIRONS   San Francisco's most congested and popular shopping mecca is centered on Union Square and bordered by Bush, Taylor, Market, and Montgomery streets. Most of the big department stores and many high-end specialty shops are here. Be sure to venture to Grant Avenue, Post and Sutter streets, and Maiden Lane. This area is a hub for public transportation; all Market Street and several other buses run here, as do the Powell–Hyde and Powell–Mason cable car lines. You can also take the Muni streetcar to the Powell Street station.

CHINATOWN   When you pass through the gate to Chinatown on Grant Avenue, say goodbye to the world of fashion and hello to a swarm of cheap tourist shops selling everything from linen and jade to plastic toys and $2 slippers. But that's not all Chinatown has to offer. The real gems are tucked away on side streets or are small, one-person shops selling Chinese herbs, original art, and jewelry. Grant Avenue is the area's main thoroughfare, and the side streets between Bush Street and Columbus Avenue are full of restaurants, markets, and eclectic shops. Stockton Street is best for grocery shopping (including live fowl and fish). Walking is the way to get around, because traffic through this area is slow and parking is next to impossible. Most stores in Chinatown are open daily from 10am to 10pm. Take bus no. 1, 9X, 15, 30, 41, or 45.

UNION STREET   Union Street, from Fillmore Street to Van Ness Avenue, caters to the upper-middle-class crowd. It's a great place to stroll, window-shop the plethora of boutiques, try the cafes and restaurants, and watch the beautiful people parade by. Take bus no. 22, 41, 45, 47, 49, or 76.

> ## ⌒Tips Just the Facts: Hours, Taxes & Shipping
>
> **Store hours** are generally Monday through Saturday from 10am to 6pm and Sunday from noon to 5pm. Most department stores stay open later, as do shops around Fisherman's Wharf, the most heavily visited area (by tourists).
>
> **Sales tax** in San Francisco is 8.5%, which is added on at the register for all goods and services purchased. If you live out of state and buy an expensive item, you might want to have the store ship it home for you. You'll have to pay for shipping, but you'll escape paying the sales tax.
>
> Most of the city's shops can wrap your purchase and **ship** it anywhere in the world. If they can't, you can send it yourself, either through **UPS** (© 800/742-5877), **FedEx** (© 800/463-3339), or the U.S. Postal Service (see "Fast Facts: San Francisco," in the appendix).

CHESTNUT STREET   Parallel and a few blocks north, Chestnut is a younger version of Union Street. It holds endless shopping and dining choices, and an ever-tanned, superfit population of postgraduate singles who hang around cafes and scope each other out. Take bus no. 22, 28, 30, 43, or 76.

FILLMORE STREET   Some of the best shopping in town is packed into 5 blocks of Fillmore Street in Pacific Heights. From Jackson to Sutter streets, Fillmore is the perfect place to grab a bite and peruse the high-priced boutiques, crafts shops, and incredible housewares stores. (Don't miss Zinc Details; p. 225.) Take bus no. 1, 2, 3, 4, 12, 22, or 24.

HAIGHT STREET   Green hair, spiked hair, no hair, or mohair—even the hippies look conservative next to Haight Street's dramatic fashion freaks. The shopping in the 6 blocks of upper Haight Street between Central Avenue and Stanyan Street reflects its clientele. It offers everything from incense and European and American street styles to furniture and antique clothing. Bus nos. 6, 7, 66, and 71 run the length of Haight Street, and nos. 33 and 43 run through upper Haight Street. The Muni streetcar N line stops at Waller Street and Cole Street.

SOMA   Although this area isn't suitable for strolling, you'll find almost all the discount shopping in warehouse spaces south of Market. You can pick up a discount-shopping guide at most major hotels. Many bus lines pass through this area.

HAYES VALLEY   It's not the prettiest area in town, with some of the shadier housing projects a few blocks away. But while most neighborhoods cater to more conservative or trendy shoppers, lower Hayes Street, between Octavia and Gough streets, celebrates anything vintage, chic, artistic, or downright funky. With new shops opening frequently, it's definitely the most interesting new shopping area in town, with furniture and glass stores, thrift shops, trendy shoe stores, and men's and women's clothiers. You can find lots of great antiques shops south on Octavia and on nearby Market Street. Take bus no. 16AX, 16BX, or 21.

FISHERMAN'S WHARF & ENVIRONS *(Overrated*   The tourist-oriented malls along Jefferson Street include hundreds of shops, restaurants, and attractions. Among them are Ghirardelli Square, PIER 39, the Cannery, and the Anchorage (see "Shopping Centers & Complexes," on p. 227).

2 Shopping A to Z

ANTIQUES

Jackson Square, a historic district just north of the Financial District's Embarcadero Center, is the place to go for the top names in fine furniture and fine art. More than a dozen dealers on the 2 blocks between Columbus and Sansome streets specialize in European furnishings from the 17th to the 19th centuries. Most shops here are open Monday through Friday from 9am to 5pm and Saturday from 11am to 4pm.

Bonhams & Butterfields   This renowned auction house holds preview weekends for upcoming auctions of furnishings, silver, antiques, art, and jewelry. Call for auction schedules. 220 San Bruno Ave. (at 16th St.). © **800/223-2854** or 415/861-7500. www.bonhams.com/us.

Therien & Co.   For the best in Scandinavian, French, and eastern European antiques, head beyond SoMa's design center to this boutique, where you can find the real thing or antique replicas, as well as made-to-order furniture from their neighboring custom furniture shop. 411 Vermont St. (at 17th St.). © **415/956-8850**. www.therien.com.

ART

The San Francisco Bay Area Gallery Guide, a comprehensive, bimonthly publication listing the city's current shows, is available free by mail. Send a self-addressed, stamped envelope to San Francisco Bay Area Gallery Guide, 1369 Fulton St., San Francisco, CA 94117 (© **415/921-1600**); or pick one up at the San Francisco Visitor Information Center at 900 Market St. Most of the city's major art galleries are clustered downtown in the Union Square area.

Catharine Clark Gallery *(Value*   Catharine Clark's is a different kind of gallery experience. Although many galleries focus on established artists and out-of-this-world prices, Catharine's exhibits works by up-and-coming contemporary as well as established artists (mainly from California). It nurtures beginning collectors by offering a purchasing plan that's almost unheard of in the art business. You can buy a piece on layaway and take up to a year to pay for it—interest free! Prices here make art a realistic purchase for almost everyone for a change, but serious collectors also frequent the shows because Clark has such a keen eye for talent. Shows change every 6 weeks. Open Tuesday through Friday 10:30am to 5:30pm and Saturday 11am to 5:30pm. Closed Sunday and Monday. 150 Minna St. ground floor (btw. Third and New Montgomery sts.). © **415/399-1439**. www.cclarkgallery.com.

Fraenkel Gallery   This photography gallery features works by contemporary American and European artists. Excellent shows change every 2 months. Open Tuesday through Friday 10:30am to 5:30pm and Saturday 11am to 5pm. Closed Sunday and Monday. 49 Geary St. (btw. Grant Ave. and Kearny St.), 4th floor. © **415/981-2661**. www.fraenkelgallery.com.

Hang *(Value*   Check out this amazingly affordable gallery for attractive pieces by yet-to-be-discovered Bay Area artists. The staff is friendly and helpful, and the gallery is designed to cater to new and seasoned collectors who appreciate original art at down-to-earth prices. 556 Sutter St. © **415/434-4264**. www.hangart.com.

Images of the North   The highlight here is one of the most extensive collections of Canadian and Alaskan Inuit art in the United States. There's also a small collection of Native American masks and jewelry. Open Tuesday through Saturday 11am to

San Francisco Shopping

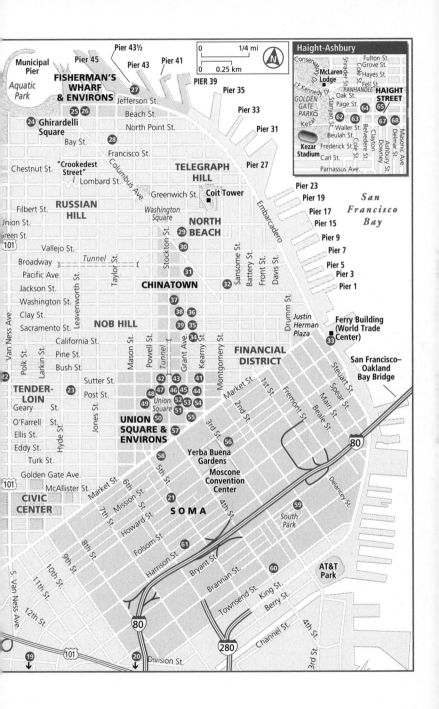

Municipal Pier

Aquatic Park

FISHERMAN'S WHARF & ENVIRONS

Pier 45
Pier 43½
Pier 43
Pier 41
Pier 39
Pier 35
Pier 33
Pier 31
Pier 27
Pier 23
Pier 19
Pier 17
Pier 15
Pier 9
Pier 7
Pier 5
Pier 3
Pier 1

PIER 39

Jefferson St.
Beach St.
North Point St.
Bay St.
Francisco St.

25 26 27 28

24 **Ghirardelli Square**

Chestnut St.
"Crookedest Street"
Lombard St.

Columbus Ave.

RUSSIAN HILL
Filbert St.
Union St.
Green St.
101
Vallejo St.
Broadway
Tunnel St.
Pacific Ave.
Jackson St.
Washington St.
Clay St.
Sacramento St.

Hyde St.
Leavenworth St.
Taylor St.
Stockton St.

TELEGRAPH HILL

Greenwich St.
Washington Square

Coit Tower

NORTH BEACH

29
30
31
32

CHINATOWN

37
38 36
39 35
34

Sansome St.
Battery St.
Front St.
Davis St.
Drumm St.

Embarcadero

Justin Herman Plaza

Ferry Building (World Trade Center)

33

San Francisco Bay

San Francisco–Oakland Bay Bridge

NOB HILL
California St.
Pine St.
Bush St.
Sutter St.
Post St.

Van Ness Ave.
Polk St.
Larkin St.
Mason St.
Powell St.
Tunnel
Grant Ave.
Kearny St.
Montgomery St.

FINANCIAL DISTRICT

TENDER-LOIN
22
23
Geary St.
O'Farrell St.
Ellis St.
Eddy St.
Turk St.

42 43 41
48 47 46 45 44
49 52 53 54
Union Square 51
50 55
57
58
56

Jones St.

UNION SQUARE & ENVIRONS

Market St.
1st St.
2nd St.
3rd St.
4th St.
Steuart St.
Spear St.
Main St.
Beale St.
Fremont St.

80

Delancey St.

Golden Gate Ave.
101
McAllister St.

CIVIC CENTER

5th St.
6th St.
7th St.
8th St.
9th St.
10th St.
11th St.
12th St.

S. Van Ness Ave.
Market St.
Mission St.
Howard St.
Folsom St.
Harrison St.
Bryant St.
Brannan St.
Townsend St.
King St.
Berry St.

Yerba Buena Gardens

Moscone Convention Center

S O M A

21
61
60
59

South Park

AT&T Park

80

101

19
20

Division St.

280

Channel St.
3rd St.
4th St.

Haight-Ashbury

Conservatory Dr.
McLaren Lodge
J.F. Kennedy Dr.
GOLDEN GATE PARK
Kezar Dr.

Shrader St.
Cole St.
Stanyan St.

Fulton St.
Grove St.
Hayes St.
Fell St.
Oak St.
Page St.
Waller St.
Beulah St.
Frederick St.
Carl St.
Parnassus Ave.

HAIGHT STREET

PANHANDLE

64 65
62 63 67 68

Clayton St.
Belvedere St.
Cole St.
Ashbury St.
Downey St.
Delmar St.
Masonic Ave.

Kezar Stadium

0 — 1/4 mi
0 — 0.25 km

N

215

5:30pm and by appointment. 2036 Union St. (at Buchanan St.). © 415/673-1273. www.images north.com.

Meyerovich Gallery   Paintings, sculptures, and works on paper here are by modern and contemporary masters, including Chagall, Matisse, Miró, and Picasso. Meyerovich's new Contemporary Gallery, across the hall, features works by Lichtenstein, Stella, Frankenthaler, Dine, and Hockney. Open Monday through Friday 10am to 6pm and Saturday 10am to 5pm. Closed Sunday. 251 Post St. (at Stockton St.), 4th floor. © 415/421-7171. www.meyerovich.com.

BODY PRODUCTS

Showroom by In Fiore *(Finds)*   I'm totally addicted to In Fiore—a high-end line of body balms, oils, perfumes, and facial serums—so I was especially thrilled when San Francisco–based founder Julie Elliott opened her by-appointment-only shop in what she calls the "Tender-Nob" (on the border of Nob Hill and the Tenderloin near Union Sq.). Come here to check out her whole line, as well as limited-edition balms, and see why celebrities like Julia Roberts and Meg Ryan are fans. Open Tuesday through Saturday and by appointment only. 868 Post St. (btw. Leavenworth and Hyde sts.). © 415/928-5661. www.infiore.net.

BOOKS

In addition to the listings below, there's a **Barnes & Noble** superstore at 2550 Taylor St., between Bay and North Point streets, near Fisherman's Wharf (© 415/292-6762); and a four-storied **Borders** at 400 Post St., at Union Square (© 415/399-1633).

Book Passage   If you're moseying through the Ferry Building Marketplace, drop into this cozy independent that emphasizes (for tourists and locals alike) local travel, boating on the Bay, food, cooking, sustainable agriculture and ecology, fiction, culinary and regional history and literature, and photo and gift books about the Bay Area. The store also hosts lots of author events: Check their website for details. Ferry Building Marketplace (at the Embarcadero and Market St.). © 415/835-1020. www.bookpassage.com.

The Booksmith   Haight Street's best selection of new books is in this large, well-maintained shop. It carries all the top titles, along with works from smaller presses, and more than 1,000 different magazines. 1644 Haight St. (btw. Clayton and Cole sts.). © 800/493-7323 or 415/863-8688.

City Lights Booksellers & Publishers *(Finds)*   Brooding literary types browse this famous bookstore owned by Lawrence Ferlinghetti, the renowned Beat Generation poet. The three-level bookshop prides itself on a comprehensive collection of art, poetry, and political paperbacks, as well as more mainstream books. Open daily until midnight. 261 Columbus Ave. (at Broadway). © 415/362-8193. www.citylights.com.

Green Apple Books *(Finds)*   The local favorite for used books, Green Apple is crammed with titles—more than 60,000 new and 100,000 used books and DVDs. Its extended sections in psychology, cooking, art, and history; collection of modern first editions; and rare graphic comics are superseded only by the staff's superlative service. 506 Clement St. (at Sixth Ave.). © 415/387-2272. www.greenapplebooks.com.

William Stout Architectural Books *(Finds)*   Step inside this shrine to all things architectural, and even if you think you're not interested in exquisite bathrooms, Southern California's modern homes, or great gardens, you can't help but bury yourself in the thousands of design books. Their recent expansion into a second level means that if they don't have what you're looking for, it probably doesn't exist. 804 Montgomery St. (at Jackson St.). ℂ **415/391-6757**. www.stoutbooks.com.

CHINA, SILVER & GLASS

Gump's *(Finds)*   Founded over a century ago, Gump's offers gifts and treasures ranging from Asian antiquities to contemporary art glass and exquisite jade and pearl jewelry. Many items are made specifically for the store. Gump's also has one of the city's most revered holiday window displays and is a huge wedding registry destination, though the staff can act very affected. 135 Post St. (btw. Kearny St. and Grant Ave.). ℂ **800/766-7628** or 415/982-1616. www.gumps.com.

CRAFTS

The Canton Bazaar   Amid a wide variety of handicrafts, here you'll find an excellent selection of rosewood and carved furniture, cloisonné enamelware, porcelain, carved jade, embroideries, jewelry, and antiques from mainland China. Open daily until 10pm. 616 Grant Ave. (btw. Sacramento and California sts.). ℂ **415/362-5750**. www.canton bazaar.com.

The New Unique Company   Primarily a calligraphy- and watercolor-supplies store, this shop also has a good assortment of books on these topics. In addition, there's a wide selection of carved stones for use as seals on letters and documents. Should you want a special design or group of initials, the store will carve seals to order. 838 Grant Ave. (btw. Clay and Washington sts.). ℂ **415/981-2036**.

DEPARTMENT STORES (DOWNTOWN)

Bloomingdale's   This massive 338,550-square-foot department store is the anchor of the Westfield San Francisco Centre at Fifth and Market streets (see "Shopping Centers & Complexes" on p. 227). It's the largest Bloomies outside of New York's flagship 59th Street store, and even sports the same black-and-white polished checkerboard marble. It's owned by the same company that runs Macy's, but fashions—for both men and women—tend to be more forward. Highlights include '60s-inspired fashions by Biba, knitwear by Sonia Rykiel, handbags by Louis Vuitton, and absurdly expensive shoes by Jimmy Choo. 845 Market St. (at Fifth St.). ℂ **415/856-5300**. www.blooming dales.com.

Macy's   The seven-story Macy's West features contemporary fashions for women, juniors, and children, plus jewelry, fragrances, cosmetics, and accessories. The sixth floor offers a "hospitality suite" where visitors can leave their coats and packages, grab a cup of coffee, or find out more about the city from the concierge. The top floors contain home furnishings, and the Cellar sells kitchenware and gourmet foods. You'll even find a Boudin Cafe (though the food is not as good compared to their food at other locations) and a Wolfgang Puck Cafe on the premises. Across the street, Macy's East has five floors of men's fashions. Stockton and O'Farrell sts., Union Sq. ℂ **415/397-3333**.

Neiman Marcus   Some call this Texas-based chain "Needless Mark-ups." But those who can afford the best of everything can't deny that the men's and women's clothes, precious gems, and conservative formalwear are some of the most glamorous in town. The Rotunda Restaurant, located on the fourth floor, is a beautiful place for lunch and afternoon tea that was recently renovated along with the rest of the store. 150 Stockton St. (btw. Geary and O'Farrell sts.), Union Sq. ℂ **415/362-3900**.

Nordstrom Located in the newly renovated San Francisco Shopping Centre (see "Shopping Centers & Complexes" on p. 227), Nordstrom is renowned for its personalized service. Equally devoted to women's and men's fashions, the store has one of the best shoe selections in the city and thousands of suits in stock. The Bistro, on the fourth floor, has a panoramic view and is ideal for an inexpensive lunch or light snack. Spa Nordstrom, on the fifth floor, is the perfect place to relax after a hectic day of bargain hunting. 865 Market St. (at Fifth St.). ℂ 415/243-8500.

DISCOUNT SHOPPING

Burlington Coat Factory As its name hints, you'll find hundreds of coats—from cheapies to designer—as well as men's and women's clothing, shoes, and accessories. But the best deal is the home section, where designer bedding, bath accessories, and housewares go for a fraction of their normal retail prices. 899 Howard St. (at Fifth St.). ℂ 415/495-7234. www.coat.com.

Jeremys *Value* This boutique is a serious mecca for fashion hounds thanks to the wide array of top designer fashions, from shoes to suits, at rock-bottom prices. There are no cheap knockoffs here, just good men's and women's clothes and accessories that the owner scoops up from major retailers that are either updating merchandise or discarding returns. 2 S. Park (btw. Bryant and Brannan sts. at Second St.). ℂ 415/882-4929. www.jeremys.com.

Loehmann's San Francisco's branch of Loehmann's—the nation's only upscale off-price specialty retailer—caters to a sophisticated white-collar crowd, offering professional clothing, shoes, and accessories at bargain prices. Be sure to check out the Back Room, where designer clothes are sold for 30% to 65% less than the Union Square department stores. 222 Sutter St. (btw. Kearny St. and Grant Ave.). ℂ 415/982-3215. www.loehmanns.com.

FABRICS

Britex Fabrics A San Francisco institution since 1952 and newly renovated, Britex offers an absurd number and variety of fabrics, not to mention a selection of more than 30,000 buttons. Closed Sundays. 146 Geary St. (btw. Stockton and Grant sts.). ℂ 415/392-2910. www.britexfabrics.com.

FASHION

See also "Vintage Clothing," later in this section.

CHILDREN'S FASHIONS

Minis Christine Pajunen, who used to design for Banana Republic, opened this children's clothing store to sell her own creations. Every piece, from shirts to pants and dresses, is made from natural fibers. Every outfit perfectly coordinates with everything else in the store. In 2004, Pajunen expanded the store so that it now includes baby gear, including functional and versatile strollers and cribs. Minis also offers educational and creative toys and books with matching dolls as well as maternity wear. 2278 Union St. (btw. Steiner and Fillmore sts.). ℂ 415/567-9537. www.minis-sf.com.

MEN'S FASHIONS

All American Boy Long known for setting the mainstream style for gay men, All American Boy is the quintessential Castro clothing shop. 463 Castro St. (btw. Market and 18th sts.). ℂ 415/861-0444.

Brooks Brothers   In San Francisco, this bulwark of tradition is 1 block east of Union Square. Brooks Brothers introduced the button-down collar and single-handedly changed the standard of the well-dressed businessman. The multilevel shop also sells traditional casual wear, including sportswear, sweaters, and shirts. 150 Post St. (at Grant Ave.). ℂ **415/397-4500. www.brooksbrothers.com.**

Cable Car Clothiers   Dapper men head to this fashion institution for traditional attire, such as three-button suits with natural shoulders, Aquascutum coats, Mc-George sweaters, and Atkinson ties. Closed Sundays. 200 Bush St. (at Sansome St.). ℂ **415/397-4740. www.cablecarclothiers.com.**

Citizen Clothing   The Castro has some of America's best men's casual clothing stores, and this is one of them. Stylish (but not faddish) pants, tops, and accessories are in stock here. Its sister store, Body, at 450 Castro St. (btw. 17th and 18th sts.), carries men's sportswear. 536 Castro St. (btw. 18th and 19th sts.). ℂ **415/575-3560.**

UNISEX

A B fits   Now in Union Square as well as North Beach, this is the place to pop in for jeans to fit all shapes, styles, and sizes, as well as smart and sassy contemporary wear for gals and guys on the go. The snugly fitting stock with over 100 styles of jeans and pants ranges from Chip & Pepper, Earnest Sewn, Edwin, Notify, and Rogan, to chic wear from the likes of Twelfth Street by Cynthia Vincent, Ya-Ya, and Twinkle by Wenlan. There's another location in North Beach at 1519 Grant Ave. (at Union and Filbert sts.) with the same phone number. 40 Grant Ave. (btw. O'Farrell and Geary sts.). ℂ **415/982-5726. www.abfits.com.**

American Rag Cie *(Finds)*   Fashionistas flock to this find, on an unlikely stretch of busy Van Ness, for vintage and new duds sure to make you look street-swank. Check it out for everything from Juicy Couture to Paul & Joe and from European vintage to modern masters such as Diesel. 1305 Van Ness Ave. (at Sutter St.). ℂ **415/474-5214.**

Gucci America   Donning Gucci's golden Gs is not a cheap endeavor. But if you've got the cash, you'll find all the latest lines of shoes, leather goods, scarves, and pricey accessories here, such as a $9,000 handmade crocodile bag. 200 Stockton St. (btw. Geary and Post sts.). ℂ **415/392-2808. www.gucci.com.**

H & M   This ever-trendy and cheap Swedish clothing chain opened in Union Square at the end of 2004 and had lines out the door all through the holiday season—and not just for their collection by Stella McCartney. Drop in anytime for trendy cuts and styles sure to satisfy the hip him and her along on the trip. 150 Powell St. (btw. Ellis and O'Farrell sts.) ℂ **415/986-4215.**

MAC *(Finds)*   No, we're not talking cosmetics. The more-modern-than-corporate stock at this hip and hidden shop (Modern Apparel Clothing) just combined its men's and women's fashion meccas in a new space next door to pastry pit stop Citizen Cake. Drop in for men's imported tailored suits and women's separates in new and intriguing fabrics as well as gorgeous ties, vibrant sweaters, and a few choice home accouterments. Lines include Belgium's Dries Van Noten and Martin Margiela, New York's John Bartlett, and local sweater sweetheart Laurie B. The best part? Prices are more reasonable than at many of the trendy clothing stores in the area. 387 Grove St. (at Gough St.). ℂ **415/863-3011.**

Amazing Grazing

There's no better way to spend a sunny Saturday morning in San Francisco than to stroll the **Ferry Building Marketplace** and **Farmers' Market,** snacking your way through some of America's finest organic produce—it's one of the most highly acclaimed farmers' markets in the United States. While foraging among the dozens of stalls crammed with Northern California fruit, vegetables, bread, shellfish, and dairy items, you're bound to bump elbows with the dozens of Bay Area chefs (such as Alice Waters) who do their shopping here. The enthusiastic vendors are always willing to educate visitors about the pleasures of organic produce and often provide free samples. It's a unique opportunity for city dwellers to buy freshly picked organic produce directly from small family-operated farms.

On Saturday mornings the market is in its full glory. Nearly the entire building is enrobed with local meat ranchers, artisan cheese makers, bread bakers, specialty food purveyors, and farmers. On Saturdays make sure you arrive by 10:30am to watch Meet the Farmer, a half-hour interview with one of the farmers, food artisans, or other purveyors who give the audience in-depth information about how and where their food is produced. Then, at 11am, Bay Area chefs give cooking demonstrations using ingredients purchased that morning from the market (you get to taste their creations then leave with the recipe in hand). Several local restaurants also have food stalls selling their cuisine—including breakfast items—so don't eat before you arrive. You can also pick up locally made vinegars, preserves, herbs, and oils, which make wonderful gifts.

If you decide you want a local foodie to lead you on a culinary excursion of the Marketplace and Farmers' Market, my friend Lisa Rogovin, an

Niketown   Here it's not "I can," but "I can spend." At least that's what the kings of sportswear were banking on when they opened this megastore in 1997. As you'd expect, inside the doors shoppers find themselves in a Nike world offering everything the merchandising team could create. 278 Post St. (at Stockton St.). ℂ 415/392-6453.

Three Bags Full   Snuggling up in a cozy sweater can be a fashionable event if you do your shopping at this pricey boutique, which carries the gamut in handmade, playful, and extravagant knitwear. Other city locations, which also close on Sunday, are 500 Sutter St., ℂ **415/398-7987;** and 3314 Sacramento St. (also closed Mon), ℂ **415/923-1454.** 2181 Union St. (at Fillmore St.). ℂ 415/567-5753. www.threebagsfull.com.

Wilkes Bashford *(Finds)*   Wilkes Bashford is one of the most expensive and best-known clothing stores in the city. In its 3-plus decades in business, the boutique has garnered a reputation for stocking only the finest clothes in the world (which can often be seen on ex-Mayor Willie Brown and current Mayor Gavin Newsom, who do their suit shopping here). Most fashions come from Italy and France; they include women's designer sportswear and couture and men's Kiton and Brioni suits (at $2,500 and up, they're considered the most expensive suits in the world). Closed Sundays. 375 Sutter St. (at Stockton St.). ℂ **415/986-4380.** www.wilkesbashford.com.

"Epicurean Concierge" and founder of **In the Kitchen with Lisa,** offers guided culinary excursions. Some of Lisa's top noshing tips include:

- Mortgage Lifter heirloom tomatoes dipped in special Rosemary Salt from **Eatwell Farm**
- Creamy and sweet Barhi dates from **Flying Disk Ranch,** spread on an épi baguette from **Acme Bread Company** with a touch of fresh Panir cheese from **Cowgirl Creamery**
- Whatever's in season at **Hamada Farms,** such as their Tahitian pomelos and Oro Blanco grapefruits
- Fleur de Sel chocolates at **Recchiuti Confections**
- **Scharffen Berger's** Bittersweet Mocha chocolate bars made with ground Sumatra coffee beans from Peet's Coffee & Tea
- Warm liquid Valrhona chocolate at **Boulette's Larder** (nirvana, she says).

For more information about Lisa's guided culinary tours, log on to her website at www.inthekitchenwithlisa.com, or call her at ℂ **415/806-5970.**

The Ferry Building Marketplace is open Monday through Friday from 10am to 6pm, Saturday from 9am to 6pm, and Sunday from 11am to 5pm. The Farmers' Market takes place year-round, rain or shine, every Tuesday and Saturday from 10am to 2pm. From spring through fall it also runs on Thursdays from 4 to 8pm and Sundays from 10am to 2pm. The Ferry Building is located on the Embarcadero at the foot of Market Street (about a 15-min. walk from Fisherman's Wharf). Call ℂ **415/693-0996** for more information or log onto www.ferryplazafarmersmarket.com or www.ferrybuildingmarket place.com.

WOMEN'S FASHIONS

The Chanel Boutique   Ever fashionable and expensive, Chanel is appropriately located on Maiden Lane, the quaint downtown side street where the most exclusive stores and spas cluster. You'll find here what you'd expect from Chanel: Clothing, accessories, scents, cosmetics, and jewelry. 155 Maiden Lane (btw. Stockton St. and Grant Ave.). ℂ 415/981-1550. www.chanel.com.

emily lee   More mature fashionistas head to the quaint shopping street of Laurel Village, a block-long strip mall of shops that includes emily lee, for everything from elegant to artsy-designer garb that tends to be stylish, sensible, and loose-fitting. Designers include the likes of Blanque, Eileen Fisher, Flax, Ivan Grundahl, and Three Dots. 3509 California St. (at Locust St.). ℂ 415/751-3443.

Métier (*Finds*)   Discerning and well-funded shoppers consider this the best women's clothing shop in town. Within its walls you'll find classic, sophisticated, and expensive creations, which include European ready-to-wear lines and designers: Fashions by Italian designers Anna Molinari, Hache, and Blumarine and by French designer Martine Sitbon. You will also find a distinguished collection of antique-style, high-end jewelry from L.A.'s Cathy Waterman as well as ultrapopular custom-designed poetry jewelry by Jeanine Payer. Closed Sunday. 355 Sutter St. (btw. Stockton and Grant sts.). ℂ 415/989-5395. www.metiersf.com.

RAG *(Finds*   If you want to add some truly unique San Francisco designs to your closet, head to RAG, or Residents Apparel Gallery, a co-op shop where around 55 local emerging designers showcase their latest creations. Prices are great; fashions are forward, young, and hip; and if you grab a few pieces, no one at home's going to be able to copy your look. 541 Octavia St. (at Hayes St.). ℂ 415/621-7718. www.ragsf.com.

FOOD

Boulangerie *(Finds*   A bit of Paris on Pine Street, this true-blue bakery sells authentically French creations, from delicious and slightly sour French country wheat bread to rustic-style desserts, including the locally famous *cannelés de Bordeaux,* custard baked in a copper mold. And if you're looking for a place to eat Boulangerie bread and pastries, visit their cafes—**Boulange de Polk,** at 2310 Polk St. near Green St. (ℂ **415/345-1107**), or **Boulange de Cole,** at 1000 Cole St. at Parnassus St. (ℂ **415/242-2442**). Closed Monday. 2325 Pine St. (at Fillmore St.). ℂ 415/440-0356, ext. 204. www.bay bread.com.

Cowgirl Creamery Cheese Shop *(Finds*   San Francisco is fanatical about cheese, and much of the local enthusiasm can be attributed to the two women who created the small-production Cowgirl Creamery, located in the Ferry Building Marketplace but still imparting the simple neighborhood shop feel. Here's how you do it: Sample, then buy a hefty slice of your favorite cheese, and then enjoy it on the waterfront with some crusty Acme Bread and a piece of fruit from Capay Farms (all within the same building). Ferry Building Marketplace, no. 17. ℂ 415/362-9354. www.cowgirlcreamery.com.

Ferry Building Marketplace *(Finds*   A one-stop shop for some of the city's finest edibles, the renovated historic Ferry Building is home to the revered Acme Bread Company, Scharffen Berger Chocolate, the Imperial Tea Court, Peet's Coffee, Cowgirl Creamery Cheese Shop (see above), Recchiuti Confections, and more. There's no better place to load up on the Bay Area's outstanding bounty. Ferry Building Plaza (at the foot of Market St. at The Embarcadero). ℂ 415/693-0996. www.ferrybuildingmarketplace.com.

Joseph Schmidt Confections *(Finds*   Here, chocolate takes the shape of exquisite sculptural masterpieces—such as long-stemmed tulips and heart-shaped boxes—that are so beautiful, you'll be hesitant to bite the head off your adorable panda bear. Once you do, however, you'll know why this is the most popular—and reasonably priced—chocolatier in town. 3489 16th St. (at Sanchez St.). ℂ **800/861-8682** or 415/861-8682. www.josephschmidtconfections.com.

Ten Ren Tea Co., Ltd. *(Finds*   At the Ten Ren Tea Co. shop, you will be offered a steaming cup of tea when you walk in the door. In addition to a selection of almost 50 traditional and herbal teas, the company stocks a collection of cold tea drinks and tea-related paraphernalia, such as pots, cups, and infusers. If you can't make up your mind, take home a mail-order form. The shop is open daily from 9am to 9pm. 949 Grant Ave. (btw. Washington and Jackson sts.). ℂ 415/362-0656. www.tentea.com.

GIFTS

Art of China   Amid a wide variety of collectibles, this shop features exquisite, hand-carved Chinese figurines. You'll also find a lovely assortment of ivory beads, bracelets, necklaces, and earrings. Pink-quartz dogs, jade figurines, porcelain vases, cache pots, and blue-and-white barrels suitable for use as table bases are just some of the many items stocked here. 839–843 Grant Ave. (btw. Clay and Washington sts.). © 415/981-1602. www.artsofchinasf.com.

Babushka   Located near Fisherman's Wharf, adjacent to the Anchorage Mall, Babushka sells only Russian products, most of which are wooden nesting dolls. Pier 39. © 415/788-7043.

Cost Plus World Market   At the Fisherman's Wharf cable car turntable, Cost Plus is a vast warehouse crammed to the rafters with Chinese baskets, Indian camel bells, Malaysian batik scarves, and innumerable other items from Algeria to Zanzibar. More than 20,000 items from 50 nations, imported directly from their countries of origin, pack this warehouse. There's also a decent wine shop here. It's open Monday through Saturday from 9am to 9pm and Sunday from 10am to 8pm. 2552 Taylor St. (btw. North Point and Bay sts.). © 415/928-6200.

Dandelion *(Finds*   Tucked in an out-of-the-way location in SoMa is the most wonderful collection of gifts, collectibles, and furnishings. There's something for every taste and budget here, from an excellent collection of teapots, decorative dishes, and gourmet foods to silver, books, cards, and picture frames. Don't miss the Zen-like second floor, with its peaceful furnishings in Indian, Japanese, and Western styles. The store is closed Sunday and Monday except during November and December, when it's open daily. Hours are 10am to 6pm. 55 Potrero Ave. (at Alameda St.). © 415/436-9500. www.tampopo.com.

Flax   If you go into an art store for a special pencil and come out $300 later, don't go near this shop. Flax has everything you can think of in art and design supplies, an amazing collection of blank bound books, children's art supplies, frames, calendars— you name it. There's a gift for every type of person here, especially you. 1699 Market St. (at Valencia and Gough sts.). © 415/552-2355. www.flaxart.com.

Good Vibrations   A laypersons' sex-toy, book, and video emporium, Good Vibrations is a women-owned, worker-owned cooperative. Unlike most sex shops, it's not a back-alley business, but a straightforward shop with healthy, open attitudes about human sexuality. It also has a vibrator museum. 603 Valencia St. (at 17th St.). © 415/522-5460 or 800/BUY-VIBE (for mail order). www.goodvibes.com. A second location is at 1620 Polk St. (at Sacramento St., © 415/345-0400); and a third is at 2504 San Pablo Ave., Berkeley ((© 510/841-8987).

Kati Koos   Need a little humor in your life? Previously called Smile, this store specializes in whimsical art, furniture, clothing, jewelry, and American crafts guaranteed to make you grin. Closed Sunday. 500 Sutter St. (btw. Powell and Mason sts.). © 415/362-3437. www.katikoos.com.

SFMOMA MuseumStore *(Finds*   With an array of artistic cards, books, jewelry, housewares, furniture, knickknacks, and creative tokens of San Francisco, it's virtually impossible not to find something here you'll consider a must-have. (Check out the FogDome!) Aside from being one of the locals' favorite shops, it offers far more tasteful mementos than most Fisherman's Wharf options. Open late (until 9:30pm) on Thursday nights. 151 Third St. (2 blocks south of Market St., across from Yerba Buena Gardens). © 415/357-4035. www.sfmoma.org.

HOUSEWARES/FURNISHINGS

Alabaster *(Finds*   Any interior designer who knows Biedermeier from Bauhaus knows that this Hayes Valley shop sets local home accessories trends with its collection of high-end must-haves. Their selection includes everything from lighting—antique and modern Alabaster fixtures, Fortuny silk shades, Venetian glass chandeliers—to other home accessories, like one-of-a-kind antiques, body products from Florence, and more. 597 Hayes St. (at Laguna St.). ⓒ **415/558-0482**. www.alabastersf.com.

Alessi Italian designer Alberto Alessi, who's known for his whimsical and colorful kitchen-utensil designs, such as his ever-popular spiderlike lemon squeezer, opened a flagship store here. Drop by for everything from gorgeous stainless-steel double boilers to corkscrews shaped like maidens. 424 Sutter St. (at Stockton St.). ⓒ **415/434-0403**. www.alessi.com.

Big Pagoda Company When I need to buy a stylish friend a gift, I head to this downtown Asian-influenced design shop for cool, unique, and contemporary finds. Within the bi-level boutique, East meets West and old meets new in the form of anything from an antique Chinese scholar's chair to a new wave table that hints at Ming or Mondrian. Its furniture and glass art is hardly cheap (an antique Tibetan dragonhead goes for $30,000), but you can get fabulous designer martini glasses at $15 a pop. Open Monday through Saturday 10am to 6pm. 310 Sutter St. (at Grant St.). ⓒ **415/296-8881**. www.bigpagoda.com.

Biordi Art Imports *(Finds* Whether you want to decorate your dinner table, color your kitchen, or liven up the living room, Biordi's Italian majolica pottery is the most exquisite and unusual way to do it. The owner has been importing these hand-painted collectibles for 60 years, and every piece is a showstopper. Call for a catalog. They'll ship anywhere. Closed Sundays. 412 Columbus Ave. (at Vallejo St.). ⓒ **415/392-8096**. www.biordi.com.

Diptyque If the idea of spending $40 on a candle makes you laugh, this isn't the place for you. But if you're the type willing to throw down good money to scentualize your living space, don't skip this French shop offering dozens of spectacular flaming fragrances. I'm such a fan that every time I went to Paris I'd weigh down my luggage with these 50-hour burners. (Before the horrible exchange rate, that is.) But now I can scoop them up in my own backyard. They also make great gifts. 171 Maiden Lane (near Stockton St.). ⓒ **415/402-0600**. www.diptyqueusa.com.

Limn For the latest in Europe's trendsetting and ultramodern furniture and lighting, go straight to SoMa celebrity Limn, which also showcases artworks in its adjoining gallery. 290 Townsend St. (at Fourth St.). ⓒ **415/543-5466**. www.limn.com.

Nest *(Finds* Don't come into Fillmore's cutest French interiors store without your credit cards. Nest carries adorable throws, handmade quilts, must-have slippers and sleepwear, and a number of other things you never knew you needed until now. 2300 Fillmore St. (at Clay St.). ⓒ **415/292-6199**.

Propeller *(Finds* This airy skylight-lit shop is a must-stop for lovers of the latest in übermodern furniture and home accessories. Owner/designer Lorn Dittfeld handpicks pieces done by emerging designers from as far away as Sweden, Italy, and Canada as well as a plethora of national newbies. Drop in to lounge on the hippest sofas; grab pretty and practical gifts like ultracool magnetic spice racks; or adorn your home with Bev Hisey's throws and graphic pillows, diamond-cut wood tables by William Earle, or hand-tufted graphic rugs by Angela Adams. 555 Hayes St. (btw. Laguna and Octavia sts.). ⓒ **415/701-7767**. www.propeller-sf.com.

Sue Fisher King *(Finds)*   For the ultimate in everything on the traditional side for the tabletop, bedroom, and beyond, head to this exclusive neighborhood boutique known by the society set as the only place to shop. It's filled with items like exquisite table linens, cashmere blankets, towels, china, silver flatware, and more. Closed Sunday. 3067 Sacramento St. (at Baker St.). ℭ **415/922-7276. www.suefisherking.com.**

Sur La Table   Cooks should beeline it to this Union Square shop specializing in all things culinary. Its two floors are packed to the rafters with pricey but stylish high-quality pots and pans, utensils, tabletop items, books, and more coupled with an extremely helpful and knowledgeable staff. A second location is at the Ferry Building Marketplace, stall no. 37 (ℭ **415/262-9970**). 77 Maiden Lane (at Grant St.). ℭ **415/732-7900. www.surlatable.com.**

The Wok Shop   This shop has every conceivable implement for Chinese cooking, including woks, brushes, cleavers, circular chopping blocks, dishes, oyster knives, bamboo steamers, and strainers. It also sells a wide range of kitchen utensils, baskets, handmade linens from China, and aprons. 718 Grant Ave. (at Clay St.). ℭ **415/989-3797** or 888/780-7171 for mail order. www.wokshop.com.

Zinc Details *(Finds)*   This contemporary furniture and knickknack shop has received accolades everywhere from *Elle Decor Japan* to *Metropolitan Home* to *InStyle* for its amazing collection of glass vases, pendant lights, ceramics from all over the world, and furniture from local craftspeople. A portion of these true works of art is made specifically for the store. While you're in the 'hood, check out their new sister store around the corner at 2410 California St. (ℭ **415/776-9002**), which showcases contemporary designer furniture. 1905 Fillmore St. (btw. Bush and Pine sts.). ℭ **415/776-2100. www.zincdetails.com.**

JEWELRY

De Vera Galleries *(Finds)*   Don't come here unless you've got money to spend. Designer Federico de Vera's unique rough-stone jewelry collection, art glass, and vintage knickknacks are too beautiful to pass up and too expensive to be a painless purchase. Still, if you're looking for a keepsake, you'll find it here. Closed Sunday and Monday. 29 Maiden Lane (at Kearny St.). ℭ **415/788-0828. www.deveraobjects.com.**

Dianne's Old & New Estates   Many local girls get engagement rings from this fantastic little shop featuring top-of-the-line antique jewelry—pendants, diamond rings, necklaces, bracelets, and pearls. For a special gift, check out the collection of platinum wedding and engagement rings and vintage watches. Don't worry if you can't afford it now—the shop offers 1-year interest-free layaway. And, if you buy a ring, they'll send you off with a thank-you bottle of celebration bubbly. 2181A Union St. (at Fillmore St.). ℭ **888/346-7525** or 415/346-7525.www.diannesestatejewelry.com.

Jeanine Payer   If you want to buy a trinket that is truly San Franciscan, stop by this boutique hidden on the street level of the beautifully ornate Phelan Building where designer Jeanine Payer showcases gorgeous, handmade contemporary jewelry that she crafts in sterling silver and 18-karat gold five stories above in her studio. All of her pieces, including fabulous baby gifts, sport engraved poetry and can even be custom done. Sound familiar? Not surprising. Celebrities such as Sheryl Crow, Debra Messing, and Ellen DeGeneres are fans. 760 Market St., Suite 533 (at O'Farrell St.). ℭ **415/788-2414. www.jeaninepayer.com.**

Pearl & Jade Empire   The Pearl & Jade Empire has been importing jewelry from all over the world since 1957. It specializes in unusual pearls and jade and offers restringing on the premises. It also has a collection of amber from the Baltic Sea. 427 Post St. (btw. Powell and Mason sts.). © 415/362-0606. www.pearlempire.com.

Tiffany & Co.   Even if you don't have lots of cash with which to buy an exquisite bauble that comes in Tiffany's famous light-blue box, enjoy this renowned store à la Audrey Hepburn in *Breakfast at Tiffany's*. The designer collection features Paloma Picasso, Jean Schlumberger, and Elsa Peretti in both silver and 18-karat gold, and there's an extensive gift collection in sterling, china, and crystal. 350 Post St. (at Powell St.). © 415/781-7000. www.tiffany.com.

Union Street Goldsmith   A showcase for Bay Area goldsmiths, this exquisite shop sells a contemporary collection of fine custom-designed jewelry in platinum and all karats of gold. Many pieces emphasize colored stones. 1909 Union St. (at Laguna St.). © 415/776-8048. www.unionstreetgoldsmith.com.

MUSIC

Amoeba Records   Don't be scared off by the tattooed, pierced, and fierce-looking employees (and other shoppers!) in this beloved new and used record store highlighting indie labels. They're actually more than happy to recommend some great music to you. If you're looking for the latest from Britney, this might not be the store for you (though they *do* have everything), but if you're into interesting music that's not necessarily on every station all the time, check this place out. You can buy, sell, and trade in this cavernous, loud Haight Street hot spot. 1855 Haight St. (btw. Shrader and Stanyan sts.). © 415/831-1200.

Recycled Records *(Finds*   Easily one of the best used-record stores in the city, this loud shop in the Haight has cases of used "classic" rock LPs, sheet music, and tour programs. It's open from 10am to 8pm daily. 1377 Haight St. (btw. Central and Masonic sts.). © 415/626-4075. www.recycled-records.com.

Streetlight Records   Overstuffed with used music in all three formats, this place is best known for its records and excellent CD collection. It also carries new and used DVDs and computer games. Rock music is cheap, and the money-back guarantee guards against defects. 3979 24th St. (btw. Noe and Sanchez sts.). © 415/282-3550. www.street lightrecords.com. A second location is at 2350 Market St., btw. Castro and Noe sts. (© 415/282-8000).

Virgin Megastore   With thousands of CDs, including an impressive collection of imports, videos, DVDs, a multimedia department, a cafe, and related books, this enormous Union Square store can make any music-lover blow his or her entire vacation fund. It's open Sunday through Thursday from 10am to 11pm and Friday and Saturday from 10am to midnight. 2 Stockton St. (at Market St.). © 415/397-4525.

SHOES

Bulo   If you have a fetish for foot fashions, you must check out Bulo, which carries nothing but imported Italian shoes. The selection is small but styles run the gamut, from casual to dressy, reserved to wildly funky. New shipments come in every 3 to 4 weeks, so the selection is ever-changing, eternally hip, and, unfortunately, ever-expensive, with many pairs going for close to $200. Men's and women's store: 437A Hayes St. (at Gough St.). © 415/864-3244. Women's store: across the street, at 418 Hayes St. (© 415/255-4939). www.buloshoes.com.

Gimme Shoes   The staff is funky-fashion snobby, the prices are steep, and the European shoes and accessories are utterly chic. 2358 Fillmore St. (at Washington St.). ℂ 415/441-3040. Additional location at 416 Hayes St. (ℂ 415/864-0691. www.gimmeshoes.com.

Kenneth Cole   This trendy shop carries high-fashion footwear for men and women. There is also an innovative collection of handbags and small leather goods and accessories. 865 Market St. (in the San Francisco Shopping Centre). ℂ 415/227-4536. www.kennethcole.com. Another shop is at 166 Grant St., at Post St. (ℂ 415/981-2653).

Paolo Shoes   This Italian import store is run by owner Paolo Iantorno, who actually designs the shoes for his hipster shops. If gorgeous, handcrafted, colorful shoes are what you're looking for, this is the shop for you. You can get your low-heeled slip-ons here—this store features men's and women's footwear and bags—but they might be in silver python. Check out the men's perforated orange slip-ons—not for the faint of heart or fashion-modest. You might not even mind that many shoes are upwards of 200 bucks when you realize that Paolo's women's shoes are so sexy and comfortable, you won't want to take them off. 524 Hayes St. ℂ 415/552-4580. A second location is at 2000 Fillmore St. (ℂ 415/771-1944). www.paoloshoes.com.

SHOPPING CENTERS & COMPLEXES

The Anchorage   This touristy waterfront mall has close to 35 stores that offer everything from music boxes to home furnishings; street performers entertain during open hours. This is not a stop for staples, but more for tourist trinkets. 2800 Leavenworth St. (btw. Beach and Jefferson sts. on Fisherman's Wharf). ℂ 415/775-6000.

Crocker Galleria   Modeled after Milan's Galleria Vittorio Emanuele, this glass-domed, three-level pavilion, about 3 blocks east of Union Square, features around 40 high-end shops with expensive and classic designer creations. Fashions include Aricie lingerie, Gianni Versace, and Polo/Ralph Lauren. Closed Sunday. 50 Post St. (at Kearny St.). ℂ 415/393-1505. www.shopatgalleria.com.

Ghirardelli Square   This former chocolate factory is one of the city's quaintest shopping malls and most popular landmarks. It dates from 1864, when it served as a factory making Civil War uniforms, but it's best known as the former chocolate and spice factory of Domingo Ghirardelli (say "Gear-ar-delly"). A clock tower, an exact replica of the one at France's Château de Blois, crowns the complex. Inside the tower, on the mall's plaza level, is the fun Ghirardelli soda fountain. It still makes and sells small amounts of chocolate, but the big draw is the old-fashioned ice-cream parlor. If you're coming to shop, think again: It's pretty lame in that department, but you can dine decently at Ana Mandara (p. 133). The main plaza shops' and restaurants' hours are 10am to 6pm Sunday through Thursday and 10am to 9pm Friday and Saturday, with extended hours during the summer. 900 North Point St. (at Polk St.). ℂ 415/775-5500. www.ghirardellisq.com.

PIER 39 *(Overrated)*   This bayside tourist trap also happens to have stunning views. To residents, that pretty much wraps up PIER 39—an expensive spot where out-of-towners go to waste money on worthless souvenirs and greasy fast food. For vacationers, though, PIER 39 does have some redeeming qualities—fresh crab (in season), playful sea lions, phenomenal views, and plenty of fun for the kids. If you want to get to know the real San Francisco, skip the cheesy T-shirt shops and limit your time here to one afternoon, if at all. Located at Beach St. and the Embarcadero.

Westfield San Francisco Centre Opened in 1988 and given a $460 million expansion in 2006, this ritzy 1.5-million-square-foot urban shopping center is one of the few vertical malls (multilevel rather than sprawling) in the United States. Its most attractive feature is a spectacular atrium with a century-old dome that's 102 feet wide and three stories high. Along with Nordstrom (p. 218) and Bloomingdale's (p. 217) department stores and a Century Theatres multiplex, there are more than 170 specialty stores, including Abercrombie & Fitch, Ann Taylor, bebe, Benetton, Footlocker, J. Crew, and Victoria's Secret. 865 Market St. (at Fifth St.). ✆ 415/512-6776. www.westfield. com/sanfrancisco.

TOYS

The Chinatown Kite Shop This shop's playful assortment of flying objects includes attractive fish kites, windsocks, hand-painted Chinese paper kites, wood-and-paper biplanes, pentagonal kites, and do-it-yourself kite kits, all of which make great souvenirs or decorations. Computer-designed stunt kites have two or four control lines to manipulate loops and dives. Open daily from 10am to 8pm. 717 Grant Ave. (btw. Clay and Sacramento sts.). ✆ 415/391-8217. www.chinatownkite.com.

TRAVEL GOODS

Flight 001 Jetsetters zoom into this space-shuttle-like showroom for hip travel accessories. Check out the sleek luggage, "security friendly" manicure sets, and other mid-air must-haves. 525 Hayes St. (btw. Laguna and Octavia sts.). ✆ 415/487-1001. www. flight001.com.

VINTAGE CLOTHING

Aardvark's One of San Francisco's largest secondhand clothing dealers, Aardvark's has seemingly endless racks of shirts, pants, dresses, skirts, and hats from the past 30 years. It's open daily from 11am to 7pm. 1501 Haight St. (at Ashbury St.). ✆ 415/621-3141.

Buffalo Exchange This large and newly expanded storefront on upper Haight Street is crammed with racks of antique and new fashions from the 1960s, 1970s, and 1980s. It stocks everything from suits and dresses to neckties, hats, handbags, and jewelry. Buffalo Exchange anticipates some of the hottest new street fashions. 1555 Haight St. (btw. Clayton and Ashbury sts.). ✆ 415/431-7733. A second shop is at 1210 Valencia St., at 24th St. (✆ 415/647-8332). www.buffaloexchange.com.

Good Byes *(Finds* One of the best new- and used-clothes stores in San Francisco, Good Byes carries only high-quality clothing and accessories, including an exceptional selection of men's fashions at unbelievably low prices (for example, $350 pre-owned shoes for $35). Women's wear is in a separate boutique across the street. 3464 Sacramento St. and 3483 Sacramento St. (btw. Laurel and Walnut sts.). ✆ 415/346-6388. www.goodbyessf.com.

La Rosa On a street packed with vintage-clothing shops, this is one of the more upscale options. Since 1978, it has featured a selection of high-quality, dry-cleaned secondhand goods. Formal suits and dresses are its specialty, but you'll also find sport coats, slacks, and shoes. The more moderately priced sister store, **Held Over,** is located at 1543 Haight St., near Ashbury (✆ **415/864-0818**); and their discount store, **Clothes Contact,** is located at 473 Valencia St., at 16th St. (✆ **415/621-3212**). 1711 Haight St. (at Cole St.). ✆ 415/668-3744.

WINE & SAKE

True Sake   Amid woven sea grass flooring, colorful backlit displays, and a so-hip Hayes Valley location are more than 140 varieties of Japanese-produced sake ranging from an $8 300ml bottle of Ohyama to an $180 720ml bottle of Kotsuzumi Rojohanaari—which, incidentally, owner Beau Timken (who is on hand to describe each wine), says is available at no other retail store in the U.S. 560 Hayes St. (btw. Laguna and Octavia sts.). © 415/355-9555. www.truesake.com.

Wine Club San Francisco *(Value*   The Wine Club is a discount warehouse that offers bargains on more than 1,200 domestic and foreign wines. Bottles cost between $4 and $1,100. 953 Harrison St. (btw. Fifth and Sixth sts.). © 415/512-9086.

11

San Francisco After Dark

For a city with fewer than a million inhabitants, San Francisco boasts an impressive after-dark scene. Dozens of piano bars and top-notch lounges augment a lively dance-club culture, and skyscraper lounges offer dazzling city views. The city's arts scene is also extraordinary: The opera is justifiably world renowned, the ballet is on its toes, and theaters are high in both quantity and quality. In short, there's always something going on in the city, and unlike in Los Angeles or New York you don't have to pay outrageous cover charges or be "picked" to be a part of the scene.

For up-to-date nightlife information, turn to the *San Francisco Weekly* (www. sfweekly.com) and the *San Francisco Bay Guardian* (www.sfbg.com), both of which run comprehensive listings. They are available for free at bars and restaurants and from street-corner boxes all around the city. *Where* (www.wheresf.com), a free tourist-oriented monthly, also lists programs and performance times; it's available in most of the city's finer hotels. The Sunday edition of the *San Francisco Chronicle* features a "Datebook" section, printed on pink paper, with information on and listings of the week's events. If you have Internet access, it's a good idea to check out www.citysearch.com or www.sf station.com for the latest in bars, clubs, and events. And if you want to secure seats at a hot-ticket event, either buy well in advance or contact the concierge of your hotel and see if they can swing something for you.

Tix Bay Area (also known as TIX; © 415/433-7827; www.tixbayarea.org) sells half-price tickets on the day of performances and full-price tickets in advance to select Bay Area cultural and sporting events. TIX is also a Ticketmaster outlet and sells Gray Line tours and transportation passes. Tickets are primarily sold in person with some half-price tickets available on their website. To find out which shows have half-price tickets, call the TIX info line or check out their website. A service charge, ranging from $1.75 to $6, is levied on each ticket depending on its full price. You can pay with cash, traveler's checks, Visa, MasterCard, American Express, or Discover Card with photo ID. TIX, located on Powell Street between Geary and Post streets, is open Tuesday through Thursday from 11am to 6pm, Friday from 11am to 7pm, Saturday from 10am to 7pm, and Sunday from 10am to 3pm. *Note:* Half-price tickets go on sale at 11am.

You can also get tickets to most theater and dance events through **City Box Office,** 180 Redwood St., Suite 100, between Golden Gate and McAllister streets off Van Ness Avenue (© 415/392-4400; www.cityboxoffice.com). MasterCard and Visa are accepted.

Tickets.com (© 800/225-2277; www. tickets.com) sells computer-generated tickets (with a hefty service charge of $3–$19 per ticket!) to concerts, sporting events, plays, and special events. **Ticketmaster** (© 415/421-TIXS; www.ticket master.com) also offers advance ticket purchases (also with a service charge).

For information on local theater, check out **www.theatrebayarea.org**. For information on major league baseball, pro basketball, pro and college football, and horse racing, see the "Spectator Sports" section of chapter 8, beginning on p. 197.

And don't forget that this isn't New York: Bars close at 2am, so get an early start if you want a full night on the town in San Francisco.

1 The Performing Arts

Special concerts and performances take place in San Francisco year-round. **San Francisco Performances,** 500 Sutter St., Suite 710 (© **415/398-6449;** www. performances.org), has brought acclaimed artists to the Bay Area for 27 years. Shows run the gamut from chamber music to dance to jazz. Performances are in several venues, including the Herbst Theater and the Yerba Buena Center for the Arts. The season runs from late September to June. Tickets cost from $12 to $50 and are available through **City Box Office** (© **415/392-4400**) or through the San Francisco Performances website.

CLASSICAL MUSIC

Philharmonia Baroque Orchestra   This orchestra of baroque, classical, and "early Romantic" music performs in San Francisco and all around the Bay Area. The season lasts September through April. Performances are in Herbst Theater, 401 Van Ness Ave. Tickets are sold through City Box Office, © 415/392-4400 (box office), or call 415/252-1288 (administrative offices). www.philharmonia.org. Tickets $29–$67.

San Francisco Symphony   Founded in 1911, the internationally respected San Francisco Symphony has long been an important part of the city's cultural life under such legendary conductors as Pierre Monteux and Seiji Ozawa. In 1995, Michael Tilson Thomas took over from Herbert Blomstedt; he has led the orchestra to new heights and crafted an exciting repertoire of classical and modern music. The season runs September through June. Summer symphony activities include a Summer Festival and a Summer in the City series. Tickets are very hard to come by, but if you're desperate, you can usually pick up a few outside the hall the night of the concert. Also, the box office occasionally has a few last-minute tickets. Performing at Davies Symphony Hall, 201 Van Ness Ave. (at Grove St.). © 415/864-6000 (box office). www.sfsymphony.org. Tickets $25–$114.

OPERA

In addition to San Francisco's major opera company, you might check out the amusing **Pocket Opera,** 469 Bryant St. (© **415/972-8930;** www.pocketopera.org). From early March to mid-July, the comic company stages farcical performances of well-known operas in English. The staging is intimate and informal, without lavish costumes and sets. The cast ranges from 3 to 16 players, supported by a chamber orchestra. The rich repertoire includes such works as *Don Giovanni, The Barber of Seville,* and over 80 other operas. Performances are Friday at 7:30pm, throughout the day on Saturday, and Sunday at 2pm. Call the box office for complete information, location (which varies), and show times. Tickets cost from $18 (students) to $35.

San Francisco Opera   The San Francisco Opera was the second municipal opera in the United States and is one of the city's cultural icons. Brilliantly balanced casts may feature celebrated stars like Frederica Von Stade and Plácido Domingo along with promising newcomers and regular members in productions that range from traditional

San Francisco After Dark

American Conservatory Theater (A.C.T.) **57**
Bambuddha Lounge **22**
BATS Improv **1**
Beach Blanket Babylon **36**
Bimbo's 365 Club **31**
Biscuits and Blues **58**
The Bliss Bar **10**
The Boom Boom Room **5**
Bottom of the Hill **75**
The Bubble Lounge **46**
Buddha Lounge **42**
Buena Vista Café **28**
The Café **11**
Cafe du Nord **13**
Caffè Greco **37**
Caffè Trieste **38**
Carnelian Room **48**
Castro Theatre **11**
Center for the Performing Arts at Yerba Buena Center **65**
The Cinch Saloon **26**
Cityscape **55**
Cobb's Comedy Club **32**
Cowell Theater **1**
Davies Symphony Hall **19**
The Eagle Tavern **72**
Edinburgh Castle **24**
Empire Plush Room **52**
The Endup **67**
Eos **8**
Equinox **52**
Eureka Theatre **43**
The Fillmore **6**
First Crush **56**
Fort Mason Center **1**
Geary Theater **57**
Gold Dust Lounge **60**
Gordon Biersch Brewery Restaurant **63**

Grant & Green Saloon **35**
Great American Music Hall **23**
Greens Sports Bar **27**
Harry Denton's Starlight Room **61**
Hemlock Tavern **24**
Herbst Theater **21**
Holy Cow **71**
Jazz at Pearl's **39**
Kimo's **25**
Levende Lounge **16**
Li Po Cocktail Lounge **42**
London Wine Bar **47**
Lone Star Saloon **69**
Lorraine Hansberry Theatre **51**
Lou's Pier 47 Club **30**
The Magic Theatre **1**
Matrix Fillmore **3**
Metro **12**
The Mint Karaoke Lounge **17**
Nectar Wine Lounge **2**
1015 Folsom **66**
ODC Theatre **15**
Perry's **4**
Philharmonia Baroque Orchestra **21**
Pied Piper Bar **62**
Pier 23 **34**
Pocket Opera **18**
Punch Line Comedy Club **44**
Rasselas **32**
The Red Room **53**
Red Vic **7**
The Redwood Room **54**
Roxie **14**
Ruby Skye **59**
The Saloon **38**

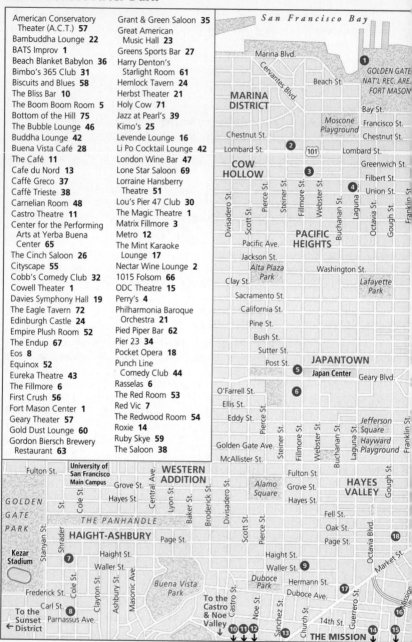

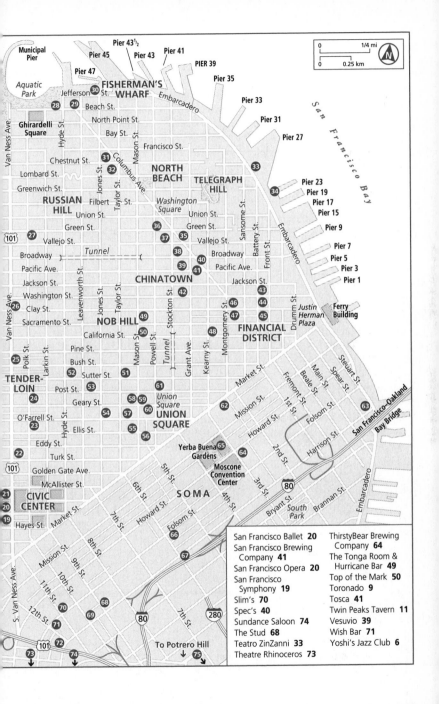

Municipal Pier

Aquatic Park

Ghirardelli Square

Pier 47
Pier 45
Pier 43½
Pier 43
Pier 41
PIER 39
Pier 35
Pier 33
Pier 31
Pier 27
Pier 23
Pier 19
Pier 17
Pier 15
Pier 9
Pier 7
Pier 5
Pier 3
Pier 1

San Francisco Bay

FISHERMAN'S WHARF
Jefferson St.
Beach St.
North Point St.
Bay St.
Francisco St.
Chestnut St.
Lombard St.
Greenwich St.
Filbert St.
Union St.
Green St.
Vallejo St.
Broadway
Pacific Ave.
Jackson St.
Washington St.
Clay St.
Sacramento St.
California St.
Pine St.
Bush St.
Sutter St.
Post St.
Geary St.
O'Farrell St.
Ellis St.
Eddy St.
Turk St.
Golden Gate Ave.
McAllister St.
Hayes St.

Embarcadero

Van Ness Ave.
Hyde St.
Columbus Ave.
Mason St.
Jones St.
Taylor St.
Leavenworth St.
Hyde St.
Larkin St.
Polk St.
S. Van Ness Ave.
Mission St.
8th St.
9th St.
10th St.
11th St.
12th St.

NORTH BEACH
TELEGRAPH HILL
Washington Square
RUSSIAN HILL
NOB HILL
CHINATOWN
Union Square
UNION SQUARE
TENDER-LOIN
CIVIC CENTER
SOMA
FINANCIAL DISTRICT
Yerba Buena Gardens
Moscone Convention Center
South Park

Sansome St.
Battery St.
Front St.
Montgomery St.
Kearny St.
Grant Ave.
Stockton St.
Powell St.
Mason St.
Drumm St.
Justin Herman Plaza
Ferry Building

Market St.
Mission St.
Howard St.
Folsom St.
Harrison St.
Bryant St.
Brannan St.
Fremont St.
1st St.
2nd St.
3rd St.
4th St.
5th St.
6th St.
7th St.
Beale St.
Main St.
Spear St.
Steuart St.

San Francisco-Oakland Bay Bridge

Embarcadero

To Potrero Hill

Tunnel

101
80
280

San Francisco Ballet **20**	ThirstyBear Brewing Company **64**
San Francisco Brewing Company **41**	The Tonga Room & Hurricane Bar **49**
San Francisco Opera **20**	Top of the Mark **50**
San Francisco Symphony **19**	Toronado **9**
Slim's **70**	Tosca **41**
Spec's **40**	Twin Peaks Tavern **11**
Sundance Saloon **74**	Vesuvio **39**
The Stud **68**	Wish Bar **71**
Teatro ZinZanni **33**	Yoshi's Jazz Club **6**
Theatre Rhinoceros **73**	

0   1/4 mi
0   0.25 km

to avant-garde. All productions have English supertitles. The season starts in September, lasts 14 weeks, takes a break for a few months, and then picks up again in June and July. During the interim winter period, future opera stars are featured in showcases and recitals. Performances are held most evenings, except Monday, with matinees on Sunday. Tickets go on sale as early as June for subscribers and August for the general public, and the best seats sell out quickly. Unless Domingo is in town, some less coveted seats are usually available until curtain time. War Memorial Opera House, 301 Van Ness Ave. (at Grove St.). (© 415/864-3330 (box office). www.sfopera.com. Tickets $24–$235; standing room $10 cash only; student rush $15 cash only.

THEATER

American Conservatory Theater (A.C.T.) *(Finds)* The Tony Award–winning American Conservatory Theater made its debut in 1967 and quickly established itself as the city's premier resident theater group and one of the nation's best. The A.C.T. season runs September through July and features both classic and experimental works. Its home is the fabulous **Geary Theater,** a national historic landmark that is regarded as one of America's finest performance spaces. The 2006–2007 season marks A.C.T.'s 40th anniversary; they haven't been resting on their laurels. In their 4-decade history, they've reached a combined audience of seven million people. Performing at the Geary Theater, 415 Geary St. (at Mason St.). (© 415/749-2ACT. www.act-sf.org. Tickets $14–$82.

Eureka Theatre Company Eureka houses contemporary performances throughout the year, usually Wednesday through Sunday. Check their website or call the theater for information on upcoming shows and how to purchase tickets (but be aware: Since they don't produce the shows themselves, they won't take reservations for any shows at the theater or sell them online). 215 Jackson St. (between Battery and Front sts.). For information, (© 415/788-7469; for tickets (© 415/255-8207. www.eurekatheatre.org. Ticket prices vary by company but are generally $22–$38.

Lorraine Hansberry Theatre San Francisco's top African-American theater group performs in a 300-seat state-of-the-art theater. It mounts special adaptations from literature along with contemporary dramas, classics, and music. Performing at 620 Sutter St. (at Mason St.). (© 415/345-3980. www.lhtsf.org. Tickets $25–$32.

The Magic Theatre The highly acclaimed Magic Theatre, which celebrated its 40th season in 2006, is a major West Coast company dedicated to presenting the works of new plays; over the years it has nurtured the talents of such luminaries as Sam Shepard and David Mamet. Shepard's Pulitzer Prize–winning play *Buried Child* had its premiere here, as did Mamet's *Dr. Faustus.* The season usually runs from October through June; performances are held Tuesday through Sunday. A perk for anyone who's been in previous years: In 2005 and 2006 they redecorated the lobby and added

---

(Value **Free Opera**

Every year, the **San Francisco Opera** stages a number of free performances. Every September, a free performance of Opera in the Park launches the season, followed by occasional free performances throughout the city as part of the Brown Bag Opera program. Schedule details can be found on the company's website at **www.sfopera.com.**

Tips **ZinZany Dinner Party**

Hungry for dinner and a damned good time? It ain't cheap, but Teatro ZinZanni is a rollicking ride of food, whimsy, drama, and song within a stunningly elegant 1926 spiegeltent on the Embarcadero. Part musical theater and part comedy show, the 3-hour dinner theater includes a surprisingly decent five-course meal served by dozens of performers who weave both the audience and astounding physical acts (think Cirque du Soleil) into their wacky and playful world. Anyone in need of a night of lighthearted laughter should definitely book a table here. Shows are held Wednesday through Sunday and tickets are $123 to $147 including dinner. The tent is located at Pier 29 on the Embarcadero at Battery Street. Call ℂ **415/438-2668** or see www.zinzanni.org for more details.

---

new seats in one of the theaters. Performing at Building D, Fort Mason Center, Marina Blvd. (at Buchanan St.). ℂ 415/441-8822. www.magictheatre.org. Tickets $20–$45; discounts for students, educators, and seniors.

Theatre Rhinoceros   Founded in 1977, this was America's first (and remains its foremost) theater ensemble devoted solely to works addressing gay, lesbian, bisexual, and transgender issues. The company presents main-stage shows and studio productions of new and classic works each year. The theater is 1 block east of the 16th St./Mission BART station. 2926 16th St. ℂ 415/861-5079. www.therhino.org. Tickets $15–$25.

DANCE

In addition to the local companies, top traveling troupes like the Joffrey Ballet and the American Ballet Theatre make regular appearances in San Francisco. Primary modern dance spaces include the **Cowell Theater,** at Fort Mason Center, Marina Boulevard at Buchanan Street (ℂ 415/345-7575; www.fortmason.org/performingarts); and the **ODC Theatre,** 3153 17th St., at Shotwell Street in the Mission District (ℂ 415/863-9834; www.odcdance.org). Tickets cost $18 to $25. Check the local papers for schedules or contact the theater box offices for more information.

San Francisco Ballet   Founded in 1933, the San Francisco Ballet is the oldest professional ballet company in the United States and is regarded as one of the country's finest. It performs an eclectic repertoire of full-length neoclassical and contemporary ballets. The Repertory Season generally runs February through May; the company performs the *Nutcracker* in December. The San Francisco Ballet Orchestra accompanies most performances. War Memorial Opera House, 301 Van Ness Ave. (at Grove St.). ℂ 415/865-2000 for tickets and information. www.sfballet.org. Tickets $10–$205.

2 Comedy & Cabaret

BATS Improv ★ *(Finds)*   Combining improvisation with competition, BATS performs hilarious improvisational tournaments in which teams of actors compete against each other in scenes, songs, and games, based on suggestions from the audience. There are also long-form shows throughout the year with improvisations of movies, musicals, and even Shakespeare; audience members supply suggestions for titles and plot points, and characters and dialogue are then made up and performed immediately onstage. Main Company shows are Fridays and Saturdays at 8pm; student performance ensemble shows on Sundays at 7pm. Reservations and discount tickets available through their website. Remaining tickets are sold at the box office the night of the show. Performing at Bayfront Theatre at the Fort Mason Center, Building B no. 350, 3rd floor. ℂ **415/474-8935.** www.improv. org. Tickets $5–$15.

Beach Blanket Babylon 🦋🦋 *(Moments)*   A San Francisco tradition, *Beach Blanket Babylon* evolved from Steve Silver's Rent-a-Freak service—a group of "party guests" extraordinaire who hired themselves out as a "cast of characters" complete with fabulous costumes and sets, props, and gags. After their act caught on, it moved into the Savoy-Tivoli, a North Beach bar. By 1974, the audience had grown too large for the facility, and *Beach Blanket* has been at the 400-seat Club Fugazi ever since. The show is a comedic musical send-up that is best known for outrageous costumes and oversize headdresses. It's been playing for over 30 years, and almost every performance sells out. The show is updated often enough that locals still attend. Those under 21 are welcome at both Sunday matinees (2 and 5pm), when no alcohol is served; photo ID is required for evening performances. Write for weekend tickets at least 3 weeks in advance, or get them through their website or by calling their box office. *Note:* Only a handful of tickets per show are assigned seating; all other tickets are within specific sections depending on price, but seating is first-come, first-seated within that section. Performances are Wednesday and Thursday at 8pm, Friday and Saturday at 7 and 10pm, and Sunday at 2 and 5pm. At Club Fugazi, Beach Blanket Babylon Blvd., 678 Green St. (btw. Powell St. and Columbus Ave.). ℂ **415/421-4222.** www.beachblanketbabylon.com. Tickets $25–$78.

Cobb's Comedy Club   Cobb's features such national headliners as Joe Rogan, Brian Regan, and Jake Johannsen. Comedy reigns Wednesday through Sunday, including a 15-comedian All-Pro Wednesday showcase (a 3-hr. marathon). Cobb's is open to those 18 and over, and occasionally to kids 16 and 17 when accompanied by a parent or legal guardian (call ahead). Shows are held Wednesday, Thursday, and Sunday at 8pm, Friday and Saturday at 8 and 10:15pm. 915 Columbus Ave. (at Lombard St.). ℂ **415/928-4320.** www.cobbscomedy.com. Cover $13–$35. 2-beverage minimum.

Punch Line Comedy Club   Adjacent to the Embarcadero One office building, this is the largest comedy nightclub in the city. Three-person shows with top national and local talent are featured here Tuesday through Saturday. Showcase night is Sunday, when 15 comics take the mic. There's an all-star showcase or a special event on Monday. Doors always open at 7pm and shows are Sunday through Thursday at 8pm, Friday and Saturday at 8 and 10pm (18 and over; two-drink minimum). They serve a full menu Thursday through Saturday (think wings, chicken sandwiches, and curiously, ravioli), and pizzas, appetizers, and salads Sunday through Wednesday. 444 Battery St. (btw. Washington and Clay sts.), plaza level. ℂ **415/397-4337** or 415/397-7573 for recorded information. www.punchlinecomedyclub.com. Cover Mon $7.50; Tues–Thurs $13–$15; Fri and Sat $18–$20; Sun $7.50. Prices are subject to change for more popular comics, maxing out at a price of $45.

3 The Club & Music Scene

The greatest legacy from the 1960s is the city's continued tradition of live entertainment and music, which explains the great variety of clubs and music enjoyed by San Francisco. The hippest dance places are South of Market Street (SoMa), in former warehouses; the artsy bohemian scene centers are in the Mission; and the most popular cafe culture is still in North Beach.

Tips **Club-Hopping Tour**

If you prefer to let someone else take the lead (and the driver's seat) for a night out, contact **3 Babes and a Bus** (© **800/414-0158**; www.threebabes.com). The nightclub tour company (the head babe is a stockbroker by day) will take you and a gaggle of 20- to 40-something partiers (mostly single women) out on the town, skipping lines and cover charges, for $39 per person.

Note: The club and music scene is always changing, often outdating recommendations before the ink can dry on a page. Most of the venues below are promoted as different clubs on various nights of the week, each with its own look, sound, and style. Discount passes and club announcements are often available at clothing stores and other shops along upper Haight Street.

Drink prices at most bars, clubs, and cafes range from about $3.50 to $9, unless otherwise noted.

ROCK & BLUES CLUBS

In addition to the following listings, see "Dance Clubs," below, for (usually) live, danceable rock.

Bimbo's 365 Club 🏵🏵 Originally located on Market Street when it opened in 1931, this North Beach destination is a fabulous spot to catch outstanding live rock and jazz (think Chris Isaak and the Brian Setzer Orchestra) and dance amid glamorous surroundings. Grab tickets in advance at the box office, which is open Monday through Friday, 10am to 4pm. 1025 Columbus Ave. (at Chestnut St.). © **415/474-0365.** www.bimbos365club.com.

Biscuits and Blues With a crisp, blow-your-eardrums-out sound system, New Orleans–speak-easy (albeit commercial) appeal, and a nightly lineup of live, national acts, there's no better place to muse the blues than this basement-cum-nightclub. From 7pm on, they serve drink specials, along with their signature fried chicken; namesake moist, flaky biscuits; some new small-plate entrees dubbed "Southern tapas"; and a newly expanded wine list. Menu items range from $7.95 to $17. 401 Mason (at Geary St.). © **415/292-2583.** www.biscuitsandblues.com. Cover (during performances) $10–$20.

The Boom Boom Room *(Finds)* The late John Lee Hooker and his partner Alex Andreas bought this Western Addition club several years back and used Hooker's star power to pull in some of the best blues bands in the country (even the Stones showed up for an unannounced jam session). Though it changed focus and is now a roots music oriented club, it's still a fun, dark, small, cramped, and steamy joint where you can hear good live tunes—ranging from New Orleans funk, soul, and new wave, to trance jazz, live drum 'n' bass, electronica, house, and more—Tuesday through Sunday until 2am. If you're going to the Fillmore (see below) to see a band, stop by here first for a drink and come back after your show for more great music. The neighborhood's a bit rough, so be sure to park in the underground lot across the street. 1601 Fillmore St. (at Geary Blvd.). © **415/673-8000.** www.boomboomblues.com. Cover varies from free to $15.

Bottom of the Hill *(Value)* Voted one of the best places to hear live rock in the city by the *San Francisco Bay Guardian,* this popular neighborhood club attracts a diverse crowd ranging from rockers to real-estate salespeople; it also offers tons of all-ages shows. The main attraction is an eclectic range of live music almost every night (focusing on indie punk with the occasional country band thrown in), but the club also offers pretty good burgers, a bar menu, and outdoor seating on the back patio Wednesday through Friday from 4pm to 2am, Saturday through Tuesday 8:30pm to 2am. Happy hour runs Wednesday to Friday from 4 to 7pm. 1233 17th St. (at Missouri St.). ✆ 415/621-4455. www.bottomofthehill.com. Cover $6–$12.

Cafe du Nord *(Finds)* If you like you clubs dim, sexy, and with a heavy dose of old-school ambience, you will definitely dig Café du Nord. This subterranean supper club has rightfully proclaimed itself as the place for a "slightly lurid indie pop scene set in a beautiful old 1907 speakeasy." It's also where an eclectic crowd gathers to linger at the front room's 40-foot mahogany bar, or dine on the likes of panko-crusted prawns and blackened mahi-mahi. The small stage hosts an eclectic mix of local and visiting artists ranging from Shelby Lynne (country) to the Dickdusters (punk) and local favorite Ledisi (R&B). 2170 Market St. (at Sanchez St.). ✆ **415/861-5016.** www.cafedunord.com. Cover $5–$25. Food $5–$15.

The Fillmore *(Finds)* Made famous by promoter Bill Graham in the 1960s, the Fillmore showcases big names in a moderately sized standing-room-only space. Check listings in papers, call the theater, or visit their website for information on upcoming events. And if you make it to a show, check out the fabulous collection of vintage concert posters chronicling the hall's history. 1805 Geary Blvd. (at Fillmore St.). ✆ **415/346-6000.** www.thefillmore.com. Tickets $17–$45.

Grant & Green Saloon The atmosphere at this historic North Beach dive bar is not that special, but Mondays feature jazz, Tuesdays are DJ and karaoke, and the local bands on Thursday through Saturday are decent. All in all, the space is an all-around great place to let your hair down. 1371 Grant Ave. (at Green St.). ✆ **415/693-9565.** www.grantandgreen.com.

Great American Music Hall *(★★)* Built in 1907 as a restaurant/bordello, the Great American Music Hall is likely one of the most gorgeous rock venues you'll encounter. With ornately carved balconies, frescoed ceilings, marble columns, and huge hanging light fixtures, you won't know whether to marvel at the structure or watch the acts, which have ranged from Duke Ellington and Sarah Vaughan to Arctic Monkeys, the Radiators, and She Wants Revenge. All shows are all ages (6 and up) so you can bring your family, too. You can buy a ticket for just the show and order bar snacks (such as nachos, black bean and cheese flautas, burgers, and sandwiches); or buy a ticket that includes a complete dinner (an extra $25), which changes nightly but always includes a salad and choice of meat, fish, or veggie entree. Alas, you can't buy your ticket via telephone, but you can download a form from their website and fax it to **415/885-5075** with your Visa or MasterCard info; there is a service charge of $2 per

---

Tips **Scope-a-Scene**

The local newspapers won't direct you to the city's underground club scene, nor will they advise you which of the dozens of clubs are truly hot. To get dialed in, check out reviews from the ravers themselves at www.sfstation.com. The far more commercial **Club Line** (✆ 415/339-8686; www.sfclubs.com) offers up-to-date schedules for the city's larger dance venues.

Drinking & Smoking Laws

The drinking age is 21 in California, and bartenders can ask for a valid photo ID, no matter how old you look. Some clubs demand identification at the door, so it's a good idea to carry it at all times. Once you get through the door, however, forget about cigarettes—smoking is banned in all California bars. The law is generally enforced and though San Francisco's police department has not made bar raids a priority, people caught smoking in bars can be—and occasionally are—ticketed and fined. Music clubs strictly enforce the law and will ask you to leave if you light up. If you must smoke, do it outside. Also, the dreaded last call for alcohol usually rings out at around 1:30am, since state laws prohibit the sale of alcohol from 2 to 6am every morning. A very important word of warning: Driving under the influence of alcohol is a serious crime in California, with jail time for the first offense. You are likely to be legally intoxicated (.08% blood alcohol) if you have had as little as one alcoholic drink an hour. When in doubt, take a taxi.

ticket. You can also stop by the box office to purchase tickets directly ($1 service charge), or buy them at Virtuous.com or Tickets.com (© **800/225-2277**). Valet parking is available for selects shows; check website for additional parking information. 859 O'Farrell (btw. Polk and Larkin sts.). © **415/885-0750**. www.musichallsf.com. Ticket prices and starting times vary; call or check website for individual show information.

Lou's Pier 47 Club   You won't find many locals in the place, but Lou's happens to be good, old-fashioned fun. It's a casual spot where you can relax with Cajun seafood (downstairs) and live blues bands (upstairs) nightly. A vacation attitude makes the place one of the more, um, jovial spots near the wharf. There's a $3 to $5 cover for bands that play between 4 and 8pm and a $3 to $10 cover for bands that play between 8 or 9pm and midnight or 1am. 300 Jefferson St. (at Jones St.). © **415/771-5687**. www.lous pier47.com.

Pier 23   If there's one good-time destination that's an anchor for San Francisco's party people, it's the Embarcadero's Pier 23. Part ramshackle patio spot and part dance floor with a heavy dash of dive bar, here it's all about fun for a startlingly diverse clientele (including a one-time visit by Bill Clinton!). The well-worn box of a restaurant with tented patio is a prime sunny-day social spot for white collars, but on weekends, it's a straight-up people zoo where every age and persuasion coexist more peacefully than the cast in a McDonald's commercial. Expect to boogie down shoulder-to-shoulder to 1980s hits and leave with a contagious feel-good vibe. Pier 23, at the Embarcadero (at Battery St.). © **415/362-5125**. www.pier23cafe.com. Cover $5–$10 during performances.

The Saloon   An authentic gold rush survivor, this North Beach dive is the oldest bar in the city. Popular with both bikers and daytime pinstripers, it schedules live blues nightly and afternoons Friday through Sunday. 1232 Grant Ave. (at Columbus St.). © **415/ 989-7666**. Cover $5–$15 Fri–Sat.

Slim's   Co-owned by musician Boz Scaggs, this glitzy restaurant and bar serves California cuisine and seats 200, but it's usually standing room only during almost nightly shows ranging from performers of homegrown rock, jazz, blues, and alternative music. An added bonus for the musically inclined family: All ages are always welcome. Call or check their website for a schedule; hot bands sell out in advance. 333 11th St. (at Folsom St.). ✆ **415/522-0333.** www.slims-sf.com. Cover free to $30.

BARS WITH DJ GROOVES

Bambuddha Lounge With a 20-foot reclining Buddha on the roof it's pretty easy to spot the Bambuddha, a reliably lively restaurant/bar/lounge adjoining the funky-cool Phoenix Hotel. The ultramodern San Francisco–meets–Southeast Asia decor includes floor-to-ceiling waterfalls and indoor/outdoor slate fireplaces in the dining room, and the city's only outdoor poolside cocktail lounge. Affordable and above-average Southeast Asian cuisine is served late into the evening, and a state-of-the-art sound system streams ambient, down-tempo, soul, funk, and house music to a mostly 20-something crowd. 601 Eddy St. (at Larkin St.). ✆ **415/885-5088.** www.bambuddhalounge.com. Cover $5–$10, $20 for special events Thurs–Sat.

The Bliss Bar Surprisingly trendy for sleepy, family-oriented Noe Valley, this small, stylish, and friendly bar is a great place to stop for a varied mix of locals, colorful cocktail concoctions, and a DJ spinning at the front window from 9pm to 2am every night except Sunday and Monday. If it's open, take your cocktail into the too-cool back Blue Room. And if you're on a budget, stop by from 4 to 7pm when martinis, lemon drops, and cosmos are only $4. 4026 24th St. (btw. Noe and Castro sts.). ✆ **415/826-6200.** www.bliss barsf.com.

Levende Lounge ✫ A fusion of fine dining, cocktailing, and DJ grooves, Levende Lounge is one of the Mission's hottest spots for young singles looking to hook up. Drop in early for happy hour Monday through Friday from 5 to 7pm, or sit down for a meal of "world-fusion" small plates (think French, Asian, and Nuevo Latino) in a more standard dinner setting amid exposed brick walls and cozy lighting. Later, tables are traded for lounge furnishings for some late-night noshing and flirting. *Tip:* Some nights have cover charges, but you can avoid the fee with a dinner reservation, and food is served until 11pm. 1710 Mission St. (at Duboce St.). ✆ **415/864-5585.** www.levendesf.com.

Wish Bar Swathed in burgundy and black with exposed cinder-block walls, cement floors, and red-shaded sconces aglow with candlelight, even you will look cool at this mellow SoMa bar in the popular night crawler area around 11th and Folsom streets. With a bar in the front, DJ spinning upbeat lounge music in the back, and seating—including cushy leather couches—in between, it's often packed with a surprisingly diverse (albeit youthful) crowd. Closed Sundays. 1539 Folsom St. (btw. 11th and 12th sts.). ✆ **415/278-9474.** www.wishsf.com.

DANCE CLUBS

The Endup This legendary party space with a huge, heated outdoor deck (complete with waterfall and fountain no less), indoor fireplace, and eclectic clientele has always thrown some of the most intense all-nighters in town. In fact, it's practically a second home to the city's DJs. There's a different theme every night: Friday Ghettodisco, Super Soul Sundayz, et cetera. The Endup is ever-popular with the sleepless dance-all-day crowd that comes here after the other clubs close, hence the name. It's open Sat morning 6am–noon and then nonstop from Sat night around 10pm until Sun night/Mon morning at 4am. Call or check the website to confirm nights—offerings change from time to time. 401 Sixth St. (at Harrison St.). ✆ **415/357-0827.** www.theendup.com. Cover free–$15.

Underground Entertainment

If you'd rather slit your wrists than visit hokey tourist attractions like Pier 39, log on to www.laughingsquid.com and see what the locals are up to during your vacation. Since 1995 Laughing Squid's **"Squid List"** has been the Bay Area's sine qua non online resource for art, culture, and technology. Along with links to local art and culture events, the Laughing Squid also hosts the Squid List, a daily event announcements list. There's some really freaky fringe stuff on this webpage, with plenty of garbage-level entertainment amongst several gems. Either way it makes for entertaining surfing.

1015 Folsom   The ginormous party warehouse—total capacity is 2,000 persons— has three levels of dance floors that make for an extensive variety of dancing venues. DJs pound out house, disco, funk, acid-jazz, and more, with lots of groovy lasers and LED lights to stimulate the eye. Each night is a different club that attracts its own crowd, ranging from yuppie to hip-hop. Open Thursday through Saturday 10pm to 2am. 1015 Folsom St. (at Sixth St.). (C) 415/431-1200. www.1015.com. Cover varies.

Harry Denton's Starlight Room *(Moments*   If that new cocktail dress is burning a hole in your suitcase, get yourself dolled up tonight and say hello to Harry, our city's de facto party host. His celestial crimson-infused cocktail lounge and nightclub, perched on the top floor of the Sir Francis Drake Hotel, is a pantheon to 1930s San Francisco, a throwback to the days when red-velvet banquettes, chandeliers, and fashionable duds were de rigueur. The 360-degree view of the city is worth the cover charge alone, but what draws tourists and locals of all ages is a night of Harry Denton–style fun, which usually includes plenty of drinking, live music, and unrestrained dancing, regardless of age. The bar stocks a pricey collection of single-malt Scotches and champagnes, and you can snack from the "Lite" menu. If you make a reservation to guarantee a table you will also have a place to rest between songs. Early evening is more relaxed, but come the weekend this place gets loose. *Tip:* Come dressed for success (no casual jeans, open-toed shoes for men, or sneakers), or you'll be turned away at the door. Atop the Sir Francis Drake Hotel, 450 Powell St., 21st floor. (C) 415/395-8595. www.harry denton.com. Cover $10 Wed–Fri after 8:30pm; $15 Sat after 8:30pm.

Holy Cow   Its motto, "Never a cover, always a party" has been the case since 1987 when this industrial SoMa nightclub opened. The local clubbers rarely come here anymore, but it's still a reliable place for tourists and geezers like me who want to break a sweat on the dance floor to DJs spinning club classics and top 40. Nightly drink specials make it difficult to leave sober, so plan your transportation accordingly. *Note:* The bar's only open Thursday through Saturday from 9pm to 2am. 1535 Folsom St. (btw. 11th and 12th sts.). (C) 415/621-6087. www.theholycow.com.

Ruby Skye   Downtown's most glamorous and colossal nightspot led a previous life as an 1890s Victorian playhouse, and many of the beautiful Art Nouveau trimmings are still in place. Mission District clubbers won't go near the place—way too disco— but for tourists it's a safe bet for a dance-filled night in the city. The light & sound system here is amazing, and on weekend nights the huge ballroom floor is packed with sweaty bodies dancing to thumping DJ beats or live music. When it's time to cool off you can chill on the mezzanine or fire up in the smoking room. Be sure to call or check the website to make sure there isn't a private event taking place. 420 Mason St. (btw. Geary and Post sts.). ℂ 415/693-0777. www.rubyskye.com. Cover $10–$25.

JAZZ & LATIN CLUBS

Jazz at Pearl's   Touted as the city's Best Jazz Club by the *San Francisco Chronicle*, Jazz at Pearl's combines a cool 1930s vibe, great live music, and excellent seating throughout this intimate North Beach venue. With a variety of jazz, blues, and Latin recording artists playing nightly there's something for everyone at this all-ages club. However, with only 25 tables, advance purchase of tickets is highly recommended. Shows start at 8 and 10pm nightly; doors open at 7:30pm. Tickets range from $25 to $150 for VIP seating, which includes preferred seating for both shows, a bottle of champagne, and a signed CD and meet-and-greet with the artist. *Note:* There's a 2-drink minimum. 256 Columbus Ave. (at Broadway). ℂ 415/291-8255. www.jazzatpearls.com.

Rasselas   Large, casual, and comfortable with couches and small tables, Rasselas is a popular locals spot for jazz, blues, soul, and R&B combos 7 days a week. The adjacent restaurant serves good Ethiopian cuisine nightly from 5 to 10pm, which, combined with the live music, makes for quite the cultural evening. 1534 Fillmore St. (at Geary Blvd.). ℂ 415/346-8696. www.rasselasjazzclub.com. Cover $10 Fri–Sat. 2-drink minimum.

Yoshi's Jazz Club 🐸🐸   What started out in 1977 as a modest sushi and jazz club in Oakland has become one of the most respected jazz venues in the world: Yoshi's. For more than three decades SF locals had to cross the Bay Bridge to listen to Stanton Moore, Branford Marsalis, and Diana Krall in such an intimate setting. With the grand opening of Yoshi's in San Francisco's Fillmore District, now locals can take a taxi. The two-story, 28,000-square-foot, state-of-the-art jazz venue features the finest local, national, and international jazz artists, as well as first-rate Japanese cuisine at the adjoining restaurant. The elegant club is awash in gleaming dark and blond woods, big sculptural Japanese lanterns, and sensuously curved walls that envelop the intimate stage. Don't worry about the seating chart; there's not a bad seat in the house. It's the perfect place for a romantic date that starts with hamachi and ends with Harry Connick Jr., so be sure the check Yoshi's website to see who playing while you're in town and make reservations ASAP—you'll be glad you did. 1330 Fillmore St. (at Eddy St.). ℂ 415/655-5600. www.yoshis.com.

4 The Bar Scene

Finding your kind of bar in San Francisco has a lot to do with which district it's in. The following is a *very* general description of what types of bars you're likely to find throughout the city:

- **Marina/Cow Hollow** bars attract a yuppie post-collegiate crowd.
- The opposite of the Marina/Cow Hollow crowd frequent the **Mission District** haunts.
- **Haight-Ashbury** caters to eclectic neighborhood cocktailers and beer-lovers.
- The **Tenderloin** is new hotspot for serious mixologists.
- Tourists mix with conventioneers at **downtown** pubs.
- **North Beach** serves all types, mostly tourists.
- **Russian Hill's** Polk Street has become the new Marina/Cow Hollow scene.
- **The Castro** caters to gay locals and tourists.
- **SoMa** offers an eclectic mix from sports bars to DJ lounges.

The following is a list of a few of San Francisco's more interesting bars. Unless otherwise noted, these bars do not have cover charges.

Buddha Lounge *(Finds)* If you like colorful dive bars you'll love the Buddha Lounge. This heart-of-Chinatown bar is a great glimpse into Chinatown's neighborhood culture. Of course, most tourists shy away from what appears to be yet another dark, seedy watering hole, but it's really just a cheery neighborhood bar. Be brave. Step inside, order a drink, and pretend you're in a Charlie Chan movie. The best part is when the Chinese woman behind the bar answers the phone: "HELLO BUDDHA!" No cover. 901 Grant Ave. (at Washington St.). ☎ 415/362-1792.

Buena Vista Café *(Moments)* "Did you have an Irish coffee at the Buena Vista?" The popular myth is that the Irish coffee was invented at the Buena Vista, but the real story is that this wharfside cafe was the first bar in the country to serve Irish coffee after a local journalist came back from a trip and described the drink to the bartender. Since then, the bar has poured more of these addictive pick-me-up drinks than any other bar in the world, and ordering one has become a San Francisco must-do. Heck, it's entertaining just to *watch* the venerable tenders pour up to 10 whiskey-laden coffees at a time (a rather messy event). The cafe is in a prime tourist spot along the wharf, so plan on waiting for a stool or table to free up on weekends. And if you need a snack to soak up the booze they serve food here as well. 2765 Hyde St. (at Beach St.). ☎ 415/474-5044. www.thebuenavista.com.

Edinburgh Castle Since 1958 this legendary Scottish pub has been known for having rare British ales on tap and one of the best selection of single-malt Scotches in the city. The homey pub is festively decorated with a mishmash of across-the-pond mementos, including an authentic Ballantine caber (a long wooden pole) used in the annual Scottish games. Fish and chips (served in newspaper of course) and other traditional British foods are available until 11pm. The Edinburgh also features author readings and performances and has hosted such noteworthy writers as Po Bronson, Beth Lisick, and Anthony Swofford. Open 5pm to 2am daily. 950 Geary St. (btw. Polk and Larkin sts.). ☎ 415/885-4074. www.castlenews.com.

Gold Dust Lounge *(Finds)* If you're staying downtown and want to head to a friendly, festive bar loaded with old-fashioned style and revelry, you needn't wander far off Union Square. This classically cheesy watering hole is all that. The red banquettes, gilded walls, dramatic chandeliers, pro bartenders, and "regulars" are the old-school real deal. Add live music and cheap drinks and you're in for a good ol' time. **Tip:** It's cash only, so come with some greenbacks. 247 Powell St. (at Geary St.). ☎ 415/397-1695.

Hemlock Tavern This former gay dance club is now one of the most popular bars on Polk Street and always packed on weekends. There's lots of dark wood, warm colors, a line for the bathroom, and an enclosed back room that's dedicated just to smokers. The crowd is a bit younger than the Edinburgh Castle crew, but there's a similar mix of locals, hipsters, musicians, and visitors who would never think of themselves as tourists. The jukebox is sweet, and you can chow down on warm peanuts (toss the shells on the floor) and wash 'em down with a good selection of beers on tap. No cover. 1131 Polk St. (at Sutter St.). ☎ 415/923-0923. www.hemlocktavern.com.

Li Po Cocktail Lounge *(Finds)* A dim, divey, and slightly spooky Chinese bar that was once an opium den, Li Po's alluring character stems from its mishmash clutter of dusty Asian furnishings and mementos, including an unbelievably huge ancient rice-paper lantern hanging from the ceiling and a glittery golden shrine to Buddha behind the bar. The bartenders, who pour a mean Li Po Special Mai Tai, love to creep out patrons with tales of opium junkies haunting the joint. Bands and DJs occasionally whip up a sweaty dance scene in the basement, but it's a hit-or-miss schedule. 916 Grant Ave. (btw. Washington and Jackson sts.). ℭ 415/982-0072.

Martuni's *Finds*   San Francisco has plenty of bars with pianos in them, but for the real sing-along piano bar experience you'll want to head to Martuni's. After a couple of stiff martinis you'll loosen up enough to join the eclectic crowd in rousing renditions of everything from Cole Porter to Elton John. If you're not up for singing, you can cuddle with your date in the dark alcoves and watch the fun; otherwise, saddle up to the piano and let 'er rip. 4 Valencia St. (at Market St.). ℭ 415/241-0205.

Matrix Fillmore   The Matrix represents the best and worst of the Marina/Cow Hollow young-n-yuppie scene: It attracts some of the city's top eye candy, but also has L.A.-style attitude in abundance (I was once asked to give up my fireplace loveseat to someone more important). Dress in black, order a mojito, say "like" a lot, and you'll do just fine. The slick lounge atmosphere is further enhanced by dyed concrete floors, flatscreen TVs, and free-standing centerpiece fireplace with its "Zen minimalist" mantel. One plus: The bar offers 10 wines by the glass and a large by-the-bottle selection including cult classics like Dalla Valle. Valet parking is available at the nearby Balboa Café (Fillmore and Greenwich sts.). 3138 Fillmore St. (btw. Greenwich and Filbert sts.). ℭ 415/563-4180. www.matrixfillmore.com.

Perry's   If you read *Tales of the City*, you may remember that this bar and restaurant has a colorful history as a pickup place for Pacific Heights and Marina singles. Although the times are not as wild today, locals still come to check out the happenings at the dark mahogany bar. A separate dining room offers breakfast, lunch, dinner, and weekend brunch. It's a good place for hamburgers, simple fish dishes, and pasta. Menu items range from $6 to $22. 1944 Union St. (at Laguna St.). ℭ 415/922-9022.

The Redwood Room   Best known for its gorgeous redwood paneling made from a single 2,000-year-old tree, the Clift Hotel's Redwood Room bar and lounge has a plush, modern feel that's illuminated by beautiful original Deco sconces. If you know who Ian Schrager and Philippe Starck are, then you know their scene: AMEX Platinum posers and randy businessmen who mix, mingle, and never balk at the high drink prices ($9–$25). But even if that's not your scene it's worth poking your head in to admire the classy decor. In the Clift Hotel, 495 Geary St. ℭ 415/775-4700. www.clifthotel.com.

Spec's *Finds*   The location of Spec's—look for a tiny nook on the east side of Columbus Ave. just south of Broadway—makes it a bit tough to find but well worth the search. Specs' historically eclectic decor—maritime flags hang from the ceiling while dusty posters, photos, and oddities like dried whale penises line the walls—offers plenty of visual entertainment while you toss back a cold Bud (sans glass of course). A "museum" displayed under glass contains memorabilia and items brought back by long-dead seamen who dropped in between voyages. There are plenty of salty and slightly pickled regulars to match the motif, so you may not want to order a cosmo while doing your nails at the bar. 12 Saroyan Place (at 250 Columbus Ave.). ℭ 415/421-4112.

The Tonga Room & Hurricane Bar *Finds*   It's kitschy as all get-out, but there's no denying the goofy Polynesian pleasures of the Fairmont Hotel's tropical oasis. Drop in and join the crowds for an umbrella drink, a simulated thunderstorm and downpour, and a heavy dose of whimsy that escapes most San Francisco establishments. If you're on a budget, you'll definitely want to stop by for the weekday happy hour from 5 to

7pm, when you can stuff your face at the all-you-can-eat bar-grub buffet (baby back ribs, chow mein, pot stickers) for $8 and the cost of one drink. Settle in and you'll catch live top-40 music after 8pm Wednesday through Sunday, when there's a $3 to $5 cover. In the Fairmont Hotel, 950 Mason St. (at California St.). ✆ 415/772-5278. www.tongaroom.com.

Toronado Gritty Lower Haight isn't exactly a charming street, but there's plenty of nightlife here, catering to an artistic/grungy/skateboarding 20-something crowd. While Toronado definitely draws in the young'uns, its 50-plus microbrews on tap and 100 bottled beers also entice a more eclectic clientele in search of beer heaven. The brooding atmosphere matches the surroundings: an aluminum bar, a few tall tables, minimal lighting, and a back room packed with tables and chairs. Happy hour runs 11:30am to 6pm every day for $1 off pints. 547 Haight St. (at Fillmore St.). ✆ 415/863-2276. www.toronado.com.

Tosca Cafe *Finds* Open Tuesday through Saturday from 5pm to 2am, Sunday 7pm to 2am, Tosca is a low-key and large popular watering hole for local politicos, writers, media types, incognito celebrities such as Johnny Depp or Nicholas Cage, and similar cognoscenti of unassuming classic characters. Equipped with dim lights, red leather booths, and high ceilings, it's everything you'd expect an old North Beach legend to be. No credit cards. 242 Columbus Ave. (btw. Broadway and Pacific Ave.). ✆ 415/986-9651.

Vesuvio Situated along Jack Kerouac Alley, across from the famed City Lights bookstore, this renowned literary beatnik hangout is packed to the second-floor rafters with neighborhood writers, artists, songsters, wannabes, and everyone else ranging from longshoremen and cab drivers to businesspeople, all of whom come for the laid-back atmosphere. The convivial space consists of two stories of cocktail tables, complemented by changing exhibitions of local art. In addition to drinks, Vesuvio features an espresso machine. 255 Columbus Ave. (at Broadway). ✆ 415/362-3370. www.vesuvio.com.

Zeitgeist The front door is black, the back door is adorned with a skeleton Playboy bunny, and inside is packed to the rafters with tattooed, pierced, and hard-core-looking partiers. But forge on. Zeitgeist is such a friendly and fun punk-rock-cum-biker-bar beer garden that even the occasional yuppie can be spotted mingling around the slammin' juke box that features tons of local bands or in the huge back patio filled with picnic tables. (There tend to be cute girls here, too.) Along with fantastic dive-bar environs, you'll find 30 beers on draft, a pool table, and pinball machines. The regular crowd, mostly locals and bike messengers, come here to kick back with a pitcher, and welcome anyone else interested in the same pursuit. And if your night turns out to, um, better than expected, there's a hotel upstairs. Cash only. 199 Valencia St. (at Duboce). ✆ 415/255-7505.

BREWPUBS

Gordon Biersch Brewery Restaurant Gordon Biersch Brewery is San Francisco's largest brew restaurant, serving decent food and tasty beer to an attractive crowd of mingling professionals. There are always several house-made beers to choose from, ranging from light to dark. Menu items run $9.50 to $26. (See p. 120 for more information.) 2 Harrison St. (on the Embarcadero). ✆ 415/243-8246. www.gordonbiersch.com.

San Francisco Brewing Company Surprisingly low key for an alehouse, this cozy brewpub serves its creations with burgers, fries, grilled chicken breast, and the like. The bar is one of the city's few remaining old saloons (ca. 1907), aglow with stained-glass windows, tile floors, skylit ceiling, beveled glass, and mahogany bar. A massive overhead fan runs the full length of the bar—a bizarre contraption crafted from brass and palm fronds. The handmade copper brew kettle is visible from the street. Most evenings the place is packed with everyday folks enjoying music, darts, chess, backgammon, cards, dice, and, of course, beer. Menu items range from $4.15—curiously, for edamame (soybeans)—to $21 for a full rack of baby back ribs with all the fixings. The happy-hour special, an 8½-ounce microbrew beer for $1.50 (or a pint for $2.75), is offered daily from 4 to 6pm and midnight to 1am. 155 Columbus Ave. (at Pacific St.). © 415/434-3344. www.sfbrewing.com.

ThirstyBear Brewing Company Nine superb, handcrafted varieties of brew are always on tap at this stylish high-ceilinged brick edifice. Good Spanish food is served here, too. Pool tables and dartboards are upstairs, and live flamenco can be heard on Sunday nights. 661 Howard St. (1 block east of the Moscone Center). © 415/974-0905. www.thirsty bear.com.

COCKTAILS WITH A VIEW

See "Dance Clubs," earlier, for a full review of **Harry Denton's Starlight Room.** Unless otherwise noted, these establishments have no cover charge.

Carnelian Room On the 52nd floor of the Bank of America Building, the Carnelian Room offers uninterrupted views of the city. From a window-front table you feel as though you can reach out, pluck up the Transamerica Pyramid, and stir your martini with it. In addition to cocktails, the restaurant serves a four-course meal ($59 per person) as well as a la carte items ($24–$49 for main entrees). Jackets are required and ties are optional for men, but encouraged. *Note:* The restaurant has one of the most extensive wine lists in the city—1,600 selections, to be exact. 555 California St., in the Bank of America Building (btw. Kearny and Montgomery sts.). © 415/433-7500. www.carnelianroom.com.

Cityscape When you sit under the glass roof and sip a drink here, it's as though you're sitting out under the stars and enjoying views of the bay. Dinner, focusing on California cuisine, is available (though not destination worthy), and there's dancing to a DJ's picks nightly from 10:30pm. The mirrored columns and floor-to-ceiling windows help create an elegant and romantic ambience here. *FYI:* They also offer a live jazz champagne brunch on Sundays from 10am to 2pm. Hilton San Francisco, Tower One, 333 O'Farrell St. (at Mason St.), 46th floor. © 415/923-5002. Cover $10 Fri–Sat nights.

Top of the Mark *Moments* This is one of the most famous cocktail lounges in the world, and for good reason—the spectacular glass-walled room features an unparalleled 19th-floor view. During World War II, Pacific-bound servicemen toasted their goodbyes to the States here. While less dramatic today than they were back then, evenings spent here are still sentimental, thanks to the romantic atmosphere. Live bands play throughout the week; a jazz pianist on Tuesdays starts at 7pm; salsa on Wednesdays begins with dance lessons at 8pm and the band starts up at 9pm; on Thursdays Stompy Jones brings a swing vibe from 7:30pm; and a dance band playing everything from '50s hits through contemporary music keeps the joint hopping Fridays and Saturdays starting at 9pm. Drinks range from $9 to $12. A $59 three-course fixed-price sunset dinner is served Friday and Saturday at 7:30pm. Sunday brunch, served from 10am to 2pm, costs $59 for adults and includes a glass of champagne; for children 4 to 12, the brunch is $30. In the Mark Hopkins Inter-Continental, 1 Nob Hill (California and Mason sts.). © 415/616-6916. www.topofthemark.com. Cover $5–$10.

A SPORTS BAR

Green's Sports Bar   If you think San Francisco sports fans aren't as enthusiastic as those on the East Coast, well, you're right. These days it's pretty easy to find an empty seat at Green's during a '49ers or Giants game. The city's de facto sports bar is a classic, cozy hangout with lots of dark wood, polished brass, windows that open onto the street, and an array of elevated TVs showing various sporting events via satellite. Highlights include 18 beers on tap, a pool table, and a boisterous happy-hour scene every Monday through Friday from 4 to 7pm. Food isn't served, but you can place an order from the various restaurants along Polk Street and eat at the bar (they even provide a selection of menus). 2239 Polk St. (at Green St.). ℂ **415/775-4287.**

WINE & CHAMPAGNE BARS

The Bubble Lounge   This two-level champagne bar—looking ever so chic with its red velvet sofas, brick walls, and floor-to-ceiling draperies—chills more than 300 Champagnes and sparkling wines, including about 30 by the glass. As one would expect at a Financial District bubbly bar, there's a soupçon of pretentiousness emanating from the BMW-driving clientele and perpetually unshaven bartenders. If you're the type that prefers beer and free pretzels you'll hate it here, particularly if you have to wait in line for a $20 flute of something you can't even pronounce, but the pickup scene really perks up as the bubbly flows into the night. 714 Montgomery St. (btw. Washington and Jackson sts.). ℂ **415/434-4204.** www.bubblelounge.com.

First Crush   If you're staying downtown and in the mood for a glass of fine wine, take a stroll to this popular restaurant and wine lounge. Amid a stylish and dimly lit interior, an eclectic mix of visitors and locals nosh on reasonably priced "progressive American cuisine" that's paired, if desired, with a large selection of all-California wines served by the glass. But plenty of folks also drop by just to sample flights of wine and talk shop with the wine-savvy staff. This also is a good late-night-bite spot, as it's open until midnight Thursday through Saturday. 101 Cyril Magnin St. (also known as Fifth St., just north of Market St., at Ellis St.). ℂ **415/982-7874.** www.firstcrush.com.

London Wine Bar   This British-style wine bar and store is a popular after-work hangout for Financial District suits. It's more of a place to drink and chat, however, than one in which to savor an array of premium wines (though they do offer a sampler). Usually 40 to 50 wines, mostly from California, are open at any given time, and about 800 are available by the bottle. It's a great venue for sampling local Napa Valley wines before you buy, and the pours are reasonably priced. 415 Sansome St. (btw. Sacramento and Clay sts.). ℂ **415/788-4811.**

Nectar Wine Lounge   Catering to the Marina's young and beautiful, this hip place to sip pours about 50 globally diverse wines by-the-glass (plus 800 choices by the bottle) along with creative small plates; pairings are optional. Soothing shades of browns lend a relaxing ambience to the lounge's industrial-slick decor that includes lots of polished woods and hexagonal highlights. 3330 Steiner St. (at Chestnut St.). ℂ **415/345-1377.** www.nectarwinelounge.com.

5 Gay & Lesbian Bars & Clubs

Just like straight establishments, gay and lesbian bars and clubs target varied clienteles. Whether you're into bears, ben wah balls, bondage, or you just want a cold bottle of Queer Beer, San Francisco has something just for you.

San Francisco Drag Shows

If you're out on a Friday night and looking for something to do that's definitely off the straight-laced path, head to the Cinch (see above) for its weekly **Charlie Horse** drag show, hosted by the sassy Miss Tranyshack 2005, Anna Conda. Every week is a different theme, such as "Valley of the Dolls Night" based on the scandalous Jacqueline Susann novel, or "What is Your Take on Old School," where the "ladies" of the evening masquerade as their favorite divas such as Dolly Parton or Joni Mitchell. There's no cover charge, no drink minimum, and the performance is free. An added bonus: The show comes with complimentary popcorn.

If you prefer your drag queens with a slice of quiche, Harry Denton's Starlight Room (see p. 241) hosts a weekly **Sunday s a Drag** brunch performance, where divas perform female impersonation acts and lip-sync Broadway tunes. The "brunch with an attitude" has two seatings every Sunday at noon and 2:30pm. The price of brunch is $40 per person which includes entertainment, brunch, coffee, tea, and fresh juices. For reservations call © **415/395-8595** or email reservations@harrydenton.com.

Check the free weeklies such as the *San Francisco Bay Guardian* and *San Francisco Weekly* for listings of events and happenings around town. The *Bay Area Reporter* is a gay paper with comprehensive listings, including a weekly community calendar. All these papers are free and distributed weekly on Wednesday or Thursday. They can be found stacked at the corners of 18th and Castro streets and Ninth and Harrison streets, as well as in bars, bookshops, and other stores around town. There are also a number of gay and lesbian guides to San Francisco. See "Gay & Lesbian Travelers," in chapter 3, beginning on p. 43, for further details and helpful information. Also check out the rather homely but very informative site titled "Queer Things to Do in the San Francisco Bay Area" at www.sfqueer.com, or www.leatherandbears.com for a plethora of gay happenings.

Listed below are some of the city's most established mainstream gay hangouts.

The Café *Finds* When this place first opened it was the only predominantly lesbian dance club on Saturday nights in the city. Once the guys found out how much fun the girls were having, they joined the party. Today, it's a hugely popular mixed gay and lesbian scene with three bars; two pool tables; a steamy, free-spirited dance floor; and a small, heated patio and balcony where smoking and schmoozing are allowed. A perk: They open at 4pm weekdays and 3pm weekends (2pm on Sunday). 2369 Market St. (at Castro St.). © **415/861-3846.** www.cafesf.com.

The Cinch Part cruisy neighborhood bar, part modern-day penny arcade, the Cinch Saloon features free Wi-Fi, two pool tables, five TVs, video games, an Internet juke box, pinball, and an outdoor smoking patio. They even have their own softball team, the Renegades. With happy hour Monday through Friday 4 to 8pm (all night on Monday), progressive music by DJs on Thursdays and Fridays nights, and a host of other fun theme nights, the bar attracts a mixed crowd of gays, lesbians, and gay-friendly straights. 1723 Polk St. (near Washington St.). © **415/776-4162.** www.thecinch.com.

The Eagle Tavern   One of the city's most established Levi's 'n' leather bars, the Eagle boasts a heated outdoor patio (where smoking is permitted), a happy hour (Mon–Fri 4–8pm), live bands every Thursday at 9pm, and the occasional mud wrestling tournament. Straight or gay, it's worth stopping in just to order a bottle of Queer Beer (although the one time I did this, the guy sitting next to me at the bar was completely naked). 398 12th St. (at Harrison St.). ✆ 415/626-0880. www.sfeagle.com.

The Endup   It's a different nightclub every night of the week, but regardless of who's throwing the party, the place is always throbbing with DJ beats and sweaty bodies. There are two pool tables, a fireplace, an outdoor patio and, on the dance floor, a mob of gyrating souls—particularly on Fridays nights. Some nights are straight or mixed, so call ahead if you care. 401 Sixth St. (at Harrison St.). ✆ 415/357-0827. www.theendup.com. Cover $5–$15.

Kimo's   This gay-owned and -operated neighborhood bar in the seedier gay section of town is a friendly oasis, decorated with plastic plants and random pictures on the walls. The bar provides a relaxing venue for chatting, drinking, and quiet cruising, and livens up with indie, punk rock, and jazz bands nightly at Kimo's Penthouse upstairs. Cover $5–$10 for live music. 1351 Polk St. (at Pine St.). ✆ 415/885-4535.

Lone Star Saloon   Expect lesbians and a heavier, furrier motorcycle crowd (both men and women) here most every night. The Thursday night and Saturday and Sunday afternoon beer busts on the patio are especially popular and cost $7 to $9 per person. 1354 Harrison St. (btw. 9th and 10th sts.). ✆ 415/863-9999. www.lonestarsaloon.com.

Metro   This bar provides the gay community with high-energy music and the best view of the Castro District from its large balcony. The bar seems to attract people of all ages who enjoy the friendliness of the bartenders and the highly charged, cruisy atmosphere. There's a Spanish restaurant on the premises in case you get hungry. 3600 16th St. (at Market St.). ✆ 415/703-9751.

The Mint Karaoke Lounge   This is a gay and lesbian karaoke bar—sprinkled with a heavy dash of straight folks on weekends—where you can get up and sing your heart out every night. Along with song, you'll encounter a mixed 20- to 40-something crowd that combines cocktails with do-it-yourself cabaret. Want to eat and listen at the same time? Feel free to bring in the Japanese food from the attached restaurant. Sashimi goes for about $7, main entrees $8, and sushi combo plates about $11. 1942 Market St. (at Laguna St.). ✆ 415/626-4726. www.themint.net. 2-drink minimum.

The Stud   The Stud, which has been around for almost 40 years, is one of the most successful gay establishments in town. The interior has an antiques-shop look. Music is a balanced mix of old and new, and nights vary from cabaret to oldies to disco-punk. Check their website in advance for the evening's offerings. Drink prices range from $3.25 to $8. Happy hour runs Monday through Saturday 5 to 9pm with $1 off well drinks. 399 Ninth St. (at Harrison St.). ✆ 415/863-6623 or 415/252-STUD for event info. www.studsf.com. Cover is $10.

Twin Peaks Tavern   Right at the intersection of Castro, 17th, and Market streets is one of the Castro's most famous (at 35 years old) gay hangouts. It caters to an older crowd but often has a mixture of patrons and claims to be the first gay bar in America. Because of its relatively small size and desirable location, the place becomes fairly crowded and convivial by 8pm, earlier than many neighboring bars. 401 Castro St. (at 17th and Market sts.). ✆ 415/864-9470.

12

Side Trips from San Francisco

The City by the Bay is, without question, captivating, but don't let it ensnare you to the point of ignoring its environs. The surrounding region contains a multitude of natural beauty such as Mount Tamalpais and Muir Woods; scenic bayside communities such as Tiburon and Sausalito; and neighboring cities such as Oakland and Berkeley.

From San Francisco, you can reach any of these points in an hour or less by car. Public transportation options are also listed throughout the chapter. Another option is to hitch a ride with **San Francisco Sightseeing** (© **888/428-6937** or 415/434-8687; www.sanfranciscosightseeing.com), which runs regularly scheduled bus tours to neighboring towns and the countryside. Half-day trips to Muir Woods and Sausalito, and full-day trips to Napa and Sonoma are available, as are excursions to Yosemite and the Monterey Peninsula. Phone for prices and schedules.

1 Berkeley

10 miles NE of San Francisco

Berkeley is best known as the home of the University of California at Berkeley, which is world-renowned for its academic standards, 18 Nobel prize winners (seven are active staff), and protests that led to the most famous student riots in U.S. history. Today, there's still hippie idealism in the air, but the radicals have aged; the 1960s are present only in tie-dye and paraphernalia shops. The biggest change the town is facing is yuppification; as San Francisco's rent and property prices soar out of the range of the average person's budget, everyone with less than a small fortune is seeking shelter elsewhere, and Berkeley is one of the top picks (although Oakland is quickly becoming a favorite, too). Berkeley is a lively city teeming with all types of people, a beautiful campus, vast parks, great shopping, and some incredible restaurants.

Pricing Categories

Note: In this chapter, hotels are organized by location, then by price range, as follows: **Very Expensive,** more than $250 per night; **Expensive,** $200 to $250 per night; **Moderate,** $150 to $200 per night; and **Inexpensive,** less than $150 per night.

Restaurants are organized by location, then by price range for a complete dinner (appetizer, entree, dessert, and glass of wine) as follows: **Very Expensive,** dinner from $75 per person; **Expensive,** dinner from $50 per person; **Moderate,** dinner from $35 per person; and **Inexpensive,** less than $35 per person for dinner.

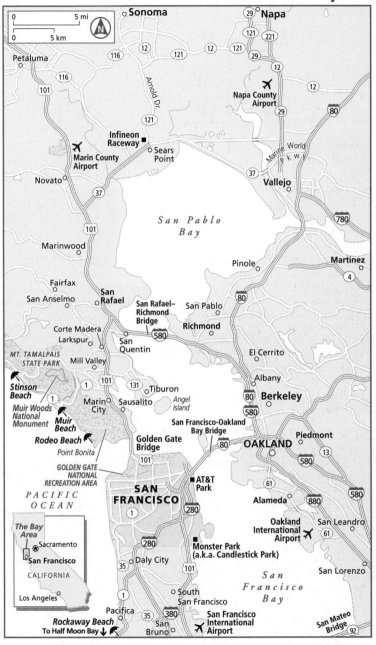

0 — 5 mi
0 — 5 km

N

Sonoma

Napa
29

121
221

Petaluma

116
12
121
12
121
29

101

116

12

12

121

Napa County Airport

Infineon Raceway

Sears Point

80

Marin County Airport

29

Marine World Pkwy

Novato

37

Vallejo

101

780

Marinwood

San Pablo Bay

Pinole

Martinez

4

Fairfax

San Anselmo

San Rafael

San Rafael–Richmond Bridge

San Pablo

Richmond

80

Corte Madera

Larkspur

580

El Cerrito

MT. TAMALPAIS STATE PARK

San Quentin

Mill Valley

Albany

Stinson Beach

1

101

131

Tiburon

80

Berkeley

Muir Woods National Monument

1

Marin City

Sausalito

Angel Island

580

Muir Beach

San Francisco–Oakland Bay Bridge

Piedmont

Rodeo Beach

Point Bonita

Golden Gate Bridge

80

OAKLAND

13

GOLDEN GATE NATIONAL RECREATION AREA

101

580

580

PACIFIC OCEAN

■ AT&T Park

61

Alameda

880

The Bay Area

SAN FRANCISCO

1

280

Oakland International Airport

61

San Leandro

Sacramento

San Francisco

280

■ Monster Park (a.k.a. Candlestick Park)

San Lorenzo

CALIFORNIA

35

Daly City

101

San Francisco Bay

Los Angeles

1

South San Francisco

San Mateo Bridge

Pacifica

35

380

San Bruno

San Francisco International Airport

92

Rockaway Beach To Half Moon Bay ↓

ESSENTIALS

The Berkeley **Bay Area Rapid Transit (BART)** station is 2 blocks from the university. The fare from San Francisco is less than $4. Call ✆ **511** or visit www.bart.gov for trip info, or fares, or to download trip planners to your iPod, mobile phone, or PDA.

If you are coming **by car** from San Francisco, take the Bay Bridge (go during the evening commute, and you'll think Los Angeles traffic is a breeze). Follow I-80 east to the University Avenue exit, and follow University until you hit the campus. Parking is tight, so either leave your car at the Sather Gate parking lot at Telegraph Avenue and Durant Street, or expect to fight for a spot.

WHAT TO SEE & DO

Hanging out is the preferred Berkeley pastime, and the best place to do it is **Telegraph Avenue,** the street that leads to the campus's southern entrance. Most of the action lies between Bancroft Way and Dwight Way, where coffee houses, restaurants, shops, great book and record stores, and crafts booths (with vendors selling everything from T-shirts and jewelry to I Ching and tarot-card readings) swarm with life. Pretend you're a local: Plant yourself at a cafe, sip a latte, and ponder something intellectual, or survey the town's unique residents.

Bibliophiles must stop at **Cody's Books,** 1730 Fourth St. (✆ **510/559-9500;** www.codysbooks.com), to peruse its gargantuan selection of titles, independent-press books, and magazines. If used and antiquarian books are your thing, stop by **Moe's Books,** 2476 Telegraph Ave. (✆ **510/849-2087;** www.moesbooks.com). After exploring four floors of new, used, and out-of-print books, you're unlikely to leave empty-handed.

UC BERKELEY CAMPUS

The University of California at Berkeley (www.berkeley.edu) is worth a stroll. It's a beautiful campus with plenty of woodsy paths, architecturally noteworthy buildings and, of course, 33,000 students. Among the architectural highlights of the campus are a number of buildings by Bernard Maybeck, Bakewell and Brown, and John Galen Howard.

Contact the **Visitor Information Center,** 101 University Hall, 2200 University Ave., at Oxford Street (✆ **510/642-5215;** www.berkeley.edu/visitors), to join a free 90-minute campus tour. Reservations are required; see website for details. Tours are available year-round Monday through Saturday at 10am and Sunday at 1pm. Weekday tours depart from the Visitor's Center and weekend tours start from Sather Bell Tower in the middle of campus. Electric cart tours are available year-round for travelers with disabilities for $40; 2 weeks' advance reservations required; no tours are given the week between Christmas and New Year's Day. Or stop by the office and pick up a self-guided walking-tour brochure or a free Berkeley map. *Note:* The information center is closed on weekends, but you can find the latest information on their website.

The university's southern, main entrance is at the northern end of Telegraph Avenue, at Bancroft Way. Walk through the entrance into Sproul Plaza, and when school is in session, you'll encounter the gamut of Berkeley's inhabitants: colorful street people, rambling political zealots, and ambitious students. You might be lucky enough to stumble upon some impromptu musicians or a heated debate. There's always something going on here, so stretch out on the grass for a few minutes and take in the Berkeley vibe. You'll also find the student union, complete with a bookstore, cafes, and an information desk on the second floor where you can pick up the student newspaper (also found in dispensers throughout campus).

Berkeley

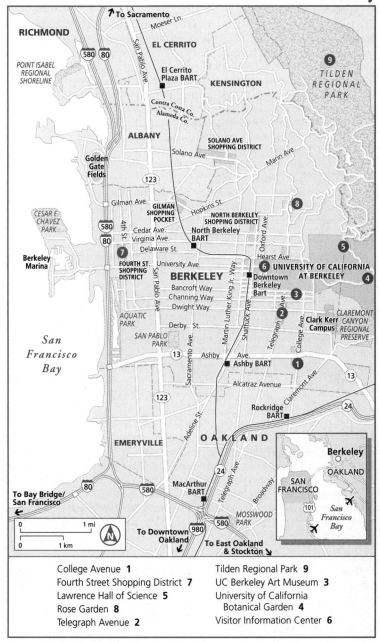

College Avenue **1**
Fourth Street Shopping District **7**
Lawrence Hall of Science **5**
Rose Garden **8**
Telegraph Avenue **2**

Tilden Regional Park **9**
UC Berkeley Art Museum **3**
University of California
  Botanical Garden **4**
Visitor Information Center **6**

For viewing more traditional art forms, there are some noteworthy museums, too. The **Lawrence Hall of Science** ⓖ (east of campus on Centennial Dr., just above the Botanical Gardens; ⓒ **510/642-5132;** www.lawrencehallofscience.org) offers hands-on science exploration. It's open daily from 10am to 5pm, and is a wonderful place to watch the sunset. Included in the admission price is an outdoor science park called Forces That Shape the Bay, which lets visitors explore ongoing geologic forces. The site includes activity stations such as earthquake simulators, a geologic uplift bench, a water feature, telescopes, BayLab programs and demonstrations, an audio tour, and picnic sites. Admission is $9.50 for adults; $7.50 for seniors 62 and over, students, and children 5 to 18; $5.50 for children 3 or 4; and free for kids 2 and under. The **UC Berkeley Art Museum** ⓖ (2626 Bancroft Way, between College and Telegraph aves.; ⓒ **510/642-0808;** www.bampfa.berkeley.edu) is open Wednesday through Sunday from 11am to 5pm. Admission is $8 for adults; $5 for seniors, non-UCB students, visitors with disabilities, and children 17 and under; and $4 for UCB students. This museum contains a substantial collection of Hans Hofmann paintings, a sculpture garden, and the Pacific Film Archive.

PARKS

Unbeknownst to many travelers, Berkeley has some of the most extensive and beautiful parks around. If you want to wear the kids out or enjoy hiking, swimming, sniffing roses, or just getting a breath of California air, jump in your car and make your way to **Tilden Park** ⓖ. On the way, stop at the colorful terraced **Rose Garden** ⓖ (ⓒ **510/981-5151**) in north Berkeley on Euclid Avenue between Bay View and Eunice Street. Then head high into the Berkeley hills to Tilden, where you'll find plenty of flora and fauna, hiking trails, an old steam train and merry-go-round, a farm and nature area for kids, and a chilly tree-encircled lake. The East Bay's public transit system, AC Transit (ⓒ **511;** www.actransit.org), runs the air-conditioned no. 67 bus line around the edge of the park on weekdays and all the way to the Tilden Visitors Center on Saturdays and Sundays. Call ⓒ **510/562-PARK** or see www.ebparks.org for further information.

Another worthy nature excursion is **The University of California Botanical Garden** (ⓒ **510/643-2755;** www.botanicalgarden.berkeley.edu), which features a vast collection of herbage ranging from cacti to redwoods. It's on campus in Strawberry Canyon on Centennial Drive. Unfortunately no public bus can take you directly there, so driving is the way to go. Call for directions. Open daily from 9am to 5pm; closed the first Tuesday of every month; docent-led tours on Thursdays, Saturdays, and Sundays at 1:30pm. Admission is $5 adults, $3 seniors 65 and over, $1 youth 3 to 17, and free for children 2 and under and UC students.

SHOPPING

If you're itching to exercise your credit cards, head to one of two places. **College Avenue** from Dwight Way to the Oakland border overflows with eclectic boutiques, antiques shops, and restaurants. The other option is **Fourth Street,** in west Berkeley, 2 blocks north of the University Avenue exit. This shopping strip is the perfect place to go on a sunny morning. Grab a cup of java, read the paper at a patio table, and then hit the **Crate & Barrel Outlet,** 1785 Fourth St., between Hearst and Virginia (ⓒ **510/528-5500**). Prices are 30% to 70% off retail. It's open daily from 10am to 6pm. This area also boasts small, wonderful stores crammed with imported and locally made housewares. Nearby is **REI,** the Bay Area's favorite outdoors outfitter, 1338 San Pablo Ave., near Gilman Street (© **510/527-4140**). It's open Monday through Friday from 10am to 9pm, Saturday from 10am to 8pm, and Sunday from 10am to 7pm.

WHERE TO STAY

Unfortunately, a little research will prove that Berkeley is not even remotely close to a good hotel town. Most accommodations are extremely basic motels and funky B&Bs. The one exception (though it's overpriced) is the **Claremont Resort & Spa,** 41 Tunnel Rd., Berkeley (© **800/551-7266** or 510/843-3000; www.claremontresort.com), a grand Victorian hotel, also on the border of Oakland, with a fancy spa and gym, three restaurants, a hip bar, and grandiose surroundings. Though it's the most luxurious thing going, it's overpriced and rooms aren't nearly as charming as the exterior. Rates range from $290 to $450 for doubles and $460 to $1,050 for suites. Or you can contact the **Berkeley & Oakland Bed and Breakfast Network** (© **510/547-6380;** www.bbonline.com/ca/berkeley-oakland), which books visitors into private homes and apartments in the East Bay area.

MODERATE

Rose Garden Inn   Like a Merchant-Ivory movie, the accommodations within this 40-room/five-building inn range from English Country to Victorian, making it a favorite for visiting grandparents and vacationing retirees. Despite your age or design sense, the stunning and expansive garden exploding with rose bushes, hydrangeas, and an abundance of flora and fauna is sure to delight as well as erase all memories that you're on a characterless stretch of Telegraph Avenue a few blocks south of the student action. Rooms, many of which have fireplaces, cable TVs, and all the basic amenities, show some wear and tend to be a little dark, but they are spacious, updated, and very clean despite the obvious age of some bathroom nooks and crannies.

2740 Telegraph Ave. (at Stuart St.), Berkeley, CA 94705. www.rosegardeninn.com. © 800/992-9005 or 510/549-2145. Fax 510/549-1085. 40 units. $125–$275 double. Breakfast included. AE, DC, DISC, MC, V. Free parking on a space-available basis. **Amenities:** Wi-Fi in lobby; coffee and afternoon cookies. *In room:* TV, high-speed Internet access in deluxe rooms, hair dryer, iron upon request.

WHERE TO DINE

East Bay dining is a relaxed alternative to San Francisco's gourmet scene. There are plenty of ambitious Berkeley restaurants and, unlike in San Francisco, plenty of parking, provided you're not near the campus.

If you want to dine student-style, eat on campus Monday through Friday. Buy something at a sidewalk stand or in the building directly behind the Student Union. There's also the **Bear's Lair Pub and Coffee House,** the **Terrace,** and the **Golden Bear Restaurant.** All the university eateries have both indoor and outdoor seating.

Telegraph Avenue has an array of small, ethnic restaurants, cafes, and sandwich shops. Follow the students: If the place is crowded, it's good, supercheap, or both.

VERY EXPENSIVE

Chez Panisse ★★★ CALIFORNIA   California cuisine is so much a product of Alice Waters's genius that all other restaurants following in her wake should be dated A.A.W. (After Alice Waters). Read the menus posted outside, and you'll understand why. Most of the produce and meat comes from local farms and is organically produced, and after all these years, Alice still tends her restaurant with great integrity and innovation. Chez Panisse is a delightful redwood and stucco cottage with a brick terrace filled with flowering potted plants. The two dining areas, the cafe and the restaurant, both serve Mediterranean-inspired cuisine.

In the upstairs cafe are displays of pastries and fruit and an oak bar adorned with large bouquets of fresh flowers. At lunch or dinner, the menu might feature delicately smoked gravlax or roasted eggplant soup with pesto, followed by lamb ragout garnished with apricots, onions, and spices and served with couscous.

The cozy downstairs restaurant, strewn with blossoming floral bouquets, is an appropriately warm environment in which to indulge in the $65 fixed-price four-course gourmet dinner, which is served Tuesday through Thursday. Friday and Saturday, it's $85 for four courses; and Monday is bargain night, with a three-course dinner for $50.

The restaurant posts the following week's menu, which changes daily, every Saturday. There's also an excellent wine list, with bottles ranging from $28 to $300.

1517 Shattuck Ave. (btw. Cedar and Vine). ℂ 510/548-5525 for main restaurant reservations, 510/548-5049 for cafe reservations. Fax 510/548-0140. www.chezpanisse.com. Reservations required for the dining room and taken 1 month prior to calendar date requested. Reservations are recommended for the cafe, but walk-ins are welcomed. Restaurant fixed-price menu $50–$85; cafe main courses $15–$25. AE, DC, DISC, MC, V. Restaurant seatings Mon–Sat 6–6:30pm and 8:30–9:15pm most times of the year (in slower months, like Jan–Mar, times vary; please call to confirm). Cafe Mon–Thurs 11:30am–3pm and 5–10:30pm; Fri–Sat 11:30am–3:30pm and 5–11:30pm. BART: Downtown Berkeley. From I-80 N, take the University Ave. exit and turn left onto Shattuck Ave.

MODERATE

Cafe Rouge ⊛ MEDITERRANEAN   After cooking at San Francisco's renowned Zuni Cafe for 10 years, chef-owner Marsha McBride launched her own restaurant, a sort of Zuni East. She brought former staff members and some of the restaurant's flavor with her, and now her sparse, loftlike dining room serves salads, rotisserie chicken with oil and thyme, grilled lamb chops, steaks, and homemade sausages. East Bay carnivores are especially happy with the burger; like Zuni's, it's top-notch. During warm days, outdoor dining overlooking the shopping square is ideal.

1782 Fourth St. (btw. Delaware and Hearst). ℂ 510/525-1440. www.caferouge.net. Reservations recommended. Main courses $14–$32. MC, V. Lunch Mon–Fri 11:30am–3pm; dinner Tues–Thurs 5:30–9:30pm; Fri–Sat 5:30–10pm; Sun 5–9:30pm; brunch Sun 10am–2:30pm.

Rivoli ⊛⊛ (Finds) CALIFORNIA   One of the favored dinner destinations in the East Bay, Rivoli offers top-notch food at amazingly reasonable prices. Aside from a few house favorites, the menu changes entirely every 3 weeks to feature whatever's freshest and in season; the wine list follows suit with around 10 by-the-glass options handpicked to match the food. While many love it, I'm not a fan of the portobello-mushroom fritter, a gourmet variation of the fried zucchini stick. However, plenty of dishes shine, including chicken cooked with prosciutto di Parma, wild mushroom chard and ricotta cannelloni, Marsala *jus*, snap peas, and baby carrots; and braised lamb shank with green garlic risotto, sautéed spinach, and oven-dried tomatoes. Finish the evening with an assortment of cheeses or a warm chocolate truffle torte with hazelnut ice cream, orange crème anglaise, and chocolate sauce.

1539 Solano Ave. ℂ 866/496-2489 or 510/526-2542. www.rivolirestaurant.com. Reservations recommended. Main courses $16–$22. AE, DC, DISC, MC, V. Mon–Thurs 5:30–9:30pm; Fri 5:30–10pm; Sat 5–10pm; Sun 5–9pm.

INEXPENSIVE

Cafe Fanny ⊛⊛ FRENCH/ITALIAN   Alice Waters's (of Chez Panisse fame) cafe is one of those local must-do East Bay breakfast traditions. Don your Birkenstocks and earth-tone apparel, grab the morning paper, and head here to wait in line for a simple

Finds Sweet Sensations at Berkeley's Chocolate Factory

If you haven't had chocolate nibs, you haven't lived—at least that's what chocoholics are likely to discover upon visiting **Scharffen Berger Chocolate Maker,** California's runaway-success chocolatier that opened its factory and retail-shop doors in Berkeley in mid-2001. Within the brick building, visitors can not only taste the nibs (crunchy roasted and shelled cocoa beans), but also see how the famous chocolate company uses vintage European equipment during regularly scheduled free tours (call or visit their website to reserve a spot as spaces are limited). All manner of chocolate-related products, from candy bars to cocoa powder to chocolate sauce, are also available in the retail shop. You can have coffee, pastries, lunch, or brunch at their restaurant, Café Cacao, which is open Monday through Friday 8am to 5pm (serving lunch 11am–3pm) and Saturday and Sunday 9am to 3pm. The factory is located at 914 Heinz Ave., Berkeley (© **510/981-4066;** www.scharffenberger.com). From I-80 E take the Ashby Avenue exit, turn left on Seventh Street, and turn right on Heinz.

yet masterfully prepared French breakfast. The menu offers such items as soft-boiled farm-fresh eggs on Levain toast, buckwheat crepes with house-made preserves, cinnamon toast, and an assortment of superb pastries. Lunch is more of an Italian experience featuring seasonal selections. Sandwiches—such as Alice's baked ham and watercress on focaccia or grilled chicken breast wrapped in prosciutto, sage, and aioli on Acme bread—might convince you that maybe Berkeley isn't such a crazy place to live after all. There's also a selection of pizzettas, salads, and soup. Eat inside at the stand-up food bar (one bench), or outside at one of the cafe tables.

1603 San Pablo Ave. (at Cedar St.). © **510/524-5447.** Most breakfast items $5; lunch $5–$7. MC, V. Mon–Fri 7am–3pm; Sat 8am–4pm; Sun 8am–3pm. Breakfast until 11am; Sun all day. Closed major holidays.

O Chamé 𝄢𝄢 JAPANESE   Spare and plain in its decor, with ocher-colored walls etched with patterns, this spot has a meditative air to complement the traditional, experimental, and extremely fresh Japanese-inspired cuisine. The menu, which changes daily, offers meal-in-a-bowl dishes ($9–$13) that allow a choice of soba or udon noodles in a clear soup with a variety of toppings—from shrimp and wakame seaweed to beef with burdock root and carrot. Appetizers include a flavorful melding of grilled shiitake mushrooms, as well as portobello mushrooms and green-onion pancakes. Their main entree selection always includes delicious roasted salmon, but you can also easily fill up on a bowl of soba or udon noodles with fresh, wholesome fixings (think roasted oysters, sea bass, and tofu skins).

1830 Fourth St. (near Hearst). © **510/841-8783.** www.themenupage.com/ochame.html. Reservations recommended Fri–Sat dinner. Main courses lunch $9–$19, dinner $18–$24. AE, MC, V. Mon–Sat 11:30am–3pm; Mon–Thurs 5:30–9pm; Fri–Sat 5:30–9:30pm.

2 Oakland

10 miles E of San Francisco

Although it's less than a dozen miles from San Francisco, Oakland is worlds apart from its sister city across the bay. Originally little more than a cluster of ranches and farms, Oakland exploded in size and stature practically overnight, when the last mile of transcontinental railroad track was laid down. Major shipping ports soon followed and, to this day, Oakland remains one of the busiest industrial ports on the West Coast.

The price for economic success, however, is Oakland's lowbrow reputation as a predominantly working-class city; it is forever in the shadow of chic San Francisco. However, as the City by the Bay has become crowded and expensive in the past few years, Oakland has experienced a rush of new residents and businesses. As a result, Oak-town is in the midst of a renaissance, and its future continues to look brighter and brighter.

Rent a sailboat on Lake Merritt, stroll along the waterfront, explore the fantastic Oakland Museum—they're all great reasons to hop the bay and spend a fog-free day exploring one of California's largest and most ethnically diverse cities.

ESSENTIALS

BART connects San Francisco and Oakland through one of the longest underwater transit tunnels in the world. Fares range from $2 to $4, depending on your station of origin; children 4 and under ride free. BART trains operate Monday through Friday from 4am to midnight, Saturday from 6am to midnight, and Sunday from 8am to midnight. Exit at the 12th Street station for downtown Oakland. Call ⓒ **511** or visit www.bart.gov for more info.

By car from San Francisco, take I-80 across the San Francisco–Oakland Bay Bridge and follow signs to downtown Oakland. Exit at Grand Avenue South for the Lake Merritt area.

For a calendar of events in Oakland, contact the **Oakland Convention and Visitors Bureau,** 463 11th St., Oakland, CA 94607 (ⓒ **510/839-9000;** www.oakland cvb.com). The city also sponsors eight free guided tours, including African-American Heritage and downtown tours held Wednesdays and Saturdays May through October; call ⓒ **510/238-3234** or visit www.oaklandnet.com/walkingtours for details.

Downtown Oakland lies between Grand Avenue on the north, I-980 on the west, Inner Harbor on the south, and Lake Merritt on the east. Between these landmarks are three BART stations (12th St., 19th St., and Lake Merritt), City Hall, the Oakland Museum, Jack London Square, and several other sights.

WHAT TO SEE & DO

Lake Merritt is Oakland's primary tourist attraction, along with Jack London Square (see below). Three and a half miles in circumference, the tidal lagoon was bridged and dammed in the 1860s and is now a wildlife refuge that is home to flocks of migrating ducks, herons, and geese. The 122-acre **Lakeside Park,** a popular place to picnic, feed the ducks, and escape the fog, surrounds the lake on three sides. Visit www.oakland net.com/parks for more info. At the **Municipal Boathouse** ✺ (ⓒ **510/238-2196**), in Lakeside Park along the north shore, you can rent sailboats, rowboats, pedal boats, canoes, or kayaks for $8 to $15 per hour (cash only). Or you can take an hour-long gondola ride with **Gondola Servizio** (ⓒ **888/737-8494;** www.gondolaservizio.com). Experienced gondoliers will serenade you, June through October, as you glide across the lake; the cost ranges from $45 to $225 for two depending on the time and gondola style.

Another site worth visiting is Oakland's **Paramount Theatre** ✺, 2025 Broadway (ⓒ **510/893-2300;** www.paramounttheatre.com), an outstanding National Historic Landmark and example of Art Deco architecture and decor. Built in 1931 and authentically restored in 1973, it's the city's main performing-arts center, hosting big-name

Oakland

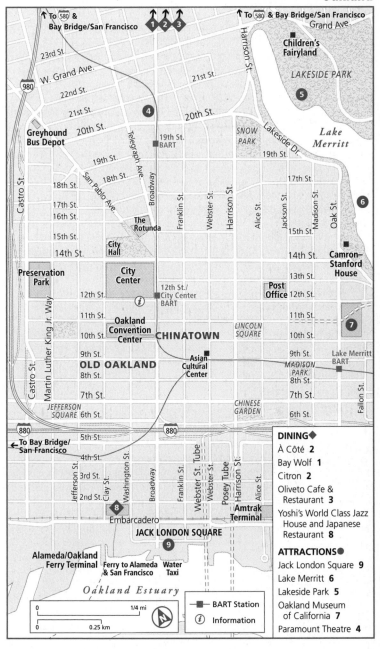

To 580 & Bay Bridge/San Francisco

To 580 & Bay Bridge/San Francisco

23rd St.

W. Grand Ave.

22nd St.

21st St.

20th St.

Greyhound Bus Depot

19th St.

18th St.

17th St.

16th St.

15th St.

14th St.

City Hall

Preservation Park

City Center

12th St.

11th St.

Oakland Convention Center

10th St.

9th St.

OLD OAKLAND

8th St.

7th St.

JEFFERSON SQUARE 6th St.

5th St.

To Bay Bridge/San Francisco

4th St.

3rd St.

2nd St.

Embarcadero

JACK LONDON SQUARE

Alameda/Oakland Ferry Terminal

Ferry to Alameda & San Francisco

Water Taxi

Oakland Estuary

Castro St.

San Pablo Ave.

Telegraph Ave.

Martin Luther King Jr. Way

Broadway

Franklin St.

Webster St.

Harrison St.

Alice St.

Jackson St.

Madison St.

Oak St.

Fallon St.

Jefferson St.

Clay St.

Washington St.

Broadway

Franklin St.

Webster St. Tube

Webster St.

Posey Tube

Harrison St.

Alice St.

Grand Ave.

Children's Fairyland

LAKESIDE PARK

Lake Merritt

SNOW PARK

Lakeside Dr.

21st St.

20th St.

19th St.

19th St. BART

The Rotunda

17th St.

15th St.

Camron-Stanford House

14th St.

13th St.

12th St./City Center BART

Post Office

12th St.

11th St.

10th St.

LINCOLN SQUARE

CHINATOWN

Asian Cultural Center

MADISON PARK

Lake Merritt BART

9th St.

8th St.

7th St.

CHINESE GARDEN

6th St.

Amtrak Terminal

DINING ◆

À Côté **2**

Bay Wolf **1**

Citron **2**

Oliveto Cafe & Restaurant **3**

Yoshi's World Class Jazz House and Japanese Restaurant **8**

ATTRACTIONS ●

Jack London Square **9**

Lake Merritt **6**

Lakeside Park **5**

Oakland Museum of California **7**

Paramount Theatre **4**

0 | 1/4 mi
0 | 0.25 km

■ BART Station
ⓘ Information

The USS *Potomac:* FDR's Floating White House

It took the Potomac Association's hundreds of volunteers more than 12 years—at a cost of $5 million—to restore the 165-foot presidential yacht *Potomac*, President Franklin D. Roosevelt's beloved "Floating White House." Now a proud and permanent memorial berthed at the Port of Oakland's FDR Pier at Jack London Square, the revitalized *Potomac* is open to the public for dockside tours, as well as 2-hour History Cruises along the San Francisco waterfront and around Treasure and Alcatraz islands. Prior to departure, a 15-minute video, shown at the nearby Potomac Visitor Center, provides background on FDR's presidency and FDR's legacy concerning the Bay Area.

The dockside tours are available year-round on Wednesdays and Fridays from 10am to 2:30pm, and on Sundays from noon to 3pm. Admission is $7 for ages 13 to 59, $5 for seniors age 60 and over, and free for children age 12 and under. The History Cruise runs on Thursdays and Saturdays from early May to mid-November; the departure time is 11am. History Cruise fares are $40 for ages 13 to 59, $35 for seniors 60 and older, $20 for children 6 to 12, and free for kids 5 and under. Due to the popularity of the cruises, advance purchase is strongly recommended.

Hours and cruise schedules are subject to change, so be sure to call the Potomac Visitor Center before arriving. Tickets for the Dockside Tour can be purchased at the Visitor Center upon arrival; tickets for the History Cruise can be purchased in advance via **Ticketweb** (© 866/468-3399; www.ticket web.com) or by calling the **Potomac Visitor Center** (© 510/627-1215; www. usspotomac.org). The Visitor Center is located at 540 Water St., at the corner of Clay and Water streets adjacent to the FDR pier at the north end of Jack London Square.

performers like Smokey Robinson and Alicia Keys. Guided tours of the 3,000-seat theater are given the first and third Saturday morning of each month, excluding holidays. No reservations are necessary; just show up at 10am at the box office entrance on 21st Street at Broadway. The tour lasts 2 hours, cameras are allowed, and admission is $5.

If you take pleasure in strolling sailboat-filled wharves or are a die-hard fan of Jack London, you might enjoy a visit to **Jack London Square** ⊛ (© 866/295-9853; www. jacklondonsquare.com). Oakland's only patently tourist area remains a relatively low-key version of San Francisco's Fisherman's Wharf, which shamelessly plays up the fact that Jack London spent most of his youth along the waterfront. The square fronts the harbor, housing a tourist-tacky complex of boutiques and eateries, as well as a more locals-friendly farmers' market year-round on Sundays from 10am to 2pm. Most shops are open daily from 11am to 6pm (some restaurants stay open later). One of the best options is live jazz at **Yoshi's World Class Jazz House & Japanese Restaurant** ⊛, 510 Embarcadero W. (© 510/238-9200; www.yoshis.com), which serves some fine sushi in its adjoining restaurant. In the center of the square is a small, reconstructed Yukon cabin in which Jack London lived while prospecting in the Klondike during the gold rush of 1897.

In the middle of Jack London Square you'll find a more authentic memorial, **Heinold's First and Last Chance Saloon** (© 510/839-6761; www.heinoldsfirstand lastchance.com), a funky, friendly little bar and historic landmark that's worth a visit. This is where London did some of his writing and most of his drinking; the corner table he used has remained exactly as it was nearly a century ago.

Jack London Square is at Broadway and Embarcadero. Take I-880 to Broadway, turn south, and drive to the end. Or you can ride BART to 12th Street station and then walk south along Broadway (about half a mile). Or take bus no. 72R or 72M to the foot of Broadway.

Oakland Museum of California ✪   Two blocks south of Lake Merritt, the Oakland Museum of California incorporates just about everything you'd want to know about the state and its people, history, culture, geology, art, environment, and ecology. Inside a low, modern building set among sweeping gardens and terraces, it's actually three museums in one: exhibitions of works by California artists from Bierstadt to Diebenkorn; collections of historic artifacts, from Pomo Indian basketry to Country Joe McDonald's guitar; and re-creations of California habitats from the coast to the Sierra Mountains. The museum holds major shows of California artists as well as exhibitions dedicated to California's rich nature and history. Recent exhibits included *Aftershock: Personal Stories from the '06 Quake and Fire* and *Baseball as America*, which showcased artifacts and photos of the nation's favorite sport. The museum also frequently shows photography from its huge collections.

Forty-five-minute guided tours leave from the gallery information desks on request or by appointment. There's a fine cafe, a **Collector's Gallery** (© 510/834-2296) that sells works by California artists, and a museum shop. The cafe is open Wednesday through Saturday from 10:30am to 4pm, Sunday from 1:30 to 4pm.

1000 Oak St. (at 10th St.). © 510/238-2200. www.museumca.org. Admission $8 adults, $5 students and seniors, free for children 5 and under. 2nd Sun of the month is free (special exhibitions excepted). Wed–Sat 10am–5pm; Sun noon–5pm; open until 9pm 1st Fri of the month. Closed Jan 1, July 4, Thanksgiving, and Dec 25. BART: Lake Merritt station; follow the signs posted in the station. From I-880 N, take the Oak St. exit; the museum is 5 blocks east. Or take I-580 to I-980 and exit at the Jackson St. ramp.

WHERE TO STAY

Two fine midrange hotel options in Oakland are the **Waterfront Plaza Hotel,** 10 Washington St., Jack London Square (© 800/729-3638 or 510/836-3800; www. waterfrontplaza.com), and the **Oakland Marriott City Center,** 1001 Broadway (© 800/228-9290 or 510/451-4000; fax 510/835-3466; www.marriott.com). Most major motel chains also have locations (and budget prices) around town and near the airport. If you want to stay near the fabulous shopping and dining neighborhood of Oakland's Rockridge and pamper yourself with a great gym, outdoor pools, and lit tennis courts, your best hotel bet (though it's undoubtedly overpriced) is the **Claremont Resort & Spa,** 41 Tunnel Rd., Berkeley (© 800/551-7266 or 510/843-3000; www. claremontresort.com), a grand Victorian hotel (with modern rooms) that borders both Berkeley and Oakland. It ain't downtown, but it's just a quick drive to all the action, and it is one of the area's prettiest options (see p. 255 for more information).

WHERE TO DINE
EXPENSIVE
Citron ✪ FRENCH/CALIFORNIA   This petite, adorable French bistro was an instant smash when it opened in 1992, and it continues to earn raves for its small yet

enticingly eclectic menu. Chef and owner Chris Rossi draws the flavors of France, Italy, and Spain together with fresh California produce for results you aren't likely to have tasted elsewhere. The menu changes every few weeks; dishes range from succulent roasted Sonoma leg of lamb, served with gigande beans, cardoons, and fennel; to spicy bayou seafood stew brimming with fried oysters, shrimp, snapper, bell peppers, and tomato sauce; to fresh chèvre lasagna with braising greens and truffled crimini mushrooms. They've also added a lunch and brunch menu. *A word of advice:* If you're into classic foods you can identify by name, head elsewhere. It's all about creative cooking here.

5484 College Ave. (north of Broadway btw. Taft and Lawton sts.). **©** 510/653-5484. www.citronrestaurant.com. Reservations recommended. Lunch and brunch main courses $8–$15; 3-course fixed-price menu $15; dinner main courses $20–$26; 3- to 5-course fixed-price menu $32–$48. AE, DC, DISC, MC, V. Tues–Fri 11:30am–4:30pm; Sat–Sun 10am–3pm; Mon–Tues 5:30–9pm; Wed–Thurs 5:30–9:30pm; Fri 5:30–10pm; Sat 5–10pm; Sun 5–9pm.

Oliveto Cafe & Restaurant 🌾🌾🌾 ITALIAN   Opened 20 years ago by Bob and Maggie Klein, and now under the helm of executive chef Paul Canales (who has been with the Kleins for 11 years, working his way up through the ranks in the kitchen), Oliveto is one of the top Italian restaurants in the Bay Area (and certainly the best in Oakland). Local workers pile in at lunchtime for wood-fired pizzas, simple salads, and sandwiches served in the lower-level cafe. The upstairs restaurant—with suave neo-Florentine decor and a partially open kitchen—is more elegant and packed nightly with fans of the mind-blowing house-made pastas, sausages, and prosciutto. Oliveto has a wood-burning oven, flame-broiled rotisserie, and a full bar which sports a high-end liquor cabinet. An assortment of pricey grills, braises, and roasts anchor the daily changing menu, but the heavenly pastas, pizzettas, and awesome salads offer the most tang for your buck. Still, the Arista (classic Italian pork with garlic and rosemary and pork *jus*) is insanely good; and no one does fried calamari, onion rings, and lemon slices better than Oliveto. *Tip:* Free parking is available in the lot at the rear of the Market Hall building.

Rockridge Market Hall, 5655 College Ave. (off the northeast end of Broadway at Shafter/Keith St., across from the Rockridge BART station). **©** 510/547-5356. www.oliveto.com. Reservations recommended for restaurant. Main courses cafe $2.50–$12 breakfast, $4–$8 lunch, $12–$15 dinner; restaurant $11–$15 lunch, $16–$30 dinner. AE, DC, MC, V. Cafe Mon 7am–9pm; Tues–Fri 7am–10pm; Sat 8am–10pm; Sun 8am–9pm. Restaurant Mon–Fri 11:30am–2pm; Tues–Wed 5:30–9:30pm; Thurs–Sat 5:30–10pm; Sun 5–9pm.

MODERATE

À Côté 🌾🌾 FRENCH TAPAS   Jack and Daphne Knowles look to chef Matthew Colgan to serve up superb rustic Mediterranean-inspired small plates at this loud, festive, and warmly lit joint. A "limited reservations" policy means there's usually a long wait during prime dining hours, but once seated, you can join locals in a nosh fest featuring the likes of croque-monsieur; *pommes frites* with aioli; wood-oven cooked mussels in Pernod; grilled pork tenderloin with creamy polenta, and pancetta; and cheese plates—and wash it down with Belgian ales, perky cocktails, or excellent by-the-glass or -bottle selections from the great wine list. *Note:* The heated and covered outdoor seating area tends to be quieter.

5478 College Ave. (at Taft Ave.). **©** 510/655-6469. www.acoterestaurant.com. Limited reservations accepted. Small plates $5–$14. MC, V. Sun–Tues 5:30–10pm; Wed–Thurs 5:30–11pm; Fri–Sat 5:30pm–midnight.

Bay Wolf 🌾 CALIFORNIA   The lifespan of most Bay Area restaurants is about a year; Bay Wolf, one of Oakland's most revered restaurants, has, fittingly, been going strong for over 3 decades. The converted brown Victorian is a comfortably familiar sight for most East Bay diners, who have come here for years to let executive chef-owner Michael Wilds and his chef de cuisine Louis Le Gassic do the cooking. Bay Wolf enjoys a reputation for simple yet sagacious preparations using only fresh ingredients. Main courses include Liberty Ranch duck three ways (grilled breast, braised leg, and crépinette) with turnips, curly endive, apples, and Calvados; flavorful seafood stew seasoned with saffron; and tender braised *osso buco* with creamy polenta and gremolata. Informal service means you can leave the tie at home. The front deck has heat lamps and a radiant heat floor, allowing for open-air evening dining year-round—a treat that San Franciscans rarely experience.

3853 Piedmont Ave. (off Broadway btw. 40th St. and MacArthur Blvd.). ✆ 510/655-6004. www.baywolf.com. Reservations recommended. Main courses $8.50–$18 lunch, $17–$24 dinner. AE, MC, V. Mon–Fri 11:30am–1:45pm; Mon–Thurs 5:30–9pm; Fri–Sat 5:30–10pm; Sun 5:30–9:30pm. Paid parking at Piedmont Ave. and Yosemite St.

3 Angel Island & Tiburon

8 miles N of San Francisco

A California State Park, **Angel Island** is the largest of San Francisco Bay's three islets (the others are Alcatraz and Yerba Buena). The island has been, at various times, a prison, a quarantine station for immigrants, a missile base, and even a favorite site for duels. Nowadays, most visitors are content with picnicking on the large green lawn that fronts the docking area; loaded with the appropriate recreational supplies, they claim a barbecue pit, plop their fannies down on the lush green grass, and while away an afternoon free of phones, televisions, and traffic. Hiking, mountain biking, and guided tram tours are other popular activities here.

Tiburon, situated on a peninsula of the same name, looks like a cross between a fishing village and a Hollywood Western set—imagine San Francisco reduced to toy dimensions. The seacoast town rambles over a series of green hills and ends up at a spindly, multicolored pier on the waterfront, like a Fisherman's Wharf in miniature. In reality, it's an extremely plush patch of yacht-club suburbia, as you'll see by the marine craft and the homes of their owners. Ramshackle, color-splashed old frame houses line Main Street, sheltering chic boutiques, souvenir stores, antiques shops, and art galleries. Other roads are narrow, winding, and hilly and lead up to dramatically situated homes. The view from here of San Francisco's skyline and the islands in the bay is a good enough reason to pay the precious price to live here.

Although there is a hotel in Tiburon, I wouldn't recommend staying there: It's a 1-block town, and the hotel is very expensive. There are no hotels on Angel Island. Both destinations are better as day trips.

ESSENTIALS

Ferries of the **Blue & Gold Fleet** (✆ 415/705-5555; www.blueandgoldfleet.com) from Pier 41 (Fisherman's Wharf) travel to both Angel Island and Tiburon. Boats run on a seasonal schedule; phone or look online for departure information. The round-trip fare is $15 to Angel Island, $8.50 for kids 6 to 12, and free for kids 5 and under. The fare includes state park fees. Tickets to Tiburon are $8.50 each way for adults, $4.50 for kids 5 to 11, and free for kids 4 and under. Tickets are available at Pier 41, online, or over the phone.

By car from San Francisco, take U.S. 101 to the Tiburon/Highway 131 exit, and then follow Tiburon Boulevard all the way downtown, a 40-minute drive from San

Francisco. Catch the **Tiburon–Angel Island Ferry** (© 415/435-2131; www.angel islandferry.com) to Angel Island from the dock at Tiburon Boulevard and Main Street. The 15-minute round-trip costs $10 for adults, $8 for children 5 to 11, and $1 for bikes. One child under 5 is admitted free of charge with each paying adult (after that it's $8 each). Boats run on a seasonal schedule, but usually depart hourly from 10am to 5pm on weekends, with a more limited schedule on weekdays. Call ahead or look online for departure information. Tickets can only be purchased when boarding and include state park fees. No credit cards.

WHAT TO SEE & DO ON ANGEL ISLAND

Passengers disembark from the ferry at **Ayala Cove,** a small marina abutting a huge lawn area equipped with tables, benches, barbecue pits, and restrooms. During the summer season, there's also a small store, a gift shop, the Cove Cafe (with surprisingly good grub), and an overpriced mountain-bike rental shop at Ayala Cove.

Angel Island's 12 miles of hiking and bike trails include the **Perimeter Road,** a paved path that circles the island. It winds past disused troop barracks, former gun emplacements, and other military buildings; several turnoffs lead to the top of Mount Livermore, 776 feet above the bay. Sometimes referred to as the "Ellis Island of the West," Angel Island was used as a holding area for detained Chinese immigrants awaiting admission papers from 1910 to 1940. You can still see faded Chinese characters on some of the walls of the barracks where the immigrants were held.

The 1-hour audio-enhanced open-air **Tram Tour** of the island costs $14 for adults, $13 for seniors, $9.50 for children 6 to 12, and is free for children 5 and under; schedules vary depending on the time of year. Your best bet is to check in at the Cove Cafe upon arrival on the island for current day's tram schedule.

Guided **Segway tours** of the island are available as well March through November. The 2½-hour interpretive tour circles the island's paved Perimeter Trail and costs $65 (there's a shorter $35 afternoon tour as well). All riders must be 16 years and older. To make tour reservations call © 415/435-3392 or visit www.segwayangelisland.com.

During the warmer months you can camp at a limited number of reserved sites; call **Reserve America** at © 800/444-7275 or visit www.reserveamerica.com to find out about environmental campgrounds at Angel Island. Reservations are taken 2 days to 7 months in advance.

Guided **sea-kayak tours** ⚐ are also available. The 2½-hour trips combine the thrill of paddling stable, two- or three-person kayaks in an informative, naturalist-led tour around the island (conditions permitting). All equipment is provided, kids are welcome, and no experience is necessary. Rates run about $75 per person. For more information, contact the Sausalito-based **Sea Trek** at © 415/488-1000; www.seatrek kayak.com. *Note:* Tours depart from Sausalito, not Angel Island.

For more information about activities on Angel Island, call © 415/897-0715 or log onto www.angelisland.com.

WHAT TO SEE & DO IN TIBURON

The main thing to do in tiny Tiburon is stroll along the waterfront, pop into the stores, and spend an easy $50 on drinks and appetizers before heading back to the city. For a taste of the Wine Country, stop at **Windsor Vineyards,** 72 Main St. (© 415/ 435-3113; www.windsorvineyards.com)—its Victorian tasting room dates from 1888. Twenty or more choices are available for a free tasting. Wine accessories and gifts—glasses, cork pullers, carry packs (which hold six bottles), gourmet sauces,

Marin County

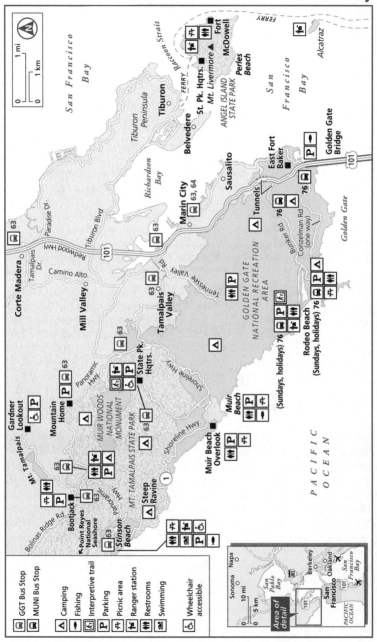

Legend:

- GGT Bus Stop
- MUNI Bus Stop
- Camping
- Fishing
- Interpretive trail
- Parking
- Picnic area
- Ranger station
- Restrooms
- Swimming
- Wheelchair accessible

San Francisco Bay

San Pablo Bay

Tiburon Peninsula

Richardson Bay

Tiburon

Belvedere

St. Pk. Hqtrs.

Mt. Livermore ▲

Fort McDowell

ANGEL ISLAND STATE PARK

Perles Beach

Alcatraz

FERRY

San Francisco Bay

Golden Gate Bridge

East Fort Baker

Sausalito

101

Marin City 63, 64

Golden Gate

Corte Madera

63

Paradise Dr.

Tamalpais Dr.

Camino Alto

Tiburon Blvd.

Redwood Hwy

63

101

Mill Valley

Tamalpais Valley

63

63

Tunnels 76

76

Bunker Rd.

Conzelman Rd. (one way)

76

GOLDEN GATE NATIONAL RECREATION AREA

Tennessee Valley Rd.

Rodeo Beach 76

(Sundays, holidays) 76

Gardner Lookout

Mt. Tamalpais

63

Mountain Home

63

Panoramic Hwy.

MUIR WOODS NATIONAL MONUMENT

State Pk. Hqtrs.

63

MT. TAMALPAIS STATE PARK

Shoreline Hwy

Muir Beach

(Sundays, holidays) 76

Muir Beach Overlook

Bootjack

Point Reyes National Seashore

Bolinas Ridge Rd.

Panoramic Hwy.

63

63

Steep Ravine

1

Stinson Beach

PACIFIC OCEAN

PACIFIC OCEAN

Sonoma Napa

San Pablo Bay

Berkeley

Oakland

80

San Francisco

San Francisco Bay

101

Area of detail

0 1 mi
0 1 km

0 10 mi
0 5 km

posters, and maps—are also available. Ask about personalized labels for your selections. The shop is open Sunday through Thursday from 10am to 6pm, Friday and Saturday from 10am to 7pm.

WHERE TO DINE IN TIBURON

Guaymas MEXICAN   Guaymas offers authentic Mexican regional cuisine and a spectacular panoramic view of San Francisco and the bay. In good weather, the two heated outdoor patios are almost always packed with diners soaking in the sun and scene. Inside the large dining room, colorful Mexican artwork and tons of colored paper cutouts strewn overhead on string brighten the beige walls. Should you feel chilled, to the rear of the dining room is a beehive-shaped adobe fireplace.

Guaymas is named after a fishing village on Mexico's Sea of Cortez, and both the town and the restaurant are famous for their *camarones* (giant shrimp). The restaurant also features ceviche, handmade tamales, and charcoal-grilled beef, seafood, and fowl. It's not fancy, nor is it gourmet, but it is a good place to come with large parties or family. In addition to a small selection of California and Central American wines, the restaurant offers an exceptional variety of tequilas and Mexican beers.

5 Main St. ℰ 415/435-6300. Reservations recommended. Main courses $13–$23. AE, DC, DISC, MC, V. Mon–Thurs 11:30am–10pm; Fri–Sat 11:30am–11pm; Sun 10:30am–10pm. Ferry: Walk about 10 paces from the landing. From U.S. 101, exit at Tiburon/Hwy. 131; follow Tiburon Blvd. 5 miles and turn right onto Main St. Restaurant is behind the bakery.

Sam's Anchor Café ⭐ *Finds* SEAFOOD   Summer Sundays are liveliest in Tiburon, when weekend boaters tie up at the docks of waterside restaurants like this one, and good-time cyclists pedal from the city to kick back here. Sam's is the kind of place where you and your cronies can take off your shoes and have a fun, relaxing time eating burgers and drinking margaritas outside on the pier. The fare is typical—sandwiches, salads, and such—but the quality and selection are inconsequential: Beer, burgers, and a designated driver are all you really need.

27 Main St. ℰ 415/435-4527. www.samscafe.com. Main courses $9–$17 brunch, $11–$24 lunch, $15–$24 dinner. AE, DC, DISC, MC, V. Mon–Fri 11am–10pm; Sat–Sun 9:30am–10pm. Ferry: Walk from the landing. From U.S. 101, exit at Tiburon/Hwy. 131; follow Tiburon Blvd. 4 miles and turn right onto Main St.

4 Sausalito

5 miles N of San Francisco

Just off the northeastern end of the Golden Gate Bridge is the picturesque little town of Sausalito, a slightly bohemian adjunct to San Francisco. With fewer than 8,000 residents, Sausalito feels rather like St. Tropez on the French Riviera (minus the beach). Next to the pricey bayside restaurants, antiques shops, and galleries you'll see hamburger joints, ice cream shops, and secondhand bookstores. Sausalito's main strip is Bridgeway, which runs along the water; on a clear day the views of San Francisco far across the bay are spectacular. After admiring the view, those in the know make a quick detour to Caledonia Street, 1 block inland; not only is it less congested, but it also has a better selection of cafes and shops. Since the town is all along the waterfront and only stretches a few blocks, it's best explored on foot and easy to find your way around.

ESSENTIALS

The **Golden Gate Ferry Service** fleet, Ferry Building (ℰ **415/923-2000;** www.golden gate.org), operates between the San Francisco Ferry Building, at the foot of Market Street, and downtown Sausalito. Service is frequent, running at reasonable intervals every day of the year except January 1, Thanksgiving, and December 25. Phone for an exact schedule. The ride takes a half-hour, and one-way fares are $6.75 for adults; $3.35 for youth 6 to 18, seniors 65 plus, and passengers with disabilities (50% off full fare); children 5 and under ride free (limit two children per full-fare adult). Family rates are available on weekends.

Ferries of the **Blue & Gold Fleet** (© **415/705-5555;** www.blueandgoldfleet.com) leave from Pier 41 (Fisherman's Wharf); the one-way cost is $8.50 for adults, $4.50 for kids 5 to 11. Boats run on a seasonal schedule; phone or log onto their website for departure information.

By car from San Francisco, take U.S. 101 N, and then take the first right after the Golden Gate Bridge (Alexander exit). Alexander becomes Bridgeway in Sausalito.

WHAT TO SEE & DO

Above all else, Sausalito has scenery and sunshine, for once you cross the Golden Gate Bridge, you're out of the San Francisco fog patch and under blue California sky (we hope). Houses cover the town's steep hills, overlooking a forest of masts on the waters below. Most of the tourist action, which is almost singularly limited to window-shopping and eating, takes place at sea level on Bridgeway.

Sausalito is a mecca for shoppers seeking handmade, original, and offbeat clothes and footwear, as well as arts and crafts. Many of the town's shops are in the alleys, malls, and second-floor boutiques reached by steep, narrow staircases on and off Bridgeway. Caledonia Street, which runs parallel to Bridgeway 1 block inland, is home to more shops.

Bay Area Discovery Museum (Kids) If you just can't stand the thought of one more trip to PIER 39 or Fisherman's Wharf and are looking for something else to do with your kids (infants to 8 years old), check out this museum. Located on 7½ acres in the Golden Gate National Recreation Area at Fort Baker, the museum offers spectacular (jaw-dropping even!) views of the city and Golden Gate Bridge (you're literally at the northern base of the bridge) and is also the ultimate indoor-outdoor interactive kids' adventure. Tot Spot is tops for crawlers and toddlers (up to 42 in.); Lookout Cove is a 2½-acre outdoor area with a scaled-down model of the GGB that kids can add rivets to, a shipwreck to explore, tidal pools, and lovely site-specific art; Art Studios splits kids into age groups 5 and under and 6 and older; and the Wave Workshop re-creates the habitat under the GGB. There's even a small cafe that serves yummy, organic food far better than typical family-friendly fare. Remi Hayashi, a California Culinary Academy grad, is at the helm here, serving up Niman Ranch hot dogs, fresh sandwiches, panini, and pizzas plus a host of snacks. *One thing to note:* If you're here alone with two kids of different ages, it can be difficult to navigate, as they do keep the little ones separate from the older ones in the Tot Spot. If you explain your situation, they'll give your older one (12 and up) a "Tot Spot Helper" sticker, and let them in, but they won't be allowed to play and will have to stick by you. But if it's a nice day, you can spend the whole time in Lookout Cove with both kids, have lunch outside, and still feel like you got your money's worth.

E. Fort Baker, 557 McReynolds Rd. © **415/339-3900.** www.baykidsmuseum.org. Admission $8.50 adults, $7.50 children, free for children under 1 and members. Discounts available to AAA members and members of reciprocal museum organizations (see website). Tues–Fri 9am–4pm; Sat–Sun 10am–5pm. Closed Mon and all major holidays. By car: Cross the Golden Gate Bridge and take the Alexander Ave. exit. Follow signs to E. Fort Baker and the Bay Area Discovery Museum.

Bay Model Visitors Center *(Kids)*   The U.S. Army Corps of Engineers once used this high-tech, 1½-acre model of San Francisco's bay and delta to resolve problems and observe the impact of changes in water flow. Today the model is strictly for educational purposes and reproduces (in scale) the rise and fall of tides and the flows and currents of water. There's a 10-minute film, self-guided and audio tours ($3 donation requested), and a 1-hour tour (free; book a reservation), but the most interesting time to visit is when the model is in operation, so call ahead.

2100 Bridgeway. ℂ 415/332-3871. www.spn.usace.army.mil/bmvc. Free admission. Labor Day to Memorial Day (winter hours) Tues–Sat 9am–4pm; Memorial Day to Labor Day (summer hours) Tues–Fri 9am–4pm, Sat–Sun and holidays 10am–5pm.

WHERE TO STAY

Sausalito is such a desirable enclave that it offers little in the way of affordable lodging. On the bright side, it's so close to San Francisco that it takes only about 15 minutes to get here, traffic permitting. Although the hotels listed below are great destinations in themselves, Sausalito itself is more day trip than destination.

VERY EXPENSIVE

The Inn Above Tide *(★★)*   Perched directly over the bay atop well-grounded pilings, this former luxury-apartment complex underwent a $4-million transformation in 2004 into one of Sausalito's—if not the Bay Area's—finest accommodations. The view clinches it: Every room affords an unparalleled panorama of the San Francisco Bay, including a postcard-quality vista of the city glimmering in the distance. Should you manage to tear yourself away from your private deck, you'll find that 23 of the sumptuously appointed rooms sport romantic little fireplaces. Soothing warm earth tones highlight the decor, which blends in well with the bayscape outside. Be sure to request that your breakfast and newspaper be delivered to your deck, and then cancel your early appointments—on sunny mornings, nobody checks out early.

30 El Portal (next to the Sausalito Ferry Landing), Sausalito, CA 94965. ℂ 800/893-8433 or 415/332-9535. Fax 415/332-6714. www.innabovetide.com. 29 units. $295–$950 double. Rates include continental breakfast and evening wine and cheese. AE, DC, MC, V. Valet parking $12. **Amenities:** Concierge; in-room massage; same-day laundry service/dry cleaning; free shoeshine. *In room:* A/C, TV/DVD, dataport, free Wi-Fi, CD player, minibar, fridge, hair dryer.

EXPENSIVE

Casa Madrona Hotel & Spa *(★★)*   Sooner or later most visitors to Sausalito look up and wonder at the ornate mansion on the hill. It's part of Casa Madrona, a hideaway by the bay built in 1885 by a wealthy lumber baron. The epitome of luxury in its day, the mansion had slipped into decay when John Gallagher purchased it in 1910 and converted it into a hotel. By 1976 it was damaged and facing the threat of demolition when John Mays acquired the property and revitalized the hotel. Successive renovations and extensions added a rambling, New England–style building to the hillside below the main house. Now listed on the National Register of Historic Places, the hotel offers whimsically decorated rooms, suites, and cottages, which are accessed by steep, gorgeously landscaped pathways. The 16 free-standing units, the seven cottages, and the rooms in the mansion have individual themes such as Lilac and Lace, Renoir, and the Artist's Loft. Some have claw-foot tubs and others have fireplaces. Rooms in the newer adjoining building have a chic contemporary decor, four-poster beds, marble bathrooms, and great marina views from some rooms. The classy Italian Poggio restaurant (see below) has been a Sausalito favorite since opening, and the hotel's full-service spa offers a wide assortment of treatments and getaway packages.

801 Bridgeway, Sausalito, CA 94965. ℂ **415/332-0502**. Fax 415/332-2537. www.casamadrona.com. 63 units. $295–$450 double; $550 suite. AE, DC, DISC, MC, V. Valet parking $20. Ferry: Walk across the street from the landing. From U.S. 101 N, take the 1st right after the Golden Gate Bridge (Alexander exit); Alexander becomes Bridgeway. **Amenities:** Restaurant; spa; concierge; room service; babysitting upon request; laundry service; dry cleaning. *In room:* TV, VCR upon availability, minibar, coffeemaker, hair dryer, robes.

WHERE TO DINE
EXPENSIVE
Horizons ⍟ SEAFOOD/AMERICAN   Eventually, every San Franciscan ends up at Horizons to meet a friend for Sunday Bloody Marys. It's not much to look at from the outside, but it gets better as you head past the 1960s-era dark-wood interior toward the waterside terrace. On warm days it's worth the wait for alfresco seating if only to watch dreamy sailboats glide past San Francisco's distant skyline. The food here can't touch the view, but it's well portioned and satisfying enough. Seafood dishes are the main items, including steamed clams and mussels, freshly shucked oysters, and a variety of seafood pastas. In fine Marin tradition, Horizons has an "herb tea and espresso" bar.

558 Bridgeway. ℂ **415/331-3232**. www.horizonssausalito.com. Reservations accepted weekdays only. Main courses $9–$21; salads and sandwiches $6–$11. AE, MC, V. Mon–Fri 11:30am–9pm; Sat 10:30am–10pm; Sun 10:30am–9pm. Valet parking $4.

Poggio ⍟⍟ ITALIAN   Sausalito has long been low on upscale dining options, but all that changed with the late-2003 opening of elegant "Poggio," which is a loose Italian translation for "special hillside place." Adjoining the Casa Madrona hotel and across the street from the marina, everything *is* special here, from the floor-to-ceiling doors opening to the sidewalk; to its interior with arches and earthen colors, mahogany accents, well-directed light, and centerpiece wood-burning oven manned by a cadre of chefs; to the wine cellar, terra-cotta-tiled floors, comfy mohair banquettes, and white linen-draped tables. The daily changing menu features items like a superb salad of endive, Gorgonzola, walnuts, figs, and honey; pizzas; addictively excellent pastas (try the spinach ricotta gnocchi with beef ragout); and entrees such as whole local petrale sole deboned and served tableside, or grilled lamb chops with roasted fennel and gremolata. With a full bar, well-priced wine list, and great desserts, this is Sausalito's premier dining destination—excluding the more casual Sushi Ran (see below).

777 Bridgeway (at Bay St.). ℂ **415/332-7771**. www.poggiotrattoria.com. Italian-style breakfast a la carte $2.50–$5.50; main courses lunch $8–$18, dinner $13–$25. AE, DC, DISC, MC, V. Continental breakfast daily 6:30–11am; lunch 11:30am–5:30pm; dinner Sun–Thurs 5:30–10pm, Fri–Sat 5:30–11pm. Free valet parking at Casa Madrona Hotel & Spa.

Sushi Ran ⍟⍟ SUSHI/JAPANESE   San Francisco isn't exactly stellar in its Japanese-food selection, but right across from the Golden Gate Bridge is a compact, but fashionable, destination for seriously delicious sushi and cooked dishes. All walks of sushi-loving life cram into the sushi bar, window seats, and more roomy back dining area for Nori Kusakabe's nigiri sushi and standard and specialty rolls. You'll also find a slew of creative dishes by Executive Chef Scott Whitman, such as generously sized and unbelievably moist and buttery miso-glazed black cod (a must-have), oysters on the half-shell with ponzu sauce and *tobiko* (fish eggs), and a Hawaiian-style ahi *poke* (Hawaiian-style minced raw fish) salad with seaweed dressing that's authentic enough to make you want to hula.

107 Caledonia St. ℂ **415/332-3620**. www.sushiran.com. Reservations recommended. Sushi $5–$14; main courses $8.50–$16. AE, MC, V. Mon–Fri 11:45am–2:30pm; Mon–Sat 5:30–11pm; Sun 5–10:30pm. From U.S. 101 N, take the 1st right after the Golden Gate Bridge (Alexander exit); Alexander becomes Bridgeway in Sausalito. At Johnson St. turn left, and then right onto Caledonia.

A Picnic Lunch, Sausalito Style

If the crowds are too much or the prices too steep at Sausalito's bay-side restaurants, grab a bite to go for an impromptu picnic in the park fronting the marina. It's one of the best and most romantic ways to spend a warm, sunny day in Sausalito. The best source for a la carte eats is the Mediterranean-style **Venice Gourmet Delicatessen** at 625 Bridgeway, located right on the waterfront just south of the ferry landing. Since 1964 this venerable deli has offered all the makings for a superb picnic: wines, cheeses, fruits, stuffed vine leaves, salami, lox, prosciutto, salads, quiche, made-to-order sandwiches, and fresh-baked pastries. It's open daily from 9am to 6pm (© 415/332-3544; www.venicegourmet.com).

INEXPENSIVE

Hamburgers BURGERS   Like the name says, the specialty at this tiny, narrow cafe is juicy flame-broiled hamburgers, arguably Marin County's best. Look for the rotating grill in the window off Bridgeway, and then stand in line and salivate with everyone else. Chicken burgers are a slightly healthier option. Order a side of fries, grab a bunch of napkins, and head to the park across the street.

737 Bridgeway. © 415/332-9471. Sandwiches $5.50–$6.50. No credit cards. Daily 11am–5pm. From U.S. 101 N, take the 1st right after the Golden Gate Bridge (Alexander exit); Alexander becomes Bridgeway in Sausalito.

5 Muir Woods & Mount Tamalpais

12 miles N of the Golden Gate Bridge

While the rest of Marin County's redwood forests were being devoured to feed San Francisco's turn-of-the-20th-century building spree, Muir Woods, in a remote ravine on the flanks of Mount Tamalpais, escaped destruction in favor of easier pickings.

MUIR WOODS

Although the magnificent California redwoods have been successfully transplanted to five continents, their homeland is a 500-mile strip along the mountainous coast of southwestern Oregon and Northern California. The coast redwood, or *Sequoia sempervirens,* is one of the tallest living things known to man (!); the largest known specimen in the Redwood National Forest towers 368 feet. It has an even larger relative, the *Sequoiadendron giganteum* of the California Sierra Nevada, but the coastal variety is stunning enough. Soaring toward the sky like a wooden cathedral, Muir Woods is unlike any other forest in the world and an experience you won't soon forget.

Granted, Muir Woods is tiny compared to the Redwood National Forest farther north, but you can still get a pretty good idea of what it must have been like when these giants dominated the entire coastal region. What is truly amazing is that they exist a mere 6 miles (as the crow flies) from San Francisco—close enough, unfortunately, that tour buses arrive in droves on the weekends. You can avoid the masses by hiking up the **Ocean View Trail,** turning left on **Lost Trail,** and returning on the **Fern Creek Trail.** The moderately challenging hike shows off the woods' best sides and leaves the lazy-butts behind.

To reach Muir Woods from San Francisco, cross the Golden Gate Bridge heading north on Highway 101, take the Stinson Beach/Highway 1 exit heading west, and follow the signs (and the traffic). The park is open daily from 8am to sunset, and the admission fee is $5 per person over 16. There's also a small gift shop, educational displays, and ranger talks. For more information, call the **National Parks Service at Muir Woods** (© 415/388-2596) or visit www.nps.gov.

If you don't have a car, you can book a bus trip with **San Francisco Sightseeing** (© 888/428-6937 or 415/434-8687; www.sanfranciscosightseeing.com), which takes you straight to Muir Woods and makes a short stop in Sausalito on the way back. The 3½-hour tour runs twice daily at 9:15am and 2:15pm and costs $47 for adults, $45 for seniors, $22 for children 5 through 11, and free for kids 4 and under. Pickup and return are offered from select San Francisco hotels. Call for information and departure times.

MOUNT TAMALPAIS

The birthplace of mountain biking, Mount Tam—as the locals call it—is the Bay Area's favorite outdoor playground and the most dominant mountain in the region. Most every local has his or her secret trail and scenic overlook, as well as an opinion on the raging debate between mountain bikers and hikers (a touchy subject). The main trails—mostly fire roads—see a lot of foot and bicycle traffic on weekends, particularly on clear, sunny days when you can see a hundred miles in all directions, from the foothills of the Sierra to the western horizon. It's a great place to escape from the city for a leisurely hike and to soak in breathtaking views of the bay.

To get to Mount Tamalpais **by car,** cross the Golden Gate Bridge heading north on Highway 101, and take the Stinson Beach/Highway 1 exit. Follow the signs up the shoreline highway for about 2½ miles, turn onto Pantoll Road, and continue for about a mile to Ridgecrest Boulevard. Ridgecrest winds to a parking lot below East Peak. From there, it's a 15-minute hike up to the top. You'll find a visitor center with a small museum, video, diorama, and store, as well as informative "Mount Tam Hosts" who are more than happy to help you plan a hike, identify plants, and generally share their love of the mountain. Visitor center admission is free; it's open Saturday and Sunday from 11am to 4pm (standard time), and Saturday and Sunday 10am to 5:30pm (daylight saving time). Park hours are 7am to 6pm daily in winter; 7am to 9pm for about 1 month during the height of summer. Two-hour, 2-mile moonlight hikes, among many others, are offered (© 415/388-2070; www.mttam.net).

6 Point Reyes National Seashore

35 miles N of San Francisco

The National Seashore system was created to protect rural and undeveloped stretches of the coast from the pressures brought by soaring real-estate values and increasing population. Nowhere is the success of the system more evident than at Point Reyes. Residents of the surrounding towns—Inverness, Point Reyes Station, and Olema— have steadfastly resisted runaway development. You won't find any strip malls or fast-food joints here, just laid-back coastal towns with cafes, country inns, and vast expanses of open, undeveloped space in between, where gentle living prevails.

Although the peninsula's people and wildlife live in harmony above the ground, the situation beneath the soil is much more volatile. The infamous San Andreas Fault separates Point Reyes—the northernmost landmass on the Pacific Plate—from the rest of

California, which rests on the North American Plate. Point Reyes is making its way toward Alaska at a rate of about 2 inches per year, but at times it has moved much faster. In 1906, Point Reyes jumped north almost 20 feet in an instant, leveling San Francisco and jolting the rest of the state. The half-mile Earthquake Trail, near the Bear Valley Visitor Center, illustrates this geological drama with a loop through an area torn by the slipping fault. Shattered fences, rifts in the ground, and a barn knocked off its foundation by the quake illustrate how alive the earth is.

ESSENTIALS

Point Reyes is only 30 miles northwest of San Francisco, but it takes at least 90 minutes to reach **by car** (it's all the small towns, not the topography, that slow you down). The easiest route is Sir Francis Drake Boulevard from Highway 101 south of San Rafael; it takes its time getting to Point Reyes, but it does so without any detours. For a much longer but more scenic route, take the Stinson Beach/Highway 1 exit off Highway 101 just south of Sausalito and follow Highway 1 north.

As soon as you arrive at Point Reyes, stop at the **Bear Valley Visitor Center** (① **415/ 464-5100;** www.nps.gov/pore) on Bear Valley Road (look for the small sign just north of Olema on Hwy. 1) and pick up a free Point Reyes trail map. The rangers are extremely friendly and helpful and can answer any questions about the National Seashore. Be sure to check out the great natural history and cultural displays while you're there. The center is open weekdays from 9am to 5pm, weekends and holidays from 8am to 5pm.

Entrance to the park is free. **Camping** is $15 per site per night for up to six people, and permits are required. All the sites range from a 1.4- to 5.5-mile hike in from the nearest trail head. Reservations can be made up to 3 months in advance by calling ① **415/663-8054** Monday through Friday from 9am to 2pm.

WHAT TO SEE & DO

When headed to any part of the Point Reyes coast, expect to spend the day surrounded by nature at its finest; however, bear in mind that as beautiful as the wilderness can be, it's also untamed. The bone-chilling waters in these areas are not only home to a vast array of sea life, including sharks, but are unpredictable and dangerous. There are no lifeguards on duty, and swimming is strongly discouraged because of the waves and rip tides. Pets are not permitted on any of the area's trails. However, if you are looking for a place to swim, consider heading toward Tomales Bay during the summer months.

By far the most popular—and crowded—attraction at Point Reyes National Seashore is the venerable **Point Reyes Lighthouse** ⭐ (① **415/669-1534**), at the westernmost tip of Point Reyes. Even if you plan to forgo the 308 steps to the lighthouse itself (sorry—no strollers or wheelchairs), the area is still worth a visit. The dramatic scenery includes thousands of common murres and prides of sea lions that bask on the rocks far below (binoculars come in handy). It's open Thursday through Monday from 10am to 4:30pm and admission is free. A parking area is designated for travelers with disabilities at the visitor center. Call ① **415/464-5100** to make arrangements.

The lighthouse is also the top spot on the California coast from which to observe **gray whales** as they make their southward and northward migrations along the coast January through April. The annual round-trip is 10,000 miles—one of the longest known mammal migrations. The whales head south in January and return north in

Finds Drake's Bay Oyster Farm

If you want to escape the crowds and enjoy some man-made entertainment, head to **Drake's Bay Oyster Farm**. Located on the edge of Drakes Estero (a uniquely pristine and nutrient-rich saltwater lagoon on the Point Reyes peninsula that produces some of the finest oysters in the world), the oyster farm doesn't look like much—it's just a cluster of wooden shacks and oyster tanks surrounded by piles of oyster shells—but there's no better place in California to buy delicious fresh-out-of-the-water oysters by the sackful. The owner is very friendly and doles out all the information you'll ever want to know about the bivalves, including a lesson on how to properly shuck them. They also have picnic tables and bottled oyster sauce so you can enjoy your recently purchased bivalves immediately (though I prefer to drive down to Point Reyes Beach), but bring your own oyster knife. Drake's Bay Oyster Farm is located at 17171 Sir Francis Drake Blvd., about 6 miles west(ish) of Inverness on the way to the Point Reyes Lighthouse. Open daily 8am to 4:30pm (© **415/669-1149**; www.drakesbayfamilyfarms.com).

March. There's never a guarantee that you will see a whale, but it's best to come during clear, calm weather. *Note:* If you plan to drive to the lighthouse to whale-watch, arrive early because parking is limited. If possible, come on a weekday. On a weekend or holiday January through the beginning of April, you have to park at the Drake's Beach Visitor Center and take the shuttle bus (weather permitting) to the lighthouse and on to Chimney Rock to watch elephant seals; the shuttle bus runs from around New Year's Day to the beginning of April and costs $5 for adults, free for children 15 and under. Dress warmly when you come here—it's often quite cold and windy—and bring binoculars. Expect to spend about 2½ hours.

Whale-watching is far from the only activity at the Point Reyes National Seashore. On weekend afternoons or daily during the summer months, many different tours are offered: You can walk along the Bear Valley Trail, spotting the wildlife at the ocean's edge; see the waterfowl at Alamere Falls; explore tide pools; view some of North America's most beautiful ducks in the wetlands of Limantour; hike to the promontory overlooking Chimney Rock to see the sea lions, harbor seals, elephant seals, and seabirds; or take a guided walk along the San Andreas Fault to observe the epicenter of the 1906 earthquake and learn about the regional geology. Tours vary seasonally; for the most up-to-date details, call the **Bear Valley Visitor Center** (© **415/464-5100**) or visit the National Park Service's website (www.nps.gov/pore), where you can also get a lay of the land and more details, including area maps, in the "Plan Your Visit" section of the site. *Note:* Many tours are suitable for travelers with disabilities.

Some of the park's best—and least crowded—highlights can be approached only on foot. They include **Alamere Falls,** a freshwater stream that cascades down a 40-foot bluff onto Wildcat Beach; and **Tomales Point Trail,** which passes through the Tule Elk Reserve, a protected haven for roaming herds of tule elk that once numbered in the thousands. Hiking most of the trails usually ends up being an all-day outing, however, so it's best to split a 2-day trip into a "by car" day and a "by foot" day.

If you're into bird-watching, you'll definitely want to visit the **Point Reyes Bird Observatory** (© 415/868-0655; www.prbo.org), one of the few full-time ornithological research stations in the United States. At the southeast end of the park on Mesa Road, this is where ornithologists keep an eye on more than 400 feathered species. Admission to the visitor center and nature trail is free, and visitors are welcome to observe the tricky process of catching and banding the birds. The observatory is open daily from sunrise to 5pm. Banding hours vary, so call the field station for exact times.

One of my favorite things to do in Point Reyes is paddle through placid Tomales Bay, a haven for migrating birds and marine mammals. **Blue Waters Kayaking** (© 415/669-2600; www.bwkayak.com) organizes nature tours and hiking and kayak trips, including 3-hour morning or sunset outings, oyster tours, day trips, and longer excursions. Instruction, private groups and classes, clinics, and boat rental are available, and all ages and levels are welcome. Prices for tours start at $68. Rentals begin at $30 per person. There are two launching points: One is on Highway 1 at the Marshall Boatworks in Marshall, 8 miles north of Point Reyes Station; and the other is on Sir Francis Drake Boulevard, in Inverness, 5 miles west of Point Reyes Station. The Inverness site is open daily from 9am to 5pm; the Marshall site is open, weather permitting, on weekends from 9am to 5pm and by appointment. Call to confirm.

WHERE TO STAY

Inns of Marin, P.O. Box 547, Point Reyes Station, CA 94956 (© 800/887-2880 or 415/663-2000; www.innsofmarin.com), is a free service that can help you find accommodations ranging from one-room cottages to inns to complete vacation homes. Many places have a 2-night minimum, but at slow times they might make an exception. The service can also refer you to restaurants, hiking trails, and attractions.

EXPENSIVE

Manka's Inverness Lodge & Restaurant ★★★ (Finds)   If there was ever a reason to pack your bags and leave San Francisco for a day or two, this is it. A former hunting and fishing lodge, Manka's looks like something out of a Hans Christian Andersen fairy tale, right down to the tree-limb bedstands. It's all terribly romantic in a Jack London-ish sort of way, and tastefully done. The lodge consists of a superb restaurant on the first floor, four rooms upstairs (room nos. 1 and 2 have large private decks), and four rooms in the Redwood Annex. Two spacious one-bedroom cabins, behind the lodge and on the water, have living rooms and bathrooms with vintage 6-foot double-ended tubs and private outdoor showers opening up to the sky. For the ultimate romantic splurge, inquire about the three secluded guesthouses: Boat House, Perch, and Cabin 125. The lodge's reputation was built on its rustic and romantic restaurant, which dominates the bottom floor and continues to make visitors swoon with house specialties of game and fish. The menu is price-fixed, ranging from $58 to $88 (Sat), and features limited selections that might include pheasant with Madeira *jus,* mashed potatoes, and wild-huckleberry jam; black-buck antelope chops with sweet-corn salsa; or, everybody's favorite, pan-seared elk tenderloin. The restaurant is open for dinner Thursday through Sunday for a single seating (7–7:30pm Thurs–Sat; 4–4:30pm Sun) except for the first 6 weeks of the year, when it's closed.

30 Callendar Way (at Argyle St., off Sir Francis Drake Blvd., ¼ mile north of downtown Inverness), P.O. Box 1110, Inverness, CA 94937. © 415/669-1034. Fax 415/669-1598. www.mankas.com. 14 units, including 4 cabins. $215–$385 double; $365–$565 cabin. AE, MC, V. **Amenities:** Restaurant; in-room massage; room service; movies on request; personal music library; free Wi-Fi. *In room:* MP3 player with CD library, phones in guesthouses, redwood soaking tubs in some rooms, massage.

INEXPENSIVE

Motel Inverness *(Kids)*   Homey, well-maintained, and fronting Tomales Bay, this is the perfect pick for the spendthrift or the outdoor adventurer who plans to spend as little time indoors as possible. All the guest rooms except one twin-bed option have queen-size beds and skylights. Attached to the hotel is a giant great room, complete with fireplace and pool table to distract the kids; parents can relax and children can play on the back lawn overlooking the bay, bird sanctuary, and rolling green hills beyond. Ideal for families is the Dacha cottage, a few miles away. On the water, it has three bedrooms, a living/dining room, sitting room, and deck with Tomales Bay views.

12718 Sir Francis Drake Blvd., Inverness, CA 94937. © 888/669-6909 or 415/669-1081. www.motelinverness.com. 8 units. $99–$175 double; $225–$275 suite; Dacha Cottage $500. MC, V. *In room:* TV, coffeemaker.

WHERE TO DINE
MODERATE

Station House Café *(Finds)* AMERICAN   For more than 2 decades, the Station House Café has been a favorite pit stop for Bay Area residents headed to and from Point Reyes. It's a friendly, low-key place with an open kitchen, an outdoor garden dining area, and live music on weekend nights. Breakfast dishes include a Hangtown omelet with local oysters and bacon, and eggs with creamed spinach and mashed-potato pancakes. Lunch and dinner specials might be fettuccine with fresh local mussels steamed in white wine and butter sauce, two-cheese polenta served with fresh spinach sauté and grilled garlic-buttered tomato, or a daily fresh salmon special—all made from local produce, seafood, and organically raised Niman Ranch beef.

11180 Hwy. 1, Main St., Point Reyes Station. © 415/663-1515. www.stationhousecafe.com. Reservations recommended. Breakfast $5.25–$9.25; main courses $7.50–$18 lunch, $9–$25 dinner. AE, DISC, MC, V. Thurs–Tues 8am–3:30pm and 5–9pm.

INEXPENSIVE

Rosie's Cowboy Cookhouse *(Finds)* MEXICAN/AMERICAN   Fresh, good, fast, cheap, and healthy: What more could you ask for in a restaurant? Taqueria La Quinta, which was a favorite lunch stop in downtown Point Reyes for years and years, is now known as Rosie's Cowboy Cookhouse. The huge selection of Mexican standards remains on the menu—try the house-made tamales—but now they've added some Tex to their Mex, such as rib-eye steak, pulled-pork sandwiches, and excellent Niman Ranch beef chili, all prepared from scratch in their kitchen using natural, free range, and organic ingredients. Oh, and watch out for the salsa—that sucker's hot.

11285 Hwy. 1 (at Third and Main sts.), Point Reyes Station. © 415/663-8868. No credit cards. Wed–Mon 11am–9pm.

The Wine Country

by Erika Lenkert

If you've got more than a few days in San Francisco or already are well-versed in the city's offerings, I highly recommend at least a quick jaunt to the Wine Country, an hour or so north by car. Amid mountains dipping into grapevine-trellised valleys, you'll experience an entirely different Northern California: fresh country air, mustard-flower–draped hillsides in spring, gloriously hot weather during summer, some of the world's finest wineries, legendary restaurants, cow-studded pastures, and virtually nothing to do but overindulge. With eating, drinking, and lounging the primary attractions, there's virtually no better example of "the good life."

To decide which of the Wine Country's two distinct valleys (Napa and Sonoma) you prefer to visit, you need to consider their differences: The most obvious is size—Napa Valley dwarfs Sonoma Valley in population, number of wineries, and sheer volume of tourism (and traffic). Napa is definitely the more commercial of the two, with many more wineries and spas to choose from, and a superior selection of restaurants, hotels, and quintessential Wine Country activities, like hot-air ballooning, wine-tasting, and shopping. Furthermore, if your goal is to really learn about the world of winemaking, Napa Valley should be your choice. World-class wineries such as Sterling and Robert Mondavi offer the most interesting and edifying wine tours in North America, if not the world (although Sonoma's Benziger Winery does give them a run for their money).

Meanwhile, Sonoma Valley is the answer for those who are in the less-is-more camp. Napa Valley's neighbor has fewer wineries (about 45), fewer big hotels and restaurants, and a less commercial feel. As a result, there are fewer crowds on the low-key country roads; more down-home charm in the country communities, B&Bs, and little family-run restaurants; and, in general, more opportunities for intimate pastoral experiences. For more on Sonoma Valley's offerings (as spectacular as Napa Valley's but more low-key), see the "Sonoma Valley" section.

If you're planning a more extensive trip to the area, consult *Frommer's Portable California Wine Country* (Wiley Publishing, Inc.).

1 Napa Valley

Just 55 miles north of San Francisco, the city of Napa and its neighboring towns have an overall tourist and big-business feel. You'll see plenty of rolling hills, flora and fauna, and vast stretches of vineyards, but they come hand-in-hand with upscale restaurants, designer discount outlets, rows of hotels and, in summer, traffic clustered more tightly than grapes on the vines. Even with hordes of visitors year-round, Napa is still pretty sleepy, focusing on daytime attractions (wine, outdoor activities, and

The Wine Country

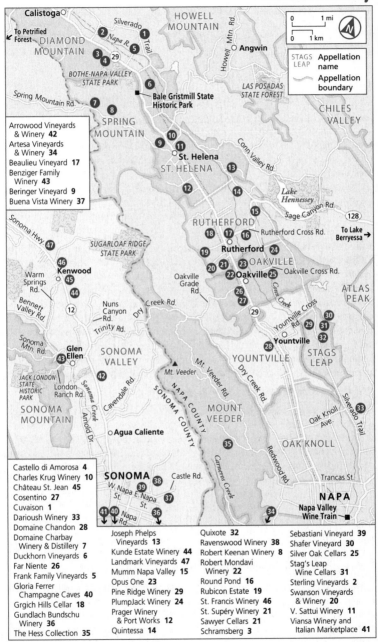

Calistoga

To Petrified Forest

DIAMOND MOUNTAIN

Silverado Trail

Napa R.

HOWELL MOUNTAIN

Howell Mtn. Rd.

Angwin

BOTHE-NAPA VALLEY STATE PARK

LAS POSADAS STATE FOREST

Spring Mountain Rd.

Bale Gristmill State Historic Park

CHILES VALLEY

SPRING MOUNTAIN

St. Helena

ST. HELENA

Conn Valley Rd.

Lake Hennessey

Sage Canyon Rd.

128

RUTHERFORD

Rutherford Cross Rd.

To Lake Berryessa

Sonoma Hwy.

SUGARLOAF RIDGE STATE PARK

Rutherford

Kenwood

Warm Springs Rd.

Bennett Valley Rd.

12

Nuns Canyon Rd.

Trinity Rd.

Dry Creek Rd.

Oakville Grade Rd.

Oakville

Oakville Cross Rd.

ATLAS PEAK

Conn Creek

Yountville Cross Rd.

STAGS LEAP

Sonoma Mtn. Rd.

Glen Ellen

JACK LONDON STATE HISTORIC PARK

London Ranch Rd.

SONOMA VALLEY

Cavedale Rd.

Mt. Veeder

Mt. Veeder Rd.

NAPA COUNTY

SONOMA COUNTY

Yountville

YOUNTVILLE

Dry Creek Rd.

Silverado Trail

SONOMA MOUNTAIN

Arnold Dr.

Sonoma Creek

MOUNT VEEDER

Oak Knoll Ave.

OAK KNOLL

Agua Caliente

SONOMA

Castle Rd.

W. Napa St.

E. Napa St.

Napa Rd.

Carneros Creek

Redwood Rd.

Trancas St.

NAPA

Napa Valley Wine Train

STAGS LEAP Appellation name

Appellation boundary

0   1 mi
0   1 km

Arrowood Vineyards & Winery 42
Artesa Vineyards & Winery 34
Beaulieu Vineyard 17
Benziger Family Winery 43
Beringer Vineyard 9
Buena Vista Winery 37

Castello di Amorosa 4
Charles Krug Winery 10
Château St. Jean 45
Cosentino 27
Cuvaison 1
Darioush Winery 33
Domaine Chandon 28
Domaine Charbay Winery & Distillery 7
Duckhorn Vineyards 6
Far Niente 26
Frank Family Vineyards 5
Gloria Ferrer Champagne Caves 40
Grgich Hills Cellar 18
Gundlach Bundschu Winery 36
The Hess Collection 35

Joseph Phelps Vineyards 13
Kunde Estate Winery 44
Landmark Vineyards 47
Mumm Napa Valley 15
Opus One 23
Pine Ridge Winery 29
PlumpJack Winery 24
Prager Winery & Port Works 12
Quintessa 14

Quixote 32
Ravenswood Winery 38
Robert Keenan Winery 8
Robert Mondavi Winery 22
Round Pond 16
Rubicon Estate 19
St. Francis Winery 46
St. Supéry Winery 21
Sawyer Cellars 21
Schramsberg 3

Sebastiani Vineyard 39
Shafer Vineyard 30
Silver Oak Cellars 25
Stag's Leap Wine Cellars 31
Sterling Vineyards 2
Swanson Vineyards & Winery 20
V. Sattui Winery 11
Viansa Winery and Italian Marketplace 41

spas) and, of course, food. Nightlife is very limited, but after indulging all day, most visitors are ready to turn in early anyway.

Although the name "Napa Valley" is larger than life, the actual area is relatively condensed and only 35 miles long. When the traffic cooperates, you can venture from the town of Napa all the way to Calistoga in half an hour.

ESSENTIALS

GETTING THERE   From San Francisco, cross the Golden Gate Bridge and continue north on U.S. 101. Turn east on California Highway 37; turn left onto the 12/121 turnoff and follow it through the Carneros District to Highway 29, the main road through the Wine Country. Head north on 29. Downtown Napa is a few minutes ahead, while Yountville, Oakville, Rutherford, St. Helena, and Calistoga are further along.

Highway 29 (the St. Helena Hwy.) runs the length of Napa Valley. You really can't get lost—there's just one north-south road, on which most of the wineries, hotels, shops, and restaurants are located. The other main thoroughfare, which parallels Highway 29, is the Silverado Trail. You'll find lots of great wineries here, too.

VISITOR INFORMATION   Once you're in Napa Valley, you can stop at the **Napa Valley Conference & Visitors Bureau,** open daily 9am to 5pm October through May and 9am to 6pm June through September, 1310 Napa Town Center, Napa, CA 94559 (© **707/226-7459,** ext. 106; www.napavalley.com). You can call or write in for the *Napa Valley Guidebook,* which includes information on lodging, restaurants, wineries, and other things to do, along with a winery map; the Bureau charges a $6 postage fee. If you don't want to pay for the official publication, point your browser to www.napavalley.org, the NVCVB's official site, which has lots of the same information for free.

Another good source is WineCountry.com, where you'll find tons of information on all of California's wine-producing regions as well as a weekly column written by *moi.*

TOURING THE NAPA VALLEY & WINERIES

Napa Valley claims more than 45,000 acres of vineyards, making it the most densely planted winegrowing region in the United States. The venture from one end to the other is easy; you can drive it in around half an hour (but expect it to take closer to 50 min. during high season, Apr–Nov). With more than 300 wineries tucked into the nooks and crannies surrounding Highway 29 and the Silverado Trail—almost all of which offer tastings and sales—it's worthwhile to research which wineries you'd like to visit before you hit the wine trails. If you'd like a map detailing the region's wineries, you can grab one from the visitor center or see *Frommer's Portable California Wine Country.*

Tips Reservations at Wineries

Plenty of wineries' doors are open to everyone, without reservations, between 10am and 4:30pm. Most wineries that require reservations for visits do so because of local permit laws, while some do so to create a more intimate tasting experience. It's always best to call ahead if you have your heart set on visiting a certain winery.

Tips Napa Valley Traffic

Travel the Silverado Trail as often as possible to avoid California Highway 29's traffic. It runs parallel to and about 2 miles east of Highway 29. You get there from the city of Napa or by taking any of the "crossroads" from Highway 29. Crossroads are not well signposted, but they're clearly defined on most maps. If you take the Trail, keep us locals happy by driving *at least* the speed limit. Slow rubberneckers are no fun to follow when you're trying to get from one end of the valley to the other. Also, avoid passing through Main Street in St. Helena (on Hwy. 29) during high season. While a wintertime ride from Napa to Calistoga can take 30 minutes, in summer you can expect the trek to take closer to 50 minutes.

Conveniently, most of the large wineries—as well as most of the hotels, shops, and restaurants—are along a single road, Highway 29. It starts at the mouth of the Napa River, near the north end of San Francisco Bay, and continues north to Calistoga and the northern limits of the grape-growing region. When planning your tour, keep in mind that most wineries are closed on major holidays.

Each of the Napa Valley establishments in this chapter—every town, winery, hotel, and restaurant—is organized below from south to north, beginning in the city of Napa, and can be reached from the main thoroughfare of Highway 29.

NAPA
55 miles N of San Francisco

The city of Napa serves as the commercial center of the Wine Country and the gateway to Napa Valley—hence the high-speed freeway that whips you right past it and on to the "tourist" towns of St. Helena and Calistoga. However, if you veer off the highway, you'll be surprised to discover a small but burgeoning community of nearly 75,000 residents with the most cosmopolitan atmosphere in the county—and some of the most affordable accommodations in the valley (Calistoga also has good deals.). It is in the process of gentrification, thanks to (relatively) affordable housing and ongoing additions of new restaurants and attractions, the latest of which is Oxbow Market, a culinary destination by the developer behind San Francisco's famed Ferry Building Marketplace. Heading north on either Highway 29 or the Silverado Trail leads you to Napa's wineries and the more quintessential Wine Country atmosphere of vineyards and wide-open country views.

Artesa Vineyards & Winery *Finds*   Views, modern architecture, seclusion, and region-specific pinot noir flights are the reasons this is one of my favorite stops. Arrive on a day when the wind is blowing less than 10 mph, and the fountains are captivating; they automatically shut off with higher winds. Step into the winery, and there's plenty to do. You can wander through the very tasteful gift shop, browse a room that outlines history and details of the Carneros region, or head to the long bar for $10 to $15 flights of everything from chardonnays and pinot noirs to cabernet sauvignon and zinfandel. Sorry, but Artesa's permits don't allow for picnicking.

1345 Henry Rd., Napa. © **707/224-1668.** www.artesawinery.com. Daily 10am–5pm; tours daily at 11am and 2pm. From Hwy. 12/121, turn north on old Sonoma Rd., turn left on Dealy Lane which becomes Henry Rd.

The Hess Collection ★★ *Finds*   Tucked into the hillside of rural Mount Veeder, this winey brings art and wine together like no other destination in the valley. Swiss art collector Donald Hess is behind the 1978 transformation of the Christian Brothers' 1903 property into a winery–art gallery exhibiting huge, colorful works by the likes of Frank Stella, Francis Bacon, and Andy Goldsworthy. A free self-guided tour leads through the collection and offers glimpses through tiny windows into the winemaking facilities. Newer guided tours and food and wine pairings, which include four to six wines and seasonal noshes, are available by appointment only Thursday through Saturday for $35 to $50 per person. But you can drop by the tasting room anytime, pay $10, and sample the current cabernet and chardonnay and one other featured wine; $15 to $20 gets you a reserve tasting. Current-release bottles start at $22 and top off at around $120. Definitely check out their gift shop; it always has gifts that go beyond the ubiquitous ceramicware and hand-painted wine goblets.

4411 Redwood Rd., Napa. ℂ **707/255-1144**. www.hesscollection.com. Daily 10am–5pm, except some holidays. From Hwy. 29 north, exit at Redwood Rd. west, and follow Redwood Rd. for 6½ miles.

Darioush Winery   Here an exotic and extremely elegant winery and visitor center accentuate the homeland of the owner, Persian-American Darioush Khaledi, who immigrated during the Islamic Revolution and found his fortune in a grocery chain. With architecture based on Persepolis, the capital city of ancient Persia, this 22,000-square-foot winery features the dazzling 16 monumental 18-foot-tall freestanding columns at the entrance, a state-of-the-art visitor center, and opulent landscaping. Tastings include a red table wine, shiraz, merlot, cabernet sauvignon, viognier, and chardonnay, and tastes of addictive Persian pistachios for $20. Opt for the appointment-only $50 private tasting with cheese pairing and you'll get to savor local Sonoma artisan cheeses with your wine and tour the facilities. Ante up $125 and you're privy to an elaborate wine and food pairing featuring old world and new world wines.

4240 Silverado Trail (south of Oak Knoll Ave.), Napa. ℂ **707/257-2345**. www.darioush.com. Daily 10:30am–5pm. Private tasting with cheese pairing daily at 2pm and 3pm by appointment only. Tours available by appointment.

Stag's Leap Wine Cellars   Founded in 1972, Stag's Leap shocked the oenological world in 1976 when its 1973 cabernet won first place over French wines in a Parisian blind tasting. Visit the charmingly landscaped, unfussy winery and its very cramped "tasting room" where, for $15 per person, you can try a selection of four current release wines. Be prepared to pay $30 to $40 for estate wines. A 1-hour tour and tasting runs through everything from the vineyard and production facilities to the ultra-swank $5-million wine caves.

5766 Silverado Trail, Napa. ℂ **707/944-2020**. www.cask23.com. Daily 10am–4:30pm. Tours by appointment only. From Hwy. 29, go east on Trancas St. or Oak Knoll Ave., and then north to the cellars.

Pine Ridge Winery   More for the serious wine taster, intimate Pine Ridge welcomes guests with a pretty hillside location, less tourist traffic than most, and highly regarded wines. Outside, vineyards surround the well-landscaped property. Across the parking lot is a demonstration vineyard, which is somewhat educational if you know something about grape growing and even more helpful if you take their $25 tour (by appointment), which also covers the cellar and barrel tastings. Otherwise, tastings, which are held inside a modest room, start at $15 and go up to $35 for their appointment-only cabernet barrel-to-bottle tasting (held at 11am, 1pm and 3pm). If you want to know about food and wine pairing, call to learn whether they're holding one of their tasty weekend cooking seminars.

Tips **Paying to Taste**

It used to be unusual to have to pay for wine tasting, and when the tides first started to change, I wasn't really for it. But over the past decade, sipping through the region has become such a pastime that in the more popular—and cheap or free—tasting spots you'll often find yourself competing for room at the bar, never mind a refill or a little wine chatter with your host. As a result, I've changed my view on paying a premium to taste. With the flash of a 10- or 20-spot per person you not only avoid crowding in with the hundreds of tipsy souls who come merely for the fun and the buzz, but you also usually get a more intimate experience, complete with attention from staff and usually far more exclusive (and sometimes even seated) surroundings.

5901 Silverado Trail, Napa. © **800/575-9777** or 707/253-7500. www.pineridgewinery.com. Daily 10:30am–4:30pm. Tours by appointment at 10am, noon, and 2pm.

Quixote *★★* *(Finds* Due to zoning laws, this spectacular and truly one-of-a-kind Stags' Leap District winery welcomes up to eight guests per day, all of whom are likely to find themselves as awestruck by the architecture as they are by the powerful petite syrahs and cabernet sauvignons. The hidden hillside property owned by longtime industry power player Carl Doumani is the only U.S. structure designed by late great European artist Friedensreich Hundertwasser. Whimsical and captivating even to those who know nothing about design, it's a structural fantasy world with undulating lines, a gilded onion dome, and a fearless use of color. During the $25-per-person reservation-only sit-down tasting visitors can fill their agape mouths with tastes of the winery's current releases.

6126 Silverado Trail, Napa. © **707/944-2659**. www.quixotewinery.com. Tastings by appointment only Monday through Saturday.

Shafer Vineyards *★★* *(Finds* For an intimate, off-the-beaten-track wine experience, make an appointment to tour and taste at this newly renovated Stags' Leap destination. Unlike many Napa wineries, this one is family owned—by John and Doug Shafer. After 23 years in publishing, John bought 209 Wine Country hillside acres and planted vines on 50 of them. Today, he and his son Doug, joined by winemaker Elias Fernandez, use sustainable farming and solar energy to make outstanding wines, including chardonnay, merlot, cabernet sauvignon, and syrah. Though they produce only 32,000 cases per year, their wines are legendary. (So much so, that anyone who gets their hands on a bottle of their Hillside Select can immediately resell it for more than $100 over the suggested retail price.) But more importantly, they share it and their winemaking philosophy with you during a truly enjoyable and relaxed $45-per-person 1½-hour tour and tasting, which is held within a bright and spacious vineyard-front room complete with fireplace and comfortable seating, and perhaps patting their yellow Lab, Tucker. Most wines go for $45 to $65, but their Hillside Select cabernet will cost you $200. *FYI:* Book your tasting tour 4 to 6 weeks in advance—online or by phone; the tours are intimate and popular.

6154 Silverado Trail, Napa. © **707/944-2877**. www.shafervineyards.com. By appointment only Mon–Fri 9am and 4pm; closed weekends and holidays.

YOUNTVILLE

68 miles N of San Francisco

Yountville (pop. 2,916) was founded by the first white American to settle in the valley, George Calvert Yount. While it lacks the small-town charm of neighboring St. Helena and Calistoga—primarily because its main street, though filling up with hotels, restaurants, and shops, doesn't feel like a center—it's still a great starting point for valley exploration. It's home to a handful of excellent wineries and inns and a small stretch of fab restaurants, including the world-renowned French Laundry.

Domaine Chandon ★★ *Finds* Founded in 1973 by French champagne house Moët et Chandon, the valley's most renowned sparkling winemaker rises to the grand occasion with truly elegant grounds and atmosphere, and more recently a hip vibe, chic decor, and after-hours music and dancing on weekends that's made it a local hot spot. Manicured gardens showcase locally made sculpture, and guests linger—their glasses fizzing with bubbly by a table loaded with snacks—in the festive tasting Salon or under its patio's umbrella shade. In the restaurant, diners indulge in a somewhat formal French-inspired meal (a more casual menu is available at lunchtime). If you can pull yourself away from the Salon's bubbly or still wine (sold in tastings for $7–$22), the comprehensive tours and tastings are interesting, very informative, and friendly. *Note:* The restaurant is closed on Tuesday and Wednesday and has even more restricted winter hours; it usually requires reservations. The Salon has become one of the hottest (and only) places to dance and party after dark; call for hours and details of evening activities.

1 California Dr. (at Hwy. 29), Yountville. ☎ **707/944-2280**. www.chandon.com. Daily 10am–6pm; hours vary by season, so call to confirm. Call or check website for free tour schedules and seasonal hours.

Cosentino Known for its friendly, laid-back atmosphere and vast selection of wines, Cosentino's tasting room is a great stop for anyone interested in covering a lot of wine-tasting ground under one roof. Pay $15 to taste current releases and $20 for reserve wines and you can taste an array of wines from their extensive brand portfolio, which includes Cosentino, CE2V, Legends, Blockheadia, and Crystal Valley Cellars. With more than 40 different wines for sale (ranging from $15 to $160), there's lots of entertainment value at the long, copper-top bar. Join the wine club for free tastings and 25% off purchases.

7415 St. Helena Hwy. (Hwy. 29), Yountville. ☎ **707/944-1220**. www.cosentinowinery.com. Daily 10am–6pm.

OAKVILLE

70 miles N of San Francisco

Driving farther north on Highway 29 brings you to Oakville, most easily recognized by Oakville Cross Road.

Far Niente ★ This storybook stone winery is a serious treat for wine, garden, and classic car lovers. Founded in 1885, it was abandoned for 60 years around prohibition, purchased in 1979 by Gil Nickel (of nearby Nickel & Nickel winery where tours and tastings are $40), and opened to the public for the first time in spring 2004. The $50 by-appointment tour here includes a walk around the beautiful historic stone property, caves, private car collection (truly stunning!), and a huge azalea garden. It finishes with a sampling of five wines (including a delicious chardonnay, cabernet sauvignon, and "Dolce"—their spectacular semillon and sauvignon blanc dessert blend that's sure to make converts of even sweet-wine naysayers). Wine prices range from $56 for chardonnay and $125 for the estate cabernet sauvignon.

1350 Acacia Dr., Oakville. © 800/363-6523 or 707/944-2861. www.farniente.com. (See also www.nickelandnickel. com and www.dolcewine.com.) Tours and tastings by appointment only daily 10am–4pm.

Silver Oak Cellars   Colorado oilman Ray Duncan and former Christian Brothers monk Justin Meyer formed a partnership and a mission to create the finest cabernet sauvignon in the world. The answer was this winery, which produces one of the valley's cabernet kings. Unfortunately, in 2006 a fire destroyed the original Mediterranean-style tasting room. But during rebuilding, which is slated to be complete in early 2009, you can toast with their wines in temporary facilities. Despite the setback, the winery still produces roughly 30,000 cases of Napa Valley cabernet sauvignon annually (an additional 70,000 cases are produced annually at their Alexander Valley winery in Geyserville). Tastings, which include a keepsake bordeaux glass, are $10. No picnic facilities are available.

915 Oakville Cross Rd. (at Money Rd.), Oakville. © 800/273-8809 or 707/944-8808. www.silveroak.com. Tasting room Mon–Sat 9am–4pm.

PlumpJack Winery   If most wineries are like a Brooks Brothers suit, PlumpJack stands out as the Todd Oldham of wine tasting: chic, colorful, a little wild, and popular with a young, hip crowd as well as a growing number of aficionados. Like the franchise's PlumpJack San Francisco restaurants and wine shop, and its Lake Tahoe resort, this playfully medieval winery is a welcome diversion from the same old same old. With Getty bucks behind what was once Villa Mt. Eden winery, the budget covers far more than just atmosphere: There's some serious winemaking going on here, too. For $10 you can sample sauvignon blanc, merlot, syrah, and chardonnay. Alas, there are no tours or picnic spots.

620 Oakville Cross Rd. (just west of the Silverado Trail), Oakville. © 707/945-1220. www.plumpjack.com. Daily 10am–4pm. Reservations required for groups of 8 or more.

Robert Mondavi Winery ★ *Finds*   At mission-style Mondavi, computers control almost every variable in the winemaking process—it's fascinating to watch, especially since Mondavi gives the most comprehensive tours in the valley. Basic jaunts, which cost $25 and last about an hour and 15 minutes, take you through the vineyards and through their winemaking facilities. Ask the guides anything; they know a heck of a lot. After the tour, you taste the results of all this attention to detail in selected current wines. If you're really into learning more about wine, ask about their myriad in-depth tours, such as the $60 "essence tasting," which explores the flavor profiles of wine by sniff-comparing varietals alongside the scents of fresh fruits, spices, and nuts, or their $110 "Celebrating California Wine and Food" tour, which includes a presentation on the history of wine, a tour of the winery, and a three-course luncheon with wine pairing. In summer, the winery also schedules some great outdoor concerts; previous performers included Buena Vista Social Club, Aimee Mann, and Chaka Kahn. Call about upcoming events.

7801 St. Helena Hwy. (Hwy. 29), Oakville. © 888/766-6328, ext. 2000, or 707/226-1395. www.robertmondavi winery.com. Daily 10am–5pm. Reservations recommended for guided tour; book 1 week ahead, especially for weekend tours. Closed Easter, Thanksgiving, Christmas Day, and New Year's Day.

Opus One   A visit to Opus One is a serious and stately affair that was developed in a partnership between Robert Mondavi and Baron Philippe de Rothschild. Today, the state-of-the-art collaboration continues between Baron Philippe de Rothschild and Constellation Brands, which bought out much of Mondavi's winery empire. Architecture buffs in particular will appreciate the tour, which takes in both the impressive Greco-Roman-meets-20th-century building and the no-holds-barred ultra-high-tech production and aging facilities.

This entire facility caters to one ultrapremium wine, which is offered here for a whopping $30 per 4-ounce taste (and a painful $180 per bottle). But wine lovers should happily fork over the cash: It's a memorable red. Grab your glass and head to the redwood rooftop deck to enjoy the view.

7900 St. Helena Hwy. (Hwy. 29), Oakville. ✆ **707/944-9442.** www.opusonewinery.com. Daily 10am–4pm. Tours daily by appointment only; in high season, book a month in advance.

RUTHERFORD

3 miles N of Oakville

If you so much as blink after Oakville, you're likely to overlook Rutherford, the next small town that borders on St. Helena. Each town in Napa Valley has its share of spectacular wineries, but you won't see most of them while driving along Highway 29.

Swanson Vineyards & Winery ☆ *Finds*   The valley's most chic and unique wine tasting is yours with a reservation and a $30 to $55 fee at Swanson. Here the shtick is to treat a tasting more like a private party, which they call a "SA-lon." You and up to seven other guests sit at a centerpiece round table in a vibrant coral parlor adorned with huge paintings, seashells, and a fireplace, and take in the uncommonly refined yet whimsical atmosphere. The table's set more for a dinner party than for a tasting, with Reidel stemware, caviar on potato crisps, slivers of a fine cheese or two, crackers, and one Alexis ganache-filled bonbon, the likes of which you will be glad to know can be purchased on the premises. Over the course of the hour-or-more snack-and-sip event, a winery host will pour four to seven wines, perhaps a bright pinot grigio, merlot, and hearty Alexis, their signature cab-syrah blend, and you're bound to befriend those at the table with you. Definitely a must-do for those who don't mind spending the money.

1271 Manley Lane, Rutherford. ✆ **707/967-3500.** www.swansonvineyards.com. Tasting appointments available Wed–Sun 10am–5pm.

Sawyer Cellars *Finds*   The most attractive thing about Sawyer, aside from its clean and tasty wines, is its dedication to extremely high quality while it maintains a humble, accommodating attitude. Step into the simple restored 1920s barn to see what I mean. Whatever you ask, the tasting-room host will answer. Whatever your request, they do their best to accommodate it. Here you can tour the property on a little tram or learn more about winemaker Brad Warner, who spent 30 years at Mondavi before embarking on this exclusive endeavor. Plunk down $7.50 to taste delicious estate-made wines: sauvignon blanc, merlot, cabernet sauvignon, and Meritage $14–$46 (for current releases), which some argue are worth twice the price. With a total production of only 4,200 cases and a friendly attitude, this winery is a rare treat.

8350 St. Helena Hwy. (Hwy. 29), Rutherford. ✆ **707/963-1980.** www.sawyercellars.com. Tasting by appointment. Tours by appointment. 10am–5pm daily.

St. Supéry Winery *Kids*   The outside looks like a modern corporate office building, but inside you'll find a functional, welcoming winery that encourages first-time tasters to learn more about oenology. On the self-guided tour, you can wander through the demonstration vineyard, where you'll learn about growing techniques. Inside, kids gravitate toward coloring books and "SmellaVision," an interactive display that teaches one how to identify different wine ingredients. Adjoining it is the Atkinson House, which chronicles more than 100 years of winemaking history during public tours at 1 and 3pm. For $20, you can sample four wines, which hopefully includes their excellent and very well priced sauvignon blanc. Even the prices make visitors feel at home: Bottles start at $19 and the tag on their high-end bordeaux red blend is $60.

8440 St. Helena Hwy. (Hwy. 29), Rutherford. (C) 800/942-0809 or 707/963-4507. www.stsupery.com. Daily 10am–5pm (until 5:30pm during summer). $10 tour at 1 and 3pm daily.

Rubicon Estate 🔗   Hollywood meets Napa Valley at Francis Ford Coppola's spectacular 1880s ivy-draped historic stone winery and grounds. Originally known as Inglenook Vineyards, then Niebaum-Coppola, it's now named after its most prestigious wine. You'll have to fork over $25 to visit the estate, but that includes valet parking, a tasting of five wines (they make a gazillion different kinds), a tour of the impeccably renovated grounds, and access to the giant wine bar and retail center and room showcasing Coppola film memorabilia, from Academy Awards to trinkets from *The Godfather* and *Bram Stoker's Dracula*. Wine, food, and gift items dominate the cavernous tasting area, where wines such as an estate-grown blend, cabernet franc, merlot, and zinfandel made from organically grown grapes are sampled. Bottles range from around $16 to more than $100. Along with the basic tour, you can pay extra for more exclusive, specialized tours as well.

1991 St. Helena Hwy. (Hwy. 29), Rutherford. (C) 800/782-4266 or 707/968-1100. www.rubiconestate.com. 10am–5pm daily. Tours daily.

Beaulieu Vineyard   Bordeaux native Georges de Latour founded the third-oldest continuously operating winery in Napa Valley in 1900. With the help of legendary oenologist André Tchelistcheff, he produced world-class, award-winning wines that have been served at the White House since Franklin D. Roosevelt was at the helm. The brick-and-redwood tasting room isn't much to look at, but with Beaulieu's (*Bowl-you*) reputation, it has no need to visually impress. Tastings range in price from $10 to $30 and a number of bottles sell for under $20. The Reserve Tasting Room offers a taste of five reserve wines for $30 and bottles that cost upwards of $100.

1960 St. Helena Hwy. (Hwy. 29), Rutherford. (C) 707/967-5233. www.bvwines.com. Daily 10am–5pm.

Grgich Hills Cellar   Croatian émigré and winemaking Hall of Famer Miljenko (Mike) Grgich (*Grr*-gitch) made his presence known to the world when his 1973 Chateau Montelena chardonnay bested the top French white burgundies at the famous 1976 Paris tasting. Since then, the master vintner teamed up with Austin Hills (of the Hills Brothers coffee fortune) and started this extremely successful and respected winery featuring estate grown wines from organically and biodynamically farmed vineyards.

The ivy-covered stucco building isn't much to behold, and the tasting room is even less appealing, but people don't come here for the scenery: As you might expect, Grgich's chardonnays are legendary—and priced accordingly. The smart buys are the outstanding zinfandel and cabernet sauvignon, which cost around $33 and $58, respectively. The winery also produces a fantastic fumé blanc for around $28 a bottle. Before you leave, be sure to poke your head into the barrel-aging room and inhale the divine aroma. Tastings cost $10 (which includes the glass). No picnic facilities are available.

1829 St. Helena Hwy. (Hwy. 29), north of Rutherford Cross Rd., Rutherford. ☎ 707/963-2784. www.grgich.com. Daily 9:30am–4:30pm. $15 tours by appointment only.

Mumm Napa Valley At first glance, Mumm, housed in a big redwood barn, looks almost humble. Once you're through the front door, however, you'll know that they mean business—big business. Just beyond the extensive gift shop (filled with all sorts of namesake mementos) is the tasting room, where you can purchase sparkling wine by the glass ($6–$15), three-wine flights ($12–$25), or the bottle ($20–$75). You can also take a 45-minute free educational tour—with your dog because this joint is pooch friendly!—and stroll the impressive fine art photography gallery, which features a permanent Ansel Adams collection and ever-changing photography exhibits. Sorry, there's no food or picnicking here.

8445 Silverado Trail (just south of Rutherford Cross Rd.), Rutherford. ☎ 800/686-6272 or 707/967-7730. www.mummnapa.com. Daily 10am–5pm. Tours offered every hr. daily 10am–3pm.

Round Pond 🍷🍷 Cruising up the palm-lined driveway of the impressive Round Pond Estate Winery seems more like a trip to Pablo Escobar's pad than a quiet winery off of Rutherford Road. Surrounded by imported blue agave, palm, and olive trees, Round Pond's sleek and minimalist digs, modeled after nearby Quintessa Winery, are the production facilities for a miniscule 3,000 annual cases of cabernet sauvignon and about 100 cases of Nebbiolo. (Here only the best grapes make the cut, and bottle prices, ranging from $29 to $125, reflect as much.) The estate also grows Spanish and Italian olives, which has resulted in award-winning oils, and red wine vinegars. Book an appointment and you can choose from three tastings, which range from the $25 estate tasting to the very sexy (and pricy) $200 twilight tasting and dinner.

875 Rutherford Rd., between the Silverado Trail and Hwy. 29, Rutherford ☎ 888/302-2575. www.roundpond.com. Winery Thurs–Mon 11am–4pm. Tours and tastings by appointment only. Olive mill is open 7days a week by appointment.

Quintessa 🍷 When you see the giant and striking crescent-shape stone wall up against a small hillside while driving along Highway 29 in Rutherford, you'll know you've arrived at Qunitessa. Beyond the stunning winery design by San Francisco–based Walker Warner Architects the draw here is simple: It's an opportunity to taste from the winery's annual 8,000 cases of one very good and well-known red wine made from a blend of the vineyard's best cabernet sauvignon, merlot, and cabernet franc. Along the way you'll learn a little background in biodynamic farming, a growing technique that takes sustainable farming a step further by basing its practices on the moon's cycles and creating a naturally symbiotic growing environment (hence the property's cows and chickens, which are believed to "calm the vines" and perhaps the crooning of Ugo, Quintessa's oldest employee, who warbles to the wine in the underground barrel caves). It may seem a bit hippie-dippy, but the $65 private tour and tasting with food pairings may just turn you into a believer. If you want to take a potable memento for the road, note that a bottle of wine costs $145.

1601 Silverado Trail, Rutherford. ☎ 707/967-1601. www.quintessa.com. Daily 10am–4pm by appointment only.

ST. HELENA
73 miles N of San Francisco

Located 17 miles north of Napa on Highway 29, this former Seventh-day Adventist village maintains a pseudo–Old West feel while catering to upscale shoppers with deep pockets—hence Vanderbilt and Company, purveyor of fine housewares, at 1429 Main

St. (© **707/963-1010;** www.vanderbiltandcompany.com). St. Helena is a quiet, attractive little town, where you'll find a slew of beautiful old homes and first-rate restaurants, boutiques, and accommodations.

V. Sattui Winery 🌟 *Kids* *Finds*   So what if it's touristy and crowded? This enormous winery is also a fun picnic-party stop thanks to a huge gourmet deli and grassy expanse. It's especially great for families since you can fill up on wine, pâté, and cheese samples without ever reaching for your pocketbook, while the kids romp around the grounds. The gourmet store stocks more than 200 cheeses, sandwich meats, pâtés, breads, exotic salads, and desserts such as white-chocolate cheesecake. (It would be an easier place to graze were it not for the continuous mob scene at the counter.) Meanwhile, the extensive wine offerings flow at the long wine bar in the back. Wines aren't distributed or particularly noteworthy, if you ask me. But if you taste something you simply must have, buy it. (A case purchase will get you membership into their private cellar and its less crowded, private tasting room.) Wine prices start at around $12, with many in the $18 neighborhood; reserves top out at around $75. ***Note:*** To use the picnic area, you must buy food and wine here. On summer weekends, check out the barbecues for $6 to $10.

1111 White Lane (at Hwy. 29), St. Helena. © 707/963-7774. www.vsattui.com. Daily 9am–6pm; winter daily 9am–5pm.

Prager Winery & Port Works *Finds*   If you want an off-the-beaten-track experience, Prager's can't be beat. Turn the corner from Sutter Home winery and roll into the small gravel parking lot; you're on the right track, but when you pull open the creaky old wooden door to this shack of a wine-tasting room, you'll begin to wonder. Don't turn back! Pass the oak barrels, and you'll quickly come upon the clapboard tasting room, made homey with a big Oriental rug, some of the most interesting "wallpaper" you've ever seen, and a Prager family host. Fork over $10 (includes a complimentary glass), and they'll pour you four samples of their wines and ports (which cost $33–$80 per bottle). Also available is "Prager Chocolate Drizzle," a chocolate liqueur sauce that tops ice creams and other desserts. If you're looking for a special gift, consider their bottles, which can be custom etched in the design of your choice for around $85, plus the cost of the wine.

1281 Lewelling Lane (just west of Hwy. 29, behind Sutter Home), St. Helena. © 800/969-7678 or 707/963-7678. www.pragerport.com. Daily 10:30am–4:30pm. Closed on Sundays.

Joseph Phelps Vineyards 🌟   Visitors interested in intimate, comprehensive tours and a knockout tasting should schedule a tour at this winery. A quick turn off the Silverado Trail in Spring Valley (there's no sign—watch for Taplin Rd., or you'll blast right by), Joseph Phelps was founded in 1973 and is a major player in both the regional and the worldwide wine market. Phelps himself accomplished a long list of valley firsts, including launching the syrah varietal in the valley and extending the 1970s Berkeley food revolution (led by Alice Waters) to the Wine Country by founding the Oakville Grocery Co. (p. 307).

A favorite stop for serious wine lovers, this modern, state-of-the-art winery and big-city vibe are proof that Phelps's annual 80,000 cases prove fruitful in more ways than one. When you pass the wisteria-covered trellis to the entrance of the redwood building, you'll encounter an air of seriousness that hangs heavier than harvest grapes. Fortunately, the mood lightens during the informal tasting for $20 or any of the "seminars" like the Blending Seminar, Le Nez Seminar, or the Wine Appreciation Seminar (all $30) that include tastings of five or six wines, mostly reds with a few whites. There's also a short film on the history of the winery. Seminars are 1½ hours on weekdays and 1 hour on weekends. Unfortunately, some wines are so popular that they sell out quickly; come late in the season, and you may not be able to taste or buy them. The three excellently located picnic tables, on the terrace overlooking the valley, are available on a first-come, first-served basis, with preference given to Phelps wine club members (join and get wine shipped a certain number of times per year) who are also able to make a reservation.

200 Taplin Rd. (off the Silverado Trail), P.O. Box 1031, St. Helena. ✆ **800/707-5789** or 707/963-2745. www. jpvwines.com. Mon–Fri 10am–5pm; Sat and Sun 10am–4pm. $30 seminars and tastings by appointment only; weekends at 10am, 11:30am, 1pm, and 2:30pm; weekdays at 11am and 2:30pm. $10 per person for 1-oz. pour of Insignia.

Robert Keenan Winery *(Finds)*

It's a winding, uphill drive to reach secluded Robert Keenan, but this far off the tourist track you're guaranteed more elbowroom at the tasting bar and a quieter, less commercial experience. When you drive in, you'll pass a few modest homes and wonder whether one of the buildings is the family winery. It's not. Keep driving (slowly—kids and dogs at play) until you get to the main building and its redwood tasting room.

The 10,000 cases produced here per year are the result of yet another fast-paced professional who left his business behind and headed for the hills. In this case, it's native San Franciscan Robert Keenan, who ran his own insurance agency for 20 years. When his company merged with another firm and was bought out in 1981, he had already purchased his "retirement property," the winery's 176 acres (48 of which are now planted with grapes), and he soon turned his fascination with winemaking into a second career. The renovated stone building has a much older history, dating back to the old Conradi Winery, which was founded in 1890.

Today, Robert Keenan Winery is known for its big, full-bodied reds, such as the Mountain cab and merlot. Chardonnay, cabernet franc, and zin sold exclusively at the winery range from $29 to $38 per bottle. Older vintages, which you won't find elsewhere, are for sale here as well. Take the tour to learn about the vineyards, production facilities, and winemaking in general. Those looking for a pastoral picnic spot should consider spreading their blankets out here. The three tables, situated right outside the winery and surrounded by vineyards, offer stunning views.

3660 Spring Mountain Rd. (off Hwy. 29), St. Helena. ✆ **707/963-9177**. www.keenanwinery.com. Open Tuesdays through Sundays; by appointment only.

Domaine Charbay Winery & Distillery

After you finally reach this mountaintop hideaway, affectionately called "the Still on the Hill," you immediately get the sense that something special is going on here. Miles Karakasevic, the owner of this family operation, considers himself more of a perfume maker than the 12th-generation master distiller he is, and it's easy to see why. The tiny distillery is crammed with bottles of his latest fragrant projects-in-the-making, such as brandy, whole-fruit-flavor-infused vodkas, grappa, and pastis. He's also become known in the valley for other elixirs: black walnut liqueur, apple brandy, a line of ports, several cabernet sauvignons, and the charter product—Charbay (pronounced Shar-*bay*)—a brandy liqueur blended with chardonnay.

The tour—which costs $20 per person and is a private and exclusive visit—centers around a small, 25-gallon copper alembic still; you'll be lovingly guided through an explanation of the distilling process by gregarious sons Miles, Jr., and Marko, or his wife Susan. You may taste their pre-made cocktails as well. It's all very low-key and laughter-filled at Domaine Charbay, one of the most unique and interesting places to visit in the Wine Country. Sadly, there are no picnic facilities. *Note:* Do not show up without an appointment; you'll be turned away.

4001 Spring Mountain Rd. (5 miles west of Hwy. 29), St. Helena. © **800/634-7845** or 707/963-9327. www.charbay. com. Open daily (except holidays) by appointment only.

Beringer Vineyards ★ *Finds*   You won't find a personal experience at this tourist-heavy stop. But you will get a taste of history within the regal 1876 estate founded by brothers Jacob and Frederick and hand-dug tunnels in the hillside. The oldest continuously operating winery in Napa Valley, Beringer managed to stay open even during Prohibition by cleverly making sacramental wines. White zinfandel is the winery's most popular seller, but plenty of other varietals are available to enjoy. Tastings of current vintages, which range from $5 to $16, are conducted in new facilities, where there's also a large selection of bottles for less than $20. Reserve wines are available for tasting in the remarkable Rhine House for $25 (applied toward purchase), and tours range from the $10 standard or $20 historical to the $35 1½-hour vintage legacy tour. There are several other tours in the $15 to $30 range; check the website for details.

2000 Main St. (Hwy. 29), St. Helena. © **707/963-7115**. www.beringer.com. Oct–May 10am–5pm (last tour 3:30pm, last tasting 4:30pm); June–Sept 10am–6pm (last tour 3:30pm, last tasting 5:30pm).

CALISTOGA
81 miles N of San Francisco

Calistoga, the last tourist town in Napa Valley, got its name from Sam Brannan, entrepreneur extraordinaire and California's first millionaire. After making a bundle supplying miners during the gold rush, he went on to take advantage of the natural geothermal springs at the north end of the valley by building a hotel and spa here in 1859. Flubbing up a speech, in which he compared this natural California wonder to New York State's Saratoga Springs resort town, he serendipitously coined the name "Calistoga," and it stuck. Today, this small, simple resort town, with 5,225 residents and an old-time main street (no building along the 6-block stretch is more than two stories high), is popular with city folk who come here to unwind. Calistoga is a great place to relax and indulge in mineral waters, mud baths, Jacuzzis, massages and, of course, wine. The vibe is more casual—and a little groovier—than you find in neighboring towns to the south.

Frank Family Vineyards ★ *Finds*   "Wine dudes" Dennis, Tim, Jeff, Rick, and Pat will do practically anything to maintain their rightfully self-proclaimed reputation as the "friendliest winery in the valley." In recent years the name may have changed from Kornell Champagne Cellars to Frank-Rombauer to Frank Family, but the vibe has remained constant; it's all about down-home, friendly fun. No muss, no fuss, no intimidation factor. At Frank Family, you're part of their family—no joke. They'll greet you like a long-lost relative and serve you all the bubbly you want (three to four varieties: blanc de blanc, blanc de noir, reserve, and rouge, at $32 to $135 a bottle). Still-wine lovers can slip into the equally casual back room to sample chardonnay and a very well-received cabernet sauvignon. Behind the tasting room is a choice picnic area, situated under the oaks and overlooking the vineyards.

1091 Larkmead Lane (just off the Silverado Trail), Calistoga. © **707/942-0859**. Daily 10am–5pm. No tours offered.

Tips The Ins & Outs of Shipping Wine Home

Perhaps the only things more complex than that $800 case of cabernet you just purchased are the rules and regulations about shipping it home. Because of absurd and forever fluctuating laws—which supposedly protect the business of the country's wine distributors—wine shipping is limited by regulations that vary in each of the 50 states. Shipping rules also vary from winery to winery.

Every single time I write this book, the rules change. This go-round the government is said to be phasing out reciprocity laws and requiring that each state be approved to ship or receive wine. Individual wineries must buy permits for each state they want to ship to, making it difficult for smaller wineries to ship to many states (so most will probably opt only for the states that brandish the most visitors or mail-order demands). Technically, only wineries with permits are allowed to ship wine; shipping stores are not supposed to ship any wine or liquor. That said, they do it anyway, so don't fret if you want to send wine.

If you do get stuck shipping illegally (not that we're recommending you do that, but believe me, it's done all the time and most shipping companies are well aware of it), you might want to package your wine in an unassuming box and head to a post office, UPS, or other shipping company outside the Wine Country area. It's less obvious that you're shipping wine from Vallejo or San Francisco than from Napa Valley.

However, you can try these companies. They are likely to help you out.

Napa Valley Shipping Companies

The UPS Store, at 3212 Jefferson St. in the Grape Yard Shopping Center (© 707/259-1398), claims to pack and ship anything anywhere. Rates for a case of wine were quoted at approximately $32 for ground shipping to Los Angeles and $65 to New York.

St. Helena Mailing Center, 1241 Adams St., at Highway 29, St. Helena (© 707/963-2686), says they will pack and ship to certain states within the U.S. Rates for pre-wrapped shipments are around $30 per case for ground delivery to Los Angeles.

Sonoma Valley Shipping Companies

The UPS Store, 19229 Sonoma Hwy., in Maxwell Village, Sonoma (© 707/935-3438), has a lot of experience with shipping wine. It claims it will ship your wine to any state. Prices vary from $34 to Los Angeles to as much as $79 to the East Coast and $155 to Hawaii and Alaska.

The **Wine Exchange of Sonoma,** 452 First St. E., between East Napa and East Spain streets, Sonoma (© 707/938-1794), will ship your wine, but there's a catch: You must buy an equal amount of any wine at the store (which they assured me would be in stock, and probably at a better rate). Shipping rates range from $19 to Los Angeles to $72 to the East Coast.

Castello di Amorosa ⭐*(Finds)* When I heard V. Sattui Winery owner Daryl Sattui built a 121,000-square-foot stone castle in Calistoga, I thought it *must* be cheesy. Boy was I wrong. The eight-level structure, complete with 90 feet of caves, a dungeon, and torture chamber, is surprisingly authentic (as evidenced by how tired and achy my legs and feet were after tromping on cobblestones). Drop by to get a glimpse of old-world grandiosity and pay $10 to sample a variety of wines, including chardonnay, merlot, cabernet, and dessert wines (bottle prices are steep at between $30 and $75). Or make a reservation for the nearly 2-hour tour, which costs $25 on weekdays and $30 on weekends ($15 for children 10 or older; 9 and under are not permitted). Though the castle is a far cry from quintessential wine country (some liken it to Disneyland), it is fun to browse this stunning architectural accomplishment.

4045 North St. Helena Hwy., Calistoga. ⓒ **707/942-8200** or 286-7273 (for events). www.castellodiamorosa.com. Tasting daily 9:30am–6pm. Tours by reservation only: on the hour weekdays 9:30am–4:30pm, and on the half-hour; weekends and holidays 9:30am–5pm.

Schramsberg ⭐⭐ *(Finds)* Though this 217-acre sparkling wine estate, a landmark once frequented by Robert Louis Stevenson and the second-oldest property in Napa Valley, has undergone its first renovation in 43 years, it still retains its wonderful old-world feel and is one of the valley's all-time best places to explore. Schramsberg is the label that presidents serve when toasting dignitaries from around the globe, and there's plenty of historical memorabilia in the front room to prove it. But the real mystique begins when you enter the sparkling wine caves, which wind 2 miles (reputedly the longest in North America) and were partly hand-carved by Chinese laborers in the 1800s. The caves have an authentic Tom Sawyer ambience, complete with dangling cobwebs and seemingly endless passageways; you can't help but feel you're on an adventure. The comprehensive, unintimidating tour ends in a charming, cozy tasting room, where you'll sample four surprisingly varied selections of their high-end bubbly. Tastings are a bit dear ($35 per person), but it's money well spent. Note that tastings are offered only to those who take the free tour, and you must make reservations in advance.

1400 Schramsberg Rd. (off Hwy. 29), Calistoga. ⓒ **707/942-2414.** www.schramsberg.com. Daily 10am–4pm. Tours and tastings by appointment only. At 10am, 11am, 1pm and 2:30pm.

Sterling Vineyards ⭐ *(Kids)* *(Finds)* No, you don't need climbing shoes to reach this dazzling white Mediterranean-style winery, perched 300 feet up on a rocky knoll. Just fork over $20 ($10 for kids—including a goodie bag) and take the aerial tram, which offers stunning bucolic views along the way. Once you're back on land, follow the self-guided tour (one of the most comprehensive in the Wine Country) of the winemaking process. Wine tastings of five varietals in the panoramic tasting room are included in the tram fare, but more sophisticated sips—limited releases or reserve flights—will set you back anywhere from $3 to $25, respectively. They also offer a guided reserve tasting and tour, limited to 10 people at 11am daily; it's $45 and reservations are highly recommended. Expect to pay anywhere from $14 to $100+ for a souvenir bottle.

1111 Dunaweal Lane (off Hwy. 29, just south of downtown Calistoga), Calistoga. ⓒ **707/942-3344.** www.sterling vineyards.com. Daily 10:30am–4:30pm.

Duckhorn Vineyards With quintessential pastoral surroundings and a unique wine-tasting program, Duckhorn Vineyards has much to offer for visitors interested in spending time to relax and taste. The airy Victorian farmhouse seems very welcoming, not only because you can stand on the veranda and look out on the surrounding meadow, but because the interior affords equally bucolic views. If you want to taste their excellent wines in their surprisingly modern tasting room, complete with cafe tables and a centerpiece bar, you'll pay $20 for a flight of four limited-release wines, or $30 for a semi-private estate-wine tasting, the latter of which you can book in advance. The fee may sound steep, but this is not your run-of-the-mill drink and dash. You'll get plenty of attention and information on their current releases of sauvignon blanc, merlot, and cabernet sauvignon.

1000 Lodi Lane (at the Silverado Trail), St. Helena. ⓒ **707/963-7108.** www.duckhorn.com. Daily 10am–4pm. Reservations recommended.

Cuvaison   In 1969, Silicon Valley engineers Thomas Cottrell and Thomas Parkhill began Cuvaison (pronounced Koo-vay-*sawn,* a French term for the fermentation of wine on the skins) with a 27-acre vineyard of Cabernet. Today, that same vineyard has expanded to 400 acres, producing 63,000 cases of premium wines every year. Known mainly for chardonnays, winemaker Steven Rogstad also produces a limited amount of merlot, pinot noir, cabernet sauvignon, and zinfandel within the handsome Spanish mission–style structure.

Tastings are $15, which includes a glass and as many as eight wines. Wine prices range from $22 for a chardonnay to as much as $80 for a cabernet sauvignon. Beautiful picnic grounds are situated amidst 350-year-old moss-covered oak trees.

4550 Silverado Trail (just south of Dunaweal Lane), Calistoga. ⓒ **707/942-6266.** www.cuvaison.com. Daily 10am–5pm. Tours at 10:30am and 11:30am daily.

BEYOND THE WINERIES: WHAT TO SEE & DO IN NAPA VALLEY
NAPA/ST. HELENA
If you have plenty of time and a penchant for Victorian architecture, seek out the **Napa Valley Conference & Visitors Bureau,** 1310 Napa Town Center, off First Street (ⓒ **707/226-7459,** ext. 106; www.napavalley.com), which offers self-guided walking tours of the town's historic buildings.

A MUSEUM   COPIA: The American Center for Wine, Food & the Arts, at 500 First St. (ⓒ **707/259-1600;** www.copia.org). This $50-million multifaceted facility tackles the topic of how wine and food influence our culture in a myriad of ways, including rotating exhibitions, vast organic vegetable and demonstration gardens, culinary programs, wine classes, concerts, films, and opportunities to dine and drink on the premises. There's not a ton to look at, but youngsters will get a kick out of the Kids' Garden with rabbits and chickens, while connoisseurs might pay extra to slip into a cooking demo. Drop by the cafe for gourmet picnic items or neighboring gift shop for accessories and food-related finds, or have a full-on feast at the adjoining restaurant Julia's Kitchen. Also, drop by Tuesday or Saturday mornings May through October for the outdoor farmers' market and check out their Thursday Outdoor Summer Concert Series for great affordable alfresco entertainment.

Copia admission is $5 for adults, $4 for seniors and students, and free for children 12 and under. Wednesday admissions are half-price for Napa and Sonoma residents. Free for Copia members everyday. The center is open Wednesday through Monday from 10am to 5pm. The restaurant is open Wednesday through Monday for lunch and dinner 11:30am to 9:30pm and Sundays for brunch from 11am until 3pm.

Marketplace ⓕ   Across the street from Copia is the new Oxbow Market, which debuted in fall 2007. A smaller version of San Francisco's Ferry Building Marketplace, the co-op features a cornucopia of tasty tenants, including a number of organic produce vendors, an exceptional rotisserie chicken (try the potatoes too!), a wine bar, yet

> **Finds**   **Enjoying Art & Nature**
>
> Anyone with an appreciation for art absolutely must visit **di Rosa Preserve** (5200 Carneros Hwy. [Hwy. 121/12]; look for the gate; © 707/226-5991; www.dirosapreserve.org). Rene and Veronica di Rosa collected contemporary American art for more than 40 years and then converted their 215 acres of prime property into a monument to Northern California's regional art and nature. Veronica has passed on, but Rene still carries the torch through his world-renowned collection featuring nearly 2,300 works in all media, by more than 900 Greater Bay Area artists. You're not likely to meet him, as the day-to-day operations are now run by a nonprofit staff, but you will be privy to his treasures, which are on display practically everywhere—along the shores of the property's 35-acre lake and in each nook and cranny of their 125-year-old winery-turned-residence, adjoining building, two newer galleries, and gardens. With hundreds of surrounding acres of rolling hills (protected under the Napa County Land Trust), this place is a must-see for both art and nature lovers. Tours range from a $10 1-hour overview at 10 and 11am Tuesday through Friday to the $15 2-hour extended home tour at 1pm to the $15 2-hour sculpture meadow tour. On Saturdays you may take a guided 2½ hour tour for $15. Reservations recommended. Drop-ins are welcome at the Gatehouse Gallery Tuesday through Friday from 9:30am to 3pm and Saturday by appointment; $3 suggested donation. Check website for times. Reservations recommended.

another outpost of Taylor's Automatic Refresher (see St. Helena restaurants for details), an outstanding organic ice cream vendor, a food-related antique shop, and many other reasons to loosen your belt and your grip on your wallet. Open daily. Check the website for hours of operation for specific vendors.

610 and 644 First Street, adjacent to Copia. © 707/226-6529. www.oxbowpublicmarket.com.

BIKING   The quieter northern end of the valley is an ideal place to rent a bicycle and ride the Silverado Trail. **St. Helena Cyclery,** 1156 Main St. (© 707/963-7736; www.sthelenacyclery.com), rents bikes for $10 per hour or $30 a day, including rear rack, helmet, lock, and bag in which you can pack a picnic.

SHOPPING   Shopaholics should make a beeline to the **Napa Premium Outlets** (© 707/226-9876; www.premiumoutlets.com), where Barneys New York can inspire even a jaded local to take the First Street exit off Highway 29 and brave the crowds. Unfortunately, Barneys now carries only cheap outlet-store stuff, but, you'll find multiple places to part with your money, including TSE (killer cashmere at bargain prices), Banana Republic, Calvin Klein, Nine West, Benetton, Jones New York, BCBG, more fashion shops, a few kitchenware and gift shops, a food court, and a decent (but expensive) sushi restaurant. Shops are open Monday through Thursday from 10am to 8pm, Friday and Saturday 10am to 9pm and Sunday from 10am to 6pm. Call for seasonal hours.

St. Helena's Main Street ℛ is the best place to go if you're suffering from serious retail withdrawal. Here you'll find trendy fashions at **Pearl** (1428 Main St.;

℃ 707/963-3236), Jimmy Choo shoes at **Footcandy** (1239 Main St.; ℃ 707/963-2040), chic pet gifts at **Fideaux** (1312 Main St.; ℃ 707/967-9935), custom-embroidered French linens at **Jan de Luz** (1219 Main St.; ℃ 707/963-1550), estate jewelry at **Patina** (1342 Main St.; ℃ 707/963-5445), and European home accessories, sample holiday table settings, and free gift-wrapping at **Vanderbilt and Company** (1429 Main St.; ℃ 707/963-1010).

Most stores are open 10am to 5pm daily; the mall is on Main Street, between Pope and Pine streets, St. Helena.

Shopaholics should also take the sharp turn off Highway 29 two miles north of downtown St. Helena to the **St. Helena Premier Outlets** (℃ **707/963-7282;** www.sthelenapremieroutlets.com). Featured designers include Escada, Brooks Brothers, and Tumi. The stores are open daily from 10am to 6pm.

One last favorite stop: **Napa Valley Olive Oil Manufacturing Company,** 835 Charter Oak Ave., at the end of the road behind Tra Vigne restaurant (℃ **707/963-4173**). The tiny market presses and bottles its own oils and sells them at a fraction of the price you'll pay elsewhere. In addition, it has an extensive selection of Italian cooking ingredients, imported snacks, great deals on dried mushrooms, and a picnic table in the parking lot. You'll love the age-old method for totaling the bill, which you simply must find out for yourself. Drop by any day between 8am and 5:30 pm.

SPA-ING IT If the Wine Country's slow pace and tranquil vistas aren't soothing enough for you, the region's diverse selection of spas can massage, bathe, wrap, and steam you into an overly pampered pulp. Should you choose to indulge, do so toward the end of your stay—when you've wined and dined to the point where you have only enough energy left to make it to and from the spa. Good choices include **Dr. Wilkinson's Hot Springs,** 1507 Lincoln Ave., Calistoga (℃ 707/942-4102); **Calistoga Spa Hot Springs,** 1006 Washington St., Calistoga (℃ 707/942-6269); and **Meadowood,** 900 Meadowood Lane, St. Helena (℃ 707/963-3646).

CALISTOGA

BIKING Cycling enthusiasts can rent bikes from **Getaway Adventures/Wine Country Adventures** (℃ **800/499-2453** or 707/568-3040; www.getawayadventures.com). Full-day group tours cost $125 per person, including lunch and a visit to four or five wineries, $105 per person for private groups of six or more. Bike rental without a tour costs $30 per day plus a $45 delivery fee to Napa Valley locations. You can also inquire about the company's kayaking and hiking tours.

MUD BATHS The one thing you should do while you're in Calistoga is what people have been doing here for the past 150 years: Take a mud bath. The natural baths

---

Tips **Sip Tip**

You can cheaply sip your way through downtown Napa without ever getting behind the wheel with the new "Taste Napa Downtown" wine card. For a mere $20, you get 10-cent tasting privileges at 10 local winecentric watering holes and tasting rooms, all of which are within walking distance of each other. Plus you'll get 10% discounts at tasting rooms. Available at the **Napa Valley Conference & Visitors Bureau** (1310 Napa Town Center, off First St.; ℃ **707/226-7459,** ext. 106). Learn more at **www.napadowntown.com.**

contain local volcanic ash, imported peat, and naturally boiling mineral hot-springs water, mulled together to produce a thick mud that simmers at a temperature of about 104°F (40°C). Sinking into a cement tub filled with hot, dense peat and mud is creepy-fun—and also a memorable travel experience.

Indulge yourself at any of these Calistoga spas: **Dr. Wilkinson's Hot Springs,** 1507 Lincoln Ave. ((©) 707/942-4102); **Golden Haven Hot Springs Spa,** 1713 Lake St. ((©) 707/942-6793); **Calistoga Spa Hot Springs,** 1006 Washington St. ((©) 707/942-6269); **Calistoga Village Inn & Spa,** 1880 Lincoln Ave. ((©) 707/942-0991); **Indian Springs Resort,** 1712 Lincoln Ave. ((©) 707/942-4913); or **Roman Spa Motel,** 1300 Washington St. ((©) 707/942-4441).

NATURAL WONDERS   Old Faithful Geyser of California, 1299 Tubbs Lane ((©) **707/942-6463;** www.oldfaithfulgeyser.com), is one of only three "old faithful" geysers in the world. It's been blowing off steam at regular intervals for as long as anyone can remember. On average, the 350°F (176°C) water spews at a height of about 40 to 60 feet every 40 minutes, day and night, and the performance lasts about 3 minutes (*Note:* Height and length of time are weather-dependent.) You can bring a picnic lunch to munch on between spews. An exhibit hall, gift shop, and snack bar are open every day. Admission is $8 for adults, $7 for seniors, $3 for children 6 to 12, and free for children 5 and under. Check the website for discount coupons. The geyser is open daily from 9am to 6pm (to 5pm in winter). To get there, follow the signs from downtown Calistoga; it's between Highway 29 and Calif. 128.

You won't see thousands of trees turned into stone, but you'll still find many interesting petrified specimens at the **Petrified Forest,** 4100 Petrified Forest Rd. ((©) **707/942-6667;** www.petrifiedforest.org). Volcanic ash blanketed this area after an eruption near Mount St. Helena 3 million years ago. You'll find redwoods that have turned to rock through the slow infiltration of silicas and other minerals, a .25-mile walking trail, a museum, a discovery shop, and picnic grounds. Admission is $6 for adults, $5 for seniors 60 and over and juniors 12 to 17, $3 for children 6 to 11, and free for children 5 and under; look on the website for discount coupons. The forest is open daily from 9am to 7pm (to 5pm in winter). Heading north from Calistoga on Calif. 128, turn left onto Petrified Forest Road, just past Lincoln Street.

WHERE TO STAY IN NAPA VALLEY

Accommodations in Napa Valley run the gamut—from motels and B&Bs to world-class luxury retreats—and all are easily accessible from the main highway. While I recommend staying in the more romantically pastoral areas such as St. Helena, there's no question you're going to find better deals in the towns of Napa or laid-back Calistoga.

When planning your trip, keep in mind that during the high season—April to November—most hotels charge peak rates and sell out completely on weekends; many also have a 2-night minimum. If you need help organizing your Wine Country vacation,

Pricing Categories

The listings in this section are arranged first by area, then by price, using the following categories: **Very Expensive,** more than $250 per night; **Expensive,** $200 to $250 per night; **Moderate,** $150 to $200 per night; and **Inexpensive,** less than $150 per night.

contact an agency. **Bed & Breakfast Inns of Napa Valley** (© **707/944-4444;** www.bbinv.com), an association of B&Bs, provides descriptions and lets you know who has rooms available. **Napa Valley Reservations Unlimited** (© **800/251-6272** or 707/252-1985; www.napavalleyreservations.com) is also a source for booking everything from hot-air balloon rides to wine-tasting tours by limousine.

NAPA

Wherever tourist dollars are to be had, you're sure to find big hotels with familiar names, catering to independent vacationers, business travelers, and groups. **Embassy Suites,** 1075 California Blvd., Napa, CA 94559 (© **800/362-2779** or 707/253-9540), offers 205 of its usual two-room suites, which here happen to be newly renovated. Each includes a galley kitchen complete with coffeemaker, fridge, microwave, and wet bar; they also have a dataport and two TVs and access to indoor and outdoor pools and a restaurant. Rates range from $189 to $344 and include cooked-to-order breakfast, 2-hour beverage reception from 5:30 to 7:30pm, complimentary passes to a nearby health club, and free parking. The 272-room **Napa Valley Marriott,** 3425 Solano Ave., Napa, CA 94558 (© **800/228-9290** or 707/253-8600; www.marriott.com), has an exercise room, a heated outdoor pool and spa, and two restaurants; rates range from $119 to $329 for rooms, $350 to $500 for suites.

Moderate

Cedar Gables Inn 𝄐𝄐 (*Finds*)   This grand, romantic B&B in Old Town Napa is in a stunning Shakespearean/Renaissance style building, built in 1892. Rooms reflect that era, with rich tapestries and stunning gilded antiques. Four have fireplaces, five have whirlpool tubs, and all feature queen-size brass, wood, or iron beds. Guests meet each evening in front of the roaring fireplace in the lower family room for wine and cheese. At other times, the family room is a perfect place to cuddle up and watch the large-screen TV. Bonuses include a three-course gourmet breakfast each morning, port in every room, and VIP treatment at many local wineries.

486 Coombs St. (at Oak St.), Napa, CA 94559. © **800/309-7969** or 707/224-7969. Fax 707/224-4838. www.cedargablesinn.com. 9 units. $199–$339 double. Rates include full breakfast, evening wine and cheese, and port. AE, DISC, MC, V. From Hwy. 29 N, exit onto First St. and follow signs to downtown; turn right onto Jefferson, and left on Oak; house is on the corner. **Amenities:** Dataport (in the shared living room). *In room:* A/C, free Wi-Fi, hair dryer, iron, ironing board, deluxe bathrobes.

Napa River Inn 𝄐𝄐   Downtown Napa's most luxurious hotel manages an old-world boutique feel throughout most of its three buildings. The main building, part of the renovated Historic Napa Mill and Hatt Market Building, is an 1884 historic landmark. Each of its fantastically appointed rooms is exceedingly romantic, with burgundy-colored walls, original brick, wood furnishings, plush fabrics, seats in front of the gas fireplace, and claw-foot tubs in the bathrooms. A newer and more modern themed addition overlooking the river and a patio boasts bright and airy accommodations. Yet another building houses the less luxurious but equally well-appointed mustard-and-brown rooms that also overlook the riverfront, but have a nautical theme and less daylight. A new river front plaza promises spacious outdoor seating in a picturesque setting. Perks abound and include instant access to downtown dining, complimentary vouchers to breakfast at adorable Sweetie Pie's bakery, and wine at the nearby swank wine bar, the Bounty Hunter. A small but excellent spa and outstanding restaurant (Angèle) are located on the property.

500 Main St., Napa, CA 94559. ℂ **877/251-8500** or 707/251-8500. Fax 707/251-8504. www.napariverinn.com. 66 units. $199–$399 double; $299–$499 suite. Rates include vouchers to a full breakfast and wine tasting at the nearby Bounty Hunter. AE, DC, DISC, MC, V. Pets $25 per night. **Amenities:** 2 restaurants; concierge; business services; same-day laundry service/dry cleaning. *In room:* A/C, TV, dataport, free Wi-Fi, fridge, coffeemaker, hair dryer, iron, CD clock radio/MP3 docking station.

Inexpensive

Chablis Inn 𝒌   There's no way around it: If you want to sleep cheaply in a town where the *average* room rate tops $200 per night in high season, you're destined for a motel. Look on the bright side: Because your room is likely to be little more than a crash pad after a day of eating and drinking, a clean bed and a remote control are all you'll really need anyway. And Chablis offers much more than that. All of the motel-style rooms are super clean, and some even boast kitchenettes or whirlpool tubs. Guests have access to a heated outdoor pool and hot tub.

3360 Solano Ave., Napa, CA 94558. ℂ **800/443-3490** or 707/257-1944. Fax 707/226-6862. www.chablisinn.com. 34 units. May to mid-Nov $99–$250 double; mid-Nov to Apr $79–$150 double. AE, DC, DISC, MC, V. **Amenities:** Heated outdoor pool; Jacuzzi. *In room:* A/C, satellite TV, dataport, free Wi-Fi, kitchenette in some rooms, fridge, coffeemaker, hair dryer, help computer at the front desk.

Château Hotel   This contemporary two-story motel complex tries to evoke the aura of a French country inn, but it isn't fooling anybody—a basic motel's a basic motel. However, the plain-Jane rooms are C-H-E-A-P and bathrooms are spacious, and have separate vanity/dressing areas. Some units have refrigerators and ten rooms are specially designed for guests with disabilities. If you're used to a daily swim, you'll be glad to know that the Château also has a heated pool and spa. Bargain travelers, be sure to ask about discounts; some special rates will knock the price down by $20.

4195 Solano Ave., Napa, CA 94558. ℂ **800/253-6272** in CA or 707/253-9300. Fax 707/253-0906. www.napavalley chateauhotel.com. 115 units. Apr–Oct $119–$169 double; Nov–Mar $99 double. Continental breakfast included. AAA, government, corporate, senior, and other discounts available. AE, DISC, DC, MC, V. From Hwy. 29 north, turn left just past Trower Ave., at the entrance to the Napa Valley wine region. **Amenities:** Restaurant; hot tub; conference facilities. *In room:* A/C, TV, coffee maker, hair dryer.

Napa Valley Travelodge 𝒱𝑎𝑙𝑢𝑒   In these parts, rarely does so much come so cheaply. This Travelodge has been around for a while, but in early 1998, the owners gutted the entire place with the intent of turning it into a "New Orleans–style" motel (including a cobblestone center courtyard/parking area). Although there are no wild partiers hanging over the balconies throwing beads, there's still plenty to celebrate. Every room has a VCR, a 25-inch TV, and a coffeemaker; some feature a Jacuzzi tub; and they are all in a great part of downtown Napa—within walking distance of the city's best dining. If you're lucky enough to secure a room, you will have gotten one of the best deals around. Ask about discounts for AAA and other clubs.

853 Coombs St., Napa, CA 94559. ℂ **800/578-7878** or 707/226-1871. Fax 707/226-1707. 45 units. $109–$189 double. DC, DISC, MC, V. **Amenities:** Heated outdoor pool; access to nearby fitness center (fee); video library; coin-operated laundry. *In room:* A/C, TV/VCR, hair dryer, iron.

YOUNTVILLE
Very Expensive
Napa Valley Lodge 𝒌 𝒇𝑖𝑛𝑑𝑠   Just off Highway 29, beyond a wall that does a good job of blocking the road, this lodge's guest rooms are large, ultraclean, and better appointed than many in the area, especially since all of the rooms were renovated in 2007 and now have spacious bathrooms with dual showerheads. Many also have vaulted ceilings, and 39 have fireplaces. Each comes with a king-size or two queen-size

beds, wicker furnishings, robes, and a private balcony or a patio. Ground-level units are smaller and get less sunlight than those on the second floor. Suites boast king-size beds and Jacuzzi tubs. Extras include a concierge, afternoon tea and cookies in the lobby, Friday-evening wine tasting in the library, and a continental breakfast—with all this, it's no wonder AAA gave the Napa Valley Lodge the four-diamond award for excellence. Ask about winery tour packages and winter discounts, the latter of which can be as high as 30%.

2230 Madison St., Yountville, CA 94599. © 800/368-2468 or 707/944-2468. Fax 707/944-9362. www.napavalley lodge.com. 55 units. $229–$575 double. Rates include champagne breakfast buffet, afternoon tea and cookies, and Fri–evening wine tasting. AE, DC, DISC, MC, V. **Amenities:** Heated outdoor pool; small exercise room; spa; Jacuzzi; redwood sauna; concierge; in-room massage. *In room:* A/C, ceiling fan, TV w/pay movies, free Wi-Fi, minibar, coffeemaker, hair dryer, iron.

Villagio Inn & Spa 🐿🐿   Set next to a small vineyard in the center of walkable Yountville, this luxury resort with immaculately maintained grounds is a choice spot if you want to lounge by a pool, indulge in spa treatments at their swank new spa, or linger over complimentary champagne breakfast (served each morning). Rooms beg to be enjoyed, too, especially if you pull the cork on the complimentary bottle of chardonnay, prop yourself up in a four-poster queen size bed, and loll in front of the flat-screen TV, on your balcony or porch, or in the bathroom's Jacuzzi for two. Most rooms also have fireplaces, and, alas, sometimes a fake-log aroma to go with them.

6481 Washington St., Yountville 94599. © 800/351-1133 or 707/944-8877. Fax 707944-8855/. www.villagio.com. 112 units. $280–$675 double. Rates include champagne breakfast buffet and complimentary wine upon arrival. AE, DISC, MC, V. **Amenities:** Pool; tennis court; spa; Jacuzzi; concierge; business center; in-room massage; laundry service; dry cleaning. *In room:* A/C, TV/VCR with on-demand movies, free Wi-Fi, fridge, coffeemaker, iron.

Inexpensive

Maison Fleurie 🐿🐿   It's impossible not to enjoy your stay at Maison Fleurie. One of the prettiest garden-set B&Bs in the Wine Country, it comprises a trio of beautiful 1873 brick-and-fieldstone buildings overlaid with ivy. The main house—a charming Provençal replica with thick brick walls, terra-cotta tile, and paned windows—holds seven rooms; the rest are in the old bakery building and the carriage house. Some feature private balconies, patios, sitting areas, Jacuzzi tubs, and fireplaces. An above-par breakfast is served in the quaint little dining room; afterward, you're welcome to wander the landscaped grounds or hit the wine-tasting trail, returning in time for afternoon hors d'oeuvres and wine.

6529 Yount St. (btw. Washington St. and Yountville Cross Rd.), Yountville, CA 94559. © 800/788-0369 or 707/944-2056. Fax 707/944-9342. www.maisonfleurienapa.com. 13 units. $135–$300 double. Rates include full breakfast and afternoon hors d'oeuvres. AE, DC, DISC, MC, V. **Amenities:** Heated outdoor pool; Jacuzzi; free use of bikes. *In room:* A/C, TV, dataport, free Wi-Fi, hair dryer, iron.

OAKVILLE & RUTHERFORD
Very Expensive
Auberge du Soleil 🐿🐿🐿 *Moments*   This spectacular Relais & Châteaux member is one of the most exclusive luxury retreats in all of California. Set high above Napa Valley in a 33-acre olive grove, contemporary California bungalow-like rooms are large enough to get lost in . . . and you might want to, once you discover all the amenities. In the private living room, oversize, cushy furniture surrounds a wood-burning fireplace—the ideal place to relax and listen to the CD selection or watch one of the room's two flatscreen TVs. Fresh flowers, original art, wood floors, and a minibar complete with drinks and snacks are the best of luxury home-away-from-home. Each sun-washed

private deck has views of the valley that are nothing less than spectacular. All guests have access to a celestial swimming pool, exercise room, and a fabulous spa. Although only guests can use the spa, you can savor Auberge's romantic grandeur without staying overnight if you have lunch on the terrace of their restaurant overlooking the valley (see p. 308 for more information). *Parents take note:* This is not a kid-friendly place.

180 Rutherford Hill Rd., Rutherford, CA 94573. ⓒ **800/348-5406** or 707/963-1211. Fax 707/963-8764. www. aubergedusoleil.com. 50 units. $525–$1,025 double; $1,000–$1,850 suite. AE, DC, DISC, MC, V. From Hwy. 29 in Rutherford, turn right on Calif. 128 and go 3 miles to the Silverado Trail; turn left and head north about 600 ft. to Rutherford Hill Rd.; turn right. **Amenities:** Restaurant; 3 outdoor pools ranging from hot to cold; tennis court; health club and full-service spa; outdoor Jacuzzi; sauna; steam room; bikes; concierge; secretarial services; free wired Internet or Wi-Fi; room service; massage; same-day laundry service/dry cleaning; art gallery and plain-air art supplies; daily newspapers. *In room:* A/C, TV/DVD w/HBO, dataport, free Wi-Fi, kitchenette, minibar, fridge, coffeemaker, hair dryer, iron, stereo, MP3 docking stations.

Moderate

Rancho Caymus Inn ⚜ This cozy Spanish-style hacienda, with two floors opening onto wisteria-covered balconies was the creation of sculptor Mary Tilden Morton (whose dad was a forestry baron; Berkeley's Tilden Park is named for him). Morton wanted each room in the hacienda to be a work of art, so she employed the most skilled craftspeople she could find. As a result you'll find Morton-designed adobe fireplaces in 22 of 26 rooms, and artifacts she gathered in Mexico and South America.

Decent-size guest rooms surround a whimsical garden courtyard with an enormous outdoor fireplace. The mix-and-match decor is on the funky side, with braided rugs and overly varnished imported carved wood furnishings. But it's hard to balk when they include wet bars, sitting areas with sofa beds and small private patios. Most of the suites have fireplaces, one has a kitchenette, and five have whirlpool tubs. Breakfast, which includes fresh fruit, granola, orange juice, and pastries, is served in the inn's dining room.

1140 Rutherford Rd., P.O. Box 78, Rutherford, CA 94573. ⓒ **800/845-1777** or 707/963-1777. Fax 707/963-5387. www.ranchocaymus.com. 26 suites. $175–$435 double; $215–$410 master suite; $275–$450 2-bedroom suite. Rates include continental breakfast. AE, MC, V. From Hwy. 29 N, turn right onto Rutherford Rd./Calif. 128 east; the hotel is on your left. **Amenities:** Restaurant. *In room:* A/C, TV, dataport, free Wi-Fi, kitchenette in 1 room, minibar, fridge, microwave in master suite, coffeemaker, hair dryer, iron in some rooms.

ST. HELENA
Very Expensive

Harvest Inn ⚜⚜ One of the valley's few sprawling resorts, this 74-unit property has wonderfully spacious accommodations, all of which are uniquely decorated with warm homey furnishings and nestled into 8 acres of flora; most have fireplaces. Extensive grounds (which include two swimming pools and hot tubs, a spa, and a wine bar) and well-appointed suites make the place popular with wedding parties and families. Although you can't reserve specific rooms in advance, request an abode away from the highway upon arrival. Also, if you're not into climbing stairs, ask for a ground-level room, as some accommodations are on a second story and don't have elevator access.

One Main St., St. Helena, CA 94574. ⓒ **800/950-8466** or 707/963-9463. Fax 707/963-5387. www.harvestinn.com. 74 units. $359–$535 double; $645–$675 suite. Rates include breakfast. AE, MC, V. From Hwy. 29 N, turn left into the driveway at the large HARVEST INN sign. **Amenities:** Complimentary parking and breakfast; evening wine tasting Sat–Sun nights; wine bar; 2 heated outdoor swimming pools; 2 hot tubs; event facilities; mountain bike rentals; in-room massage. *In room:* A/C, TV/DVD, dataport, free Wi-Fi, fridge, coffeemaker, hair dryer, iron, clock radio, twice-daily maid service.

Meadowood Napa Valley ★★ *Finds* At this spectacular resort surrounded by 250 secluded acres of pristine mountainside, freestanding luxury accommodations, which vary in size depending on the price, are scattered amid the expansive hillside grounds. Rooms are freshly furnished with warm colors, lush fabrics, and American country classic furnishings and include beamed ceilings, private patios, stone fireplaces, and forest views. Many are individual suite-lodges so far removed from the common areas that you must drive to get to them—and hike a bit to get to the restaurant or spa. Lazier folks can opt for more centrally located rooms.

The resort offers a wealth of activities: golf on a challenging 9-hole course, tennis on seven championship courts, and croquet (yes, croquet) on two international regulation lawns. There are private hiking trails, a health spa, yoga, two heated pools, and two whirlpools. An added bonus for lazy travelers: Their formal restaurant has great talent cranking out delicious multi-course meals that focus on the seasons and local ingredients.

900 Meadowood Lane, St. Helena, CA 94574. © 800/458-8080 or 707/963-3646. Fax 707/963-3532. www. meadowood.com. 85 units. $475–$825 double; $775–$1,250 1-bedroom suite; $1,275–$2,075 2-bedroom suite; $1,775–$2,900 3-bedroom suite; $2,275–$3,725 4-bedroom suite. Ask about promotional offers and off-season rates. 2-night minimum stay on weekends. AE, DC, DISC, MC, V. **Amenities:** 2 restaurants; 2 large heated outdoor pools (adult and family pools); golf course; 7 tennis courts; health club and full-service spa; Jacuzzi; sauna; concierge; business center; room service; same-day laundry service/dry cleaning weekdays only; 2 croquet lawns. *In room:* A/C, TV, dataport, free high-speed Internet access and Wi-Fi, kitchenette in some rooms, minibar, coffeemaker, hair dryer, iron.

Moderate

Wine Country Inn ★★ Just off the highway behind Freemark Abbey vineyard is one of Wine Country's most personable choices. The attractive wood-and-stone inn, complete with a French-style mansard roof and turret, overlooks a pastoral landscape of vineyards. The individually decorated rooms contain antique furnishings and handmade quilts; most have fireplaces and private terraces overlooking the valley, and others have private hot tubs. The five luxury cottages include king-size beds, a single bed (perfect for the tot in tow), sitting areas, fireplaces, private patios, and three-headed walk-in showers. Suites come with two-person jetted tubs, stereos, plenty of space, and lots of privacy. The family that runs this place puts personal touches everywhere and makes every guest feel welcome. They serve wine and plenty of appetizers nightly, along with a big dash of hotel-staff hospitality in the inviting living room. A full buffet breakfast is served there, too. *Note:* TV junkies book elsewhere. There are no tubes in rooms here.

1152 Lodi Lane, St. Helena, CA 94574. © 888/465-4608 or 707/963-7077. Fax 707/963-9018. www.winecountry inn.com. 29 units, 12 w/shower only. $215–$405 double; $535–$660 for cottages. Rates include breakfast and appetizers. MC, V. **Amenities:** Heated outdoor pool; spa services; Jacuzzi; concierge; free Wi-Fi; big-screen TV in common room. *In room:* A/C, hair dryer, iron.

Inexpensive

El Bonita Motel ★ *Kids* *Value* This 1940s Art Deco motel is a bit too close to Highway 29 for comfort, but the 2½ acres of beautifully landscaped gardens behind the building (away from the road) help even the score. The rooms, while small and nothing fancy (think motel basic), are spotlessly clean and decorated with newer furnishings and kitchenettes; some have a whirlpool bathtub. It ain't heaven, but it is cheap for St. Helena.

195 Main St. (at El Bonita Ave.), St. Helena, CA 94574. © 800/541-3284 or 707/963-3216. Fax 707/963-8838. www.elbonita.com. 41 units. $94–$289 double. Rates include continental breakfast. AE, DC, DISC, MC, V. **Amenities:** Heated outdoor pool; spa; Jacuzzi; free high-speed Internet access in lobby. *In room:* A/C, TV, free Wi-Fi, fridge, microwave, coffeemaker, hair dryer, iron.

CALISTOGA
Very Expensive
Calistoga Ranch ⭐⭐⭐   Tucked into the eastern mountainside on 157 pristine hidden-canyon acres, the 46 rural-chic free-standing luxury cottages may cost more than $700 per night, but if you've got the cash, it's worth the expense. Auberge's sister property boasts stunning grounds and rooms packed with every conceivable amenity (including fireplaces, patios along a wooded area, and cushy outdoor furnishings). Reasons not to leave include a giant swimming pool, a reasonably large gym, an incredibly designed indoor-outdoor spa with a natural thermal pool, and individual pavilions with private-garden soaking tubs, as well as a breathtakingly beautiful restaurant with stunning views of the property's Lake Lommel. Need more enticement? They offer free activities like watercolor painting, yoga, biking, and hiking. Add the startlingly good food (that can be experienced only by guests) to the resort architecture that intentionally tries to blend with the natural surroundings, and you've got a romantically rustic slice of Wine Country heaven.

580 Lommel Rd., Calistoga, CA 94515. ℂ **707/254-2800.** Fax 707/254-2888. www.calistogaranch.com. 46 cottages. $600–$3,200 double. AE, DC, DISC, MC, V. **Amenities:** Restaurant; large heated outdoor pool; gym; activities; spa; Jacuzzi; steam room; concierge; Wi-Fi throughout; room service; massage; laundry service; dry cleaning (next-day). *In room:* A/C, TV/DVD w/DVDs, fax upon request, dataport, free Wi-Fi, 1 lodge w/full kitchen, minibar, fridge, coffeemaker, hair dryer, iron, safe.

Expensive
Cottage Grove Inn ⭐   Standing in two parallel rows at the end of the main strip in Calistoga are adorable cottages that, though on a residential street (with a paved road running between two rows of accommodations), seem removed from the action once you've stepped across the threshold. Each compact guesthouse has a wood-burning fireplace, homey furnishings, a king-size bed with down comforter, and an enormous bathroom with a skylight and a deep, two-person Jacuzzi tub. Guests enjoy such niceties as gourmet coffee, a flat-screen TV, a stereo with CD player, a DVD (the inn has a complimentary DVD library), and a wet bar. Several local spas are within walking distance. This is a top pick if you want to do the Calistoga spa scene in comfort and style. Smoking is allowed only in the gazebos. Bicycles are provided for cruises around town, and guests can recoup a few bucks by using the complimentary tasting passes to more than a dozen nearby wineries.

1711 Lincoln Ave., Calistoga, CA 94515. ℂ **800/799-2284** or 707/942-8400. Fax 707/942-2653. www.cottagegrove.com. 16 cottages. $250–$395 double. Rates include continental breakfast and evening wine and cheese. AE, DC, DISC, MC, V. *In room:* A/C, TV/DVD, dataport, fridge, coffeemaker, hair dryer, iron, safe, robes, wet bar, 40 digital music channels.

Moderate
Christopher's Inn ⭐ *Kids*   A decade of renovations and expansions by architect-owner Christopher Layton has turned sweet old homes at the entrance to downtown into hotel rooms with a little pizzazz. Options in this non-smoking spot range from somewhat simple but tasteful rooms with colorful and impressive antiques and small bathrooms to huge lavish abodes with four-poster beds, rich fabrics and brocades, and sunken Jacuzzi tubs facing a fireplace. Most rooms have fireplaces, and some have flatscreen TVs and DVDs (with cable). Those who prefer homey accommodations will feel comfortable here, since the property doesn't have corporate polish or big-business blandness. The lobby features a 6-foot high fireplace and cappuccino machine,

making it a great place for an afternoon pick-me-up pit stop. The two rather plain but very functional two-bedroom units are ideal for families, provided you're not expecting the Ritz. An expanded continental breakfast is delivered to your room daily.

1010 Foothill Blvd., Calistoga, CA 94515. © **866/876-5755** or 707/942-5755. Fax 707/942-6895. www.christophers inn.com. 24 units. $185–$465 double; $330–$350 house sleeping 5 or 6. Rates include expanded continental breakfast. AE, MC, V. **Amenities:** Non-smoking; 2-person massage studio. *In room:* TV, dataport, free Wi-Fi, free computer hookups.

Euro Spa & Inn ⚘⚘   In a quiet residential section of Calistoga, this small inn and spa provides a level of solitude and privacy that few other spas can match. The horseshoe-shaped inn consists of 13 stucco bungalows, a spa center, and an outdoor patio, where an expanded continental breakfast and snacks are served. The rooms, although small, are pleasantly decorated and come equipped with whirlpool tubs, decks, gas wood stoves, and kitchenettes. Spa treatments range from foot reflexology to minifacials.

1202 Pine St. (at Myrtle), Calistoga, CA 94515. © **707/942-6829.** Fax 707/942-1138. www.eurospa.com. 13 units. $119–$298 double. Rates include expanded continental breakfast. 7 package discounts available. AE, DC, DISC, MC, V. **Amenities:** Outdoor heated pool; Jacuzzi. *In room:* A/C, TV, free Wi-Fi, kitchenette, hair dryer, iron, robes.

The Silver Rose Inn and Spa closed in June 2008 to undergo a complete transformation into an ultra-premium five-star resort under new management. It is slated to open in 2010.

Inexpensive

Calistoga Spa Hot Springs ⚘ *Kids* *Value*   Very few hotels in the Wine Country cater specifically to families with children, which is why I recommend Calistoga Spa Hot Springs if you're bringing the little ones: They classify themselves as a family resort and are accommodating to visitors of all ages. In any case, it's a great bargain, offering unpretentious yet comfortable rooms, as well as a plethora of spa facilities. All of Calistoga's best shops and restaurants are within easy walking distance, and you can even whip up your own grub at the barbecue grills near the large pool and patio area.

1006 Washington St. (at Gerard St.), Calistoga, CA 94515. © **866/822-5772** or 707/942-6269. www.calistogaspa. com. 57 units. $136–$196 double. Discounted rates available weekdays November through February, excluding holidays. MC, V. **Amenities:** 3 heated outdoor pools; kids' wading pool; exercise room; spa. *In room:* A/C, TV, kitchenette, fridge, coffeemaker, hair dryer, iron.

Dr. Wilkinson's Hot Springs Resort ⚘   This spa/"resort," in the heart of Calistoga, is one of the best deals in Napa Valley. The rooms range from attractive Victorian-style accommodations to cozy, recently renovated guest rooms in the main 1960s-style motel. All rooms, which have flat-screens and iPod players, are spiffier than most of the area's other hotels, with surprisingly tasteful textiles and basic motel-style accoutrements. Larger rooms have refrigerators and/or kitchens. Facilities include three mineral-water pools (two outdoor and one indoor), a Jacuzzi, a steam room, and mud baths. All kinds of body treatments are available in the spa, including famed mud baths, steams, and massage—all of which I highly recommend. Be sure to inquire about their excellent packages and their sister property, Hideaway Cottages, which offers fully equipped multi-room cottages at amazingly good prices.

1507 Lincoln Ave. (Calif. 29, between Fairway and Stevenson aves.), Calistoga, CA 94515. © **707/942-4102.** www.drwilkinson.com. 42 units. $139–$299 double; $164–$600 for the Hideaway cottages. Weekly discounts and packages available. AE, MC, V. **Amenities:** 3 pools; spa; Jacuzzi; steam room; mud baths; free Wi-Fi in lobby. *In room:* A/C, TV, dataport, coffeemaker, hair dryer, iron, voice mail.

WHERE TO DINE IN NAPA VALLEY

Napa Valley's restaurants draw as much attention to the valley as its award-winning wineries. Nowhere else in the state are kitchens as deft at mixing fresh seasonal, local, organic produce into edible magic, which means that menus change constantly to reflect the best available ingredients. Add that to a great bottle of wine and stunning views, and you have one heck of an eating experience. To best enjoy Napa's restaurant scene, keep one thing in mind: Reserve in advance—especially for a seat in a famous room.

NAPA
Moderate
Angèle ⭑⭑ COUNTRY FRENCH   I love this riverside spot for two reasons: The food is great, and the surroundings are some of the best in the valley. Its cozy combo of raw wood beams, taupe-tinted concrete-block, concrete slab floors, bright yellow leather bar stools, candlelight, and a heated, shaded patio (weather permitting) has always been great for intimate dining. New chef Aaron Meneghelli, previously at Calistoga Ranch, is keeping the same level of quality that former chef Tripp Mauldin instilled with his fabulous crispy roast chicken with summer corn, chanterelles, lardons, baby potatoes, and *jus;* outstanding burgers; and tasty seafood such as king salmon with arugula salad, heirloom tomatoes, olives, basil, and Parmesan. During winter eves, opt for the rustic-chic indoors; for summer, settle into one of the outdoor seats. And if you're a banana fan, definitely try their cobbler version for dessert; with fresh banana slices submerged in pastry cream and topped with crisp crumbly topping, it's deliciously decadent.

540 Main St. (in the Hatt Building). © 707/252-8115. Reservations recommended. Main courses $18–$32. AE, MC, V. Daily 11:30am–10pm.

Bistro Don Giovanni ⭑⭑⭑ *Value* REGIONAL ITALIAN   Donna and Giovanni Scala own this bright, bustling, and cheery Italian restaurant, which also happens to be one of my favorite restaurants in Napa Valley. Fare prepared by chef/partner Scott Warner highlights quality ingredients and California flair and never disappoints, especially when it comes to the thin-crusted pizzas and house-made pastas. Every time I grab a menu, I can't get past the salad of beets and *haricots verts* or the pasta with duck Bolognese. On the rare occasion that I do, I am equally smitten with outstanding classic pizza Margherita fresh from the wood-burning oven, seared wild salmon filet perched atop a tower of buttermilk mashed potatoes, and steak frites. My only complaint: Over the past few years the appetizers have been getting skimpier and more expensive and the staff has been more aloof. But don't let these drawbacks deter you. Alfresco dining in the vineyards is available—and highly recommended on a warm, sunny day. Midwinter, I'm a fan of ordering a bottle of wine (always expensive here) and dining at the bar. Desserts seriously rock, so be sure to partake.

4110 Howard Lane (at St. Helena Hwy.). © 707/224-3300. www.bistrodongiovanni.com. Reservations recommended. Main courses $12–$24. AE, DC, DISC, MC, V. Sun–Thurs 11:30am–10pm; Fri–Sat 11:30am–11pm.

Inexpensive
Alexis Baking Company ⭑ BAKERY/CAFE   Alexis (also known as ABC) is a quaint, casual stop for residents and in-the-know tourists. On weekend mornings—especially Sunday, which is when you'll find me devouring their out-of-this-world huevos rancheros and classic eggs Benedict—the line stretches out the door. Once you order (from the counter during the week and at the table on Sun) and find a seat, you

Pricing Categories

The restaurants listed in this section are classified first by town, then by price, using the following categories: **Very Expensive,** dinner from $75 per person; **Expensive,** dinner from $50 per person; **Moderate,** dinner from $35 per person; and **Inexpensive,** less than $35 per person for dinner. These categories reflect prices for an appetizer, a main course, a dessert, and a glass of wine.

can relax and enjoy the coffeehouse atmosphere. Start your day with spectacular pastries, coffee drinks, and breakfast goodies like pumpkin pancakes with sautéed pears. Lunch also bustles with locals who come for simple, fresh fare like grilled hamburgers with Gorgonzola, grilled-chicken Caesar salad, roast lamb sandwich with minted mayo and roasted shallots on rosemary bread, and lentil bulgur orzo salad. (Sorry, fries lovers; you won't find any here.) Desserts run the gamut; during the holidays, they include a moist and magical steamed persimmon pudding. Oh, and the pastry counter's cookies and cakes beg you to take something for the road.

1517 Third St. (btw. Main and Jefferson sts.). © **707/258-1827.** www.alexisbakingcompany.com. Main courses $6–$13 breakfast, $7–$11 lunch. MC, V. Mon–Fri 6:30am–4pm; Sat 7:30am–3pm; Sun 8am–2pm.

Pizza Azzurro ✿ ITALIAN   This casual, cheery, family-friendly restaurant, serves the best fancy thin-crust pies in downtown Napa. Unlike many Valley dining rooms, the place has an authentic neighborhood feel thanks to a very low-key atmosphere, and the continual presence of chef/owner Michael Gyetvan who spent 10 years in the kitchens of Tra Vigne, One Market, and Lark Creek Inn. While killer thin-crust pizzas—such as the incredible *Salsiccia* (tangy tomato sauce, rustic Sonoma-made fennel pork sausage, crunchy red onion, and mozzarella) star here, they've got great salads, too. Pastas, such as rigatoni in red sauce with hot Italian sausage and mushrooms, play it safe, while *manciatas*—soft, lightly cooked pizza dough meant to be folded and eaten like a soft taco—are very satisfying. (Try the B.B.L.T. version.) Although Bistro Don Giovanni is king of fancy pasta and pizza fixes, Azzurro is cheaper and far better if you've got the kids in tow or want to have a low-key or fast dinner.

1260 Main St. (at Clinton St.). © **707/255-5552.** No reservations except for 8 or more. Main courses $9.95–$12. AE, MC, V. Mon–Fri 11:30am–11pm; Sat–Sun 5–11pm.

Villa Corona ✿ MEXICAN   The best Mexican food in town is served in this bright, funky, and colorful restaurant hidden in the southwest corner of a strip mall behind an unmemorable sports bar and restaurant. The winning plan here is simple: Order and pay at the counter, sit at either a table inside or at one of the few sidewalk seats, and wait for the huge burritos, enchiladas, and chimichangas to be delivered to your table. Those with pork preferences shouldn't miss the carnitas, which are abundantly flavorful and juicy. My personal favorites are hard-shell tacos or chicken enchiladas with light savory red sauce, a generous side of beans, and rice. Don't expect to wash down your menudo, or anything else for that matter, with a margarita. The place serves only beer and wine. Don't hesitate to come for a hearty breakfast, too. Excellent *chilaquiles* (eggs scrambled with salsa and tortilla) and huevos rancheros are part of the package.

3614 Bel Aire Plaza, on Trancas St.. © **707/257-8685.** Breakfast, lunch, and dinner $6–$10. MC, V. Tues–Fri 9am–9pm; Sat 8am–9pm; Sun 8am–8pm.

ZuZu ★★ TAPAS A local place to the core, ZuZu lures neighborhood regulars with a no-reservation policy, a friendly cramped wine and beer bar, and affordable Mediterranean/Latin American small plates, which are meant to be shared. The comfortable, warm, and not remotely corporate atmosphere extends from the environment to the food, which includes sizzling mini-skillets of tangy and fantastic paella, addictive prawns with chipotle and paprika, light and delicate sea scallop seviche salad, and Moroccan barbecued lamb chops with a sweet-and-spicy sauce. Desserts aren't as fab, but with a bottle of wine and more tasty plates than you can possibly devour, who cares?

829 Main St.. ℂ **707/224-8555.** Reservations not accepted. Tapas $3–$13. MC, V. Mon–Thurs 11:30am–10pm; Fri 11:30am–11pm; Sat 4–11pm; Sun 4–9pm.

YOUNTVILLE
Very Expensive
The French Laundry ★★★ CLASSIC AMERICAN/FRENCH It's almost futile to include this restaurant, because you're about as likely to secure a reservation—or get through on the reservation line, for that matter—as you are to drive Highway 29 without passing a winery. Several years after renowned chef-owner Thomas Keller bought the place and caught the attention of epicureans worldwide (including the judges of the James Beard Awards, who named him "Chef of the Nation" in 1997), this discreet restaurant is one of the hottest dinner tickets *in the world.*

Plainly put, the French Laundry is unlike any other dining experience, period. Part of it has to do with the intricate preparations, often finished tableside and always presented with uncommon artistry and detail, from the food itself to the surface it's delivered on. Other factors are the service (superfluous, formal, and attentive) and the sheer length of time it takes to ride chef Keller's culinary magic carpet. The atmosphere is as serious as the diners who quietly swoon over the ongoing parade of bite-size delights. Seating ranges from downstairs to upstairs to seasonal garden tables, where you also might wait to be seated, sip some champagne, or puff a cigar. Technically, the prix-fixe menu offers a choice of nine courses (including a vegetarian menu), but after a slew of cameo appearances from the kitchen, everyone starts to lose count. Signature dishes include Keller's "tongue in cheek" (a marinated and braised round of sliced lamb tongue and tender beef cheeks) and "macaroni and cheese" (sweet butter-poached Maine lobster with creamy lobster broth and orzo with mascarpone cheese). The truth is, the experience defies description, so if you absolutely love food, you'll simply have to try it for yourself. Portions are small, but only because Keller wants his guests to taste as many things as possible. Trust me, nobody leaves hungry.

The staff is well acquainted with the wide selection of regional wines; there's a $50 corkage fee if you bring your own bottle, which is only welcome if it's not on the list. *Hint:* If you can't get a reservation, try walking in as soon as lunch or dinner service begins—on occasion folks don't keep their reservation and tables open up, especially during lunch on rainy days. Reservations are accepted 2 months in advance of the date, starting at 10am. Anticipate hitting redial many times for the best chance. Also, insiders tell me that fewer people call on weekends, so you have a better chance at getting beyond the busy signal.

6640 Washington St. (at Creek St.). ℂ **707/944-2380.** www.frenchlaundry.com. Reservations required. Nine-course tasting menu (including vegetarian option) $240. AE, MC, V. Fri–Sun 11am–1pm; daily 5:30–9pm. Dress code: no jeans, shorts, or tennis shoes; men should wear jackets; ties optional.

Expensive

Redd 🍴🍴 CONTEMPORARY AMERICAN   Chef Richard Reddington may have put his name on the culinary map at nearby resort Auberge du Soleil, but he secured a spot among the valley's very best chefs when he opened his own restaurant at the end of 2005. Though the modern and stark dining room is a wee too stark and white-on-white for my taste, the menu is definitely full-flavored. Not that I am surprised. Expect exceptional appetizers such as a delicate sashimi hamachi with edamame, cucumber, ginger, and sticky rice, as well as a cold foie gras trio with pistachios and brioche. For entrees, the Atlantic cod with chorizo, clams, and curry sauce is a dream dish that simultaneously manages to be rich *and* light. The new pastry chef promises to sweeten the offerings with the likes of a citrus trio of Meyer lemon cake, tangerine float, and grapefruit s'mores. If your budget allows, definitely let the sommelier wine-pair the meal for you. He's bound to turn you on to some new favorites. Also, if you're looking for a lush brunch spot, this is it!

6480 Washington St.. ℂ 707/944-2222. Reservations recommended. Main courses brunch $14; main course lunch $21–$25, main courses dinner $23–$29; 5-course tasting menu $70. AE, DISC, MC, V. Mon–Sat 11:30am–2:30pm, Sun 11am–2pm; dinner daily 5:30–10pm; bar menu served 2:30pm–midnight nightly.

Moderate

Bistro Jeanty 🍴 FRENCH BISTRO   This casual, warm bistro, with muted buttercup walls, two dining rooms divided by the bar, and patio seats, is where chef Philippe Jeanty creates seriously rich French comfort food for legions of fans. The all-day menu includes legendary tomato soup in puff pastry, foie gras pâté, steak tartare, and home-smoked trout with potato slices. No meal should start without a paper cone filled with fried smelt (it's often on the list of specials), and none should end without the crème brûlée, made with a thin layer of chocolate cream between classic vanilla custard and a caramelized sugar top. In between, it's a rib-gripping free-for-all including coq au vin; cassoulet; and juicy, thick-cut pork chop with *jus,* spinach, and mashed potatoes. Alas, quality has suffered since Jeanty has branched out to three restaurants, but when the kitchen is on it's still a fine place to sup.

6510 Washington St.. ℂ 707/944-0103. www.bistrojeanty.com. Reservations recommended. Appetizers $8.50–$13; most main courses $15–$29. AE, MC, V. Daily 11:30am–10:30pm.

Bouchon 🍴🍴 FRENCH BISTRO   If you're looking for a delicious, moderately priced meal in city-chic, lovely environs, this is your best bet. Perhaps to appease the crowds who never get a reservation at French Laundry, Thomas Keller opened this far more casual, but still delicious, and very sexy French brasserie. Along with a raw bar, expect superb renditions of steak frites, mussels meunière, grilled-cheese sandwiches, and other heavenly French classics (try the expensive and rich foie gras pâté, which is made at Bouchon). My all-time favorite must-orders: the Bibb lettuce salad (seriously, trust me on this), French fries (perhaps the best in the valley), and roasted chicken bathed in wild mushroom ragout. A bonus, especially for restless residents and off-duty restaurant staff, is the late hours, although they offer a more limited menu when the crowds dwindle.

6534 Washington St. (at Humboldt). ℂ 707/944-8037. www.frenchlaundry.com. Reservations recommended during the week, required on weekends. Main courses $16–$30. AE, MC, V. Daily 11:30am–12:30am.

(Tips) Where to Stock Up for a Gourmet Picnic

You can easily plan your whole trip around restaurant reservations, but gather one of the world's best gourmet picnics, and the valley's your oyster.

One of the finest gourmet-food stores in the Wine Country, if not all of California, is the **Oakville Grocery Co.**, 7856 St. Helena Hwy., at Oakville Cross Road, Oakville (© **707/944-8802;** www.oakvillegrocery.com). You can put together the provisions for a memorable picnic or, with at least 24 hours' notice, the staff can prepare a picnic basket for you. The store, with its small-town vibe and claustrophobia-inducing crowds, can be quite an experience. You'll find shelves crammed with the best breads and choicest cheeses in the northern Bay Area, as well as pâtés, cold cuts, crackers, top-quality olive oils, fresh foie gras (domestic and French, seasonal), smoked Norwegian salmon, and, of course, an exceptional selection of California wines. The store is open daily from 9am to 6pm. There's also an espresso bar tucked in the corner (open Mon–Fri 7am–6pm; Sat–Sun 8am–6pm), offering lunch items, a complete deli, and house-baked pastries.

Another of my favorite places to fill a picnic basket is New York's version of a swank European marketplace, **Dean & DeLuca**, 607 S. St. Helena Hwy. (Hwy. 29), north of Zinfandel Lane and south of Sulphur Springs Road, St. Helena (© **707/967-9980;** www.deananddeluca.com). The ultimate in gourmet grocery stores is more like a world's fair of foods, where everything is beautifully displayed and often painfully pricey. As you pace the barn-wood plank floors, you'll stumble upon more high-end edibles than you've probably ever seen under one roof. They include local organic produce (delivered daily); 300 domestic and imported cheeses (with an on-site aging room to ensure proper ripeness); shelves and shelves of tapenades, pastas, oils, hand-packed dried herbs and spices, chocolates, sauces, cookware, and housewares; an espresso bar; one hell of a bakery section; and more. Along the back wall, you can watch the professional chefs prepare gourmet takeout, including salads, rotisserie meats, and sautéed vegetables. You can also snag a pricey bottle from the wine section's 1,400-label collection. The store is open daily from 9am to 8pm (the espresso bar is open daily at 7am).

Mustards Grill ☆☆ CALIFORNIA Mustards is one of those standby restaurants that everyone seems to love because it's dependable and its menu has something that suits any food craving. Housed in a convivial, barn-style space, it offers 300 wines and an ambitious chalkboard list of specials. Options go from exotic offerings like smoked duck or Mongolian style pork chop with hot mustard sauce, to a sautéed lemon-garlic half-chicken with mashed potatoes and fresh herbs. The menu includes something for everyone, from vegetarians to good old burger lovers, and the wine list features nothing but "New World" wines.

7399 St. Helena Hwy. (Hwy. 29). © **707/944-2424.** www.mustardsgrill.com. Reservations recommended. Main courses $11–$25. AE, DC, DISC, MC, V. Mon–Thurs 11:30am–9pm; Fri 11:30am–10pm; Sat 11am–10pm; Sun 11am–9pm.

RUTHERFORD
Expensive

Auberge du Soleil ⭐ *Finds* WINE COUNTRY CUISINE Perched high atop a hill overlooking Napa Valley, this is the spot to come to if an afternoon or early evening of alfresco romance is on your itinerary. The primary reason to choose this place over other big-ticket restaurants is the view, which is only afforded during daylight from the terrace, so skip dinner and come for lunch, sunset cocktails, or early dinner and request an outdoor table.

Chef Robert Curry, previously at Domaine Chandon and the nearby Culinary Institute, serves well-prepared cuisine that focuses on the very best of local seasonal ingredients. His forage for freshness pays off in dishes such as risotto with lobster, sunchokes, and hazelnut emulsion; or Liberty Farm duck with chestnuts, verjus, braised radicchio, and caramelized shallot sauce. Add to this the impressive (and very pricy) wine list, with over 30 available by the glass, and you're in for a treat. At dinner you can opt for a four-course fixed-price feast (with a vegetarian option) or the tasting menu for the whole table. For lighter fare, grab a seat at the bar, a cozy room wrapped around the remains of an ancient tree, where you can sample ahi tuna tartare, grilled chicken panini, and oysters on the half-shell, along with 25 wines by the glass.

180 Rutherford Hill Rd.. ✆ **707/967-3111**. www.aubergedusoleil.com. Reservations required. Main courses $19–$25 lunch; 4-course fixed-price dinner $90; 6-course $125, $213 with wine pairings per person; vegetarian tasting menu $90; bar menu $7–$32. AE, DISC, MC, V. Breakfast 7–11am, lunch 11:30am–2:30pm, and dinner 5:30–9:30pm.

ST. HELENA
Expensive

Go Fish ⭐⭐ SEAFOOD/SUSHI There are not words to describe the joy I felt when Ken Tominaga of Sonoma County's Hana Japanese Restaurant teamed up with Cindy Pawlcyn to bring stellar sushi and seafood to Napa Valley. By the looks of the crowds, I'm not the only one who overlooks lackadaisical service for killer specialty rolls that are so big and yummy they're worth the $20 price tag, fantastic ahi poke, and nigiri along with designer cocktails, sake, a raw bar, and a tasty main menu overseen by talented young chef Victor Scargle. (Try the miso-marinated black cod with shiitake broth or crispy whole snapper with shelling bean ragout and spicy greens.) The vibe is good here, too. The long bar welcomes last-minute diners and revelers, tables are well dispersed amid the large dining area (so you can easily converse even at a large table), and the vibe, while more steakhouse than seafood, feels like a relatively fun place to be—especially since it's a rare night that the joint isn't packed.

641 Main St. (just south of downtown St. Helena). ✆ **707/963-0700**. www.gofishrestaurant.net. Reservations recommended. Sushi $5–$20; main courses $17–$35. AE, DC, MC, V. Sun–Thurs 11:30am–9:30pm, Fri–Sat 11:30am–10pm.

Terra ⭐⭐⭐ CONTEMPORARY AMERICAN Quiet and intimate, Terra manages to be humble even though it serves some of the most extraordinary food in Northern California. The creation of Lissa Doumani and her husband, Hiro Sone, a master chef who hails from Japan, is a culmination of talents brought together nearly 20 years ago, after the duo worked at L.A.'s Spago. Today, the menu reflects Sone's full use of the region's bounty and his formal training in classic European and Japanese cuisine. Dishes—all of which are incredible and are served in the rustic-romantic dining room— range from understated and refined (two must-tries: rock shrimp salad, or broiled sake-marinated cod with shrimp dumplings and shiso broth) to rock-your-world flavorful. I cannot express the importance of saving room for dessert (or forcing it even if you don't). Doumani's recipes, which includes to-die-for tiramisu, are heavenly.

1345 Railroad Ave. (between Adams and Hunt sts.). ℂ **707/963-8931**. www.terrarestaurant.com. Reservations recommended. Main courses $20–$32. AE, DC, MC, V. Wed–Mon dinner starting at 6pm. Closed 2 weeks in early Jan.

Moderate

Tra Vigne Restaurant ⭐ ITALIAN   As much as I want to love everything about this famous, absurdly scenic restaurant, I can't—anymore. With lots of chef changes over the years and meals that range from barely so-so to totally rockin', it's just not the sure thing it used to be. If you sit in the Tuscany-evoking courtyard, however, you'll likely enjoy yourself regardless of whether the kitchen is on the money or missing the mark. Inside, the bustling, cavernous dining room and happening bar are fine for chilly days and eves, but they're not nearly as magical. You can also count on wonderful bread (served with house-cured olives); a menu of robust California dishes, cooked Italian-style; a daily oven-roasted pizza special; lots of pastas; and tried-and-true standbys like short ribs and fritto misto.

1050 Charter Oak Ave.. ℂ **707/963-4444**. www.travignerestaurant.com. Reservations recommended. Main courses $15–$26. DC, DISC, MC, V. Summer daily 11:30am–10pm; winter Sun–Thurs 11:30am–9pm, Fri–Sat 11:30am–10pm.

Inexpensive

Gillwoods Café AMERICAN   In a town like this—where if you order mushrooms on your burger, the waiter's likely to ask, "What kind?"—a plain old American restaurant can be a godsend. In St. Helena, the land of snobs and broccoli rabes, Gillwoods is that place. At this homey haunt, with its wooden benches and original artwork, it's all about the basics. You'll find a breakfast of bakery goods, fruit, pancakes, omelets (with pronounceable ingredients), and a decent eggs Benedict; and a lunch menu of burgers, sandwiches, lots of salads, and chicken-fried steak. Lunch is available starting at 10:30am, but late risers can order breakfast all day. A second location is in downtown Napa at 1320 Napa Town Center, ℂ **707/253-0409**.

1313 Main St. (Hwy. 29, at Spring St.). ℂ **707/963-1788**. Breakfast $9–$12; lunch $9–$13. AE, MC, V. Daily 7am–3pm. Napa location daily 8am–3pm.

Market AMERICAN   In past editions I've highly recommended this upscale but cheap ode to American comfort food. But ever since the chef departed to open Cyrus, a high-end sister restaurant in Northern Sonoma County's town of Healdsburg, the food quality has been unpredictable (though it's incredible at Cyrus: 29 North St., Healdsburg—that's a 45-min. drive from St. Helena; ℂ **707/433-3311;** www.cyrusrestaurant. com; 3- to 5-course menus $58–$95). Still, if you're in expensive St. Helena and want some casual glamour with your burger, you'll find it here with fancy stone-wall and Brunswick bar surroundings paired with clunky steak knives and simple white-plate presentations. At lunch, you can also opt for a three-course meal—a steal at a measly $20.

1347 Main St.. ℂ **707/963-3799**. www.marketsthelena.com. Most main courses $7–$20. AE, MC, V. Daily 11:30am–10pm.

Taylor's Automatic Refresher (Overrated) DINER   Yet another winner to slip from sublime status to buyer beware, this gourmet roadside burger shack built in 1949 still draws huge lines of tourists who love the notion of ordering at the counter and feasting alfresco. But the last few meals I had there left me knowing the $80 I coughed up for lunch for five would have been better spent at Oakville Grocery's deli. The burger, onion rings, and fries were mediocre at best, the iceberg salad was unwieldy, and only the shake left me satisfied. (How hard is it to make a great shake, after all?) Perhaps it's that the owners now have a closer eye on their San Francisco outpost, which is great, by the way. No matter. It's still the only casual burger joint in St. Helena (it also offers ahi tuna burgers and various sandwiches, tacos, soups and salads) and its ever-bustling status proves everyone knows it. A second location in Napa at 644 First St. (near Soscal Ave.) is open daily 10:30am to 9pm

933 Main St.. ℂ 707/963-3486. www.taylorsrefresher.com. Main courses $5–$14. AE, MC, V. Daily 11am–8:30pm (9pm in summer).

CALISTOGA
Moderate
All Seasons Café ✿✿ CALIFORNIA   All Seasons successfully balances old-fashioned down-home dining charm with today's penchant for sophisticated, seasonally inspired dishes. It also happens to have perhaps the best food in downtown Calistoga. Vibrant bouquets, large framed watercolors, and windows overlooking busy Lincoln Avenue soften the look of the black-and-white checkered flooring, brick-red ceiling, and long, marble wine bar. The laid-back atmosphere and service make the quality of crispy skin chicken with white truffle chicken *jus* and herb-roasted monkfish with fennel nage that much more of a delicious surprise. Don't forget to take advantage of the fact that they have 400-plus wines available from their adjoining wine shop (with a $15 corkage fee, buy next door and drink for far cheaper than at most restaurants). Alas, the kitchen was a wee bit slow on my last visit, but all was forgiven when the food far surpassed my expectations.

1400 Lincoln Ave. (at Washington St.). ℂ 707/942-9111. www.allseasonsnapavalley.net. Reservations recommended on weekends. Main courses $9–$11 lunch, $19–$28 dinner. DISC, MC, V. Lunch Fri–Sun noon–2:30pm; dinner nightly 6–9pm (times vary in winter, please call or go online to confirm).

Inexpensive
Wappo Bar & Bistro GLOBAL   One of the best alfresco dining venues in the Wine Country is under Wappo's giant jasmine-and-grapevine-covered arbor. I used to shrug off the mediocre food, reasoning that much can be forgiven when the wine's flowing and you're surrounded by pastoral splendor. But the globally influenced menu has been better of late. Anticipate the likes of Thai noodles and green papaya salad, tandoori chicken, rosemary-scented rabbit with gnocchi and mustard cream sauce. Desserts of choice are black-bottom coconut cream pie and strawberry rhubarb pie.

1226 Washington St. (off Lincoln Ave.). ℂ 707/942-4712. www.wappobar.com. Main courses $14–$24. AE, MC, V. Wed–Mon 11:30am–2:30pm and 6–9:30pm.

2 Sonoma Valley

A pastoral contrast to Napa, Sonoma manages to maintain a backcountry ambience, thanks to its far lower density of wineries, restaurants, and hotels. Small, family-owned wineries are Sonoma's mainstay; tastings are low-key and come with plenty of friendly banter with the winemakers. Basically, this is the valley to target if your ideal vacation includes visiting a handful of wineries along quiet woodsy roads, avoiding shopping outlets and Napa's high-end glitz, and simply enjoying the laid-back country atmosphere.

The valley is some 17 miles long and 7 miles wide, and it's bordered by two mountain ranges: the Mayacamas to the east and the Sonomas to the west. Unlike in Napa Valley, you won't find much in the way of palatial wineries with million-dollar art collections or aerial trams. Rather, the Sonoma Valley offers a refreshing dose of family-owned winery reality, where modestly sized wineries are integrated into the community. If Napa Valley feels like a fantasyland, where everything exists to service the almighty grape and the visitors it attracts, then the Sonoma Valley is its antithesis, an unpretentious gaggle of ordinary towns, ranches, and wineries that welcome tourists but don't necessarily rely on them. The result is a chance to experience what Napa Valley must have been like long before the Seagrams and Moët et Chandons of the world turned the Wine Country into a major tourist destination.

As in Napa, you can pick up *Wine Country Review* throughout Sonoma. It gives you the most up-to-date information on wineries and related area events.

ESSENTIALS

GETTING THERE   From San Francisco, cross the Golden Gate Bridge and stay on U.S. 101 north. Exit at Highway 37; after 10 miles, turn north onto Highway 121. After another 10 miles, turn north onto Highway 12 (Broadway), which takes you directly into the town of Sonoma.

VISITOR INFORMATION   While you're in Sonoma, stop by the **Sonoma Valley Visitors Bureau,** 453 First St. E. (℮ **866/996-1090** or 707/996-1090; www.sonoma valley.com). It's open Monday through Saturday from 9am to 5pm (6pm in summer on Fridays and Saturdays) and Sunday 10am to 5pm. An additional **Visitors Bureau** is a few miles south of the square at Cornerstone Festival of Gardens at 23570 Arnold Dr. (Hwy. 121; ℮ **866/996-1090**); it's open daily from 9am to 4pm, 5pm during summer.

If you prefer advance information from the bureau, you can contact the Sonoma Valley Visitors Bureau to order the free *Sonoma Valley Visitors Guide,* which lists almost every lodge, winery, and restaurant in the valley.

TOURING THE SONOMA VALLEY & WINERIES

Sonoma Valley is currently home to about 45 wineries (including California's first winery, Buena Vista, founded in 1857) and 13,000 acres of vineyards. It produces roughly 76 types of wines, totaling more than five million cases a year. Unlike the rigidly structured tours at many of Napa Valley's corporate-owned wineries, on the Sonoma side of the Mayacamas Mountains, tastings are usually low-key and tours free.

The towns and wineries covered below are organized geographically from south to north, starting at the intersection of Highway 37 and Highway 121 in the Carneros District and ending in Kenwood. The wineries tend to be a little more spread out here than they are in Napa Valley, but they're easy to find. Still, it's best to decide which wineries you're most interested in and devise a touring strategy before you set out, so you don't do too much backtracking.

I've reviewed some of my favorite Sonoma Valley wineries here—more than enough to keep you busy tasting wine for a long weekend. If you'd like a complete list of local wineries, be sure to pick up one of the free guides available at the Sonoma Valley Visitors Bureau (see "Visitor Information," above).

For a map of the wineries below, please see "The Wine Country" map on p. 277.

THE CARNEROS DISTRICT

As you approach the Wine Country from the south, you must first pass through the Carneros District, a cool, windswept region that borders San Pablo Bay and marks the entrance to both the Napa and Sonoma valleys. Until the latter part of the 20th century, this mixture of marsh, sloughs, and rolling hills was mainly used as sheep pasture (*carneros* means "sheep" in Spanish). However, after experimental plantings yielded slow-growing, high-quality grapes—particularly chardonnay and pinot noir—several Napa and Sonoma wineries expanded their plantings here. They eventually established the Carneros District as an American Viticultural Appellation, a legally defined wine-grape growing area. Although about a dozen wineries are spread throughout the region, there are no major towns or attractions—just plenty of gorgeous scenery as you cruise along Highway 121, the major route between Napa and Sonoma.

Viansa Winery and Italian Marketplace *Finds* The first major winery you'll encounter as you enter Sonoma Valley from the south, this sprawling Tuscan-style villa perches atop a knoll overlooking the entire lower valley. Viansa is the brainchild of Sam and Vicki Sebastiani, who left the family dynasty to create their own temple to food and wine. (*Viansa* is a contraction of "Vicki and Sam.") Here you'll find a large room crammed with a cornucopia of high-quality mustards, olive oils, pastas, salads, breads, desserts, Italian tableware, cookbooks, and wine-related gifts as well as tasting opportunities.

The winery, which does an extensive mail-order business through the Tuscan Club, has established a favorable reputation for its Italian varietals. Tastings, which cost $5 per person, are offered at the east and west end of the marketplace, and the self-guided tour includes a trip through the underground barrel-aging cellar adorned with colorful hand-painted murals. Guided tours, held at 11am, 2pm and 3pm, cost $10.

Viansa is also one of the few wineries in Sonoma Valley that sells deli items—the focaccia sandwiches are delicious. You can dine alfresco under the grape trellis while you admire the bucolic view.

25200 Arnold Dr. (Calif. 121), Sonoma. *C* **800/995-4740** or 707/935-4700. www.viansa.com. Daily 10am–5pm. Daily self–guided tours. Guided tours daily 11am, 2pm, and 3pm, $10.

Gloria Ferrer Champagne Caves *Finds* When you have had it up to here with chardonnays and pinots, it's time to pay a visit to Gloria Ferrer, the grande dame of the Wine Country's sparkling-wine producers. Who's Gloria? She's the wife of José Ferrer, whose family has made sparkling wine for 5 centuries. The family business, Freixenet, is the largest producer of sparkling wine in the world; Cordon Negro is its most popular brand. That equals big bucks, and certainly a good chunk of them went into building this palatial estate. Glimmering like Oz high atop a gently sloping hill, it overlooks the verdant Carneros District. On a sunny day, enjoying a glass of dry brut while soaking in the magnificent views is a must.

If you're unfamiliar with the term *méthode champenoise,* be sure to take the free 30-minute tour of the fermenting tanks, bottling line, and caves brimming with racks of yeast-laden bottles. Afterward, retire to the elegant tasting room, order a glass of one of seven sparkling wines ($4–$10 a glass) or tastes of their eight still wines ($2–$3 per taste), find an empty chair on the veranda, and say, "Ahhh. *This* is the life." There are picnic tables, but it's usually too windy for them to be comfortable, and you must buy a bottle (from around $20–$50) or glass of sparkling wine to reserve a table. Tours are $10 per person and include two tastings.

23555 Carneros Hwy. (Calif. 121), Sonoma. *C* **707/996-7256.** www.gloriaferrer.com. Daily 10am–5pm. Tours daily; call day of visit to confirm schedule.

SONOMA

At the northern boundary of the Carneros District along Highway 12 is the centerpiece of Sonoma Valley. The midsize town of Sonoma owes much of its appeal to Mexican general Mariano Guadalupe Vallejo, who fashioned this pleasant, slow-paced community after a typical Mexican village—right down to its central plaza, Sonoma's geographical and commercial center. The plaza sits at the top of a T formed by Broadway (Hwy. 12) and Napa Street. Most of the surrounding streets form a grid pattern

Tips A Garden Detour

Garden lovers should pull over for a gander at the latest Sonoma addition, **Cornerstone Festival of Gardens**, 23570 Arnold Dr., Sonoma (© **707/933-3010;** www.cornerstonegardens.com). Modeled in part after the International Garden festival at Chaumont-sur-Loire in France's Loire Valley and the Grand-Métis in Quebec, Canada, the 9-acre property is the first gallery-style garden exhibit in the United States and includes a series of 22 ever-changing gardens designed by famed landscape architects and designers. With a recently added children's garden featuring a brightly colored water tower surrounded by a sand moat and buckets, shovels, and plastic plumbing fittings, this is a great spot for the whole family. When you get hungry, stop by the **Blue Tree Café,** which offers light breakfasts, pastries, and espresso drinks along with a seasonal lunch menu including soups, salads, and sandwiches. It's all served on nifty metal trays, perfect for carrying out to the gardens; there's also seating indoors and out in front. Another plus for those with kids: The gardens include a cleverly installed willow reed maze that's about 3 feet high and only has one entrance/exit right in front of the cafe, so if you're sitting out front and the kids get bored, you can safely let them run through the maze. If you get inspired, you can load up on loot here that will help your own garden grow—from furniture and gifts to plants, garden art, and books, as there are several interesting shops here, too. Open 10am–5pm daily (gardens close at 4pm), year-round (Café opens at 9am). April through November the price for admission to the gardens is $9 adults, $7.50 seniors 65 plus, $6.50 college students, $3 youth 4 to 17, and free for kids 3 and under (check for locals' discounts); December through March, tickets are half-price. You can take a self-guided tour anytime; installations are marked with descriptive plaques. Docent tours are available for groups of 10 or more by appointment.

around this axis, making Sonoma easy to negotiate. The plaza's Bear Flag Monument marks the spot where the crude Bear Flag was raised in 1846, signaling the end of Mexican rule; the symbol was later adopted by the state of California and placed on its flag. The 8-acre park at the center of the plaza, complete with two ponds populated by ducks, is perfect for an afternoon siesta in the cool shade.

Gundlach Bundschu Winery ✿✿   If it looks like the people working here are actually enjoying themselves, that's because they are. Gundlach Bundschu (pronounced *Gun*-lock *Bun*-shoe) is the quintessential Sonoma winery—nonchalant in appearance but obsessed with wine: The GB clan are a nefarious lot, infamous for wild stunts such as holding up Napa's Wine Train on horseback and—egad!—serving Sonoma wines to their captives; the small tasting room looks not unlike a bomb shelter, the Talking Heads is their version of Muzak, and the "art" consists of a dozen witty black-and-white posters promoting GB wines.

This is the oldest continually family-owned and operated winery in California, going into its sixth generation since Jacob Gundlach harvested his first crop in 1858. Drop in to sample chardonnay, pinot noir, merlot, cabernet, and more. Prices for the 14 distinct wines range from $24 per bottle for the Mountain Cuvee to $90 for the Vintage reserve cabernet sauvignon. Tastings are $5 and tours, which include a trip into the 430-foot cave, start at $20 and are by appointment only.

Gundlach Bundschu has the best picnic grounds in the valley, though you have to walk to the top of Towles' Hill to earn the sensational view. They also have great activities (Midsummer Mozart Festival, film fests), so call or check the website if you want to join the fun.

2000 Denmark St. (off 8th St. E.), Sonoma. Ⓒ **707/938-5277.** www.gunbun.com. Daily 11am–4:30pm. Tours last 1 hour and are by appointment only. Groups of seven or more should make an appointment.

Buena Vista Winery Count Agoston Haraszthy, the Hungarian émigré who is universally regarded as the father of California's wine industry, founded this historic winery in 1857. A close friend of General Vallejo, Haraszthy returned from Europe in 1861 with 100,000 of the finest vine cuttings, which he made available to all growers. Although Buena Vista's winemaking now takes place at an ultramodern facility in the Carneros District, the winery maintains a tasting room inside the restored 1862 Press House. The beautiful stone-crafted room brims with wines, wine-related gifts, and accessories.

Tastings are $5 for four wines, $10 for a flight of three library wines. You can take the self-guided tour any time during operating hours; their $20 "Carneros Experience" requires a reservation and pairs five wines with a small plate of food, including cheeses. After tasting, grab your favorite bottle, a selection of cheeses from the Sonoma Cheese Factory, salami, bread, and spreads (all available in the tasting room), and plant yourself at one of the many picnic tables in the lush, verdant setting.

18000 Old Winery Rd. (off E. Napa St., slightly northeast of downtown), Sonoma. Ⓒ **800/926-1266** or 707/265-1472. www.buenavistawinery.com. Daily 10am–5pm.

Sebastiani Vineyards & Winery The name Sebastiani is practically synonymous with Sonoma. What started in 1904, when Samuele Sebastiani began producing his first wines, has in three generations grown into a small empire, producing some 350,000 cases a year. The original 1904 property is open to the public with educational tours ($5–$7.50 per person), an 80-foot S-shaped tasting bar, and lots of gift shopping opportunities. In the contemporary tasting room's mini-museum area you can see the winery's original turn-of-the-20th-century crusher and press, as well as the world's largest collection of oak-barrel carvings, crafted by bygone local artist Earle Brown. If it's merely wine that interests you, you can sample three Sonoma County wines for $5 or a flight of four for $10. Bottle prices are reasonable, ranging from $13 to $75. A picnic area adjoins the cellars; a far more scenic spot is across the parking lot in Sebastiani's Cherryblock Vineyards.

389 Fourth St. E., Sonoma. Ⓒ **800/888-5532** or 707/933-3200. www.sebastiani.com. Daily 10am–5pm. Tours daily at 11am, 1pm, and 3pm, with an additional tour at noon Sat–Sun.

Ravenswood Winery Compared to old heavies like Sebastiani and Buena Vista, Ravenswood is a relative newcomer to the Sonoma wine scene. Nevertheless, it quickly established itself as the sine qua non of zinfandel, the versatile red grape that's known in these parts for being big, ripe, juicy, and powerful. The first winery in the United States to focus primarily on zins, which make up about three-quarters of its astonishing 1-million-case production, Ravenswood underscores zins' zest with their motto, "No Wimpy Wines." But they also produce merlot, cabernet sauvignon, Rhone varietals, and a small amount of chardonnay.

The winery is smartly designed—recessed into the hillside to protect its treasures from the simmering summers. Tours ($15 per person) follow the winemaking process from grape to glass, and include a visit to the aromatic oak-barrel aging rooms. You're

Moments **Touring the Sonoma Valley by Bike**

Sonoma and its neighboring towns are so small, close together, and relatively flat that it's not difficult to get around on two wheels. In fact, if you're in no great hurry, there's no better way to tour the Sonoma Valley than by bicycle, even though there are no great bike routes (it's all along the road for the most part). You can rent a bike from the **Goodtime Bicycle Company** (© **888/525-0453** or 707/938-0453; www.goodtimetouring.com). The staff will happily point you to easy bike trails, or you can take an organized excursion to Kenwood-area wineries, south Sonoma wineries, or even northern Sonoma's Russian River and Dry Creek areas. Goodtime also provides a gourmet lunch featuring local Sonoma products. If you purchase wine along the way, Goodtime will carry it for you and help with shipping arrangements. Lunch rides start at 10:30am and end around 3:30pm. The cost, including food and equipment, is $125 per person (that's a darn good deal). Rentals cost $25 a day, and include helmets, locks, everything else you'll need, and delivery and pickup to and from local hotels.

Mountain bikes, helmets, and locks are also available for rent from **Sonoma Valley Cyclery,** 20093 Broadway, Sonoma (© **707/935-3377**), for $35 to $55 a day. Hybrid bikes (better for casual wine-tasting cruisers) are $25 per day, helmet and lock included.

welcome to bring your own picnic basket to any of the tables, and don't forget to check their website or call to find out if they're having one of their famous ongoing barbecues or winter celebrations. Regardless, tastings are $10 for four wines to $15 for the Vineyard Designate series, both of which are refundable with purchase. Bottles average around $35.

18701 Gehricke Rd. (off Lovall Valley Rd.), Sonoma. © **888/669-4679** or 707/933-2332. www.ravenswood winery.com. Labor Day to Memorial Day 10am–4:30pm; Memorial Day to Labor Day 10am–5pm. Tours at 10:30am; reservations recommended.

GLEN ELLEN

About 7 miles north of Sonoma on Highway 12 is the town of Glen Ellen. Although just a fraction of the size of Sonoma, Glen Ellen is home to several of the valley's finest wineries, restaurants, and inns. Aside from the addition of a few new restaurants, this charming town hasn't changed much since the days when Jack London settled on his Beauty Ranch, about a mile west. Other than the wineries, you'll find few real signs of commercialism; the shops and restaurants, along one main winding lane, cater to a small, local clientele—that is, until the summer tourist season begins and traffic nearly triples on the weekends. If you haven't decided where you want to set up camp during your visit to the Wine Country, I highly recommend this lovable little rural region.

Arrowood Vineyards & Winery   Richard Arrowood had already established a reputation as a master winemaker at Château St. Jean when he and his wife, Alis Demers Arrowood, set out on their own in 1986. Their picturesque winery stands on a gently rising hillside lined with perfectly manicured vineyards. Tastings take place in the Hospitality House, the newer of Arrowood's two stately gray-and-white buildings.

They're fashioned after New England farmhouses, complete with wraparound porches. Richard's focus is on making world-class wine with minimal intervention, and his results are impressive: More than one of his recent releases scored over 90 points in *Wine Spectator, Wine Advocate,* or *Wine Enthusiast.* Mind you, excellence isn't free: a taste here is $5 or $10 for four limited-production wines, while a winery tour is $15 and vineyard and cellar tour is $30, but if you're curious about what near-perfection tastes like, it's well worth it. *Note:* No picnic facilities are available here.

14347 Sonoma Hwy. (Calif. 12), Glen Ellen. ℭ 707/935-2600. www.arrowoodvineyards.com. Daily 10am–4:30pm. Tours by appointment only.

Benziger Family Winery ✿ *Finds*   A visit here confirms that this is indeed a family winery. At any given time, two generations of Benzigers (*Ben*-zigger) may be running around tending to chores, and they instantly make you feel as if you're part of the clan. The pastoral, user-friendly property features an exceptional self-guided tour of the certified biodynamic winery ("The most comprehensive tour in the wine industry," according to *Wine Spectator*), gardens, and a spacious tasting room staffed by amiable folks. Definitely pay the $15 for adults and $5 for kids under 21 for the 45-minute tram tour, pulled by a beefy tractor. Both informative and fun, it winds through the estate vineyards and to caves, and ends with a tasting. *Tip:* Tram tickets—a hot item in the summer—are available on a first-come, first-served basis, so either arrive early or stop by in the morning to pick up afternoon tickets.

Tastings of the standard-release wines are $5. Tastes including several limited-production wines or reserve or estate wines cost $15. The winery also offers several scenic picnic spots.

1883 London Ranch Rd. (off Arnold Dr., on the way to Jack London State Historic Park), Glen Ellen. ℭ 888/490-2739 or 707/935-3000. www.benziger.com. Tasting room daily 10am–5pm. Tram tours daily (weather permitting) $10 adults, $5 children, every half-hour, 10:30am–3:30pm.

KENWOOD

A few miles north of Glen Ellen along Highway 12 is the tiny town of Kenwood, the valley's northernmost outpost. Although Kenwood Vineyards' wines are well known throughout the United States, the town itself consists of little more than a few restaurants, wineries, and modest homes on the wooded hillsides. The nearest lodging, the luxurious Kenwood Inn & Spa (p. 322), is about a mile south of the vineyards. Kenwood makes for a pleasant half-day trip from Glen Ellen or downtown Sonoma. Take an afternoon tour of Château St. Jean (see below) and have dinner at Kenwood Restaurant (p. 328).

Kunde Estate Winery   Expect a friendly, unintimidating welcome at this scenic winery, run by five generations of the Kundes since 1904. One of the largest grape suppliers in the area, the Kunde family (pronounced *Kun*-dee) has devoted 700 acres of its 2,000-acre ranch to growing ultrapremium-quality grapes, which it provides to many Sonoma and Napa wineries. This abundance allows the Kundes to make nothing but estate wines (wines made from grapes grown on the Kunde property, as opposed to also using grapes purchased from other growers).

The tasting room is located in a spiffy 17,000-square-foot winemaking facility, which features specialized crushing equipment that enables the winemaker to run whole clusters to the press—a real advantage in white-wine production. Tastings of four estate releases are $10 (refunded with purchase) and reserve tastings will set you back $20; bottle prices range from $16 for a Magnolia Lane sauvignon blanc to $60 for a Drummond Vineyards cabernet sauvignon; most labels sell in the high teens.

The tasting room also has a gift shop and large windows overlooking the bottling room and tank room.

The tour of the property's extensive wine caves includes a history of the winery. Private tours are available by appointment, but most folks are happy to just stop by for some vino and to relax at one of the many patio tables placed around the man-made pond. Animal lovers will appreciate Kunde's preservation efforts: The property has a duck estuary with more than 50 species (which can be seen by appointment only).

9825 Sonoma Hwy., Kenwood. ℂ 707/833-5501. www.kunde.com. Tastings daily 10:30am–4:30pm. Complimentary Cave tours Tues–Thurs 11am, Fri–Mon on the hour 11am–3pm.

Château St. Jean ⭐ Finds
Château St. Jean is notable for its wines, but also for its exceptionally beautiful buildings, expansive landscaped grounds, and gourmet marketlike tasting room. Among California wineries, it's a pioneer in vineyard designation—the procedure of making wine from, and naming it for, a single vineyard. A private drive takes you to what was once a 250-acre country retreat built in 1920; a well-manicured lawn overlooking the meticulously maintained vineyards is now a picnic area, complete with a fountain and tables.

In the huge tasting room—where there's also a charcuterie shop and plenty of other fun stuff for sale—you can sample Château St. Jean's wide array of wines. They range from chardonnays and cabernet sauvignon to fumé blanc, merlot, riesling, and gewürztraminer. Tastings are $10 per person, $15 per person for reserve wines.

8555 Sonoma Hwy. (Calif. 12), Kenwood. ℂ 800/543-7572 or 707/833-4134. www.chateaustjean.com. Tasting daily 10am–4:30pm. Tour times vary depending on the weather, so call ahead to confirm. At the foot of Sugarloaf Ridge, just north of Kenwood and east of Hwy. 12.

St. Francis Winery
Although St. Francis Winery makes commendable chardonnay, zinfandel, and cabernet sauvignon, they're best known for their highly coveted merlot. Winemaker Tom Mackey, a former high-school English teacher from San Francisco, has been hailed as the "Master of Merlot" by *Wine Spectator* for his uncanny ability to craft the finest merlot in California.

If you've visited before, but haven't been back in a while, don't follow your memory to the front door. In 2001, St. Francis moved a little farther north to digs bordering on the Santa Rosa County line. The original property was planted in 1910 as part of a wedding gift to Alice Kunde (scion of the local Kunde family) and christened St. Francis of Assisi in 1979 when Joe Martin and Lloyd Canton—two white-collar executives turned vintners—completed their long-awaited dream winery. Today the winery still owns the property, but there's new history in the making at their much larger facilities, which include a tasting room and upscale gift shop. Tastings are $10 per person for a choice of four wines from a selection of nationally known brands and wines only available at the winery. Wine and food pairings range from $25 for flight of four wines paired with seasonal hors d'oeuvres to $50, which includes four plated pairings in the elegant dining room. Now that St. Francis is planning more special activities, it's worthwhile to call or check their website for their calendar of events.

100 Pythian Rd. (Calif. 12/Sonoma Hwy.), Santa Rosa (at the Kenwood border). ℂ 800/543-7713, ext. 242; or 707/833-4666. www.stfranciswinery.com. Daily 10am–5pm.

Landmark Vineyards
One of California's oldest exclusively chardonnay estates was first founded in 1972 in the Windsor area of Northern Sonoma County. When new housing development started encroaching on the winery's territory, proprietor Damaris Deere W. Ethridge (great-great-granddaughter of John Deere, the tractor

baron) moved her operation to Northern Sonoma Valley in 1990. The winery, which produces 27,000 cases annually, is housed in a modest, mission-style building set on 11 acres of vineyards. The tasting room offers $5 samples of current releases and pours reserve tastings for $10. (Notice the wall-to-wall mural behind the tasting counter painted by noted Sonoma County artist Claudia Wagar.) Wine prices range from $27 for the Overlook chardonnay to $65 for a reserve pinot noir.

The winery has a pond-side picnic area, as well as what is probably the only professional bocce court in the valley (yes, you can play, and yes, they provide instructions). Also available from Memorial Day to Labor Day are free Belgian horse–drawn wagon tours through the vineyards, offered every Saturday from 11:30am to 3pm.

101 Adobe Canyon Rd. (just east of Hwy. 12), Kenwood. © **800/452-6365** or 707/833-1144. www.landmarkwine. com. Daily 10am–4:30pm. Tours available by appointment.

WHERE TO STAY IN SONOMA VALLEY

Keep in mind that during the peak season and on weekends, most B&Bs and hotels require a minimum 2-night stay. Of course, that's assuming you can find a vacancy; make reservations as far in advance as possible. If you are having trouble finding a room, call the **Sonoma Valley Visitors Bureau** (© **866/996-1090** or 707/996-1090; www.sonomavalley.com). The staff will try to refer you to a lodging that has a room to spare but won't make reservations for you. Another option is the **Bed and Breakfast Association of Sonoma Valley** (© **800/969-4667**), which can refer you to a B&B that belongs to the association. You can also find updated information on their website, **www.sonomabb.com**.

SONOMA
Very Expensive
Fairmont Sonoma Mission Inn & Spa ★★★ Set on 12 meticulously groomed acres, the Fairmount Sonoma Mission Inn consists of a massive three-story replica of a California mission (well, aside from the pink paint job) built in 1927, an array of satellite wings housing numerous superluxury suites, and world-class spa facilities. It's a popular retreat for the wealthy and well known, so don't be surprised if you see a famous face. Since Fairmont took over the resort in 2002, the resort has spent around $100-million on room and spa renovations, which included completely redoing the Heritage Rooms in understated country elegance and enhancing the property's original draw: naturally heated artesian mineral pools and whirlpools. Fancier digs include more modern rooms with plantation-style shutters, ceiling fans, down comforters, and over-size bath towels. The Wine Country rooms feature king-size beds, desks, refrigerators, and huge limestone and marble bathrooms; some offer wood-burning fireplaces, too, and many have balconies or patios. For the ultimate in luxury, the opulently appointed Mission Suites are the way to go. Golfers will be glad to know the resort is also home to the nearby Sonoma Golf Club, host of the PGA championship every October.

Pricing Categories

Hotel listings in this section are arranged first by area, then by price, using the following categories: **Very Expensive,** more than $250 per night; **Expensive,** $200 to $250 per night; **Moderate,** $150 to $200 per night; and **Inexpensive,** less than $150 per night.

101 Boyes Blvd., corner of Boyes Blvd. and Calif. 12, P.O. Box 1447, Sonoma, CA 95476. ℭ 800/441-1414 or 707/938-9000. Fax 707/938-4250. www.fairmont.com/sonoma. 226 units. $259–$1,259 double. AE, DC, MC, V. Valet parking is free for day use (spa-goers) and $14 for overnight guests. From central Sonoma, drive 3 miles north on Hwy. 12 and turn left on Boyes Blvd. **Amenities:** 2 restaurants; 3 large, heated outdoor pools; golf course; health club and spa; Jacuzzi; sauna; bike rental; concierge; business center; salon; room service; babysitting; same-day laundry service/dry cleaning; free wine tasting (4:30–5:30pm). *In room:* A/C, TV, dataport, high-speed Internet access ($13 per day), minibar, hair dryer, iron, safe, free bottle of wine upon arrival.

MacArthur Place ✦✦   A recommended alternative to the Fairmont Sonoma Mission Inn & Spa (see above) is this much smaller and more intimate luxury property and spa located 4 blocks south of Sonoma's plaza. The 5½-acre "country estate" is replete with landscaped gardens and tree-lined pathways, free-standing accommodations, a spa, and heated swimming pool and whirlpool. Most of the individually decorated guest rooms are Victorian-modern attached cottages scattered throughout the resort; all are exceedingly well stocked. Some suites come with fireplaces, porches, wet bars, six-speaker surround sound, and whirlpool tubs that often have shutters opening to the bedroom. Everyone has access to complimentary wine and cheese in the evening and the DVD library anytime. The full-service spa offers a fitness center, body treatments, skin care, and massages. Within the resort's restored century-old barn is Saddles, Sonoma's only steakhouse specializing in grass-fed beef, organic and sustainably farmed produce, and whimsically classy Western decor. An array of other excellent restaurants—as well as shops, wineries, and bars—is within biking distance. *Note:* All rooms are nonsmoking.

29 E. MacArthur St., Sonoma, CA 95476. ℭ 800/722-1866 or 707/938-2929. www.macarthurplace.com. 64 units. Sun–Thurs $349–$650 double; Fri–Sat $399–$699 double. Rates include continental breakfast. AE, MC, V. Free parking. **Amenities:** Restaurant and bar specializing in martinis; outdoor heated pool; exercise room; full-service spa; outdoor Jacuzzi; steam room; rental bikes; concierge; room service; massage; laundry service; same-day dry cleaning. *In room:* A/C, TV/DVD, dataport, free Wi-Fi throughout, minibar, wet bar and coffeemaker in suites, hair dryer, iron.

Expensive

Best Western Sonoma Valley Inn *Kids*   Perfect for the traveling family, this simple inn with recently updated rooms offers plenty for kids along for the ride. There's room to run around, plus a large, heated outdoor saltwater pool, gazebo-covered spa, and sauna to play in. The rooms come with a few nice perks, such as continental breakfast delivered to your room each morning, and satellite TV with HBO (they also offer a host of paid movies). Recently all rooms were newly furnished with loveseats, new window treatments, and brand-new designer bedding. Most rooms have either a balcony or a deck overlooking the inner courtyard. An added bonus: If you need someone to help you get the kinks out, you can reserve one of the two new spa rooms and have the staff book an outside company to come in and give you an on-site massage. The inn is also in a convenient location, just a block from Sonoma's plaza.

550 Second St. W. (1 block from the plaza), Sonoma, CA 95476. ℭ 800/334-5784 or 707/938-9200. Fax 707/938-0935. www.sonomavalleyinn.com. 80 units. $114–$369 double. Rates include continental breakfast. AE, DC, DISC, MC, V. **Amenities:** Heated outdoor pool; exercise room; Jacuzzi; sauna; steam room; free Wi-Fi. *In room:* A/C, TV, dataport, Wi-Fi, fridge, coffeemaker, hair dryer, iron.

The Renaissance Lodge at Sonoma ✦✦   Downtown Sonoma's only large scale hotel takes into account its surroundings, offering some country charm in its 182 rooms. At the center of this resort is a U-shaped building with a classic big-hotel lobby and a large courtyard swimming pool with plenty of lounge chairs. The tasteful and spacious accommodations in the main building are decorated in earth tones and come complete with prints by local artists, artistic lighting fixtures, balconies or patios, and some fireplaces and tubs with shutters that open from the bathroom to the bedroom. The two-story cottages along the property are especially appealing because they're surrounded by trees, flowers, and shrubs and offer a sense of seclusion. The Raindance Spa, where I've consistently had exceptional massages, makes excellent use of its outdoor public space, with a number of small pools surrounded by lush plants. And as a bonus after your treatment, you get to hang around the pool all day if you want to.

1325 Broadway, Sonoma, CA 95476. ℂ 888/710-8008 or 707/935-6600. Fax 707/935-6829. www.thelodgeat sonoma.com. 182 units. $249–$449 double. AE, MC, V. **Amenities:** Restaurant; large heated outdoor pool; health club and spa; Jacuzzi; concierge; business center; limited room service. *In room:* A/C, TV w/pay movies, dataport, wet bar in suites and some rooms, coffeemaker, hair dryer, iron, iPod docks.

Moderate
El Dorado Hotel ★★ This 1843 mission revival building may look like a 19th-century Wild West relic from the outside, but inside it's all 21st-century deluxe. Each modern, handsomely appointed guest room has French windows and tiny balconies. Some rooms offer lovely views of the plaza; others overlook the private courtyard and heated lap pool. Most rooms are on the second floor and there's no elevator. However, if you're against hoofing it you can request one of the four so-called bungalows on the ground floor, which were upgraded in 2006 and have partially enclosed patios. A new "market," opened late 2007, serves light breakfast and lunch fare, coffee, and ice cream. Though prices reflect its prime location on Sonoma Square, this is still one of the more charming options within its price range—especially when you factor in instant access to the ground-floor El Dorado Kitchen, which is one of the valley's best restaurants.

405 First St. W., Sonoma, CA 95476. ℂ 800/289-3031 or 707/996-3030. Fax 707/996-3148. www.eldorado sonoma.com. 27 units. Summer $195–$225 double; winter $145–$185 double. 2-night minimum weekends and holidays. AE, MC, V. **Amenities:** Restaurant; coffee and organic teas; heated outdoor pool; laundry service; daily newspapers; fireplace lodge. *In room:* A/C, flatscreen TV, DVD/CD player, dataport, fridge, hair dryer, iron, environmentally safe bath products, cordless phone, voice mail.

El Pueblo Inn Located on Sonoma's main east-west street, 8 blocks from the center of town, this isn't Sonoma's fanciest hotel, but it is well cared for and offers some of the best-priced accommodations around. The rooms here are pleasant enough, with individual entrances, post-and-beam construction, exposed brick walls, light-wood furniture, down comforters, recliners, and geometric prints. A new addition in 2002 resulted in 20 new larger rooms with high ceilings, DVDs, and fireplaces in some rooms. They also recently made each room open to a courtyard with a fountain. Their new reception area doubles as a breakfast room for their continental breakfast and leads to a small meeting room. Reservations should be made at least a month in advance for the spring and summer months.

896 W. Napa St., Sonoma, CA 95476. ℂ 800/900-8844 or 707/996-3651. Fax 707/935-5988. www.elpuebloinn. com. 53 units. May–Oct $184–$299 double; Nov–Apr $154–$214 double. AE, DC, DISC, MC, V. Corporate, AAA, and senior discounts available. **Amenities:** Seasonal heated outdoor pool; fitness room; Jacuzzi; in-room massage. *In room:* A/C, TV, DVD (newer rooms only), high-speed Internet access, fridge, coffeemaker and biscotti, hair dryer, iron.

Inexpensive
Sonoma Hotel ★★ This cute little historic hotel on Sonoma's tree-lined town plaza emphasizes 19th-century elegance and comfort. Built in 1880 by Swiss immigrant Henry Weyl, it has attractive guest rooms decorated in early California style, with French country furnishings, wood and iron beds, and pine armoires. In a bow to modern luxuries, recent additions include private bathrooms, cable TV, phones with dataports, and (this is crucial) air-conditioning. Perks include fresh coffee and pastries in the morning

and wine in the evening. Its lovely restaurant, the girl & the fig (p. 323), serves California-French cuisine. *Tip:* For a quieter stay, request a room that doesn't front the street.

110 W. Spain St., Sonoma, CA 95476. © 800/468-6016 or 707/996-2996. Fax 707/996-7014. www.sonoma hotel.com. 16 units. Summer $110–$248 double; winter $99–$210 double. 2-night minimum required for summer weekends. Rates include continental breakfast and evening wine. AE, DC, MC, V. *In room:* A/C, TV, dataport.

Victorian Garden Inn   A small picket fence, a wall of trees, and an acre of gardens enclose an adorable Victorian garden brimming with violets, roses, camellias, and peonies, all shaded under flowering fruit trees. It's truly a marvelous sight in the springtime. The guest units—three in the century-old water tower and one in the main building (an 1870s Greek Revival farmhouse), as well as a cottage—continue the Victorian theme, with white wicker furniture, floral prints, padded armchairs, and claw-foot tubs. The most popular units are the Top o' the Tower and the Woodcutter's Cottage. Each has its own entrance and a garden view; the cottage boasts a sofa and armchairs set in front of the fireplace. After a hard day of wine tasting, spend the afternoon cooling off in the pool or on the shaded wraparound porch, enjoying a mellow merlot while soaking in the sweet garden smells. *New parents, take note:* The property recommends you leave young tots behind.

316 E. Napa St., Sonoma, CA 95476. © 800/543-5339 or 707/996-5339. Fax 707/996-1689. www.victoriangarden inn.com. 4 units, 1 cottage. $186–$359 double. Rates include continental breakfast. AE, DC, MC, V. **Amenities:** Outdoor pool; hot tub; concierge; business center w/free Internet access; laundry service. *In room:* A/C, fireplaces in some rooms.

GLEN ELLEN
Expensive
Gaige House Inn ★★★ *Finds*   Recently taken over by the slick Thompson hotel group, this remains Wine Country's finest B&B. Within the 1890 Queen Anne–Italianate building and Garden Annex you'll find a level of service, amenities, and decor normally associated with luxury resorts. Spacious rooms offer everything you could want—firm mattresses, silky-soft Sferra linens, premium comforters and stylish plantation-style decor with Asian and Indonesian influences. All have king- or queen-size beds; four rooms have Jacuzzi tubs, one has a Japanese soaking tub, and the 13 spa garden suites have, among other delights, granite soaking tubs. For chilly country nights, fireplaces (in 17 rooms) definitely come in handy. Bathrooms are equally luxe, range in size, and are stocked with Aveda products and slippers.

But wait, it gets better. The inn is set on a 3-acre oasis with perfectly manicured lawns and gardens, a 40-foot-long heated pool, and an inviting creek-side hammock shaded by a majestic Heritage oak. Evenings are best spent in the reading parlor, sipping premium wines. Appetizers at wine hour might include freshly shucked oysters or a sautéed scallop served ready-to-slurp on a Chinese soupspoon. Breakfast is a momentous event, accented with herbs from the inn's garden. On sunny days, the meal can be served at individual tables on the large terrace.

13540 Arnold Dr., Glen Ellen, CA 95442. © 800/935-0237 or 707/935-0237. Fax 707/935-6411. www.thompson hotels.com. 23 units. Summer $365–$375 double, $395–$695 suite; winter $200–$325 double, $300–$595 suite. Rates include evening wines. AE, DC, DISC, MC, V. **Amenities:** Large heated pool; free Wi-Fi; in-room massage. *In room:* A/C, TV/DVD, dataport, DSL and Wi-Fi, fridge, hair dryer, iron, safe.

Inexpensive
Beltane Ranch ★ *Finds*   The word *ranch* conjures up a big ole' two-story house in the middle of hundreds of rolling acres, the kind of place where you laze away the day in a hammock watching the grass grow or in the garden pitching horseshoes. Well, friend, you can have all that and more at the well-located Beltane Ranch, a century-old

buttercup-yellow manor that's been everything from a bunkhouse to a brothel to a turkey farm. You simply can't help but feel your tensions ease away as you prop your feet up on the shady wraparound porch overlooking the quiet vineyards, sipping a cool, fruity chardonnay while reading *Lonesome Dove* for the third time. Each room is uniquely decorated with American and European antiques; all have sitting areas and separate entrances. A big and creative country breakfast is served in the garden or on the porch overlooking the vineyards. For exercise, you can play tennis on the private court or hike the trails meandering through the 105-acre estate. The staff here is knowledgeable and helpful. *Tip:* Request one of the upstairs rooms, which have the best views.

11775 Sonoma Hwy./Hwy. 12, P.O. Box 395, Glen Ellen, CA 95442. © 707/996-6501. www.beltaneranch.com. 5 units, 1 cottage. $150–$220 double. Rates include full breakfast. No credit cards; personal checks accepted. **Amenities:** Outdoor, unlit tennis court. *In room:* No phone.

Glenelly Inn and Cottages 🏆 Perhaps the best thing about this rustic retreat is its reasonable rates. But equally important, this former railroad inn, built in 1916, is positively drenched in serenity. Located well off the main highway on an oak-studded hillside, the peach-and-cream inn comes with everything you would expect from a country retreat. Long verandas offer Adirondack-style chairs and views of the verdant Sonoma hillsides; breakfast is served beside a large cobblestone fireplace; and bright units contain old-fashioned claw-foot tubs, Scandinavian down comforters, and ceiling fans (though cottages have whirlpool tubs and air-conditioning). Downsides include thin walls, the usual laugh lines that come with age, and depending on your perspective, lack of TV and phone in every room. However, the staff understands that it's the little things that make the difference—hence the firm mattresses, good reading lights, and a simmering hot tub in a grapevine- and rose-covered arbor. All rooms are decorated with antiques and country furnishings, and have terry robes and private entrances. Top picks are the Vallejo and Jack London family suites, both with large private patios, although I also like the rooms on the upper veranda—particularly in the spring, when the terraced gardens below are in full bloom. The new free-standing garden cottages (the best option) are for those who want to splurge; they come with fireplaces, TV/VCRs, CD players, coffeemakers, and fridges.

5131 Warm Springs Rd. (off Arnold Dr.), Glen Ellen, CA 95442. © 707/996-6720. Fax 707/996-5227. www.glenelly.com. 9 units. $175–$205 double/suite; $320 cottage. Rates include full breakfast. AE, DISC, MC, V. **Amenities:** Outdoor Jacuzzi; TV in common room. *In room:* TV in some rooms, free Wi-Fi.

KENWOOD
Very Expensive
Kenwood Inn & Spa 🏆🏆 Inspired by the villas of Tuscany, the Kenwood Inn's honey-colored Italian-style buildings, flower-filled flagstone courtyard, and pastoral views of vineyard-covered hills are enough to make any northern Italian homesick. The friendly staff and luxuriously restful surroundings made this California girl feel right at home. What's not to like about a spacious room lavishly and exquisitely decorated with imported tapestries, velvets, and antiques, plus a fireplace, balcony (except on the ground floor), private bathroom (many with spa tubs), feather bed, CD player, and down comforter? With no TV in the rooms, relaxation is inevitable—especially if you book treatments at their Caudalie Vinotherapie Spa. A minor caveat is road noise, which you're unlikely to hear from your room but can be slightly audible over the tranquil pumped-in music around the courtyard and decent-size pool.

An impressive three-course gourmet breakfast is served in the courtyard or in the Mediterranean-style dining room. A note for traveling families: Kenwood Inn doesn't welcome kids under 16.

10400 Sonoma Hwy., Kenwood, CA 95452. © **800/353-6966** or 707/833-1293. Fax 707/833-1247. www.kenwood inn.com. 30 units. Apr–Oct from $425 double; Nov–Mar from $375 double. Rates include gourmet breakfast. 2-night minimum on weekends. AE, MC, V. No pets allowed. Children under 16 not recommended. **Amenities:** Heated outdoor pool; 2 outdoor hot tubs; indoor steam room and soaking tub; full-service spa; concierge. *In room:* A/C, CD player, high-speed Internet access, hair dryer, iron, Caudalie bath products.

WHERE TO DINE IN SONOMA VALLEY
SONOMA
Moderate

Cafe La Haye ☆☆ ECLECTIC   Everything about this cafe-like restaurant is charming. The atmosphere within the small split-level dining room is smart and intimate. The vibe is small business—a welcome departure from Napa Valley's big-business restaurants. The straightforward, seasonally inspired cuisine, which chefs bring forth from the tiny open kitchen, is delicious and wonderfully well-priced. Although the menu is small, it offers just enough options. Expect a risotto special; pasta such as fresh tagliarini with butternut squash, prosciutto, sage, and garlic cream; and pan-roasted chicken breast, perhaps with goat cheese–herb stuffing, caramelized shallot *jus,* and fennel mashed potatoes. Meat eaters are sure to be pleased with filet of beef seared with black pepper and lavender and served with Gorgonzola-potato gratin.

140 E. Napa St.. © **707/935-5994**. www.cafelahaye.com. Reservations recommended. Main courses $15–$24. AE, MC, V. Tues–Sat 5:30–9pm.

El Dorado Kitchen ☆☆ CALIFORNIA   Downtown Sonoma's most hip and contemporary restaurant, which has sexy seating indoors and out, entices with a seasonal menu ("Mediterranean-inspired bistro cuisine") of familiar items with unfamiliar twists—such as griddled prosciutto and Vermont cheddar with San Marzano tomato soup, curry fritto misto (lightly battered and fried apples, cauliflower and fall squash served with curry salt and aioli), and a Caesar salad that pays homage to Southern France with the addition of niçoise olives. Entrees might include Pacific salmon with white bean cassoulet, prosciutto, and sage; or lamb loin with rosemary polenta, piquillo peppers, Swiss chard and niçoise olive sauce. Don't hesitate to order the white truffle and parmesan French fries and one of their house drinks. In an area where dinner prices can run upwards the cost of some people's monthly house payments, El Dorado Kitchen's prices are surprisingly reasonable and portions are generous.

405 First St. W.. © **707/996-3030**. www.eldoradosonoma.com. Reservations recommended. Lunch $8–$17, dinner $8–$26, brunch $8–$18. Daily 11:30am–2:30pm and 5:30–9pm.

the girl & the fig ☆ COUNTRY FRENCH   Well established in its downtown Sonoma digs (it used to be in Glen Ellen), this modern, attractive, and cozy eatery, with lovely patio seating, is the home for Sondra Bernstein's (the girl) beloved restaurant. Here the cuisine, orchestrated by chef de cuisine Chris Jones from Chicago who recently replaced Matt Murray, is nouveau country with French nuances, and yes, figs are sure to be on the menu in one form or another. The wonderful fig and arugula salad contains pancetta, pecans, dried figs, Laura Chenel goat cheese, and fig-and-port vinaigrette. Murray uses garden-fresh produce and local meats, poultry, and fish whenever possible, in dishes such as grilled pork chops or duck confit. For dessert, try the butterscotch pot de creme, a glass of Cave des Vigneron muscat, and a sliver of one of their delicious offerings from the cheese list. Sondra knows her wines, features Rhone varietals, and will be happy to choose the best accompaniment for your meal. Looking for brunch? Head here on Sunday when it's served until 3pm.

Pricing Categories

The restaurants listed in this section are classified first by town, then by price, using the following categories: **Expensive**, dinner from $50 per person; **Moderate**, dinner from $35 per person; and **Inexpensive**, dinner less than $35 per person. (*Note:* The "Very Expensive" category—dinner from $75 per person—has been omitted since no restaurants in this chapter fall under its umbrella.) These categories reflect prices for an appetizer, a main course, a dessert, and a glass of wine.

110 W. Spain St.. (C) **707/938-3634.** www.thegirlandthefig.com. Reservations recommended. Main courses $13–$24. AE, DISC, MC, V. Daily 11:30am–10pm; Sun brunch 10am. Late night brasserie menu until 11pm Fri–Sat.

Harmony Lounge (finds) CONTINENTAL   Fronting Sonoma Square, the Harmony Club is not just a looker, with its elegant Italianate dining room with dark woods, high ceilings, marble flooring, and a wall of giant doors opening to sidewalk seating and Sonoma's plaza. It also delivers in food and live entertainment. Drop in for a seasonal menu, which features hearty winter rib-grippers such as veal osso bucco with creamy roast garlic mushroom polenta and braised greens or somewhat lighter warm-weather fare such as cumin-crusted ahi tuna with beluga lentils, roasted vegetables, and red wine sauce. Go for sidewalk seating during warmer weather (they also have heat lamps), sit inside, or hang at the carved wood bar. Either way you'll want to face the piano when the restaurant hosts a special-occasion performer, often one of the region's better talents singing jazz standards. Alas, the only letdown is the wine list, which leaves little in the way of options as this spot, owned by Steve Ledson of Ledson Winery, naturally features Ledson wines almost exclusively.

480 1st St. E. (at the plaza). (C) **707/996-9779.** Reservations accepted. Entrees $6–$12. AE, MC, V. Daily 11am–11pm.

Harvest Moon REGIONAL SEASONAL AMERICAN   Napa may have better restaurants in general, but the feasts to the east have nothing on this new downtown Sonoma restaurant. Chef/owner Nick Demarest's experience at Berkeley's world-famous Chez Panisse is evidenced by his use of outstanding ingredients combined into dishes of clean, pure, and glorious flavors. His chicory salad with mustard vinaigrette, house-cured bacon, and Gruyère is a case-in-point appetizer that's easily backed up by entrees such as pan-fried local rock cod with Swiss chard, fingerling potatoes, and beurre rouge. Sweetening the already delicious deal, his wife Jen is a pedigreed pastry chef with experience at Napa's fancy La Toque. The space itself is quirky, which means you can expect great seats at the wine bar and a scattering of tables tucked within a cramped and warm historic adobe room. Inside you'll see the chef hard at work within the shoebox open kitchen. Outside, weather permitting, is a spacious garden dining area. Regardless, if it's a good meal you're after, you will not find a better on this side of the Mayacamas.

487 1st St W. (C) **707/933-8160.** www.harvestmoonsonoma.com. Reservations recommended. Main courses $17–$25. AE, DISC, MC, V. Sun–Thurs 5:30–9pm; Fri–Sat 5:30–9:30pm.

Meritage SOUTHERN FRENCH/NORTHERN ITALIAN   Chef-owner Carlo Cavallo, formerly executive chef for Giorgio Armani, combines the best of southern French and northern Italian cuisines (hence "Meritage," after a blend made with traditional bordeaux varieties), giving Sonomans yet another reason to eat out. The menu, which changes twice daily, is a good read: foie gras ravioli with sage truffle sauce; seafood stew with tiger prawns, Manila clams, mussels, and mixed fresh fish in a spicy tomato saffron broth; and wild boar chops in white truffle sauce with mashed potatoes. Shellfish fans can't help but love the oyster raw bar with options of fresh crab and lobster, and cocktailers revel in the new martini bar. A lovely garden patio is prime positioning for sunny brunches and lunches and summer dinners. Such edible enticement—combined with reasonable prices, excellent service, a stellar wine list, and Carlo's practiced charm—make Meritage a trustworthy option.

165 W. Napa St.. (©) 707/938-9430. www.sonomameritage.com. Reservations recommended. Main courses $10–$36. Chef tasting menu $50; vegetarian tasting menu $45. AE, MC, V. Brunch 10am–3pm Sat–Sun only; lunch 11:30am–3pm Mon and Wed–Sun; dinner 5–9pm Mon and Wed–Thurs, 5–9:30 pm on weekends.

Shiso ASIAN/SUSHI   Named for a Japanese mint leaf that's referenced throughout the restaurant, this modern, airy spot is the place to come for sushi and Japanese cuisine with Americanized flair. Browse the menu and you'll find the likes of miso-glazed butterfish with Chinese long beans and miso emulsion, braised beef short ribs with glazed daikon and carrots, and local skate with sautéed stinging nettles and uni cream sauce. Sushi ranges from traditional nigiri, sashimi, hand rolls, and rolls (tuna, negi hama, California) to creative combinations (the Oregon roll has salmon, cream cheese, and cucumber). If it's on the specials menu (it usually is), don't miss the tempura-fried Kobe beef roll with hot Chinese mustard aioli, spinach, and avocado. Although the food is satisfying, it's the little touches like coffee served in a French press that makes this place a real standout. Finish the evening with ginger snap and macadamia nut–crusted tempura-fried coconut ice cream or ginger crème brûlée.

522 Broadway (just off the plaza). (©) 707/933-9331. www.shisorestaurant.com. Reservations accepted. Main courses $9–$13 lunch, $15–$45 dinner; $3.75–$50 sushi and sashimi. AE, DISC, MC, V. Winter hours Wed–Sun 5:30–9:30pm; summer hours Wed–Sun noon–2pm, Tues–Sun 5:30–9:30pm; hours are seasonal, so please call to confirm.

Swiss Hotel CONTINENTAL/NORTHERN ITALIAN   With its slanting floors and beamed ceilings, the historic Swiss Hotel, located right in the town center, is a Sonoma landmark and very much the local favorite for fine food served at reasonable prices. The turn-of-the-20th-century oak bar at the left of the entrance is adorned with black-and-white photos of pioneering Sonomans. The bright white dining room and sidewalk patio seats are pleasant spots to enjoy lunch specials such as penne with chicken, mushrooms, and tomato cream; hot sandwiches; and California-style pizzas fired in a wood-burning oven. But the secret spot is the atmospheric back garden patio, a secluded oasis shaded by a wisteria-covered trellis and adorned with plants, a fountain, gingham tablecloths, and a fireplace. Dinner might start with a warm winter salad of radicchio and frisée with pears, walnuts, and bleu cheese. Main courses run the gamut; I like the linguine and prawns with garlic, hot pepper, and tomatoes; the bleu cheese–encrusted filet mignon; and roasted rosemary chicken. The food may not knock your socks off, but it's all simply satisfying.

18 W. Spain St (at First St. W.). (©) 707/938-2884. www.swisshotelsonoma.com. Reservations recommended. Main courses lunch $8–$17, dinner $13–$28. AE, MC, V. Daily 11:30am–2:30pm; Sun–Thurs 5–9pm; Fri–Sat 5–10pm. (Bar daily 11:30am–2am.)

Inexpensive
Basque Boulangerie Café BAKERY/DELI   If you prefer a lighter morning meal and strong coffee, stand in line with the locals at the Basque Boulangerie Café, the most popular gathering spot in Sonoma Valley. Most everything—sourdough Basque breads, pastries, quiche, soups, salads, desserts, sandwiches, cookies—is made in-house and made well. Daily lunch specials, such as a grilled-veggie sandwich ($6.25), are listed on

the chalkboard out front. Seating is scarce, and if you can score a sidewalk table on a sunny day, consider yourself one lucky person. A popular option is ordering to go and eating in the shady plaza across the street. The cafe also sells wine by the glass, as well as a wonderful cinnamon bread by the loaf that's ideal for making French toast.

460 1st St. E.. © 707/935-7687. Menu items $3–$10. Credit cards accepted with a $5 minimum, local checks only. Daily 7am–6pm.

Black Bear Diner (Kids DINER   When you're craving a classic American breakfast with all the cholesterol and the fixin's (perhaps to counterbalance that wine hangover), make a beeline for this old-fashioned diner. First, it's fun, with its over-the-top bear paraphernalia, gazette-style menu listing local news from 1961 and every possible diner favorite, and absurdly friendly waitstaff. Second, it's darned cheap. Third, helpings are huge. What more could you want? Kids get a kick out of coloring books, old-timers reminisce over Sinatra playing on the jukebox, and everyone leaves stuffed on omelets, scrambles, and pancakes. Lunch and dinner feature steak sandwiches, salads, and comfort food faves like barbecued pork ribs, Cobb salad, fish and chips, and burgers—they grind their own beef. But unless you like old-school run-of-the-mill diner fare, your best bet is to dine elsewhere.

201 W. Napa St. (at Second St.). © 707/935-6800. www.blackbeardiner.com. Main courses breakfast $5–$8.50, lunch and dinner $5.50–$17. AE, DISC, MC, V. Daily 6am–9:30pm (closing varies on weekends, depending on business).

Della Santina's 🖈🖈 TUSCAN   For those of you who just can't swallow another expensive, chichi California meal, follow the locals to this friendly, traditional Italian restaurant. How traditional? Ask father-and-son team Dan and Robert: When I last dined here, they pointed out Signora Santina's hand-embroidered linen doilies as they proudly told me about her Tuscan recipes. And their pride is merited: Every dish my party tried was refreshingly authentic and well flavored, without overbearing sauces or one *hint* of California pretentiousness. Be sure to start with traditional antipasti, particularly sliced mozzarella and tomatoes, or delicious, traditional tortellini in brodo (home-made tortellini in broth). The nine pasta dishes are, again, wonderfully authentic (gnocchi lovers, rejoice!). The spit-roasted meat dishes are a local favorite (although I found them a bit overcooked); for those who can't choose between chicken, pork, turkey, rabbit, or duck, there's a selection that offers a choice of three. Don't worry about breaking your bank on a bottle of wine, because many choices here go for under $40. Portions are huge, but be sure to save room for a wonderful dessert, like the creamy panna cotta. Though the inside's small, a huge back patio covered in blooming trellises is full practically every night in the summer (the wait's never too bad), and they've recently tented part of it, so you can eat back there in winter, too, weather permitting.

133 E. Napa St. (just east of the square). © 707/935-0576. www.dellasantinas.com. Reservations recommended. Main courses $11–$18. AE, DISC, MC, V. Daily 11:30am–3pm and 5–9:30pm.

Juanita Juanita MEXICAN   Everyone loves this roadside shack hawking fresh Mexican specialties and hearty sides of who-gives-a-heck attitude. Lines out the door during weekends prove the point. But if you've gotta have a killer quesadilla, nachos, enchiladas, tacos, and their fabulous "plate" specials (think grilled chicken with chipotle cream sauce on a bed of spinach and avocado with rice, beans, and tortillas) it's worth the wait. Besides, the place is fun. Here the decor and vibe is about as casual as you can get. Plop down at the counter, pull up a chair at one of the mix-and-match tables, or grab a table on the patio, kick up your heels, dig into the plastic bucket of tortilla chips and side o' salsa, sip on an ice cold beer, and revel in the oh-so-Sonoma-casual vibe as you fill up on the huge portions. Kids dig the place, too, and have their own specialties offered at pint-sized prices of $4.75.

19114 Arnold Dr. (just north of W. Napa St.). ℂ **707/935-3981**. www.juanitajuanita.com. No reservations. Main courses $7.50–$17. No credit cards. Wed–Mon 11am–8pm.

GLEN ELLEN
Moderate
the fig café & wine bar *✶✶* NEW AMERICAN   The girl & the fig's (p. 323) sister restaurant is more casual than its downtown Sonoma sibling. But don't let the bucolic neighborhood vibe, airy environs, and soothing sage-and-mustard color scheme fool you. From his open kitchen, general manager and chef de cuisine Bryan Jones brings you the kind of rustic sophistication more commonly associated with urban restaurants. Consider starting with a thin-crust pizza, fried calamari with spicy lemon aioli, a cheese plate, or the signature fig and arugula salad; move on to braised pot roast with mashed potatoes or mussels in a garlic, leek, and tarragon sauce with fries; and finish with a fantastic chocolate brownie with vanilla ice cream. A perk: the "Rhone Alone" wine selections are available by the flight, glass, or bottle, free corkage.

13690 Arnold Dr. (at Madrone Rd). ℂ **707/938-2130**. www.thefigcafe.com. Reservations not accepted. Main courses $10–$18. AE, DISC, MC, V. Sun–Thurs 5:30–9pm; Fri–Sat until 9:30pm. Brunch offered Sat–Sun 9:30am–2:30pm.

Glen Ellen Inn Oyster Grill & Martini Bar *✶* CALIFORNIA   Christian and Karen Bertrand have made this place so quaint and cozy that you feel as if you're dining in their home, and that's exactly the place's charm. Garden seating is the favored choice on sunny days, but the covered, heated patio is also always welcoming. The first course from Christian's open kitchen might be a ginger tempura calamari with wasabi or a brie fondue with sourdough toast points. Main courses, which change with the seasons, range from spinach and Stilton ravioli to grilled salmon with blood oranges, watercress, and lemon aioli. Other favorites include pork tenderloin with sun-dried cranberries, mozzarella, caramelized onions, and polenta; and utterly tender filet mignon with Maytag blue cheese and garlic frites. On my last visit, the Sonoma Valley mixed-green salad, seared ahi tuna, and homemade French vanilla ice cream floating in bittersweet caramel sauce made a lovely meal. They've recently added the eponymous oyster grill and martini bar, including half-size taster martinis and, of course, oysters any way you want 'em. If that doesn't do it for you, the 550-plus wine selection list offers numerous bottles from Sonoma, as well as more than a dozen wines by the glass. *Tip:* There's a small parking lot behind the restaurant.

13670 Arnold Dr. (at O'Donnell Lane). ℂ **707/996-6409**. www.glenelleninn.com. Reservations recommended. Main courses $16–$25. AE, DISC, MC, V. Fri–Tues 11:30am–9pm (dinner from 5pm); Wed–Thurs 5:30–9pm. Closed 1 week in Jan.

Wolf House *✶* ECLECTIC   The most polished-looking dining room in Glen Ellen is elegant yet relaxed, whether you're seated in the handsome dining room—smartly adorned with maple floors, gold walls, dark-wood wainscoting, and a corner fireplace—or outside on the multilevel terrace under the canopy of trees with serene views of adjacent Sonoma Creek. The lunch menu adds fancy finishes to old favorites such as the excellent chicken Caesar salad, fresh grilled ahi tuna niçoise sandwich, or juicy half-pound burger with Point Reyes Original Blue cheese. During dinner, skip the soggy beer-battered prawns and head straight for seared roasted Liberty Farms duck breast with wild stewed plums, cipollini onions, barley risotto, baked pears, and plum demi; or pan-roasted salmon with sweet asparagus, baby arugula salad, and sunchoke mash. The reasonably priced wine list offers many by-the-glass options as well as a fine selection of

Sonoma wines. At brunch locals love the *nepalas rancheros* (chorizo, pinto beans, roasted chiles, and fried eggs), Dungeness crab cake Benedict, omelets, and almond crusted French toast. During my visits, service was rather languid, but well meaning.

13740 Arnold Dr. (at London Ranch Rd.). *C* **707/996-4401**. www.jacklondonlodge.com/rest.html. Reservations recommended. Main courses brunch and lunch $11–$15, dinner $15–$25. AE, MC, V. Lunch Mon–Fri 11am–3pm; dinner daily 5:30–9pm; brunch Sat and Sun 11am–3pm.

KENWOOD
Moderate
Kenwood Restaurant & Bar ★★ CALIFORNIA/CONTINENTAL   This is what Wine Country dining should be—but often, disappointingly, is not. From the terrace of the Kenwood Restaurant, diners enjoy a view of the vineyards set against Sugarloaf Ridge as they imbibe Sonoma's finest at umbrella-covered tables. On nippy days, you can retreat inside to the Sonoma-style roadhouse, with its vibrant artwork and cushioned rattan chairs at white cloth–covered tables. Regardless of where you pull up a chair, expect first-rate cuisine, perfectly balanced between tradition and innovation, complemented by a reasonably priced wine list. Great starters are Dungeness crab cake with herb mayonnaise; superfresh sashimi with ginger, soy, and wasabi; and a wonderful Caesar salad. The main dish might be poached salmon in salsa beurre blanc, or prawns with saffron Pernod sauce. But the Kenwood doesn't take itself too seriously: Great sandwiches and burgers are also available.

9900 Sonoma Hwy. (just north of Dunbar Rd.). *C* **707/833-6326**. www.kenwoodrestaurant.com. Reservations recommended. Main courses $13–$30. MC, V. Wed–Sun 11:30 am–9pm.

Inexpensive
Café Citti NORTHERN ITALIAN   If you're this far north into the Wine Country, then you're probably doing some serious wine tasting. If that's the case, then you don't want to spend half the day at a fancy, high-priced restaurant. What you need is Café Citti (pronounced *Cheat*-ee), a roadside do-it-yourself Italian trattoria that is both good and cheap. You order from the huge menu board displayed above the open kitchen. Afterward, you grab a table (the ones on the patio, shaded by umbrellas, are the best on warm afternoons), and a server will bring your meal. It's all hearty, home-cooked Italian. Standout dishes are the green-bean salad, tangy Caesar salad, focaccia sandwiches, and roasted rotisserie chicken stuffed with rosemary and garlic. Wine is available by the bottle, and the espresso is plenty strong. Everything on the menu board is available to go, which makes Café Citti an excellent resource for picnic supplies.

9049 Sonoma Hwy.. *C* **707/833-2690**. Main courses $12–$16. MC, V. Lunch daily 11am–3:30pm; dinner Sun–Thurs 5–8:30pm, Fri–Sat 5–9pm.

Taste of the Himalayas ★ NEPALESE/INDIAN   You might wonder how this group of Nepalese friends (including a sherpa!), ended up in this small restaurant just off the square in Sonoma, but then you taste their food and you're just happy they did. If you're looking for something other than the usual pizzas, pastas and burritos, this is your spot. Just what does a Nepalese meal entail? Start with crisp *samosas* (a mild blend of potatoes and peas served with mint sauce,) or *momos* (small steamed dumplings stuffed with either lamb or veggies). Move on to entrees such as curry or Tandoori dishes, which wash down nicely with Indian Taj Mahal beer. All entrees come with a delicious bowl of mild *daal bhat,* the traditional Indian lentil soup, your choice of basmati rice or naan, and casual but attentive service.

464 First St. E. *C* **707/996-1161**. Reservations recommended, but walk-ins welcome. Main courses $10–$18. Daily 11am–2:30pm and 5–10pm.

Appendix: Fast Facts

AMERICAN EXPRESS For travel arrangements, traveler's checks, currency exchange, and other member services, there's an office at 455 Market St., at First Street (☎ **415/536-2600**), in the Financial District, open Monday through Friday from 9am to 5:30pm and Saturday from 10am to 2pm. To report lost or stolen traveler's checks, call ☎ **800/221-7282.** For American Express Global Assist, call ☎ **800/554-2639.**

AREA CODES The area code for San Francisco is **415;** for Oakland, Berkeley, and much of the East Bay, **510;** for the peninsula, generally **650.** Napa and Sonoma are **707.** Most phone numbers in this book are in San Francisco's 415 area code, but there's no need to dial it if you're within city limits.

ATM NETWORKS/CASHPOINTS See "Money & Costs," p. 39.

AUTOMOBILE ORGANIZATIONS Motor clubs will supply maps, suggested routes, guidebooks, accident and bail-bond insurance, and emergency road service. The **American Automobile Association (AAA)** is the major auto club in the United States. If you belong to a motor club in your home country, inquire about AAA reciprocity before you leave. You may be able to join AAA even if you're not a member of a reciprocal club; to inquire, call AAA (☎ **800/222-4357;** www.aaa.com). AAA is actually an organization of regional motor clubs, so look under "AAA Automobile Club" in the White Pages of the telephone directory. AAA has a nationwide emergency road service telephone number (☎ 800/AAA-HELP).

BUSINESS HOURS Most banks are open Monday through Friday from 9am to 5pm as well as Saturday mornings. Many banks also have ATMs for 24-hour banking. (See the "Money & Costs" section beginning on p. 39.) Most stores are open Monday through Saturday from 10 or 11am to at least 6pm, with shorter hours on Sunday. But there are exceptions: Stores in Chinatown, Ghirardelli Square, and Pier 39 stay open much later during the tourist season, and large department stores, including Macy's and Nordstrom, keep late hours. Most restaurants serve lunch from about 11:30am to 2:30pm and dinner from about 5:30 to 10pm. They sometimes serve later on weekends. Nightclubs and bars are usually open daily until 2am, when they are legally bound to stop serving alcohol

CAR RENTALS See p. 37.

DRINKING LAWS The legal age for purchase and consumption of alcoholic beverages is 21; proof of age is required and often requested at bars, nightclubs, and restaurants, so it's always a good idea to bring ID when you go out. Supermarkets and convenience stores in California sell beer, wine, and liquor.

Most restaurants serve alcohol, but some only serve beer and wine—it depends on the type of liquor license they own. By law all bars, clubs, restaurants, and stores cannot sell or serve alcohol after 2am, and "last call" tends to start at 1:30am. There are no county or calendar alcohol restrictions in California.

Do not carry open containers of alcohol in your car or any public area that isn't zoned for alcohol consumption. The police can fine you on the spot. And nothing will ruin your trip faster than getting a citation for DUI ("driving under the influence"), so don't even think about driving while intoxicated.

DRIVING RULES   See "Getting There & Getting Around," p. 32.

EARTHQUAKES   There will always be earthquakes in California, most of which you'll never notice. However, in case of a significant shaker, there are a few basic precautionary measures you should know. When you are inside a building, seek cover; do not run outside. Stand under a doorway or against a wall, and stay away from windows. If you exit a building after a substantial quake, use stairwells, not elevators. If you are in your car, pull over to the side of the road and stop—but not until you are away from bridges, overpasses, telephone poles, and power lines. Stay in your car. If you're out walking, stay outside and away from trees, power lines, and the sides of buildings. If you're in an area with tall buildings, find a doorway in which to stand.

ELECTRICITY   Like Canada, the United States uses 110 to 120 volts AC (60 cycles), compared to 220 to 240 volts AC (50 cycles) in most of Europe, Australia, and New Zealand. Downward converters that change 220–240 volts to 110–120 volts are difficult to find in the United States, so bring one with you.

EMBASSIES & CONSULATES   All embassies are located in the nation's capital, Washington, D.C. Some consulates are located in major U.S. cities, and most nations have a mission to the United Nations in New York City. If your country isn't listed below, call for directory information in Washington, D.C. (© **202/555-1212**) or check **www. embassy.org/embassies**.

The embassy of **Australia** is at 1601 Massachusetts Ave. NW, Washington, DC 20036 (© **202/797-3000;** www.

austemb.org). There are consulates in New York, Honolulu, Houston, Los Angeles, and San Francisco.

The embassy of **Canada** is at 501 Pennsylvania Ave. NW, Washington, DC 20001 (© **202/682-1740;** www.canadian embassy.org). Other Canadian consulates are in Buffalo (New York), Detroit, Los Angeles, New York, and Seattle.

The embassy of **Ireland** is at 2234 Massachusetts Ave. NW, Washington, DC 20008 (© **202/462-3939;** www. irelandemb.org). Irish consulates are in Boston, Chicago, New York, San Francisco, and other cities. See website for complete listing.

The embassy of **New Zealand** is at 37 Observatory Circle NW, Washington, DC 20008 (© **202/328-4800;** www. nzemb.org). New Zealand consulates are in Los Angeles, Salt Lake City, San Francisco, and Seattle.

The embassy of the **United Kingdom** is at 3100 Massachusetts Ave. NW, Washington, DC 20008 (© **202/588-7800;** www.britainusa.com). Other British consulates are in Atlanta, Boston, Chicago, Cleveland, Houston, Los Angeles, New York, San Francisco, and Seattle.

EMERGENCIES   Call © **911** to report a fire, call the police, or get an ambulance anywhere in the United States. This is a toll-free call (no coins are required at public telephones).

GASOLINE (PETROL)   At press time, in the U.S., the cost of gasoline (also known as gas, but never petrol), is abnormally high (about $4 per gallon at press time). Taxes are already included in the printed price. One U.S. gallon equals 3.8 liters or .85 imperial gallons. Fill-up locations are known as gas or service stations.

HOLIDAYS   Banks, government offices, post offices, and many stores, restaurants, and museums are closed on the following legal national holidays: January 1 (New Year's Day), the third Monday in January

(Martin Luther King, Jr., Day), the third Monday in February (Presidents' Day), the last Monday in May (Memorial Day), July 4 (Independence Day), the first Monday in September (Labor Day), the second Monday in October (Columbus Day), November 11 (Veterans' Day/ Armistice Day), the fourth Thursday in November (Thanksgiving Day), and December 25 (Christmas). The Tuesday after the first Monday in November is Election Day, a federal government holiday in presidential-election years (held every 4 years, and next in 2008).

For more information on holidays see "Calendar of Events," earlier in this chapter.

HOSPITALS **Saint Francis Memorial Hospital,** 900 Hyde St., between Bush and Pine streets on Nob Hill (© **415/ 353-6000**), provides emergency service 24 hours a day; no appointment is necessary. The hospital also operates a **physician-referral service** (© **800/333-1355** or 415/353-6566).

INSURANCE Medical Insurance Although it's not required of travelers, health insurance is highly recommended. Most health insurance policies cover you if you get sick away from home—but check your coverage before you leave.

International visitors to the U.S. should note that unlike many European countries, the United States does not usually offer free or low-cost medical care to its citizens or visitors. Doctors and hospitals are expensive, and in most cases will require advance payment or proof of coverage before they render their services. Good policies will cover the costs of an accident, repatriation, or death. Packages such as **Europ Assistance's "Worldwide Healthcare Plan"** are sold by European automobile clubs and travel agencies at attractive rates. **Worldwide Assistance Services, Inc.** (© **800/777-8710;** www. worldwideassistance.com) is the agent for Europ Assistance in the United States.

Though lack of health insurance may prevent you from being admitted to a hospital in nonemergencies, don't worry about being left on a street corner to die: The American way is to fix you now and bill the daylights out of you later.

If you're ever hospitalized more than 150 miles from home, **MedjetAssist** (© **800/ 527-7478;** www.medjetassistance.com) will pick you up and fly you to the hospital of your choice in a medically equipped and staffed aircraft 24 hours day, 7 days a week. Annual memberships are $225 individual, $350 family; you can also purchase short-term memberships.

Canadians should check with their provincial health plan offices or call **Health Canada** (© **866/225-0709;** www.hc-sc.gc.ca) to find out the extent of their coverage and what documentation and receipts they must take home in case they are treated in the United States.

Travelers from the U.K. should carry their European Health Insurance Card (EHIC), which replaced the E111 form as proof of entitlement to free/reduced cost medical treatment abroad (© **0845/ 606-2030;** www.ehic.org.uk). Note, however, that the EHIC only covers "necessary medical treatment," and for repatriation costs, lost money, baggage, or cancellation, travel insurance from a reputable company should always be sought (www.travelinsuranceweb.com).

Travel Insurance The cost of travel insurance varies widely, depending on the destination, the cost and length of your trip, your age and health, and the type of trip you're taking, but expect to pay between 5% and 8% of the vacation itself. You can get estimates from various providers through **InsureMyTrip.com**. Enter your trip cost and dates, your age, and other information, for prices from more than a dozen companies.

U.K. citizens and their families who make more than one trip abroad per year may find an annual travel insurance policy works out cheaper. Check **www.money supermarket.com**, which compares prices across a wide range of providers for single- and multi-trip policies.

Most big travel agents offer their own insurance and will probably try to sell you their package when you book a holiday. Think before you sign. **Britain's Consumers' Association** recommends that you insist on seeing the policy and reading the fine print before buying travel insurance. **The Association of British Insurers** (© **020/7600-3333**; www.abi. org.uk) gives advice by phone and publishes Holiday Insurance, a free guide to policy provisions and prices. You might also shop around for better deals: Try **Columbus Direct** (© **0870/033-9988**; www.columbusdirect.net).

Trip Cancellation Insurance Trip-cancellation insurance will help retrieve your money if you have to back out of a trip or depart early, or if your travel supplier goes bankrupt. Trip cancellation traditionally covers such events as sickness, natural disasters, and State Department advisories. The latest news in trip-cancellation insurance is the availability of **expanded hurricane coverage** and the **"any-reason"** cancellation coverage—which costs more but covers cancellations made for any reason. You won't get back 100% of your prepaid trip cost, but you'll be refunded a substantial portion. **TravelSafe** (© **888/ 885-7233**; www.travelsafe.com) offers both types of coverage. Expedia also offers any-reason cancellation coverage for its air-hotel packages. For details, contact one of the following recommended insurers: **Access America** (© 866/807-3982; www.accessamerica.com); **Travel Guard International** (© 800/826-4919; www. travelguard.com); **Travel Insured International** (© 800/243-3174; www.travel insured.com); and **Travelex Insurance Services** (© 888/457-4602; www.travelex-insurance.com).

LEGAL AID If you are "pulled over" for a minor infraction (such as speeding), never attempt to pay the fine directly to a police officer; this could be construed as attempted bribery, a much more serious crime. Pay fines by mail, or directly into the hands of the clerk of the court. If accused of a more serious offense, say and do nothing before consulting a lawyer. Here the burden is on the state to prove a person's guilt beyond a reasonable doubt, and everyone has the right to remain silent, whether he or she is suspected of a crime or actually arrested. Once arrested, a person can make one telephone call to a party of his or her choice. International visitors should call your embassy or consulate.

LOST & FOUND Be sure to tell all of your credit card companies the minute you discover your wallet has been lost or stolen and file a report at the nearest police precinct. Your credit card company or insurer may require a police report number or record of the loss. Most credit card companies have an emergency toll-free number to call if your card is lost or stolen; they may be able to wire you a cash advance immediately or deliver an emergency credit card in a day or two. Visa's U.S. emergency number is © **800/ 847-2911** or 410/581-9994. American Express cardholders and traveler's check holders should call © **800/221-7282.** MasterCard holders should call © **800/ 307-7309** or 636/722-7111. For other credit cards, call the toll-free number directory at © **800/555-1212.**

If you need emergency cash over the weekend when all banks and American Express offices are closed, you can have money wired to you via **Western Union** (© **800/325-6000**; www.westernunion. com).

MAIL At press time, domestic postage rates were 27¢ for a postcard and 42¢ for a letter. For international mail, a first-class letter of up to 1 ounce costs 94¢ (72¢ to Canada and Mexico); a first-class postcard costs the same as a letter. For more information go to **www.usps.com** and click on "Calculate Postage."

If you aren't sure what your address will be in the United States, mail can be sent to you, in your name, c/o General Delivery at the main post office of the city or region where you expect to be. (Call ⓒ **800/ 275-8777** for information on the nearest post office.) The addressee must pick up mail in person and must produce proof of identity (driver's license, passport, and so on). Most post offices will hold your mail for up to 1 month, and are open Monday to Friday from 8am to 6pm, and Saturday from 9am to 3pm.

Always include zip codes when mailing items in the U.S. If you don't know your zip code, visit www.usps.com/zip4.

MEASUREMENTS   See the chart on the inside front cover of this book for details on converting metric measurements to nonmetric equivalents.

MEDICAL CONDITIONS   If you have a medical condition that requires **syringe-administered medications,** carry a valid signed prescription from your physician; syringes in carry-on baggage will be inspected. Insulin in any form should have the proper pharmaceutical documentation. If you have a disease that requires treatment with **narcotics,** you should also carry documented proof with you—smuggling narcotics aboard a plane carries severe penalties in the U.S.

NEWSPAPERS & MAGAZINES   The city's main daily is the *San Francisco Chronicle,* which is distributed throughout the city. Check out the *Chronicle's* massive Sunday edition that includes a pink "Datebook" section—an excellent preview of the week's upcoming events. The free weekly *San Francisco Bay Guardian* (www.sfbg.com) and *San Francisco Weekly* (www.sfweekly.com), tabloids of news and listings, are indispensable for nightlife information; they're widely distributed through street-corner kiosks and at city cafes and restaurants.

Of the many free tourist-oriented publications, the most widely read are *San Francisco Guide* (www.sfguide.com), a handbook-size weekly containing maps and information on current events, and *Where San Francisco* (www.wheremagazine.com), a glossy regular format monthly magazine. You can find them in most hotels, shops, and restaurants in the major tourist areas.

POLICE   For emergencies, dial ⓒ **911** from any phone; no coins are needed. For other matters, call ⓒ **415/553-0123.**

SMOKING   If San Francisco is California's most European city in looks and style, the comparison stops when it comes to smoking in public. Each year, smoking laws in the city become stricter. Since 1998, smoking has been prohibited in restaurants and bars. Hotels are also offering more nonsmoking rooms, which often leaves those who like to puff out in the cold—sometimes literally.

TAXES   In the United States, there is no value-added tax (VAT) or other indirect tax at the national level. Every state, county, and city has the right to levy its own local tax on all purchases, including hotel and restaurant checks, airline tickets, and so on, and is not included in the price tags you'll see on merchandise. This tax is not refundable. Sales tax in San Francisco is 8.5%. Hotel tax is charged on the room tariff only (which is not subject to sales tax) and is set by the city, ranging from 12% to 17% around Northern California.

TELEPHONES   Many convenience groceries and packaging services sell **prepaid calling cards** in denominations up to $50; for international visitors these can be the least expensive way to call home. Many public pay phones at airports now accept American Express, MasterCard, and Visa credit cards. **Local calls** made from pay phones in most locales cost either 25¢ or 35¢ (no pennies, please).

Most long-distance and international calls can be dialed directly from any phone. **For calls within the United States and to Canada,** dial 1 followed by the area code and the seven-digit number. **For other international calls,** dial 011 followed by the country code, city code, and the number you are calling.

Calls to area codes **800, 888, 877,** and **866** are toll-free. However, calls to area codes **700** and **900** (chat lines, bulletin boards, "dating" services, and so on) can be very expensive—usually a charge of 95¢ to $3 or more per minute, and they sometimes have minimum charges that can run as high as $15 or more.

For **reversed-charge or collect calls,** and for person-to-person calls, dial the number 0 then the area code and number; an operator will come on the line, and you should specify whether you are calling collect, person-to-person, or both. If your operator-assisted call is international, ask for the overseas operator.

For **local directory assistance** ("information"), dial 411; for long-distance information, dial 1, then the appropriate area code and 555-1212.

TIME   San Francisco is in the Pacific Standard Time zone, which is 8 hours behind Greenwich Mean Time and 3 hours behind Eastern Standard Time. The continental United States is divided into **four time zones:** Eastern Standard Time (EST), Central Standard Time (CST), Mountain Standard Time (MST), and Pacific Standard Time (PST). Alaska and Hawaii have their own zones. For example, when it's 9am in Los Angeles (PST), it's 7am in Honolulu (HST),10am in Denver (MST), 11am in Chicago (CST), noon in New York City (EST), 5pm in London (GMT), and 2am the next day in Sydney.

Daylight saving time is in effect from 1am on the second Sunday in March to 1am on the first Sunday in November, except in Arizona, Hawaii, the U.S. Virgin Islands, and Puerto Rico. Daylight saving time moves the clock 1 hour ahead of standard time.

TIPPING   Tips are a very important part of certain workers' income, and gratuities are the standard way of showing appreciation for services provided. (Tipping is certainly not compulsory if the service is poor!) In hotels, tip **bellhops** at least $1 per bag ($2–$3 if you have a lot of luggage) and tip the **chamber staff** $1 to $2 per day (more if you've left a disaster area for him or her to clean up). Tip the **doorman** or **concierge** only if he or she has provided you with some specific service (for example, calling a cab for you or obtaining difficult-to-get theater tickets). Tip the **valet-parking attendant** $1 every time you get your car.

In restaurants, bars, and nightclubs, tip **service staff** 15% to 20% of the check, tip **bartenders** 10% to 15%, tip **checkroom attendants** $1 per garment, and tip **valet-parking attendants** $1 per vehicle.

As for other service personnel, tip **cab drivers** 15% of the fare; tip **skycaps** at airports at least $1 per bag ($2–$3 if you have a lot of luggage); and tip **hairdressers** and **barbers** 15% to 20%.

TOILETS   Those weird, oval-shaped, olive-green kiosks on the sidewalks throughout San Francisco are high-tech self-cleaning public toilets. They've been placed on high-volume streets to provide relief for pedestrians. French potty-maker JCDecaux gave them to the city for free—advertising covers the cost. It costs 25¢ to enter, with no time limit, but I don't recommend using the ones in the sketchier neighborhoods such as the Mission because they're mostly used by crackheads and prostitutes. Toilets can also be found in hotel lobbies, bars, restaurants, museums, department stores, railway and bus stations, and service stations. Large hotels and fast-food restaurants are often the best bet for clean facilities. Restaurants and bars in resorts or heavily visited areas may reserve their restrooms for patrons.

Index

See also Accommodations and Restaurant indexes, below.

RESTAURANTS